Empirically Oriented Theoretical Morphology and Syntax

Chief Editor: Stefan Müller
Consulting Editors: Berthold Crysmann, Laura Kallmeyer

In this series:

1. Lichte, Timm. Syntax und Valenz: Zur Modellierung kohärenter und elliptischer Strukturen mit Baumadjunktionsgrammatiken

2. Bîlbîie, Gabriela. Grammaire des constructions elliptiques: Une étude comparative des phrases sans verbe en roumain et en français

3. Bowern, Claire, Laurence Horn & Raffaella Zanuttini (eds.). On looking into words (and beyond): Structures, Relations, Analyses

ISSN: 2366-3529

On looking into words (and beyond)

Structures, Relations, Analyses

Edited by

Claire Bowern
Laurence Horn
Raffaella Zanuttini

Claire Bowern, Laurence Horn & Raffaella Zanuttini (eds.). 2017. *On looking into words (and beyond)*: *Structures, Relations, Analyses* (Empirically Oriented Theoretical Morphology and Syntax 3). Berlin: Language Science Press.

This title can be downloaded at:
http://langsci-press.org/catalog/book/151
© 2017, the authors
Published under the Creative Commons Attribution 4.0 Licence (CC BY 4.0):
http://creativecommons.org/licenses/by/4.0/
ISBN: 978-3-946234-92-0 (Digital)
      978-3-946234-97-5 (Hardcover)
      978-3-946234-81-4 (Softcover)
ISSN: 2366-3529
DOI:10.5281/zenodo.495467

Cover and concept of design: Ulrike Harbort
Typesetting: Claire Bowern, Parker Brody, Jun Chen, Dolly Goldenberg, Maggie Kandel, and Jason Zentz
Proofreading: Claire Bowern, Laurence Horn, and Sharon Klein
Editors: Claire Bowern, Laurence Horn, and Raffaella Zanuttini, in collaboration with Ryan Bennett, Bob Frank, Maria Piñango, Jason Shaw, and Jim Wood
Fonts: Linux Libertine, Arimo, DejaVu Sans Mono
Typesetting software: X⅂ᴀTEX

Language Science Press
Unter den Linden 6
10099 Berlin, Germany
langsci-press.org

Storage and cataloguing done by FU Berlin

Language Science Press has no responsibility for the persistence or accuracy of URLs for external or third-party Internet websites referred to in this publication, and does not guarantee that any content on such websites is, or will remain, accurate or appropriate.

Contents

Preface   vii

I   Phonology

1. Between natural and unnatural phonology: The case of cluster-splitting epenthesis
Juliette Blevins   3

2. The domain of stress assignment: Word-boundedness and frequent collocation
Ellen Kaisse   17

3. Compensatory lengthening and structure preservation revisited yet again
Darya Kavitskaya   41

4. Phonological exceptionality is localized to phonological elements: the argument from learnability and Yidiny word-final deletion
Erich R. Round   59

5. U-umlaut in Icelandic and Faroese: Survival and death
Höskuldur Thráinsson   99

II   Morphology

6. Word-based Items-and-processes (WoBIP): Evidence from Hebrew morphology
Outi Bat-El   115

7. Root-based syntax and Japanese derivational morphology
Brent de Chene   135

8. Morphological complexity and Input Optimization
Michael Hammond   155

Contents

9	Multiple exponence in the Lusoga verb stem Larry M. Hyman & Sharon Inkelas with Fred Jenga	171
10	Romansh allomorphy (Again!) Martin Maiden	189
11	How to wake up irregular (and speechless) Charles Yang	211

III Syntax and Morphosyntax

12	Special clitics and the right periphery in Tsotsil Judith Aissen	235
13	Another way around causatives in Chamorro Sandra Chung	263
14	Preliminaries to the investigation of clitic sequencing in Greek and Indo-Iranian Mark Hale	289
15	Nominal verbs and transitive nouns: Vindicating lexicalism Paul Kiparsky	311
16	On mechanisms by which languages become [nominative-]accusative Ashwini Deo	347
17	OF as a phrasal affix in the English determiner system Randall Hendrick	369
18	Split-morphology and lexicalist morphosyntax: The case of transpositions Andrew Spencer	385
19	Rules and blocks Gregory Stump	421

IV Language and Linguistic Theory

20	Darwinism tested by the science of language Mark Aronoff	443
21	Temporal patterning in speech and birdsong Louis Goldstein	457

22 "Constructions" and grammar: Evidence from idioms
   Julia Horvath & Tal Siloni   471

23 A-morphous iconicity
   Ryan Lepic & Carol Padden   489

24 Iconicity chains in sign languages
   Donna Jo Napoli   517

25 Where, if anywhere, are parameters? A critical historical overview of
   parametric theory
   Frederick J. Newmeyer   547

26 Saussure's Dilemma: Parole and its potential
   Alan Timberlake   569

Indexes   587

Preface

While linguistic theory is in continual flux as progress is made in our ability to understand the structure and function of language, one constant has always been the central role of the word. *On Looking into Words* is a wide-ranging volume spanning current research into word-based morphology, morphosyntax, the phonology-morphology interface, and related areas of theoretical and empirical linguistics. The 26 papers that constitute this volume extend morphological and grammatical theory to signed as well as spoken language, to diachronic as well as synchronic evidence, and to birdsong as well as human language. Central concerns of the volume's authors include morphological gaps, learnability, increases and declines in productivity, and the interaction of different components of the grammar.

The contributions in the volume explore linked synchronic and diachronic topics in phonology, morphology, and syntax (in particular, inflection and cliticization) and their implications for linguistic theory, and are informed by data from a wide range of language families. Languages discussed in the contributions include Ancient and Modern Greek (Hale, Kavitskaya), Macedonian (Kaisse), Sanskrit, Finnish, and Sakha (Kiparsky), Middle Indo-Aryan (Deo), Rumantsch (Maiden), Latin and French (Timberlake), Russian (Spencer), Icelandic and Faroese (Thráinsson), Welsh (Hammond), Hebrew (Bat-El, Horvath & Siloni), Limbu and Southern Sotho (Stump), Lusoga (Hyman & Inkelas), Yidiny (Round), Japanese (de Chene), and Tsotsil Mayan (Aissen), as well as ASL and other signed languages (Lepic & Padden, Napoli), as well as English.

The papers are offered as a tribute to Stephen R. Anderson, the Dorothy R. Diebold Professor of Linguistics at Yale, who is retiring at the end of the 2016–2017 academic year and who has long been a major figure in several of the fields under investigation in the volume: phonology and morphology (and the history of scholarship on those topics), the of morphology-syntax interface, the relation of theory to data, the evolution of human language and its relation to animal communication systems. The contributors – friends, colleagues, and former students of Professor Anderson – are all important contributors to linguistics in their own right. The central contributions that Anderson has made to so many areas of linguistics and cognitive science, drawing on synchronic and diachronic phenomena in diverse linguistic systems, are represented through the papers in the volume.

The papers in Part I of the volume focus on phonology at the level of the word and below. Ellen Kaisse draws on evidence from literary Macedonian to investigate why stress assignment is word-bounded, despite the existence of higher-level prosodic interactions – that is, she discusses the reasons why lexical stress is specifically *lexical*. Dasha Kavitskaya revisits a robust generalization from work by de Chene and Anderson that

Preface

predicts compensatory lengthening should be structure preserving. She argues that a class of apparent exceptions to this generalization have independently motivated analyses consistent with the generalization. Juliette Blevins looks at the role of language contact in determining cross-linguistic strategies for the resolution of stop + liquid clusters through vowel epenthesis as a recurrent feature of loan-word phonology. Erich Round's contribution addresses issues of learnability in determining the class of possible grammars. He discusses the implications of word-final deletion in Yidiny (Pama-Nyungan) for the theory of exceptionality, which he shows cannot be represented in purely phonological or purely diacritic terms. Like several papers in the collection, Höski Thráinsson's examines the diachronic underpinnings of synchronic linguistic structure. He uses contrastive evidence from alternations in Modern Icelandic and Modern Faroese to argue for different trajectories in historical change in u-umlaut and accounts for differing degrees of synchronic productivity and transparency of the umlaut rules in the two languages.

The papers in Part II concentrate on issues in morphological theory, in several cases also drawing on the interaction of synchronic and diachronic factors. Martin Maiden argues for the use of comparative and historical evidence in deciding between possible synchronic interpretations of phenomena. He revisits paradigmatic phenomena in Rumantsch and investigates whether allomorphy in verb stems is phonologically conditioned or is evidence for paradigm autonomy. Brent de Chene's paper looks at an apparent argument for a syntactic approach to derivational stem morphology (as proposed in the theory of Distributed Morphology) in languages like Japanese and shows that a closer examination of the facts supports the approach defended by Anderson on which it is just inflectional (and not derivational) processes that lend themselves to a syntactic analysis. Anderson's A-Morphous Morphology is an item-and-process approach that takes words to be related to each other by morphological processes; Semitic languages, with their celebrated triconsonantal roots, were explicitly excluded from the purview of Anderson's analysis. In her contribution, Outi Bat-El – invoking data from both adult and child language – argues that in fact the Anderson-style item-and-process framework can be naturally extended to provide an empirically grounded account of word relations in Modern Hebrew, with the word/stem taken as basic and the putative triconsonantal root seen as a mere residue of phonological elements. Mike Hammond applies data from English and Welsh to the examination and measurement of morphological complexity, applying the statistical framework of Input Optimization developed by Hammond himself in earlier work to questions arising in morphological investigation. Larry Hyman and Sharon Inkelas (with Fred Jenga) address a different type of question for morphological theory, the nature of and motivation for multiple exponence. Lusoga, a Bantu language spoken in Uganda, exhibits multiple exponence of causative, applicative, subjunctive and perfective suffixes and the apparent intermingling of derivational and inflectional affixation processes, properties which Hyman & Inkelas see as posing challenges for theories of morphology that seek to minimize redundancy and treat derivation as distinct from (and invariably ordered before) inflection. Finally, Charles Yang's paper examines a different issue for morphological theory, that of morphological defectiveness arising when a productive process fails to be recognized by the language learner.

He reconsiders the *amn't problem – the absence (in most dialects of English) of an inflected negation for the first person singular copula – through the lens of his Tolerance Principle, a corollary of the Elsewhere Principle motivated by the behavior of speakers with respect to paradigm gaps in English, Russian, Spanish, and other languages. As in other papers in this section (and in the volume more generally), Yang extends his view to consider the implications of the processes he describes for language acquisition, variation, and change.

Part III encompasses a set of issues relating morphology to syntax, drawing on complex synchronic and diachronic evidence from a diverse set of languages. Sandy Chung's paper returns to the interaction of causative marking and number agreement in Chamorro, which has been recognized as a challenge for the traditional view that inflectional affixes invariably attach outside derivational ones. While Anderson proposed taking number agreement to be derivational, Chung argues that the apparent causative prefix is actually a prosodically deficient verb, thus dissolving the apparent counterexample to the inflection-outside-derivation while preserving the intuition that number agreement is inflectional. Another contribution to morphosyntactic investigation in this section is Randy Hendrick's argument for analyzing the English preposition of (appearing in degree inversion expressions like *more complex of a theory*) as a phrasal affix rather than a syntactic head, thus predicting certain distributional features of the construction and allowing an explanation of the appearance of *of* in fractional expressions (*one third of a cup*).

Several of the papers in this section examine the nature of clitics. Mark Hale investigates the syntax underlying the distribution of clitics that fall under Wackernagel's Law, which describes the tendency of clitics to appear in second (or, now, "Wackernagel") position in the sentence. Utilizing diachronic data from Ancient Greek and Indo-Iranian, Hale provides a detailed examination of cases in which there are multiple demands on a Wackernagel position and of the devices for resolving those conflicts, ultimately taking Wackernagel's Law to be epiphenomenal on other phenomena. Judith Aissen similarly considers exceptional clitic placement, but in Tsotsil (Mayan); while Hale argues for syntactic constraints on exceptionality based primarily on Attic Greek, Aissen focuses on the role of phonology, and in particular prosodic constraints, in the determination of the placement of clitics on the right periphery (rather than in the syntactically conditioned second position). Like Hale, Deo and Kiparsky examine diachronic shifts in Indo-Aryan, albeit toward different ends. Ashwini Deo's article traces the morphosyntax of ergative alignment loss in Indo-Aryan. Anderson and others have While much work, including a seminal paper by Anderson, has sought to describe how languages develop ergative case marking, Deo turns the tables by seeking to develop an understanding of how nominative-accusative marking can emerge in historically ergative systems, as in the gradual de-ergativization of Middle Indo-Aryan based on independent shifts in argument realization in that language. Paul Kiparsky leverages a synchronic analysis of gerunds and nominalizations across a variety of languages (Vedic Sanskrit, Finnish, Sakha (Yakut), English) to argue for a lexicalist rather than syntactically derived analysis of agent nominalizations; gerunds, on the other hand, are argued to be verbal at all levels of the syntactic derivation. Thus, we have a neatly symmetrical system: while gerunds are verbs that bear a Case feature (via their INFL head), transitive nominalizations (*pace* Baker) are nouns with an Aspect feature. The final two papers in the (Morpho)syntax component of the volume bear on the status of inflectional morphology within the general theory of grammar. Like other authors in the volume, Andy Spencer takes as a jumping off point Anderson's "split morphology" hypothesis – the view that derivational morphology is lexically mediated while inflectional morphology is syntactically mediated. Along with the gerunds and nominalizations explored in Kiparsky's contribution, another test case for this view is posed by participles. Spencer investigates Russian participles and other transpositions utilizing a generalized version of Stump's Paradigm Function Morphology. He concludes that while the participle's actual lexical entry is that of an adjective (as lexicalist theory predicts), it realizes the verbal properties of voice/aspect, sharing the semantic properties and lexemic index of its verbal base, just as in the case of verb inflection. In his paper, Greg Stump focuses on the viability of Anderson's conception of rule block for inflectional processes within a grammar and on rule interaction. His evidence is provided by multiple exponence in Limbu, a Tibeto-Burman language of Nepal, and by polyfunctionality in Southern Sotho, a Bantu language of southern Africa. He develops principles of rule conflation that are independently motivated and converge to explain the outcome when a single rule participates in more than one block.

The volume concludes with a set of papers that explore linguistic theory from a broad perspective, while also extending the issues of words and rules from the structure and evolution of spoken language to the properties of signed languages and birdsong. Mark Aronoff, who is (along with Anderson) a key figure in the development of word-based morphology, turns his attention here to the mismatch between the nature of linguistic rules and that of biological evolution (despite the influence of the results of neogrammarians on Darwin and other prime movers in the establishment of the principles of natural selection). This mismatch led Saussure to abandon his earlier productive focus on diachrony in favor of a single-minded characterization of synchronic linguistics. Aronoff borrows Gause's principle of competitive exclusion from evolutionary ecology as a means for reviving the evolutionary approaches of Saussure and his 19th century predecessors. Besides the dichotomy of diachrony and synchrony, Saussure is also celebrated for his distinction between *langue* and *parole*, the latter notion often dismissed by generative linguists as a matter of peripheral interest. Alan Timberlake revisits Saussure's treatment of the shift in stress rules from Latin to French and points to the crucial role of parole in accounting for the relevant shifts not only in that case but in the alternations dictating the appearance of intrusive /r/ (*the idear of it*) and reanalysis (*a napron > an apron*) in English. The papers by Newmeyer and Horvath & Siloni reconsider theoretical issues in generative grammar and its rivals. While parameters have long been adduced in grammatical theory as a means to account for cross-linguistic variation, Fritz Newmeyer's paper re-examines the role of parametric explanation and argues that despite its success in leading generative scholars to the discovery of cross-linguistic generalizations, macro- and micro-parameters rest on shaky ground empirically and conceptually in current theoretical scholarship. Newmeyer goes on to survey some promising alternative approaches for capturing the relevant insights. Julia Horvath and Tal Siloni compare two theoretically distinct approaches to idioms. They argue that the distributional differences between phrasal and clausal idioms with respect to the diatheses with which they co-occur represent a serious problem for the approach of Construction Grammar, which treats linguistic knowledge as a network of stored constructions, while generative grammar, which allows for a computational system (providing unstored derivational outputs) as well as a storage module, is more capable of offering an empirically adequate account of these phenomena.

The of iconicity in sign languages representations is explored in the papers by Lepic & Padden and Napoli. On the a-morphous theory of word structure proposed by Anderson, the word and not the morpheme is the fundamental building block of morphology. As earlier posited by Jackendoff and Aronoff, the task of Word Formation Rules is analysis rather than creation; the speaker's knowledge encompasses the complex relationships among the words in her lexicon. Ryan Lepic and Carol Padden provide further support for this theory by drawing on the properties of lexical iconicity (and the gradual loss of iconicity) in American Sign Language. Donna Jo Napoli's paper also deals with iconicity in non-spoken linguistic modalities, although she extends her domain from ASL to a wide range of the world's signed languages. She uncovers biologically motivated "chains of iconicity" consisting of mappings from perceptual systems into visual realizations that evolve along semantic lines, a natural development that helps explains why unrelated signed languages exhibit similar signs for abstract concepts. The final contribution is by Louis Goldstein, a pioneer in the development of articulatory phonology, a gesture-based approach to the problem of how messages in the mind of the sender are transferred to the mind of the receiver through actions of the body. In his paper, Goldstein explores the ways such messages are conveyed by humans (through spoken or signed words) and by birds; his study demonstrates that despite their real and instructive differences, birdsong, like speech, is a complex motor behavior with an essential role played by temporal patterning.

The word has always been at the crux of descriptive and theoretical research on phonology, morphology, syntax, and semantics. By looking into words, the contributors to this volume shed light on both specific subfields and the interfaces among them, on how languages work and how they change over time. The papers in this volume, in addressing linguistic structure and linguistic relationships, help further our understanding of individual languages and of language as a unified phenomenon.

Part I

Phonology

Chapter 1

Between natural and unnatural phonology: The case of cluster-splitting epenthesis

Juliette Blevins
The Graduate Center, CUNY

A widely recognized feature of loan-word phonology is the resolution of clusters by vowel epenthesis. When a language lacking word-initial clusters borrows words from a language with initial #TRV sequences, T an oral stop and R a liquid, it is common to find vowel epenthesis, most typically vowel-copy, as in, for example: Basque <gurutze> 'cross' from Latin <cruce(m)>; Q'eqchi' <kurus> 'cross' from Spanish <cruz> 'cross', or Fijian <kolosi> 'cross' from English <cross>. The phonological rule or sound change responsible for this pattern is sometimes called "cluster-splitting epenthesis": #TRV$_i$ > #TV$_{(i)}$RV$_i$. The most widely accepted explanation for this pattern is that vowel epenthesis between the oral stop and the following sonorant is due to the vowel-like nature of the TR transition, since #TRV$_i$ is perceptually similar to #TV$_{(i)}$RV$_i$. A fact not often appreciated, however, is that cluster-splitting epenthesis is extremely rare as a language-internal development. The central premise of this chapter is that #TRV$_i$ in a non-native language is heard or perceived as #TV$_{(i)}$RV$_i$ when phonotactics of the native language demand TV transitions. Without this cognitive component, cluster-splitting epenthesis is rare and, as argued here, decidedly unnatural.

1 Introduction

Diachronic explanations have been offered for both natural and unnatural sound patterns in human spoken languages. Building on the Neogrammarian tradition, as well as the experimental research program of Ohala (e.g. 1971; 1974; 1993), it is argued that natural sound patterns, like final obstruent devoicing, nasal place assimilation, vowel harmony, consonant lenition, and many others, arise from regular sound changes with clear phonetic bases (Blevins 2004, 2006, 2008, 2015; Anderson 2016). Unnatural sound patterns, in contrast, cannot be explained in terms of simple phonetic processes. Case studies of unnatural patterns show more complex histories: in some cases more than one natural change has been collapsed; in others, a natural change is reanalyzed or inverted;

Juliette Blevins. 2017. Between natural and unnatural phonology: The case of cluster-splitting epenthesis. In Claire Bowern, Laurence Horn & Raffaella Zanuttini (eds.), *On looking into words (and beyond)*, 3–16. Berlin: Language Science Press. DOI:10.5281/zenodo.495434

in still others, analogy has extended a sound pattern whose origins are morphological, not phonological; and combinations of all of these paths can also be observed (Bach & Harms 1972; Anderson 1981; Buckley 2000; Vaux 2002; Blevins 2008b,a,c; Garrett & Blevins 2009; Anderson 2016).

However, typological study of regular sound change reveals certain kinds of sound change that are neither wholly natural nor wholly unnatural. For example, the shift of *#kl > #tl, documented in at least three different language families, appears to have a natural basis in perception, since [kl] and [tl] clusters are acoustically similar and confused with each other. However, the rarity of this sound change is associated with structural factors: misperception of [kl] as [tl] is strongly associated with the absence of phonological /tl/ clusters in a language. In this case, the absence of a sound pattern, /tl/, influences cognition, making listeners more likely to perceive [kl] as [tl] (Blevins & Grawunder 2009). The presence of a contrast can also facilitate particular types of sound change. As first argued by de Chene & Anderson (1979), compensatory lengthening sound changes are strongly associated with pre-existing vowel length contrasts. This statistical tendency is argued to arise from phonetically natural vowel lengthening in pre-sonorant and open syllable contexts (Kavitskaya 2002), combined with the cognitive effects of structural analogy, where pre-existing categories act as attractors in the course of language acquisition (Blevins 2004: 150–155 and Kavitskaya, this volume).

In this contribution, I offer another example of regular sound change that is neither wholly natural nor wholly unnatural, and highlight the role of human cognition in cases where it has occurred. Cluster-splitting epenthesis is of interest, not only because of its rarity as a regular sound change, but in how it advances our understanding of sound patterns compared to 20th century models (Anderson 1985), and emphasizes the extent to which historical linguists, phonologists, and phoneticians still need the cognitive scientist (Anderson 2001).

2 Cluster-splitting epenthesis in loanword phonology

A widely recognized feature of loanword phonology is the resolution of clusters by vowel epenthesis. When a language lacking word-initial clusters borrows words from a language with initial #TRV sequences, T an oral stop and R a liquid, it is common to find vowel epenthesis, most typically vowel-copy, as illustrated in (1).[1]

If loanword phonology is taken as evidence for properties of phonological grammars (Hyman 1970), a phonological rule describing this pattern can be stated as in (2).

---

[1] For these and other examples, see: Blevins & Egurtzegi (2016) on Latin loans in Basque; Casparis (1997) on Sanskrit loans in Indonesian; Campbell (2013) on Colonial Spanish loans into Mayan languages; and Kenstowicz (2007) on Fijian loanword phonology. A reviewer notes that some varieties of Q'eqchi' permit initial /CR/ clusters. Proto-Mayan had only *CVC syllables, and Mayan *kurus* arguably reflects borrowing of Colonial Spanish *cruz* into a language which lacked initial CR clusters.

1 Between natural and unnatural phonology: The case of cluster-splitting epenthesis

(1) Cluster-splitting epenthesis in loanword phonology
    a.   Source language   Latin   *crucem*   'cross'
          Target language   Basque   gurutze   'cross'

    b.   Source language   Sanskrit   *klēśa*   'defilement'
          Target language   Indonesian   kelesa   'indolent'

    c.   Source language   Spanish   *cruz*   'cross'
          Target language   Q'eqchi'   kurus   'cross'

    d.   Source language   English   *cross*   'cross'
          Target language   Fijian   kolósi   'cross'

(2) Cluster-splitting vowel-epenthesis
$$\#TRV_i \rightarrow \#TV_{(i)}RV_i$$

Within the structuralist and generative traditions detailed in Anderson (1985), the locus of explanation for this type of epenthesis lies in phonotactic differences between the source language and the target language. Under this general account, the speaker of the target language hears a word pronounced in the source language, constructs a phonological representation with an initial #TR cluster based on this hearing, but then alters this phonological representation in line with the phonotactics of the speaker's native language which lacks initial #TR clusters (e.g. Broselow 1987; Itô 1989).

Typological studies of loanword phonology and advances in our understanding of speech perception have given rise to 21st century treatments of these patterns that are more explanatory in accounting not only for a "repair" but for the specific type of sound pattern that results. At present, the most widely accepted explanation for the sound pattern in (2) combines two new findings in speech perception, one related to perceptual similarity, and the other related to perceptual illusions. A first component of the analysis is that vowel-epenthesis between the oral stop and following sonorant is due to the vowel-like nature of the TR transition (Fleischhacker 2001; 2005; Kang 2011; Berent 2013; Broselow 2015). Fleischhacker (2001; 2005) argues that the general pattern is determined by perceptual similarity: initial TR clusters are more perceptually similar to TVR than VTR. An important aspect of her work is the distinction between initial #TR clusters and initial #sT clusters, which rarely show vowel-splitting epenthesis, and defy purely phonotactic accounts. A second component of the analysis relates to specific structural differences between the source and target languages. Under the perceptual account, perception of #TR by native speakers of languages that lack initial #TR is biased: these speakers will tend to hear a vowel between the oral stop and the following liquid, even if no vowel is present. Experimental work supporting the existence of illusionary vowels for Japanese speakers presented with CC clusters was presented in Dupoux et al. (1999), and has been supported by much subsequent work (see Peperkamp & Dupoux

2002; Kang 2003; 2011; Kabak & Idsardi 2007; Davidson & Shaw 2012), including a range of studies showing vowel percepts in TR clusters (Berent 2013, and works cited there).[2]

Given this evidence, one might conclude that the sound pattern described in (2) is both natural and common, having a clear phonetic explanation (Blevins 2004; 2008b; 2015). As a natural, phonetically-based sound pattern one might expect many instances of reconstructed word-initial *TR clusters to be resolved by a sound change parallel to the synchronic rule in (2). A sound change of this kind might be even more common than expected on phonetic grounds due to markedness proposals stating that complex onsets are less preferred than simple onsets (Prince & Smolensky 1993; Kager 1999). As I show below, these expectations are not borne out, suggesting that cognitive bias in the context of novel stimuli plays a central role in cluster-splitting epenthesis.

3 Cluster-splitting epenthesis as regular sound change

Very few well-studied and widely agreed upon proto-languages are reconstructed with initial *TR clusters at the oldest stages. One exception is Proto-Indo-European, reconstructed with *TR clusters as well as other initial cluster types (Fortson 2010: 64–65). Some widely agreed upon Proto-Indo-European reconstructions with initial *TR clusters are shown in (3).

(3) Word-initial *TR in Proto-Indo-European
    a. *gras- 'eat'   Cf. Vedic grásate 'eats, feeds', Greek grástis 'green fodder, grass', Latin grāmen (< *gras-men) 'grass, fodder'

    b. *prek^j- 'ask'   Cf. Vedic pṛccháti 'asks', Latin precor 'I entreat', German fragen, Tocharian B prek-

    c. *trejes 'three'   Cf. Lycian tri-, Vedic tráyas, Greek treîs, Avestan θrayō, Latin trēs

The Indo-European language family is relatively large, relatively diversified, and relatively well-studied in comparison with other language families of the world. According to *Ethnologue*, there are approximately 445 living Indo-European languages at present, and linguists agree that the major subgroups of Anatolian, Indo-Iranian, Greek, Italic, Celtic, Armenian, Tocharian, and Balto-Slavic have had long independent developments. If cluster-splitting vowel-epenthesis in (2) has a natural phonetic basis in perceptual similarity as outlined above, then a sound change like (3) might be expected to have occurred numerous times in the Indo-European language family.

(4) Cluster-splitting vowel-epenthesis as sound change
    #TRV$_i$ > #TV$_{(i)}$RV$_i$

---

[2] This approach is not agreed upon by all researchers. See Uffmann (2007) and Hall (2011) for discussion.

1 Between natural and unnatural phonology: The case of cluster-splitting epenthesis

However, cluster-splitting vowel epenthesis as a regular sound change is rare in the Indo-European language family. *TR clusters are inherited intact in all of the major subgroups, and sound changes affecting these clusters at later stages of development are of distinct types (e.g. palatalization of *l in Romance *Tl clusters; loss of *p in Celtic).

Indeed, within the entire Indo-European language family, there appears to be only one clear instance of a regular sound change like (3).[3] The sound change in question appears to have occurred in relatively recent times, in the transition from Middle Persian to Modern Persian (aka New Persian, Farsi, Dari, Tajiki), or, perhaps more generally, from Middle to Early New Iranian.[4] While the specific sound change is rarely stated as in (3), it is implied. For example in their chapter on modern Persian and Tajik phonology, Windfuhr & Perry (2009: 427–428) describe the language as having syllable onsets consisting of only a single consonant, and note that "The inherited initial clusters have been resolved by prothetic or epenthetic vowels, either of which could become standardized, e.g. st-: *stār* 'star' > *setāre/sitora*, br: *brādar* 'brother' > *barādar/barodar*..." (Windfuhr & Perry 2009: 428). The epenthesis process described is identical to that schematized in (3), and it is also characteristic in loanword phonology, on which much more has been written (see, e.g. Strain 1968, Karimi 1987). Illustrative examples comparing Middle Persian inherited clusters to Modern Persian #CVC sequences are shown in (5).

(5) One case of cluster-splitting epenthesis in Indo-European: Modern Persian

	Middle Persian	Modern Persian	gloss	PIE
a.	brādar	barādar	'brother'	*bʰréh₂ter-
b.	griftan	gereftan, giriftan	'grab, takc'	*gʰrebh₂-
c.	draxt	daraxt	'tree'	*drew- 'wood'
d.	griy-	geri-	'to cry'	*gʰreh₂d-

A second case of cluster-splitting epenthesis sound change is found in the Siouan-Catawba language family, a small group of languages in North America that includes Crow, Hidatsa, Mandan, Lakota, Dakota, Assiniboine, Yanktonai, Stoney, Sioux Valley, Chiwere (aka Iowa-Missouria-Otoe), Hoocąk (aka Winnebago), Omaha-Ponca, Ponca, Kanza/Kaw, Osage, Quapaw, Biloxi, Ofo, Tutelo, Saponi, Catawba and Woccon. The diachronic process known as Dorsey's Law (Dorsey 1885) is a sound change taking Proto-

---

[3] Fortson (2010: 302–303) mentions evidence for a sound change similar to cluster-splitting epenthesis in Oscan, an extinct Italic language known from inscriptions from approximately 400 BC - 100 CE, as in *aragetud* 'with money' (cf. Lat. *argentō*) and *sakarater* 'it is consecrated' (cf. Lat. *sacratūr*). However, the *rg cluster continued in *aragetud* was arguably heterosyllabic R.T (as opposed to tautosyllabic TR) and initial TR clusters are continued intact in Oscan as in *tristaa, triíbúm, prúfatted* (op cit.).

[4] In his discussion of East and West Iranian dialectology, Windfuhr (2009: 21) states the reflexes of initial #CC-clusters as showing a distinct areal distribution: "insertion of a short vowel, CVC-, along the Zagros, including the NW tier I from Kurdish, Zazaki to the SW Fars and Larestan dialects, as opposed to initial vowel, VCC-, elsewhere", while in the east, Balochi and most East Iranian languages allow initial clusters.

Siouan *TRV to #TV$_i$RV$_i$ in Hoocąk (aka Winnebago).[5] Examples from Rankin et al. (2015) are shown in (3).

(6) One case of cluster-splitting epenthesis in Siouan: Dorsey's Law in Hoocąk

	Chiwere	Hoocąk	Proto-Mississippi-Valley	gloss
a.	églųñį	waki/kųnųnį	*krų́rį	'forget'
b.	glé	keré	*kre	'go back to'
c.	wa/brú	ru/purú 'plough'	*prú	'powder'

While the time-depth of Siouan-Catawba is thought to be 2,000–3,000 years (Parks & Rankin 2001), Hoocąk and Chiwere are considered to be closely related and even sometimes treated as dialects of a single language (Miner 1979).[6] Given this, Dorsey's Law must be a relatively recent development.

Outside of the Persian and Hoocąk cases, it is difficult to find convincing cases of cluster-splitting epenthesis as a diachronic development. And here lies the central point of interest. Given that cluster-splitting epenthesis is common in loanword phonology (2), and appears to be a natural phonetically-motivated process, why is it rarely attested as a regular sound change? Why, out of more than 440 Indo-European languages, is there only one clear case of a #TRV$_i$ > #TV$_{(i)}$RV$_i$ sound change? And how should we understand the Siouan sister-languages Chiwere and Hoocąk, where Chiwere continues #TRV, but Hoocąk does not?

I suggest that cluster-splitting epenthesis is neither wholly natural nor wholly unnatural: non-phonetic structural and cognitive factors are involved. The structural condition is that cluster-splitting epenthesis occurs only when speakers of a language that *lacks* initial TR clusters begin to acquire a language that *has* initial TR clusters. It is only under this circumstance that the perceptual illusion of #TRV as #TVRV arises (cf. Dupoux et al. 1999), with this perceptual illusion constituting the cognitive catalyst for phonological change. An important component of this model is that regular sound changes of this kind will only occur under special types of language contact, where speakers dominant in a language that lacks initial consonant clusters suddenly (or without extensive exposure) acquire a language with #CR-clusters.[7] If extensive exposure occurs, perceptual illusions of phantom vowels will weaken, lowering the probability of epenthesis as regular sound change. Let us now evaluate this proposal with respect to the two cases of diachronic cluster-splitting epenthesis documented above.

---

[5] Dorsey's Law also refers to the resulting synchronic sound pattern in Hoocąk. It also applies to medial clusters. Since the syllabification of medial TR is ambiguous cross-linguistically, discussion is limited here to initial #TR where, at least utterance-initially, sequences constitute unambiguous complex onsets.

[6] Miner (1979: 25) begins his article with the statement that: "Winnebago and Chiwere ... are, in spite of their geographical separation in historical times, very closely related and enjoy a high degree of mutual comprehensibility." He also notes on the same page (footnote 1) that "Winnebago-Chiwere is sometimes referred to in the literature simply as Chiwere."

[7] For a similar proposal regarding paragoge (final vowel insertion), see Ng (2015), a dissertation supervised by Steve Anderson.

1 Between natural and unnatural phonology: The case of cluster-splitting epenthesis

Modern Persian phonology has had significant influence from Arabic and Turkic. Arabic loans constitute about half of the lexicon, and some estimate that of the most frequent vocabulary, at least 25% is Arabic (Perry 2004; 2005). Turkic loans also exist and there is a long history of Persian-Turkic bilingualism as well as Turkic "Persianization". Could acquisition of Persian by Arabic or Turkic speakers be the source of Modern Persian cluster-splitting epenthesis? I believe the answer is yes. More specifically, I suggest that the Persianization of Turkic people, such as the one occurring during the Ghaznavid dynasty (977–1186), and extending over large parts of Iran, was a critical factor in the evolution of cluster-splitting epenthesis in Modern Persian. Turkic languages have phonotactics that appears to be most important in triggering cluster-splitting-epenthesis: they disallow complex onsets in word-initial position (and elsewhere). Under this scenario, Middle Persian underwent rapid phonological change, as it was acquired by native speakers of Turkic languages across Iran. How early the process began is unknown, though it could have begun as early as the 10th century when Turkic speakers came to the area, or in the 11th and 12th centuries, when a large migration of Oghuz Turks resulted in the gradual "Turkification" of Azerbaijan and Anatolia (Frye 2004). Key (2012), who focuses on morphosyntactic effects of contact, suggests that Turkic influence may date from the Safavid state (1501–1736) "the rulers of which were Persianized Turks who spoke a variety of Middle Azerbaijanian that might actually have been a mixed language incorporating Ottoman elements (Stein 2005: 228)."[8] Frye (2004) presents a distinct view of the Safavids as Turkicized Iranians, but most seem to agree that it was the post-Islamic migration of Turks, as opposed to Arabic speakers, that had the most linguistic influence in the area: " ...the Turks who came, especially beginning from the tenth century, moved in sufficient numbers to change the linguistic map of the whole area. (op cit.)"

Though Classical Arabic also disallows onset clusters, there are several reasons to doubt Arabic as the source of cluster-splitting epenthesis in Modern Persian. First, evidence from early loans into Classical Arabic shows common prothetic vowels, with epenthesis the exception (cf. Arabic ʔiklīl 'crown , wreath' from Syriac klīlo, Arabic ʔiqlīm 'region' from Greek klīma; but also Arabic dirham 'money' from Greek drakhmi; Bueasa 2015). Second, the influence of Arabic on Middle Iranian languages came, primarily, through translation of religious texts into Arabic, and through acquisition of Arabic by writers and thinkers who used it as a prestige language. This socialization process was notably different from the Persianization of Turkic people referred to above, and resulted in significant loans, but no obvious evidence of Arabic influence on Persian grammar.

I hypothesize that cluster-splitting epenthesis in the history of Persian arose as a result of contact between speakers of Turkic languages, which did not allow complex onsets, and speakers of Middle Iranian languages with initial #TR-clusters. As Turks became Persianized, they acquired Persian (and, perhaps, other Middle Iranian languages). In this process, cognitive effects of CV(C) syllable structure resulted in the perception of illusory vowels in #TR-initial words (cf. Dupoux et al. 1999), giving rise to the change in

---

[8] Key's (2012) study of differential object marking in Turkic and Persian identifies Iranian Azerbaijan as an isogloss for this feature.

pronunciation schematized in (3). Under this account, the rarity of sound changes like (3) is attributed to three factors: first, initial #TR clusters are relatively stable over time, so (3) is unexpected as a language-internal development; second, a sound change of this kind requires contact between two distinct language types, one language which lacks complex onsets and another which has word-initial #TR; a third factor is the nature of the language contact involved, which must include social factors that demand rapid and full acquisition of the language with #TR clusters despite minimal previous exposure.[9] Only when these last two conditions are met will cluster-splitting epenthesis occur as a regular sound change.[10]

Can the same hypothesis involving language contact of a very specific type account for the evolution of Dorsey's Law in Hoocąk (Winnebago)? I believe so. Oral histories suggest that the split between Hoocąk, traditionally spoken between Green Bay and Lake Winnebago in present-day Wisconsin, and Chiwere, once spoken south and west of Hoocąk territory, occurred sometime in the mid-16th century, a time-line consistent with the great similarity between the two languages.[11] This would make the mid-16th century the earliest time at which Hoocąk could have developed cluster-splitting epenthesis, an innovation not found in Chiwere (3). By the time Jean Nicolet made contact with the "Ho-Chunk" in 1634, with an estimated population of 8,000 or more, their culture was very similar to that of surrounding Algonquian tribes, they were completely encircled by speakers of Algonquian languages, and the language had a significant number of borrowings from Central Algonquian languages (Radin 1990; Pfister 2009: 17).[12] I suggest that sometime between the mid-16th and mid-17th centuries, (pre-)Hoocąk was acquired by speakers of neighboring Algonquian languages. Since none of the Central Algonquian languages had initial #TR clusters, cognitive effects of #CV(C) syllable structure resulted in the perception of illusory vowels in #TR-initial words (cf. Dupoux et al. 1999), giving rise to Dorsey's Law. As with the contact scenario sketched for Modern Persian above, the evolution of cluster-splitting epenthesis is associated not only with these structural-cognitive factors, but also with a specific type of language contact: external social factors demanding rapid and full acquisition of a language, (pre-)Hoocąk, with initial #TR clusters by speakers of a language Central Algonquian language with only simple #C-onsets word-initially.

---

[9] This process is distinct from creolization, since the starting point here is not a pidgin. Interestingly, many Creoles show initial complex onsets (Klein 2013), consistent with the view here, that they are relatively stable, and not particularly "marked".

[10] An anonymous reviewer notes that if future generations have access to the donor language, and that language is prestigious, one may see a shift involving adoption of the donor phonotactics.

[11] Though the homeland of the Siouan-Catawba language family is widely debated, oral histories and archeological remains are consistent with (pre)-Hoocąk occupation of land between Green Bay and Lake Winnebago (in present-day northeast Wisconsin) in pre-contact times.

[12] By the late 1650s, the Hoocąk population may have been as few as 500 people, with great cultural devastation. This drastic decrease in population is attributed to a storm-related accident, epidemics (due to European contact), and/or battle losses to neighboring tribes (Edmunds 1978; Radin 1990).

4 Concluding remarks

The typology of sound change may seem like an odd place to uncover significant evidence of cognitive forces that are independent of universal phonetics, or evidence against widely assumed markedness constraints.[13] Yet, this study of cluster-splitting epenthesis as regular sound change suggests that typological studies of this kind may illuminate our understanding of the role of human cognition in shaping sound patterns, and the extent to which general aspects of memory, category formation, similarity metrics, and analogy contribute to their evolution (Blevins & Blevins 2009). Contrary to widely assumed markedness constraints treating all complex onsets as marked or dispreferred, the typology of sound change suggests that word-initial #TR clusters are phonotactically stable. On the other hand, in the rare cases where these clusters undergo regular cluster-splitting epenthesis, this epenthesis is not a simple case of "syllable-repair". Rather, native-language #CV-structure in language-contact situations results in the perception of phantom vowels which take on phonological status when speakers of #CV-initial languages must quickly, and with little earlier familiarity, acquire a language with #TR clusters. This, I suggest, was the original situation of Turkic speakers acquiring Persian, and of Central Algonquians acquiring Hoocąk. Unlike many other common sound patterns, regular cluster-splitting epenthesis does not have a simple phonetic explanation, and is not known as a purely language-internal development. By examining other sound changes with this profile, we may, unexpectedly, learn even more about the human mind.

References

Anderson, Stephen R. 1981. Why phonology isn't "natural". *Linguistic Inquiry* 12(4). 493–539.
Anderson, Stephen R. 1985. *Phonology in the Twentieth century: Theories of Rules and Theories of Representations*. Chicago: University of Chicago Press.
Anderson, Stephen R. 2001. Why linguistics needs the cognitive scientist. *Psychiatry* 64(1). 11–13.
Anderson, Stephen R. 2016. Synchronic versus diachronic explanation and the nature of the language faculty. *Annual Review of Linguistics* 2. 11–31.
Bach, Emmon & Robert Harms. 1972. How do languages get crazy rules? In Robert Stockwell & Ronald Macaulay (eds.), *Linguistic change and generative theory*. Bloomington: Indiana University Press.
Berent, Iris. 2013. *The phonological mind*. Cambridge: Cambridge University Press.
Blevins, James & Juliette Blevins. 2009. *Analogy in grammar: Form and acquisition*. Oxford: Oxford University Press.

---

[13] Though other instances of non-phonetic cognitive forces have been suggested. See, for example, Blevins & Wedel (2009), where lexical competition is argued to play an active role in shaping the typology of sound change.

Blevins, Juliette. 2004. *Evolutionary phonology: The emergence of sound patterns.* Cambridge: Cambridge University Press.

Blevins, Juliette. 2006. New perspectives on English sound patterns: 'Natural' and 'unnatural' in Evolutionary Phonology. *Journal of English Linguistics* 34. 6–25.

Blevins, Juliette. 2008a. Consonant epenthesis: Natural and unnatural histories. In Jeff Good (ed.), *Language universals and language change*, 79–107. Oxford: Oxford University Press.

Blevins, Juliette. 2008b. Natural and unnatural sound patterns: A pocket field guide. In Klaas Willems & Ludovic De Cuypere (eds.), *Naturalness and iconicity in language*, 121–48. Amsterdam: John Benjamins.

Blevins, Juliette. 2008c. Phonetic explanation without compromise: The evolution of Mussau syncope. *Diachronica* 25. 1–19.

Blevins, Juliette. 2015. Evolutionary phonology: A holistic approach to sound change typology. In Patrick Honeybone & Joseph Salmons (eds.), *Handbook of historical phonology*, 485–500. Oxford: Oxford University Press.

Blevins, Juliette & Ander Egurtzegi. 2016. The nature of obstruent loss in Basque borrowings with initial OR clusters. In *CUNY Phonology Forum*. The Graduate Center, New York.

Blevins, Juliette & Sven Grawunder. 2009. *K1 > T1 sound change in Germanic and elsewhere: Descriptions, explanations, and implications. *Linguistic Typology* 13. 267–303.

Blevins, Juliette & Andrew Wedel. 2009. Inhibited sound change: An evolutionary approach to lexical competition. *Diachronica* 26. 143–183.

Broselow, Ellen. 1987. Non-obvious transfer: on predicting epenthesis errors. In Georgette Ioup & Steven H. Weinberger (eds.), *Interlanguage phonology: the acquisition of a second language sound system*, 269–280. Rowely, MA: Newbury House Publishers.

Broselow, Ellen. 2015. The typology of position-quality interactions in loanword vowel insertion. In Y. Hsiao & L-H. Wee (eds.), *Capturing phonological shades*, 292–319. Cambridge: Cambridge Scholars Publishing.

Buckley, Eugene. 2000. On the naturalness of unnatural rules. *Santa Barbara Papers in Linguistics* 9. 16–29.

Bueasa, Noor Mohammed. 2015. *The adaptation of loanwords in Classical Arabic: The governing factors.* University of Kentucky MA thesis.

Campbell, Lyle. 2013. *Historical linguistics: An introduction.* Third Edition. Edinburgh: Edinburgh University Press.

Casparis, Johannes de. 1997. *Sanskrit loan-words in Indonesian: An annotated check-list of words from Sanskrit in Indonesian and traditional Malay.* Badan Penyelenggara Seri NUSA, Universitas Katolik Indonesia Atma Jaya.

Davidson, Lisa & Jason Shaw. 2012. Sources of illusion in consonant cluster perception. *Journal of Phonetics.* 234–248.

de Chene, Brent E. & Stephen R. Anderson. 1979. Compensatory lengthening. *Language* 55(3). 505–535.

Dorsey, J. Owen. 1885. On the comparative phonology of four Siouan languages. *Annual Report of the Board of Regents of the Smithsonian Institution* 919-929.

Dupoux, Emmanuel, Kazuhiko Kakehi, Yuki Hirose, Christophe Pallier & Jacques Mehler. 1999. Epenthetic vowels in Japanese: A perceptual illusion? *Journal of Experimental Psychology: Human Perception and Performance* 25. 1568–1578.

Edmunds, David. 1978. *The Potawatomis: Keepers of the fire*. Norman: University of Oklahoma Press.

Fleischhacker, Heidi. 2001. Cluster-dependent epenthesis asymmetries. In Adam Albright & Taehong Cho (eds.), *UCLA working papers in linguistics 7, Papers in phonology 5*, 71–116.

Fleischhacker, Heidi. 2005. *Similarity in phonology: Evidence from reduplication and loanword adaptation*. UCLA PhD thesis.

Fortson Benjamin W., IV. 2010. *Indo-European language and culture: An introduction*. Second Edition. London: John Wiley & Sons.

Frye, Richard. 2004. Peoples of Iran (1): A general survey. *Encyclopaedia Iranica* XIII(3). 321–326.

Garrett, Andrew & Juliette Blevins. 2009. Analogical morphophonology. In Sharon Inkelas & Kristin Hanson (eds.), *The Nature of the Word: Essays in honor of Paul Kiparsky*, 527–46. MIT Press.

Hall, Nancy. 2011. Vowel epenthesis. In Marc van Oostendorp, Colin Ewen, Elizabeth Hume & Keren Rice (eds.), *The Blackwell companion to phonology*, 1576–1596. Oxford: Wiley-Blackwell.

Hyman, Larry. 1970. The role of borrowing in the justification of phonological grammars. *Studies in African Linguistics* 1. 1–48.

Itô, Junko. 1989. A prosodic theory of epenthesis. *Natural Language and Linguistic Theory* 7(2). 217–259.

Kabak, Barış & William J. Idsardi. 2007. Perceptual distortions in the adaptation of English consonant clusters: syllable structure or consonantal contact constraints? *Language and Speech* 50(1). 23–52.

Kager, René. 1999. *Optimality theory*. Cambridge: Cambridge University Press.

Kang, Yoonjung. 2003. Perceptual similarity in loanword adaptation: English postvocalic word-final stops in Korean. *Phonology* 20. 219–273.

Kang, Yoonjung. 2011. Loanword phonology. In Marc van Oostendorp, Colin J. Ewen, Elizabeth Hume & Keren Rice (eds.), *The Blackwell companion to phonology*, 2258–2282. Wiley-Blackwell.

Karimi, Simin. 1987. Farsi speakers and the initial consonant cluster in English. In Georgette Ioup & Steven H. Weinberger (eds.), *Interlanguage phonology: the acquisition of a second language sound system*, 305–318. Rowely, MA: Newbury House Publishers.

Kavitskaya, Darya. 2002. *Compensatory lengthening: Phonetics, phonology, diachrony*. New York: Routledge.

Kenstowicz, Michael. 2007. Salience and similarity in loanword adaptation: A case study from Fijian. *Language Sciences* 29. 316–340.

Key, Greg. 2012. Differential object marking in Turkic and Persian as a contact phenomenon. In *Proceedings of the Annual Meeting of the Berkeley Linguistics Society*, vol. 38, 239–252.

Klein, Thomas. 2013. Typology of creole phonology: Phoneme inventories and syllable templates. In Parth Bhatt & Tonjes Veenstra (eds.), *Creole languages and linguistic typology*, 207–244. Amsterdam: John Benjamins.

Miner, Kenneth. 1979. Dorsey's Law in Winnebago-Chiwere and Winnebago accent. *International Journal of American Linguistics* 45. 25–33.

Ng, E-Ching. 2015. *The phonology of contact: Creole sound change in context*. Yale University PhD thesis.

Ohala, John. 1971. The role of physiological and acoustic models in explaining the direction of sound change. *Project on Linguistic Analysis Reports (Berkeley)* 15. 25–40.

Ohala, John. 1974. Experimental historical phonology. In J. M. Anderson & C. Jones (eds.), *Historical linguistics II. Theory and description in phonology [Proceedings of the 1st International Conference on Historical Linguistics]*, 353–389. Amsterdam: North Holland.

Ohala, John. 1993. The phonetics of sound change. In Charles Jones (ed.), *Historical linguistics: Problems and perspectives*, 237–278. London: Longman.

Parks, Douglas & Robert Rankin. 2001. The Siouan languages. In Raymond DeMallie & William Sturtevant (eds.), *Handbook of North American Indians: Plains*, vol. 13, 94–114. Washington, D.C.: Smithsonian Institution.

Peperkamp, Sharon & Emmanuel Dupoux. 2002. A typological study of stress "deafness". *Laboratory phonology* 7. Carlos Gussenhoven & Natasha Warner (eds.). 203–240.

Perry, John. 2004. Arabic elements in Persian. *Encyclopaedia Iranica* 2. online version, www.iranicaonline.org/articles., 229–36.

Perry, John. 2005. Lexical areas and semantic fields of Arabic loanwords in Persian and beyond. In Carina Jahani, Bo Isaksson & Éva Ágnes Csató (eds.), *Linguistic convergence and areal diffusion: Case studies from Iranian, Semitic and Turkic*, 97–110. New York: Routledge.

Pfister, Joel. 2009. *The Yale Indian: The education of Henry Roe Cloud*. Chapel Hill: Duke University Press.

Prince, Alan & Paul Smolensky. 1993. *Optimality Theory: Constraint interaction in generative grammar*. Oxford: Blackwell Publishing.

Radin, Paul. 1990. *The Winnebago tribe*. Lincoln: University of Nebraska Press.

Rankin, Robert, Richard Carter, A. Welsey Jones, John Koontz, David Rood & Iren Harmann (eds.). 2015. *Comparative Siouan dictionary*. Leipzig: Max Planck Institute for Evolutionary Anthropology.

Stein, Heidi. 2005. Traces of Türki-yi Acemi in Pietro della Valle's Turkish Grammar (1620). In Éva Ágnes Csató, Bo Isaksson & Carina Jahani (eds.), *Linguistic convergence and areal diffusion: Case studies from Iranian, Semitic and Turkic*. New York: Routledge Curzon.

Strain, Jeris. 1968. A contrastive sketch of the Persian and English sound systems. *International Review of Applied Linguistics* 6. 55–62.

Uffmann, Christian. 2007. *Vowel epenthesis in loanword adaptation*. Tübingen: Max Niemeyer Verlag.

Vaux, Bert. 2002. *Consonant epenthesis and the problem of unnatural phonology*. Department of Linguistics, Harvard University MA thesis.

1 Between natural and unnatural phonology: The case of cluster-splitting epenthesis

Windfuhr, Gernot. 2009. Dialectology and topics. In Gernot Windfuhr (ed.), *The Iranian languages*, 5–42. New York: Routledge.

Windfuhr, Gernot & John Perry. 2009. Persian and Tajik. In Gernot Windfuhr (ed.), *The Iranian languages*, 416–544. New York: Routledge.

Chapter 2

The domain of stress assignment: Word-boundedness and frequent collocation

Ellen Kaisse
University of Washington

> Phenomena that a theory of the human language faculty ought to accommodate might well happen never to be attested because there is no course of change or borrowing by which they could arise. (Anderson 1992: 336)

The linguistic literature treats hundreds of processes that apply between adjacent, open class content words. Overwhelmingly, these processes are local, segmental adjustments applying between the last segment of one word and the first segment of the next, such as voicing or place assimilation. Most other kinds of processes are profoundly underrepresented. Notably, iterative processes that eat their way across words such as vowel harmony, consonant harmony, or footing (assignment of rhythmic stress) typically do not extend beyond the word or count material outside the word when locating a particular stressable syllable, such as the penult. This result becomes more understandable when one considers how processes are phonologized from their phonetic precursors. Precursors are articulatorily or perceptually motivated and are strongest in temporally adjacent segments; they lose their force as the distance between segments increases, so there are no strong precursors for iteration outside of a word. Furthermore, frequent repetition leads to phonologization (Bybee 2006). Any content word in a lexicon occurs next to any other content word much less frequently than do roots plus their affixes, hosts plus clitics, or any combination that includes at least one closed class item. So we should expect roots and affixes or hosts and clitics to be much more common as domains for stress assignment or other iterative rules than are strings of independent lexical items. In this paper, I concentrate on the near non-existence of stress assignment rules that span a domain larger than a morphological word plus clitics. We look at one revealing case that does treat some pairs of content words as a single span: stress assignment in literary Macedonian (Lunt 1952). The spans involve frequent collocations –

Ellen Kaisse. 2017. The domain of stress assignment: Word-boundedness and frequent collocation. In Claire Bowern, Laurence Horn & Raffaella Zanuttini (eds.), *On looking into words (and beyond)*, 17–41. Berlin: Language Science Press. DOI:10.5281/zenodo.495437

groups of already frequent words that are frequently heard together, sometimes to the extent that they have developed a lexicalized meaning. The other interword Macedonian cases involve closed class item such as prepositions and interrogatives. Finally, we consider evidence that rhythm can be evidenced statistically in the syntactic choices speakers make (Anttila, Adams & Speriosu 2010; Shih 2016), concluding that there may be rhythmic pressures from the lexicon to make phrases eurhythmic as well as eurhythmic pressures from phrases that can be phonologized to create rules of lexical stress assignment.

1 Introduction: what kinds of processes are postlexical and where do stress rules fit in?

Some types of phonological processes seem always to apply solely within a single word, not taking into account any material in adjacent words, while other types can apply between words. In work to appear (Kaisse Forthcoming) I surveyed the literature on lexical (word-bounded) and postlexical (non-word-bounded) rules, sampling about 70 careful descriptions of non-tonal processes that make up their focus and environment from material that spans more than one content word.[1] Only a few involve anything other than strictly local adjustments between the last segment of one word and the first segment of the next. They might require agreement in voicing, place of articulation, or other features. Or they might avoid onset-less syllables by deleting or desyllabifying a word final vowel when the next word begins with a vowel, or by moving a word final consonant into the onset of the next, vowel-initial word. (1) contains some fairly familiar examples from Spanish. (1a) illustrates postlexical voice assimilation of /s/ to [z] before voiced consonants and assimilation of continuancy (/g/ → [ɣ] and /b/ → [β]) after that /s/; (1b) shows place assimilation of a nasal to a following consonant and the retention of an underlying stop after non-continuant /n/; (1c) shows reduction of hiatus; and (1d) shows resyllabification of a word-final consonant:

(1) Spanish (personal knowledge)
  a. /los ˈgato-s ˈbjen-en/ → [loz ˈɣatoz ˈβjenen]
   the cat-PL come-3PL
   'The cats are coming.'

  b. /ˈbjen-en ˈgato-s/ → [ˈbjeneŋ ˈgatos]
   come-3PL cat-PL
   'Cats are coming.'

---

[1] Some tonal processes are well known to span large numbers of syllables, both within and between words (Hyman 2011), though many are also word-bounded. In Kaisse (forthcoming) I endorse David Odden's (p.c. 2015) speculation about the long-distance behavior of tonal adjustments in Bantu languages, which offer the most numerous and robust examples of processes where several tones in one word can be affected by a distant tone in an adjacent word. Odden cites the perceptual difficulty of locating tone in Bantu, with its long words and subtle cues for tone, and tone's low functional load there, since only H, not L tone needs to be marked.

2 The domain of stress assignment: Word-boundedness and frequent collocation

c. /ˈteŋ-o ˈotro-s/ → [ˈteŋ ˈotros]
have-1SG other-PL
'I have others.'

d. /ˈtjen-es ˈotro-s/ → [ˈtje.ne.ˈso.tros]
have-2SG other-PL
'You have others.'

Really, any local adjustment that is found within words can be found between words. This exuberance of types is probably due to the fact that most phonologized processes start life as natural local effects and these effects are not sensitive to grammatical information but rather to temporal adjacency (Kiparsky 1982 et seq.). However, I found almost no vowel harmony processes that extended into an adjacent content word, no consonant harmony processes (Hansson 2010), and, crucially for the current paper, no stress rules with a domain larger than the morphological word or the morphological word plus clitics. Compare the familiar types of examples in (1) with the fanciful ones in (2), where something resembling the English rule that constructs moraic trochees from the end of a word takes a whole noun phrase as its domain, resulting in feet that span syllables belonging to different words and in wide-scale allomorphy:

(2) Fanciful English with noun phrase as initial domain of footing

a. ×
   (×)(× .)
   / taj ni dag /
   [ˌtajˈnidəg]
   'tiny dog'

b.   ×
   (× .)(× .)
   / taj ni kɪ tɛn/
   [ˌtajniˈkɪrən]
   'tiny kitten'

c.   ×
   (×)(× .)(× .)
   / taj ni pɪ ɹa na /
   [ˌtajˌnipəˈɹanə]
   'tiny piranha'

In this paper, I will describe the continuum of stress behavior of cohering and non-cohering affixes (i.e. affixes that do and do not interact phonologically with their bases), clitics of varying degrees of stress-interaction with their hosts, compound words, and the one detailed presentation of a stress rule I have encountered where initial stress assignment takes some strings of content words and treats them as a single domain, ignoring any stress the component words might otherwise have in isolation. That case comes from literary Macedonian (Lunt 1952; Franks 1987; 1989).

Before continuing, I should make it clear that there are many rhythmic adjustments that do apply between content words – cases like the Rhythm Rule in English (Hayes 1984) which is responsible for the retraction of the secondary stress in ˌJapanese 'language (vs. ˌJapa'nese) or ˌMississippi 'mud vs. ˌMissi'ssippi. These kinds of cases are postlexical and involve prosodically self-sufficient content words that have had their own stresses assigned lexically, independent of the larger context in which they find themselves. There is then a rhythmic adjustment that demotes or moves a nonprimary stress in order to avoid stress clash. Like the invented example (2), the Macedonian case that I will look at instead involves assigning a single antepenultimate stress to a string of two content words which, in other syntactic contexts, would each receive a stress of their own. Often the single stress does not fall on any of the syllables that would have been stressed in isolation. This is clearly different from the way a rhythm rule works.

Another example of postlexical stress adjustment, as opposed to the first pass of stress assignment, involves compound stress rules. Again, these are not relevant to my claim that pairs of content words are almost never the domain of the first pass of stress assignment. The most well-known of these compound stress rules, like that of English, also simply adjust the relative primary stresses of the members, rather than treating them as a single unit for the lexical footing process. Thus, if we put together *lin'guistics* and *'scholar* we get *lin'guistics ˌscholar*, with the primary stress of *'scholar* subordinated to that of *lin'guistics*, but we do not stress the whole string as a single prosodic word, which might result in antepenultimate stress falling on the last syllable of the first member, with the bizarre (for English) output *lingui'stics scholar*. We shall see, however, that occasionally languages (such as Modern Greek) do take compound words as the initial domain of stress assignment. So while prosodically independent content words are not commonly the domain for the first pass of stress assignment, some languages stretch that domain to include both members of a compound word.

Yet another aspect of the postlexical adjustment of stress is offered by Newman's (1944: 28–29) insightful early discussion of stress domains in Yokuts, pointed out to me by an anonymous referee. Nouns and verbs maintain their lexical stresses in connected speech but function words tend to lean on them and to lack stresses of their own, and the faster the speech, the bigger the phrasing groups and the fewer the perceived stresses. Newman's description is perforce rather general and impressionistic, but it summarizes well the plasticity of postlexical stress adjustments, which favor cliticization of function words and variable rhythmic groupings dependent on tempo and number of syllables.[2]

While truly grammaticized rhythmic stress assignment almost never takes an initial domain beyond a word and its affixes and clitics, there are now known to be gradient rhythmic effects that extend beyond the word. They simply don't seem to be able to rise to the level of phonologization in that larger domain. Martin (2007), Anttila, Adams & Speriosu (2010), and Shih (2016) have found that vowel harmony (Martin) and optimization of rhythm can have statistical reflections in Turkish compound words and in

---

[2] I cannot tell from Newman's description how content words that are not nouns or verbs might behave. I tentatively conclude that he is referring only to lack of stress on function words in rapid connected speech, not to complete loss of stress on open class modifiers or other content words.

English word order. That is, to use Martin's felicitous phrasing, lexical generalizations that are part of the grammar can "leak" into larger domains, causing statistical preferences for outputs that are consonant with the phonology of a language's words. I would add that it is hard to know what the primary direction of leakage really is: the leakage Martin and Shih posit from smaller domains to larger ones probably co-exists with the direction of larger-to-smaller domain phonologization, which I posit in Kaisse (Forthcoming) and which is the staple view of Lexical Phonology and its descendants (Kiparsky 1982; Bermudez-Otero 2015) and of most traditional approaches to sound change. In Kaisse (Forthcoming) I used the example of the phonetic precursor of vowel harmony, namely the vowel-to-vowel coarticulation that peters out as one gets farther away from the source vowel (Öhman 1966; Ohala 1992; Flemming 1997), which can be grammaticized within words because stems and their affixes are in frequent collocation (Bybee 2006)[3]. Classical Lexical Phonology postulates this one-way direction (from postlexical and variable or gradient to lexical and regular and obligatory), but there is no reason that once a rule is lexicalized, it cannot then generalize postlexically again (Kaisse 1993). One can imagine a feedback loop, where small postlexical variation in favor of alternating stresses and avoidance of stress clash starts to be phonologized as iterative footing, while iterative footing starts to make syntactic phrases that are eurhythmic more desirable as choices for speakers in real time.

There is a continuum of likely domains for foot-construction. Selkirk (1995), Peperkamp (1997) and Anderson (2011) demonstrate that there are various types of clitics that range from more to less rhythmically cohesive (interactive) with their hosts. I will extend the continuum, showing that in literary Macedonian (Lunt 1952; Franks 1987; 1989) the lexical stress rule assigning antepenultimate stress has stretched its domain to include even two content words, but only when they are in frequent collocation and, in some of the cases, have taken on a more lexicalized, semantically less compositional meaning. This is the "exception that proves the rule." In general, only the supremely frequent collocation of a closed class bound morpheme – an affix – with another affix or the root it can attach to provides the frequent collocation that allows for phonologization. However, occasionally even two content words can appear together so frequently that they become subject to the first pass of the lexical stress rules of the language; they act like a single word for the purposes of building a foot at the edge of a word. Clitics and function words in Macedonian also form part of the initial domain for this foot-building. This accords with the general observation that the phonology of clitics is like the phonology of affixes in many cases – they are 'phrasal affixes' (Anderson 1992). Clitics are usually less cohering than stem-level affixes but, as we shall illustrate in §2, there are even a few that act like they are inside the phonological word for the purpose of foot-construction. But basic foot building algorithms do not typically extend beyond the morphological word.

---

[3] Barnes (2006) cites Inkelas et al. (2001) for evidence that phonetic vowel-to-vowel coarticulation is problematic as a simple, unaided source for vowel harmony. Their argument comes from Turkish, where anticipatory phonetic effects are stronger than perseveratory ones, but the phonologized harmony system is perseveratory. He instead attributes the phonologization of vowel harmony to vowel-to-vowel coarticulation coupled with lengthening of the trigger syllable and paradigm uniformity effects allowing longer-distance effects on distant affixes.

Occasionally they extend even less far than that, as in the case of non-cohering (stress neutral) suffixes of English, and occasionally they extend into the larger phonological word, which can include clitics and other function words that can have stressless variants – i.e. be prosodically deficient, in Anderson's (2011)'s terms. Indeed, the failure of an affix to participate in the lexical footing domain is one of the main ways in which non-cohering affixes have been defined. Note for instance that Chomsky & Halle (1968: 84ff) use the term "stress neutral" for the group of suffixes which, to anticipate the later interpretation of their intentions, are outside the prosodic word. These suffixes, which include all the inflectional affixes, as well as a number derivational affixes such as #*ly*, #*ness*, agentive #*er*, #*ful*, and many others, not only fail to affect stress but also don't induce word-internal rules like Trisyllabic Shortening and Sonorant Syllabification. (See Kiparsky 1982 for a full discussion of Trisyllabic Laxing and Kaisse 2005 for a summary of the characteristics of English cohering suffixes.) Indeed, we might ask why stress is one of the most typical diagnostics for cohering suffixes, and not only in English. I would speculate that rhythm is hard to grammaticize as a phonological process without frequent repetition of the same strings. Like clitics, word-level suffixes have less stringent subcategorization restrictions. Fabb (1988), which we will discuss in a bit more detail in §2 discovered that the possible combinations of English stem-level suffixes with other suffixes or with roots are very restricted. On the other hand, word-level suffixes can combine freely with many suffixes and words, and therefore are not in as frequent collocation as the stem level ones, which are heard over and over again with the same preceding morpheme, be it an affix or a root. Clitics are even less demanding of the preceding host – indeed in some cases, such as special clitics, the host can belong to any part of speech and can even be a phrase – so they are less likely to be phonologized as part of the stress domain. But because they are prosodically unable to stand on their own, they must lean on a host and thus may sometimes be phonologized as part of the stress domain.

2 Clitics and the stress domain continuum

There has been considerable attention paid to the various ways that clitics – prosodically deficient items that must lean on a host in some fashion – interact with the lexical stress assignment rules of a language and fall into their domain. I will summarize some recent results here because I believe that the insights from clitics can help us understand how compound words and even some phrases can come to behave in the same way as clitics do with respect to their hosts.

It is worth reviewing some of the typical diagnostics of clitics (paraphrased from Zwicky & Pullum 1983):

(3) Characteristics of clitics
   a. clitics have a low degrees of selection with respect to their hosts; affixes have a higher degree of selection.

b. affixed words are more likely to have idiosyncratic semantics than host + clitic combinations
c. affixed words are treated as a unit by the syntax while hosts plus their clitics are not.

To these we can add that while the boundary between a root and stem-level (cohering) affix is the most favorable position for phonological interactions to occur, and the boundary between base and word-level (non-cohering) suffixes somewhat less favorable, clitics are sometimes phonologically even less connected – less cohesive – with their hosts; they might fail, for instance, to undergo vowel harmony, the last segment of their hosts might undergo word-final devoicing, as if there were no following segment, and as we shall see, in some languages, the clitics might not be visible to the lexical stress rules or at least to the first pass of those rules.

Beginning with Anderson's (1992) classification of clitics as phrasal affixes as a foundation, Selkirk (1995) and Peperkamp (1997), elaborated in Anderson (2011), propose a hierarchy of clitic types. Ranked from least-cohering to most cohering with respect to phonological interaction with their host, we have the continuum in (4):

(4) The clitic continuum
prosodic word clitic > free clitic > affixal clitic > internal clitic
a. Prosodic Word Clitic
b. Free Clitic
c. Affixal Clitic
d. Internal Clitic

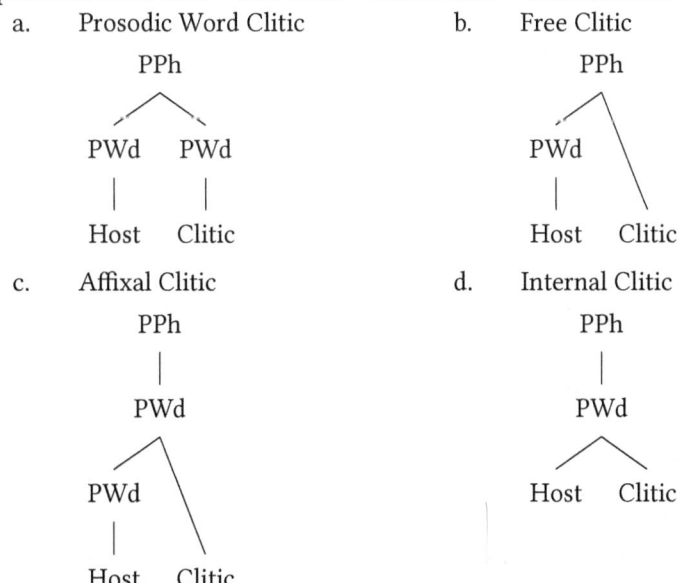

Intuitively speaking, we know that clitics usually fall somewhere in between the phonological cohesiveness of stem-level, highly cohering affixes and the phonological non-cohesiveness of independent prosodic words. But in this elaborated hierarchy, not all clitics do. There are clitics termed 'internal' by Selkirk that act, at least for some processes, exactly like stem-level affixes. We will extend this notion to the compound words of

Modern Greek and the extended stress domains of Macedonian – these involve normally prosodically independent words that nonetheless act as a single domain and receive one stress as if they were a single word. On the other end, there are clitics that Selkirk terms 'prosodic word clitics;' these are forced in some cases to behave like independent prosodic words despite their underlying prosodic deficiency. In (5), I illustrate the internal type with the example of verbal clitics in Formentera Catalan (Torres-Tamarit & Pons-Moll 2015), where the whole verb-clitic complex is used to assign moraic trochees from the right. This can result in no stress falling on the verb stem itself if there are two monosyllabic clitics (5d) or one monosyllabic clitic followed by a clitic consisting of a single consonant that makes a heavy syllable (5e). The raising of the root /o/ of the imperative verb in (5b–5e), which only occurs to unstressed mid vowels, suggests that stress is not assigned cyclically to the root and then again to the host-clitic complex, but rather all in one go to the entire string:

(5) Formentera Catalan (Torres-Tamarit & Pons-Moll 2015) internal clitics
/kompr-ə/

    a. ˈkompr-ə
       buy   -2SG.IMP
       'Buy!'

    b. kumˈpr-ə   =l
       buy   -2SG.IMP=3SG.M.ACC
       'Buy it/him!'

    c. kumˈpr-ə   =n
       buy   -2SG.IMP=PART
       'Buy some!'

    d. kumpr-ə   =ˈmə =lə
       buy   -2SG.IMP=1SGDAT=3SG.F.ACC
       'Buy it/her for me!'

    e. kumpr-ə   =ˈmə =l
       buy   -2SG.IMP=1SG.DAT=3M.ACC
       'Buy it/him for me!'

Internal clitics meet the criteria of low selection, predictable semantics, and so forth, but phonologically they are unusual – they act like stem-level affixes. The situation in Formentera is similar to that described for Lucanian Italian clitics by Peperkamp (1997). Formentera and Lucanian internal clitics are wholly included within the phonological word and count from the outset in the calculation of where a right edge trochaic foot should be built.

    More generally speaking, internal clitics are prosodically deficient words that act more cohesively in their phonological interaction with their host than their other characteristics would suggest they should. This is captured in Selkirk's framework by having them form a single prosodic word in combination with their host. Their hallmark is that they

2 The domain of stress assignment: Word-boundedness and frequent collocation

are stressed and generally processed by the word-bounded on the first pass, acting just like a stem-level affix. This means that they can never receive a second stress all their own, but they may happen to be in position to take the stress of the whole host-clitic string, as illustrated in the Formentera form (5d) [kumprə='mə=lə], where the clitic /mə/ receives the penultimate stress for the whole host-clitic complex. I suggest that we can profitably extend this insight onto bigger, more independent words than clitics. We will see in §3 that Modern Greek treats the otherwise independent pieces of a compound word as a single domain for stress assignment – a comparatively rare phenomenon. And Macedonian (§4) treats prepositions, even polysyllabic ones, as a single stress domain with their objects and treats certain common collocations of adjective + noun as a single stress domain as well. To put it another way, one occasionally encounters situations where a pair of words that should be expected to be prosodically independent can act like 'internal words,' parallel to the notion of internal clitics. I will link this unusual phenomenon to frequency of collocation. The more exemplars there are of a string of words, repeatedly heard together, the more likely they are to be internalized as a rhythmic group and to be reified as a domain for the assignment of a single stress.

At the other end of the continuum of independence of clitics lie the Prosodic Word clitics, which receive postlexical treatment as independent prosodic words even though they are underlyingly prosodically deficient. They are illustrated by the prevocalic clitics of Bilua (Obata 2003, reported in Anderson 2011), where preconsonantal proclitics are normally free – they are outside the domain of stress assignment, which targets the first syllable of the word:

(6) Bilua (Obata 2003, Anderson 2011: 2004) free clitic
 o= 'βουβαε=k   =a
 3SG.M=kill   =3SG.FEM.OBJ=TNS
 'He killed it.'

When a host word begins with a vowel, however, the usually stressless clitics instead take on a derived prosodic word-hood of their own and receive an independent stress:

(7) Bilua (Obata 2003, Anderson 2011) PWd clitic under duress
 'o= 'οdiε=k   =a
 3SG.M=call =3SG.FEM.OBJ=TNS
 'He called her.'

In this case, the clitic is forced to act like content words do normally.

A referee has expressed some doubt about the proper analysis of Bilua clitics and, by extension, whether the category of prosodic clitics needs to exist at all. But it is useful to suspend our skepticism and contemplate such an entity because it illustrates the opposite side of a prosodic coin. The putative prosodic clitics are elements that are inherently prosodically deficient, but that can be forced under certain circumstances to act as independent prosodic words with their own stress. Macedonian nouns and adjectives in certain frequent collocations are inherently prosodically independent elements that can be forced under certain circumstances to act as prosodically deficient pieces of a single prosodic word, as are the words that make up a compound in Modern Greek.

To complete the hierarchy, there are clitics whose characteristics of independence place them between internal and Prosodic Word clitics. The affixal clitics and the free clitics are probably the ones that linguists are most used to encountering. An affixal clitic shows some prosodic independence from its host: it is not included in the domain of footing on the first pass. In Selkirk's framework it forms a recursive prosodic word with that host, and it therefore may receive or induce an additional stress or stress shift once it is included in a second pass of stress assignment. When word stress falls on the penult or antepenult of a content word, we find an additional stress added to a string of clitics if they can form a foot, as shown in the third column of (8) (Binary footing is indicated with parentheses.):

(8) Neapolitan Italian (Peperkamp 1997) affixal clitics
 a. ˈkonta ˈkonta=lə (ˈkonta)=(ˈti=llə)
    tell.IMP tell.IMP=it tell.IMP=you=it
 b. ˈpettina ˈpettina =lə (ˈpetti)na=(ˈti=llə)
    comb.IMP comb.IMP=it comb.IMP=you=it

Neapolitan Italian treats the morphological word, sans clitics, as the basic, initial domain of footing, but clitics are partially cohering, falling into a larger domain that still follows the basic principles of word-internal stress assignment. In Neapolitan, if the stress assigned to the clitic sequence clashes with the stress of the host, the host's stress is lost:

(9) Neapolitan Italian (Peperkamp 1997) affixal clitics with clash reduction
 ˈfa ˈfal =lə fa =ˈtti =llə
 do.IMP do.IMP=it do.IMP=you=it

The parallel for us here is that the pieces of compound words and larger phrases usually receive stress treatment individually for their component parts, but a postlexical pass of stress assignment can promote, move, or demote one of the stresses once the two elements are considered together in a larger domain. In English compounding, as we have mentioned, the component prosodic words each receive a lexical stress but the rhythm of the two is adjusted when they come together, promoting the first stress to primary:

(10) English compound
 linˈguistics deˈpartment → linˈguistics deˌpartment

And in English phrases, which typically have the most prominent stress on the final content word, the Rhythm Rule (Hayes 1984) adjusts the tertiary and secondary stresses of the first word in that phrase to avoid stress clash with the primary stress.

(11) English phrase

```
                 ×                        ×
       ×    ×                   ×         ×
   (× .)(×) (×    .)          (× .)(×) (×    .)
   [Japanese] [language]  →   [Japanese] [language]
```

2 The domain of stress assignment: Word-boundedness and frequent collocation

The last type of clitic we need to discuss is 'free.' Such clitics simply do not interact with their host for the purposes of stress assignment. They are not themselves independent prosodic words but do not fall inside of any prosodic word and thus are invisible to every pass of footing. For instance, Barcelona Catalan verbs (Torres-Tamarit & Pons-Moll 2015) show the same stress whether or not they have enclitics, and the stress can fall three or even four syllables from the end of the word, in contravention to the generalization that there is a three-syllable final stress window and that stress is typically penultimate.

(12) Barcelona Catalan (Torres-Tamarit & Pons-Moll 2015)
    a. 'kompr-ə
        buy   -2SG.IMP
        'Buy!'
    b. 'kompr-ə   =mə   =lə
        buy   -2SG.IMP=1SGDAT=3SG.F.ACC
        'Buy it/her for me!'
    c. 'kompr-ə   =mə   =l
        buy   -2SG.IMP=1SGDAT=3SG.M.ACC
        'Buy it/him for me!'

The parallel for larger units is this: in §4.4 we will see that while some Macedonian prepositions are inherently stressless and are included in a stress-assignment domain with their objects (i.e. they are 'internal'), others always remain stressless and do not form a domain with their objects (i.e. they are free).

Even though stress is very often iterative within a word and its stem-level affixes, it can be unable to cross even the relatively weak boundary of a word level suffix. Consider for instance the lack of movement of stress from the base in English words suffixed by word-level suffixes such as #hood and #ly, and the concomitant location of stress outside the lexically mandated window of the last three syllables:

(13) English
    a. 'dialect#hood (c.f. 'dialect, 'dia'lect-al)
    b. 'manifestly (c.f. 'manifest, ˌmanifes'tation)

If even an affix can be outside the domain of stress assignment and other phonological processes, it is not surprising that stress assignment often does not count clitics on the initial pass (or ever), let alone treat them as single domain compound words, words plus function items leaning on them, or the strings of prosodically independent content words.

Let us tie these increasingly unlikely domains for stress assignment to frequency of collocation. Cohesive affixes are typically less productive and more selective with respect to the stems they combine with than are non-cohesive affixes, which are somewhat clitic-like. There is thus a hierarchy of selectiveness tied to frequency of collocation:[4]

(14) Hierarchy of selectiveness
- stem-level cohering affixes
- word-level non-cohering affixes
- clitics
- compound words
- words in fixed expressions
- collocations involving closed class items, such as prepositions, even if they are polysyllabic
- truly novel or unpredictable collocations that are clearly not listed in the lexicon

For instance, Fabb (1988) discovered that the English stem-level adjective-forming suffix *-ous* has very narrow sectional restrictions. It cannot attach after any other affix at all. It's clear that *-ous* is stem level because it affects the stress of its base (*'moment, mo'mentous*), triggers Trisyllabic Laxing (*'ōmen, 'ŏminous*) and meets the various other tests for cohesion in the literature. Similarly, the stem-level adjective-forming suffix *-ic* attaches only after the suffix *-ist* (*capitalistic*), and the stem-level adjective-forming suffix *-ary* attaches only after the suffix *-ion* (*revolutionary*). On the other hand, word-level adjective-forming #*y* can attach productively to virtually any noun (*chocolate#y*, or *protein#y*, recently heard on a yoghurt commercial), and it can occur in novel coinages after most other noun-forming suffixes (*musi-cian#y, profess-or#y*.) Like clitic-host semantics, the meanings of words with word-level affixes are usually transparent. Finally, notice that *'chocolate#y* has primary stress in the same place as the base *'chocolate*, even though, if *'chocolate* is pronounced with three syllables, stress in *'chocolate#y* falls in an otherwise impossible pre-antepenultimate position. The same is true for *'manifestly* (13b). Non-cohesive affixes are in a sense invisible to the lexical phonology of the language and can violate various of its requirements.

Clitics are even less selective than word-level affixes. For example, many Romance, Greek and Slavic clitics attach to any verb and after any set of affixes. Similarly, the English contracted auxiliary =*s* can be found leaning leftward on words of almost any category.

(15) English
    a. That man's a linguist;
    b. The thing you are leaning on's not safe;
    c. What you think's not important;

---

[4] A referee raises the excellent question of "whether this hierarchy predicts an implicational typology of stress domains, e.g. if a language treats compound words as a single stress domain, then clitics and all affixes should be parsed within the same stress domain as their host." I do not know the answer to this question, though it does seem to be true for Modern Greek (discussed for instance in Anderson 2011 as having affixal clitics which affect the stress of their hosts) and for Macedonian.

d. Skin that looks pink's an indication of good circulation.

And both within compounds and within sentences almost any word can be followed by almost any other word – there are almost no selectional requirements. However, some words belong to closed classes – prepositions, relative and interrogative elements, and other function words and therefore will recur sequences more frequently. This cline lines up with the likelihood of two elements being taken into a single stress domain.

The hierarchy in (14) will take us through the extended domain cases of Macedonian, where prepositions – even polysyllabic and semantically rich ones – are unstressable on their own, always forming a stress domain with their complements or being unstressable, and where frequent collocations of content words, particularly involving frequent words or collocations with unpredictable or frozen semantics, are stressed as if they were single words.

3 Compounds and the stress domain continuum

The continuum of domain size we have observed for clitics continues outward into compounds. To review, there are clitics of various sorts: the 'internal' type which is considered in the first pass of stress assignment, the more familiar type which figures in a second pass that takes into account previously assigned stresses, and a third, free type, which is never counted for stress. My impression is that it is even more uncommon to find compound words – i.e. words made of otherwise prosodically independent elements – forming a single domain for the first pass of footing. Rather, as we noted earlier, members of a compound are rather like affixal clitics, where a postlexical instantiation of rhythm may adjust the stresses on the basis of the newly available material but does not erase earlier, lexically assigned footing. But this is not always the case.

Modern Greek demonstrates the comparatively rare type of compounding where a compound word is stressed as a single domain. It has been shown instrumentally by Athanasopoulou & Vogel (2014) that the well-known traditional description, sharpened in Ralli (2013), of a single, usually antepenultimate primary stress, is correct. The stress is placed without regard to where the stresses would fall in the individual members in isolation. A compounding morpheme -o is often inserted at the end of the first member (replacing any final inflectional ending) and stress falls on one of the last three syllables of the whole compound, most commonly the antepenult:

(16)   Modern Greek (Athanasopoulou & Vogel 2014; Ralli 2013)
   a. ˈlik -os
      wolf-M.SG.NOM
   b. ˈskil-os
      dog-M.SG.NOM
   c. lík -o-   skil-o
      wolf-CMPD-dog-N.SG.NOM
      'wolfhound'

d. ˈriz -i
rice-N.SG.NOM

e. ˈɣala
milk

f. riˈz -o- ɣal -o
rice-CMPD-milk-N.SG.NOM
'rice pudding'

Tokyo Japanese (Poser 1990; Kubozono 2008) has a similar phenomenon whereby a single pitch accent is assigned within a compound based, they argue, on foot structure.

A referee points out that English compounds, especially those ending in the element *-man,* can sometimes have only a single stress, reminiscent of the Greek case here and of some Macedonian cases to come. While I have not found a published study on this phenomenon, *Language Log* (Liberman 2015) has an informative post that discusses the unstressed, hence reduced, final vowels in such words as *fireman, clansman, gentleman* versus the full final vowels in words like *caveman, handyman,* and *weatherman.* A lively set of reader responses about which words have a schwa versus the expected compound stress and full final vowel seems to lead to the conclusion that the longer a *-man* compound has been in English, the more likely it is to have a single stress. The situation here may be the demotion of a compound to a single word over time rather than a Greek-like treatment of a compound word as a single stress domain, but it falls under the general rubric of familiarity breeding unitary stress domains. However, the reader consensus is that there is no simple connection to actual contemporary frequency in the behavior of *-man.*

I had believed that the Greek case was as far as regular stress domains ever extend. However, there is at least one case I am now aware of where the domain extends into some combinations of prosodically independent words – Literary Macedonian.[5]

4 Enlarged stress domains in Macedonian

4.1 Overview

We have seen that while stem level affixes virtually always are taken into account in the first pass of foot building, many languages have stress neutral word-level affixes like English *#ly, #ness,* that are not part of the stress domain. Indeed, stress neutrality seems to be a recurrent, if not definitional characteristic of non-cohesiveness. This suggests that rhythm is not easily maintained or phonologized over large domains. Continuing along this cline, we saw that there are clitics of various sorts, some of which are considered in the first pass of stress assignment, some in a second pass that takes into account previously assigned stresses, and some of which are never counted for stress. Finally, we saw that compound words are only rarely the domain of initial footing.

---

[5] I am very grateful to Ryan Bennett for bringing case to my attention.

2 The domain of stress assignment: Word-boundedness and frequent collocation

A survey of stress assignment, beginning with the compendious Hayes (1995) confirms the general impression that stress-assigning processes are lexical, not postlexical. But there is an exception, well-known among Slavicists, that in a sense proves the rule. Macedonian as described by Lunt (1952) and Koneski (1976) (analyzed in generative terms by Franks 1987; 1989 can build initial feet over certain units larger than the word. The example treated by Lunt and Koneski comes from what is termed 'Literary Macedonian.' At first I was concerned that this might be an artificial language and that the cases of large domain stress could be the creation of scholars. However, Lunt (1952: 5–6) and Franks (1987) explain that the literary language is simply a pan-dialectal creation-by-commission that takes features from several western and central dialects but does not invent them. The large domain stress effects are found in several dialects, though some of the details differ from spoken dialect to spoken dialect.

Literary Macedonian has regular antepenultimate stress:

(17) Literary Macedonian (Lunt 1952; Franks 1987; 1989)
    a. 'beseda
         lecture
    b. be'seda-ta
         lecture-DEF
    c. vo'denitʃar
         miller
    d. vodeni'tʃar-i -te
         miller   -PL-DEF

As is usual in such systems, monosyllables are stressed and disyllables are stressed on the penult. (See Halle & Vergnaud 1987: 53 for a full analysis.) But some syntactically complex strings can be stressed as single units, termed 'enlarged stress domains'. These domains are not, for the most part, unfamiliar to phonologists, as they involve potentially prosodically deficient function words such as negative or interrogative particles and pronouns plus the following word. However, there are also some strings of modifiers plus nouns. There are also polysyllabic propositions, which are cross-linguistically unlikely to be prosodically deficient (i.e., to be clitics), yet are stressed as a unit with their objects. I summarize Lunt's list in (18):

(18) Literary Macedonian enlarged domains (Lunt 1952: 23–25)
    a. monosyllabic words which have no accent of their own, both proclitic and enclitic. The proclitics include personal pronouns, particles and prepositions. The enclitics include definite articles and certain indirect personal pronouns.
    b. the negative particle plus the verb, and any elements that fall between them, such as the present tense of the verb 'to be,' even though these normally have their own accent.
    c. the interrogatives meaning 'what,' 'how,' 'where,' and 'how many,' plus the following verb, and any stressless elements between them.

d. prepositions and their pronominal objects.
e. prepositions "when used with concrete, spatial meanings" "and in a number of set phrases" when their object is non-definite.
f. a numeral and the noun it modifies.
g. some combinations of adjectives and the nouns they modify.

Let us begin with (18g), which is the most typologically unusual. We will return to the also-surprising prepositions 18d) in §4.3.

4.2 Prenominal adjectives

It is worth quoting Lunt's remarks about the combination of adjectives and nouns in their entirety.

> The combination of adjective+substantive under a single accent is common to many, but not all, of the central dialects on which the literary language is based, and in any case it is not productive. Such a shift of accent is impossible if either the noun or adjective come from outside the narrow sphere of daily life. Therefore this usage is not recommended. Conversational practice is extremely varied. Place names tend to keep the old [i.e. single domain, antepenultimate-EMK] accent... Often used combinations tend to keep the single accent: 'soured milk' [yoghurt], 'dry grapes= raisins', 'the left foot', 'the lower door', '(he didn't see a) living soul'. Still one usually hears [the words stressed as separate domains]. Only with the numbers and perhaps a few fixed phrases [dry grapes] is the single stress widespread in the speech of Macedonian intellectuals. (Lunt 1952: 24–25)

What we should note then, is that open class content words are only grouped into a single stress domain when the words are frequent ("narrow sphere of everyday life"), especially when such words are also in frequent collocation with one another ("often-used combinations"). And even though this system arose in some of the dialects on which the new literary language was based, it apparently is not easily learned. Lunt here reports that the single domain stress on attributive adjective plus noun has not been taken up by the educated speakers who adopted it.

Franks (1987; 1989) combines Lunt's examples with those of Koneski (1976) and others he and colleagues elicited. Here are several representative ones, including those mentioned in the above quotation.

(19) Literary Macedonian (Lunt 1952; Franks 1987: 989)
  a. dolna'ta porta
     lower   gate
  b. kise'lo mleko
     sour   milk
     'yoghurt'

c. suˈvo grozje
   dry grapes
   'raisins'
d. Crˈvena voda
   red water
   'name of a village'
e. ˈstar tʃovek
   old man
f. novaˈta kukʲa
   new   house

The examples in (19) are not argued to be compound words by the various sources, probably because they have the regular syntax of noun phrases and many such as (a), (e) and (f) have compositional semantics; however, they are strings that that are in frequent collocation and may have come to take on a specialized, less predictable meaning. Given the silence of the sources on the question of compound versus phrase, perhaps the most noncommittal and appropriate term for them is Erman and Warren's (2000) "prefabs." Prefabs are not idioms or lexicalized compounds with unpredictable meaning and peculiar syntax but simply common and conventional collocations that can be stored in the lexicon while having compositional meaning and normal syntax.

The matter of whether a string of words that occur together frequently is a compound or a phrase is a vexed one, even for well-studied languages like English. (See Plag et al. 2008 for an overview of the controversy.)

4.3 Another compound or adjective-noun case

Ryan Bennett informs me that some dialects of Modern Irish show a similar phenomenon in their adjective plus noun pairs. For instance, Mhac An Fhailigh & Éammon (1968) states for the dialect of Erris that while such a phrase typically has word stress on each element, frequent collocations can show a single stress. Thus the infrequent [ˈdrɑx ˈxlɑdəx] 'bad shore' has stress on each member, but [ˈʃan vʲan] 'old woman,' has only a single stress. Mhac An Fhailigh calls these 'loose' versus 'close' compounds, rather than phrases vs. compounds, but does not give clear criteria for what defines a compound versus a phrase. I have not yet found an extended description of this phenomenon in Irish so I mention it only in passing here.

The adjective plus noun enlarged domains of Macedonian (and perhaps of Erris Irish) are the exception that proves the rule – phrases are not normally the domain of stress assignment. If what leads to phonologization of rhythmic tendencies within words is frequent collocation, it is gratifying that the only extensively described example of an enlarged domain that I could find is one involving frequent collocation of common words, and it is consistent with my hypothesis that the Erris Irish seems to accord with the same generalization. But Lunt tells us that the Macedonian example is hard to learn and is being eliminated over time. Stress rules really don't like to apply outside a single content word, its affixes (or some of them) and, sometimes, its clitics.

4.4 Macedonian prepositions and their objects

The stress behavior of prepositions in Macedonian is also worth looking at in a bit of detail. Since prepositions are the heads of phrases and especially since they can be polysyllabic in Macedonian, one might expect they would be independent prosodic words on their own. Looking at a more familiar case, English monosyllabic prepositions like *to* and *for* are optionally proclitic on their complements, but polysyllabic prepositions like *behind* and *above* are not. But Macedonian prepositions, regardless of their apparent prosodic heft in terms of syllable count, never receive stress as a domain on their own. They are, apparently, as prosodically deficient as clitics. Lunt devotes several pages (??–??) to the individual behavior of some two dozen prepositions because their stress behaviors are somewhat idiosyncratic. The basic generalization is that prepositions have or receive no accent of their own. They either form a single stress domain with their nominal or pronominal complement, acting like internal clitics (20a); or, in some cases, they behave like free clitics, never receiving a stress of their own nor receiving the single stress of the enlarged domain (20b).

(20) Literary Macedonian (Franks 1989)
    a. oko'lu selo
       near   village

       'near the village'

    b. otkaj 'gradot
       from direction

       'from the direction (of)'

Prosodic deficiency in prepositions makes sense from the point of view of the frequency of collocations. Prepositions are closed class items and they require a nominal or pronominal complement. Thus, when they are heard, they are always in collocation with a noun phrase.

4.5 Summary

As we mentioned earlier, it is helpful to think of the Macedonian collocations of full words that are stressed as a single word as the inverse of the Prosodic Word clitics of Bilua in (7), re-illustrated below in (21). PWd clitics are underlyingly prosodically deficient but can receive their own stress under duress. The Macedonian adjectives are elements that are *not* inherently prosodically deficient, even in Macedonian, yet in certain common collocations, they are being treated as a piece of a single prosodic word, like internal clitics. This is illustrated in (22). From a cross-linguistic perspective, the Macedonian polysyllabic prepositions are a bit unexpected in being inherently prosodically deficient, parallel either to internal (20a) or free (20b) proclitics. These are illustrated in the second line of (22) and in (23).

(21) Prosodic independence of underlyingly prosodically deficient clitic

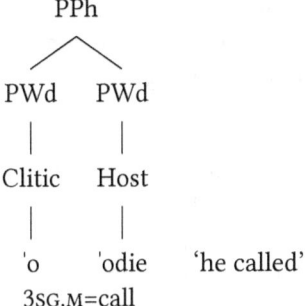

'o   'odie   'he called'
3SG.M=call

(22) Prosodic dependence of underlyingly prosodically independent words and of 'internal' prepositions

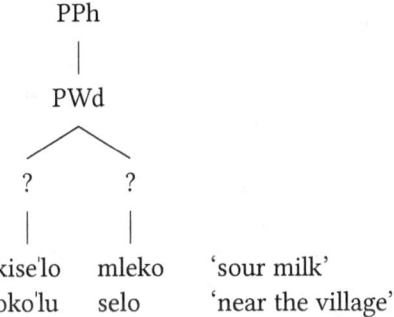

kise'lo   mleko   'sour milk'
oko'lu   selo   'near the village'

(23) Macedonian unstressable preposition parallel to free proclitic

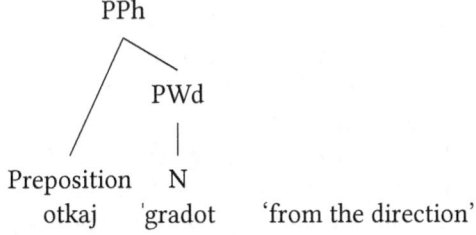

Preposition   N
otkaj   'gradot   'from the direction'

5 Conclusion

Why is stress assignment almost always word-bounded? Why is it restricted only to cohering affixes in some languages, and how does it manage to extend outward to clitics in others? The hypothesis offered in this paper and in Kaisse (forthcoming) is that rhythm, like long-distance harmony, is grammaticized when certain syllables are heard together over and over.[6] This usually only happens within words, including their affixes, and, occasionally, with words plus slightly more independent closed class items such as clitics. Because word-level affixes have fewer selectional restrictions than stem-level ones, stem-level affixes are the most likely to be included in the initial domain of footing. And since clitics have even fewer selectional restrictions than word-level affixes, they are even less likely to be included. Since there are thousands of independent content words, the collocation of any two is much less likely to have many exemplars. However, both compound words (as in Modern Greek) and 'prefabs' – collocations of frequent words in frequently heard phrases like 'old man' – are more prone to becoming a single domain than just any sequence of content words. Similarly, collocations of closed class items like prepositions may cross the border and form a single initial stress domain.

There may also be a functional motivation for the prosodic independence of content words. Extending the domain for the initial building of feet would eliminate the demarcative function linguists often ascribe to stress. Because stress is culminative, with exactly one primary stressed syllable per content word, it allows us to identify the independent lexical words of a phrase. And because stress is often predictably located on an initial, final, or penultimate syllable, it also allows us to identify word boundaries, helping the listener locate the end of one word and the beginning of the next.

Let us return to a question I raised in §??. Does the regular, alternating stress assignment found within words stem from the grammaticization of rhythmic tendencies in sentences? Or are rhythmic tendencies in sentences the result of "leakage" from regular phonology within the word? The counterparts of word-bounded phonological processes are present and, in the current century, detectable, as statistical, gradient tendencies in larger domains such as compounds and phrases. Shih (2016) shows that syntactic choices are gradiently influenced by the rhythmic principles that we see operating obligatorily inside words as alternating stress assignment, rhythm rules, stress clash avoidance, lapse avoidance, and so on. She argues that word order and construction choice can be recruited in response to these phonological pressures from inside the lexical phonology, unearthing small effects in the choice of optional syntactic variants that favor more eurhythmic outputs. Thus she finds that the genitive constrictions *X's Y* and *Y of X* are skewed toward avoidance of stress clashes and lapses. Similarly, the dative alternation *verb IO DO* vs. *verb DO to IO* trends in a small but discoverable way towards phrases that are more eurhythmic (Anttila, Adams & Speriosu 2010; Shih 2016). Along the same lines, Hammond (2013) finds that the Brown and the Buckeye corpora contain statistically fewer instances of underlyingly clashing prenominal adjective-noun pairs than would be expected, so that adjectives like *aloof* and *unknown,* with final primary stress, are underrepresented when they are prenominal, while adjectives like *happy* and *finite,* with initial primary stress are not. Here we run into a chicken and egg problem. The more traditional view in historical linguistics is the Neogrammarian one: these pressures

---

[6] Although tone rules are more powerful in their ability to escape the word, for reasons that, as far as I know, are not well understood (see footnote 2), word-boundedness is nonetheless certainly robustly attested for tone rules as well as other iterative processes, and I would propose that the same factors of frequent collocation should underlie that domain restriction.

are there all along as variation, with the syntax reflecting them before they are phonologized. This is how I envisioned the progression in Kaisse (forthcoming). Along the same lines, Myers & Padgett (2015) note the tendency of learners to extend phenomena like utterance-final devoicing to the word-level. Participants in their artificial language-learning experiments generalized beyond the training data, applying word-final devoicing inside of utterances in novel strings, not just the kind of utterance-final devoicing they were trained on. Myers & Padgett (2015: 399) conclude that "learners are biased towards word-based distributional patterns." They speculate that this is because we hear and store many more exemplars of words than we do of utterances. Baumann & Ritt (2012) take a similar view of the direction of development of lexical stress patterns, investigating through game theoretic simulations the lexicalization of stress in English bisyllabic words, which can have either initial (*'lentil, 'research$_N$*) or final (*ho'tel, re'search$_V$*) prominence. They argue that "words adopt, on average, those stress patterns that produce, on average, the best possible phrasal level rhythm." But Shih and Martin's views are equally plausible: the obligatory, regular stress system of the language spreads from words into gradient choices in the syntax. I suspect that both directions are operating at the same time, since language change results from a constant push and pull of variation and optimization.

Whatever the direction of change, we have seen that it is rare for rhythmic tendencies beyond the word to become phonologized and to be reflected as foot construction processes that take material outside of words as their domain. I have argued that there are simply not enough exemplars of adjacent words heard repeatedly together to result in the reification of such a large domain.

Acknowledgements

I am grateful to Ryan Bennett, Larry Hyman, Andrew Livingston, David Odden, the referees for this paper, and the audience at the Annual Meeting on Phonology 2015 (University of British Columbia).

References

Anderson, Stephen R. 1992. *A-morphous morphology*. Cambridge: Cambridge University Press.

Anderson, Stephen R. 2011. Clitics. In Marc van Oostendorp, Colin J. Ewen, Elizabeth Hume & Keren Rice (eds.), *The Blackwell companion to phonology*, 2002–2018. Chichester: Wiley-Blackwell.

Anttila, Arto, Matthew Adams & Michael Speriosu. 2010. The role of prosody in the English dative alternation. *Language and Cognitive Processes* 25(7–9). 946–981.

Athanasopoulou, Angeliki & Irene Vogel. 2014. Compounds in Modern Greek. *Journal of the Acoustical Society of America* 136(4). 2176.

Barnes, Jonathan. 2006. *Strength and weakness at the interface: Positional neutralization in phonetics and phonology.* Berlin: Mouton de Gruyter.

Baumann, Andreas & Nikolaus Ritt. 2012. Transferring mathematics to English Studies. In Manfred Markus & Herbert Schendl (eds.), *Transfer in English Studies,* 219–239. Wien: Braumüller.

Bermudez-Otero, Ricardo. 2015. Amphichronic explanation and the life cycle of phonological processes. In Patrick Honeybone & Joseph Salmons (eds.), *The Oxford handbook of historical phonology,* 374–399. Oxford: Oxford University Press.

Bybee, Joan. 2006. From usage to grammar: The mind's response to repetition. *Language* 82(4). 711–733.

Chomsky, Noam & Morris Halle. 1968. *The sound pattern of English.* New York: Harper & Row.

Erman, Britt & Beatrice Warren. 2000. The idiom principle and the open choice principle. *Text* 20(1). 29–62.

Fabb, Nigel. 1988. English suffixation is constrained only by selectional restrictions. *Natural Language and Linguistic Theory* 6(4). 527–539.

Fhailigh, Mhac An & Éammon. 1968. *The Irish of Erris, Co. Mayo: A phonemic study.* Dublin: Dublin Institute for Advanced Studies.

Flemming, Edward. 1997. Phonetic detail in phonology: Towards a unified account of assimilation and coarticulation. In K. Suzuki & D. Elzinga (eds.), *Proceedings of the 1995 Southwestern Workshop in Optimality Theory (SWOT).* Tucson: University of Arizona.

Franks, Steven L. 1987. Regular and irregular stress in macedonian. *International Journal of Slavic Linguistics and Poetics* 35–36. 93–142.

Franks, Steven L. 1989. The monosyllabic head effect. *Natural Language and Linguistic Theory* 7(4). 551–563.

Halle, Morris & Jean-Roger Vergnaud. 1987. *An essay on stress.* Cambridge, MA: MIT Press.

Hammond, Michael. 2013. Data input optimization in English. *Journal of the Phonetic Society of Japan* 17. 26–38.

Hansson, Gunnar Ó. 2010. *Consonant harmony: Long-distance interaction in phonology.* University of California Publications in Linguistics, 145. Berkeley, CA: University of California Press.

Hayes, Bruce. 1984. The phonology of rhythm in English. *Linguistic Inquiry* 15(1). 33–74.

Hayes, Bruce. 1995. *Metrical stress theory: Principles and case studies.* Chicago: University of Chicago Press.

Hyman, Larry. 2011. Tone is different. In John Goldsmith, Jason Riggle & Alan C. L. Yu (eds.), *The handbook of phonological theory,* 197–239. Somerset, NJ: Wiley.

Inkelas, Sharon, Jonathan Barnes, Jeffrey Good, Darya Kavitskaya, Orhan Orgun, Ronald Sprouse & Alan Yu. 2001. Stress and vowel-to-vowel coarticulation in Turkish. Presented at the annual meeting of the Linguistic Society of America.

Kaisse, Ellen M. 1993. Rule reordering and rule generalization in lexical phonology: A reconsideration. In Sharon Hargus & Ellen M. Kaisse (eds.), *Studies in lexical phonology,* 343–363. San Diego: Academic Press.

Kaisse, Ellen M. 2005. Word formation and phonology. In Pavel Štekauer & Rochelle Lieber (eds.), *Handbook of word-formation*, 25–47. Studies in natural language and linguistic theory 64. New York: Springer Verlag.

Kaisse, Ellen M. Forthcoming. What kinds of processes are postlexical? And how powerful are they? In Hongming Zhang (ed.), *Prosodic studies: Challenges and prospects*. London: Routledge.

Kiparsky, Paul. 1982. Lexical morphology and phonology. In Linguistic Society of Korea (ed.), *Linguistics in the morning calm: Selected papers from SICOL–1981*, 3–91. Seoul: Hanshin.

Koneski, Bozidar. 1976. *Gramatika na makedonskiot literaturen jazik*. Skopje: Kultura.

Kubozono, Haruo. 2008. Japanese accent. In Shigeru Miyagawa & Mamoru Saito (eds.), *The Oxford handbook of Japanese linguistics*, 165–191. Oxford: Oxford University Press.

Liberman, Mark. 2015. *Man: reduced or not? Language Log*. Accessed January 18, 2017. http://languagelog.ldc.upenn.edu/nll/?p=18451.

Lunt, Horace G. 1952. *A grammar of the Macedonian literary language*. Skopje: Drzavno Knigoizdatelstvo na NR Makedonija.

Martin, Andrew T. 2007. *The evolving lexicon*. Los Angeles, CA: University of California dissertation.

Myers, Scott & Jaye Padgett. 2015. Domain generalization in artificial language learning. *Phonology* 31(3). 399–433.

Newman, Stanley. 1944. *Yokuts language of California*. Vol. 2 (Viking Fund publications in anthropology). New York.

Obata, Kazuko. 2003. *A grammar of Bilua: A Papuan language of the Solomon Islands*. Vol. 540. Canberra: Pacific linguistics.

Ohala, John J. 1992. What's cognitive, what's not, in sound change. In Günter Kellermann & Michael Morrissey (eds.), *Diachrony within synchrony: Language history and cognition*, 309–355. Frankfurt: Peter Lang.

Öhman, Sven E. G. 1966. Coarticulation in CVC utterances: Spectrographic measurements. *Journal of the Acoustical Society of America* 39(1). 151–168.

Peperkamp, Sharon. 1997. *Prosodic words* (HIL dissertations 34). The Hague: Holland Academic Graphics.

Plag, Ingo, Gero Kunter, Sabine Lappe & Maria Braun. 2008. The role of semantics, argument structure, and lexicalization in compound stress assignment in English. *Language* 84(4). 760–794.

Poser, William. 1990. Evidence for foot structure in Japanese. *Language* 66(1). 78–105.

Ralli, Angela. 2013. *Compounding in Modern Greek*. New York: Springer Verlag.

Selkirk, Elisabeth O. 1995. The prosodic structure of function words. In Jill N. Beckman, Laura Walsh Dickey & Suzanne Urbanczyk (eds.), *University of Massachusetts occasional papers 18: papers in Optimality Theory*, 439–469. Amherst: GLSA.

Shih, Stephanie S. 2016. Phonological influences in syntactic alternations. In Vera Gribanova (ed.), *The morphosyntax-phonology connection*. (pages not yet available). Oxford: Oxford University Press.

Torres-Tamarit, Francesc & Clàudia Pons-Moll. 2015. *Enclitic-triggered stress shift in Catalan*. Paper delivered at Going Romance, 29. Nijmegen: Radboud University.

Zwicky, Arnold M. & Geoffrey K. Pullum. 1983. Cliticization vs. inflection: English N'T. *Language* 59(3). 502–513.

Chapter 3

Compensatory lengthening and structure preservation revisited yet again

Darya Kavitskaya
University of California, Berkeley

> In their seminal paper, de Chene & Anderson (1979) make a strong claim that pre-existing vowel length contrast is a necessary condition for the phonologization of vowel length through compensatory lengthening. Compensatory lengthening is thus predicted to be always a structure-preserving change. Since that time, the claim has been challenged in numerous works (Gess 1998; Hock 1986; Morin 1992, among others). A closer examination of the cited counterexamples to de Chene and Anderson's claim reveals certain generalizations. Some apparent counterexamples, such as Samothraki Greek (Kiparsky 2011), involve the full vocalization stage of the consonant with the subsequent coalescence of that consonant with the preceding vowel. In other cases, such as Old French (Gess 1998) and Komi Ižma (Hausenberg 1998), heterosyllabic or heteromorphemic identical vowel sequences are attested elsewhere in the language. The former cases involve the reanalysis of vowel length before weakened consonants that is indeed strengthened by the independent existence of the vowel length contrast in the languages in question, in support of de Chene and Anderson's claim. The former cases are not truly compensatory, and phonemic vowel length is introduced into the language through coalescence.

1 Introduction

In their seminal paper on compensatory lengthening (CL), de Chene & Anderson (1979) make a strong claim that the independent existence of a vowel length contrast is a necessary condition for the phonologization of vowel length through compensatory lengthening. CL is thus predicted to be always a structure-preserving change that cannot introduce contrastive vowel length into a language. Since that time, the generalization in its stronger version (certain sound changes are always structure preserving) or in its weaker version (structure preservation is a tendency in sound change) has been accepted and developed by linguists otherwise advocating very diverse and sometimes incompatible approaches to sound change, in particular, in research programs by Paul Kiparsky

Darya Kavitskaya. 2017. Compensatory lengthening and structure preservation revisited yet again. In Claire Bowern, Laurence Horn & Raffaella Zanuttini (eds.), *On looking into words (and beyond)*, 41–58. Berlin: Language Science Press. DOI:10.5281/zenodo.495438

(Kiparsky 1995; 2003) and Juliette Blevins (Blevins 2004a; 2009). However, the generalization has also been challenged in several works. For instance, Gess (1998) takes issue with de Chene and Anderson's claim, suggesting that in general, "structure preservation is irrelevant as a theoretical construct" and proceeds to argue that de Chene and Anderson's interpretation of the Old French data, which is their main example, is incorrect, and that in Old French compensatory lengthening happened before the introduction of the other sources of length distinction into the language, contrary to de Chene and Anderson's analysis. CL through onset loss, such as in Samothraki Greek (Topintzi 2006; Kiparsky 2011; Katsika & Kavitskaya 2015), is also a potential counterexample to the claim that CL is a structure-preserving change, along with the case of Occitan (Morin 1992). In other languages without pre-existing vowel length contrast, such as Andalusian Spanish (Hock 1986), Ilokano (Hayes 1989) and the Ngajan dialect of Dyirbal (Dixon 1990), vowel length that is the result of CL remains allophonic and predictable. In yet another type of cases, such as Komi Ižma (Harms 1967; 1968; Hausenberg 1998), vowel length from CL appears to be quasi-phonemic and on its way to phonologization.

CL is a common sound change that has occurred independently in many languages across the world, and only a few potential counterexamples to de Chene and Anderson's claim have been reported. In principle, we could have been done simply restating this observation that supports a weaker but less controversial claim that there is a tendency for CL to occur in languages with pre-existing vowel length, in the spirit of proposals about structure-preserving sound change by either Kiparsky (2003) or Blevins (2009), but we will proceed to examining the most widely discussed counterexamples to de Chene and Anderson's claim. A closer examination of these counterexamples reveals certain generalizations. The working analyses of some cases proposed in the literature involve the full vocalization stage of the consonant with the subsequent coalescence with the preceding vowel, such as in Samothraki Greek (Sumner 1999; Kiparsky 2011). In other cases, such as Old French (Gess 1998) and Komi Ižma (Hausenberg 1998), heterosyllabic or heteromorphemic long vowels (or rather vowel sequences) are attested elsewhere in the language. We shall argue that the cases of CL that do not involve full vocalization (Hayes 1989; Kavitskaya 2002) are in a sense truly compensatory, as opposed to instances of consonant vocalization and subsequent vowel coalescence. The former cases involve the reanalysis of vowel length before weakened consonants that is indeed strengthened by the independent existence of the vowel length contrast in the languages in question. In the latter cases, phonemic vowel length is introduced into the language through coalescence.

2 The problem

CL through consonant loss is defined as a process whereby a vowel lengthens in compensation for the loss of a tautosyllabic consonant. CL through coda loss is the most typologically wide spread process, as either a diachronic change or a synchronic alternation.[1] An example of this kind of CL in the Ižma dialect of Komi (a Uralic language

---

[1] I do not address CL through vowel loss in this paper.

3 Compensatory lengthening and structure preservation revisited yet again

of the Permian subgroup) is shown in Table 1 (Harms 1967; 1968; de Chene & Anderson 1979).

Table 1: CL through coda loss in Komi Ižma (after Harms 1968: 104).

	Stem	Past 1SG	Infinitive	
a.	lɨj-	lɨj-i	lɨj-nɨ	'shoot'
	mun-	mun-i	mun-nɨ	'go'
b.	kɨl-	kɨl-i	kɨː-nɨ	'hear'
	sulal-	sulal-i	suloː-nɨ	'stand'

In Komi Ižma, the lateral /l/ deletes in the coda position with the lengthening of the preceding vowel, as illustrated in (b) of Table 1.[2] De Chene & Anderson (1979) propose that CL through consonant loss should be analyzed as an instance of the conversion of coda consonants, /l/ in the case of Komi Ižma, to glides (either semivocalic or laryngeal), /w/ in the case of Komi Ižma, with the subsequent monophthongization of the resulting vowel-glide sequence in the syllable nucleus, as in, for example, *kɨl.nɨ > *kɨw.nɨ > kɨː.nɨ 'to hear', with the intermediate stage unattested in Komi Ižma but present in other dialects of Komi, such as Vychegda Komi (Lytkin 1966; Lytkin & Teplyashina 1976).

De Chene and Anderson (1979: 508) emphasize that their account is phonetic in nature and accounts for CL as a historical sound change, and not as a synchronic alternation:

> We will argue that these processes can be understood as the transition of the consonant, through loss or reduction of its occlusion, to an eventual glide G. It is the monophthongization of the resulting sequence (X)VG(Y) which gives rise to a syllable nucleus that is interpreted as distinctively long. In consequence, cases of apparent compensatory lengthening can be analysed (as far as their phonetic bases are concerned) as a combination of consonantal weakening in certain positions followed by monophthongization; and compensatory lengthening per se can be eliminated as an independent member of any inventory of phonetic process-types.

This insight into the phonetics of CL serves as the basis for the analysis developed in Kavitskaya (2002), who maintains that CL is the result of the reanalysis of the longer phonetic duration of vowels as phonological length with the loss of tautosyllabic consonants. Kavitskaya (2002) maintains that vowels are more likely to be reanalyzed as phonologically long in the environment of more sonorous consonants after the loss of the said consonants, which makes the differences in vowel length unpredictable. De Chene and Anderson's (1979) analysis of CL as a process whereby consonants weaken to glides supports Kavitskaya's phonetic analysis, which is shown in Table 2.

The schematic representation in Table 2 considers two possible situations where the consonants X and Y are lost. Prior to the deletion of the consonants, both vowels are

---

[2] The lengthened /a/ surfaces as [oː].

Table 2: CL through coda loss (Kavitskaya 2002: 9).

	Stage 1 (before consonant loss)	Stage 2 (consonant loss)	Phonologization
CVX	C V C	C V	C V:
CVY	C V C	C V	C V

correctly analyzed as phonologically short. In the case when the listener mishears the more sonorous consonant X as absent, the longer transitions are reinterpreted as a part of the vowel, which is subsequently reanalyzed as long. The vocalic transitions to the less sonorant consonant Y are shorter, and with the loss of this consonant, there is no reinterpretation of vowel length based on its duration. The divide between X and Y is arbitrary, and the more sonorous the deleting consonant is, the more likely its deletion to be compensated by the lengthening of the vowel.

Several later accounts of CL are mostly phonological. The most well-known of those is an account by Hayes (1989), who analyzes CL through consonant loss as the deletion of a weight-bearing coda while preserving its weight and reassigning it to the preceding vowel, as illustrated in (1) for Komi Ižma. The account holds that when the underlying coda /l/ is deleted, its mora is left behind (in an intermediate stage) and spreads to the preceding vowel, making it bimoraic and thus long:

(1) CL through coda loss in Komi Ižma (after Hayes 1989)

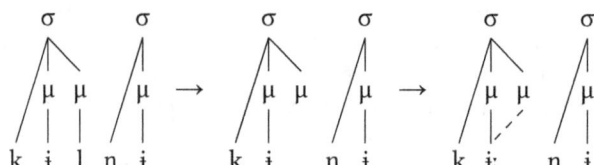

The reason for the necessity of the phonetic explanation in de Chene and Anderson's analysis and its conspicuous absence from Hayes analysis lies in the difference between the general approaches to CL taken by these two accounts. De Chene and Anderson's account carefully distinguishes between a sequence of phonetic processes that comprises the weakening of occlusion followed by a monophthongization of the resulting vowel-glide sequences and the phonological reinterpretation of some of the outputs of this monophthongization as long vowels. While Hayes uses historical examples to illustrate his points (one of the examples being Attic Greek, where CL is arguably only a historical process with no synchronic alternations), the account he proposes is synchronic in nature and does not consider either phonetic or phonological stages of the sound change analyzed by de Chene and Anderson.

3 Compensatory lengthening and structure preservation revisited yet again

One of the important predictions of de Chene and Anderson's account concerns the systemic constraints on the phonologization of vowel length. They propose that the phonologization of vowel lengthening as a result of CL can happen if and only if the language in question has a pre-existing vowel length contrast. This prediction does not follow directly from de Chene and Anderson's analysis, nor it is necessary for the accounts in the spirit of Hayes. It a sense, it is not a prediction per se, but rather a generalization about the nature of CL as a sound change. In the following sections, I will consider several counterexamples to this claim, discuss the similarities among these examples, and offer some speculation on why de Chene and Anderson's generalization is at least a tendency in the languages of the world.

3 CL with no pre-existing vowel length: Apparent counterexamples

As can be inferred from an (admittedly small) survey of languages with CL in Kavitskaya (2002), CL is more often a structure-preserving sound change. In the majority of the cases of CL, this tendency indeed holds: out of 80 languages with historical CL sound changes listed in Kavitskaya's (2002) survey, 72 or 90% occur in languages with pre-existing long/short vowel contrasts, while only 8 or 10% are found in languages without a pre-existing vowel length contrast.[3] These 8 languages constitute counterexamples to the stronger version of the claim, which holds that CL as a sound change is always structure-preserving. However, first, the presence of counterexamples does not make the tendency false (it is just not a universal). Second, there seems to be an important difference between the cases that are structure-preserving and the cases in which vowel length (mostly allophonic) is potentially introduced into a language through CL.

3.1 Old French

Old French is the central example used by de Chene and Anderson to illustrate that CL as a sound change does not happen unless contrastive vowel length is independently present in the language. According to de Chene & Anderson (1979: 527–528), stated after Pope (1934: 79, 191), the diphthong [aw], inherited both from Indo-European and from Vulgar Latin, monophthongized to a short [o] in French by the middle of the 9th century, as in (2a). The loss of other consonants, such as velars before *l* and *n* and *p/b* and *t/d* before *p/b*, *t/d*, and *s*, that took place at approximately the same time, was not accompanied by CL either, as exemplified in (2b):

---

[3] This information is not explicitly present in Kavitskaya (2002) and was compiled by Blevins (2009).

(2) a. Monophthongization of [aw] to [o] in Old French (circa 850 AD)
or < *aurum* 'gold'
oser < *ausare* 'to dare'
forge 'forge' < **faurga* < *fabrica* 'workshop'
parole < *paraula* < *parab(o)la* 'word'

b. Loss of consonants g, k, p, and d in Old French (before 850 AD)
agneau [aɲo] < *agnellum* 'lamb'
maille [may] < *mac(u)lam* 'stain'
route 'road' < *(via) rupta* 'broken road'
après 'after' < *adpressum* 'near'

Another wave of monophthongization, presumably through the weakening of the coda [l] to a labiovelar glide, happened in Old French by the 16th century, this time resulting in a long [oː], as illustrated in (3a). The loss of other pre-consonantal consonants, such as nasals (complete by the middle of the 16th century) and fricatives *s* and *z* (earlier), was accompanied by CL. Examples of the loss of fricatives are in (3b), and CL through the loss of nasals is illustrated in (3c).

The examples in (3b) show the orthographic *s* that was preserved in such words until 1740 (de Chene & Anderson 1979: 520). However, Pope (1934: 151) mentions that 12th century poetry suggests that the fricative had begun to drop before voiced consonants by this period. French loanwords in English, such as *blame, male,* and *isle,* do not have a pronounced [s], which adds more support to this conclusion:

(3) a. Monophthongization of [aw] < [al] to [oː] in Old French (16th century)
autre [oːtr] < *alterum* 'other'
aube [oːb] 'dawn' < *alba* 'white' (fem.sg.)

b. Loss of fricatives with CL in Old French (12th century)
mêler (ModFrench) < *mesler* (Old French) < *misculāre* 'to mix'
île (ModFrench) < *isle* (Old French) < *insula* 'island'

c. Loss of nasals with CL in Old French (16th century)
fendre [fãːdr] < *findere* 'to split'
rompre [rɔ̃ːpr] < *rumpere* 'to break'

De Chene and Anderson claim that the difference between the outcomes of the two Old French monophthongizations, as well as between the loss of consonants without and with vowel lengthening, lies in the fact that in the 9th century, the Old French vowel system did not exhibit contrastive vowel length, and so vowels did not lengthen as a response to the loss of consonants, while by some time in the 12th to 16th century a vowel length distinction was introduced into the system independently, and this pre-existing vowel length contrast made it possible for the reanalysis of the vowels that preceded the lost consonants as long.

It is argued in de Chene (1985) that languages typically acquire vowel length through vowel coalescence (dubbed as vowel hiatus or geminate vowel clusters, de Chene & Anderson 1979: 520). De Chene and Anderson (1979) state that French obeys this rule

3 Compensatory lengthening and structure preservation revisited yet again

and acquires long vowels through the deletion of intervocalic consonants and subsequent vowel coalescence in the period between the changes exemplified in (2) and (3). The examples of consonant loss and vowel coalescence are presented in Table 3.

Table 3: Intervocalic consonant loss between identical vowels (de Chene & Anderson 1979 after Pope 1934).

Modern French	Old French	Latin	
bâiller	baailler	bataculare	'to yawn'
	graal	gradalem	'dish'
	aates	adaptas	'suitable' (fem.acc.pl)
sceau	seel	sigillum	'seal'

Gess (1998) takes issue with de Chene and Anderson's claim that CL is only possible in languages with a preexisting vowel length contrast. He argues with the claim on the basis of the evidence from Old French. The objection is that the putative long vowels are treated as disyllabic in 12th and 13th century poetry in Old French, as shown in (4) for one of the examples in Table 3. From the scansion of the octosyllabic line in (4), it is evident that *graal* 'dish' consists of two syllables for the purposes of poetic syllabification:

(4) Le Roman de Perceval, late 12th century (Roach 1959: 3, 11, 76–77; Gess 1998: 357)
Ce est le contes de GRAAL,
 1 2 3 4 5 6 7 8
'This is the story of the Grail,'
Dont li quens li bailla le livre.
'About which the count gave him the book.'

The evidence from the scansion provided by Gess (1998) is questionable since syllabification in poetry is often conservative and reflects an earlier stage of the language. The scansion is also consistent with the possibility that vowel coalescence has already happened and long vowels scan as two syllables, with a poetic line becoming mora-counting rather than syllable-counting (see discussion in de Chene (1985: 76, 84ff) about such developments in Japanese and Tongan).[4] If this is the case, then Old French does not constitute a counterexample to de Chene and Anderson's generalization.

The metrical evidence presented by Gess (1998) is thus inconclusive. However, even if Gess' interpretation is correct and indeed his examples illustrate that at the time of CL in Old French there were heterosyllabic sequences of identical vowels, it could have been sufficient to strengthen the possibility of CL, as we shall further discuss for another example in the next section.

---

[4] I am grateful to a reviewer for the discussion of this point.

3.2 Komi Ižma

It would be informative now to return to Komi Ižma, which does not have contrastive long vowels in the inventory, or any other allophonically long vowels, except for those that are derived by CL (Lytkin 1966; Lytkin & Teplyashina 1976; Hausenberg 1998). Thus, in principle, Komi Ižma constitutes a counterexample to de Chene and Anderson's claim interpreted broadly, as noticed by Gess (1998). The forms in Table 4 illustrate CL alternations in Komi Ižma:

Table 4: CL through coda loss in Komi Ižma (after Harms 1968: 104–105).

Stem	Past 1SG	Infinitive	
kɨl-	kɨli	kɨːni	'to hear'
sulal-	sulali	suloːnɨ	'to stand'
Indefinite	Definite	Dative	
pi	pijɨs	pilɨ	'son'
piː	pilɨs	piːlɨ	'cloud'
vəː	vəlɨs	vəːlɨ	'horse'

The deletion of *l* in Komi Ižma went through the stage of the loss of the occlusion of the liquid to the labiovelar glide *w*, followed by the monophthongization of the *Vw* sequence.[5] The diphthongal stage is synchronically attested in related dialects of Komi, spoken in Vychegda and Syktyvkar, and there is also a dialect group in Komi that preserves the lateral (cf. vəː /vəl/ 'horse' in Komi Ižma vs. vəv /vəl/ 'horse' in Vychegda Komi vs. vəl /vəl/ 'horse' in Komi Yazva) (Lytkin 1966: 44–49, Lytkin & Teplyashina 1976: 106–115).[6]

De Chene and Anderson (1979) maintain that Komi Ižma data do not counterexemplify their generalization since the language has heteromorphemic long vowels (or vowel sequences), so sufficient contrast in vowel duration is present for CL to go through. Hausenberg (1998: 309) states that in dialects long vowels may develop through assimilation in forms like *una-an* < *una-ën* 'many', *baba-as* < *baba-ïs* 'his wife'.

In a narrower sense, Komi Ižma is not a counterexample since CL does not introduce vowel length contrast into the language: vowel length is allophonic and predictable, and even though 'son' and 'cloud' look like a minimal pair, they are underlyingly /pi/ 'son' vs. /pil/ 'cloud'. Abondolo (1998: 13) calls vowel quantity in Komi Ižma "nascent", thus interpreting vowel length distinction in the language as quasi-phonemic and possibly on its way to phonemicization. However, another view on the facts of Komi Ižma CL is possible that provides additional evidence in support of de Chene and Anderson's claim.[7]

---

[5] Syllable-final /l/ frequently undergoes vocalization; cf., for instance, *l*-vocalization in BCS (South Slavic): beo /bel/ 'white-MASC' (vs. bela 'white-FEM'), video /videl/ 'see-PAST.MASC' (vs. videla 'see-PAST-FEM').

[6] Yet another dialect of Komi, Komi Inva, vocalizes /l/ into [w] in all positions (Lytkin 1966: 44–49).

[7] I am much indebted to a reviewer for the following discussion of vowel length and morphology.

These long vowels can arise through either inflection, as in Table 4, or derivation, as in (5):

(5) CL in Komi Ižma (Collinder 1957: 309 via de Chene & Anderson 1979: 525)
perna-al-as
cross-verb-3sg.pres
'he hangs (TRANS), as a cross on one's breast'

In an important paper that defines the place of morphology in grammar, Anderson (1982) proposes that the traditional category of inflection is the subset of morphology that is relevant to the syntax. As a consequence, inflection depends on the results of syntactic operations and is post-syntactic, while derivation happens before syntax. Thus, according to Anderson's model, the units of lexical storage are stems that "include all internal structure of a derivational sort" (Anderson 1982: 592). Endorsing this approach amounts to saying that, since long vowels resulting from the addition of derivational material are robustly attested in Komi Ižma, the language has lexical long vowels even if none of them are morpheme-internal.

3.3 Samothraki Greek

One of the languages in which CL introduces phonemic vowel length into a system without pre-existing vowel length contrast is a dialect of Greek spoken on the island of Samothraki (Newton 1972a,b; Hayes 1989; Katsanis 1996; Sumner 1999; Kavitskaya 2002; Topintzi 2006; Kiparsky 2011; Katsika & Kavitskaya 2015). Samothraki Greek is not a usual case of CL in yet another respect since it is the loss of the onset, not the coda, that triggers tautosyllabic vowel lengthening, as illustrated in Table 5.

In Samothraki Greek, the prevocalic *r* deletes with the lengthening of the following vowel in a) the word-initial onset of either stressed or unstressed syllable, as in Table 5a, and b) after a consonant in a complex onset, both in biconsonantal clusters, as in Table 5b, and triconsonantal clusters, as in Table 5c, both in stressed and unstressed word-initial and word-medial/final syllables:

Table 5: CL through onset loss in Samothraki Greek (after Katsika & Kavitskaya 2015).[8]

	Standard Greek	Samothraki Greek	
a.	ˈri.zɐ	ˈiː.zɐ	'root'
	rɛˈvi.θçɐ	iːˈvi.θçɐ	'chickpeas'
	rɔˈðɐ.ci.nɐ	uːˈðɐ.ci.nɐ	'peaches'
b.	ˈvri.si	ˈviːs	'faucet'
	ˈθri.mi	ˈθiːm	'shard'
c.	ˈɐ.sprɔs	ˈɐ.spuːs	'white'

The examples in Table 6 show the synchronic status of *r*-deletion in Samothraki Greek: the rhotic surfaces in the coda and as a first consonant in a complex onset, but deletes intervocalically. On the basis of such alternations, Kiparsky (2011) argues that the presence of r-zero alternations constitutes evidence for the synchronic status of CL in the language:

Table 6: Alternations in Samothraki Greek (Katsika & Kavitskaya 2015: 7).

ˈçɛɾ	'hand'	pɔˈðɐɾ	'foot'
ˈçɛ.rjɐ	'hands'	pɔˈðɐ.rjɐ	'feet'
çiˈu.ðjɐ	'little hands'	pɔ.ðɐˈu.ðjɐ	'little feet'

However, as Katsika & Kavitskaya (2015) point out, there are no synchronic alternations where the deletion of /r/ is accompanied by vowel lengthening. In other words, there are no attested examples in which one member of a semantically related pair has a surface [ɾ], while the other exhibits a long vowel as a consequence of the *r*-deletion. On the basis of this, Katsika & Kavitskaya (2015) conclude that it would be more accurate to analyze r-zero alternation as a synchronic process, and CL through the loss of *r* as a sound change in Samothraki Greek.

CL through onset loss presents a problem for the theories that treat CL as weight conservation (such as Hayes 1989), which predict that only the deletion of coda consonants can result in vowel lengthening. It is generally assumed that, unlike codas, onsets cannot bear weight and do not count as moraic.[9] Several such problematic cases, including CL through onset loss in Samothraki Greek, are reanalyzed in Hayes (1989). Hayes extends Newton's (1972) idea that *rC* clusters underwent vowel epenthesis of the form VrC → VriC → ViC and proposes that identical vowel epenthesis happened in *Cr* clusters as well, yielding $CrV_i → CV_irV_i → CV_{i:}$. The deletion of the intervocalic *r* could then be followed by vowel coalescence, just like in other VrV → V: cases in Samothraki Greek.

However, as shown by Topintzi (2006), the Samothraki Greek CL resists such a reanalysis since the deletion of the word-initial *r* cannot be accounted for by metathesis. In addition, Kiparsky (2011) claims that Hayes' analysis is problematic because it incorrectly predicts the merger of the outputs of the *r*-deletion from CrV and VrV. While after the loss of *r*, the original *rV sequence where the vowel is accented becomes a long vowel accented on the first mora, as in *θrími* → *θíim* 'shard', the original *VrV sequence where the second vowel is accented becomes a long vowel accented on the second mora, as in *xará* → *xaá* 'joy'. However, Heisenberg (1934: 91) notes that if *r*-deletion results in a sequence of identical vowels with the stress on the second vowel, the stress shifts from the second vowel to the first one, as in /karávi/ → [káav] 'ship'. Newton (1972a: 79)

---

[8] In Samothraki Greek, unstressed high vowels /i/ and /u/ delete unless the deletion creates phonotactically unacceptable structures. Unstressed mid vowels /ɛ/ and /ɔ/ raise to [i] and [u] (Newton 1972a: 79).

[9] Ryan (2014) presents statistical evidence from stress and meter showing that onsets are factors in syllable weight, though they are subordinate to the rhyme with respect to weight. For the discussion of the possibility of moraic onsets, see Curtis (2003), Davis (1999), among others.

interprets the stress shift as evidence for vowel contraction (coalescence), while Heisenberg (1934: 90) and Margariti-Rogka & Tsolaki (2011) ascertain that the vowels remain separate and belong to different syllables in such cases.

While the moraic weight approach does not seem to account for the Samothraki Greek CL, Kavitskaya (2002) proposes a phonetic/historical account. According to Kavitskaya (2002: 99), r is vocalic enough to be reinterpreted as additional vowel length. Kiparsky (2011) argues that neither purely phonetic models nor purely phonological (weight conservation) models are sufficient to account for CL in Samothraki Greek. He develops an account that relies on the observation that r is excluded from the onset position cross-linguistically (Zec 2007). Typologically, high sonority segments are dispreferred in the onset, which is evident from the fact that many languages, such as Korean, various Turkic languages, Basque, Piro, Telefol, etc., do not allow rhotics in word-initial or syllable-initial positions (de Lacy 2001; Smith 2003) even though they have some type of r in their consonant inventories. Languages employ different strategies to avoid onset rhotics, such as prothesis, deletion, fortition, anti-gemination, and incorporation into the nucleus (Kiparsky 2011: 26). Specifically, in Samothraki Greek the prohibition on the rhotic in the onset is resolved through the latter strategy: the rhotic is syllabified as a part of the nucleus so that the r and the following vowel form a rising diphthong, and then deletes with CL. Katsika & Kavitskaya (2015) develop an articulatory phonetic account of Samothraki Greek CL that builds both on Kavitskaya (2002) and Kiparsky (2011). To resolve the dispreference for the onset rhotic, the tongue tip constriction of the r is deleted, but the tongue body constriction is kept, preserving some of the segmental and temporal information of the r. The resulting segment is highly vocalic and is subsequently incorporated into the nucleus. Thus, Katsika and Kavitskaya's (2015) account provides articulatory motivation to Kiparsky's idea that in Samothraki Greek, the onset r goes through a vocalic stage followed by the coalescence with the following vowel.

We can thus conclude that the best analysis of Samothraki Greek CL treats it as a two-stage process, under which the vocalization of the onset r happens first, followed by the coalescence of the two vocalic elements.[10]

3.4 Towards the explanation of CL as a sound change

From the point of view of contrast maintenance and loss, CL can be described as the loss of contrast in a certain position. In the case of CL through the loss of consonants, it is usually the coda consonant that deletes with the lengthening of the tautosyllabic

---

[10] A reviewer points out that there are cases when the deletion of a coda consonant happens simultaneously with intervocalic deletion of the same consonant, as, for example, in Turkish (de Chene & Anderson 1979, Kavitskaya 2002: 23). The reviewer suggests that this renders such examples consistent with de Chene and Anderson's generalization. If the same was the case in Samothraki Greek, and the coalescence was phonetically complete at the time of r-deletion, this, by itself, would be enough to exclude Samothraki Greek from potential counterexamples to de Chene and Anderson's generalization. I believe, however, that CL through onset loss in Samothraki Greek is best re-analyzed as vowel coalescence, in the spirit of Kiparsky (2011).

vowel. In a system with no phonologically long vowels, the result of this process could in principle be the introduction of a new vowel length contrast (the phonologization of vowel length in a narrow sense). However, in the case of the pre-existing vowel length distinction, the result is the introduction of the merger of the new long vowels with existing long vowels (the phonologization of vowel length in a certain position, in a broader sense of phonologization).

On the basis of the examples discussed above as well as other instances of CL, it an be argued that CL as a sound change should indeed be defined as the lengthening of the vowel after the loss of the tautosyllabic consonant as a result of the phonological reanalysis of the additional vowel length, either in the spirit of de Chene & Anderson (1979) or of Kavitskaya (2002). De Chene & Anderson (1979) dub this process "monophthongization", that is, roughly, a vowel shift under which a monosyllabic vowel of two vowel qualities becomes a monosyllabic vowel of one vowel quality (as exemplified by Old French and Komi Ižma, among many others). From our admittedly incomplete survey of CL, some kind of a pre-existing length contrast is a necessary condition for CL in the cases where such reanalysis is involved, and no clear cases that counterexemplify this prediction have yet been found if this contrast is interpreted as including heterosyllabic and heteromorphemic sequences of identical vowels. Thus, CL is best described as phonologization in a broader sense, that is, a merger of existing long vowels with new long vowels that are the result of CL. It is possible that Samothraki Greek could also be reanalyzed along these lines (as discussed in footnote 10), but, according to Kiparsky's (2011) account and the phonetic evidence amounted in Katsika & Kavitskaya (2015), it stands out since the sound change goes through an intermediate stage, whereby the consonant becomes a full vocalic entity. CL in this case is a misnomer, and Samothraki Greek is really an instance of vowel coalescence, which is a well-known and uncontroversial source of vowel length in the languages of the world.

We can thus conclude that Samothraki Greek is not a counterexample to the generalization because the lost consonant vocalizes completely and then vowel coalescence happens, with the result that is reminiscent of CL as it has the initial stage of consonant plus vowel and a final stage of a long vowel, but is not, in fact, CL, but rather an instance of VV > V: coalescence. In turn, Old French is not a counterexample because, even if Gess's analysis of the Old French on the basis of the metrical scansion is correct, the presence of a sequence of identical heterosyllabic vowels, which are likely to be phonetically identical to long vowels, provides sufficient contrast. Finally, Komi Ižma is not a counterexample to the most restricted version of the generalization because the presence of a sequence of identical heteromorphemic vowels is sufficient contrast.

4 Sound change, mergers, splits, and contrast

A broad question that remains to be discussed is the reason for why the CL sound change that proceeds by gliding followed by monophthongization (de Chene & Anderson 1979) tends to be structure-preserving, that is, is more likely to acquire vowel length in certain positions with the loss of the consonant if vowel length is already contrastive elsewhere in the system?

3 Compensatory lengthening and structure preservation revisited yet again

Two distinct proposals in the literature address the question of the relevance of structure preservation to sound change. One view on the structure-dependence of sound change is expressed in Kiparsky (1995; 2003) and is to various extent present in other work by Paul Kiparsky. Another view on structure-preserving sound change is presented in Blevins (2004a) and developed in Blevins (2009). As Anderson (2016) notes, Blevins and Kiparsky advocate quite different views on the explanation of sound change. While Blevins (2004a; 2006) puts the main burden of explanation of the sound change on the phonetic factors, Kiparsky (2006) in a critique of Blevins' program views individual grammars as a result of both "what change can produce and of what the theory of grammar allows" (Anderson 2016: 17). Interestingly, both Blevins and Kiparsky see a place for structure preservation in the theory of sound change, either as belonging to the grammar (Kiparsky 1995; 2003) or emerging through acquisition (Blevins 2004a; 2009).

Kiparsky (2003: 328) comments on "the textbook story" of phonologization, where redundant features become phonemic with the loss of conditioning environment (e.g., in the CL sound change, vowel length phonologizes with the loss of the tautosyllabic consonant). However, as Kiparsky (2003) points out, in many similar cases the redundant features fail to phonologize and disappear with the loss of the conditioning environment. Kiparsky goes on to posit a priming effect, which is a diachronic manifestation of structure preservation, formulated as in (6):

(6) Priming effect in phonologization (Kiparsky 2003: 328)
Redundant features are likely to be phonologized if the language's phonological representations have a class node to host them.

Kiparsky (2003) distinguishes between the two types of sound change, perception-based and articulation-based, and claims that while perception-based changes, such as CL, metathesis, tonogenesis, and assimilation, are more likely to be structure-preserving (phonologization in a broad sense, as defined in §3.4), articulation-based changes, such as lenition, umlaut, etc., are usually structure-changing (phonologization in a narrow sense, as defined in §3.4). Among the structure-changing processes that create long vowels are vowel coalescence and also vowel lengthening in specific prosodic conditions (for instance, under stress). Kiparsky (2003: 329) notes that Korhonen (1969: 333–335) suggested that only certain allophones have a functional load that allows for the phonemicization with the loss of conditioning environment. Korhonen (1969) dubs these allophones *quasi-phonemes*. Having claimed that the classical phoneme is "something of a straightjacket" when it comes to understanding of the introduction and loss of phonological contrast, Kiparsky (2013) proposes a system, where he distinguishes between contrastiveness, as a structural notion, and distinctiveness, as a perceptual notion, as shown in Table 7.

By the system in Table 7, quasi-phonemes are not contrastive, but distinctive, and thus they represent a necessary stage to the secondary split. Since distinctiveness is a perceptually-defined notion, only those sound changes that are perceptually-based are predicted to follow this pattern. As was discussed in §3.3, vowel length in Komi Ižma is quasi-phonemic and thus is a likely candidate for the phonologization of vowel length in the language.

Table 7: Contrastiveness vs. distinctiveness (Kiparsky 2013).

	Contrastive	Non-contrastive
Distinctive	Phonemes	Quasi-phonemes
Non-distinctive	Near contrasts	Allophones

Blevins (2004a; 2009) pursues a research agenda that is very different from Kiparsky's theory of sound change. However, she also notes that certain sound changes tend to be structure-preserving, and that these changes tend to be perceptually-based. Blevins (2004a) posits a principle of structural analogy, stated in (7):

(7) Structural Analogy (Blevins 2004a: 154)
In the course of language acquisition, the existence of a (non-ambiguous) phonological contrast between A and B will result in more instances of sound change involving shifts of *ambiguous elements* to A or B than if no contrast between A and B existed.

The consequence of such principle for sound change is a tendency towards structure preservation. Blevins (2009) presents an overview of two known cases of sound changes that have this tendency, such as CL (de Chene & Anderson 1979; Kavitskaya 2002) and metathesis (Blevins & Garrett 1998; Blevins 2004a,b; Hume 2004) and then proceeds to a case study of the Principle of Structural Analogy, unstressed vowel syncope in Austronesian.

According to Blevins (2009), unstressed vowel syncope in the Austronesian languages discussed is a perceptually-based sound change that is the result of the ambiguous vocalic status of hypoarticulated short unstressed vowel. The loss of the second vowel in a CV.CV.CV sequence creates a structure CVC.CV where the first syllable is closed. The Principle of Structural Analogy predicts that languages that contrast open and closed syllables will have a stronger tendency towards this kind of syncope. Indeed, as Blevins (2009) shows, the prediction is borne out.

Blevins' (2009) example is different from the case of CL in an interesting and fundamental way. While CL as a sound change amounts to the introduction of a new allophone and potentially a new phoneme with a positional loss of a segment, unstressed vowel syncope is the introduction of a new prosodic structure with a positional loss of a segment.[11] This example provides additional support to the generalization that the presence of contrast in the system affects sound change that potentially creates similar structures.

---

[11] As a reviewer notes, length is prosodic structure as well, and in this sense, there is little difference between the case discussed by Blevins and the cases of CL. However, while CL (potentially) introduces a new element to the inventory of phonemes, Blevins discusses an example that introduces a new structure to the inventory of syllables.

5 Conclusions

De Chene and Anderson (1979) had an important insight about the structure-preserving nature of CL that holds in the majority of the languages with this sound change and thus cannot be ignored. I have presented examples in which systemic considerations play an important role in the phonologization of newly introduced phonetic detail in perception-based sound changes, such as vowel duration in CL. I have shown a way to address potential counterexamples to the generalization, reanalyzing CL in Samothraki Greek as vowel coalescence and arguing that in the cases of Old French and Komi Ižma the presence of identical tautosyllabic vowels elsewhere in the system might have constituted a sufficient contrast for the phonologization of vowel length through CL.

References

Abondolo, Daniel (ed.). 1998. *The Uralic languages*. London/New York: Routledge.
Anderson, Stephen R. 1982. Where's morphology? *Linguistic Inquiry* 13(4). 571–612.
Anderson, Stephen R. 2016. Synchronic versus diachronic explanation and the nature of the language faculty. *Annual Review of Linguistics* 2. 11–31.
Blevins, Juliette. 2004a. *Evolutionary phonology: The emergence of sound patterns*. Cambridge: Cambridge University Press.
Blevins, Juliette. 2004b. Phonetic explanations for recurrent sound patterns: D iachronic or synchronic? In Eric Raimy & Charles Cairns (eds.), *Phonological theory: Representations and architecture*. Paper presented at CUNY Symposium on Phonology Theory. Cambridge, MA: MIT Press.
Blevins, Juliette. 2006. New perspectives on English sound patterns: 'Natural' and 'unnatural' in Evolutionary Phonology. *Journal of English Linguistics* 34. 6–25.
Blevins, Juliette. 2009. Structure-preserving sound change: A look at unstressed vowel syncope in Austronesian. In Andrew Pawley & Alexander Adelaar (eds.), *Austronesian historical linguistics and culture history: A festschrift for Bob Blust*, 33–49. Canberra: Pacific Linguistics.
Blevins, Juliette & Andrew Garrett. 1998. The origins of consonant-vowel metathesis. *Language* 74(3). 508–556.
Collinder, Björn. 1957. *Survey of the Uralic languages*. Stockholm: Almqvist & Wiksell.
Curtis, Emily. 2003. *Geminate weight: Case studies and formal models*. University of Washington Ph.D. Dissertation.
Davis, Stuart. 1999. On the representation of initial geminates. *Phonology* 16. 93–104.
de Chene, Brent E. 1985. *The historical phonology of vowel length*. New York: Garland.
de Chene, Brent E. & Stephen R. Anderson. 1979. Compensatory lengthening. *Language* 55(3). 505–535.
de Lacy, Paul. 2001. Markedness in prominent positions. In Ora Matushansky, A. Costa, Javier Martin-Gonzalez, Adam Szczegielniak & Lance Nathan (eds.), *Proceedings of HUMIT 2000, MIT Working Papers in Linguistics 40*, 53–66. Cambridge, MA: MITWPL.

Dixon, Robert M. W. 1990. Compensating phonological change: An example from the northern dialects of Dyirbal. *Lingua* 80. 1–34.

Gess, Randall. 1998. Compensatory lengthening and structure preservation revisited. *Phonology* 15. 353–366.

Harms, Robert T. 1967. Split, shift, and merger in the Permic vowels. *Ural-Altaische Jahrbücher* 39. 163–198.

Harms, Robert T. 1968. *Introduction to phonological theory*. Englewood Cliffs, NJ: Prentice-Hall.

Hausenberg, Anu-Reet. 1998. Komi. In Daniel Abondolo (ed.), *The Uralic languages*, 305–326. London/New York: Routledge.

Hayes, Bruce. 1989. Compensatory lengthening in moraic phonology. *Linguistic Inquiry* 20(2). 253–306.

Heisenberg, August. 1934. *Neugriechische Dialekttexte*. Leipzig, Germany: Harrassowitz.

Hock, Hans Henrich. 1986. Compensatory lengthening: In defense of the concept 'mora'. *Folia Linguistica* 20. 431–460.

Hume, Elizabeth. 2004. The indeterminacy/attestation model of metathesis. *Language* 80(2). 203–237.

Katsanis, Nicolaos. 1996. *Το γλωσσικό ιδίωμα της σαμοθράκης*. Thessaloniki, Greece: Aristotle University of Thessaloniki Press.

Katsika, Argyro & Darya Kavitskaya. 2015. The phonetics of /r/ deletion in Samothraki Greek. *Journal of Greek Linguistics* 15. 34–65.

Kavitskaya, Darya. 2002. *Compensatory lengthening: Phonetics, phonology, diachrony*. New York: Routledge.

Kiparsky, Paul. 1995. The phonological basis of sound change. In John Goldsmith (ed.), *The handbook of phonological theory*, 640–670. Oxford: Blackwell Publishing.

Kiparsky, Paul. 2003. The phonological basis of sound change. In Brian D. Joseph & Richard D. Janda (eds.), *The handbook of historical linguistics*, 313–342. Oxford: Blackwell Publishing.

Kiparsky, Paul. 2006. The Amphichronic Program vs. Evolutionary Phonology. *Theoretical Linguistics* 32(2). 217–236.

Kiparsky, Paul. 2011. Compensatory lengthening. In Eric Raimy & Charles Cairns (eds.), *Handbook of the syllable*, 33–69. Leiden: Brill.

Kiparsky, Paul. 2013. Phonologization. In Patrick Honeybone & Joseph Salmons (eds.), *Handbook of historical phonology*. Oxford: Oxford University Press.

Korhonen, Mikko. 1969. Die Entwicklung der morphologischen Methode im Lappischen. *Finnisch-Urgische Forschungen* 37. 203–262.

Lytkin, V. I. (ed.). 1966. *The contemporary Komi language*. Syktyvkar.

Lytkin, V. I. & T. I. Teplyashina. 1976. *Permskie iazyki. Osnovy finno-ugorskogo iazykoznaniia*. Moskva: Nauka.

Margariti-Rogka, Marianna & Maria Tsolaki. 2011. Τα μακρά φωνήεντα στο ιδίωμα της σαμοθράκης. In C. Mpasea-Mpezantakou, I. Manolessou, A. Afroudakis, S. Mpeis & G. Katsouda (eds.), *Νεοελληνική διαλεκτολογία 6*, 273–294. Athens, Greece: Academy of Athens.

Morin, Yves-Charles. 1992. *Phonological interpretations of historical lengthening.* Paper presented at the 7th International Phonology Meeting. Krems.

Newton, Brian. 1972a. *Generative interpretation of the dialect.* Cambridge: Cambridge University Press.

Newton, Brian. 1972b. Loss of /r/ in a Modern Greek dialect. *Language* 48. 566–572.

Pope, Mildred K. 1934. *From Latin to Modern French with especial consideration of Anglo-Norman: Phonology and morphology.* Manchester: Manchester University Press.

Roach, William (ed.). 1959. *Chrétien de Troyes – Le Roman de Perceval ou Le Conte du Graal.* Geneva: Droz.

Ryan, Kevin. 2014. Onsets contribute to syllable weight: Statistical evidence from stress and meter. *Language* 90. 309–341.

Smith, Jennifer. 2003. Onset sonority constraints and subsyllabic structure. *Rutgers Optimality Archive* 608.

Sumner, Megan. 1999. Compensatory lengthening as coalescence: Analysis and implications. In Sonya Bird, Andrew Carnie, Jason D. Haugen & Peter Norquest (eds.), *WCCFL 18 proceedings*, 532–544. Somerville, MA: Cascadilla Press.

Topintzi, Nina. 2006. A (not so) paradoxical instance of compensatory lengthening: Samothraki Greek and theoretical implications. *Journal of Greek Linguistics* 7. 71–119.

Zec, Draga. 2007. The syllable. In Paul de Lacy (ed.), *The Cambridge handbook of phonology*, 161–194. Cambridge: Cambridge University Press.

Chapter 4

Phonological exceptionality is localized to phonological elements: the argument from learnability and Yidiny word-final deletion

Erich R. Round
University of Queensland

> Anderson (2008) emphasizes that the space of possible grammars must be constrained by limits not only on what is cognitively representable, but on what is learnable. Focusing on word final deletion in Yidiny (Dixon 1977a), I show that the learning of exceptional phonological patterns is improved if we assume that Prince & Tesar's (2004) Biased Constraint Demotion (BCD) with Constraint Cloning (Pater 2009) is subject to a Morphological Coherence Principle (MCP), which operationalizes morphological analytic bias (Moreton 2008) during phonological learning. The existence of the MCP allows the initial state of Con to be simplified, and thus shifts explanatory weight away from the representation of the grammar per se, and towards the learning device.
>
> I then argue that the theory of exceptionality must be phonological and diacritic. Specifically, I show that co-indexation between lexical forms and lexically indexed constraints must be via indices not on morphs but on individual phonological elements. Relative to indices on phonological elements, indices on morphs add computational cost for no benefit during constraint evaluation and learning; and a theory without indices on phonological elements is empirically insufficient. On the other hand, approaches which represent exceptionality by purely phonological means (e.g. Zoll 1996) are ill-suited to efficient learning. Concerns that a phonologically-indexed analysis would overgenerate (Gouskova 2012) are unfounded under realistic assumptions about the learner.

1 Exceptionality

What is the nature of representations which are passed from the morphology to the phonology? Anderson (1992) demonstrates that the processes that create those representations can be elaborate and complex. Operations that act upon morphological forms, to realize units of morphologically-relevant meaning, involve not only the concatenation

Erich R. Round. 2017. Phonological exceptionality is localized to phonological elements: the argument from learnability and Yidiny word-final deletion. In Claire Bowern, Laurence Horn & Raffaella Zanuttini (eds.), *On looking into words (and beyond)*, 59–98. Berlin: Language Science Press. DOI:10.5281/zenodo.495439

of formatives, but also selection among alternatives and non-concatenative modifications to intermediate representations (see also Anderson 2015; 2016; 2017). However, what of the final result, which comprises some number of morphs that must then be interpreted phonologically? A constant concern of generative phonology since its inception has been to account adequately for patterned phonological exceptionality, the phenomenon in which segments in a restricted class of morphs exhibit phonologically distinctive behavior as triggers, targets or blockers of alternations, or as participants in exceptional featural, phonotactic or prosodic surface structures. For example, in Yidiny (Dixon 1977a,b) vowels delete word-finally, if that deletion would prevent the word from surfacing with an unfooted syllable. This is seen in the root *gaɟara-* 'possum' in (1a) and the suffix *-ɲa* ACCUSATIVE in (1b), where feet are marked by parentheses. However, in a restricted set of morphs the final vowel behaves exceptionally, resisting deletion, as in the root *guɟara-* 'broom' (2a) and the suffix *-na* PURPOSIVE (2b).

(1) a. 'possum.ABS' /gaɟara/ → (ga ɟa:r)
    b. 'father-ACC' /bimbi-ɲa/ → (bim bi:ɲ)

(2) a. 'broom.ABS' /guɟara/ → (gu ɟa:) ra
    b. 'go-PURP' /gali-na/ → (ga li:) na

In order for the phonology to treat morph-specific, exceptional segments appropriately, it must receive from the morphology some kind of discriminating information which it can act upon. For much of the generative period it has been argued that this information is associated with morphs as a whole, and not with their individual phonological elements. Here I present an argument for the contrary view. The contribution, then, is to clarify the nature of one important aspect of the interaction between the morphological and phonological components of grammar. The principle line of evidence is learnability, namely the learnability of an optimality-theoretic grammar for phonological exceptionality. Anderson (2008) has emphasized that the space of possible human grammars must be constrained not only by limits on what is cognitively representable, but also on what is learnable. The crux of the argument here relies not on specifics, but ultimately on general properties of learnable grammars, and thus I would hope should remain valid even as specific theories undergo refinement as they move closer to answering Anderson's (2008) challenge.[1]

The chapter falls into two broad parts. In §2–§5 I discuss the processes and principles required to learn exceptionality. This leads to the positing of a Morphological Coherence

---

[1] A reviewer asks whether the machinery presented here is necessary if one assumes an exemplar-based model of phonology. I assume that learners do store rich, exemplar-like representations of linguistic experiences. However, natural language morphology in general has enough combinatorial complexity that reliance upon retrieved episodes will not be sufficient to reproduce the full range of creative behavior that humans display. Consequently some generative machinery is necessary, which performs not merely simple analogies and concatenations, but which can reproduce with precision the complex patterns generated by a realizational morphology such as Anderson's (1992), and by a formal phonological grammar such as entertained here.

Principle in §6, which operationalizes a morphological bias that ensures successful learning for certain cases. In §7–§9 I am concerned with the underlying theory of these processes and principles. I evaluate two broad approaches to phonological exceptionality: PHONOLOGICAL approaches, which represent exceptionality as a property of individual segments (Bloomfield 1939; Kiparsky 1982a; Inkelas 1994; Zoll 1996), and MORPHOLOGICAL approaches which represent it as a property of morphs (Chomsky 1964; Chomsky & Halle 1968; Zonneveld 1978; Pater 2000). The result is an argument in favor of a DIACRITIC PHONOLOGICAL approach. On this account, exceptionality is represented at the level of individual phonological elements, not morphs; however the means of marking it is by diacritics which are visible to the phonology but not manipulable by it, in contradistinction to the CONCRETE PHONOLOGICAL approach, where the crucial representations are themselves phonological elements. As I show, the function of these "Φ-indices" is essentially identical to "M-indices" which would mark morphs, only there is no assumption that all exponents of a morph *m* be indexed identically. As we shall see, freedom from that assumption is both coherent theoretically and desirable, computationally and empirically. The discussion is illustrated throughout by the facts of word final deletion in Yidiny, to which we turn now in §2.

2 Word-final deletion in Yidiny

2.1 The phenomenon

Yidiny (Dixon 1977a) belongs to the Yidinyic subgroup of the Pama-Nyungan language family. Traditionally it was spoken in the rainforest region southwest of Cairns, in Northeastern Australia. Most examples below are from Dixon's (1977) detailed descriptive grammar; examples marked † are from Dixon's (1991) dictionary and texts. An inventory of underlying segments is in Table 1.

Table 1: Yidiny underlying segments, after Dixon (1977a: 32).

	Labial	Apical	Laminal	Dorsal
Stop	b	d	ɟ	g
Nasal	m	n	ɲ	ŋ
Lateral, trill		l, r		
Approximant	w	ɻ	y	
Vowels	i, a, u, iː, aː, uː			

Syllable shapes are tightly constrained. Onsets are obligatory and simple. Codas permit only sonorants other than /w/. Codas in word-final position are simple; word-internal codas also permit disegmental, continuant–nasal sequences. Morphologically, the language is almost entirely suffixing and largely agglutinative. Roots are minimally disyllabic and suffixes are maximally disyllabic (Dixon 1977a: 35,90). An online appendix[2] discusses the morphological constituency of verbal inflection.

Of Yidiny's phonological alternations, those to receive the greatest attention have been stress placement, vowel length and to a lesser extent, word-final deletion (Dixon 1977a,b; Hayes 1982; 1985; Kager 1993; Crowhurst & Hewitt 1995; Halle & Idsardi 1995; Hall 2001; Pruitt 2010; Hyde 2012; Bowern, Round & Alpher in revision, *inter alia*). Yidiny's stress and length alternations in particular have featured in significant theoretical works on meter and prosody over the past four decades, and both are nontrivial topics in themselves. Word-final deletion, however, can be studied largely independently of them for reasons that follow.

Although stress placement in Yidiny has proven contentious (Pruitt 2010; Bowern, Round & Alpher in revision), word-final deletion is not sensitive to stress *per se*, but rather only to the position of foot boundaries. These have been uncontroversial since their analysis by Hayes (1982): feet in Yidiny are disyllabic and left-aligned within the phonological word.

Many words with word-final deletion also exhibit vowel lengthening; however the phenomena show little to no mutual interaction. In a rule-based theory permitting simultaneous application (Anderson 1974) lengthening and deletion would apply simultaneously; neither rule feeds or bleeds the other.[3] See Round (in progress) for an analysis of Yidiny lengthening.

Word-final deletion is sensitive to foot placement, and foot placement is sensitive to phonological word boundaries. In Yidiny, phonological words commence at the left edge of each root and each disyllabic suffix (Dixon 1977a: 88–98).[4] Phonological words therefore begin with either a polysyllabic root or a disyllabic suffix and are followed by zero or more monosyllabic or entirely consonantal suffixes. Word-final deletion targets unfooted syllables and therefore only affects prosodic words which, *modulo* deletion, would be at least trisyllabic. As a consequence, we are interested here in three kinds of phonological word: those comprised of bare roots of three or more syllables; those comprised of roots plus one or more monosyllabic suffixes; and those comprised of a disyllabic suffix plus one or more additional, monosyllabic suffixes. The third kind is rare,[5] and so discussion will focus on the first two.

Word-final deletion applies only if the word thereby avoids surfacing with an unfooted syllable. For example, the roots *gindanu-* 'moon' and *gubuma-* 'black pine' both contain three vowels, each of which is a potential syllabic nucleus at the surface. In (3a,4a) they have undergone deletion of their final vowel to prevent it from surfacing in an unfooted syllable; compare (3b,4b) where the roots are non-final in the word, and the final vowels surface.

---

[2] Available from 10.6084/m9.figshare.4579696
[3] Deletion counter-bleeds lengthening, thus in a strictly serial analysis lengthening would precede word-final deletion (Dixon 1977a,b; Hayes 1985; Crowhurst & Hewitt 1995).
[4] Yidiny's only prefix, [ɟa:-] 'in a direction' occupies its own phonological word (Dixon 1977a: 98,162).
[5] For an illustration, see example (25).

4 Phonological exceptionality is localized to phonological elements

(3) a. 'moon[ABS]' /gindanu/ → (gin da:n)
       *(gin da:) nu
   b. 'moon-ERG' /gindanu-ŋgu/ → (gin da) (nuŋ gu)

(4) a. 'black pine[ABS]' /gubuma/ → (gu bu:m)
       *(gu bu:) ma
   b. 'black pine-PURP' /gubuma-gu/ → (gu bu) (ma gu)

Final vowel deletion may also affect suffixes. In (5a,c,6a), the vowels of the nominal comitative suffix -*yi* and verbal comitative suffix -*ŋa* have undergone deletion, thereby preventing the surfacing of an unfooted syllable. In (5b,6b) the suffixes are non-final in the word, and the vowel surfaces.

(5) a. 'woman-COM' /buɲa-yi/ → (bu ɲa:y)
       *(bu ɲa:) yi
   b. 'woman-COM-ERG' /buɲa-yi-ŋgu/ → (bu ɲa) (yiŋ gu)
   c. 'black bream-COM' /gulugulu-yi/ → (gu lu) (gu lu:y)
       *(gu lu) (gu lu:) yi

(6) a. 'come-COM[IMP]' /gada-ŋa/ → (ga da:ŋ)
       *(ga da:) ŋa
   b. 'come-COM-PST' /gada-ɲa-lɲu/ → (ga da:) (ɲal ɲu)

Word-final deletion interacts with restrictions on word-final consonants, and the interaction plays out differently in roots versus suffixes. In roots, deletion will fail to apply if the result would be an illicit word-final coda, containing either a stop or /w/ (7) or a cluster (8). One conceivable alternative, to also delete the consonant, is not attested in roots (7–8).[6]

(7) a. 'man[ABS]' /waguɟa/ → (wa gu:) ɟa
       *(wa guɟ)
       *(wa gu:)
   b. 'dog[ABS]' /gudaga/ → (gu da:) ga
       *(gu da:g)
       *(gu da:)
   c. 'sugar ant[ABS]' /balawa/ → (ba la:) wa
       *(ba la:w)
       *(ba la:)
   d. 'place name[ABS]' /ɲalumba/ → (ɲa lu:m) ba
       *(ɲa lu:mb)
       *(ɲa lu:m)

---

[6] Neither Dixon's grammar (1977) nor dictionary (Dixon 1991, which cites underlying forms) records a surface form for the roots in (7c) and (7d), or for roots illustrating the same pre-final consonant or comparable consonant clusters. However, Dixon (1977a: 57–58) specifically reports that the roots *balawa*- and *gindalba*- do not undergo deletion; the surface forms provided here are what we would expect if this is so.

(8) 'warn[IMP]' /binarŋa/ → (bi na:r) ŋa
                                *(bi na:rŋ)
                                *(bi na:r)

In contrast, deletion in suffixes applies not only to the final vowel, but also to a single consonant that precedes it, if that consonant would be illicit word-finally, as in (9). This form of CV deletion respects phonotactic constraints while also avoiding unfooted syllables.[7]

(9) a. 'grey possum-ERG'   /margu-ŋgu/   → (mar gu:ŋ)
    b. 'see-PST'   /wawa-lɲu/   → (wa wa:l)
    c. 'warn-DAT.SUB'   /binarŋa-lɲu-nda/ → (bi nar) (ɲal ɲu:n)

However, word-final deletion never deletes the initial segment of a suffix (and consequently, it will never delete an entire suffix), as illustrated in (10).

(10) a. 'woman-SET'   /buɲa-ba/   → (bu ɲa:) ba
                                         *(buɲ ba)
     b. 'bandicoot-GEN'   /guygal-ni/ → (guy ga:l) ni
                                         *(guy ga:ln)
                                         *(guy ga:l)

Deletions do not occur word internally (11a,b), nor do word-final, licit codas delete (11b). All Yidiny roots and suffixes that are consonant-final end underlyingly with licit coda consonants, so no morph undergoes spontaneous deletion of an underlyingly-final consonant (11c).

(11) a.   'woman-SET' /buɲa-ba/   → (bu ɲa:b)
                                      *(bu ɲa:)
     b.[†] 'name[ABS]' /bagiram/   → (ba gi:) ram
                                      *(ba gi:rm)
                                      *(ba gi:r)
     c.   */bagirag/ → *(ba gi:r)

To summarize, word-final deletion applies only so as to avoid the surfacing of unfooted syllables. It may delete the final vowel from a root and the final (C)V sequence from a suffix, but will not delete a suffix-initial segment. Deletion is blocked (in roots) or expanded (in suffixes, from V deletion to CV deletion) in order to obey phonotactic restrictions on word-final codas. These are the regular conditions under which word-final deletion occurs.

In addition to its regular application, Yidiny contains roots and suffixes which are exceptional non-undergoers of word-final deletion. In (13), the non-undergoer roots

---

[7] The "dative subordinate" is marked by what Round (2013: 26) has called "compound suffixation", comprising two monosyllabic suffixal morphs, /-lɲu; -nda/. That these are not a single, disyllabic suffix is evident in the fact that they fail to be parsed into a their own phonological word, separate from the root.

4 Phonological exceptionality is localized to phonological elements

mulari-, guɟara-, ɟudulu-, baŋgamu- all resist word-final deletion despite their pre-final consonant being permissible as a coda, and despite the fact that the consequence is an unfooted, word-final syllable.

(12) a. 'initiated man[ABS]'   /mulari/   → (mu la:) ri
        *(mu la:r)
     b. 'broom[ABS]'   /guɟara/   → (gu ɟa:) ra
        *(gu ɟa:r)
     c. 'brown pigeon[ABS]'   /ɟudulu/   → (ɟu du:) lu
        *(ɟu du:l)
     d. 'potato[ABS]'   /baŋgamu/   → (baŋ ga:) mu
        *(baŋ ga:m)

Dixon (1977a: 59) reports 115 trisyllabic roots whose phonotactic shape would, under regular conditions, expose them to word-final deletion. Of these, 34, or around 30%, are exceptional non-undergoers. The distinction is idiosyncratic; neither Dixon (1977a: 58) nor subsequent researchers have found any phonological, semantic or grammatical factor that categorically determines whether a root will be a non-undergoer.[8]

Suffixes also may be exceptional non-undergoers. In (17) the non-undergoer suffixes *-nda, -lɟi* and *-na* resist word-final deletion and allow an unfooted syllable to surface. Avoidance of regular, word-final CV deletion is seen in (13a,b) and V deletion in (13c).

(13) a. 'grey possum-DAT'   margu-nda   → (mar gu:n) da
        *(mar gu:n)
     b. 'see-LEST[ADS]'   wawa-lɟi   → (wa wa:l) ɟi
        *(wa wa:l)
     c. 'go-PURP'   gali-na   → (ga li:) na
        *(ga li:n)

Tables 2 and 3 list all suffixal allomorphs in Yidiny which, on phonotactic grounds, could plausibly delete.[9] Regular undergoers are in Table 2 and non-undergoers in Table 3.

---

[8] Historically speaking, borrowed forms may account for many of these items (Barry Alpher p.c.); synchronically, however, their motivation is opaque.

[9] Such suffixes must be vowel-final and monosyllabic. If just the final vowel is to delete, then it must leave behind a single, licit-coda consonant in word final position. This will require the suffix to be -CV, and be preceded by a vowel, not a consonant. Alternatively, if the final CV is to delete, then the suffix must be -CCV, since suffix-initial segments do not delete, and it too must attach to a vowel-final stem. Data here is from a comprehensive search of Dixon (1977a), in which relevant information can be found on pp.50–54, 151. "Emphatic" *-ɲa* (Dixon 1977a: 151) is excluded. It behaves as a phonological clitic that occupies a distinct phonological word, and does not undergo final deletion.

Table 2: Monosyllabic suffixes which undergo word-final deletion.

Function		-CV	-CCV
Case	ERGATIVE		-ŋgu
	LOCATIVE	-la	
	ACCUSATIVE	-ɲa	
	COMITATIVE	-yi	
	GENITIVE	-ni, -nu	
Verbal	PAST tense inflection	-ɲu	-lɲu, -ɻɲu
	COMITATIVE derivation	-ŋa	
	DATIVE SUBORDINATE inflection		-nda[10]

Table 3: Monosyllabic suffixes which escape word-final deletion.

Function		-CV	-CCV
Case	DATIVE		-nda
Verbal	PURPOSIVE inflection	-na	-lna, -ɻna
	LEST nominalizing derivation		-nɟi, -lɟi, -ɻɟi

Exceptional non-undergoers, both roots and suffixes, only block the deletion of their own segments; the exceptionality does not spread to neighboring morphs. Accordingly in (14), the exceptional non-undergoer LEST does not block deletion in the following, regular undergoer, ERGATIVE suffix.

(14) wiwi-:ɟi-nɟi-ŋgu 'give-ANTIP-LEST-ERG' → (wi wi:) (ɟin ɟi:ŋ)
     *(wi wi:) (ɟin ɟi:ŋ) gu

Likewise, the presence of a regular undergoer will not undo the blocking effect of an exceptional non-undergoer. In (15) the regular undergoer COMITATIVE does not undermine the blocking of deletion in the exceptional non-undergoer PURPOSIVE, which follows it.

(15) maɟinda-ŋa-lna 'walk up-COM-PURP' → (ma ɟin) (da ŋa:l) na
     *(ma ɟin) (da ŋa:l)

It will be recalled that roots in Yidiny can undergo word-final deletion of vowels, but not of the consonants that precede them. More specifically, roots that end in CCV do not delete final CV, whereas some suffixes do, and nor does final C'V delete from roots that end in VC'V, where C' is an impermissible coda. Two conceivable accounts for this

---

[10] The dative subordinate is marked by a string of two monosyllabic suffixes -lɲu-nda, cf. fn.7.

may be distinguished. On one account, the grammar of Yidiny expressly prohibits root-final CV deletion. On the other, it happens just by chance that all CCV-final and VC'V-final roots are exceptional non-undergoers. On the latter account, the grammar WOULD enforce CV deletion from roots, if only the lexicon provided the right inputs; on the former account it would not. The level of empirical support for these hypotheses can be assessed statistically. Table 4 compares counts of CCV- and VC'V-final roots and CCV-final suffixes which either do or do not delete. The distribution is strongly unbalanced, and we can reject with confidence the null hypothesis that it is due to chance ($\chi^2_{df=1}$ = 47.9 $p < 10^{-10}$). Table 5 compares counts of roots that are CCV- and VC'V-final with those that are VCV-final, i.e., where C is a permissible coda. Again, the counts are highly unbalanced and we reject the hypothesis that the absence of deletion in CCV- and VC'V-finals is by chance ($\chi^2_{df=1}$ = 125.8. $p < 10^{-10}$). The only empirically-supported conclusion is that the lack of consonant deletion in Yidiny roots is systematic, not due to chance. A satisfactory formal analysis should reflect this.[11]

Table 4: Deletion of coda-ilicit pre-final C in roots versus suffixes.

	CCV- and VC'V-final roots	CCV-final suffixes
No deletion	116	6
Deletion	0	4

Table 5: Deletion in roots with pre-final coda-illicit C versus prefixal coda-licit C.

	CCV- and VC'V-final roots	VCV-final suffixes
No deletion	116	34
Deletion	0	81

2.2 Constraint rankings

A briefly sketch now follows of how the facts above would be analysed in OT. Foot placement in Yidiny is due to FOOTBINARITY ≫ PARSESYLLABLE ≫ ALIGN(FT,L,PRWD,L) (Prince & Smolensky 2004[1993], McCarthy & Prince 1993a, McCarthy & Prince 1995). Of these, only PARSESYLLABLE (PRS) will be of interest for our purposes; I assume that other prosodic constraints are satisfied optimally. Absolute re-

---

[11] As a reviewer observes, there is an interesting historical background to be clarified here, and an account of it is planned. Naturally, the object of a synchronic analysis differs ontologically from that of a historical one. The two are complementary, but neither account would substitute for or serve as a counter-analysis to the other.

strictions against obstruents and /w/ in codas are due to SONORANT/CODA (e.g. Lombardi 2002) and *w/CODA; I assume these are unviolated.

Regular word-final deletion in Yidiny can be analysed straightforwardly by ranking PRS ≫ MAXIMALITY (MAX, McCarthy & Prince 1995). This causes deletion of final vowels in preference to the surfacing of unfooted syllables, but not if an illicit coda results.

Segments may delete from the right edge of the word only, not the left or word-internally. High-ranking ANCHOR-LEFT(morph) penalizes deletion from the left edge of any morph and CONTIG-IO(PRWD) penalizes deletion internally (McCarthy & Prince 1995).

Yidiny permits complex codas word-internally, but not word-finally. Ranking CNTG ≫ *COMPLEXCODA (Bernhardt & Stemberger 1998) accounts for this; ranking both above PRS accounts for the absence of deletion after pre-final clusters in roots and the defeat of candidates which delete only a final vowel from word-final CCV suffixes.

Word-final deletion applies differently to roots and suffixes. Roots will not undergo consonant deletion, even if the consequence is an unfooted syllable. The ranking of un-dominated MAX-C/ROOT (McCarthy & Prince 1995) above PRS accounts for this. Suffixes do not violate MAX-C/RT and consequently are free to undergo consonant deletion, however highly-ranked ANC penalizes the deletion of morph-initial segments. This accounts for the fact that a consonant may delete from a -CCV suffix but not from -CV.

At this point, regular word-final deletion occurs whenever satisfaction of the markedness constraint PRS requires the violation of the lower-ranked faithfulness constraint MAX. Deletion is blocked unexceptionally whenever PRS itself is violated in order to satisfy higher-ranking constraints, which are of two kinds: those which penalize marked codas, SON/CODA, *w/CODA, *CPLX; and those which penalize deletion in specific morphological contexts, namely at left edges of morphs, ANC, and consonants in roots, MAX-C/RT. We see that the driver of word-final deletion in Yidiny is the ranking of PRS ≫ MAX. Deletion occurs when PRS is satisfied but MAX is not. Regular blocking results when PRS must be violated, in which case MAX can be satisfied.

Exceptional non-undergoers avoid deletion. For them, MAX is always satisfied, even at the expense of PRS. Consequently, while regular undergoers are subject to a ranking of PRS ≫ MAX, exceptional non-undergoers must be subject to MAX ≫ PRS. In §4 I consider two approaches that will ensure this is the case, one morphological and one phonological. First though, a remark about constraint violations.

3 Relativized constraint violation

I introduce here a simple expression for relating the violations of certain pairs of constraints, which will aid discussion in later sections.

For any constraint C and candidate CAND, there will be zero or more violations of C. Given the definition of C, those violations will be due to certain parts, or loci, in CAND, either in the output of CAND or in the correspondences between input and output elements (McCarthy & Prince 1995). We can define the set of LOCI OF VIOLATION, V(C, CAND), as the loci in CAND which cause violations of C (McCarthy 2003, Łubowicz 2005). Now, some pairs of constraints C_1, C_2 are related such that for any CAND, the loci of violation of C_2 are a subset of the loci of violation of C_1. In many cases, the latter are precisely those members of the former which also contain some particular kind of phonological element. For example V(MAX-C, CAND) are those members of V(MAX, CAND) which also contain input consonants. In that case, we can express V(C_2, CAND) terms of the INTERSECTION of the set V(C_1, CAND) and some appropriately defined second set, that picks out loci containing the criterial elements. Let us define the set of "φ-loci", $L_\varphi(D(\varphi),$ CAND), as the set of loci in CAND that contain a phonological element φ of the kind denoted by predicate $D(\varphi)$. For example, V(MAX-C, CAND) can be defined in relative terms, as in (16), where the predicate INPUT_CONSONANT(φ) denotes input consonants. (For brevity I omit the "CAND" from the expression for each set.)

(16) V(MAX-C) $=_{def}$ V(MAX) $\cap$ L_φ(INPUT_CONSONANT(φ))

This relativized method will be used below to define new constraints C_N in terms of a reference constraint, C_R, and a set of phonological elements which restrict the violations of C_N relative to those of C_R.

4 Preliminary analysis of word-final deletion

4.1 A morphological approach

We now consider an OT implementation of the morphological approach to Yidiny exceptionality, using lexically indexed constraints (Pater 2000; 2006; 2009). A lexically indexed constraint C_M behaves precisely like its unindexed counterpart, C, except that it can be violated only by structures which contain exponents of a specific set M of morphs, each of which has been assigned a diacritic mark which I will term a LEXICAL M-INDEX, that co-indexes it to C_M. The definition can be expressed relatively as in (17), following a similar formulation by Finley (2010).

(17) V(C_M) $=_{def}$ V(C) $\cap$ $L_\varphi(m \in M$ & EXP(φ, m)), where:
    M is the set of morphs co-indexed to C_M.
    EXP(φ, m) states that element φ is an exponent of morph m

If we now define two sets of Yidiny morphs, U the set of regular undergoers of word-final deletion, and N the set of exceptional non-undergoers, then either of the rankings in (18) will ensure that the correct sets of morphs is subject to the desired partial ranking of PRS and MAX.

(18) a. PRS$_U$ $\gg$ MAX $\gg$ PRS
      b. MAX$_N$ $\gg$ PRS $\gg$ MAX

In (18a), all phonological exponents of undergoer morphs will be subject to PRS$_U$ $\gg$ MAX, and non-undergoers to MAX $\gg$ PRS. In (18b), all phonological exponents of non-undergoer morphs will be subject to MAX$_N$ $\gg$ PRS, and undergoers to PRS $\gg$ MAX. For

69

now I will use ranking (18a); the reason for this will become clear in §5.[12,13] Examples in (19a–19b) illustrate word-final deletion of regular undergoers which are indexed U, the root *malanu-$_U$* and suffix ERGATIVE *-ŋgu$_U$*, while (19c–19d) show the absence of deletion for exceptional non-undergoers *mulari-* 'initiated man' and DATIVE *nda*.

(19)			PRS$_U$	MAX	PRS
	a.	/malanu$_U$/ 'right hand[ABS]' (ma la:n) > (ma la:) nu	W	L	W
	b.	/margu-ŋgu$_U$/ 'grey possum-ERG' (mar gu:ŋ) > (mar gu:ŋ) gu	W	L	W
	c.	/mulari/ 'initiated man[ABS]' (mu la:) ri > (mu la:r)		W	L
	d.	/margu-nda/ 'grey possum-DAT' (mar gu:n) da > (mar gu:n)		W	L
	e.	/maɟinda-ŋa$_U$-lna/ 'walk up-COM-PURP' (ma ɟin) (da ŋa:l) na > (ma ɟin) (da ŋa:l)		W	L

Example (19e) illustrates the fact that violations of PRS$_U$ require not merely the presence of a U-indexed morph in the word, but a locus of violation which contains a phonological exponent of a U-indexed morph (17). Namely, the final syllable of (19e), *na*, is unfooted. However since that syllable contains no phonological exponent of a U-indexed morph, no violation of PRS$_U$ results. This is true despite the presence of a U-indexed morph elsewhere in the word.

4.2 A phonological approach

The phonological approach correlates the (un)exceptionality of a segment with representational properties of the segment itself. Implementations differ as to which property is used. Zoll (1996) analyses segments which resist deletion as having root nodes in their input, whereas segments that delete more readily lack root nodes, and are termed SUBSEGMENTS. Under these assumptions, a ranking MAX(SEG) ≫ PRS ≫ MAX(SUBSEG) ensures that segments with input root nodes are subjected to MAX(SEG) ≫ PRS, while those without are subjected to PRS ≫ MAX(SUBSEG).[14] Examples are in (20), where segments without root nodes are underlined.

---

[12] Briefly, procedures for learning OT grammars improve in performance if they opt to rank markedness higher than faithfulness when given a choice. Consequently the ranking in (18a) will be learned in preference to (18b); see §5.

[13] An early proposal that only faithfulness constraints be indexable (Benua 1997; Itô & Mester 1999; Fukazawa 1999) has proven untenable (Pater 2000; 2006; Flack 2007b; Flack 2007a; Inkelas & Zoll 2007; Gouskova 2007; Mahanta 2008; Jurgec 2010).

[14] Assuming undominated *FLOAT (Myers 1997), which prohibits surface subsegments, and low-ranked DEP(ROOT) (Zoll 2001).

4 Phonological exceptionality is localized to phonological elements

(20)

		Max(Seg)	Prs	Max(Subseg)
a.	/malanu̱/ (ma la:n) > (mu la:) nu̱		W	L
b.	/marguŋgu̱/ (mar gu:ŋ) > (mar guŋ) gu̱		W	L
c.	/mulari/ (mu la:) ri > (mu la:r)	W	L	W
d.	/margu-nda/ (mar gu:n) da > (mar gu:n)	W	L	W

I wish to draw a distinction now between two conceivable kinds of phonological analysis. A CONCRETE phonological analysis represents exceptionality using regular phonological material, such as features, root nodes and prosodic units, or perhaps their absence. An ABSTRACT phonological analysis uses diacritic lexical indices, which I will term LEXICAL Φ-INDICES, on segments, much like the morphological analysis uses lexical M-indices on morphs. Some objections which have been raised to phonological analyses are specific to the concrete approach. These include doubts over whether sufficiently many concrete phonological contrasts would be available in languages with very many exceptional patterns (Gouskova 2012), and concerns over whether learners can choose between multiple, alternative concrete representations (Kiparsky 1973, Pater 2009). I will set these concrete-specific concerns aside for now, and instead assume an abstract phonological approach. I return to the concrete approach in §9, where I argue on independent grounds that it is poorly adapted to efficient learning.

Accordingly, I will use lexical Φ-indices u and n to index undergoer and non-undergoer segments respectively, and define Φ-indexed constraints, C_Φ, in relative terms as in (21).

(21) $V(C_\Phi) =_{def} V(C) \cap L_\varphi(\varphi \in \Phi)$, where:
Φ is the set of phonological elements co-indexed to C_Φ.

Returning to the phonological account of Yidiny exceptionality, a constraint ranking Max-n ≫ Prs ≫ Max, or Prs-u ≫ Max ≫ Prs, will be sufficient for our purposes. Tableau (22) shows examples using the latter ranking; u-indexed segments are underlined.

(22)

		Prs-u	Max	Prs
a.	(ma la:n) > (mu la:) nu̱	W	L	W
b.	(mar gu:ŋ) > (mar guŋ) gu̱	W	L	
c.	(mu la:) ri > (mu la:r)		W	L
d.	(mar gu:n) da > (mar gu:n)		W	L
e.	(ma ɟin) (da ŋa:l) na > (ma ɟin) (da ŋa:l)		W	L

A recent criticism of the phonological approach to exceptionality in OT is that it overgenerates (Gouskova 2012). Adapting Gouskova's arguments to the facts of Yidiny: if we adopt the ranking P$_{RS}$-*u* ≫ M$_{AX}$ ≫ P$_{RS}$, then it is no longer necessary to assign a high ranking to the morphologically-sensitive constraints A$_{NC}$ and M$_{AX}$-C/R$_T$, which penalize the deletion of morph-initial segments and root consonants. Rather, so long as all morph-initial segments and all root consonants lack a lexical *u*-index, then by virtue of the partial ranking M$_{AX}$ ≫ P$_{RS}$, they will resist deletion irrespective of the ranking of A$_{NC}$ and M$_{AX}$-C/R$_T$. By the same token however, if A$_{NC}$ and M$_{AX}$-C/R$_T$ do receive a low ranking, then the analysis will fare poorly in the context of Richness of the Base (Prince & Smolensky 2004-1993]), since without high-ranked A$_{NC}$ and M$_{AX}$-C/R$_T$ ensuring that morph-initial and root-consonant deletion is impossible, there is nothing to prevent segments from deleting in those positions if they are *u*-indexed in the lexicon. For example, a root such as **binarŋa* could undergo CV deletion; a suffix **-ni* could delete entirely; and **mulari* could delete from the left, thereby failing to capture the generalization that the absence of such forms is not an accident of the lexicon, but a systematic property of the grammar. This is perhaps the most significant apparent flaw of the phonological approach: it fails to rule out unattested patterns. This is in contrast to the morphological approach, which does rule them out. Or at least, so it would seem. In §5 I show that the true situation can be otherwise, once learning is taken into account.

4.3 Alternatives

Before proceeding to learning, I mention two OT alternatives to the analysis of exceptionality in Yidiny word-final deletion.

Co-phonological approaches handle exceptionality as a type of cyclicity effect (Orgun 1996, Kiparsky 2000, Inkelas & Zoll 2007, Bermúdez-Otero 2016). On each morphological cycle the result of a morphological operation is submitted to an appropriate phonological subgrammar, of which the language may possess many. Problematic for any cyclicity-based approach to exceptionality in Yidiny word-final deletion is that the Yidiny case is non-cyclic. Instead, undergoers are subject to deletion only if word-final. For example, in building both words in (23a,b) the first step would be to introduce the undergoer root *bigunu-* 'shield'. However at that point, the "deleting" subgrammar should only be applied if the root will end up word final, as in (23a) but not in (23b).

(23) a. 'shield[ABS]'   /bigunu/   →   (bi gu:ŋ)
    b. 'shield-comit-ERG' /bigunu-yi-ŋgu/ →   (bi gu) (nu yi:ŋ)
                                                                                                          *(bi gun) (yiŋ gu)

Selecting the correct subgrammar in (23) thus requires information about the next step in the derivation. Crucially though, it requires forewarning, not only of whether or not there is more morphology to come, but also of what the PHONOLOGICAL ramifications will be. This is because the relevant domain for word final-deletion in Yidiny is not the morphological word but the prosodic word. For example, in (24) the roots *gaɟula-* 'dirty' and *gumaɻi-* 'red' are followed by suffixes. Since the suffixes are monosyllabic, just one

4 Phonological exceptionality is localized to phonological elements

prosodic word results and the roots are non-final in their prosodic word. In (25) however, the roots are followed by the disyllabic INCHOATIVE suffix *daga*, which commences a second prosodic word. As a consequence, the roots are final in their prosodic word and deletion is possible: the undergoer *gaɟula-* deletes while the non-undergoer *gumaɻi-* does not.

(24)   a.   'dirty-CAUS-PST'
             /gaɟula-ŋa-lɲu/   →   [(ga ɟu) (la ŋaːl)ₚWd]
        b.   'red-CAUS-PST'
             /gumaɻi-ŋa-lɲu/   →   [(gu ma) (ɻi ŋaːl)ₚWd]

(25)   a.   'dirty-INCHO-PST'
             /gaɟula-daga-ɲu/   →   [(ga ɟuːl)ₚWd] [(da gaːɲ)ₚWd]
        b.   'red-INCHO-PST'
             /gumaɻi-daga-ɲu/   →   [(gu maː) ɻi ₚWd] [(da gaːɲ)ₚWd]

Any cyclic, look-ahead mechanism in Yidiny would therefore need to know how the word would be prosodically parsed on the NEXT cycle, before it can decide whether or not to apply the "deleting" subgrammar on the current cycle. The look-ahead mechanism would therefore require the power of a subgrammar itself, yet if the theory were augmented in this manner, then other core mechanisms such as scope, or "bracket erasure", effects (Inkelas & Zoll 2007) would be undermined. I conclude that co-phonology theory as it stands cannot analyse exceptionality in Yidiny word-final deletion.

Another approach would be to lexically list two allomorphs for all undergoer morphs in the language, and have the grammar select them either optimally (Mester 1994, Kager 1996, Mascaró 1996, and Tranel 1996a,b) or with some degree of stipulation (Bonet, Lloret & Mascaró 2007; Round 2013; Wolf 2015). On this approach, "deletion" is apparent only, due in reality to the selection between two input allomorphs, one of which contains only a subset of the segments in the other (for a proposal not unlike this for Yidiny, see Hayes 1997). An example is shown in (26), where the grammar optimally selects between two input allomorphs of the undergoer root *bigunu-* 'shield'.

(26)

{/bigunu/, /bigun/} 'shield[ABS]'	ANC	MAX-C/RT	PRS	MAX
a. ☞ /bigun/ ∷ (bi guːn)				
b. /bigun/ ∷ (bi guː) nu			*W	
c. /bigunu/ ∷ (bi guːn)				*W
d. /bigunu/ ∷ (bi guː) nu			*W	

Two objections can be raised. First, because the approach simply lists alternant pairs, it misrepresents their resemblances as accidents, rather than relating them systematically. Relatedly, in the context of Richness of the Base, the analysis would allow the apparent deletion of morph-initial and -medial segments as well as root consonants, by leaving them out of an underlying allomorph, in a pair such as {/bigunu/, /gunu/}. Ranking ANC and MAX-C/ROOT highly would not ameliorate the problem, as shown in (27).

73

(27)

		{/biɟunu/, /gunu/}	Anc	Max-C/root	Prs	Max
a.	☞	/gunu/ ∷ (gu nu)				
b.		/biɟunu/ ∷ (bi gu:) nu			*W	

Second, it is unclear how the analysis would prevent apparent deletion in word medial positions in the event that it is optimising, as in (28), where the true output *buɟala-ŋa:-lna* violates Prs while the more optimal false winner *buɟal-ŋa-lna* does not. The constraint Cntg will not prevent this occurring.

(28)

		†{/buɟala, buɟal/}-ŋa-lna/ 'finely ground-CAUSE-PURP'	Cntg	*Cplx	Prs	Max
a.	☞	/buɟala-ŋa-lna/ ∷ (bu ɟa) (la ŋa:l) na			*L	
b.	*	/buɟal-ŋa-lna/ ∷ (bu ɟal) (ŋal na)				

I conclude that neither the co-phonological approach nor the allomorph-selection approach offers a viable alternative for Yidiny word-final deletion.

5 Learning exceptionality

5.1 Biased Constraint Demotion

I turn now to consider how exceptionality is, or isn't, learned. After introducing Prince and Tesar's (2004) Biased Constraint Demotion (BCD) algorithm and adaptations of it for the learning of indexed constraints, I show that the learning of Yidiny word-final deletion does not proceed as one might expect from the discussion in §4. A solution is then offered in §6.

Prince and Tesar's BCD is a computationally efficient algorithm for the learning of OT grammars. It builds upon Tesar's earlier Recursive Constraint Demotion (RCD) algorithm (Tesar 1995, Tesar & Smolensky 2000), deterministically learning a grammar, conditional on the data, by ranking constraints in a series of steps, or recursions. At the first step, one or more constraints is assigned to the highest-ranked CONSTRAINT STRATUM in the grammar. A stratum is a set of constraints whose relative ranking against one another is indeterminate given the data, but whose ranking relative to constraints in other strata is significant. The act of assigning constraints to a stratum is termed INSTALLATION. At each subsequent step, one or more additional constraints are installed in the next-highest stratum, and so on, until all constraints are ranked. The determination of which constraint(s) are installed next is based on evidence from winner–loser pairs (WLPs). For each WLP, any constraint yet to be installed will favor the winner in the pair, the loser, or neither. The full table of WLPs and constraints yet to be installed is termed the SUPPORT. A fragment of a support is shown in (29). The relative order of constraints and WLPs in a support is inconsequential, though for ease of inspection I set out markedness constraints to the left of a vertical double line, and faithfulness to the right.

(29)

		FtBin	Prs-u	Prs	*Cplx	Max	Cntg	Anc
a.	/margu-ni̱/ (mar gu:n) > (mar gu:) ni		W	W		L		
b.	/guygal-ni̱/ (guy ga:l) ni > (guy ga:l)		L	L		W		W
c.	/guygal-ni̱/ (guy ga:l) ni > (guy ga:ln)		L	L	W	W		
d.	/guygal-ni̱/ (guy ga:l) ni > (guy ga:l ni)	W	L	L				
e.	/bulmba/ (bulm ba) > (bul ba)			L	L	W	W	

In the original RCD algorithm, the sole criterion for installing a constraint was that it favor no losers. This is true of the constraints FtBin, Cntg and Anc in (29). When a constraint, C, is installed, all of the WLPs for which C favors the winner are removed from the support, since the constraint ranking has now accounted for them. In the RCD, all constraints meeting this criterion at any recursion are installed, and the result at the end of all recursions is a correct grammar for the data. Nevertheless, the grammars inferred by the RCD are not optimal (Prince & Tesar 2004). The suboptimality relates to the subset problem (Baker 1979; Angluin 1980), a general problem in algorithmic learning from positive evidence, namely that the system which results from learning will correctly assess as grammatical all attested items, but will fail to rule out certain systematically unattested items. This in turn relates to the notion of restrictiveness: a learning algorithm ought ideally to learn the most restrictive grammar consistent with the data. The RCD does not do this. In practice, meeting this desideratum is challenging for an efficient algorithm. However Prince & Tesar (2004) demonstrate that good headway can be made by enhancing the RCD with a small set of biases, hence the name Biased Constraint Demotion, or BCD. The BCD differs from the RCD in two main respects. The first is the principle of FAITHFULNESS DELAY. According to this, at every recursion faithfulness constraints are not installed, even when they favor no losers, unless there are no other installable constraints. In (29) for example, the BCD would install the markedness constraint FtBin but not the faithfulness constraints Cntg and Anc. If we do this, and remove from (29) all the WLPs for which FtBin favors the winner, namely (29d), and remove FtBin, we have (30), in which only faithfulness constraints, Cntg and Anc favor no losers; under these conditions, faithfulness delay would permit the installation of Cntg and Anc.

(30)

		P$_{RS}$-u	P$_{RS}$	*C$_{PLX}$	M$_{AX}$	C$_{NTG}$	A$_{NC}$
a.	/margu-ni̱/ (mar guːn) > (mar guː) ni	W	W		L		
b.	/guygal-ni̱/ (guy gaːl) ni > (guy gaːl)	L	L		W		W
c.	/guygal-ni̱/ (guy gaːl) ni > (guy gaːln)	L	L	W	W		
e.	/bulmba/ (bulm ba) > (bul ba)			L	L	W	W

However, there is a second principle to consider also. A principle of "freeing up markedness" states that when there is a choice between installing several faithfulness constraints, the algorithm should install the smallest subset possible, whose installment would cause a markedness constraint to become installable in the next recursion. For example, in (30), installing C$_{NTG}$ would remove WLP (30e), thereby freeing up the markedness constraint *C$_{PLX}$ at the next recursion; no comparable gain would flow from installing A$_{NC}$. On those grounds, from (30) the BCD would install C$_{NTG}$.

5.2 A support for learning Yidiny exceptionality

I now consider several learning scenarios for Yidiny exceptionality. Each begins directly after the installation of undominated constraints. Table 6 contains a set of WLPs that is representive of all combinations of roots and suffixes which are relevant to the grammar of word-final deletion: it is not the complete support, but it represents the complete support well. Segments which can delete are underlined. To economize on space below, WLPs will be referred to by the letters in the first column of Table 6.

5.3 Learning the phonological account (preliminary version)

We begin with the learning of the phonological account of Yidiny exceptionality described previously in §4.2. For the moment, I assume that input segments are already lexically Φ-indexed as u or n. We begin after undominated constraints have been installed, with a support as in (31).

4 Phonological exceptionality is localized to phonological elements

Table 6: Support for learning Yidiny exceptionality.

a.	/margu-ni̲/	(mar gu:n)	>(mar gu:) ni	
b.	/guygal-ni̲/	(guy ga:l) ni	>(guy ga:l)	
c.	/guygal-ni̲/	(guy ga:l) ni	>(guy ga:ln)	
d.	/margu-ŋgu̲/	(mar gu:ŋ)	>(mar gu:ŋ) gu	
e.	/margu-ŋgu̲/	(mar gu:ŋ)	>(mar gu:ŋg)	
f.	/bigunu̲-yi-ŋgu̲/	(bi gu) (nu yi:ŋ)	>(bi gun) (yiŋ gu)	
g.	/wawa-lɲu̲/	(wa wa:l)	>(wa wa:l) ɲu	
h.	/gali-ɲa̲/	(ga li:ŋ)	>(ga li:) ɲa	
i.	/gaɟara̲/	(ga ɟa:r)	>(ga ɟa:) ra	
k.	/margu-nda/	(mar gu:n) da	>(mar gu:n)	
l.	/wawa-lna/	(wa wa:l) na	>(wa wa:l)	
m.	/gali-na/	(ga li:) na	>(ga li:n)	
n.	/guɟara/	(gu ɟa:) ra	>(gu ɟa:r)	
o.	/maɟinda-ŋa-lna/	(ma ɟin) (da ŋa:l) na	>(ma ɟin) (da ŋa:l)	
p.	/bulmba/	(bulm ba)	>(bul ba)	

(31)

	Prs-*u*	Prs	*Cplx	Max	Max-C	Cntg	Anc
a, h, i.	W	W		L			
b.	L	L		W	W		W
c.	L	L	W	W			
d, g.	W			L	L		
e.			W	L	L		
f.				L	L	W	
j, k, l, o.		L		W	W		
m, n.		L		W			
p.			L	W		W	

Support (31) does not contain any markedness constraints that favor no losers. Two faithfulness constraints favor no losers: Cntg, which would free up *Cplx if installed, and Anc, which would not free up any markedness constraints. Consequently, Cntg is installed next, removing WLPs (f) and (p) from the support. After that, the newly freed-up *Cplx is installed, removing WLPs (c) and (e), and leaving (32).

(32)

	Prs-u	Prs	Max	Max-C	Anc
a, h, i.	W	W	L		
b.	L	L	W	W	W
d, g.	W	W	L	L	
j, k, l, o.		L	W	W	
m, n.		L	W		

In 32 only Anc favors no losers, and so is installed. This removes (b), freeing up Prs-u, which is installed next, removing (a,h,i) and (d.,g), leaving (33). From (33), Max will be installed since it frees up Prs. This leaves Prs and Max-C, which according to faithfulness delay, will be ranked last as Prs ≫ Max-C, as in (34).

(33)

	Prs	Max	Max-C
j, k, l, o.	L	W	W
m, n.	L	W	

(34) Cntg ≫ *Cplx ≫ Anc ≫ Prs-u ≫ Max ≫ Prs ≫ Max-C

Some comments are in order. First, the BCD algorithm has learned the key constraint ranking Prs-u ≫ Max ≫ Prs responsible for the core of Yidiny exceptionality. Secondly however, it has also ranked Anc ≫ Prs-u, in which case the learned grammar expressly prohibits morph-initial deletion. Indeed, had Max-C/RT been included in (31), it would also have been ranked highly since it only ever favors winners, meaning the grammar would also expressly prohibit CV deletion in roots (the reasons for my excluding Max-C/RT are clarified in §6). This means that the algorithm is learning precisely the rankings required to prevent the phonological solution from overgenerating, thereby voiding the major criticism of the phonological approach which was introduced in §4.2. This is perhaps surprising, so why is the ranking learned? It is learned because the BCD algorithm attempts to construct a restrictive grammar. The typical assumption, that grammars implementing a phonological approach would not assign redundant, high rankings to constraints like Anc, is predicated on an implicit assumption that the learner would be seeking a PERMISSIVE grammar; doing so leads to overgeneration. However no successful learner would adopt that assumption, because successful learning in general requires a restrictive approach. For the theory of exceptionality, this is significant. It means the result obtained here, in which a phonological approach to exceptionality has been learned without overgeneration, is not dependent on some minor detail of the BCD, or the constraints used, or even OT. Rather, it follows from a general principle of learning. Consequently, the adoption of realistic assumptions about learning narrows the performance gap between the phonological and morphological approaches. I will examine the phonological approach further in §7.3.

5.4 Learning indexed constraints and the morphological analysis

We consider next the learning of the morphological approach. The support begins, after installation of undominated constraints, as (35). These are the same constraints and WLPs as in the previous section, but without PRS-u. The support begins with no lexically indexed constraints; how they are learned is considered shortly. I also do not include MAX-C/RT in the support. MAX-C/RT is essentially a variant of MAX-C, indexed to all root morphs. This is the kind of constraint we might reasonably expect the morphological approach to learn.

(35)

	PRS	*CPLX	MAX	MAX-C	CNTG	ANC
a, h, i.	W		L			
b.	L		W	W		W
c.	L	W	W			
d, g.	W		L	L		
e.		W	L	L		
f.			L	L	W	
j, k, l, o.	L		W	W		
m, n.	L		W			
p.		L	W	W	W	

Turning now to the BCD algorithm, neither of the markedness constraints in support (35) favors no losers. CNTG does, and would free up *CPLX. ANC also does, but would not free up any markedness constraints. Accordingly, CNTG is installed next, removing WLPs (f) and (p) are from the support, and *CPLX after that, removing (c) and (e), leaving (36).

(36)

	PRS	MAX	MAX-C	ANS
a, h, i.	W	L		
b.	L	W	W	W
d, g.	W	L	L	
j, k, l, o.	L	W	W	
m, n.	L	W		

ANC is installed next, removing WLP (b), which leaves (37), a support in which there is no constraint which favors no losers.

(37)

	Prs	Max	Max-C
a, h, i.	W	L	
d, g.	W	L	L
j, k, l, o.	L	W	W
m, n.	L	W	

Supports in this state are said to have reached INCONSISTENCY. An inconsistency, however, is not a failure.

Inconsistencies indicate that the combination of data and assumptions currently under consideration have not led to a working grammar. Accordingly (assuming the data is correct), a revision of the assumptions is warranted. Suppose, in this case, that a revision could be made which leaves intact all previously installed constraints and their rankings, and the validity of all previously accounted-for WLPs, that is, a revision that would change only what is in the support. Suppose also that as a result of this revision the support came to contain a constraint that favors no losers. Such a revision would resolve the inconsistency. The BCD could restart and, one hopes, lead to a working grammar. Revisions that meet these criteria can be considered a type of learning. One such revision is to add a new, lexically M-indexed constraint to CON.

Pater (2009) describes a method for learning M-indexed constraints and assigning co-indices to morphs, which takes a BCD inconsistency as its starting point. Coetzee (2009) extends this to Output-Output constraints, which I will not consider here. Becker's modifications (Becker 2009; Becker, Ketrez & Nevins 2011) are addressed in §8.

Central to Pater's method is the operation of CONSTRAINT CLONING, a process I describe informally here and return to in detail in §8. Within the stalled support, a constraint C is sought which, if it were indexed to some set M of morphs, would (i) favor at least one winner[15] and (ii) favor no losers. Assuming such a constraint C can be identified, it is then cloned, which is to say, a lexically M-indexed version of it, C_M, is added to the support. Because C_M favors no losers, it is installed next. For example, support (38) is the same as (37) but now displays information about which morphs are involved. I have annotated relevant undergoers as U and non-undergoers as N.

According to the criteria for cloning, all three of PRS, MAX and MAXC are candidates for cloning (indexed to sets U, N and N respectively). I assume that owing to faithfulness delay, markedness constraints are cloned in preference to faithfulness when both are available, in which case PRS will be cloned. In (39) the cloned, lexically M-indexed constraint PRS_U is added to the support. Installing it removes WLPs (a,d,g,h,i) which frees up MAX, whose installation is followed by PRS and MAX-C. The resulting ranking is (40), which requires comment.

---

[15] The new constraint needs to favor at least one winner to have any chance of freeing up another constraint once it is installed.

4 *Phonological exceptionality is localized to phonological elements*

(38)

		Prs	Max	Max-C
a.	/margu-ni$_U$/	W	L	
d.	/margu-ni$_U$/	W	L	L
g.	/margu-ŋgu$_U$/	W	L	L
h.	/gali-ɲa$_U$/	W	L	
i.	/gaɟara$_U$/	W	L	
j.	/binarŋa/	L	W	W
k.	/margu-nda$_N$/	L	W	W
l.	/wawa-lna$_N$/	L	W	W
m.	/gali-na/	L	W	
n.	/guɟara$_N$/	L	W	
o.	/maɟinda-ŋa-lna$_N$/	L	W	W

(39)

	Prs-$_U$	Prs	Max	Max-C
a, h, i.	W	W	L	
d, g.	W	W	L	L
j, k, l, o.		L	W	W
m, n.		L	W	

(40)   Cntg ≫ *Cplx ≫ Anc ≫ Prs$_U$ ≫ Max ≫ Prs ≫ Max-C

The algorithm has successfully learned the key constraint ranking Prs$_U$ ≫ Max ≫ Prs. However, it did not create an indexed version of Max-C for roots, and thus has not learned to expressly prohibit CV deletion in roots. To be sure, no individual roots ending in CCV or VC'V (where C' would be an illicit coda) will have been co-indexed to Prs$_U$ during the cloning operation (see §8 for details) and so none of those roots will be subject to CV deletion, however the ranking in (40) predicts that if the lexicon did contain a root such as *binarŋa$_U$, then that root and any like it would undergo CV deletion. This is overgeneration of the same kind which was believed to beset phonological accounts. Thus, while §5.3 showed that grammars learned for the phonological account may suffer less than expected from overgeneration once learning is taken into consideration, §5.4 shows that grammars for the morphological account may suffer from overgeneration more than expected. In the next section, I propose a solution.

6 Morphological analytic bias: the Morphological Coherence Principle

In §5.4 the grammar which was learned for a morphological analysis of Yidiny exceptionality suffers from a manifestation of the subset problem. Although the algorithm correctly handled all attested data, it did not learn the more restrictive generalization which applies also to unattested data, that roots in Yidiny do not undergo consonant deletion. The problem arises because the cloning procedure assesses morphology on a morph-by-morph basis only, whereas the true generalization in Yidiny applies to a class of morphs, in this instance, to roots. The remedy to be pursued here has two parts. It adds a new kind of constraint cloning, which indexes a constraint not to an idiosyncratic lexical list of morphs, but to a general class. It then biases constraint cloning so that class-indexed (or K-INDEXED) cloning is preferred over lexically indexed cloning. Effectively, this introduces an analytic bias (Moreton 2008) from morphology to phonological learning at BCD inconsistencies.

Now, supposing that the algorithm is seeking a constraint that it will clone and K-index to some non-idiosyncratic class of morphs, which classes should be available for the learner to consider? Important here is the fact that human phonological learning will need to proceed in parallel with, and interleaved with, morphological learning (Tesar 2007, Merchant 2008: 6). Accordingly, I assume the learner has access both to universally-defined classes such as "root", and those classes which have been morphologically learned, such as ERGATIVE CASE. The biasing principle, which I term the Morphological Coherence Principle is stated in (41), where criterion 2 provides an additional bias towards maximal restrictiveness.

(41) The Morphological Coherence Principle:
  1. At a BCD inconsistency, attempt to create a K-indexed constraint, co-indexed to some universal or learned morphological class K, before attempting to create a lexically-indexed constraint.
  2. If multiple constraints are eligible for K-indexation, select the one whose co-indexed class is most general.

The MCP has some desirable theoretical properties. If the universal state of CON at the commencement of learning is CON$_{init}$, then the MCP obviates the need for CON$_{init}$ to contain any constraints that are relativized to universal or learned morphological classes, since such constraints will be learned on demand, if and only if needed. In effect, this reduces the size of CON$_{init}$ without any change in the explanatory capacity of the theory. And, since it allows the grammar to BUILD constraints for language-specific morphological classes it makes those constraints available to the learner without problematically assuming them universal (Russell 1995, Hammond 2000, see also Smith 2004, Flack 2007b). The MCP operationalizes, in a specific manner, the kind of insight into linguistic theory that Anderson (2008) argues ought to follow from an improved understanding of the learning device.

Let us now return to Yidiny exceptionality, equipped with the MCP. Learning begins and proceeds as in §5.4 until the inconsistency in (38), at which point a constraint is sought for cloning. The MCP states that if possible, a constraint should be cloned and K-indexed. In (38) MAX-C would favor no losers if it were K-indexed to the entire class of roots, so it is cloned and accordingly K-indexed. This is the functional equivalent of adding MAX-C/RT to CON, and the reason why in §5 I did not include MAX-C/RT in the support at the outset. Adding Max-C/rt to the support results in (42). From (42), Max-C/rt is installed and WLP (j) is removed, whereupon we return to inconsistency, in (51). As in §5.4, the process from that point results in the cloning of Prs and the installation of Prs$_U$, then Max, Prs and Max-C, yielding the desired constraint ranking (43).

(42)

	Prs	Max	Max-C/rt	Max-C
a, h, i.	W	L		
d, g.	W	L		L
j.	L	W	W	W
k, l, o.	L	W		W
m, n.	L	W		

(43)

	Prs	Max	Max-C
a, h, i.	W	L	
d, g.	W	L	L
k, l, o.	L	W	W
m, n.	L	W	

(44)   Cntg ≫ *Cplx ≫ Anc ≫ Max-C/rt ≫ Prs$_U$ ≫ Max ≫ Prs ≫ Max-C

To summarize, results from §5.3 suggested that, provided a learner is seeking a restrictive grammar, the phonological approach to exceptionality may not suffer from overgeneration. This contradicts recent arguments, which on examination appear to adopt the implausible assumption that a learner would be seeking a permissive grammar. That being said, I have not yet clarified how the learner would arrive at the requisite Φ-indices required by the phonological approach. That will be discussed in §7.3. Meanwhile, §5.4 revealed that without further refinement, the BCD is prone to learning grammars that overgenerate even in a morphological approach to exceptionality, due to an overly atomistic method of morphological generalization. This was remedied in §6 by the Morphological Coherence Principle (41), which solves the learning problem and simplifies Con$_{init}$.

7 The theoretical status of lexical indices

In §7 I set Yidiny to one side and consider some matters of theory.

7.1 Lexical M-indices

Lexical M-indices are representations which are visible to the phonology, but they are not phonological elements *per se*. In OT, Gen cannot alter M-indices. It cannot add or remove them, or displace them from one morph to another. There is therefore no need for mechanisms such as M-index "faithfulness", rather it is simply assumed that the lexical affiliation of a morph m with an M-index M is identical in the input and output. This set of properties is shared with other kinds of lexical affiliation, such as the affiliation of a phonological element with its morph, and is termed Consistency of Exponence (McCarthy & Prince 1993b, Van Oostendorp 2007).

Taking a historical view, M-indices closely resemble the RULE FEATURES and ALPHABET FEATURES of early generative phonology (GP) (Chomsky & Halle 1968, Lakoff 1970, Coats 1970, Zonneveld 1978, *inter alia*). Both sets of formalisms fulfill the function of determining for cases of exceptionality whether a morph m participates in certain phonological patterns or not, by ensuring that m is visible or not visible as required, to OT's constraints or GP's phonological rules. Diacritic features were investigated extensively in GP. It was argued that the theory should not allow the phonology to manipulate diacritic features (Kiparsky 1973, Zonneveld 1978). The same applies to M-indices in OT. It was argued that not all idiosyncrasies in the phonology can be analysed satisfactorily in terms of rule exception features, and that there is an additional role for cyclicity (Chomsky & Halle 1968, Kiparsky 1982b) and the same has been recognized for M-indices (Pater 2009). In GP, it was also assumed that the diacritic features of morph m were distributed across, and directly characterized, each of the phonological elements (namely, segments) in m. We might ask whether this is also true of M-indices in OT. Suppose that it is, so that the M-indices of a morph m directly characterize each phonological element φ that is lexically affiliated with m (that is all φ which are EXPONENTS of m). In that case, the relative definition of an M-indexed constraint (25), repeated here as (45), can be revised and simplified as (46).

(45) $V(C_M) =_{def} V(C) \cap L_\varphi(m \in M$ & $\text{Exp}(\varphi, m))$, where:
M is the set of morphs co-indexed to C_M.
$\text{Exp}(\varphi, m)$ states that element φ is an exponent of morph m

(46) $V(C_M) =_{def} V(C) \cap L_\varphi(\varphi \in \Phi_M)$, where:
Φ_M is the set of phonological elements co-indexed to C_M.

It will be recalled that the relative definition of a constraint C_M is expressed as the set intersection between the loci of variation of the unindexed constraint C, written V(C), and the set of loci, $L_\varphi(D(\varphi))$ which contain some criterial type of phonological element φ, described by predicate $D(\varphi)$. Importantly, this means that M-indexed constraints are defined DIRECTLY in terms of phonological elements, φ, and only indirectly in terms of morphs m. The indirectness shows up in the complexity of $D(\varphi)$ in (45), which links morphs to their exponent φ elements via the function $\text{Exp}(\varphi, m)$. This is in contrast with (46), where the assumption is that all φ elements are directly characterized by the M-index borne by their affiliated morph. The constraint definition no longer refers to the morph itself, and so the predicate $D(\varphi)$ is simpler.

At risk of laboring the point, the phonology itself assesses violations of M-indexed constraints directly in terms of φ elements, not morphs. While it is possible to refer to the morphs in the definitions of M-indexed constraints as in (17/45), it is not necessary. Nor is it possible to refer only to the morphs and not to the φ elements, since the loci of violation of these constraints are defined inherently at a sub-morphological, phonological level.

7.2 Lexical Φ-indices

Let us now consider the nature of lexical Φ-indices of the type I invoked in §4.2 and §5.3. My proposal is that these are exactly like M-indices: they are non-phonological indices of lexical affiliation, visible to, but not manipulable by, the phonology and used for making particular phonological elements visible or not, as required, to OT's constraints in order to provide a coherent account of exceptionality. The only distinction between Φ-indices and M-indices lies in the supplementary assumption attached to M-indices, in (47).

(47) The M-index assumption:
A lexical index which characterizes phonological element φ_i will also characterize all other phonological elements φ_j affiliated with the same morph m.

Φ-indices are not subject to this redundancy; they are affiliated with only those φ elements for which the affiliation makes any difference to the analysis of language. As I will show in §8, that makes Φ-indices somewhat simpler to learn, since they correspond more directly to the evidence in the data.

The reader may also have noticed that the definition of a Φ-indexed constraint in (21) is almost exactly like the simplified definition of an M-indexed constraint in (46). This reflects the fact that for the operation of the phonology, it is φ elements, and the indexation of specific φ elements, that matter. Whether or not one chooses to adopt supplementary assumption (47) in fact has no material consequence for the evaluation of an individual indexed constraint. The question of whether there are other consequences, and whether they are desirable, is taken up in §9.

7.3 Learning lexical Φ-indices

Given the proposal above, the learning of Φ-indices is quite parallel to the learning of M-indices. I assume that the MCP still applies, so that class-based exceptionality and K-indexed constraints continue to be learned with priority over idiosyncratic exceptionality, even though the latter will now be accounted for by Φ-indexed constraints, not M-indexed. This is a coherent assumption to make. The MCP is concerned with the learning of class-based generalizations, whereas Φ- and M-indexed constraints are alternative devices for learning idiosyncrasies. Accordingly, in a stalled support once there are no K-indexed constraints available for cloning, the algorithm seeks a constraint C which, were it indexed to some set Φ of phonological elements, would (i) favor at least one winner and (ii) favor no losers. All else proceeds as for M-indexed constraints. In the learning of Yidiny word-final deletion, the process begins as in §6, leading to a first inconsistency resolved by the addition of Max-C/RT to Con, and proceeding from there to the second inconsistency (43), repeated here in part and in more detail as (48).

(48)

		Prs	Max	Max-C
a.	/margu-ni̱/ (mar gu:n) > (mar gu:) ni	W	L	
d.	/margu-ŋg̱u/ (mar gu:ŋ) > (mar gu:ŋ) gu	W	L	L
h.	/gali-ɲa̱/ (ga li:ɲ) > (ga li:) ɲa	W	L	
i.	/gaɟara̱/ (ga ɟa:r) > (ga ɟa:) ra	W	L	
k.	/margu-nda/ (mar gu:n) da > (mar gu:n)	L	W	W
m.	/gali-na/ (ga li:) na > (ga li:n)	L	W	
n.	/guɟara/ (gu ɟa:) ra > (gu ɟa:r)	L	W	
o.	/maɟinda-ɲa̱-lna/ (ma ɟin) (da ɲa:l) na > (ma ɟin) (da ɲa:l)	L	W	W

In (48), no K-indexed constraint is available for cloning.[16] Turning to potential Φ-indexed constraints, we see that the constraint Prs would, if it were co-indexed to all underlined phonological elements, favor at least one winner and favor no losers, and so it is cloned and co-indexed resulting in (49).

(49)

		Prs	Prs-u	Max	Max-C
a.	/margu-ni̱/	W	W	L	
d.	/margu-ŋg̱u/	W	W	L	L
h.	/gali-ɲa̱/	W	W	L	
i.	/gaɟara̱/	W	W	L	
k.	/margu-nda/	L		W	W
m.	/gali-na/	L		W	
n.	/guɟara/	L		W	
o.	/maɟinda-ɲa̱-lna/	L		W	W

(50) Cntg ≫ *Cplx ≫ Anc ≫ Max-C/rt ≫ Prs-u ≫ Max ≫ Prs

---

[16] Actually this is not strictly true. All PAST suffixes for example are undergoers, in which case the MCP would generate and rank Prs_PST. Notwithstanding this, the essential argument remains, since other morphological classes exist, such as ERGATIVE and "root", that are not uniformly (non)undergoers, and still need to be handled by lexically-indexed, not K-indexed, constraints. This minor correction applies equally to the learning process in §6.

From there the algorithm proceeds in the now-familiar fashion, resulting in grammar (50). With its high-ranking Max-C/rt and Anc, (50) does not overgenerate. Moreover, given the argument in §7.2, that for Eval there is no detectable difference between M-indexed and Φ-indexed constraints, we can see that grammar (50) is in all material aspects identical to grammar (44) learned in §6.

8 Constraint cloning

8.1 Assessing eligibility for cloning

It is necessary now to examine more precisely the processes by which constraints are deemed eligible for cloning (§8.1), by which a viable set of co-indexed elements is identified (§8.2), and by which a selection is made between multiple eligible constraints (§8.3).

Earlier, I introduced criteria by virtue of which a constraint becomes eligible for cloning. These are restated in (51) in a generalized from, so that the set S is: a coherent class of morphs for K-indexing; an idiosyncratic set of morphs for M-indexing; or an idiosyncratic set of lexical phonological elements for Φ-indexing.

(51) A constraint should be sought for cloning which, if it were indexed to set S, would (i) favor at least one winner, and (ii) favor no losers.

Criterion (??ii) ensures that once the cloned constraint is added to the support, it can be installed; (51i) ensures that its installation will remove at least one WLP from the support, and thereby have some hope of freeing up other constraints. The formulation in (51) improves upon Pater's (2009: 144) criterion, which is to seek a constraint that favors no losers "for all instances" of some morph.[17] To see why Pater's criterion fails, consider WLPs (h,l,o) from the stalled support (38), reproduced in part and in detail in (52). For the purposes of discussion, I assume we are attempting to learn an M-indexed constraint, though the argument generalizes to other kinds.

(52)			Prs	Max	Max-C
	h.	/gali-ŋa/ 'go-COM[IMP]' (ga li:ŋ) > (ga li:) ŋa	W		
	l.	/wawa-lna/ 'see-PURP' (wa wa:l) na > (wa wa:l)	L	W	W
	o.	/maɟinda-ŋa-lna/ 'walk up-COM-PURP' (ma ɟin) (da ŋa:l) na > (ma ɟin) (da ŋa:l)	L	W	W

In (52), WLPs (h) and (o) both contain the suffix -ŋa, a regular undergoer which our procedure ought to co-index to the M-indexed constraint Prs$_U$. In WLP (h) word-final ŋa is subject to deletion, and Prs favors the winner. In WLP (o) non-final ŋa is parsed

---

[17] Pater's phrase "favors only winners" is equivalent to my "favors no losers".

into a foot and escapes deletion. Nevertheless, for WLP (o) Prs favors the loser. This has nothing to do with *ŋa*, but is due to the non-deletion of the unparsed, word-final non-undergoer *-lna*. Pater's co-indexing criterion asks whether Prs favors no losers "for all instances" of *-ŋa* in the support. The answer is "no", because (o) contains an instance of *-ŋa* and Prs favors the loser for (o). This is the wrong result; the suffix *-ŋa* ought to get co-indexed to Prs$_U$. It comes about because Pater's criterion does not discriminate between morphs that contribute to violations and those which are present in the word, but do not contribute. The criteria in (51) avoid this problem because they refer directly to how the co-indexed constraint would perform, were it created. The next two sections detail how to operationalize them.

8.2 Specifying co-indexed sets

The question considered here is which set S ought to be co-indexed to a given constraint C if we wish to clone C? The answer varies depending on which kind of indexed constraint we are constructing. One possible answer is that no such set exists, and C cannot be cloned. Seen from that angle, the question here is also: is C eligible for cloning?

K-indexed constraints can be co-indexed only to the morphological classes $K_1, K_2...K_n$ in the language (§6). In (41) I suggested that the preferred class for co-indexation is the MOST GENERAL one. Thus, to efficiently assess if constraint C is eligible for cloning and K-indexing, the learner should proceed stepwise through the available classes, ordered by decreasing generality. The process is one of trial and error. At each step, the constraint C_K is built and applied to all WLPs in the support. If C_K meets criteria (51) then it is successful; the process halts and C_K is used, otherwise the trial and error continues. If by the end, no successful constraint $C_{K1}...C_{Kn}$ is found, then C is ineligible for cloning.

For M-indexed and Φ-indexed constraints, the desired set S can be identified by focusing attention on loci of violation. Suppose we are considering constraint C for cloning. For any WLP, p, its loci of violation of constraint C fall into three classes: the class w(p), responsible for violations of C that favor the winner (i.e., the locus occurs in the loser only), class L(p) which favor the loser (locus occurs in the winner only) and class N(p) which favor neither (occurs in both). Next define $\Phi_{w(p)}$ as the set of phonological elements φ contained in any of the loci in w(p), and $\Phi_{L(p)}$ as the set of φ elements contained in any of the loci in L(p). Finally, define Φ_W as the union of $\Phi_{w(p)}$ for all WLPs, $p_1, p_2 ... p_n$, in the support, and Φ_L as the union of all $\Phi_{L(p)}$ in the support. Now, consider the set $(\Phi_W - \Phi_L)$, the set difference between Φ_W and Φ_L. This is the set of all φ elements which both (i) appear in at least one locus that in at least one WLP causes C to favor a winner, and (ii) never appear in a locus that causes C to favor a loser. For a Φ-indexed constraint this is an optimal set S. If for a given constraint C, $(\Phi_W - \Phi_L)$ is the null set, then we may conclude that C is ineligible for cloning.[18]

---

[18] To be precise, if $(\Phi_W - \Phi_L)$ is the null set then it is possible that there still exists some additional, viable set S which contains fortuitous elements φ_i which are elements of both Φ_W and Φ_L such that in EVERY WLP p in which φ_i is contained in some number n of the loci w(p) there are at least n offsetting loci in L(p) which contain other elements φ_j which are also in S. Identifying these fortuitous elements φ_i, or even determining if any exist, would very likely be prohibitively expensive computationally.

4 Phonological exceptionality is localized to phonological elements

To find the equivalent for an M-indexed constraint, it is necessary to extrapolate from Φ_W and Φ_L to morphs: set S will be the set $(M_W - M_L)$ where M_W is the set of all morphs m_w, such that any of m_w's phonological exponents is an element of Φ_W; and M_L is the set of all morphs m_l, such that any of m_l's phonological exponents is an element of Φ_L. Note that M_W and M_L can be calculated only after the calculation of Φ_W and Φ_L is performed.

In §7.1 I considered what is involved computationally in assessing violations of Φ- and M-indexed constraints, and argued that the calculations for both are essentially concerned with φ elements, not morphs. Here we see that the same is true when learning the co-indexed set. As in §7.1, one can bring morphs into the picture, to be sure, but in both cases doing so requires additional computational effort, for no effective difference in how the grammar will work. In §9 I will argue the theory to be preferred is one which admits lexically Φ-indexed constraints, but not M-indexed.

8.3 Selecting among eligible constraints

Suppose there are multiple lexically-indexed constraints which are eligible for cloning; which do we choose? The principles of faithfulness delay and freeing-up of markedness constraints will eliminate some options (§5.1). Beyond that, I suggest the learner chooses the constraint which favors the most winners, and whose installment would therefore remove the greatest number of WLPs. A desirable consequence will be a bias toward restrictiveness. For example, suppose MAX is eligible. If so, then so too is MAX-C, MAX-V, MAX-p, etc. This "maximize-winners" criterion would select MAX, and increase the restrictiveness of the grammar, relative to the other options.

Interestingly, Becker (2009) proposes a MINIMIZE-winners criterion, whose effect is to generate many, very specific cloned constraints, each indexed to highly specific subclasses in the lexicon. The aim is to account for a particular phenomenon, which I describe here. I argue that other accounts are possible, and that Becker's solution has undesirable consequences.

When language learners assign novel words to existing grammatical categories, they do so on the basis of statistical correlations that exist in the lexicon, for example between category membership and aspects of the members' phonological forms (Poplack, Pousada & Sankoff 1982; Albright 2002). One such task is to assign a word as exceptional or non-exceptional, given evidence which underdetermines that choice. The key question here is, what existing statistical knowledge do speakers use, and what do they ignore? In Turkish, speakers appear to ignore correlations between the (non)alternation of a stop's laryngeal features and the quality of its neighboring vowel. It is proposed (Becker 2009; Becker, Ketrez & Nevins 2011) that this is because speakers do not access lexical statistics *per se*, rather they attend to the statistics of constraint indexation. Importantly, CON lacks constraints such as *[+HIGH]tV which refer to a stop and the quality of its vocalic neighbor. Consequently, no such constraint can be indexed, making such correlations invisible and hence irrelevant to a speaker when she assigns a novel word to a (non)exceptional lexical category. Assuming this is the case, then in order for fine-grained knowledge to be available to speakers, an atomizing, "minimize-winners" criterion for cloning is needed. However, this solution would seem neither necessary nor warranted.

Notwithstanding the facts of Turkish, speakers in other languages and performing other novel-word tasks do use lexical correlations which lack a corresponding constraint in Con (Moreton & Amano 1999, Albright 2002, Albright & Hayes 2002, Ernestus & Baayen 2003), indicating that speakers are capable of such computation. In that case, atomized indexed constraints alone are not enough to produce the Turkish results. An additional stipulation is required, that this ability is suppressed when assigning novel words to exceptionality classes; yet this leads to a curious view of phonology. Whereas the grammar is usually the store of generalizations, just in the case of exceptionality, it is a store of highly detailed idiosyncrasy, and just in that case speakers ignore their usual, lexical store of idiosyncrasy and turn to the grammar. More satisfying would be to find some other explanation of the Turkish data. While that would take us well beyond this scope of this paper, it can be noted that what is required is a mechanism that can filter the lexical information in some way. That mechanism needn't be part of the OT grammar. Indeed, if it is true that learners build certain constraints during learning (Flack 2007b, Hayes & Wilson 2008, Hayes 2014), then there must exist EXTRA-grammatical generalization devices, which may provide the lexicon-filtering power needed. For now I conclude that that Becker's proposal follows from just one possible solution to an interesting puzzle, however both the puzzle and solution are outliers relative to what else we know. In contrast, a "maximize-winners" criterion leads to the learning of restrictive grammars, and on those general grounds would appear correct.

9 Discussion

9.1 The case against concrete accounts

Throughout this paper, I have considered only the ABSTRACT phonological approach to analyzing exceptionality, gradually building the argument that its superiority to the morphological approach lies in the fact that it localizes exceptionality to specific φ elements, which are the elements in terms of which the relevant computation must be carried out. CONCRETE phonological approaches also localize exceptionality at a sub-morphological level, but compared to the abstract approach they are ill-suited to learning, and to seriality, as follows.

Lexical indexation is an ideal response to BCD inconsistency, because it annotates the lexicon with indices which are invisible to all previously installed constraints. This guarantees, without needing to check, that all previously accounted-for WLPs remain accounted for. Even if some of them contain lexical φ elements which acquire a new index, their violations of all previously ranked constraints remain unchanged, since no previously-ranked constraint is sensitive to the new index. In contrast, the alteration of phonological form — for example, removing a root node from certain segments — may very well alter the evaluation of WLPs by already-ranked constraints, thus it requires a re-evaluation of the entire ranking. It is not possible to simply repair an inconsistency and resume the BCD process. An ABSTRACT phonological account is therefore easier to learn.

In serial theories, concrete phonological approaches face the problem that in non-initial strata, it is possible that a preceding stratum will have removed, altered, moved or introduced, those aspects of phonological form which should function as pseudo-indices, which lack Consistency of Exponence. This opens up the possibility of all manner of phonological manipulations of exceptionality, for which I am unaware of any evidence.

Taking a more historical view, Chomsky (1964) criticized concrete phonological accounts espoused by structuralists (e.g. Bloomfield 1939) for the proliferation of underlying segments that they entailed. To the extent that such concerns matter to modern phonological theories, Φ-indexation avoids such proliferation by augmenting representations with non-phonological indices (cf §7), rather than additional underlying phonological distinctions.

9.2 The case against M-indexing

In §7 and §8 I showed that for both constraint evaluation and constraint learning, exceptionality is calculated in terms of phonological elements, not morphs. Morphs can be brought into the picture, but at additional computational cost and to no effect. Perhaps, however, it is nevertheless empirically true that exceptionality is inherently morph-bound. If that were so, then phonological exceptionality in any morph m would always be either (i) uniform throughout all phonological exponents of m or (ii) entirely predictably located within m. Yet this is not the case. If we accept something along the lines of Anderson's (1982) analysis of French schwa as an exceptionally-deleting /ø/ vowel, then that exceptional property is neither uniform throughout morphs nor does it have a predictable location. Similarly, in Turkish, non-high round vowels are phonotactically exceptional outside the first syllable (Clements & Sezer 1982; Hulst & Weyer 1991), yet the location of the exception is not predictable, as seen in a comparison of *otoban* 'highway', *monoton* 'monotone', *fenomen* 'phenomenon' and *paradoks* 'paradox'. There is no doubt that in most known cases, exceptionality does happen to be either uniform or predictable within a morph, but this follows uninterestingly from the fact that most exceptional morphs are short, or that most phonological alternations are either local, in which case their location inside a morph is predictably restricted to an edge, or domain-spanning, in which case the morph acts uniformly. However, when such uninformative cases are set aside, the small, informative residue of evidence does not support the morph-based view.

A second argument in defense of M-indices might be that morphs, and not φ elements, belong to lexical strata, and that a single morphological diacritic can therefore coherently index a whole set of phonological exceptionality patterns, patterns which impact different parts of the morph and which therefore would be only incoherently represented by individual diacritics on φ elements. Yet the empirical falsity of this claim has long been recognized. SPE (Chomsky & Halle 1968) permitted both stratal diacritics, later labeled MORPHOLOGICAL FEATURES (Postal 1968) and more specific RULE FEATURES (Lakoff 1970), in view of the fact that distinct phonological patterns associated with strata are not uniformly attested in all morphs. For more recent work, see for example Labrune (2012: 71,72,85ff) on Japanese.

A third argument in defense of M-indices might be that since some kinds of phonological exceptionality are cyclic (§7.1), and since cycles are inherently tied to morphology, not φ elements, then something like M-indices are required anyhow, in which case Φ-indices are redundant. I would suggest that this is a category mistake. While it is true that cycles are inherently tied to morphology, they are tied not to morphs, but to morphological operations. Some operations are non-concatenative and hence morph-free (Anderson 1992). Cyclicity effects, therefore, are about how phonological subgrammars correlate with OPERATIONS; in contrast, Φ-indices are about correlation with FORMS. M-indices fall uncomfortably in between. Since they are inherently attached to morphs, they will be unavailable for the triggering of cyclicity effects associated with non-concatenative operations. And, as we have seen above, they are inefficient, and in all likelihood insufficient, devices for exceptionality of forms.

10 Conclusion

For most of the generative period, an implicit assumption has been that we must choose between a concrete phonological and a diacritic morphological approach to phonological exceptionality.[19] But the argument from learning is that the correct theory is phonological and diacritic, based on lexical phonological indices which are visible to the phonology but not manipulable by it. The concrete phonological approach, whose pseudo-indices are manipulable by the phonology, is ill-suited to efficient learning (§9.1). Diacritic approaches are well suited to learning; however the computation of exceptionality is simply not carried out in terms of morphs, rather its currency is lexical phonological elements. This is true for both constraint evaluation (§7.1) and the learning of co-indexation (§8.2). Concurrently, plausible assumptions about learning ensure that a diacritic phonological account does not suffer from overgeneration (§5.3), and reveal the need for a morphological analytic bias, operationalized here as the Morphological Coherence Principle (§6). Finally, a morph-based diacritic theory appears empirically insufficient in the inevitably small number of cases that are informative (§9.2). No doubt there is much more to be said on the topic of exceptionality, but I hope to have established that the nature of exceptionality is, in essence, phonological and diacritic.

Abbreviations

Abbreviations conform with the Leipzig glossing rules; in addition are: LEST 'lest' and SET 'inclusion/one of a group' (Dixon 1977a).

---

[19] Except, trivially, in purely abstract theories (e.g. Lamb 1966, Fudge 1967).

References

Albright, Adam. 2002. Islands of reliability for regular morphology: evidence from Italian. *Language* 78(4). 684–709.

Albright, Adam & Bruce Hayes. 2002. Modeling English past tense intuitions with minimal generalization. In *Proceedings of the ACL-02 workshop on Morphological and phonological learning-Volume 6*, 58–69. Association for Computational Linguistics.

Anderson, Stephen R. 1974. *The organization of phonology*. New York: Academic Press.

Anderson, Stephen R. 1982. Where's morphology? *Linguistic Inquiry* 13(4). 571–612.

Anderson, Stephen R. 1992. *A-morphous morphology*. Cambridge: Cambridge University Press.

Anderson, Stephen R. 2008. Phonologically conditioned allomorphy in the morphology of Surmiran (Rumantsch). *Word Structure* 1(2). 109–134.

Anderson, Stephen R. 2015. Morphological change. In Claire Bowern & Bethwyn Evans (eds.), *The Routledge handbook of historical linguistics*, 264–285. New York: Routledge.

Anderson, Stephen R. 2016. The role of morphology in transformational grammar. In Andrew Hippisley & Gregory T. Stump (eds.), *The Cambridge handbook of morphology*, 587–608. Cambridge: Cambridge University Press.

Anderson, Stephen R. 2017. Words and paradigms: Peter H. Matthews and the development of morphological theory. *Transactions of the Philological Society* 115. 1–13.

Angluin, Dana. 1980. Inductive inference of formal languages from positive data. *Information and control* 45(2). 117–135.

Baker, Carl L. 1979. Syntactic theory and the projection problem. *Linguistic Inquiry* 10(4). 533–581.

Becker, Michael. 2009. *Phonological trends in the lexicon: The role of constraints*. Amherst, MA: University of Massachusetts Ph.D. dissertation.

Becker, Michael, Nihan Ketrez & Andrew Nevins. 2011. The surfeit of the stimulus: Analytic biases filter lexical statistics in Turkish laryngeal alternations. *Language* 87(1). 84–125.

Benua, Laura. 1997. *Transderivational identity: phonological relations between words*. University of Massachusetts, Amherst PhD thesis.

Bermúdez-Otero, Ricardo. 2016. Stratal Phonology. In S.J. Hannahs & Anna R. K. Bosch (eds.), *The Routledge handbook of phonological theory*. Abingdon: Routledge.

Bernhardt, Barbara H. & Joseph P. Stemberger. 1998. *Handbook of phonological development from the perspective of constraint-based nonlinear phonology*. Academic press.

Bloomfield, Leonard. 1939. Menomini morphophonemics. *Travaux du Cercle Linguistique de Prague* 8. 105–115.

Bonet, Eulàlia, Maria-Rosa Lloret & Joan Mascaró. 2007. Allomorph selection and lexical preferences: Two case studies. *Lingua* 117(6). 903–927.

Bowern, Claire, Erich R. Round & Barry J. Alpher. in revision. The Phonetics and Phonology of Yidiny Stress.

Chomsky, Noam. 1964. *Current issues in linguistic theory*. Mouton: The Hague.

Chomsky, Noam & Morris Halle. 1968. *The sound pattern of English*. New York: Harper & Row.

Clements, George N. & Engin Sezer. 1982. Vowel and consonant disharmony in Turkish. In Harry Van der Hulst & Norval Smith (eds.), *The structure of phonological representations*, vol. 2, 213–255.

Coats, Herbert S. 1970. Rule environment features in phonology. *Papers in Linguistics* 2(?). 110–140.

Coetzee, Andries W. 2009. Learning lexical indexation. *Phonology* 26(1). 109–145.

Crowhurst, Megan & Mark Hewitt. 1995. Prosodic overlay and headless feet in Yidiny. *Phonology* 12(1). 39–84.

Dixon, Robert M. W. 1977a. *A grammar of Yidiny*. Cambridge: Cambridge University Press.

Dixon, Robert M. W. 1977b. Some Phonological Rules in Yidiny. *Linguistic Inquiry* 8(1). 1–34.

Dixon, Robert M. W. 1991. *Words of our country: stories, place names and vocabulary in Yidiny, the Aboriginal language of the Cairns-Yarrabah region*. Brisbane: University of Queensland Press.

Ernestus, Mirjam & R. Harald Baayen. 2003. Predicting the unpredictable: interpreting neutralized segments in dutch. *Language* 79(1). 5–38.

Finley, Sara. 2010. Exceptions in vowel harmony are local. *Lingua* 120(6). 1549–1566.

Flack, Kathryn. 2007a. Templatic morphology and indexed markedness constraints. *Linguistic Inquiry* 38(4). 749–758.

Flack, Kathryn G. 2007b. *The sources of phonological markedness*. Amherst, MA: University of Massachusetts Ph.D. dissertation.

Fudge, Eric C. 1967. The nature of phonological primes. *Journal of Linguistics* 3(1). 1–36.

Fukazawa, Haruka. 1999. *Theoretical implications of OCP effects on features in Optimality Theory*. University of Massachusetts, Amherst Ph.D. Dissertation. https://rucore.libraries.rutgers.edu/rutgers-lib/38461/.

Gouskova, Maria. 2007. The reduplicative template in Tonkawa. *Phonology* 24(3). 367–396.

Gouskova, Maria. 2012. Unexceptional segments. *Natural Language & Linguistic Theory* 30(1). 79–133.

Hall, Nancy. 2001. Max-Position drives iterative footing. In Karine Megerdoomian & Leora A. Bar-el (eds.), *Proceedings of the 20th West Coast Conference on Formal Linguistics*. Cascadilla Press.

Halle, Morris & William J. Idsardi. 1995. General properties of stress and metrical structure. In John Goldsmith (ed.), *The handbook of phonological theory*, 403–443. Oxford: Blackwell Publishing.

Hammond, Michael. 2000. There is no lexicon. *Coyote Papers* 10. 55–77.

Hayes, Bruce. 1982. Metrical structure as the organizing principle of Yidiny phonology. In Harry Van der Hulst & Norval Smith (eds.), *The Structure of Phonological Representations, Part I*, 97–110. Dordrecht: Foris.

Hayes, Bruce. 1985. *A metrical theory of stress rules*. New York: Garland.

Hayes, Bruce. 1997. Anticorrespondence in Yidiɲ. Ms., University of California, Los Angeles.

Hayes, Bruce. 2014. Comparative phonotactics. In. Second International Workshop on Phonotactics. Pisa: Dept. of Linguistics Scuola Normale Superiore.

Hayes, Bruce & Colin Wilson. 2008. A maximum entropy model of phonotactics and phonotactic learning. *Linguistic Inquiry* 39(3). 379–440.

Hulst, Harry van der & Jeroen van de Weyer. 1991. Topics in Turkish Phonology. In R. Boeschoten & L. Verhoeven (eds.), *Turkish Linguistics Today*, 11–159. Leiden: Brill.

Hyde, Brett. 2012. The odd-parity input problem in metrical stress theory. *Phonology* 29(3). 383–431.

Inkelas, Sharon. 1994. The consequences of optimization for underspecification. In Jill Beckman (ed.), *Proceedings of NELS 25*, 287–302. Amherst: GLSA.

Inkelas, Sharon & Cheryl Zoll. 2007. Is grammar dependence real? A comparison between cophonological and indexed constraint approaches to morphologically conditioned phonology. *Linguistics* 45(1). 133–171.

Itô, Junko & Armin Mester. 1999. The phonological lexicon. In Natsuko Tsujimura (ed.), *The handbook of Japanese linguistics*, 62–100. Oxford: Blackwell Publishing.

Jurgec, Peter. 2010. Disjunctive lexical stratification. *Linguistic Inquiry* 41(1). 149–161.

Kager, René. 1993. Alternatives to the iambic-trochaic law. *Natural Language & Linguistic Theory* 11(3). 381–432.

Kager, René. 1996. On affix allomorphy and syllable counting. In Ursula Kleinhenz (ed.), *Interfaces in phonology* (Studia Grammatica 41), 155–171. Berlin: Akademie-Verlag.

Kiparsky, Paul. 1973. *Abstractness, opacity and global rules*. Bloomington: Indiana University Linguistics Club.

Kiparsky, Paul. 1982a. From cyclic phonology to lexical phonology. In Harry van der Hulst & Norval Smith (eds.), *The structure of phonological representations*, 131–175. Dordrecht: Foris.

Kiparsky, Paul. 1982b. From cyclic phonology to lexical phonology. In Harry Van der Hulst & Norval Smith (eds.), *The Structure of Phonological Representations, Part I*, 131–175. Dordrecht: Foris.

Kiparsky, Paul. 2000. Opacity and cyclicity. *The Linguistic Review* 17(2–4). 351–366.

Labrune, Laurence. 2012. *The Phonology of Japanese*. Oxford: Oxford University Press.

Lakoff, George. 1970. *Irregularity in syntax*. New York: Holt, Rinehart & Winston.

Lamb, Sydney M. 1966. Prolegomena to a theory of phonology. *Language* 42(2). 536–573.

Lombardi, Linda. 2002. Coronal epenthesis and markedness. *Phonology* 19(02). 219–251.

Łubowicz, Anna. 2005. Locality of conjunction. In John Alderete, Chung-hye Han & Alexei Kochetov (eds.), *Proceedings of the 24th West Coast Conference on Formal Linguistics*, 254–262.

Mahanta, Shakuntala. 2008. *Directionality and locality in vowel harmony: With special reference to vowel harmony in Assamese*. Netherlands Graduate School of Linguistics Ph.D. Dissertation.

Mascaró, Joan. 1996. External allomorphy and contractions in Romance. *Probus* 8(2). 181–206.

McCarthy, John & Alan Prince. 1993a. Generalized alignment. In Geert Booij & Jaap van Marle (eds.), *The yearbook of morphology 1993*, 79–153. Dordrecht: Kluwer Academic Press.

McCarthy, John & Alan Prince. 1993b. Prosodic morphology i: constraint interaction and satisfaction. Ms., University of Massachusetts, Amherst.

McCarthy, John & Alan Prince. 1995. Faithfulness and reduplicative identity. In *University of Massachusetts occasional papers 18: Papers in Optimality Theory*, 249–384. Amherst: Graduate Linguistic Student Association, UMass.

McCarthy, John J. 2003. Comparative markedness. *Theoretical linguistics* 29(1-2). 1–51.

Merchant, Nazarré Nathaniel. 2008. *Discovering underlying forms: Contrast pairs and ranking*. New Brunswick, NJ: Rutgers University PhD thesis.

Mester, Armin. 1994. The quantitative trochee in Latin. *Natural Language and Linguistic Theory* 12(1). 1–61.

Moreton, Elliott. 2008. Analytic bias and phonological typology. *Phonology* 25(1). 83–127.

Moreton, Elliott & Shigeaki Amano. 1999. Phonotactics in the perception of Japanese vowel length: evidence for long-distance dependencies. In *Proceedings of the 6th European Conference on Speech Communication and Technology*, 82. https://pdfs.semanticscholar.org/f76d/0ebc91f9414ecc23bc36420662cc33776267.pdf.

Myers, Scott. 1997. OCP effects in Optimality Theory. *Natural Language and Linguistic Theory* 15(4). 847–892.

Orgun, Cemil. 1996. *Sign-based morphology and phonology with special attention to Optimality Theory*. Berkeley, CA: University of California, Berkeley PhD thesis.

Pater, Joe. 2000. Non-uniformity in English secondary stress: the role of ranked and lexically specific constraints. *Phonology* 17(2). 237–274.

Pater, Joe. 2006. The locus of exceptionality: morpheme-specific phonology as constraint indexation. In Leah Bateman & Adam Werle (eds.), *University of Massachusetts Occasional Papers 32: Papers in Optimality Theory*, 1–36. Amherst, MA: GLSA.

Pater, Joe. 2009. Morpheme-specific phonology: Constraint indexation and inconsistency resolution. In Steve Parker (ed.), *Phonological Argumentation: Essays on Evidence and Motivation*, 123–154.

Poplack, Shana, Alicia Pousada & David Sankoff. 1982. Competing influences on gender assignment: Variable process, stable outcome. *Lingua* 57(1). 1–28. http://www.sciencedirect.com/science/article/pii/0024384182900687, accessed 2016-10-02.

Postal, Paul. 1968. *Aspects of phonological theory*. New York: Harper & Row.

Prince, Alan & Paul Smolensky. 2004. *Optimality Theory: Constraint interaction in generative grammar*. Malden, MA: Wiley-Blackwell.

Prince, Alan & Bruce Tesar. 2004. Learning phonotactic distributions. In René Kager, Joe Pater & Wim Zonneveld (eds.), *Constraints in phonological acquisition*, 245–291. Cambridge: Cambridge University Press.

Pruitt, Kathryn. 2010. Serialism and locality in constraint-based metrical parsing. *Phonology* 27(3). 481–526.

Round, Erich R. 2013. *Kayardild Morphology and Syntax*. English. Oxford: Oxford University Press.

Round, Erich R. in progress. Unsyllabified moras and length in Yidiny.

Russell, Kevin. 1995. Morphemes and candidates in Optimality Theory.

Smith, Jennifer L. 2004. Making constraints positional: toward a compositional model of CON. *Lingua* 114(12). 1433–1464.

Tesar, Bruce & Paul Smolensky. 2000. *Learnability in Optimality Theory*. Cambridge: MIT Press.

Tesar, Bruce B. 1995. *Computational optimality theory*. Boulder: University of Colorado Ph.D. dissertation.

Tesar, Bruce B. 2007. Learnability. In Paul de Lacy (ed.), *The Cambridge handbook of phonology*, 555–574. Cambridge: Cambridge University Press.

Tranel, Bernard. 1996a. Exceptionality in Optimality Theory and final consonants in French. In Karen Zagona (ed.), *Grammatical Theory and Romance Languages*, 275–293. Amsterdam: John Benjamins.

Tranel, Bernard. 1996b. French liaison and elision revisited: A unified account within Optimality Theory. In Claudia Parodi, Carlos Quicoli & Mario Saltarelli (eds.), *Aspects of Romance linguistics*, 433–455. Washington, DC: Georgetown University Press.

Van Oostendorp, Marc. 2007. Derived environment effects and consistency of exponence. In Sylvia Blaho, Patrick Bye & Martin Krämer (eds.), *Freedom of analysis?*, 123–148. Berlin/New York: Mouton de Gruyter.

Wolf, Matthew. 2015. Lexical insertion occurs in the phonological component. In Eulàlia Bonet, Maria-Rosa Lloret & Joan Mascaró (eds.), *Understanding Allomorphy: Perspectives from Optimality Theory*, 361–407. London: Equinox Publishing.

Zoll, Cheryl. 2001. Constraints and representation in subsegmental phonology. In Linda Lombardi (ed.), *Segmental phonology in Optimality Theory: Constraints and representations*, 46–78.

Zoll, Cheryl C. 1996. *Parsing below the segment in a constraint based framework*. Berkeley, CA: University of California, Berkeley Ph.D. dissertation.

Zonneveld, Wim. 1978. *A formal theory of exceptions in generative phonology*. Lisse: Peter de Ridder.

Chapter 5

U-umlaut in Icelandic and Faroese: Survival and death

Höskuldur Thráinsson
University of Iceland

> Although Icelandic and Faroese are closely related and very similar in many respects, their vowel systems are quite different (see e.g. Anderson 1969b; Árnason 2011). This paper compares *u*-umlaut alternations in Icelandic and Faroese and shows that the Faroese umlaut has a number of properties that are to be expected if the relevant alternations are morphological (or analogical) rather than being due to a synchronic phonological process. In Icelandic, on the other hand, *u*-umlaut has none of these properties and arguably behaves like a living phonological process. This is theoretically interesting because the quality of the vowels involved (both the umlaut trigger and the target) has changed from Old to Modern Icelandic. In addition, *u*-umlaut in Modern Icelandic is more opaque (in the sense of Kiparsky 1973) than its Old Icelandic counterpart, i.e. it has more surface exceptions. An epenthesis rule inserting a (non-umlauting) /u/ into certain inflectional endings is the cause of many of these surface exceptions. Yet it seems that *u*-umlaut in Icelandic is still transparent enough to be acquired by children as a phonological process. In Faroese, on the other hand, *u*-umlaut became too opaque and died out as a phonological rule. It is argued that this has partly to do with certain changes in the Faroese vowel system and partly with the fact that the *u*-epenthesis rule was lost in Faroese.

1 Introduction

Anderson put the process of *u*-umlaut in Icelandic on the modern linguistic map with the analysis he proposed in his dissertation (Anderson 1969b) and several subsequent publications (Anderson 1969a; 1972; 1973; 1974; 1976). Because of changes in the vowel system from Old to Modern Icelandic, the nature of the umlaut process changed somewhat through the ages (see e.g. Benediktsson 1959). The most important part of *u*-umlaut, and the only part that is alive in the modern language, involves /a/ ~ /ǫ/ alternations in the old language (phonetically [a] ~ [ɔ], as shown in 2), which show up as /a/ ~ /ö/ alternations in the modern language (phonetically [a] ~ [œ], cf. 2). This is illustrated in (1) with the relevant vowel symbols highlighted:

(1)   Old Icelandic: Modern Icelandic:
      saga 'saga', OBL sǫgu, PL sǫgur   saga, OBL sögu, PL sögur
      hvass 'sharp', DAT hvǫssum   hvass, DAT hvössum
      tala 'speak', 1.PL tǫlum   tala, 1PL tölum

As these examples suggest, the quality of the root vowel /a/ changes when a /u/ follows in the next syllable. The relevant proecesses can be illustrated schematically as in (2). For the sake of simplicity I use conventional orthographic symbols to represent the vowels and only give IPA-symbols for the vowels that are important for the understanding of the umlaut processes. The umlaut-triggering vowels are encircled:[1]

(2)   a. *u*-umlaut in Old Icelandic and the system of short vowels:

	[-back]		[+back]	
	[-round]	[+round]	[-round]	[+round]
[+high]	i	y		ⓤ [u]
	e	ø		o
[+low]	ę		a [a] ⟶ ǫ [ɔ]	

b. *u*-umlaut in Modern Icelandic and the system of monophthongs:[2]

	[-back]		[+back]	
	[-round]	[+round]	[-round]	[+round]
[+high]	í			ú [u]
	i	ⓤ [ʏ]		
[+low]	e	ö [œ] ⟵ a [a]	o [ɔ]	

The gist of Anderson's analysis of *u*-umlaut can then be illustrated semi-formally as in the traditional generative phonological notation in (3), with the assimilating features highlighted (see also Rögnvaldsson 1981: 31, Thráinsson 2011: 89–90):[3]

(3)   a. *u*-umlaut in Old Icelandic:
      $$/a/ \rightarrow [\text{+round}] \;/\; \_C_0V \begin{bmatrix} \text{+round} \\ \text{+high} \\ \text{+back} \end{bmatrix}$$

      b. *u*-umlaut in Modern Icelandic:
      $$/a/ \rightarrow \begin{bmatrix} \text{+round} \\ \text{-back} \end{bmatrix} \;/\; \_C_0V \begin{bmatrix} \text{+round} \\ \text{-back} \\ \text{-low} \end{bmatrix}$$

---

[1] Note that in the representation of the Modern Icelandic vowel system, the accents over vowel symbols have nothing to do with quantity but simply denote separate vowel qualities. Thus /í/ is [i], /i/ is [ɪ], /ú/ is [u] and /u/ is [ʏ], as the schematic representation in (2) suggests.

[2] I am assuming here, like Thráinsson (1994) and Gíslason & Thráinsson (2000: 34), for instance, that Modern Icelandic only distinguishes between three three vowel heights and that /e/ [ɛ] and /ö/ [œ] are both phonologically [+low], like /a/ [a] and /o/ [ɔ]. For different assumptions see e.g. Árnason (2011: 60).

[3] Here, and elsewhere in this paper, I will use the kinds of formulations of rules and conditions familiar from classical generative phonology since much of the work on *u*-umlaut has been done in that kind of framework. For analyses employing more recent frameworks see Gibson & Ringen 2000, Hansson 2013 and Ingason 2016. Most of the argumentation in this paper should be relatively framework-independent, however.

As the illustration in (3) shows, the modern version of the umlaut is somewhat more complex than the old one, assimilating two features rather than one. Nevertheless, it is still arguably a phonologically (or phonetically) natural assimilation process, assimilating rounding and backness.

Although the *u*-umlaut discussion was most lively on the international scene in the 1970s (see e.g. Iverson 1978; Iverson & Anderson 1976; Orešnik 1975; 1977, cf. also Valfells 1967), the topic keeps popping up to this day, e.g. in journals and conferences dedicated to Scandinavian linguistics (see e.g. Gibson & Ringen 2000; Indriðason 2010; Thráinsson 2011; Hansson 2013) and even in recent master's theses and doctoral dissertations (see Markússon 2012; Ingason 2016). The main reason is that while *u*-umlaut in Modern Icelandic is obviously very productive, being applied consistently to new words and loanwords, it shows a number of intriguing surface exceptions. These have been discussed extensively in the literature cited but here I will concentrate on the most common and widespread one, namely the lack of umlaut before a /u/ that has been inserted between the inflectional ending /r/ and a preceding consonant. This epenthesis did not exist in Old Icelandic as illustrated in (4):

(4) Old Icelandic: Modern Icelandic:
     dalr 'valley', *latr* 'lazy'   *dal**u**r, lat**u**r*

If *u*-umlaut is a phonological rule in the modern language, this *u*-epenthesis has to follow it, as it did historically. This is one of the properties of *u*-umlaut that have been used to argue for the necessity of relatively abstract phonological representations and derivations (e.g. Anderson 1969b; 1974; Rögnvaldsson 1981; Thráinsson 2011; Hansson 2013) while others have maintained that *u*-umlaut is not a phonological process anymore in Modern Icelandic and the relevant alternations are morphologized and purely analogical (see e.g. Markússon 2012) or at least "morpheme-specific", i.e. triggered by particular morphemes that may or may not contain a /u/ (Ingason 2016).[4]

In this paper I will compare *u*-umlaut alternations in Modern Icelandic and Modern Faroese. This comparison will show very clearly that *u*-umlaut in Modern Faroese has a

---

[4] Ingason (2016: 220) formulates his umlaut rule as follows:

Realize an underlying /a/ as /ö/ in the syllable which precedes the morpheme which triggers the umlaut.

As can be seen here, no mention is made of a triggering /u/ in the rule. The reason is that Ingason wants to derive all all paradigmatic /a/ ~ /ö/ alternations the same way, including the ones where /u/ has been syncopated historically. Thus he argues that the NOM.SG. morpheme -ø in feminine nouns like *sök* 'guilt, case' and the NOM./ACC.PL. morpheme -ø in neuter nouns like *börn* 'children' triggers umlaut the same way that the DAT.PL. morpheme *-um* does in *sökum* and *börnum*. But many researchers have wanted to distinguish between morphologically conditioned umlaut, where there is no triggering /u/, and phonologically conditioned umlaut triggered by /u/, e.g. Rögnvaldsson (1981). One reason for doing so comes from the behavior of loanwords like the adjective *smart* 'smart, chic'. Here the NOM.SG.F and the NOM/ACC.PL.N can either be *smart* or *smört*, i.e. a morphologically conditioned umlaut may or may not apply. But once an umlauting inflectional ending containing /u/ is added to the loanword *smart*, the *u*-umlaut becomes obligatory. Thus DAT.PL can only be *smört-um* and not **smart-um* and the NOM.PL.WK form has to be *smört-u* and not **smart-u*. This suggests that the morphologically conditioned umlaut is more prone to exceptions than the phonologically conditioned one, which is actually to be expected. Thanks to Eiríkur Rögnvaldsson for pointing this out to me.

number of properties (e.g. paradigm levelling, various kinds of exceptions, total absence from certain paradigms, inapplicability to loanwords ...) that are to be expected if the relevant alternations are no longer due to a synchronic process. In Modern Icelandic, on the other hand, *u*-umlaut has none of these properties and behaves more like a phonological rule. This is of general theoretical interest since it illustrates how phonological rules can survive (in the case of Icelandic) despite reduced transparency (in the sense of Kiparsky 1973) and how changes in the phonological system can cause the death of a phonological rule (in the case of Faroese) and what the consequences can be.

The remainder of the paper is organized as follows: In §2 I first illustrate how the *u*-epenthesis works in Modern Icelandic and then present a couple of arguments for the phonological (as opposed to morphological) nature of Modern Icelandic *u*-umlaut. §?? first describes some facts about the Faroese vowel system that must have been important for the development of *u*-umlaut and then shows that *u*-epenthesis does not exist anymore as a phonological process in Modern Faroese. It is then argued that these developments led to the death of *u*-umlaut as a phonological process in Faroese. §?? then contains a systematic comparison of *u*-umlaut alternations in Modern Icelandic and Faroese, concluding that the Faroese ones must be analogical (and morphological) in nature as they do not exhibit any of the crucial phonological properties that Modern Icelandic *u*-umlaut alternations show. In Icelandic, on the other hand, *u*-umlaut does not show the non-phonological properties listed for its Faroese counterpart. §?? concludes the paper.

2 u-epenthesis and u-umlaut in Modern Icelandic

2.1 The epenthesis rule

The phoneme /r/ frequently occurs in Old Icelandic (Old Norse) as a marker of various morphological categories, including NOM.SG of strong masculine nouns and adjectives as illustrated in (5). It sometimes assimilated to a preceding consonant, e.g. /s, l, n/ (cf. 5c),[5] but it was deleted after certain consonant clusters, such as /gl, gn, ss/ (cf. 5d):

(5)   a.   *stór-r* 'big', *mó-r* 'peat', *há-r* 'high'

       b.   *dal-r* 'valley', *lat-r* 'lazy', *tóm-r* 'empty', *harð-r* 'hard'

       c.   *ís-s* 'ice', *laus-s* 'loose', *stól-l* 'chair', *fín-n* 'fine'

       d.   *fugl* 'bird', *vagn* 'wagon', *foss* 'waterfall' (stem *foss-*)

It is likely that the /r/ in words of type (5b) was syllabic in Old Icelandic. There are no syllabic consonants in Modern Icelandic, on the other hand. Instead a /u/ appears between the /r/ and the preceding consonant in the modern version of words of type (5b). There is historical evidence for this *u*-insertion from the late thirteenth century and

---

[5] Assimilation to stem-final /l, n/ only happened in Old Icelandic if these consonants were preceded by long vowels, i.e. Old Icelandic diphthongs and vowels that are standardly represented by accented vowel symbols in Old Icelandic orthography, cf. *stól-l* 'chair' vs. *dal-r* 'valley', *fín-n* 'fine' vs. *lin-r* 'soft, limp', *heil-l* 'whole' vs. *hol-r* 'hollow'.

onwards (see e.g. Kristinsson 1992 and references cited there) and many linguists have argued that *u*-epenthesis is still a productive phonological process in Modern Icelandic (e.g. Anderson 1969b,a; Orešnik 1972; Rögnvaldsson 1981; Kiparsky 1984).[6] This implies that speakers distinguish between a *-ur*-ending where the underlying morpheme is #-r# and the /u/ is epenthetic (and does not trigger *u*-umlaut) and a *-ur*-ending where the /u/ is not epenthetic and the underlying morpheme is #-ur# (and the /u/ triggers *u*-umlaut). This contrast is illustrated in (??) vs. (??) (see also the examples in 1 and 4 above):

(6) a. #dal+r# 'valley' NOM.SG.M → *dal-ur* by epenthesis no umlaut
   #lat+r# 'lazy' NOM.SG.M → *lat-ur* by epenthesis no umlaut
b. #sag+ur# 'sagas' NOM.PL.F → *sög-ur* *u*-umlaut
   #tal+ur# 'numbers' NOM.PL.F → *töl-ur* *u*-umlaut

Thus the NOM.SG ending #-r#, which is both found in strong masculine nouns like *dalur* 'valley' and in the strong masculine form of adjectives like *latur* 'lazy', does not have the same properties as the NOM.PL ending #-ur# which is found in feminine nouns like *sögur* 'sagas' and *tölur* 'numbers'. Despite their surface similarities in certain environments, speakers can clearly distinguish these endings. A part of the reason must be that the NOM.SG.M ending #-r# only shows up as *-ur* in phonologically definable environments, i.e. the modern version of words with stems of type (5b), whereas the NOM.PL.F ending #-ur# is not so restricted and always shows up as *-ur*. This is illustrated in Table 1 (compare the examples in 5).

Comparison of Table 1 and the Old Icelandic examples in (5) reveals a slight extension of *r*-deletion: The /r/ of the morphological ending #-r# is now deleted after /r/ (compare line d of the table to 5a) and after all instances of /s/, not just /ss/ (compare line d of the table to (5c,d)). The *u*-epenthesis illustrated in line b of Table 1 is an innovation, of course. Otherwise the NOM.SG.M ending behaves in much the same way as in Old Icelandic. The different behavior of the morphemes compared in Table 1 can be seen as an argument for distinguishing them in the underlying form, e.g. for not analyzing the N.SG.M ending as #-ur#.

2.2 Some phonological properties of Modern Icelandic u-umlaut

In this section I will mention two sets of facts which show that *u*-umlaut still has certain properties in Modern Icelandic that are to be expected if it is a phonologically conditioned process.

---

[6] Orešnik later maintained that *u*-epenthesis could not be a synchronic rule in Modern Icelandic because of the existence of exceptional word forms like *klifr* 'climbing' (from the verb *klifra* 'climb'), *sötr* 'slurping' (from the verb *sötra* 'slurp'), *pukr* 'secretiveness' from the verb *pukra(st)* 'be secretive about', etc. (Orešnik 1978; see also the discussion in Kjartansson 1984). In words of this kind one would have expected *u*-epenthesis to apply. The importance of these exceptions is not very clear since this is a very special class of words (all derived from verbs ending in *-ra*) and it is typically possible or even preferred to apply the epenthesis rule to these forms, giving *klifur, sötur, pukur*, etc. For the sake of completeness it should be noted that the final *-r* in word forms like *sötr, pukr* has to be voiceless and this may be related to the fact that there are no syllabic consonants in Modern Icelandic, as stated above.

Table 1: Phonological realization of the inflectional endings #-r# and #-ur# in Modern Icelandic.

	type of stem	phonological realization of the NOM.SG.M ending #-r#	phonological realization of the NOM.PL.F ending #-ur#
a.	ending in a vowel	-r (*mó-r* 'peat', *há-r* 'high')	-ur (*ló-ur* 'golden plovers')
b.	ending in a single consonant (but see c)	-*ur* (*dal-ur* 'valley', *lat-ur* 'lazy')	-ur (*sög-ur* 'sagas', *töl-ur* 'numbers')
c.	ending in a high vowel + /l,n/	assimilation (*stól-l* 'chair', *fín-n* 'fine')	-ur (*spús-ur* 'wives', *súl-ur* 'columns', *dýn-ur* 'mattresses')
d.	ending in /s, r/ or consonant clusters ending in /l, n/ such as /gl, gn/	deletion (*ís* 'ice', *laus* 'loose', *foss* 'waterfall' *bjór* 'beer', *stór* 'big', *fugl* 'bird', *vagn* 'wagon')	-ur (*ýs-ur* 'haddocks', *aus-ur* 'scoops', *hór-ur* 'whores', *ugl-ur* 'owls', *hrygn-ur* 'spawning fish', *byss-ur* 'guns')

First, if *u*-umlaut was morphologically conditioned and not phonologically, we would expect it to be restricted to certain morphological categories or parts of speech. It is not. It applies in the paradigms of nouns, adjectives and verbs when a /u/ follows in the inflectional ending (with the exception of the epenthetic /u/ already mentioned). This is illustrated in (7):

(7) a. *saga* 'saga', OBL.SG *sög-u*, NOM/ACC.PL *sög-ur*, DAT.PL *sög-um*
    b. *snjall* 'smart', DAT.SG.M *snjöll-um*, NOM.PL.WK *snjöll-u*
    c. *kalla* 'call', 1.PL.PRS *köll-um*, 3.PL.PST *kölluð-u*

The so-called *i*-umlaut is very different in this respect. It is clearly not alive as a phonological rule anymore but its effects can still be observed in the modern language in certain morphologically definable environments. As a result we can find near-minimal pairs of word forms where *i*-umlaut has applied in one member but not the other although the phonological conditions seem identical. Some examples are given in (8):

(8) a. *háttur* 'mode', DAT.SG *hætt-i*/*hátt-i*, NOM.PL *hætt-ir*/*hátt-ir*
    b. *sáttur* 'satisfied', NOM.SG.M.WK **sætt-i/sátt-i*, NOM.PL.M **sætt-ir/sátt-ir*

In (8a) we see examples of the paradigmatic alternation /á ~ æ/ (phonetically [au] ~ [ai] in the modern language, probably [aː] ~ [ɛː] in Old Icelandic) originally caused by *i*-umlaut.

5 U-umlaut in Icelandic and Faroese: Survival and death

In the NOM.SG we have /á/ in the stem but in the DAT.SG the only acceptable form is *hætti* and the "non-umlauted" version **hátti* is unacceptable. Similarly, in the NOM.PL only *hættir* is acceptable and **háttir* is not. At a first glance we might think that an /i/ in the inflectional ending is still causing this "umlaut" but a comparison with the adjectival forms in (8b) indicates that this cannot be the case. Here the only acceptable weak NOM.SG.M form is *sátti* and not **sætti* and the only NOM.PL.M form is *sáttir* and not **sættir*. So the *i*-umlaut alternations in Modern Icelandic are clearly morphologically conditioned and not phonological anymore (see also Thráinsson 2011: 93 for further examples of this kind).

Second, recall that standard generative phonology formulations of *u*-umlaut in Icelandic of the kind illustrated in (3b) above state explicitly that /u/ only triggers umlaut of /a/ in the immediately preceding syllable. This is illustrated by examples like the following:

(9) a. *bakki* 'bank' DAT.PL *bökk-um/*bakk-um*
     b. *akkeri* 'anchor' DAT.PL **ökker-um/akker-um*

In (9a) the *u*-umlaut obligatorily applies to the root vowel /a/ in the immediately preceding syllable. In (9b), on the other hand, the /u/ in the (same) inflectional ending cannot apply to the root vowel /a/ because there is a syllable intervening. An interesting and much discussed case, e.g. by Anderson in several of the publications cited above, involves trisyllabic words with two instances of /a/ in the stem. Consider the examples in (10):

(10) a. *kallu* 'call'
        1.SG.PST *kalla-ð-i*, 1.PL.PST **kallö-ð-um/köllu-ð-um/*kallu-ð- um/*kölla-ð-um*
     b. *banan-i* 'banana'
        DAT.PL *banön-um/bönun-um/*banun-um/*bönan-um*

Consider first the conceivable 1.PL.PST forms of the verb *kalla* 'call'. Based on the formulation (3b) of the *u*-umlaut rule, one might have expected the form **kallöðum*, where the /u/ in the inflectional ending triggers *u*-umlaut of the /a/ in the preceding syllable. This is not an acceptable form, however. The reason is that in forms of this sort a "weakening" of unstressed /ö/ to /u/ is obligatory. This weakening is found in in many words, e.g. the plural of the word *hérað* 'district', plural *héröð* or (preferred) *héruð*, *meðal* 'medicine', plural *meðöl* or (preferred) *meðul*. It is not always obligatory but it seems that in the past tense of verbs of this sort it is. But once the (umlauted) /ö/ in **kallöðum* has been weakened to /u/ it obligatorily triggers *u*-umlaut of the preceding /a/ so *kölluðum* is acceptable but **kalluðum* is not. Finally, the form **köllaðum* is not acceptable either, since there *u*-umlaut would be applied across an intervening syllable, which is not possible, as we have seen (cf. 9b). The *u*-umlaut works in a similar fashion in the word *banani*, except that here the weakening of the second (and unstressed) syllable from /ö/ to /u/ is not obligatory. Hence *banönum* is an acceptable form, with the /u/ in the final syllable triggering *u*-umlaut of the preceding /a/ to /ö/. But if this /ö/ is further weakened to

/u/, then *u*-umlaut of the first /a/ is obligatory and *bönunum* is an acceptable form but **banunum* is not.[7] As predicted by the formulation of the *u*-umlaut rule in (3b) a form like **bönanum* is unacceptable because there the *u*-umlaut would have applied across an intervening syllable. Facts of this sort have been interpreted as showing that *u*-umlaut in Modern Icelandic is of a phonological nature since it depends on syllabic structure (no syllables can intervene between the umlaut trigger and the target) and it can be applied iteratively (a /u/ which itself is derived by *u*-umlaut and subsequent independently needed weakening can trigger *u*-umlaut).

3 The conditions for u-umlaut in Modern Faroese

3.1 u-umlaut and the Modern Faroese vowel system

Modern Faroese has preserved some *u*-umlaut-like vowel alternations. A couple of examples are given in (11) (see also Thráinsson et al. 2012: 78, 100, passim):

(11) *dag-ur* 'day', DAT.PL *døg-um*; *spak-ur* 'calm', NOM.PL.WK *spøk-u*

At first glance, these alternations seem very similar to the Icelandic ones described in the preceding sections. But while the *u*-umlaut alternations are arguably phonologically (or phonetically) natural in Modern Icelandic (see the diagram in 2b and the formulation in 3b), it will be claimed below that this is not the case in Faroese. To demonstrate this, it is necessary to look closely at the Faroese vowel system. Consider first the following schematic representation of Faroese *u*-umlaut of the type just illustrated, where the alleged umlaut trigger is encircled (cf. Thráinsson 2011: 98, Thráinsson et al. 2012: 33, compare Árnason 2011: 248–250):[8]

(12) *u*-umlaut in Modern Faroese and the system of monophthongs:

	[-back]		[+back]	
	[-round]	[+round]	[-round]	[+round]
[+high]	i	y		ⓤ [uː/ʊ]
	e ⟶ ø [øː/œ]			o
[+low]	æ [ɛaː/a]		a	ɔ

Something like (13) would seem to be a possible formulation of a process of this kind in traditional generative phonology terms (compare 3b):

---

[7] It is sometimes claimed that *bönönum* is also an acceptable form for some speakers. If this is so, it is possible that the /ö/ in the next-to-last syllable triggers *u*-umlaut (i.e. ö-umlaut!) of the /a/ in the first syllable. That would simply mean that the feature [-low] in the definition of the environment of the *u*-umlaut in (3b) would be omitted. But since there are no derivational (nor inflectional) morphemes containing an underlying /ö/ (i.e. an /ö/ that cannot have been derived by *u*-umlaut), this proposal cannot be tested independently of the iterative rule application, as pointed out by a reviewer.

[8] Vowel length is predictable in Faroese, as it is in Icelandic: Vowels are long in stressed open syllables, otherwise short. As illustrated in the brackets in (12), there is often a considerable difference in the phonetic realization of the long and short variants. This will be illustrated below. — It should be noted that Árnason (2011: 76) assumes a different analysis of Faroese monophthongs.

5 U-umlaut in Icelandic and Faroese: Survival and death

(13) Possible phonological formulation of *u*-umlaut in Modern Faroese:

$$/æ/ \rightarrow \begin{bmatrix} \text{+round} \\ \text{-low} \end{bmatrix} / \_C_0V \begin{bmatrix} \text{+round} \\ \text{+back} \\ \text{-low} \end{bmatrix}$$

Presented this way, *u*-umlaut in Faroese looks like a fairly natural assimilation rule at a first glance.[9] But the facts are somewhat more complicated.

First, the alleged trigger /u/ is not too stable in Modern Faroese. The reason is that unstressed /i,u/ are not distinguished in all Faroese dialects. In some dialects they merge into an [ɪ]-like sound, in others into an [ʊ]-like sound but some dialects distinguish them as [ɪ] and [ʊ] (see Thráinsson et al. 2012: 27, and references cited there). This situation has clearly added to the phonological opacity of *u*-umlaut alternations for speakers acquiring Faroese.

Second, the target of the *u*-umlaut in Faroese is arguably a "moving" one. As indicated in (12), the umlaut affects the phoneme represented there as /æ/. As the orthography suggests, it is a descendant of Old Norse /a/ in words like *dagur*, *spakur* (see 11). It is realized phonetically as [ɛa:] when long and [a] when short, as shown in (12), cf. *spakur* [spɛaːʰkʊɹ] 'calm', SG.N *spakt* [spakt] (see Thráinsson et al. 2012: 34 passim). But in the history of Faroese Old Norse /a/ [a] and /æ/ [ɛː] merged so the phoneme represented here as /æ/ can also be a descendant of Old Norse /æ/ and then it is represented in the spelling as 'æ', cf. *trælur* [tʰɹɛaːlʊɹ] 'slave', *æða* [ɛaːva] 'eider duck'. Words written with 'æ' show the same alternation between long [ɛa:] and short [a] as demonstrated for *spakur* and *spakt* above (e.g. *vænur* [vɛaːnʊɹ] 'beautiful' SG.M vs. *vænt* [vant̥], cf. Thráinsson et al. 2012, p. 34). Yet it seems that *u*-umlaut is rarely if ever found in the 'æ'-words. Thus the DAT.PL of *trælur* is *trælum* and not **trølum* (compare DAT.PL *dølum* of *dalur* 'valley') and although the words *æða* 'eider duck' and *aða* '(big) mussel' sound the same, i.e. as [ɛa:va], the DAT.PL of the former has to be *æðum* [ɛaːvʊn] and *øvum* [øːvʊn] can only be DAT.PL of *aða*.[10]

To further complicate matters, the development of Old Norse /a/ in Faroese has left "room" for a "regular /a/" in the Faroese vowel system, as shown in the diagram in (12). It occurs in loanwords and is realized as [a:] when long and [a] when short, cf. *Japan* [ˈjaːʰpan], *japanskur* [jaˈpʰanskʊɹ] 'Japanese'.[11] It does not seem that this vowel ever undergoes *u*-umlaut in Faroese (for further discussion see §4).

---

[9] A reviewer suggests, however, that a process changing rounding and height as formulated for Faroese in (13), might be less natural from the point of view of acoustic phonetics than a process changing rounding and backness the way the *u*-umlaut rule in Modern Icelandic does according to (3): The former affects both F1 (for the height difference) and F2 (for rounding) whereas the latter affects F2 in opposite directions (raising it for fronting but lowering it for rounding). Thus the Modern Icelandic *u*-umlaut rule would "generate more similar input-output mappings", which may be preferred to less similar ones.

[10] A reviewer points out that the fact that *u*-umlaut does not apply do 'æ'-words in Faroese suggests that "*u*-umlaut had already taken on a morphological character before /a/ and /æ/ merged." But since there are no written records of Faroese from 1400–1800, the historical development of the language is very murky.

[11] In the noun *Japan* the stress falls on the first syllable, in the adjective *japanskur* it falls on the second one as indicated. Hence the quantity alternation in the first vowel.

Finally, there is no *u*-epenthesis in Modern Faroese to "explain away" apparent exceptions to *u*-umlaut as will be shown in the next section.

3.2 The lack of u-epenthesis in Modern Faroese

Now recall that the most obvious surface exception to *u*-umlaut in Modern Icelandic is due to the *u*-epenthesis described above. This rule creates -*ur*-endings that do not trigger *u*-umlaut. It was argued that this epenthesis rule is still productive in Icelandic, witness the fact that it only applies in phonologically definable environments. Hence there is a clear distributional difference between -*ur*-endings produced by the epenthesis rule (and not triggering *u*-umlaut) and -*ur*-endings where the /u/ is a part of the underlying form (and triggers umlaut). This is not the case in Faroese, where the ending -*ur* as a marker of the NOM.SG of strong masculine nouns and adjectives, with a /u/ that was historically inserted by epenthesis, has been generalized to all environments. Hence it has become distributionally indistinguishable from other -*ur*-endings. Table 2 compares the phonological realization of the NOM.SG.M #-r#-ending in Modern Icelandic to its Modern Faroese counterpart (see also Thráinsson 2011: 100):

Table 2: Phonological realization of a strong NOM.SG.M-ending in Modern Icelandic and Modern Faroese.

	type of stem	phonological realization of a strong NOM.SG.M ending in Modern Icelandic	phonological realization of a strong NOM.SG.M ending in Modern Faroese
a.	ending in a vowel	-*r* (*mó-r* 'peat', *há-r* 'high')	-*ur* (*mó-ur/mógv-ur* 'peat', *há-ur* 'high')
b.	ending in a single consonant (but see c)	-*ur* (*dal-ur* 'valley', *lat-ur* 'lazy')	-*ur* (*dal-ur* 'valley', *lat-ur* 'lazy')
c.	ending in a high vowel + /l,n/	assimilation (*stól-l* 'chair', *fín-n* 'fine')	-*ur* (*stól-ur* 'chair', *fín-ur* 'fine')
d.	ending in /s, r/ or consonant clusters like /gl, gn/	deletion (*ís* 'ice', *laus* 'loose', *foss* 'waterfall', *stór* 'big', *fugl* 'bird', *vagn* 'wagon')	-*ur* (*ís-ur* 'ice', *leys-ur* 'loose', *foss-ur* 'waterfall', *stór-ur* 'big', *fugl-ur* 'bird', *vagn-ur* 'wagon')

This has clearly made the *u*-umlaut rule in Faroese more opaque since now the non-umlauting and umlauting *ur*-endings occur in the same phonological environments. It seems very likely that this has contributed to the death of *u*-umlaut as a phonological process in Faroese.

4 Testing the predictions

In the preceding discussions I have described /a ~ ö/ alternations in Modern Icelandic and their Modern Faroese counterparts. I have argued that the Icelandic alternations are still governed by a synchronic phonological process. Although these alternations are still found in Modern Faroese, I have argued that they cannot be governed by a phonological rule. Instead they must be morphologically governed or analogical. This analysis makes several testable predictions (see Thráinsson 2011: 100–102).

First, we do not a priori expect phonologically conditioned alternations to be restricted to particular morphological categories whereas morphologically conditioned alternations obviously are, by definition. As we have already seen, the Icelandic *u*-umlaut occurs in the inflectional paradigms of nouns, adjectives and verbs and in various grammatical categories (cases, numbers, tenses, persons …). Its Faroese counterpart behaves differently. It is found in the inflectional paradigms of nouns and adjectives, as we have seen (cf. 11), but not in the past tense forms of verbs, where it would be expected on phonological grounds. Thus we have *við kölluðum* in Icelandic vs. *vit kallaðu* in Faroese for 1.PL.PST 'we called', and *við frömdum* vs. *vit framdu* in Faroese for 1.PL.PST 'we did, made'.

Second, a phonological rule should not allow analogical extensions to forms that do not fit its structural conditions. Such extensions are not found for Icelandic *u*-umlaut but in Faroese they are very common. Thus the /ø/ of the oblique cases *søgu* 'saga' has been analogically extended to the NOM.SG form *søga* and many other words of a similar type. The corresponding form **söga* is unacceptable in Icelandic.[12]

Third, a phonologically conditioned rule should apply whenever its structural conditions are met. Thus we would not expect to find inflectional forms in Icelandic where *u*-umlaut fails to apply in an appropriate environment. Such examples are very common in Faroese, on the other hand. Thus the DAT.PL of the noun *rakstur* 'shave' in Faroese is *rakstrum* and not the expected **røkstrum*, the DAT.PL of *spakur* 'calm' can either be *spøkum* or *spakum*, etc. (see Thráinsson et al. 2012: 79, 100, passim). Corresponding unumlauted forms are unacceptable in Icelandic.

Fourth, there is evidence for "iterative" application of *u*-umlaut in Icelandic, with one application of the *u*-umlaut rule feeding another. This was discussed above (second part of §2.2) in connection with forms like 1.PL.PST *kölluðum* '(we) called' and DAT.PL *bönunum* 'bananas'. No such evidence is found in Faroese, where the corresponding forms are *kallaðum* and *bananum*.[13]

---

[12] As a reviewer reminds me, the Icelandic neologism for *computer* is interesting in this connection. It was supposed to be *tölva* (related to the word *tala* 'number' — this was when computers were mainly used for computing) in NOM.SG, oblique singular cases *tölvu*. In Proto-Nordic time /v/ could trigger umlaut of /a/ to /ǫ/ so we have Old Norse words like *vǫlva* 'sooth-sayer, witch'. But since /v/ is not a trigger of umlaut in Modern Icelandic (witness loanwords like *salvi* 'salve, cream'), speakers tend to use the form *talva* for NOM.SG, thus in a way undoing the underlying /ö/ in the nominative as if they are "assuming" that the /ö/ in the oblique cases is derived by a synchronic *u*-umlaut from /a/, as in words like *saga* 'saga', oblique *sögu* (for some discussion see Thráinsson 1982).

[13] The latter form may be related to the fact that *banan* 'banana' is a loanword and contains the vowel /a/ (long variant [a:]) and not /æ/, cf. the discussion in §3.1. See also the next paragraph.

Finally, Icelandic *u*-umlaut is so productive that it is naturally applied in loanwords, as we have seen. This is not so in Faroese. Thus the word *app* (for a small program) has been adopted into both languages. In Icelandic the DAT.PL has to be ***öppum*** whereas the natural form is ***appum*** in Faroese. This can easily be verified by searching for the word combinations *með öppum* and *við appum* 'with apps' on Google. For the first variant one finds a number of Icelandic hits, for the second Faroese ones.

The general conclusion, then, is that *u*-umlaut in Modern Icelandic has a number of properties that are to be expected if it is a phonological process but none of the properties one might expect of morphologically conditioned or analogical alternations.

5 Concluding remarks

While it has often been argued that phonology need not be "natural" (see e.g. Anderson 1981), there must obviously be limits to the "unnaturalness" and opacity of phonological processes. Once they become too unnatural and opaque, they can no longer be acquired as such and the phonological alternations originally created by them will be relegated to morphology. Then their productivity will be limited and it will at best survive to some extent by analogy, but analogical processes are known to be irregular and unpredictable. The fate of *i*-umlaut in Icelandic is a case in point, as described above (see the discussion of the examples in 8). But whereas we do not have detailed information about how *i*-umlaut died as a phonological process, comparison of the development of *u*-umlaut in Icelandic and Faroese sheds an interesting light on how a phonological rule can die and how it can survive despite changing conditions.

Acknowledgements

Many thanks to Steve Anderson for introducing me to the wonders of synchronic *u*-umlaut way back when. Thanks are also due to the editors and to two anonymous reviewers for help, useful comments, suggestions and corrections.

References

Anderson, Stephen R. 1969a. An outline of the phonology of Modern Icelandic vowels. *Foundations of Language* 5. 53–72.
Anderson, Stephen R. 1969b. *West Scandinavian vowel systems and the ordering of phonological rules.* Cambridge, MA: Massachusetts Institute of Technology PhD thesis.
Anderson, Stephen R. 1972. Icelandic u-umlaut and breaking in a generative grammar. In Evelyn S. Firchow, Karen Grimstad, Wayne A. O'Neil & Nils Hasselmo (eds.), *Studies for Einar Haugen*, 13–30. Mouton: The Hague.
Anderson, Stephen R. 1973. U-umlaut and scaldic verse. In Stephen R. Anderson & Paul Kiparsky (eds.), *A Festschrift for Morris Halle*, 3–13. New York: Holt, Rinehart & Winston.

Anderson, Stephen R. 1974. *The organization of phonology*. New York: Academic Press.
Anderson, Stephen R. 1976. On the conditioning of icelandic u-umlaut. *Language Sciences*. 26–27.
Anderson, Stephen R. 1981. Why phonology isn't "natural". *Linguistic Inquiry* 12(4). 493–539.
Árnason, Kristján. 2011. *The phonology of Icelandic and Faroese*. Oxford: Oxford University Press.
Benediktsson, Hreinn. 1959. The vowel system of Icelandic: A survey of its history. *Word* 15. [Also published in Guðrún Þórhallsdóttir, Höskuldur Þráinsson, Jón G. Friðjónsson and Kjartan Ottosson (eds.), *Linguistic studies, historical and comparative, by Hreinn Benediktsson*, 50–73. Reykjavík, Iceland: Institute of Linguistics, University of Iceland], 282–312.
Gibson, Courtenay St John & Catherine O. Ringen. 2000. Icelandic umlaut in Optimality Theory. *Nordic Journal of Linguistics* 23(1). 49–64.
Gíslason, Indriði & Höskuldur Thráinsson. 2000. *Handbók um íslenskan framburð*. *['handbook on Icelandic pronunciation']*. 2nd edn. Reykjavík: Rannsóknarstofnun Kennaraháskóla Íslands.
Hansson, Gunnar. 2013. *Alternations, allomorphy and abstractness: Icelandic u-umlaut revisited*. Paper presented at the 25th Scandinavian Conference of Linguistics, Reykjavík.
Indriðason, Þorsteinn G. 2010. Til varnar hljóðkerfisreglu. Nokkrar athugasemdir við umræðugrein. ['In defence of a phonological rule. Some comments on a discussion article.'] *Íslenskt mál* 32. 137–149.
Ingason, Anton Karl. 2016. *Realizing morphemes in the Icelandic Noun Phrase*. Philadelphia: University of Pennsylvania PhD thesis.
Iverson, Gregory. 1978. Synchronic umlaut in Old Icelandic. *Nordic Journal of Linguistics* 1. 121–139.
Iverson, Gregory & Stephen R. Anderson. 1976. Icelandic u-umlaut: An exchange of views. *Language Sciences*. 28–34.
Kiparsky, Paul. 1973. Phonological representations. In Osamu Fujimura (ed.), *Three dimensions of linguistic theory*, 1–135. Tokyo: TEC.
Kiparsky, Paul. 1984. On the lexical phonology of Icelandic. In Iréne Johansson Claes-Christian Elert & Eva Strangert (eds.), *Nordic prosody III*, 135–164. Umeå: University of Umeå.
Kjartansson, Helgi Skúli. 1984. *U*-innskot, lífs eða liðið? ['*u*-epenthesis, alive or dead?'] *Íslenskt mál* 6. 182–185.
Kristinsson, Ari Páll. 1992. *U*-innskot í íslensku. ['*u*-epenthesis in Icelandic.'] *Íslenskt mál* 14. 15–33.
Markússon, Jón Símon. 2012. *Eðli u-hljóðvarpsvíxla í íslenskri málsögu*. ['The nature of u-umlaut alternations in the history of Icelandic.'] Reykjavík: University of Iceland Master's thesis.
Orešnik, Janez. 1972. On the epenthesis rule in Modern Icelandic. *Arkiv för nordisk filologi* 87. 1–32.

Orešnik, Janez. 1975. The Modern Icelandic u-umlaut rule. In Karl-Hampus Dahlstedt (ed.), *The Nordic languages and modern linguistics 3*, 621–633. Almqvist & Wiksell, Stockholm.

Orešnik, Janez. 1977. Modern Icelandic u-umlaut from the descriptive point of view. *Gripla* 2. 151–182.

Orešnik, Janez. 1978. The Modern Icelandic epenthesis rule revisited. *Arkiv för nordisk filologi* 93. 166–173.

Rögnvaldsson, Eiríkur. 1981. *U*-hljóðvarp og önnur a ~ ö víxl í íslensku. ['*u*-umlaut and other a ~ ö alternations in Icelandic.']. *Íslenskt mál* 3. 25–58.

Thráinsson, Höskuldur. 1982. Bölvuð talvan. ['The damned computer.'] *Íslenskt mál* 4. 293–294.

Thráinsson, Höskuldur. 1994. Icelandic. In Johan van der Auwera & Ekkehard König (eds.), *The germanic languages*, 142–189. Routledge, London.

Thráinsson, Höskuldur. 2011. Um dauðans óvissan tíma: *u*-hljóðvarp lífs og liðið. ['Uncertain time of death: On *u*-umlaut alive and dead.'] *Íslenskt mál* 33. 85–107.

Thráinsson, Höskuldur, Hjalmar P. Peterson, Jógvan í Lon Jacobsen & Zakaris Svabo Hansen (eds.). 2012. 2nd edn. Tórshavn & Reykjavík: Faroe University Press – Fróðskapur & Linguistic Institute, University of Iceland.

Valfells, Sigrid. 1967. *Umlaut alternations in Modern Icelandic.* Cambridge, MA: Harvard University PhD thesis.

Part II

Morphology

Chapter 6

Word-based Items-and-processes (WoBIP): Evidence from Hebrew morphology

Outi Bat-El
Tel-Aviv University

> In his seminal book *A-Morphous Morphology*, Anderson provides ample evidence supporting the item-and-process approach to morphology, whereby relations between words, and thus the derivation of one word from another is expressed in terms of processes. Although Anderson excluded Semitic languages from the paradigm, I argue in this paper for the advantage of item-and-process in the analysis of Modern Hebrew word relations. Under this approach, the word/stem is the base, and the putative consonant root is just a residue of phonological elements, which are lexically prominent as are consonants in non-Semitic languages. The empirical basis of the arguments is drawn from natural and experimental data of adult Hebrew as well as child Hebrew.

1 Introduction

"Items vs. processes in morphology" is the title of §3.4 in Anderson's (1992) seminal book *A-Morphous Morphology*. In this section, Anderson compares two models of morphology – item-and-arrangement and item-and-process (attributed to Hockett 1954) – and argues in favor of the latter. Taking apophony (or ablaut; e.g. *sing – sang*) as one of the many problems encountered with the item-and-arrangement model, Anderson claims that "what presents {PAST} in *sang* is … the *relation* between *sang* and *sing*, expressed as the **process** by which one is formed from the other" (Anderson 1992: 62; emphasis original). The process in this case is replacement (or stem modification); "the PAST form of *sing* is formed by replacing /ɪ/ with /æ/." Crucially, /æ/ is not the morpheme designating PAST, and *sang* is not derived by combining bound morphemes, i.e. *s-ŋ* and *-æ-*.

The section which immediately follows in Anderson's book (§3.5) is titled "Word-based vs. morpheme-based morphology". The issues addressed in these two sections are always considered together, since one is contingent upon the other. A root-based morphology is usually analyzed within the item-and-arrangement model. However, if

Outi Bat-El. 2017. Word-based Items-and-processes (WoBIP): Evidence from Hebrew morphology. In Claire Bowern, Laurence Horn & Raffaella Zanuttini (eds.), *On looking into words (and beyond)*, 115–135. Berlin: Language Science Press. DOI:10.5281/zenodo.495441

morphology is word-based, the debate between item-and-arrangement and item-and-process still holds (see §2). This debate is particularly heated in the study of Semitic morphology, where a consonantal root has been claimed to be the core morphological unit in the word.

Paradigms like *sing – sang* are relatively rare in English, but abundant in Semitic languages, such as Hebrew, where the relation between words is often expressed with apophony; e.g. *χam – χom* 'hot – heat', *limed – limud* 'to teach – learning', *ʃuman – ʃémen* 'fat – oil', *gadol –gódel* 'big – size' (stress is final unless otherwise specified). Since item-and-arrangement has been the traditional approach to Semitic morphology, and has been supported by traditional Semiticists (see, however, §6) and generative linguists, Anderson contemplates whether *sing – sang* can be analyzed as a root *s-ŋ* plus the markers /ɪ/ 'PRESENT' and /æ/ 'PAST'. He, however, rejects this analysis due to the absence of "substantive evidence in its favor" (Anderson 1992: 62), and adds in parentheses "as there clearly is ... for something like McCarthy's analysis of Arabic and other Semitic languages" (ibid). That is, Anderson accepts the common view that item-and-arrangement is the appropriate model for Semitic morphology.

While I support Anderson's approach to morphology, I do not agree with the exclusion of Semitic languages from the paradigm. On the basis of data from Modern Hebrew, I provide in this paper evidence supporting the word-based item-and-process (WoBIP) model for Semitic morphology. That is, English is not like Hebrew, but rather Hebrew is like English.

In the context of Semitic morphology, I outline in the following §2 the possible morphological models that can be derived from the four different approaches: word-based, morpheme-based, item-and-process, and item-and-arrangement. Then, in §§3–5 I provide supporting evidence for the word-based item-and-process model, but due to space limitation, I do not dwell on arguments against competing models. Each piece of evidence supports only part of the model, but together we get a well-motivated model of morphology. Given Anderson's commitment to the history of linguistics (see, in particular, Anderson 1985), I devote §6 to two principal Semiticists from the 19th century, whose grammar books support the word-based item-and-process model. Concluding remarks are given in §7.

2 Models of morphology

Research in morphology often concentrates on two questions: What is listed in the lexicon and how are words derived? Each of these questions is associated with competing approaches. The *what*-question is related to the root-based vs. word-based debate, which is of particular interest in the study of Semitic morphology, where the root is always bound. The *how*-question is related to the item-and-process vs. item-and-arrangement debate. Together, they give rise to three models of morphology, shown in Figure 1: root-based item-and-arrangement, word-based item-and-arrangement, and word-based item-and-process.

6 Word-based Items-and-processes (WoBIP): Evidence from Hebrew morphology

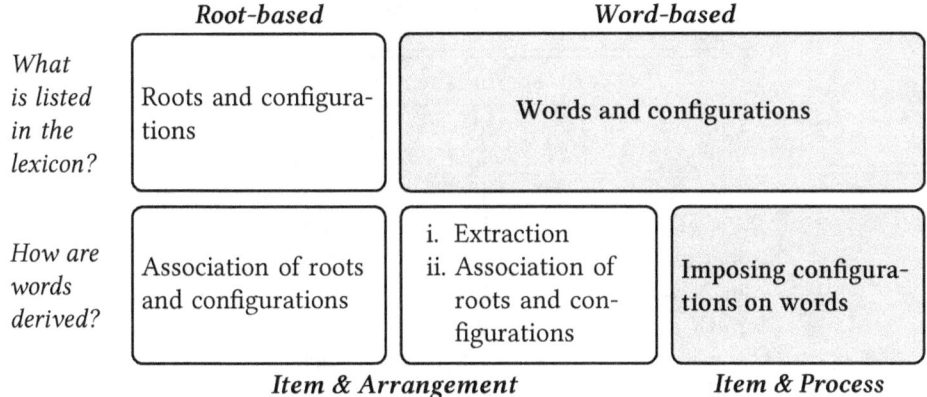

Figure 1: Models of morphology.

In this paper I support the word-based item-and-process (WoBIP) model. Before displaying the supporting arguments, a short review of the three models is given in the three ensuing subsections.[1]

2.1 Root-based item-and-arrangement

In the context of Semitic morphology, the root-based morphology teams up with item-and-arrangement. According to the traditional approach, the root in Hebrew and other Semitic languages consists of 2–4 consonants (3 in most cases) and is combined with a configuration (Bat-El 2011), where the latter, traditionally termed *mishkal* for nouns and *binyan* for verbs, is a shorthand for the grouping of prosodic structure, vocalic pattern, and affixes (if any).[2] In a configuration like *miCCéCet*, for example, the C-slots host the root consonants, the specified consonants (*m* and *t*) are affixes, and the vowels are part of the vocalic pattern (e.g. *mivʁéʃet* 'brush', *mizχélet* 'sleigh', *miʃméʁet* 'guard'). Table 1 shows examples of words sharing a root and examples of words sharing a configuration.

The classical studies seem to suggest a lexical representation consisting of morphemes, as can be inferred from Moscati's (1980: 71) account of the Semitic morphological system:

---

[1] I do not consider here the pluralistic approaches, whereby some words are derived from roots and others from words (McCarthy 1979; Arad 2005; Berman 2012), because all phenomena can be accounted for within the WoBIP model reviewed in §2.2.

[2] Each of these elements (i.e. the prosodic structure, the vocalic pattern, and the affix) is independent (McCarthy 1979; 1981), but here reference to the configuration suffices. In this context, we should note that the term "Semitic morphology" refers to morphology that employs configurations consisting of at least a vocalic pattern and prosodic structure. Of course, Hebrew and other Semitic languages employ the more conventional affixal morphology, but this type of morphology does not concern us here.

[3] Some words get additional, idiomatic meaning. For example, *siduʁ* carries the general meaning 'arrangement' and the more specific one referring to 'a prayer book'. Similarly, *sédeʁ* carries the general meaning 'order' and the more specific one referring to 'Passover ceremony' (*sédeʁ pésaχ*).

[4] As in other studies, the exponent of the 3rd person masculine past serves as the citation form because it is structurally neutral, i.e. it has no affixes. The gloss is still in the infinitive, implying reference to the lexeme.

117

Table 1: Roots and configurations.

Words sharing the root √sdʁ			
CiCeC	√sdʁ	sideʁ	'to arrange'
CaCiC		sadiʁ	'regular'
CiCuC		siduʁ	'arrangement'[3]
CeCeC		sédeʁ	'order'
meCuCaC		mesudaʁ	'arranged'
miCCaC		misdaʁ	'military parade'
miCCeCon		misdeʁon	'corridor'
CaCCan		sadʁan	'usher'
CiCCa		sidʁa	'series'
Words sharing a configuration[4]			
CaCCan	√sdʁ	sadʁan	'usher'
	√ʁkd	ʁakdan	'dancer'
	√btl	batlan	'lazy'
CeCeC	√bgd	béged	'garment'
	√jld	jéled	'boy'
	√dgl	dégel	'flag'
CiCeC	√xps	xipes	'to search'
	√btl	bitel	'to cancel'
	√χbʁ	χibeʁ	'to connect'

"The Semitic languages present a system of consonantal roots (mostly triconsonantal), each of which is associated with a basic meaning range common to all members of that root: e.g. *ktb* 'to write', *qbr* 'to bury', *qrb* 'to approach', etc. These roots (root morphemes) constitute a fundamental category of lexical morphemes." If roots are listed, so are the configurations, and word formation thus consists of associating roots and configurations, i.e. item-and-arrangement.

As Hoberman (2006: 139) notes, "students of Semitic languages find the concept of the root so convenient and useful that one finds it hard to think about Semitic morphology without it." However, researchers vary with respect to the definition of the term "root". Lipiński (1997: 202), for example, assumes that "Semitic roots are *continuous* morphemes which are instrumental in derivation but subject to vocalic and consonantal change ... based on continuous or discontinuous 'pattern morphemes'" (emphasis original). The "continuous morphemes", which Lipiński calls roots, are not the traditional consonantal roots, but rather stems consisting of vowels and consonants; the "pattern morphemes" are what I call configurations. Aronoff (2007) drains the original morphological (structural and semantic) properties from the root, claiming that it does not have to be linked to meaning and its phonology can be vague. Yet another use of the term "root" is found

2.2 Word-based item-and-process (WoBIP)

Within this approach, the word or the stem is the core element to which all the required processes apply (Aronoff 1976). As a core element, it does not have an internal morphological structure. The processes are *operations* (Anderson 1992: 72) that *modify* the basic form (Matthews 1974: 97). Indeed, the most common process in languages is the one deriving *bats* from *bat*, i.e. affixation, but there are other processes, such as apophony, which derives *teeth* from *tooth*.

Also in the context of Semitic morphology, the input is a word/stem to which several processes apply (see §3.1.2 for word vs. stem as the base). The processes vary according to the goal, and the goal is that the output fits into a configuration. Such a goal- or output-oriented phenomenon, called *stem modification* (Steriade 1988; McCarthy & Prince 1990), is best analyzed within the framework of Optimality Theory (Prince & Smolensky 1993/2004), as shown in analyses of Semitic morphology, such as McCarthy & Prince (1993); Ussishkin (1999; 2000); Gafos (2003); Bat-El (2003).

The details of the required modification depend on the structural similarity between the base and the output; the more similar they are, the fewer the required adjustments. Any element in the configuration can be modified – the vocalic pattern, the prosodic structure, and/or the affix. The modification, however, is contingent upon the configuration of the output.

Table 2: Stem modification – modifying elements in the configuration.

Base form			Derived form		Modified elements
sabon	'soap'	→	siben	'to soap'	vocalic pattern
tipel	'to take care of'	→	me-tapel	'caretaker'	vocalic pattern, affix
matok	'sweet'	→	ma-mtak	'candy'	vocalic pattern, affix, prosodic structure

Within this approach, there is no morphological element consisting solely of three consonants, and the emphasis here is on a "morphological element". Of course, related words share consonants, but these are *stem consonants*, where the stem is a morphological unit (e.g. *tapél* in *me-tapel* 'caretaker'), but the consonants are phonological elements.

2.3 Word-based item-and-arrangement

Item-and-arrangement can also be applied within the word-based approach, but only if a root is extracted from the base word (Ornan 1983; Bolozky 1978). That is, the base is the word but the root is an intermediate morphological element in the derivation. The derivation proceeds in two stages – extraction and association (Bat-El 1986; 1989). For example, the word *sabón* 'soap' serves as the base for the verb *sibén* 'to soap', which is derived in two stages: (i) extraction of the consonants *s,b,n*, which automatically become the root √*sbn* (traditionally called a secondary root), and (ii) association of this newly formed root with the verb configuration *CiCeC*. The assumption is that the extracted consonants carry the semantic properties of their base, which are, in turn, carried over to the derived form.

However, root extraction is necessary only when one is limited to the root-based approach, and thus to item-and-arrangement. In this model, all words are derived via association of a root with a configuration, regardless of whether the base is a word or a root. Not only is there no independent reason to prefer root extraction to stem modification (§2.2), but also there is empirical evidence refuting root extraction. These are cases of phonological transfer (§3.1), whereby properties that cannot be carried over by the consonants are transferred from the base to the derived form.

3 Phonological and morphological relations

3.1 Transfer of phonological structure

The most striking evidence for a direct relation between words, without an intermediate stage that derives a root, is provided by cases exhibiting phonological transfer (Clements 1985; Hammond 1988; McCarthy & Prince 1990). As shown below, there are cases where structural information, which cannot be encoded in the consonantal root, is transferred from the base to the derived form. In the case of Hebrew, the structural information is both prosodic and segmental (Bat-El 1994).

3.1.1 Prosodic transfer

Prosodic transfer includes transfer of the entire configuration or of a consonant cluster.

Configurations are often assigned a grammatical function (Doron 2003), but the question is whether this grammatical function is a property of the configuration or just a property shared by many (but not all) words within a morphological class. In general, words that share meaning are often structurally similar, but it does not necessarily mean that this shared meaning is a property of a morphological unit. One striking example is displayed by the nouns in Table 3 below, most of which are creative innovations (drawn from http://www.dorbanot.com). These nouns share the configuration *CoCCa* and the meaning 'related to a computer program'.

Since these nouns share a configuration and meaning, the traditional Semitic morphology would assign the meaning to the configuration. This is, of course, erroneous because there are other nouns with the configuration *CoCCa* that do not carry this meaning; e.g. *joʃva* 'dignity' (cf. *jaʃav* 'honest'), *χoχma* 'wisdom' (cf. *χaχam* 'smart'), *oʦma* 'strength' (cf. *aʦum* 'huge'), *jozma* 'enterprise' (cf. *jazam* 'to initiate'). In addition, this meaning is too specific to function as a morpho-semantic feature.

6 Word-based Items-and-processes (WoBIP): Evidence from Hebrew morphology

Table 3: Nouns sharing a configuration.

CoCCa noun		Related word	
toχna	'computer program'	toχnit	'program'
gonva	'stolen computer program'	ganav	'to steal'
poʁna	'computer program with porno pop-ups'	poʁna	'pornography'
tsoʁva	'illegally burned computer program'	tsaʁav	'to burn'
gomla	'old computer program'	gimlaot	'pension'

What we actually have here is a Semitic-type blending. The last four words in the first column of Table 3 use the first word *toχna* as a base form, from which the configuration is drawn, along with the basic meaning. That is, *toχna* provides the configuration *CoCCa* and the meaning 'relating to a computer program'. The stem consonants are drawn from the related words in the third column of Table 3, along with some specific meaning denoted by this word. Crucially, such a derivation must be word-based, and the fact that these words are creative innovations suggests that this model is active in the Hebrew speakers' grammar.

Other creative examples are found in a children's story written by Meir Shalev (*ʁoni venomi vehadov jaakov* 'Roni and Nomi and the bear Jacob'). Each invented word in the first column of Table 4 has two bases, one providing the configuration and another the consonants.

Table 4: Meir Shalev's invented words.

Invented word		Source of configuration		Source of consonants	
koféfet	'she wears gloves'	lovéʃet	'she wears'	kfafot	'gloves'
mogéfet	'she puts on boots'	noélet	'she puts on shoes'	magaf	'boot'
lehitmaheʁ	'to hurry/rush'	lehizdaʁez	'to hurry'	lemaheʁ	'to rush'
laχuts	'to run out'	laʁuts	'to run'	haχutsa	'outside'

Given that the invented words draw semantic properties from the two base words, as is usually the case with blends, direct access to the base must be assumed. That is, the configuration of one of the base words is imposed on the other.

Cluster transfer is often found in denominative verbs like *tʁansfeʁ* → *tʁinsfeʁ* 'to transfer' and *faks* → *fikses* 'to fax' (Bolozky 1978; McCarthy 1984; Bat-El 1994). In such cases, the distribution of the sequential order of vowels and consonants, thus including the clusters, is preserved in the derived form. For example, *filteʁ* 'filter' is the base of the

121

verb *filteʁ* (preserved cluster – *lt*), while *fliʁt* 'flirt' is the base of *fliʁtet* (preserved clusters – *fl, ʁt*), and not **filʁet*. Note that the higher the structural similarity between the base and the derived form, the closer the semantic relation (Raffelsiefen 1993), and thus, the fewer the structural amendments required in the course of stem modification (§2.2), the greater the semantic similarity.

3.1.2 Segmental transfer

Segmental transfer includes vowel transfer as well as the transfer of an affix consonant to the stem (Bat-El 1994).

In *vowel transfer*, an exceptional configuration is selected because its vowel is identical to that of the base (e.g. *kod* 'code' → *koded* 'to codify', *ot* 'sign' → *otet* 'to signal'). It should be noted that in most cases, the regular configuration is also possible (e.g. *kided* 'to codify'). However, the exceptional configuration is used only when the base has an *o*. That is, there is output-output correspondence between the base noun *kod* and the derived form, and *koded* is segmentally more faithful to *kod* then *kided* (Bat-El 2003).

In *affix transfer*, the consonant that serves as an affix in the base becomes a stem consonant in the derived form. This is common with the suffix *-n*, as in *paʁʃan* 'commentator' → *piʁʃen* 'to commentate' (cf. *peʁeʃ* 'to interpret') and the prefix *m-*, as in *maχzoʁ* 'cycle' → *miχzeʁ* 'to recycle' (cf. *χazaʁ* 'to return'). Note that speakers' morphological knowledge allows them to strip the word of its affixes (more so in regular forms), and therefore the inclusion of an affix consonant in the derived words has its purpose, mostly to preserve a semantic contrast, as in *χizeʁ* 'to court' vs. *miχzeʁ* 'to recycle' (from *maχzoʁ* 'cycle'). But in the paradigm of *ʃamaʁ* 'to guard' – *miʃmaʁ* 'guard' there is no **miʃmeʁ* (though it is a potential verb).

3.2 Semantic distance

One crucial property distinguishing among the three approaches reviewed in §3 is the semantic "distance" between related words; among these, only the WoBIP model (1c) allows a direct relation between a base and its derived form.

(1) The distance factor

    a. *Root-based item-and-process*

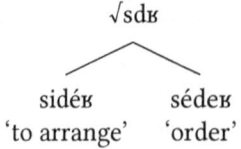

          √sdʁ

      sidéʁ   sédeʁ
   'to arrange' 'order'

b. *Word-based item-and-process*

   séderוּ ——— √sdʁ
   'order'   │
                    │
                  sidérוּ
                  'to arrange'

   c. *Word-based item-and-arrangement*

   séderוּ ——— sidérוּ
   'order'   'to arrange'

The advantage of the direct relation (1c) is that information can be carried over from input to output, be it structural (§3.1) or semantic. It is often the case that within a group of words sharing stem consonants, there is 1st, 2nd or higher degree of separation between words, as illustrated in Figure 2.

Such a network can express different degrees of semantic relations, depending on how far one word is from another. Needless to say, such a network cannot be expressed if all words are derived from a single root. Of course, one can claim that the three words at the middle of the network (*takdím, kidómet,* and *mikdamá*), which are not directly related to one another, are derived from a root, while all other words are derived from words (McCarthy 1979; Arad 2005). However, this is an unsupported and unnecessary burden on the system. All words in the network are connected to one another, directly or indirectly, where some words are basic and others are derived. The fact that all the words in Figure 2 share the stem consonants is due to the important role of consonants in conveying lexical information and lexical relations (see §5.2).

3.3 Derivation without a configuration

A fundamental element of the traditional root-based item-and-arrangement model is that every word consists of a root and a configuration, where every configuration is a function. This is particularly essential in the verbal paradigms, where the configurations are claimed to carry grammatical categories, such as transitivity (Doron 2003; Arad 2005). Such a theory predicts that the transitivity relation must involve a change in the configuration. This is true for most cases (e.g. *katáv* 'to write' – *hitkatév* 'to correspond', *ʃalax* 'to send' – *niʃlax* 'to be sent', *laxats* 'to press' – *hilxíts* 'to cause to feel pressured'), but not all.

In an extensive study of labile alternations in Hebrew, Lev (2016: 114–115) lists 91 verbs where transitivity does not involve a change of the configuration; three of his examples are provided in Table 5. As Lev argues, a root-based morphology cannot accommodate labile verbs because under this approach the root has to associate with two different con-

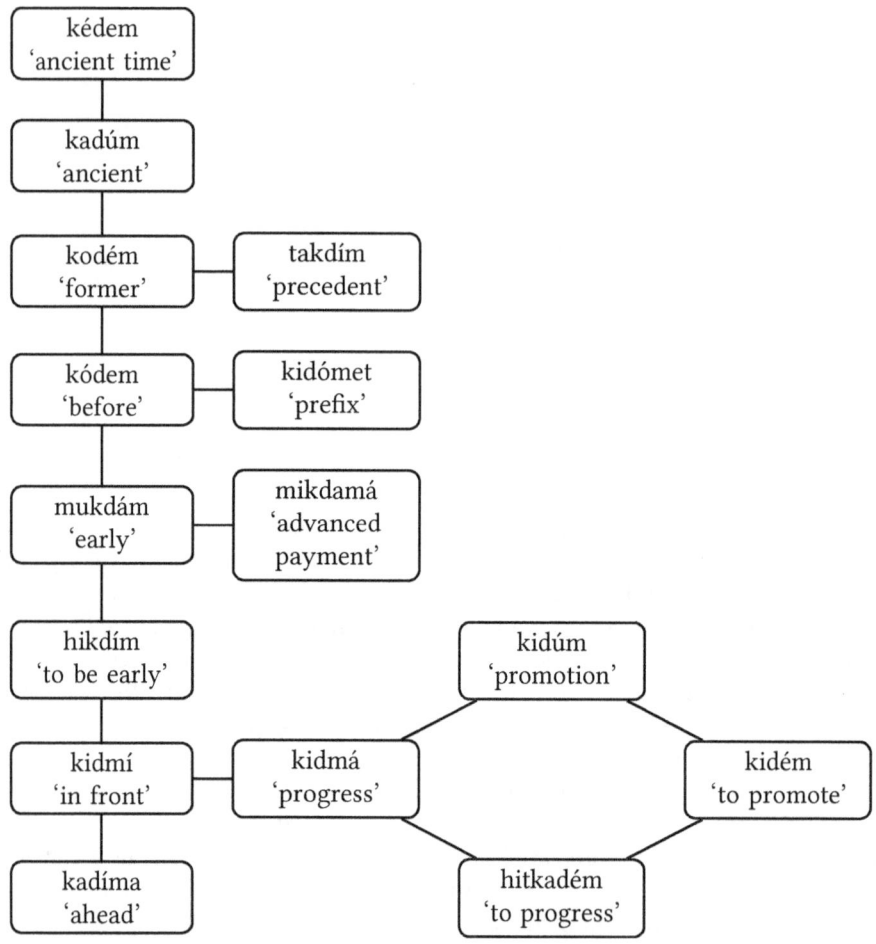

Figure 2: Degrees of separation.

figurations in order to derive verbs contrasting in transitivity. The word-based approach, on the other hand, can incorporate labile verbs, assuming that transitivity in such verbs is not lexically specified but rather derived from the syntactic context. That is, some verbs are specified for [± transitive] and others, i.e. the labile verbs, are [ø transitive]. Many of the examples in Lev's list are recent innovations, i.e. where verbs with transitivity specification become labile. For example, the verb *tijel* used to have one meaning only, 'to walk', but today it also means (at least for some speakers) 'to walk someone (usually a dog)'. This change can be viewed as a loss of transitivity specification, i.e. [– transitive] >[ø transitive]. Crucially, it is the verb that loses its specification for transitivity, not the configuration. That is, in historical change too, as shown in the ensuing §4, it is the word that changes, and not some putative consonantal root.

Table 5: Labile verbs (Lev 2016: 114–115).

Verb	Transitive	Intransitive
hiʃχiʁ	'to make black'	'to become black'
hivʁik	'to polish'	'to shine'
hivʁi	'to cure'	'to recuperate'

4 Historical change

4.1 Configuration change

Over the course of time, words may change their meaning or their structure. In his study of instrumental nouns in Hebrew, Laks (2015) shows that quite a few instrumental nouns undergo change in their configuration, in particular within a compound, as illustrated in Table 6. As Laks shows, the change always goes towards the participial configuration, and it never occurs when the instrumental noun does not have a verbal counterpart. That is, while both *maχded* 'pencil sharpener' and *mazleg* 'fork' have the same configuration, only the former adopts the participial configuration *meχaded*, given its verbal counterpart *χided* 'to sharpen'; the latter cannot adopt a participial configuration because it does not have a verbal counterpart.

Table 6: Change of configuration in instrumental nouns (Laks 2015).

Old configuration		New configuration – participle		
maχded	maCCeC	meχaded	meCaCeC	'pencil sharpener'
nakdan	CaCCan	menaked (tekstim)	meCaCeC	'text vocalizer'
masχeta	maCCeCa	soχet (mitsim)	CoCeC	'juicer (juice squeezer)'

In order for this restriction to hold, an instrumental noun must be linked to its verb, from which it can draw its participial configuration. Otherwise, as Laks argues, the instrumental noun could adopt any of the five participial configurations, not necessarily the one associated with its verb. That is, we get the instrumental noun *meχaded* 'pencil sharpener' because *meCaCeC* is the participial configuration of *χided* 'to sharpen'. Similarly, we get the instrumental nouns *soχet* (*mitsim*) 'juicer' because *CoCeC* is the participial configuration of *saχat* 'to squeeze'. Such a change is possible only in a word-based lexicon; a root-based lexicon does not account for the restrictive generalization as it allows options that are not attested.

4.2 Semantic change

Over the course of time, the meaning of words also changes; crucially, the semantic change affects words and not putative roots. For example, the verbs *nimlat* and *himlit* used to differ in transitivity only, with the former meaning 'to escape' and the latter 'to help someone to escape'. Nowadays, these verbs are not related, since *himlit* means 'to give birth (for non-humans)'. Similarly, *kalat* and *hiklit* used to be related, with the former meaning 'to absorb' and the latter 'to cause to absorb'. However, the meaning of *hiklit* is now 'to record', and the two verbs are vaguely related, if at all. For the traditional root-based approach (§2.1), it would be rather strange that the change in meaning does not affect the element that carries it, i.e. the root. This inconsistency does not arise within the word-based approach.

It is quite feasible that the root does not undergo semantic change because its meaning is just "a basic meaning range", according to Moscati (1980) and other Semiticists, or underspecified, according to Arad's (2005) analysis within the theory of Distributed Morphology (Halle & Marantz 1993 and subsequent studies). That is, semantic specification of roots may have at least three degrees of specification: fully specified (e.g. *boy*), underspecified (e.g. Hebrew roots), and unspecified (e.g. the roots in *refer, remit,* and *resume*; Aronoff 1976).

The major problem is that the specific meaning of words is derived, according to Arad (2005), from the morpho-syntactic context, i.e. the configurations. This works nicely for some words but not for others. Consider, for example, the pairs *zaʁak* 'to throw' – *hizʁik* 'to inject' and *maʃaχ* 'to pull' – *himʃiχ* 'to continue'. It is not clear which semantic property can be assigned to the configurations *CaCaC* and *hiCCiC* such that the relation within these pairs would be consistent.

4.3 Segmental change

Like semantic change, segmental change also affects words and not consonantal roots, even when the change is in the stem consonants. This is seen in the case of stop-fricative alternation, which due to its opacity, suffers from a great degree of change-oriented variation (Adam 2002).

As shown in Table 7, normative verb inflectional paradigms are changing under the force of paradigm uniformity. Although the change affects consonants, it certainly does not affect a consonantal root because derivationally related words are hardly ever affected; nonetheless they change, and sometimes they even undergo independent change. For example, while χ can change to k in *katav* – *jiktov* (normative *jiχtov*) 'to write PAST – FUTURE', it never changes to k in *miχtav* (*miktav*) 'letter'. Note also that while the direction of change in this paradigm is from a fricative to a stop (*jiχtov* → *jiktov*), the change in a related pair is towards a fricative, as in *ktav* → *χtav* 'handwriting'.

Table 7: Change of configuration in instrumental nouns (Adam 2002).

Old paradigm			New paradigm			
k–χ	kisa	jeχase	χ–χ	χisa	jeχase	'to cover PAST – FUTURE'
k–χ	katav	jiχtov	k–k	katav	jiktov	'to write PAST – FUTURE'
b–v	bitel	jevatel	v–v	vitel	jevatel	'to cancel PAST – FUTURE'

5 Other supporting sources

5.1 Children's words

During the early stages of acquisition, verbs in the production lexicon of children acquiring Hebrew are not derivationally related, i.e. they do not share stem consonants. Derivationally related verbs start appearing later on, where the new verbs "are learnt as versions of, and based upon, the verbs known from before" (Berman 1988: 62).

This direct derivation in children's speech is not surprising given Ravid et al.'s (2016) study on the distribution of verbs in spoken and written Hebrew corpora: child-directed speech (to toddlers age 1;8–2;2) and storybooks (for preschoolers and 1st–2nd grade). In both corpora, the average number of verbs per root was below two: 684 verbs for 521 root types in the spoken corpus (1.3) and 1,048 verbs for 744 roots in the written corpus (1.4). Only around 30% of the verb types in each corpus share a root with another verb, and most such verbs share a root with only one other verb.

These results mean, as the authors admit, that at least until the age of 7, the children have very little input supporting a root-based morphology. Nevertheless, the authors insist that the children must "eventually construe the root as a structural and semantic morphological core" (Ravid et al. 2016: 126). As argued in the current paper and elsewhere, starting with Bat-El (1994), Hebrew speakers are free from this burden since Hebrew morphology (and Semitic morphology in general) is not root-based, but rather word/stem-based.

Previous studies that attribute children and adults' innovations to root extraction (§2.3 – word-based item-and-arrangement) must now reconsider their conclusion at least for children below the age of 7. In an experimental study reported in Berman (2003), children at the age of 4–6 years old had a rather high success rate (84–88%) of morphological innovation (forming novel verbs from nouns or adjectives) with a very high percentage of well-formed innovations (91–99%). If children can form verbs from nouns/adjectives at the stage where they still do not have sufficient input that allows them to form a root-based morphology (Ravid et al. 2016), they probably use another strategy – the modification strategy employed within the WoBIP model (§2.3). And if they can use this model successfully until the age of 7, they have no reason whatsoever to shift to a root-based model later on. Of course, as I have argued here and elsewhere, they do not – Hebrew speakers employ WoBIP at all ages.

5.2 Experimental studies

There are quite a few experimental studies supporting the consonantal root in Hebrew. Most notable are Berent's studies with the acceptability rating paradigm (Berent & Shimron 1997; Berent, Everett & Shimron 2001, inter alia) and Frost's studies with the priming paradigm (Frost, Forster & Deutsch 1997; Frost et al. 2000, inter alia).[5] However, most experimental studies supporting the consonantal root in Hebrew morphology adopted a visual modality. As such, they cannot tease apart the effect of orthography, which is primarily consonantal (Bat-El 2002 and Berrebi 2017 for a critical view).

A fresh look on the matter is provided in Berrebi's (2017) auditory priming study, which controlled semantic relatedness and orthographic identity. Word pairs sharing phonological stem consonants were either semantically related (e.g. *kibel* 'to receive' – *hitkabel* 'to be accepted') or semantically unrelated (e.g. *ʁigel* 'to spy' – *hitʁagel* 'to get used to'); and when semantically unrelated, either orthographically identical with respect to the consonants (e.g. *ʁigel* 'to spy' – *hitʁagel* 'to get used to') or orthographically different (e.g. *ʃikeʁ* 'to lie' – *hiʃtakeʁ* 'to get drunk', where *k* is spelled differently). The results showed that all conditions had a priming effect, i.e. whether or not the prime and the target were orthographically identical or semantically related. As the property shared by the prime and the target in all conditions was phonological, i.e. stem consonants, the results suggest that there is a phonological priming effect among words sharing stem consonants. Crucially, the stem consonants are not a morphological unit since there was also a priming effect when the words were semantically unrelated and orthographically different (e.g. *ʃikeʁ* – *hiʃtakeʁ*).

If we assume that priming effects reflect the organization of the lexicon, then we can conclude that words are also phonologically organized according to the stem consonant. As emphasized in §2.2, the stem consonants are phonological elements (consonants) within a morphological unit (stem); they do not carry meaning and they do not constitute a morphological unit.

Stem consonants, and not vowels, serve to identify relations between words because consonants are lexically prominent, while vowels have syntactic functions (Nespor, Peña & Mehler 2003; Berent 2013); this is true not only for Hebrew but also for non-Semitic languages. In their experimental study, Cutler et al. (2000) asked the participants: "Is a *kebra* more like *cobra* or *zebra*?". They found that speakers identify similarity between a nonce word (*kebra*) and an existing word on the basis of shared consonants (*kebra* – *cobra*) rather than shared vowels (*kebra* – *zebra*). That is, the consonants serve as the core of similarity between words in English, French, Swedish, and Dutch as much as they do in Hebrew and other Semitic languages (see also Ooijen 1996; New, Araujo & Nazzi 2008; Carreiras & Molinaro 2009; Winskel & Perea 2013).

Consonants are lexically prominent from the very early stages of language development. This is reported in Nazzi & New's (Nazzi & New) study, where French 16–20 month old infants could learn in a single trial two new nonce words if they differed by one con-

---

[5] In an additional study, which was design to ask "is it a root or a stem?" (rather than "is it a root?"), Berent, Vaknin & Marcus (2007) note that although their results do not falsify the root-based account, they strongly suggest that the stem can account for the restrictions on identical consonants.

sonant (*pize* – *tize*), but not if they differed by one vowel (*pize* – *paze*). That is, although vowels are acoustically more prominent than consonants, when it comes to lexical contrast, consonants are employed. This is true for children and adults, regardless of the ambient language, whether it is Semitic or non-Semitic.

Consonants are prominent not only in speech perception and lexical relations but also in the association between sound and shape revealed by the *bouba-kiki* effect (Köhler 1929), whereby people pair labial consonants with round shapes and dorsal consonants with spiky shapes. One of the many subsequent studies of the *bouba-kiki* effect is Fort, Martin & Peperkamp (2015), which found that the sound–shape association remains constant regardless of the vowels. That is, *lomo* was associated with a round shape as much as *limi*, and *toko* with a spiky shape as much as *tiki*. Fort, Martin & Peperkamp (2015) conclude that consonants have a greater effect than vowels in sound – shape association.

6 19th century Semitic grammarians

The root-based item-and-arrangement model of Semitic morphology has been deeply entrenched for generations, thus presenting the advocates of the word-based item-and-process approach as revolutionary (see Horvath 1981; Lederman 1982; Heath 1987; Hammond 1988; McCarthy & Prince 1990; Bat-El 1994; 2002; 2003; Ratcliffe 1997; Ussishkin 1999; 2000; 2005; Laks 2011; 2015; Lev 2016).

However, WoBIP has its seeds in the studies of the orientalists Wilhelm Gesenius (1786–1842) and William Wright (1830–1889), who wrote the seminal grammar books of Hebrew and Arabic respectively. It is important to note that both Gesenius and Wright were not native speakers of a Semitic language (Gesenius was German and Wright British), and thus not biased like the other Semitic grammarians by the consonantal script of Hebrew and Arabic.

Gesenius (1813) distinguishes between "primitive" verbs, which consist of a stem only and are not derived from any other form, and derived verbs, among which there are verbal derivatives and denominative verbs. Gesenius used the term "internal modification" when addressing the processes involved in the derivation. He indicates two types of "changes in the primitive form" (Gesenius 1813: 115): internal modification (cf. stem modification; §2.2) and repetition (i.e. reduplication) of one or two of the stem consonants. Within the internal modification, he includes vowel change like *gadal* 'to grow' – *gidel* 'to raise', and gemination as in Biblical Hebrew *ga:dal* 'to grow' – *giddel* 'to raise' (there is no gemination in Modern Hebrew). Crucially, Gesenius compares vowel modification in Hebrew to that in English *lie* – *lay* and *fall* – *fell*, and does not find them different. That is, Gesenius finds stem modification to be identical in both Hebrew and English, but unlike Anderson (1992) who contemplates whether English is like Hebrew, Gesenius actually claims that Hebrew is like English.

A similar approach is found in Wright's (1859) grammar book of Arabic, where he describes the relation between verbs within the WoBIP model. For example, "the third form … is formed from the first by lengthening the vowel sound after the first radical" (p. 32) or "[T]he second form … is formed from the first … by doubling the second radical"

(p. 31). This is the format of Wright's description of each and every binyan in Arabic, and it specifically says that (i) one form is derived from another, i.e. word-based derivation, and (ii) the derivation involves some process, doubling, lengthening, etc., i.e. item-and-process. Note that Wright uses the term "radical" to refer to a consonant in the stem, without reference to the stem consonants being an independent morphological unit.

That is, although it has always been said that the root-based approach is the one assumed by traditional Semiticists, it is important to emphasize that the two great 19th century Semiticists, Gesenius and Wright, were proponents of the WoBIP model of Semitic morphology.[6]

7 Concluding remarks

In §3.6, Anderson (1992: 71) concludes: "... the morphology of a language consists of a set of Word Formation Rules which operates on lexical stems to produce other lexical stems ..." In this paper I extended the scope of this model to Semitic morphology. That is, in Semitic languages too, words are derived from words/stems via modification of the base.

The modification in Semitic morphology is output oriented, as the output has to fit into a configuration. The constraint-based framework of Optimality Theory (Prince & Smolensky 1993) allows for output-oriented grammar, where the constraints impose certain configurations (structural constraints) as well as output-output identity of consonants (faithfulness constraints). A configuration is imposed by several constraints, referring to syllabic structure (usually a foot), syllable structure, and vocalic patterns (where the latter ones are language specific). Identity among the stem consonants is imposed by the faithfulness constraints, where preservation of segmental identity ensures preservation of morphological relation among words.

That is, the stability of the stem consonants is due to phonological faithfulness constraints that require identity among stem consonants. Phonological faithfulness enhances morphological relations. "Any given *focal* word (that is, a specific word in which we are interested) is thus surrounded by a vaguely defined family of words which are more or less acoustically similar to it. The members of the family will in general have the widest variety of meaning, and yet it may often happen that some members of the family will resemble the focal word not only in acoustic shape, but also in meaning" (Hockett 1958: 297, 1987: 86). That is, within an acoustic family of words there is a morphological

---

[6] A reviewer suggested that Gesenius and Wright adopted the word-based approach, which was used for Latin grammar, because they worked prior to the introduction of the term morpheme. Kilbury (1976) and Anderson (1985) attribute the term morpheme to Baudouin de Courtenay's student H. Ułaszyn, in his articles from 1927 and 1931. However, it is possible to have a notion without a specific term. Sibawayhi (760–796), who wrote the first known Arabic grammar *Al-kitab*, used the term *kalima* 'word' in the sense of a morpheme (e.g. the suffix -*ta*) and referred to the radicals that make up the words (Levin 1986). Gesenius notes that the Jewish grammarians call the stem root and the stem consonants radical letters. That is, there was a reference to morphological units (stem, affixes), but the stem consonants did not constitute a morphological unit.

family, where the words are not only acoustically similar but also semantically related. For the purpose of membership in a morphological family, the consonants are more important than the vowels. This status does not grant the consonants morphological status, neither in English nor in Hebrew.

Acknowledgements

As my advisor and mentor, Steve Anderson set the foundations for my approach to Semitic morphology presented in this paper.

References

Adam, Galit. 2002. *From Optimal Grammar to Variable Grammar: Evidence from language acquisition and change*. Tel-Aviv University PhD thesis.
Anderson, Stephen R. 1985. *Phonology in the Twentieth century: Theories of Rules and Theories of Representations*. Chicago: University of Chicago Press.
Anderson, Stephen R. 1992. *A-morphous morphology*. Cambridge: Cambridge University Press.
Arad, Maya. 2005. *Roots and patterns: Hebrew Morpho-syntax*. Dordrecht: Springer.
Aronoff, Mark. 1976. *Word formation in generative grammar*. Cambridge, MA: MIT Press.
Aronoff, Mark. 2007. In the beginning was the word. *Language* 83. 803–830.
Bat-El, Outi. 1986. *Extraction in Modern Hebrew Morphology*. University of California, Los Angeles MA thesis.
Bat-El, Outi. 1989. *Phonology and word structure in Modern Hebrew*. University of California, Los Angeles PhD thesis.
Bat-El, Outi. 1994. Stem modification and cluster transfer in Modern Hebrew. *Natural Language and Linguistic Theory* 12(4). 571–593.
Bat-El, Outi. 2002. *Semitic verb structure within a universal perspective*. Joseph Shimron (ed.). Amsterdam: John Benjamins.
Bat-El, Outi. 2003. The fate of the consonantal root and the binyan in Optimality Theory. *Recherches Linguistiques de Vincennes* 32. 31–60.
Bat-El, Outi. 2011. Semitic templates. In Marc van Oostendorp, Colin Ewen, Elizabeth Hume & Keren Rice (eds.), *Blackwell companion to phonology*, 2586–2608. Malden, MA: Wiley-Blackwell.
Berent, Iris. 2013. *The phonological mind*. Cambridge: Cambridge University Press.
Berent, Iris, Daniel Everett & Joseph Shimron. 2001. Do phonological representations specify variables? Evidence from the Obligatory Contour Principle. *Cognitive Psychology* 42(1). 1–60.
Berent, Iris & Joseph Shimron. 1997. The representation of Hebrew words: Evidence from the obligatory contour principle. *Cognition* 64. 39–72.
Berent, Iris, Vered Vaknin & Gary Marcus. 2007. Roots, stems and the universality of lexical representations: Evidence from Hebrew. *Cognition* 104. 254–286.

Berman, Ruth. 1988. Word class distinction in developing grammars. In Izchak Schlesinger & Yonata Levy (eds.), *Categories and processes in language acquisition*, 45–72. Hillsdale, NJ: Erlbaum.

Berman, Ruth. 2003. Children's lexical innovations: Developmental perspectives on Hebrew verb-structure. In Joseph Shimron (ed.), *Language processing and language acquisition in a root-based morphology*, 243–291. Amsterdam: John Benjamins.

Berman, Ruth. 2012. Revisiting roots in Hebrew: A multi-faceted view. In Malka Muchnik & Zvi Sadan (eds.), *Studies on Modern Hebrew and Jewish Languages*, 132–158. Jerusalem: Carmel.

Berrebi, Si. 2017. *The roots of consonant bias: A psycholinguistic study of phonological facilitation in Hebrew*. Tel-Aviv University M.A. Thesis.

Bolozky, Shmuel. 1978. Word formation strategies in Modern Hebrew verb system: Denominative verbs. *Afroasiatic Linguistics* 5. 1–26.

Carreiras, Manuel Jon Andoni Duñabeitia & Nicola Molinaro. 2009. Consonants and vowels contribute differently to visual word recognition: ERPs of relative position priming. *Cerebral Cortex* 19. 2659–2670.

Clements, George. 1985. The problem of transfer in nonlinear phonology. *Cornell Working Papers in Linguistics* 5. 38–73.

Cutler, Ann, Nuria Sebastiín-Gallés, Olga Soler-Vilageliu & Brit van Ooijen. 2000. Constraints of vowels and consonants on lexical selection: Cross-linguistic comparisons. *Memory and Cognition* 28. 746–755.

Doron, Edit. 2003. Agency and voice: The semantics of the Semitic templates. *Natural Language Semantics* 11. 1–67.

Fort, Mathilde, Alexander Martin & Sharon Peperkamp. 2015. Consonants are more important than vowels in the bouba-kiki effect. *Language and Speech* 58. 247–266.

Frost, Ram, Kenneth I. Forster & Avital Deutsch. 1997. What can we learn from the morphology of Hebrew? a masked-priming investigation of morphological representation. *Journal of Experimental Psychology: Learning, Memory, and Cognition* 23(4). 829–856.

Frost, Ram, Avital Deutsch, Oran Gilboa, Michael Tannenbaum & William Marslen-Wilson. 2000. Morphological priming: Dissociation of phonological, semantic, and morphological factors. *Memory & Cognition* 28. 1277–1288.

Gafos, Adamantios I. 2003. Greenberg's asymmetry in Arabic: a consequence of stems in paradigms. *Language* 79(2). 317–355.

Gesenius, Wilhelm. 1813. *Gesenius' Hebrew grammar*. Oxford: Clarendon Press.

Halle, Morris & Alec Marantz. 1993. Distributed morphology and the pieces of inflection. In Kenneth Hale & Samuel Jay Keyser (eds.), *The view from Building 20: Essays in linguistics in honor of Sylvain Bromberger*, 111–176. Cambridge, MA: MIT Press.

Hammond, Michael. 1988. Templatic transfer in Arabic broken plurals. *Natural Language & Linguistic Theory* 6. 247–270.

Heath, Jeffrey. 1987. *Ablaut and ambiguity: Phonology of a Moroccan Arabic Dialect*. Albany: SUNY Press.

Hoberman, Robert. 2006. Semitic triradicality or prosodic minimality? Evidence from sound change. In Cynthia Miller (ed.), *Studies in Semitic and Afroasiatic linguistics* presented to Gene B. Gragg, 139–154. Chicago: The Oriental Institute of the University of Chicago Studies in Ancient Oriental Civilization.

Hockett, Charles F. 1954. Two models of grammatical description. *Word* 10. 210–234.

Hockett, Charles F. 1958. *A course in modern linguistics*. London: Macmillan.

Hockett, Charles F. 1987. *Refurbishing our foundations*. Amsterdam: John Benjamins.

Horvath, Julia. 1981. On the status of vowel patterns in Modern Hebrew: Morphological rules and lexical representations. *Extended Word-and-Paradigm Theory. UCLA Occasional Papers in Linguistics* 4. 228–261.

Kilbury, James. 1976. *The Development of Morphophonemic Theory*. Amsterdam: John Benjamins.

Köhler, Wolfgang. 1929. *Gestalt psychology*. New York: Liveright.

Laks, Lior. 2011. *Morpho-phonological and morpho-thematic relations in Hebrew and Arabic verb formation*. Tel-Aviv University PhD thesis.

Laks, Lior. 2015. Variation and change in instrument noun formation in Hebrew and its relation to the verbal system. *Word Structure* 8. 1–28.

Lederman, Shlomo. 1982. Problems in a prosodic analysis of Hebrew morphology. *Studies in the Linguistic Sciences* 12. 141–163.

Lev, Shaul. 2016. *Hebrew labile alternations*. Tel-Aviv University MA thesis.

Levin, Aryeh. 1986. The medieval Arabic term kalima and the modern linguistic term morpheme: Similarities and differences. In Dāwid Ayyālôn & Šārôn (eds.), *Studies in Islamic history and civilization: In honour of Professor David Ayalon*, 423–446. Leiden: Brill.

Lipiński, Edward. 1997. *Semitic languages: Outline of comparative grammar*. Leuven: Uitgeverij Peeters en Department Oostersc Studies.

Matthews, Peter H. 1974. *Morphology: An introduction to the theory of word-structure*. Cambridge: Cambridge University Press.

McCarthy, John. 1984. Prosodic organization in morphology. In Mark Aronoff & Richard Oehrle (eds.), *Language Sound Structure*, 299–317. Cambridge, MA: MIT Press.

McCarthy, John & Alan Prince. 1990. Foot and word in Prosodic Morphology: the Arabic broken plural. *Natural Language and Linguistic Theory* 8. 209–283.

McCarthy, John & Alan Prince. 1993. Prosodic morphology i: constraint interaction and satisfaction. Ms., University of Massachusetts, Amherst.

McCarthy, John J. 1979. *Formal problems in Semitic phonology and morphology*. MIT PhD thesis.

McCarthy, John J. 1981. A prosodic theory of nonconcatenative morphology. *Linguistic Inquiry* 12(3). 373–418.

Moscati, Sabatino. 1980. *An introduction to the comparative grammar of the Semitic languages*. Wiesbaden: Otto Harrassowitz.

Nazzi, Thierry & Boris New. 2007. Beyond stop consonants: Consonantal specificity in early lexical acquisition. *Cognitive Development* 22. 271–279.

Nespor, Marina, Marcela Peña & Jacques Mehler. 2003. On the different roles of vowels and consonants in speech processing and language acquisition. *Lingue e Linguaggio* 2. 221–247.

New, Boris, Veronica Araujo & Thierry Nazzi. 2008. Differential processing of consonants and vowels in lexical access through reading. *Psychological Science* 19. 1223–1227.

Ooijen, Brit van. 1996. Vowel mutability and lexical selection in English: Evidence from a word reconstruction task. *Memory & Cognition* 24. 573–583.

Ornan, Uzzi. 1983. How is the Hebrew word formed? In Moshe Bar-Asher, Aron Dotan, Davic Tene & Gad B. Sarfatti (eds.), *Language studies*, 13–42. in Hebrew. Jerusalem: Magnes.

Prince, Alan & Paul Smolensky. 1993. *Optimality Theory: Constraint interaction in generative grammar*. Oxford: Blackwell Publishing.

Prince, Alan & Paul Smolensky. 1993/2004. *Optimality Theory: Constraint interaction in generative grammar*. Oxford: Blackwell Publishing.

Raffelsiefen, Renate. 1993. Relating words: A model of base recognition. *Linguistic Analysis* 23. 3–139.

Ratcliffe, Robert R. 1997. Prosodic templates in a word-based morphological analysis of Arabic. In Mushira Eid & Robert Ratcliffe (eds.), *Perspectives on Arabic Linguistics X*, 147–171. Amsterdam: John Benjamins.

Ravid, Dorit, Orit Ashkenazi, Ronit Levie, Galit Zadok, Tehila Grunwald, Ron Bratslavsky & Steven Gillis. 2016. Foundations of the early root category: Analyses of linguistic input to Hebrew-speaking children. In Ruth Berman (ed.), *Acquisition and development of Hebrew, from infancy to adolescence*, 95–134. Amsterdam: John Benjamins.

Steriade, Donca. 1988. Reduplication and syllable transfer in Sanskrit and elsewhere. *Phonology* 5(1). 73–155.

Ussishkin, Adam. 1999. The inadequacy of the consonantal root: Modern Hebrew denominal verbs and output-output correspondence. *Phonology* 16(3). 401–442.

Ussishkin, Adam. 2000. Root-and-pattern morphology without roots or patterns. In Masako Hirotani, Andries W. Coetzee, Nancy Hall & Ji-yung Kim (eds.), *Proceedings of the 30th meeting of the North East Linguistic Society*, 655–670. Amherst, MA: GLSA.

Ussishkin, Adam. 2005. A fixed prosodic theory of nonconcatenative templatic morphology. *Natural Language and Linguistic Theory* 23(1). 169–218.

Winskel, Heather & Manuel Perea. 2013. Consonant/vowel asymmetries in letter position coding during normal reading: Evidence from parafoveal previews in Thai. *Journal of Cognitive Psychology* 25. 119–130.

Wright, William. 1859. *A grammar of the Arabic language*. Cambridge: Cambridge University Press.

Chapter 7

Root-based syntax and Japanese derivational morphology

Brent de Chene

Waseda University

> This paper argues that the formation of transitive and intransitive verb stems in Japanese, a process that has been widely seen as supporting the Distributed Morphology view of derivational stem-formation as performed by the syntax, cannot in fact be analyzed as syntactic. The Japanese data are thus consistent with Anderson's (1982) claim that it is precisely that morphology traditionally classified as inflectional that reflects syntactic operations.

1 Introduction

In a well-known paper, Anderson (1982: 587) proposes that "Inflectional morphology is what is relevant to the syntax," where syntactically relevant properties are those "assigned to words by principles which make essential reference to larger syntactic structures." He claims further that a delimitation of inflection on this basis closely mirrors the traditional understanding of where the boundary between inflection and derivation lies. In contrast, the Distributed Morphology literature, in treating syntax as root-based and stem formation of all types as syntactic, denies significance to the traditional distinction between inflection and derivation and renders vacuous the claim that inflection is just that portion of morphology that realizes elements and properties manipulated by the syntax.[1] The present paper takes up the formation of transitive and intransitive verb stems in Japanese, a case that has been widely seen as supporting the DM view of stem-formation as performed by the syntax, and argues that a closer look reveals that the derivational processes in question cannot in fact be analyzed as syntactic. In the

---

[1] The founding paper of the DM framework, Halle & Marantz (1993), presents DM as a theory of inflection and makes no explicit claims about derivation, but the adoption of root-based syntax and the rejection of the inflection/derivation distinction are clear at least by Marantz (1997; 2001). See below for further references.

end, then, the Japanese data is consistent with Anderson's view that there is a fundamental distinction between inflection and derivation and that the criterion of syntactic relevance picks out just that morphology traditionally classified as inflectional.[2]

In recent years, the derivational morphology of the Japanese verb has become a standard example (as in Harley 2012) illustrating the DM claim that syntax is root-based – the claim, that is, that along with functional morphemes, the atoms of syntactic computation are roots rather than (inflectable) stems or (inflected) words (Embick & Marantz 2008: 5). In particular, it has become widely accepted (Marantz 2013: 106) that the Japanese suffixes that create transitive and intransitive verb stems are instances of little v, causative and inchoative, that attach to roots and thus that the verb stems themselves are syntactic constructions – much like, say, the combination of a verb stem with a tense element or a main verb with an auxiliary. Here, I note first that these claims about the constituency of Japanese verb stems rest on a restricted database that masks the fact that a significant number of stems involve sequences of two transitivity-determining suffixes. I then present the failure of two nested suffixes to interact in the way expected of syntactic elements – in particular, the fact that an inner suffix must be taken as invisible for purposes of semantic interpretation and argument structure – as the first of several related arguments casting doubt on the proposal to generate Japanese verb stems syntactically.

The data on which DM theorists base their claim that the verbal derivational suffixes of Japanese are instances of little v attaching to roots is the appendix of Jacobsen (1992), which represents a light revision of the appendix of Jacobsen (1982), and in turn appears lightly revised as Appendix I in Volpe (2005). That appendix consists of roughly 350 pairs of isoradical intransitive and transitive verbs presented in their citation forms (Imperfect/Nonpast Conclusive) and sorted into sixteen classes depending on the derivational suffixes that appear at the right edge of their stems. The fact that the Jacobsen/Volpe appendix is limited to verb stems presented pairwise means that using it as a basis for the identification of root requires assuming for each transitivity pair that there are neither stems of other lexical categories nor verb stems outside the transitivity pair that provide information about the relevant root. §2 below, in the context of presenting background information on Japanese derivation, introduces a number of cases in which this assumption is unjustified. The following three sections, building on the observations of §2, present reasons for doubting that verb stems are syntactically derived. While for concreteness I refer throughout to the DM literature cited above and related work, the argumentation is intended to apply to any proposal to generate Japanese verb stems syntactically.

§3, first, shows that a substantial minority of verb stems involve two transitivizing (T) or intransitivizing (I) suffixes (with the four orders TT, TI, IT, II all attested), but that an outer suffix must be taken to render an inner one null and void for purposes of argument structure and semantic interpretation. §4 shows that the same is true for the suffix

---

[2] On a personal note, while I have taken the idea that inflection is precisely the syntactically relevant morphology as a guiding principle for many years, it was anything but obvious to me at the time Steve proposed it. It ranks high in my personal inventory of the many things I have learned from Steve, and I am happy to have this opportunity to reaffirm it in a volume dedicated to him.

pair *-m-* (verbal) and *-si-* (adjectival), with the additional complication that the order in which those two suffixes appear relative to a root R is an idiosyncratic function of R. §5, finally, argues against a syntactic account of stem formation on the basis of semantic change, claiming, for lexical causatives in particular, that the diachronic instability of the putatively compositional causative interpretation (much as if a phrase like *kick the bucket* were to lose its compositional interpretation, retaining only the idiosyncratic one) shows that that interpretation cannot have been based on a syntactic derivation in the first place. In all of these cases, the behavior of the derivational suffixes under consideration is contrasted with that of inflectional and uncontroversially syntactic elements. §6, a brief conclusion, sketches two possible non-syntactic approaches to derivational morphology and speaker knowledge thereof and suggests that the choice between them for cases like the one considered here remains a topic for further research.

2 Background

In considering the shortcomings of Jacobsen's (1982; 1992) appendix as a database for Japanese verbal derivation, the first thing to note is that the pairwise presentation of the data does not always adequately represent the relations of isoradicality that hold among verb stems. This is because a number of roots underlie three or (in at least one case) four verb stems rather than two; in such cases, Jacobsen either lists two pairs in separate places or, as we will see below, omits one of the stems. In several cases involving three stems on a single root, there are two pairs of stems differentiated at least roughly by root alloseme, with a formal contrast for either transitives or intransitives but not both. For example, the difference between the allosemes 'solve' and 'dissolve, melt' of the root *tok-* corresponds to a formal distinction for transitives but not for intransitives, as shown in (1) and (2).[3]

(1)   a.   *tok-e-* 'be solved'
       b.   *tok-* 'solve'

(2)   a.   *tok-e-* 'melt (i)'
       b.   *tok-as-* 'melt (t)'

In other cases, as in (3) and (4), there is no alloseme-dependent pairing, simply a triplet of isoradical stems.

(3)   a.   *tunag-ar-* 'be connected'
       b.   *tunag-e-* 'connect (t)'
       c.   *tunag-* 'connect (t)'

---

[3] Below, taking the distinction between inflection and derivation in Japanese to be uncontroversial, I use *stem* in the traditional meaning "morpheme (sequence) subject to inflection" and cite bare stems rather than inflected forms; "(i)" and "(t)" in glosses indicate intransitive and transitive meanings, respectively.

(4) a. *uk-* 'float (i)'
　　 b. *uk-ab-* 'float (i)'
　　 c. *uk-ab-e-* 'float (t)'

In these last two cases, the policy of pairwise listing results in one stem of each isoradical set (specifically, 3b and 4a) being left out of the database.

In fairness to Jacobsen, it must be noted that morphological analysis was not his aim in compiling his appendix. Most crucially for our purposes, he nowhere refers to the notion "root", and it is only with Volpe's (2005) DM treatment that the root becomes a central concept in the interpretation of the appendix data. Volpe's (2005: 121 (note 27)) procedure for root extraction, however, amounts to simply peeling off the outermost derivational suffix and labeling the residue a root, and he has been followed implicitly in this practice by other DM theorists.

We should observe before proceeding that there are many cases, illustrated by (5) below, in which Volpe's procedure does in fact yield a root.

(5) a. *nao-r-* 'get better (illness, injury); get repaired'
　　 b. *nao-s-* 'cure; repair'

(5) is clearly the kind of case Marantz (2013: 106) has in mind when he says about Japanese that "there seems overwhelming support for analyzing the suffixes signaling either the lexical causative as opposed to the inchoative or the inchoative as opposed to the lexical causative as realizations of a little *v* head attaching to the root." As we will now see, however, there are a number of respects in which the properties of (5) do not generalize to the Japanese derivational system as a whole. Most crucially, there is reliable evidence for a number of Volpe's "roots" that they are actually morphologically complex, with the result that many verb stems contain two derivational suffixes rather than one. Given that, as we have already noted, Volpe's procedure for root extraction involves no attempt to compare verb stems with stems of other lexical classes or with verb stems outside the transitivity pair under consideration, this result is unsurprising. Let us examine a few representative cases.

Consider the sequence *tunag-* of (3) above. Comparison of that sequence, roughly meaning 'connect', with the noun *tuna* 'rope' suggests that the former is underseg-mented, and in particular that the transitive stem *tunag-* consists of the noun stem *tuna* (or the root that underlies it) suffixed with *-g-*. This suggestion is confirmed when we observe that *-g-* is suffixal in a number of other stems as well, with a core subset ((6–7 below and the three of note 3) displaying a very specific semantics: *-g-* takes as input a noun stem denoting a tool T and returns a verb stem with the meaning "to make typical use of T". Three examples that occasion resegmentation of entries of the Jacobsen/Volpe appendix are given in (6) through (8), with both a transitive and an intransitive stem noted in each case.[4]

---

[4] Three further examples whose status in the contemporary language might be thought questionable are *tumu-g-* 'spin (thread)' (*tumu* 'spindle'), *ha-g-* 'fletch (arrow)' (*ha* 'feather'), and, with an irregular alternation of *t* with *s*, *husa-g-* 'cover, stop up' (*huta* 'cover').

(6) a. *tuna* 'rope'
     b. *tuna-g-* 'tie together, tie up'
     c. *tuna-g-ar-* 'get connected'[5]

(7) a. *to(-isi)* 'whetstone'
     b. *to-g-* 'whet'
     c. *to-g-ar-* 'become pointed'

(8) a. *mata* 'crotch, fork'
     b. *mata-g-* 'step over, straddle (t)'
     c. *mata-g-ar-* 'straddle (i)'

The derivational relationships postulated in (6–8) appear unimpeachable in both formal and semantic terms: the roots are nonalternating, and the semantic relationship between nominal and verbal meanings is unmistakable.

More common as a stem-forming suffix than -g- is -m-, which can be shown to be a stem formant in several dozen verbs. (9–11) display three cases in which recognition of suffixal -m- forces resegmentation of strings that Volpe takes to be roots (the (a) items of (9) and (10) are adjective stems, and that of (11) is an adjectival noun, a stem with adjectival meaning but essentially nominal inflection).

(9) a. *ita-* 'painful'
     b. *ita-m-* 'be painful, get injured'
     c. *Ita-m-e-* 'injure'

(10) a. *yuru-* 'slack'
     b. *yuru-m-* 'slacken (i)'
     c. *yuru-m-e-* 'slacken (t)'

(11) a. *hiso-ka* 'stealthy, secret'
     b. *hiso-m-* 'be hidden, lurk'
     c. *hiso-m-e-* 'conceal, mask'

We have seen that in addition to verb stems formed with the common suffixes -r- and -s-, illustrated in (5), there are verb stems formed with -g- and -m-. In fact, of the nine occurring stem-final consonants, all but *n* can be shown to be suffixal in some stems. Suffixal -b- has been illustrated in (4b) above; (12) through (14) display one example each for -k-, -t-, and -w- (w deletes in the phrasal phonology before nonlow vowels; here and below, I take reference to a suffix -C(V)- to subsume reference to its post-consonantal allomorph -aC(V)-).

---

[5] Kunio Nishiyama (personal communication) suggests the possibility that -g- in (6) is a (transitivity-neutral) verbalizer, with the transitivity of (6b) resulting from a null transitivizer parallel to the intransitive -ar- of (6c). A fully general form of this proposal will require the postulation of a very large number of morphological zeros.

(12) a. *na-k-* 'make characteristic sound' (animal); 'weep' (human)
    b. *na-r-* 'sound (i)' (inanimate subject)
    c. *na-r-as-* 'sound (t)'

(13) a. *hana-re-* 'move (i) away (from); be released'
    b. *hana-s-* 'move (t) away (from); release'
    c. *hana-t-* 'release forcefully, discharge'

(14) a. *muk-* 'face, look (in a direction)'
    b. *muk-e-* 'cause to face, turn (t) (in a direction)'
    c. *muk-aw-* 'face, proceed toward'
    d. *muk-aw-e-* '(go to) meet, receive (a visitor)'

We see, then, that the inventory of suffixes that create verb stems of determinate transitivity is a good deal larger than envisioned in the Jacobsen/Volpe appendix, where, apart from idiosyncratic formations, the relevant set is essentially limited to *-r-*, *-s-*, *-re-*, *-se-*, *-e-*, *-i-*, and zero. In closing this introductory section, let us consider two semantic issues that arise with respect to the Jacobsen/Volpe appendix data. The first involves the interpretation of roots, the second the interpretation of suffixes.

Quite apart from the question of whether or not roots are taken to be elements that are manipulated by the syntax, no attempt to segment stems into roots and suffixes synchronically is a fully grounded project in the absence of a criterion for isoradicality – a criterion, that is, for determining when two given stems share a root and when they do not. The semantic lability of individual stems over time that will be illustrated in §5 makes this by no means an idle question. It is, however, a question that neither Jacobsen nor Volpe engage with seriously; Jacobsen (1982: 38)[6] says only that the members of a transitivity pair must exhibit "a certain degree of semantic affinity", and Volpe (2005: 32) confines himself to observing that "Root semantics is a wide-open area for further research". The question of isoradicality is essentially coextensive with the traditional problem of distinguishing homophony from polysemy, a problem that may ultimately be illuminated by psycholinguistic and neurolinguistic research (see Marantz 2013: 103). It is worth keeping in mind, however, that any program involving the synchronic identification of roots requires innumerable provisional decisions on this matter.

Turning now to the interpretation of the stem-forming suffixes of which we have seen a number of examples, let us note first that while Volpe (2005) follows Jacobsen (1982; 1992) in referring to the two members of a transitivity pair as "intransitive" and "transitive", more recent literature such as Harley (2008; 2012) and Marantz (2013) use the more specific "inchoative" and "causative". In fact, cases like *ka-r-* (Western Japan; cf. Eastern *ka-ri-*) 'borrow' versus *ka-s-* 'lend' and *azuk-ar-* 'take on deposit' versus *azuk-e-* 'deposit' show that even the former pair of terms is too specific to be accurate in general. This is because the first member of each of those pairs shows "intransitive" morphology in spite of displaying what, under Burzio's generalization, are the twin hallmarks of causative little

---

[6] See also note 5, p.34 and the corresponding note 30 of Jacobsen 1992 (pp. 248–249).

v, namely an agentive external argument and accusative case-marking. Cross-linguistic parallels[7] suggest that the treatment of 'borrow' as the intransitive counterpart of 'lend' is by no means accidental or exceptional. The phenomenon of a stem with causative meaning but "intransitive" morphology appears to show that if the semantics of the two morphological types are specified separately, they will have to overlap. Let us briefly note another type of example that suggests the same conclusion.

The stems *too-r-* 'pass through' and *mata-g-* 'step over, pass over, straddle' (8b above) are closely parallel in both their semantics and their case-marking. When the subject is animate, as in (15) (where stem-internal segmentation is suppressed), that subject (marked nominative but omitted in the examples) is both an agent and a theme moving along a path, and the accusative object is an intermediate point on that path.

(15) a. Syootengai   o   toot-te   eki   ni modot-ta.
     shopping.district ACC pass.through-CJ station DAT return-PF
     'I passed through the shopping district and returned to the station.'

  b. Saku o   matai-de   hodoo   ni hait-ta.
     barrier ACC step.over-CJ sidewalk DAT enter-PF
     'I stepped over the barrier and onto the sidewalk.'

In other uses, the agent of examples (15) may be replaced by an inanimate theme, with *matag-* in the meaning 'pass over', or by a path argument, as in *The road passes through the tunnel/over the train tracks.*

In spite of the close semantic parallelism between *too-r-* and *mata-g-*, however, the two stems differ in their transitivity status: *too-r-* is the intransitive corresponding to transitive *too-s-* 'pass though (t)', while *mata-g-* is the transitive corresponding to intransitive *mata-g-ar-* 'straddle' (8c above), the latter differing from *mata-g-* in taking a dative rather than an accusative object. Unless *too-r-* and *mata-g-* are semantically distinct in a way we have failed to identify, this fact shows that the transitivity status of a stem cannot be a function of that stem's semantics alone, and a fortiori cannot be a function of the semantics of that stem's suffix. An alternative possibility, which considerations of space preclude developing here, is that there is a continuum of degrees of transitivity, as suggested by Hopper & Thompson (1980) and subsequent work, and that what transitivity pairs have in common is that the "transitive" member has a higher degree of transitivity than the "intransitive" member.[8] In any case, however, the evidence we have seen here is sufficient to establish that there is no simple, general account of the semantics of the suffixes that create transitivity-specific Japanese verb stems, and that, as was the case regarding the question of a criterion for isoradicality, much work remains to be done in this area.

Above, we have seen that the data of the Jacobsen/Volpe appendix is a good deal more complex and irregular, both formally and semantically, than consideration of examples

---

[7] See Kuo (2015: 59, 84–85, 107) for the Taiwanese languages Amis, Puyama, and Seediq, respectively; other languages for which the relationship can be easily verified include Tagalog and Swahili.

[8] Jacobsen (1992: 73–74) develops a scalar concept of transitivity but does not suggest that the common point of transitivity pairs is a transitivity differential in favor of the morphologically transitive member.

like (5) might suggest. Nothing in the present section, however, is intended as an argument for or against any particular treatment of that data. Taking our discussion of the Jacobsen/Volpe appendix as a starting point, we now turn, in Sections 3 through 5, to arguments against proposals to generate Japanese verb stems syntactically.

3 Sequences of verbal suffixes

As we have already noted, one consequence of the resegmentations that are entailed by comparing the stems that participate in transitivity pairs with stems of other lexical categories (as well as with other verb stems) is that many stems can be seen to display a sequence of two suffixes attached successively to a root rather than a single transitivity-determining suffix. For example, the (c) examples of (6) through (8) above all involve the sequence -g-ar-, where the first suffix creates a transitive stem and the second an intransitive. Similarly, the (c) examples of (9) through (11) all involve -m-e-, where the first suffix creates an intransitive stem and the second a transitive. Suffix sequences are also observed in (12c) and (14d).

Sequences of two transitivizing suffixes and two intransitivizing suffixes are observed as well. For example, (16d) below, where (16) is an expansion of (6), involves the sequence -g-e-, where both suffixes create transitive stems, and (17c) involves the sequence -m-ar-, where both suffixes create intransitive stems.

(16) a. *tuna* 'rope'
 b. *tuna-g-* 'tie together, tie up'
 c. *tuna-g-ar-* 'get connected'
 d. *tuna-g-e-* 'tie together, connect'
(17) a. *yasu-raka* 'peaceful, calm'
 b. *yasu-m-* 'rest (i)'
 c. *yasu-m-ar-* 'become rested, at ease'
 d. *yasu-m-e-* 'rest (t)'

Recall now the DM claim that Japanese transitivity-determining suffixes are instances of little v, with at least an inchoative and a causative "flavor" (Marantz 2013: 107) to be distinguished. Abstracting away from the fact that (at a minimum) both types of little v will have to be polysemous, and writing the inchoative version as "v_i" and the causative version as "v_c", the structure of the two stems of (5), for example, will be as shown in (18) (simplified glosses given).

(18) a. *nao-r-* [[R]v_i] 'get better'
 b. *nao-s-* [[R]v_c] 'make better'

In the same way, the structure of the stems (16c–16d) will be as in (19), and that of the stems (17c–17d) will be as in (20). (Here and below, I take the fact that -g- and -m- (and also -b-, -k-, -t-, -w-) in isolation are entirely parallel in function to the suffixes the DM literature treats as little v (notably -r-, -s-, and -e- (see e.g. Marantz 2013: 108) to license a parallel treatment for them in the DM framework we are taking as representative of syntactic treatments of derivation.)

(19)   a.   *tuna-g-ar-* $[[[R]v_c]v_i]$ 'connect (i)'
        b.   *tuna-g-e-* $[[[R]v_c]v_c]$ 'connect (t)'

(20)   a.   *yasu-m-ar-* $[[[R]v_i]v_i]$ 'get rested'
        b.   *yasu-m-e-* $[[[R]v_i]v_c]$ 'rest (t)'

If the representations of (19–20) are constructed in the syntax, in line with the proposal that roots and functional morphemes are the primitives of syntactic derivation, we will expect them to be interpreted compositionally, with the meaning of the outer little v combining with the result of composing the meaning of the inner little v with that of the root. In fact, no verb stem has an interpretation that involves two units of "little v meaning", either two instances of "inchoative" or two instances of "causative" or one of each; for interpretive purposes, the only little v that matters in representations like those of (19–20) is the outer one.[9] This is as if, when the Perfect auxiliary occurs outside of the Progressive in English or the Passive outside of the (productive) Causative in Japanese, as illustrated in (21), the outer auxiliary were to nullify the interpretation of the inner one rather than composing with it semantically.

(21)   a.   have been eating   [PERF[PROG[V]]]
        b.   *tabe-sase-rare-*   [[[V]CAUS]PASS] 'be made to eat'

It would seem that in uncontroversially syntactic constructions like those of (21), this kind of nullification never occurs, and thus that we can assume that the syntactic computational system includes no mechanism for opting out of compositional interpretation in this way. The structures of (19–20) therefore pose a major problem for the idea that the suffixes deriving Japanese verb stems are syntactic elements.

We have seen that the syntactic status of constructions like (19–20) is called into question by their interpretive properties. The representations of (19) pose a second problem as well, namely that the internal v_c will introduce an external argument that must ultimately remain unrealized.[10] In the remainder of this section, I concentrate on documenting further instances of the construction (19a), verb stems that introduce no external argument in spite of containing a transitivizing suffix.

---

[9] While the v_i of (20b) could be taken to be semantically active, the meaning of such causatives would have to coincide with that of causatives derived from roots, as in (18b). The semantic inertness of the inner little v thus follows for this case as for the others. (In DM, identification of category-determining elements with phase heads requires that lexical causatives, being monophasal, be root-based (Marantz 2007).)

[10] The causative interpretation and the external argument may in fact be introduced by separate heads (Pylkkänen 2008: chapter 3); what is important for our purposes is that in the data at hand they are both present when a transitivizing suffix appears alone but absent when it appears inside another transitivity-determining suffix.

Consider first the isoradical sets (22–25), all of which illustrate the suffix sequence *-r-e-*.[11]

(22) a. *mak-* 'roll up, wind around'
 b. *maku-r-* 'roll up, tuck up'
 c. *maku-r-e-* 'get turned up, ride up'

(23) a. *nezi* 'screw'
 b. *nezi-r-* 'twist'
 c. *nezi-r-e-* 'get twisted'

(24) a. *yabu-k-* 'rip (t)'
 b. *yabu-r-* 'rip (t)'
 c. *yabu-r-e-* 'rip (i)'

(25) a. *kasu-ka* 'faint, at the limits of perception'
 b. *kasu-m-* 'become hazy, dim'
 c. *kasu-m-e-* 'cloud (the vision of), deceive; graze, skim over; skim off, steal'
 d. *kasu-r-* 'graze (touch lightly in passing)'
 e. *kasu-r-e-* 'become faint or discontinuous (printing, writing); become hoarse (voice)'

The stems of (22–25) are all in common use in contemporary Japanese; a final parallel set that is particularly transparent semantically but for which the verb stems are obsolete is *kubi* 'neck', *kubi-r-* 'strangle', *kubi-r-e-* 'die by hanging oneself'.

Examples of the construction (19a) involving the suffix sequence *-m-ar-* can also be cited, as in (26–28). (26a) reflects the fact, not previously exemplified, that bare roots not infrequently occur reduplicated as adverbial items of the mimetic vocabulary.

(26) a. *kurukuru* 'round and round (rotation, winding)'
 b. *kur-* 'reel in, wind'
 c. *kuru-m-* 'wrap by rolling'
 d. *kuru-m-ar-* 'be rolled up, wrapped up'
 e. *kuru-m-e-* 'lump together'

(27) a. *tuka* 'hilt, handle'
 b. *tuka-m-* 'grasp' (accusative object)
 c. *tuka-m-ar-* 'be caught, captured'; 'hold on to' (dative object)
 d. *tuka-m-aw-e-* 'catch, capture'

---

[11] Taking the root to be *maku-* in (22) obviates postulating a new suffix allomorph for the (b) and (c) examples but requires a rule deleting a root-final vowel in a zero-derived verb stem for (22a). Given also a rule *a + i > e*, mirroring the presumed historical development (see Ono 1953 and subsequent literature), many apparently consonant-final roots could be reanalyzed along parallel lines; for example, the stems of (1–2) above could be *tok-*, *toka-i-*, *toka-s-* (√*toka*) rather than *tok-*, *tok-e-*, *tok-as-* (√*tok*).

(28) a. *haza-ma* 'gap, interstice' (< *hasa-ma* (*ma* 'interval'))
   b. *hasa-m-* 'insert between'
   c. *hasa-m-ar-* 'get caught between'

In (6–8) and (22–28), then, we have seen examples in which intransitivizing suffixes appear outside transitivizing suffixes, resulting in stems of the shape (19a). These are structures for which, as a result of the internal v_c, both a causative interpretation and an external argument are predicted, but do not materialize. We have already argued that the syntactic status of all four constructions (19–20) is called into question by the fact that the inner little v of those constructions is never interpreted. Regarding the unrealized external argument of stems of the shape (19a), similarly, it is clear that there is no way, in a system of syntactic derivation based on selectional features and the Merge operation and restricted by a "no tampering" condition (Chomsky 2008: 138), for a specifier introduced by one head to be deleted or ignored as a consequence of merger of a higher head. The conclusion seems inescapable, then, that a system of stem-formation that allows stems of the form (19a), and stems of the form (19–20) more generally, cannot be the result of the syntactic computational system.

4 Verbal *-m-* and adjectival *-si-*

In (19–20) above, we saw that transitivizing and intransitivizing suffixes, characterized as v_c and v_i respectively, can occur in any of the four logically possible orders following a root. We have not seen any examples, however, in which the members of an individual pair of suffixes appear in a given order after one set of roots but in the opposite order after another set. For example, the suffixes of the sequence *-g-e-* always occur in that order regardless of their status as transitivizing or intransitivizing. In fact, there are three possibilities in that regard: both suffixes can be transitivizing, as in (16d), the first can be intransitivizing and the second transitivizing, as in *yawa-ra-g-e-* 'soften (t)' (cf. *yawa-ra-g-* 'soften (i)'), or the first can be transitivizing and the second intransitivizing, as in *hisya-g-e-* ~ *hisi-g-e-* 'be crushed' (cf. *hisya-g-* ~ *hisi-g-* 'crush'). In this section we will observe two suffixes, one deriving verb stems and the other adjective stems, for which there are four modes of attachment to a root: direct affixation of each suffix, verbal suffix preceding adjectival, adjectival suffix preceding verbal, and both orders with the same root. It will be argued that both the fact that only the outer suffix is interpreted, parallel with what we saw in §3, and the fact that the relative position of the suffixes is an idiosyncratic function of the individual root militate against treating the suffixes as syntactic elements.

Many Japanese roots support both a verb stem in *-m-*, exemplified in §3, and an adjective stem formed with the suffix *-si-*. While adjective stems in *-si-* are not treated in the DM literature on Japanese derivation, that suffix has a natural DM analysis as a category-determining little a, where the latter is a stative counterpart of inchoative v_i and causative v_c (Marantz 2013: 103). In the examples of (29–30), both suffixes attach directly to a root, making those examples parallel, as the displayed structure shows, to the verb stems *nao-r-* and *nao-s-* that we saw in (5) and (18) (the root of 30 also supports a stem *kuy-i-* that is a close synonym of (30b); *y* deletes before a front vowel in the phrasal phonology).

(29) a. *suzu-si-* [[R]a] 'cool, refreshing'
     b. *suzu-m-* [[R]v$_i$] 'cool off, refresh oneself'
(30) a. *kuy-asi-* [[R]a] 'causing chagrin, regret'
     b. *kuy-am-* [[R]v$_c$] 'rue, regret'

There are a number of roots supporting both types of stem seen in (29–30), however, for which the verb stem in *-m-* is derived from the adjective stem in *-si-*. This is illustrated in (31–32) (I take *-si-* to be suffixal in an otherwise unsegmentable CVCV *si-* adjective stem).

(31) a. *kuru-si-* [[R]a] 'painful, uncomfortable, difficult'
     b. *kuru-si-m-* [[[R]a]v$_i$] 'suffer'
(32) a. *kana-si-* [[R]a] 'sad'
     b. *kana-si-m-* [[[R]a]v$_i$] 'grieve, sorrow'

And there are roots for which, in contrast, the verb stem in *-m-*, whether transitive (as in 33b) or intransitive (as in 34b) serves as the base for derivation of the adjective stem in *-si-*:[12]

(33) a. *uto-* [[R]a] 'distant, ill-informed'
     b. *uto-m-* [[R]v$_c$] 'shun, ostracize'
     c. *uto-m-asi-* [[[R]v$_c$]a] 'unpleasant, repugnant'
(34) a. *ita-* [[R]a] 'painful'
     b. *ita-m-* [[R]v$_i$] 'be painful; get damaged'
     c. *ita-m-asi-* [[[R]v$_i$]a] 'pitiable, pathetic'

Finally, there is at least one root for which both the verb stem in *-m-* and the adjective stem in *-si-* contain both suffixes, in the opposite order in the two cases:

(35) a. *tutu-m-asi-* [[[R]v$_c$]a] 'modest, unpretentious'
     b. *tutu-si-m-* [[[R]a]v$_c$] 'be cautious regarding; abstain from'

What conclusions can we draw from the data of (29–35)? First of all, with regard to interpretation, those examples support the same observation that was made in §3 for stems of the four types in (19–20), namely that when a stem contains two derivational suffixes, the inner one is interpretively inert.[13] The semantic relations of the two stems

---

[12] For an English parallel to the three types (29–30), (31–32), (33–34), consider *ambigu-ous/ity, duplic-it-ous, monstr-os-ity*.

[13] While one might imagine for some of the doubly suffixed stems of (31–35) that the interpretation of the whole depends in some way on that of the inner suffix, there is evidence against this idea in some cases. With respect to (34), for example, the root-reduplicated adjective *itaita-si-* 'pitiable, pathetic' shows that the occurrence of that meaning for the stem *ita-m-asi-* has nothing to do with the inner suffix *-m-*.

7 Root-based syntax and Japanese derivational morphology

to each other and to the root in (35), for example, are roughly the same as in (29–30), even though the stems of (35) each contain two suffixes and the stems of (29–30) only one. This observation, as we have seen, casts doubt on the proposal that the suffixes in question are syntactic elements.

A parallel argument can be made regarding the relative position of suffixes. (19–20) have already shown, of course, that if suffixes are divided into transitivizing ("causative") and intransitivizing ("inchoative") types, there are no constraints on their relative order when two of them occur in the same stem, so that their actual order in particular cases becomes a function of the individual root. As suggested by the discussion of the suffix sequence -*g-e-* at the beginning of this section, though, if we classify suffixes on strictly distributional grounds, without reference to transitivity value, it is possible to set up two position classes that will obviate conditioning of suffix order by roots in the great majority of cases: roughly speaking, the suffixes recognized by the Jacobsen/Volpe segmentation of stems will belong to the outer layer, with the inner layer being composed of suffixes such as -*g*-, -*m*-, -*w*-, and (transitivity-neutral) -*r*-.

For the data of (29–35), however, conditioning of suffix order by individual roots is inescapable. This, then, constitutes a second way, independent of the interpretive inertness of the inner suffix, in which the behavior of -*m*- and -*si*- fails to conform to what we would expect of syntactic elements. Returning to the analogy with auxiliary verbs that we appealed to in §3 (see 21 above), the positional relations of those two suffixes are as if the Perfect and the Progressive auxiliaries (say) both appeared adjacent to the stem for one class of verbs, but the Perfect was formed by placing the Perfect auxiliary outside the Progressive for a second class of verbs, and the Progressive was formed by placing the Progressive auxiliary outside the Perfect for a third class. The reason, of course, that this is difficult to imagine is that we expect unambiguously syntactic elements to appear in a fixed order with respect to a verbal or nominal stem. Indeed, since the 1990s, a great deal of work in cartographic syntax (notably Cinque 1999) has developed the idea that the (hierarchical) ordering of syntactic functional heads is fixed not only internally to a single language, but universally. From that perspective, the radical failure of Japanese verbal -*m*- and adjectival -*si*- to display a consistent ordering makes it extremely difficult to view them as syntactic heads.

5 Compositional meanings and semantic change

We have claimed that the syntactic computational system includes no mechanism for opting out of compositional interpretation, in particular by allowing a higher head to nullify the interpretation of a lower one. More generally, it seems reasonable to assume that the compositional interpretation of structures generated by the syntax is automatic, so that there is no way to block the compositional interpretation of a syntactic constituent.[14] We expect it to be true, in other words, that no instance of a syntactically generated structure or construction can idiosyncratically fail to display the compositional

---

[14] I will assume that this principle is not compromised by the delayed transfer to the interfaces characteristic of phase-based derivation (Chomsky 2001).

semantic interpretation associated with that structure or construction.[15] As a result, a phrase like *kick the bucket* that is demonstrably generated by the syntax will automatically have the compositional interpretation predicted by its lexical items and its syntactic structure, independently of whether it has one or more listed interpretations as well. As a diachronic corollary, we can infer that loss of the compositional interpretation of a syntactically generated constituent is not a possible change, assuming that the grammar and the lexicon have remained stable in the relevant respects. Thus, it would not be possible for *kick the bucket* to lose its compositional interpretation over time, retaining only the idiomatic one. When a phrase that was once generated by the syntax does have only a listed interpretation, it is either because the component words have dropped out of the lexicon, as is probably the case for the phrase *to plight one's troth* for most contemporary English speakers, or because the grammar no longer generates phrases of the type in question, as is the case for the phrase *till death do us part*.

What is true for manifestly phrasal constituents is true for inflected forms as well. Lexicalization (i.e. idiomatization) of *guts* in the meaning 'courage' and *balls* in the meaning 'audacity' has no effect on the status of those forms as regular plurals as long as the relevant stems and the rules for forming and interpreting plurals are diachronically stable. In Japanese, many verbal Gerund forms in *-te* are lexicalized as adverbs: *sitagatte, yotte* 'consequently' (*sitagaw-* 'obey', *yor-* 'be due to'), *kiwamete, itatte* 'extremely' (*kiwame-* 'reach, carry to extremity', *itar-* 'reach'). As long as the relevant verb stems remain in the lexicon and *-te* remains an inflectional suffix, however, there is no way that these idiomatic meanings can replace the compositional meanings that the forms have by virtue of their inflectional (ultimately, syntactic) status. The same is true of verbal Conjunctive forms that have been lexicalized as nouns: *nagasi* 'sink' (*naga-s-* 'make flow'), *nagare* 'flow, course of events' (*naga-re-* 'flow').[16]

If loss of a compositional interpretation is not a possible semantic change, assuming stability of grammar and lexicon, then demonstrating that the predicted compositional meaning of a putatively syntactic construction is subject to loss over time will support the conclusion that the construction in question is not syntactic after all, since if it were, its compositional meaning should be diachronically stable. In the present section, I will make this argument with respect to the Japanese lexical causative in *-s-*, exemplified by stems like *nao-s-* 'cure, repair', seen in (5b) and (18b) above. Specifically, I will document a number of cases in which the construction [R[s]] can be shown to have had the predicted interpretation CAUS(‖R‖) (‖R‖ the interpretation of R) originally but later to have lost that interpretation in spite of the fact that ‖R‖ itself has remained constant.

---

[15] Correspondingly, establishing that some phrase P is a counterexample to this principle will require (a) displaying P's syntactic structure; (b) displaying the rule of interpretation associated with that structure; and (c) showing that P idiosyncratically lacks the predicted interpretation.

[16] The semantics of these nouns has been treated in the DM literature since Volpe (2005) as involving selection of root allosemes by a noun-forming suffix ("special meanings of the root triggered across the little *v* head" (Marantz 2013: 107). The extreme semantic distance that separates many of the nouns from their corresponding roots (abundantly documented by Volpe), however, makes idiom-formation a more plausible basis for the nominal meanings than alloseme choice (for the distinction between the two mechanisms, see Marantz 2013: 105).

7 Root-based syntax and Japanese derivational morphology

As a first example, consider the stem *yurus-* 'allow, forgive'. In Old Japanese (see Omodaka et al. 1967), the primary meaning of this stem is 'slacken (t)', with secondary meanings 'let go of'; 'allow, comply with, tolerate'; and 'forgive, exempt'. *Yurus-*, in other words, is historically the causative in *-s-* on √yuru 'slack' (see ??) above), a root that in modern Japanese underlies the adjective stem *yuru-* 'slack', the nominal adjective *yuru-yaka* 'slack, gradual', and the verb stems *yuru-m-* 'slacken (i)' and *yuru-m-e-* 'slacken (t)'. As is clear from these four stems, the root has been completely stable semantically over thirteen centuries, and the same can be assumed for causative *-s-*. There is no trace in the modern meaning of *yurus-*, however, of the original concrete primary meaning 'slacken'. That meaning, in other words, has been completely replaced by the originally secondary or extended meanings 'allow' and 'forgive'. If *yuru-s-* had been a syntactic construction, with the meaning 'slacken (t)' the compositional result of a semantic rule of interpretation, this replacement should have been impossible, just as we have suggested that it would be impossible for *kick the bucket* to lose its compositional meaning and retain only the idiomatic one.

The history of the stem *itas-* 'do (humble)' is broadly parallel. In Old Japanese, it is the causative corresponding to *itar-* 'reach a limit', as explicitly noted in Omodaka et al. (1967), and thus means 'bring to a limit'. In the modern language, while intransitive *itar-* has retained its original meaning, *itas-* is for the most part, bleached of concrete content, simply a suppletive humble variant of *suru* 'do'. A third case in which a *s*-stem has lost a putatively compositional causative meaning involves *konas-* 'deal with, take care of; be skilled at', whose primary meaning was originally 'break up, pulverize' and which is based historically on *ko* 'powder' (Ono, Satake & Maeda 1974). Like many other original monosyllables, *ko* has been replaced as a freestanding noun by a bisyllabic form, in this case *kona*, which is attested starting around 1700. The only serious proposal for the origin of *kona* (see NKD) appears to be that it is a backformation based on *konas-*. If the backformation theory is correct, *kona* and *konas-* were unquestionably isoradical at the relevant point in time, so that *konas-* consisted of √kona 'powder' plus causative *-s-*. Today, however, while the root noun remains in the language, the meaning 'break up, pulverize' for the verb is extinct.[17]

Two further stems in *-s-* for which the predicted causative meaning appears to have been lost over time are *hatas-* 'carry out, perform, accomplish' and *kuras-* 'make a living; live, spend (time)'. The roots appear in the zero-derived noun *hata* 'edge, perimeter; outside' and the zero-derived adjective stem *kura-* 'dark', respectively, and are semantically identifiable in the intransitives *hate-* 'end (i)' and *kure-* 'darken (day), end (i)' (for the *a* ~ *e* alternation, see note 11 above). The expected primary meaning 'end (t)' of *hatas-* appears in the gloss 'bring to a conclusion' in Omodaka et al. (1967); for *kuras-*, similarly, Omodaka et al. record the expected primary meaning 'spend the time until evening' (i.e. 'let the day darken'). In both cases, however, this compositional meaning is absent from the modern stems, neither of which stands in a purely causative relation to the corresponding intransitive or to the root. The meaning of *hatas-*, as the above

---

[17] While dictionaries retain examples like *tuti o konasu* 'break up dirt (clods)', the speakers I have consulted deny knowledge of such a usage.

definition indicates, inherently includes an element of purposive activity (carrying out a command, achieving a goal, fulfilling an obligation) that is absent from that of *hate-*. While the semantic difference between *kuras-* and *kure-* is more subtle, the basic fact preventing the former from functioning as the causative of the latter is that, unlike *kure-* ('come to an end'), *kuras-* ('spend (time)') is atelic. Both *hatas-* and *kuras-*, then, like *yurus-, itas-, and konas-,* are cases in which the predicted interpretation CAUS(‖R‖) of the construction [R[s]] has been lost over time.

In this section, we have seen an argument against the syntactic derivation of Japanese verb stems based on semantic change, using causatives in -*s*- as a representative stem-type. It goes without saying, we should emphasize, that perhaps the most common type of semantic change, the addition of idiomatic or extended meanings, does not count against the hypothesis of syntactic generation: as is well known, linguistic units of any size can be idiomatized, with the tendency to undergo idiomatization inversely proportional, roughly speaking, to size (Di Sciullo & Williams 1987: 14). But loss of a putatively compositional meaning, we have claimed, does count against syntactic generation, because there is no reason to take the compositional interpretation of syntactic structure to be anything but automatic and exceptionless. In order for a compositional meaning M to be lost, the syntactic structure underlying it would first have to be exempted from compositional interpretation, with M being lexicalized at the same time; M could then be lost from the lexicon. If this sequence of events is impossible because exemptions of the required type are never granted, however, a putatively compositional meaning that is in fact subject to loss cannot have been based on a syntactic derivation in the first place.

6 Conclusion

Above, I have attempted to evaluate the proposal that the derivational suffixes that create transitive and intransitive verb stems in Japanese are syntactic heads, in particular varieties of little v. Crucial evidence in this regard has come from identifying an inner layer of derivational suffixation (-*g*-, -*m*-, etc.) in addition to the well-known outer layer whose main members are -*r*-, -*s*-, -*re*-, -*se*-, -*e*-, -*i*-, and zero, since this has allowed us to raise the question of how two derivational suffixes interact when they occur together in the same stem. We saw in §3 that in such a case, the inner suffix is always inert for purposes of argument structure and semantic interpretation, casting doubt on the position that the suffixes are syntactic elements. In §4, we saw that the same is true for combinations of the verbal suffix -*m*- and the adjectival suffix -*si*-, with the added complication that the order in which those two suffixes occur is an idiosyncratic function of the root. Finally, in §5, we argued, without reference to suffix sequences, that the combination of a root and a transitivity-determining suffix, taking causative -*s*- as a representative example, cannot be a syntactic construction because its putatively compositional interpretation is unstable over time. All the evidence we have seen, then, points toward the conclusion that the derivational suffixes under consideration are not syntactic elements. Equivalently, if one wishes in the face of this evidence to generate Japanese verb and adjective stems syntactically, one will require relaxation of otherwise well-motivated constraints on structure-building and interpretation precisely for the domain of the stem. As suggested at the outset, our conclusions in this regard support Anderson's (1982: 594) position on the place of morphology in the grammar: derivation is pre-syntactic, and the units of lexical storage are inflectable stems; inflection, in contrast, is the post-syntactic spellout of morphological elements and morphosyntactic properties that are treated by syntactic operations.

The conclusion that Japanese derivational suffixes, in contrast with suffixes like the Passive and the productive Causative, are not syntactic elements is supported at a more impressionistic level by the fact that, as is easily confirmed, the two sets of suffixes differ sharply in their degree of regularity, both formal and semantic. Formally, while variation in the shape of the Passive suffix -(r)are- is limited to phonologically conditioned alternation of r with zero at the left edge, and variation in the shape of the Causative suffix -(s)as(e)- is limited to phonologically conditioned alternation of s with zero at the left edge and non-phonological alternation of e with zero at the right, variation in the realization of what under a DM analysis will be v_i and v_c is highly unconstrained, with multiple unrelated allomorphs for each of the suffixes and almost complete overlap between the two allomorph sets. Semantically, while the meaning of Passivepassive stems in -(r)are- and (apart from occasional idioms) Causative stems in -(s)as(e)- is both regular and relatively straightforward to characterize, the meaning of stems in v_i and v_c is in most cases multiply polysemous and highly idiosyncratic; the glosses we have given above, while aiming at a marginal increase in accuracy over the labels in Jacobsen (1992) and Volpe (2005), in many cases only scratch the surface of the problem of specifying stem meaning. With regard to semantics, it should also be remembered that, as we noted in §2, morphological analysis internal to the stem proceeds on the basis of an unredeemed promissory note regarding the criterion for isoradicality and that equally serious questions arise about how the meaning of transitivity suffixes is to be specified, given the apparent semantic overlap between transitivizing and intransitivizing morphology.

If Japanese verb and adjective stems are not, then, created by the syntactic computational system, how should we conceive of their structure and, crucially, the knowledge that speakers have about that structure? Broadly speaking, there are two types of answer that could be given to this question. On one of them, derivational morphology of the type we have seen here would be the result of a combinatory system roughly parallel to syntax but less regular both in terms of the hierarchical relationships holding among grammatical elements and the semantic interpretation of complex structures. From the standpoint of theoretical parsimony, of course, this would seem like an unattractive proposal; surely, if possible, we would prefer to maintain that the language faculty involves a "single generative engine" (Marantz 2001; 2005). Viewing language as a biological object, however, there would appear to be no grounds for excluding a priori the possibility that our linguistic capacities include a combinatory stem-formation module of the sort in question. In evolutionary terms, such a module might have provided a vastly expanded repertory of named concepts in advance of the emergence of a fully regular and productive syntax, representing a sort of half-way house on the road to discrete infinity.

The second type of answer that could be given to the question of the form taken by speaker knowledge of the relations among isoradical stems, assuming that those relations are not mediated by the syntactic computational system, is that that knowledge is frankly non-generative – that is, non-combinatory. In this case, all stems will be lexically listed, with relations among them captured by redundancy rules, for example, those of the type pioneered by Jackendoff (1975) (see also Jackendoff 2002: 53). What is unsatisfying about this type of answer is that it provides no insight into why derivational morphology should exist at all – why, that is, stems (setting aside compounds) are not all atomic. While we have seen evidence that at least some derivational morphology cannot be syntactic, then, there is no unambiguously attractive alternative account of the structure of speaker knowledge in this area. As a result, the place of derivational morphology in our linguistic competence remains very much an open question.

Acknowledgments

I would like to express my appreciation to Takayuki Ikezawa, in conversations with whom the idea for this paper emerged. I am also grateful to Kunio Nishiyama and Yoko Sugioka for comments on a presentation of some of this material at the 152nd meeting of the Linguistic Society of Japan (Tokyo, June 2016). Finally, I am indebted to several reviewers for comments that have resulted in a number of clarifications and improvements. Remaining errors of fact or interpretation are my responsibility.

Abbreviations

CJ (second or perfective) conjunctive
PF perfective

References

Anderson, Stephen R. 1982. Where's morphology? *Linguistic Inquiry* 13(4). 571–612.
Chomsky, Noam. 2001. Derivation by phase. In Michael Kenstowicz (ed.), *Ken Hale: A life in language*, 1–52. Cambridge, MA: MIT Press.
Chomsky, Noam. 2008. On phases. In Robert Freidin, Carlos P. Otero & Maria Luisa Zubizarreta (eds.), *Foundational issues in linguistic theory*, 133–166. Cambridge, MA: MIT Press.
Cinque, Guglielmo. 1999. *Adverbs and functional heads*. Oxford: Oxford University Press.
Di Sciullo, Anna-Maria & Edwin Williams. 1987. *On the definition of word*. Cambridge, MA: MIT Press.
Embick, David & Alec Marantz. 2008. Architecture and blocking. *Linguistic Inquiry* 39(1). 1–53.
Halle, Morris & Alec Marantz. 1993. Distributed morphology and the pieces of inflection. In Kenneth Hale & Samuel J. Keyser (eds.), *The view from Building 20: Essays in linguistics in honor of Sylvain Bromberger*, 111–176. Cambridge, MA: MIT Press.

Harley, Heidi. 2008. On the causative construction. In Shigeru Miyagawa & Mamoru Saito (eds.), *The Oxford handbook of Japanese linguistics*, 20–53. Oxford: Oxford University Press.

Harley, Heidi. 2012. Lexical decomposition in modern syntactic theory. In Markus Werning, Wolfram Hinzen & Edouard Machery (eds.), *The Oxford handbook of compositionality*, 328–350. Oxford: Oxford University Press.

Hopper, Paul J. & Sandra A. Thompson. 1980. Transitivity in grammar and discourse. *Language* 56. 251–299.

Jackendoff, Ray. 1975. Morphological and semantic regularities in the lexicon. *Language* 51(3). 639–671.

Jackendoff, Ray. 2002. *Foundations of language*. Oxford: Oxford University Press.

Jacobsen, Wesley M. 1982. *Transitivity in the Japanese verbal system*. Bloomington: Indiana University Linguistics Club.

Jacobsen, Wesley M. 1992. *The transitive structure of events in Japanese*. Tokyo: Kurosio Publishers.

Kuo, Jonathan Cheng-Chuen. 2015. *Argument alternation and argument structure in symmetrical voice languages: A case study of transfer verbs in Amis, Puyama, and Seediq*. University of Hawai'i at Manoa Dissertation (pre-defense draft).

Marantz, Alec. 1997. No escape from syntax: Don't try morphological analysis in the privacy of your own lexicon. *University of Pennsylvania Working Papers in Linguistics* 4(2). 201–225.

Marantz, Alec. 2001. Words. Handout for invited lecture. 20th West Coast Conference on Formal Linguistics, University of Southern California. http://babel.ucsc.edu/~hank/mrg.readings/Marantzwords.pdf.

Marantz, Alec. 2005. Generative linguistics within the cognitive neuroscience of language. *The Linguistic Review* 22(2–4). 429–445.

Marantz, Alec. 2007. Phases and words. In Sook-Hee Choe (ed.), *Phases in the theory of grammar*, 191–222. Seoul: Dong In.

Marantz, Alec. 2013. Locality domains for contextual allomorphy across the interfaces. In Ora Matushansky & Alec Marantz (eds.), *Distributed Morphology today*, 95–115. Cambridge, MA: MIT Press.

Nihon kokugo daiziten dainihan hensyuu iinkai/Syoogakukan kokugo ziten hensyuubu [Great dictionary of the Japanese language second edition editorial committee/Syoogakukan Japanese dictionary editorial division] (ed.). 2000–2002. *Nihon kokugo daiziten [Great dictionary of the Japanese language]*. 2nd ed. Tokyo: Syoogakukan.

NKD (Nihon kokugo daiziten) = Nihon kokugo daiziten dainihan hensyuu iinkai/Syoogakukan kokugo ziten hensyuubu 2000–2002.

Omodaka, Hisataka, Toru Asami, Teizo Ikegami, Itaru Ide, Haku Ito, Yoshiaki Kawabata, Masatoshi Kinoshita, Noriyuki Kojima, Atsuyoshi Sakakura, Akihiro Satake, Kazutami Nishimiya & Shiro Hashimoto (eds.). 1967. *Zidaibetu kokugo daiziten. Zyoodaihen [Great historical dictionary of Japanese. Nara period]*. Tokyo: Sanseidoo.

Ono, Susumu. 1953. Nihongo no doosi no katuyookei no kigen ni tuite [On the origin of the inflected forms of Japanese verbs]. *Kokugo to Kokubungaku [Japanese Language and Literature]* 350. 47–56.

Ono, Susumu, Akihiro Satake & Kingoro Maeda (eds.). 1974. *Iwanami kogo ziten [Iwanami historical dictionary of Japanese]*. Tokyo: Iwanami Syoten.

Pylkkänen, Liina. 2008. *Introducing arguments*. Cambridge, MA: MIT Press.

Volpe, Mark. 2005. *Japanese morphology and its theoretical consequences: Derivational morphology in Distributed Morphology*. New York: Stony Brook University Dissertation.

Chapter 8

Morphological complexity and Input Optimization

Michael Hammond
University of Arizona

> In this paper, we examine morphological complexity through the lens of Input Optimization. We take as our starting point the dimensions of complexity proposed in Anderson (2015). Input Optimization is a proposal to account for the statistical distribution of phonological properties in a constraint-based framework. Here we develop a framework for extending Input Optimization to the morphological domain and then test the morphological dimensions Anderson proposes with that framework.
>
> The dimensions we consider and the framework we develop are both supported by empirical tests in English and in Welsh.

1 Introduction

Anderson (2015) lays out a number of dimensions of morphological complexity, ways that we might evaluate how complex different morphological systems are, e.g. number of morphemes in the system, complexity of principles governing combinations of morphemes, complexity of exponence, complexity of allomorphy, etc.

These are clearly the right kinds of dimensions for evaluating the complexity of morphological systems, and we might be inclined to use them as part of a typology of morphology. However, if we adopt these as our dimensions for calculating complexity, what follows? As I learned from Steve Anderson years ago in graduate school, typology without implications is bad typology. (For discussion, see, for example, Anderson 1999.)

In this paper, I consider the implications of these dimensions of morphological complexity for the theory of Input Optimization (Hammond 2013; 2014; 2016). This theory develops a notion of phonological complexity which languages "attempt" to minimize statistically. To the extent that different phonological representations are complex, they are under-represented statistically. This complexity shows up in the markedness of surface representations and in the complexity of input–output mappings. For example, marked segments or syllable structures are under-represented compared with their less marked counterparts. In addition, outputs that are distinct from their inputs are underrepresented with respect to outputs that are identical with their inputs.

Interestingly, there are morphological effects as well, effects that sometimes work in the opposite direction. For example, initial consonant mutation in Welsh causes a mismatch between output and input, but is over-represented. I argue that this is because phonological complexity includes morphological mapping. Specifically, to the extent that morphological distinctions are not made in the surface form, a representation is more complex. This is formalized in OT-based terms using a constraint deriving from work by Kurisu (2001).

This general approach is supported by the facts of haplology, e.g. English adjectives in *-ly* like *weekly* not getting double-marked with adverbial *-ly* and plurals like *kings* not getting double-marked with genitive *-s*. The absence of double-marking means that a morphological distinction is not made on the surface; thus these cases are under-represented as expected.

These morphological cases beg the larger question: should phonological complexity be generalized further? Should there be a more general notion of morphological complexity, built on dimensions of the sort cited above, where forms that are more complex morphologically are statistically under-represented? In this paper, I pursue just this course, formalizing a notion of morphological complexity and then testing it with cases from English and Welsh with respect to the dimensions of morphological complexity identified in Anderson (2015).

The organization of this paper is as follows. I first review some of the dimensions of complexity presented in Anderson (2015). I then outline the theory of Input Optimization and a framework for a constraint-based theory of morphology that we can assess Input Optimization with respect to. With these in hand, we then consider the predictions made by the Input Optimization framework and turn to the English and Welsh data.

2 Dimensions of complexity

Anderson (2015) discusses a number of dimensions of morphological complexity and we will not review them all here.

We explicitly set aside those systemic dimensions that cannot distinguish options within a language. For example, Anderson cites the number of elements in the morphological system as a measure of its complexity. Thus, for example, if one language has one way of marking noun plurals and another has ten ways, we might think of the first as less complex. Input Optimization makes no predictions about systemic differences like these, as we will see in the next section, so we don't consider them any further.

Anderson cites the number of morphemes in a word as a dimension of complexity.[1] This can be taken in several ways. One possibility is that one might compare across different languages, which seems to be Anderson's intent. Another possibility though

---

[1] This, of course, begs the question of what is a morpheme, an issue at the forefront of much of Steve's own work.

would be to compare across words in the same language and we investigate this possibility below.

Another dimension Anderson identifies is whether the morphemes present in a word depend on each other in some way. We might think of this in two ways. Some morpheme may only occur when "licensed" by some other. Gender in Spanish is an example of this. If gender is marked on a noun, then that gender marking must be present in the plural as well, e.g. *mes+a+s* 'tables' table + feminine + plural. Another example might be verbal theme vowels in Romance; person/number marking depends on the presence of the theme vowel.

The other side of this coin would be cases where the presence of some morpheme blocks another. Haplology is an example of this. For example, adverbial *-ly* in English cannot occur on an adjective that already ends in *-ly*. Thus we have *happily*, but not *weeklyly*.

Anderson also distinguishes among morpheme types in terms of complexity. Simple prefixation or suffixation is less complex than circumfixion or infixation. Presumably, non-concatenative morphology like templatic operations, ablaut, umlaut, truncation are also more complex.

Lastly, Anderson cites the complexity of allomorphy as an instance of general morphological complexity. We take this to mean that a system is more complex when there is more allomorphy. We interpret allomorphy as generously as possible to include cases where the phonology seems to be involved, say, in the different pronunciations of the English plural *-s* as [s, z, əz], but also plurals that differ on some other basis, e.g. *geese, criteria, sheep*, etc.

Anderson treats some other possibilities as well, but the ones above are quite simple and can be examined within a single language. We list them together below.

1. Number of morphemes in a word

2. Principles of morphological combination, e.g. scope, haplology, etc.

3. Complexity of exponence, e.g. circumfixes, infixes, etc.

4. Complexity of allomorphy

In the following section, we review the Input Optimization proposal and sketch out the predictions it makes for these. Our interest in Input Optimization is that it provides a mechanism by which we can assess the dimensions of morphological complexity we've just considered.

3 Input Optimization

The problem that Input Optimization addresses is that certain phonological configurations occur less often than we might otherwise expect. For example, if we look at the distribution of stress on two-syllable adjectives, we see that adjectives with final stress like *alert* [əlɪ́t] or *opaque* [òpʰék] are less frequent overall. Strikingly, both are even less frequent when they occur prenominally.

Hammond (2013) argues that this effect is driven by the English Rhythm Rule (Liberman & Prince 1977; Hayes 1984). Certain stress configurations in English are avoided by shifting a primary stress leftward onto a preceding secondary. Thus we have alternations like *Mìnnesóta* vs. *Mínnesòta Míke*; *thìrtéen* vs. *thírtèen mén*; etc. When an adjective with final stress occurs in prenominal position, the relevant configuration is quite likely to occur. In addition to following context, there is a restriction on preceding context. With an adjective like *òpáque*, stress shift leftward is possible because of the preceding stress, e.g. *ópàque stóry*, but with an adjective like *alért*, such a shift is impossible and the offending configuration must surface, e.g. *alért pérson*. Both kinds of cases are statistically under-represented in English. Specifically, these configurations arise significantly less frequently than we might expect based on the overall distribution of adjectives with these stress patterns.

Input Optimization is a proposal to account for statistical skewings like these that occur in the phonologies of languages. The idea is developed in Hammond (2013; 2014; 2016). The basic idea is that markedness and faithfulness violations are avoided in the phonology so as to reduce the complexity of the phonological system. Input Optimization is a generalization of the notion of Lexicon Optimization Prince & Smolensky (1993):

(1) **Lexicon Optimization:**
Suppose that several different inputs $I_1, I_2, \ldots, I_n$ when parsed by a grammar G lead to corresponding outputs $O_1, O_2, \ldots, O_n$, all of which are realized as the same phonetic form Φ—these inputs are all *phonetically equivalent* with respect to G. Now one of these outputs must be the most harmonic, by virtue of incurring the least significant violation marks: suppose this optimal one is labelled O_k. Then the learner should choose, as the underlying form for Φ, the input I_k.

The idea is that if there are multiple ways to produce an output form consistent with the facts of a language, the learner chooses the input that produces the fewest constraint violations. There are no empirical consequences to Lexicon Optimization by itself. In fact, it is defined to apply only when there are no consequences.

To refine this into something we can use, we define a notion of *Phonological complexity* that applies to individual input–output pairings, but also to entire phonological systems. (The basic logic of this is that the complexity of a phonological system is proportional to the number of asterisks in its tableaux.)

We define the output/surface forms of a language as a possibly infinite set of forms.

(2) $O = \{O_1, O_2, \ldots, O_n, \ldots\}$

Each output form has a corresponding input:

(3) $I = \{I_1, I_2, \ldots, I_n, \ldots\}$

The phonology is comprised of a finite sequence or vector of constraints:

8 Morphological complexity and Input Optimization

(4) $C = \langle C_1, C_2, \ldots, C_n \rangle$

Any input–output pairing, (I_i, O_i), then defines a finite vector of violation counts, some number of violations for each constraint earned by the winning candidate for that input.

(5) $\langle n_{C_1}, n_{C_2}, \ldots, n_{C_n} \rangle$

With these notions, Phonological Complexity (PC) is defined as follows:

(6) **Phonological Complexity** (PC)
The phonological complexity of some set of forms is defined as the vector sum of the constraint violation vectors for surface forms paired with their respective optimal inputs.

To produce a *relative* measure of PC given some set of *n* surface forms, divide the PC score for those forms by *n*.

Hammond (2016) exemplifies this with a hypothetical example of nasal assimilation. Imagine we have the forms in (7) we wish to compute the PC for. Given the inputs provided in column 2, we have the constraint violations for winning candidates in columns 3 and 4.

(7)

	Input	Output	NC	IO-Faith
a.	/on pi/	om pi		*
b.	/an ba/	am ba		*
c.	/un bo/	um bo		*
d.	/en do/	en do		
e.	/on ta/	on ta		
f.	/un ti/	un ti		
g.	/an ku/	aŋ ku		*
h.	/in ga/	iŋ ga		*
i.	/on ke/	oŋ ke		*
			0	6

The relative complexity of this first system is: $\langle 0, 6 \rangle / 9 = \langle 0, .66 \rangle$. We can compare the system in (7) with the one below in (8). Here we have a different array of output forms, but the same logic for inputs and constraint violations.

(8)

	Input	Output	NC	IO-Faith
a.	/on pi/	om pi		*
b.	/an ba/	am ba		*
c.	/en do/	en do		
d.	/on ta/	on ta		
e.	/un ti/	un ti		
f.	/in di/	in di		
g.	/an ku/	aŋ ku		*
h.	/in ga/	iŋ ga		*
			0	4

The relative complexity of the second system is: $\langle 0, 4 \rangle / 8 = \langle 0, 0.5 \rangle$, less than the first. As argued by Hammond (2016), this notion extends obviously to weighted constraint systems. For example, in a system with strict ranking, $\langle 0.1, 0.4 \rangle$ is more complex than $\langle 0, 0.5 \rangle$.

The proposal then is that all phonological systems are skewed to be less complex.

(9) **Input Optimization**
All else being equal, phonological inputs are selected that minimize the phonological complexity of the system.

Note that (9) alters the frequency of input–output pairings and does not change the input–output mapping of any particular form. For example, this principle prefers (8) to (7), though both systems contain the same pairings. The difference is in the relative frequency of the pairings that occur.

Our goal in this paper is to see if it is profitable to extend this system to include morphology. In point of fact, Hammond (2016) addresses this question partially in response to statistical effects in Welsh. In particular, Welsh initial consonant mutation is statistically over-represented when, based on what we have seen so far, we might have expected the opposite.

Consonant mutation in Welsh refers to a set of phonological changes that apply to initial consonants in specific morpho-syntactic contexts. For example, the *Soft Mutation* makes the following changes:

(10)

Orthographic		Phonological	
Input	Output	Input	Output
p	b	p	b
t	d	t	d
c	g	k	g
b	f	b	v
d	dd	d	ð
g	∅	g	∅
m	f	m	v
ll	l	ɬ	l
rh	r	r̥	r

There are many contexts where this occurs, e.g. after certain prepositions, direct object of an inflected verb, after certain possessives, feminine singular nouns after the article, etc. The following figure gives some examples after the preposition *i* [i] 'to'.

(11)
pen [pʰɛn] 'head' i ben [i bɛn] 'to a head'
cath [kʰaθ] 'cat' i gath [i gaθ] 'to a cat'
mis [mis] 'month' i fis [i vis] 'to a month'
nai [naj] 'nephew' i nai [i naj] 'to a nephew'
siop [ʃɔp] 'shop' i siop [i ʃɔp] 'to a shop'

The chart above also includes examples of non-mutating consonants. Note that words with these occur in mutation contexts with no change.

The Input Optimization framework would seem to predict that mutation should be under-represented. After all, mutation entails a faithfulness violation and, all else being equal, the system is less complex to the extent that such violations are avoided. This, however, is not what occurs. Instead, we get over-representation in mutation contexts. Words that begin with consonants that can mutate are over-represented in mutation contexts compared with words that begin with consonants that do not mutate.

To capture this, Hammond (2016) proposes the (revised) Realize Morpheme constraint (12). This is a slight revision of a constraint that Kurisu (2001) motivates on other (non-statistical) grounds. This constraint basically militates for the expression of morphological information.

(12) REALIZE MORPHEME (*revised*) (RM')
Let α be a *morpheme*, β be a morphosyntactic category, and F(α) be the phonological form from which F(α+β) is used to express a morphosyntactic category β. Then RM' is satisfied with respect to β iff F(α+β) ≠ F(α) phonologically.

With this in hand, the reason why Welsh mutation is over-represented is to reduce phonological complexity by minimizing violations of RM'.

The RM' constraint is also invoked by Hammond (2016) to account for haplology in English. We've already cited the fact that forms like *weeklyly* are blocked. Similarly, we find overt marking of the genitive in English does not occur on plural forms marked with -*s*; the genitive plural of *cat* is *cats'*, not something like *catses*. Both kinds of cases are statistically under-represented in English: they are avoided to minimize violations of RM'.

While RM' (12) does what's required, it begs the question of whether a more general version of PC is appropriate. In other words, beyond the effects of RM', do we expect Input Optimization to apply to morphology?

4 Constraint-based morphology

To assess this, we need a constraint-based theory of morphology. There have been a number of proposals over the years for how to deal with morphology generally in an OT-like framework. The earliest we know of are Russell (1993; 1995); Hammond (2000), but see Aronoff & Xu (2010); Xu & Aronoff (2011) for more recent and fuller proposals. A full-on theory of this sort is well beyond the scope of this paper, but let's lay out what such a theory might look like, at least in sufficient detail so we can assess whether it makes the right predictions about Input Optimization.

Let us assume that morphology—like phonology—is a constraint-based system mapping inputs to outputs. Inputs are denuded of any morphological marking, but have sufficient featural information so that we can evaluate whether morphologically marked candidate forms satisfy relevant constraints. For example, we might imagine that plural marking in English comes about by taking a stem marked [+plural] and adding various affixes or performing other operations that do or do not express that feature. The idea is that the syntax provides a featurally complex object that the morphology can then interpret. Morphological operations like affixation, reduplication, mutation, etc. add features which do or do not match those required by the syntax. Following is a schematic partial tableau to give a sense of this.

(13)

/[cat +pl]/	...
[cat +pl]	
☞ [cat +pl] + [-s +pl]	
[cat +pl] + [-ed +past]	

We would want constraints that force the correct morphological operation to take place. Presumably there would be one or more constraints that enforce a correspondence between the features required by the stem and the features offered by any affixes or other changes; to the extent that those don't match, we would have violations. For convenience, let's call this FEATURES (Fs). The RM' constraint above, or constraints that get the same effects, should fall in this class.

We also need constraints that militate against gratuitous morphological operations. Some of this might be achieved by featural correspondence imposed by Fs, but we surely need something to account for the relative markedness of morphological operations generally. Perhaps something like this:

(14) *ABLAUT ≫ *INFIX ≫ *PREFIX ≫ *SUFFIX

The basic idea is to posit constraints that militate against *any* morphological operation. These constraints are ranked with respect to each other, presumably in a universal fashion. This hierarchy would then be interleaved with the Fs constraint. For example, we might have:

(15) *ABLAUT ≫ *INFIX ≫ FEATURES ≫ *PREFIX ≫ *SUFFIX

The effect of such a ranking is that the featural needs of a stem can be met by prefixation and suffixation, but not by other operations.

This system is woefully incomplete and, in its present form, cannot do justice to the full range of effects we see in morphological systems. See, for example, Anderson (1982;

1992). It is, in some ways, quite similar to these proposals in treating affixation as an instance of more general morphological operations that interpret syntactically-motivated features. However, our goal here is not to develop a full-on constraint-based morphological theory. Rather, the point is to build enough of such a theory so that we can test Input Optimization with respect to the dimensions of morphological complexity identified above.

Let's now return to our dimensions and consider one by one what our theoretical skeleton in conjunction with Input Optimization predicts. First, we have the number of morphemes. All else being equal, the system certainly as developed militates for as few morphemes, or other morphological operations, as possible. Additional morphology entails violations of the constraints in (14) and Input Optimization predicts these should be avoided statistically.

The second dimension of complexity refers to principles of morphological combination. The system we've developed says nothing (so far) about the licensing side of this, but it does address morphological haplology. To the extent that haplology occurs, it entails violations of RM' (12) and of Fs. Previous work cited above has already established that Input Optimization applies in these cases.

The third dimension is the complexity of exponence, that certain morphological operations are intrinsically more complex than others. This is captured by the ranking, e.g. in (14). We expect morphologies to be statistically skewed against violations of the higher-ranked constraints.

The fourth dimension is complexity of allomorphy, allomorphy that is a consequence of phonology or morphophonology like English plural [s, z, əz], but also plurals that differ on some other basis, e.g. *geese*, *criteria*, *sheep*, etc. The phonological cases fall under the core Input Optimization proposal. In fact, Hammond (2013) shows statistical skewing for English plural and past allomorphy in just the expected directions. The other case cited is also accommodated by the proposal. Internal modifications like *geese* or truncation+suffixation like *criteria* violate higher-ranked constraints than simple plural suffixation; hence they should exhibit under-representation. Similarly, plurals with no change like *sheep* should violate RM' and Fs and be under-represented.

Summarizing, a constraint-based morphological theory of the sort sketched out, in conjunction with Input Optimization, makes the following predictions:

(16) 1 Words should have fewer morphemes.
2 Haplology should be avoided. (This has already been established by Hammond 2016.)
3 More marked morphological operations (per the hierarchy above) should be avoided.
4 Morphophonology should be avoided. (This has already been established by Hammond 2013.)
5 Ablaut, umlaut, truncation, etc. should be avoided. (This is essentially the same as #3 above.)
6 Zero-marking should be avoided.

We must therefore examine #1, #3/5, and #6 empirically. In the next sections, we look at all three cases with data from English and Welsh.

5 Number of morphemes

The first prediction of Input Optimization applied to our toy constraint-based theory of morphology is that a form is more complex if it has more morphemes. This is a bit tricky to test. In many cases, having fewer morphemes is not necessarily the less complex option. For example, consider the plural form *sheep* which lacks an overt plural suffix. Is this less complex than a form like *cat+s*? Probably not. The most reasonable analysis given the framework above is that the plural *sheep* surfaces with an undischarged plural feature. On that view, it is not clearly less complex than a form like *cat+s*.

We might also think of strong verb forms like *spoke*, as compared with *look+ed*. Here, however, it would be a mistake to view *spoke* as having fewer morphemes than *look+ed*. Rather, there is some operation, perhaps mostly lexical, for creating or selecting strong verb forms when available. Presumably, this would add to the complexity of *spoke*.

To find a case without these alternative analyses, we turn to Welsh plurals. Welsh has a number of ways of forming plurals. For example:

(17)
Singular			Plural	
ysgol	[ə́sgɔl]	'school'	ysgolion	[əsgɔ́ljɔn]
cyfarfod	[kʰəvárvɔd]	'meeting'	cyfarfodydd	[kʰəvarvɔ́dið]
cynllun	[kʰə́nɬin]	'plan'	cynlluniau	[kʰənɬínjaɨ]
problem	[pʰrɔ́blɛm]	'problem'	problemau	[pʰrɔblɛ́maɨ]
panel	[pʰánɛl]	'panel'	paneli	[pʰanɛ́li]
pwnc	[pʰʊ́ŋk]	'subject'	pynciau	[pʰə́ŋkʰjaɨ]
angen	[áŋɛn]	'need'	anghenion	[aŋhɛ́njɔn]
gorchymyn	[gɔrχə́min]	'order'	gorchmynion	[gɔrχmə́njɔn]
alarch	[álarχ]	'swan'	elyrch	[ɛ́lirχ]
castell	[kʰástɛɬ]	'castle'	cestyll	[kʰɛ́stɨɬ]

Note that there are different suffixes and stem changes.

There is another class of nouns, however, where it is the singular that is marked rather than the plural. The singular is always marked with either *-yn* in the masculine gender or *-en* in the feminine gender. For example:

(18) Singular   Plural
      mochyn   [mɔ́χin]   'pig'   moch   [mɔ́χ]
      blewyn   [bléwin]   'hair'   blew   [bléw]
      morgrugyn   [mɔrgrɨ́gin] 'ant'   morgrug   [mɔ́rgrɨg]
      marworyn   [marwɔ́rin]   'ember'   marwor   [márwɔr]
      eginyn   [ɛgínin]   'sprout'   egin   [ɛ́gɪn]
      mefusen   [mɛvísɛn]   'strawberry'   mefus   [mévɨs]
      coeden   [kʰɔ́ɯdɛn]   'tree'   coed   [kʰɔɯd]
      derwen   [dɛ́rwɛn]   'oak'   derw   [déru]
      madarchen   [madárχɛn]   'mushroom'   madarch   [mádarχ]
      moronen   [mɔrɔ́nɛn]   'carrot'   moron   [mɔ́rɔn]

There are some blended cases as well, where nouns marked for the singular co-occur with stem changes or take plural suffixes as well. For example:

(19) Singular   Plural
      merlyn   [mɛ́rlin]   'pony'   merlod   [mɛ́rlɔd]
      oedolyn   [ɔɯdɔ́lin]   'adult'   oedolion   [ɔɯdɔ́ljɔn]
      taten   [tʰátʰɛn]   'potato'   tatws   [tʰátʰʊs]
      (a)deryn   [(a)dérin]   'bird'   adar   [ádar]
      gwreiddyn   [gwréjðin]   'root'   gwraidd   [gwrájð]
      deilen   [déjlɛn]   'leaf'   dail   [dájl]
      hwyaden   [hujádɛn]   'duck'   hwyaid   [hújajd]
      cneuen   [kʰnéɯɛn]   'nut'   cnau   [kʰnáɯ]

The existence of the pairs where the singular is marked instead of the plural allows us to test the number of morphemes prediction without the problems of the English cases above.[2] On one hand, we take nouns which mark the plural with -(i)au, the most frequent plural suffix, and no associated stem changes. On the other, we take nouns which mark the singular with -en or -yn, and no associated stem changes or plural marking. In other words: *problem/problemau*, etc. vs. *coeden/coed*, etc. What we're interested in is whether there is a difference in the relative frequency of singular and plural forms in the two classes as a function of whether the form has an extra morpheme. Since we have both types of marking in Welsh, we can do this independent of the relative frequency of singulars and plurals in the language.

Individual lexical items have different frequencies of occurrence, so we must equalize for this. We therefore take the ratio of singular to plural as a measure of the relative frequency of singular and plural. Since this is a ratio, it abstracts away from the overall frequency of each pair.

---

[2] One might counter that it's possible to treat these as instances of subtractive morphology. There are two arguments against this. First, the singulatives are always marked with the suffixes -yn or -en (depending on gender). Second, there are cases where nouns end in these phonetic sequences where they are not suffixes. In these cases, normal plural formation occurs. For example: *emyn/emynau* 'hymn', *terfyn/terfynau* 'boundary', *ffenomen/ffenomenau* 'phenomenon', *awen/awenau* 'inspiration, muse', etc.

For this investigation, we use the CEG corpus (Ellis et al. 2001). This is a tagged written corpus of 1223501 words. For each word form, it also includes lemmas, so it is possible to determine singular–plural pairs fairly easily. In this corpus, we find 885 distinct pairs where the plural is marked with -(i)au and 41 distinct pairs where the singular is marked with -en or -yn. (As above, in both cases, we exclude pairs where stem changes are involved.)

When the plural is marked, the ratio of singulars to plurals is 11.08; when the singular is marked, the ratio is 1.26. Singulars greatly outnumber plurals that are marked, but singulars occur far less frequently when they are marked instead. This difference is significant: $t(920.287) = -8.267, p < .001$. This is consistent with the hypothesis that forms with more morphemes are more complex.

6 Marked morphological operations

Let's now consider the question of whether more marked morphological operations are under-represented. If they are, this would be consistent with Anderson's typology and Input Optimization.

To test this, let's look at the distribution of plurals in English using the tagged Brown corpus (Kučera & Francis 1967). The Brown corpus is a fairly old written corpus of 928181 words. The advantage of using it here is that it is tagged, so identification of singular and plural nouns is relatively easy, and it is widely used and available.

Focusing on plural nouns, we can separate them into regular plurals marked with -s vs. other plural forms, e.g. *men, stigmata, radii, oxen*, etc. When we pair these up with their respective singular forms, we get the following overall counts:

(20)
Type	Pl. tokens	Sg. tokens	Pairs/types
-s	46083	111904	4266
Irregular	2891	2517	79

Overall, there are far more regular than irregular forms, but this is, of course, to be expected by the very definition of "irregular". It is, however, also consistent with Input Optimization. The complexity of a system can be enhanced by limiting the number of forms that exhibit marked properties. It can also be enhanced by limiting the distribution of forms that do have those properties.

Is there a difference in the likelihood of a plural form given its regularity? If irregular forms are more complex, then we would expect their use to be statistically under-represented because of Input Optimization. To test this, we calculate the ratio of singular to plural tokens for each noun pair. This ratio allows us to examine the relative distribution of singular and plural forms, abstracting away from the overall frequency of any specific lexical item. The difference is plotted in Figure 1.

Strikingly, the difference goes in the wrong difference here: irregular plurals are more frequent relative to their singular forms than regular -s plurals with respect to their singular forms. This difference is significant: $t(90.318) = 3.151, p = 0.002$.

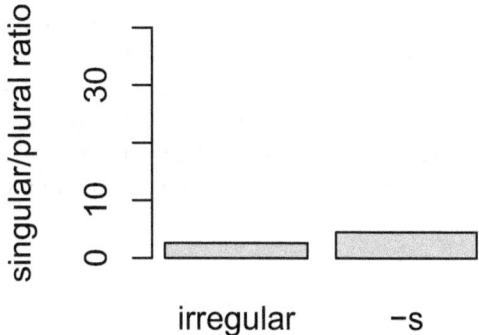

Figure 1: Singular-to-plural ratios for regular and irregular plurals in English

We conclude that the distribution of irregular plurals is ambiguous. In terms of relative frequency of singulars and plurals, the distribution goes in the wrong direction. In terms of overall distribution, however, it goes in the right direction. There are 2891 instances of irregular plurals in Brown and 46083 instances of regular plurals. If we were to assume that both types were equally likely, the difference is certainly significant: $X^2(4344, N = 48974) = 425346.797, p < .001$.

7 Zero marking

Let's now turn to zero marking. The claim is that zero marking is more complex and therefore the prediction is that zero marking should be under-represented.

We examine this with respect to plurals in English in the Brown corpus. Zero-marked plurals in English includes examples like: *deer, aircraft, buffalo*, etc. The difference in ratios between regular plurals in -s and zero plurals is shown in Figure 2.

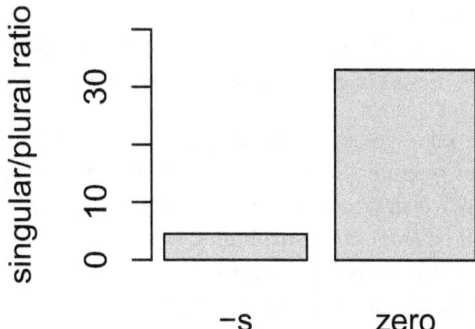

Figure 2: Singular-to-plural ratios for regular and zero plurals in English

Zero-marked plurals are far more frequent—relatively speaking—than regular plurals. Unfortunately, the variance is quite high—there is a lot of variation within each category—and though the mean difference is large, it is not significant: $t(19.002) = -1.416$, $p = 0.173$. As with the irregular plurals, however, the absolute difference is significant. There are 184 instances of zero plurals in Brown and 46083 instances of regular plurals. If we were to assume that both types were equally likely, the difference is certainly significant: $X^2(4285, N = 46267) = 311130.115$, $p < .001$. Again then, though the relative count is not significant, the absolute count goes in the right direction.

8 Summary

Our goal here has been to test the dimensions of morphological complexity proposed in Anderson (2015) with the theory of Input Optimization. As reviewed above, Input Optimization maintains that grammatical complexity, as assessed through constraint violation, is minimized at the input level of the grammar. Specifically, we should see under-representation of more marked morphological structures.

We picked out several dimensions of morphological complexity to examine, some of which have already been treated with respect to Input Optimization. The following list is repeated from Section 3 and annotated to reflect our results.

(21)   1   Words should have fewer morphemes. *This is borne out by the distribution of marked plurals and marked singulars in Welsh.*
        2   Haplology should be avoided. (This has already been established by Hammond 2016.)
        3   More marked morphological operations (per the hierarchy above) should be avoided. *This was tested with respect to English plurals and is borne out in an absolute comparison, but not in a relative comparison.*
        4   Morphophonology should be avoided. (This has already been established by Hammond 2013.)
        5   Ablaut, umlaut, truncation, etc. should be avoided. (This is essentially the same as #3 above.)
        6   Zero-marking should be avoided. *This was tested with respect to English plurals and is borne out in an absolute comparison, but not in a relative comparison.*

First, all else being equal, we expect forms with more morphemes to be dispreferred to forms with fewer morphemes. We saw that this was borne out in a comparison of singular–plural pairs in Welsh where in some cases the singular has an extra morpheme and in others the plural has an extra morpheme.

Second, we predict that morphological haplology should be under-represented. This was established in previous work with respect to the English genitive plural and adjectives in *-ly*.

Third, more marked morphological operations should be under-represented with respect to less marked morphological constructions. We saw an overall effect here with English irregular noun plurals. We also saw that the relative distribution of plurals with respect to singulars went in the opposite direction.

Fourth, we predict that morphophonology should be avoided. This was established in previous work with respect to morphophonology associated with English past *-ed* and plural *-s*.

The fifth point is the same as the third.

Finally, zero-marking should be under-represented. We saw an overall effect here with English zero-marked noun plurals. We also saw that the relative distribution of plurals with respect to singulars went in the opposite direction.

We conclude that the parameters of complexity developed in Anderson (2015) tested here and in previous work are correct.

We have seen that there is some divergence in the absolute and relative representation of plural marking, but we leave investigation of that for future work.

Acknowledgements

Thanks to Nick Kloehn and Diane Ohala for useful discussion. All errors are my own.

References

Anderson, Stephen R. 1982. Where's morphology? *Linguistic Inquiry* 13(4). 571–612.
Anderson, Stephen R. 1992. *A-morphous morphology*. Cambridge: Cambridge University Press.
Anderson, Stephen R. 1999. A formalist's reading of some functionalist work in syntax. In Michael Darnell, Edith A. Moravcsik, Frederick J. Newmeyer, Michael Noonan & Kathleen Wheatley (eds.), *Functionalism and formalism in linguistics*, vol. 1, 111–135. Amsterdam: John Benjamins.
Anderson, Stephen R. 2015. Dimensions of morphological complexity. In Matthew Baerman, Dunstan Brown & Greville G. Corbett (eds.), *Understanding and measuring morphological complexity*, 11–26. Oxford: Oxford University Press.
Aronoff, Mark & Zheng Xu. 2010. A Realization Optimality-Theoretic approach to affix order. *Morphology* 20. 381–411.
Ellis, N. C., C. O'Dochartaigh, W. Hicks, M. Morgan & N. Laporte. 2001. Cronfa Electroneg o Gymraeg (CEG): A 1 million word lexical database and frequency count for Welsh. http://www.bangor.ac.uk/canolfanbedwyr/ceg.php.en.
Hammond, Michael. 2000. There is no lexicon! *Coyote Papers* 10. ROA #43 (1995), 55–77.
Hammond, Michael. 2013. Input optimization in English. *Journal of the Phonetic Society of Japan* 17. 26–38.
Hammond, Michael. 2014. Phonological complexity and input optimization. *Phonological Studies* 17. 85–94.
Hammond, Michael. 2016. Input optimization: Phonology and morphology. *Phonology* 33. 459–491.
Hayes, Bruce. 1984. The phonology of rhythm in English. *Linguistic Inquiry* 15. 33–74.

Kurisu, Kazutaka. 2001. *The phonology of morpheme realization*. University of California, Santa Cruz PhD thesis.
Kučera, Henry & W. Nelson Francis. 1967. *Computational analysis of present-day American English*. Providence: Brown University Press.
Liberman, Mark & Alan Prince. 1977. On stress and linguistic rhythm. *Linguistic Inquiry* 8(2). 249–336.
Prince, Alan & Paul Smolensky. 1993. Optimality Theory. University of Massachusetts and University of Colorado.
Russell, Kevin. 1993. *A constraint-based approach to phonology*. University of Southern California PhD thesis.
Russell, Kevin. 1995. Morphemes and candidates in Optimality Theory. ROA #44.
Xu, Zheng & Mark Aronoff. 2011. A Realization Optimality Theory approach to blocking and extended morphological exponence. *Journal of Linguistics* 47(3). 673–707.

Chapter 9

Multiple exponence in the Lusoga verb stem

Larry M. Hyman
University of California, Berkeley

Sharon Inkelas
University of California, Berkeley

with Fred Jenga
University of Texas, Austin

> In this paper we address an unusual pattern of multiple exponence in Lusoga, a Bantu language spoken in Uganda, which bears on the questions of whether affix order is reducible to syntactic structure, whether derivation is always ordered before inflection, and what motivates multiple exponence in the first place. In Lusoga, both derivational and inflectional categories may be multiply exponed. The trigger of multiple exponence is the reciprocal suffix, which optionally triggers the doubling both of preceding derivational suffixes and of following inflectional suffixes. In these cases, each of the doubled affixes appear both before (closer to the root) and after the reciprocal. We attribute this pattern to restructuring, arguing that the inherited Bantu stem consisting of a root + suffixes has been reanalyzed as a compound-like structure with two internal constituents, the second headed by the reciprocal morpheme, each potentially undergoing parallel derivation and inflection.

1 Introduction

Among the most important contributions of Steve Anderson's realizational approach to morphology have been his early insistence that morphology is not reducible to syntax, his argument that formal theoretical models of morphology need to take different approaches to derivation and inflection ("split morphology"), his development of morphological rule ordering as the mechanism of ordering affixes, and his postulation that redundant (inflectional) morphological exponence is actively avoided by grammars. According to Anderson (1992), derivational morphology takes place in the lexicon, while

inflectional morphology takes place in the syntax. Inflectional morphology is realized by the application of ordered rules which spell out features supplied by syntactic principles such as agreement. The best evidence that the ordering of inflectional affixes cannot simply be read off of syntactic structure comes from morphotactics which have no analogue or simple justification in syntax.

In this paper we address some rather unusual facts from Lusoga, a Bantu language spoken in Uganda, which bear on the questions of whether affix order is reducible to syntactic structure, and whether derivation is always ordered before inflection, particularly as concerns multiple exponence. In §2 we introduce the Bantu verb stem and briefly summarize what has been said about the ordering of derivational suffixes within it. After reviewing the findings that much of this ordering is strictly morphotactic, not following from syntactic scope or semantic compositionality, in §3 we discuss multiple exponence among the Lusoga derivational verb extensions. In §4 we then turn to the original contribution of Lusoga, which shows multiple exponence of inflectional agreement as well as unexpected intermingling of inflectional and derivational affixation. We present our analysis in §5 and conclude with a few final thoughts in §6.

2 The Bantu verb stem

Most overviews of the Bantu verb stem assume a structure with an obligatory verb root followed by possible derivational suffixes ("extensions"), and ending with an inflectional final vowel (FV) morpheme. As shown in (1), the verb stem may in turn be preceded by a string of inflectional prefixes to form a word:

(1)

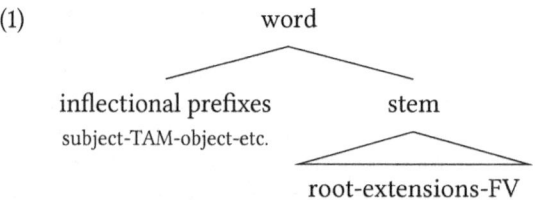

While this structure has been reconstructed for Proto-Bantu (Meeussen 1967), there is much variation on how the different derivational "verb extensions" are ordered. As shown in Hyman (2003b), most Bantu languages show at least a tendency to favor the "CARP" template in (2), for which we give reflexes in several Bantu languages:

(2)

	C(ausative)	A(pplicative)	R(eciprocal)	P(assive)
Shona	-is-	-il-	-an-	-w-
Makua	-ih-	-il-	-an-	-iw-
Chichewa	-its-	-ir-	-an-	-idw-
Lusoga	-is-	-ir-	-agan-	-(ib)w-
Proto-Bantu	*-ic-	*-ɪd-	*-an-	*-ɪC-ʊ-

The arguments for recognizing the CARP template include the following:

(i) Certain pairs of co-occurring suffixes must appear in a fixed surface order. This is true of the causative + applicative (CA), which can co-occur only in this order, independent of their relative scope. Compare the following two examples from Chichewa, in which applicative *-ir-* introduces an instrument (Hyman & Mchombo 1992; Hyman 2003b). Scope (schematized on the right) varies across the two examples, but surface order is the same:

(3) a. applicativized causative:
     lil-its-ir-   'cause to cry with'   [[cry] -cause-with]
    b. causativized applicative:
     takas-its-ir- 'cause to stir with'   [[stir-with] -cause]

(ii) Non-templatic orders which are driven by scope can occur with certain sets of suffixes, but are typically limited and show a "compositional asymmetry": The a-templatic order is restricted to the reading in which the surface order corresponds to relative scope, while the templatic order can be interpreted with either possible scope relations (e.g. reciprocalized causative, causativized reciprocal). The two orders of causative and reciprocal (CR, RC) illustrate this property in (4), again from Chichewa:

(4) a. templatic CR:
     mang-its-an-   'cause each other to tie'   [[tie] -cause-e.o.]
                    'cause to tie each other'   [[tie-e.o.] -cause]
    b. a-templatic RC:
     mang-an-its-   'cause to tie each other'   [[tie-e.o.] -cause]
                  * 'cause each other to tie'

As seen in (4a), the templatic CR order allows either scope interpretation, while the a-templatic RC order in (4b) can only be used to express a causativized reciprocal. The same facts are observed in cases where the a-templatic order of applicative and reciprocal is reinforced by an A-B-A "copied" sequence:

(5) a. templatic AR:
     mang-ir-an-   'tie (sth.) for each other'   [[tie] -for-e.o.]
                    'tie each other for (s.o.)'   [[tie-e.o.] -for]
    b. a-templatic RAR:
     mang-an-ir-an- 'tie each other for (s.o.)'   [[tie-e.o.] -for]
                  * 'tie (sth.) for each other'

Again, as seen in (5a), the templatic AR order can have either scope (reciprocalized applicative, applicativized reciprocal), while in (5b) the a-templatic (RA) + copy (R) sequence can only be compositional, hence an applicativized reciprocal. (We will see such A-B-A sequences in Lusoga in §3.)

(iii) A third argument for CARP is that at least one language, Chimwiini, allows only this order, whereas no Bantu language allows verb extensions to be freely ordered by scope. Thus, Abasheikh (1978: 28) writes:

"In Chimwi:ni, unlike some other Bantu languages, the order of the extensions is restricted. The following ordering of the extensions mentioned above is as follows: - Verb Stem - Causative - Applied - Reciprocal - Passive. It is not possible to put these extensions in any other order."

Other than stative -ik-, which is more restricted in its co-occurrence with other suffixes, the above summarizes the general picture for the productive extensions which are involved in valence. Even given the occasional variations, e.g. Kitharaka (Muriungi 2003), which reverses the applicative and reciprocal, hence the order CRAP, the evidence points unequivocally to the fact that extension order is determined primarily by template.

The importance of templaticity is also seen from the existence of one other valence-related suffix, the short causative -i- (I) which typically occurs between the reciprocal and passive, hence CARIP (see also Bastin 1986, Good 2005). Although both *-ɪc- (> -ɪs-, -is-) and *-i- were present in Proto-Bantu, *-ɪc- occurred only in combination with *-i-, hence *-ɪc-i- (cf. Bastin (1986). However, as summarized in (6), the current distribution of the two extensions (as well as the productivity of -i-) varies considerably across different Bantu languages (Hyman 2003b: 261):

(6) a. -is-i- and -i-   : Kinande, Luganda, Lusoga
    b. -is- only   : Chichewa, Shona, Zulu
    c. -i- only (or almost only) : Nyamwezi, Nyakyusa

The fact that -is- is the linearly first extension and -i- a quite later extension in CARIP, for reasons not motivated by scope, presents one more reason to accept a templatic, rather than compositional approach to Bantu verb extensions. However, this conclusion is not without interesting complications. As shown in such studies as Hyman (1994; 2003a) and Downing (2005), -i- frequently produces frication of a preceding consonant (a.k.a. Bantu spirantization) with potential multiple (cyclic) effects, as seen from the following examples in which -i- co-occurs with the (non-fricativizing) applicative -il- suffix in (7) from Cibemba:

(7) lub-   'be lost'   lil-   'cry'   UR
    lub-i-   'lose'   lil-i-   'make cry'   Morphology (I)
    luf-i-   lis-i-   Phonology
    luf-il-i- 'lose for/at' lis-il-i-   'make cry for/at'   Morphology (A)
    luf-is-i-   lis-is-i-   Phonology

In both outputs, the applicative and short causative exhibit the expected surface AI order. However, the frication of *lub-* 'be lost' and *lil-* 'cry' to *luf-* and *lis-* suggests that at some level of representation, -i- is root adjacent. Hyman (1994) adopts the above cyclic analysis in which morphology and phonology are interleaved (see e.g. Kiparsky 1982): -i- combines with the root on the first morphological cycle, triggering a phonological application of frication on the root. When the applicative is added on the next cycle of morphology, it is "interfixed" between the root and the short causative, in conformity with the AI order required by the CARIP template. This example illustrates the surface nature of the template.

Although it is not part of the CARIP template of valence-changing derivational suffixes, the "final vowel" (FV) inflectional ending position is also templatic in that it is required in most Bantu languages. The set of suffixes that may appear in the FV position includes past tense *-ɪ-, subjunctive *-ɛ, and (in most other contexts) default *-a. The -ɛ portion of perfective *-il-ɛ, which we will encounter in §4, is also in this slot, even as the -il- portion is sometimes considered to be part of the extension system. The customary reason for assuming bimorphemic *-il-ɛ is that the short causative (I) and passive (P) occur between the two parts, hence *-il-i-ɛ and *-il-ʊ-ɛ (Bastin 1983). If we assumed that *-il-ɛ was monomorphemic, we would have to assume some kind of exfixation or metathesis of the causative and passive with the [il] portion of -ilɛ. There is a second argument from Lusoga (and Luganda): Whenever causative -i- or passive -u- is present, the FV of the perfective complex is -a (see (9) and note 5 below). We assume that -il- occurs in the template ordered before -I-P- with the function of perfectivizing the extended derivational base so it can accept -ɛ or -a (cf. §4).) With this established, we are ready to go on to the issues that arise in Lusoga.

3 Lusoga verb extensions

As mentioned above, Lusoga is spoken in Uganda and is the Bantu language most closely related to Luganda. The data cited in this study were contributed by Fr. Fred Jenga, a native speaker from Wairaka (Jinja District).

3.1 Long and Short Causatives

Lusoga exhibits the CARIP template discussed above, where C refers to the long causative -is- and I refers to the short causative extension -i-. In fact, Lusoga uses both -is-i- and -i- productively and often interchangeably, to express both causation and instrumentals: -lim-is-i-, -lim-i- 'cause to cultivate, cultivate with (sth.)'. As indicated, -is- cannot occur without -i-, while the reverse is possible. The two causative morphs are quite consistent in their CARIP templatic ordering with respect to the applicative, namely, -is-il-i- (CAI), -il-i- (AI), which are realized as -is-iz- and -iz- by the following processes:

(8) 'make cultivate for/at'
    lim-is-il-i-a   lim-il-i-a   UR
    lim-is-iz-i-a   lim-iz-i-a   frication
    lim-is-iz-y-a   lim-iz-y-a   gliding
    lim-is-iz-a   lim-iz-a   glide-absorption

3.2 Reciprocal + Short Causative

Challenges to the CARIP template arise with the reciprocal suffix, which in Lusoga has the long reflex -*agan*- of Proto-Bantu *-*an*-.[1] In the next few subsections we will consider how the reciprocal combines with its fellow extensions in the CARIP template, including both ordering flexibility as well as affix doubling.

We begin with the short causative, -*i*-. When used alone, without the long causative, we observe flexible ordering possibilities, well beyond what would be expected from the CARIP template. In these and subsequent examples, a left bracket indicates the boundary between inflectional prefixes and the beginning of the verb stem:

(9) 'they make each other sew'
    a. bà-[tùùng-ágán-y-á   /tùùng-agan-i-a/   RI
    b. bà-[tùùnz-ágán-á   /tùùng-i-agan-a/   IR
    c. bà-[tùùnz-ágán-y-á   /tùùng-i-agan-i-a/ IRI

In none of (9a-c) does the short causative -*i*- surface as a vowel. Nonetheless, its presence is clearly felt. In (9a) it glides, preceding a following vowel; in (9b) and (9c) it spirantizes the final /g/ of /-tùung-/ 'sew' to [z] by a general process in the language, and is otherwise deleted before the following vowel (of the reciprocal). The reciprocal suffix -*agan*- does not trigger compensatory lengthening when vowels glide or delete before it, as also seen in the examples with root-final vowels immediately followed by -*agan*-, below:

(10) a. bà-[mw-àgán-á   'they shave each other'   /-mo-/   'shave'
     b. bà-[ty-àgán-á   'they fear each other'   /-tì-/   'fear'

Note that (9c) appears to exhibit *two* instances of the short causative: root spirantization indicates a following short causative, and the glide following the reciprocal also indicates a following short causative. These two surface reflexes of the short causative could result from input suffix doubling, something that is attested elsewhere in Lusoga, as shown in the UR given for (9c). Alternatively, the double reflex of the short causative could be the result of a-templatic IR order, in which the single short causative spirantizes the root and then the reciprocal is interfixed inside of it, an analysis Hyman has supported for Chibemba (7). On this account, short causative doubling (IRI) is illusory. We leave open for now whether the IRI ordering is required; what is clear is that both RI and IR are possible.

3.3 Reciprocal + Long Causative

We turn next to the long causative -*is*-, which, as we have seen, must co-occur with the short causative -*i*-. The most common realization when reciprocal and long causative

---

[1] While it is marginally possible for the reciprocal and passive to co-occur in some Bantu languages, typically with an impersonal subject, e.g. Ndebele *kw-a-sik-w-an-a* ~ *kw-a-sik-an-w-a* 'there was stabbing [stabbed] of each other' (Sibanda 2004: 66), we have thus far not been able to get the two to co-occur in Lusoga and will therefore ignore the passive extension in what follows.

are both present is for *-agan-* to appear between *-is-* and *-i-*, as in (11a), exhibiting the CRI order expected given the CARIP template. However, two other surface realizations are also possible:[2]

(11) 'they make each other sew'
    a. bà-[tùùng-ís-ágán-y-á   /tùùng-is-agan-i-a/   CRI
    b. bà-[tùùng-ís-ágán-á   /tùùng-is-i-agan-a/   CIR
    c. bà-[tùùng-ágán-ís-á   /tùùng-agan-is-i-a/   RCI

In (11b), *-agan-* follows *-is-i-* (CIR). In (11c) *-agan-* precedes *-is-i-* (RCI). This variation reveals the same freedom with respect to the ordering of the long causative and reciprocal extensions that we observed in §?? with respect to the ordering of the short causative and reciprocal extensions.

Note that for phonological reasons, it is impossible to distinguish between the inputs *-is-* and *-is-i-* before *-agan-*. The reason is that, sandwiched between long causative *-is-* and following vowel-initial *-agan-*, short causative *-i-* would glide to *-y-* and then get absorbed into the preceding [s], without leaving a trace. As was seen in (10), compensatory lengthening is not expected before *-agan-*. However, it can be detected between *-i-* and a FV when an enclitic such as locative class 17 *=kò* 'on it, a little' is added:

(12) 'they make each other sew a little'
    a. bà-[tùùng-ís-ágán-y-áá =kò   /tùùng-is-i-agan-i-a =kò/   CIRI + encl
    b. bà-[tùùng-ís-ágan-á =kò   /tùùng-is-i-agan-a =kò/   CIR + encl
    c. bà-[tùùng-ágán-ís-áá =kò   /tùùng-agan-is-i-a =kò/   RCI + encl

In (12a), the final length on *-aa* can be directly attributed to the gliding of the preceding *-i-*, since there is a surface [y], as can be the final length in (12c), where the glide has been absorbed into the preceding [s]. Although (12b) does not show a surface reflex of the internal *-i-*, we continue to assume that *-is-* must be accompanied by *-i-*, as also reconstructed for Proto-Bantu (Bastin 1986).

While there are three possible realizations when reciprocal *-agan-* combines with the long and short causative suffixes, the preferred surface orders are IRI in (9c), and CRI, in (11a). RI and CRI are of course predicted straightforwardly from CARIP, while the IR of IRI is not. Both early placement of C (*-is-*) in the CARIP template and the early realization of the first *-i-* of the hypothesized a-templatic IRI ordering discussed in this section are consistent with a generalization that Hyman (2003b: 272) has characterized as "causativize first!": Both *-is-* and *-i-* are spelled out early, but later affixation may result in two surface reflexes of *-i-*, either because of interfixation of subsequently added extension suffixes or because of outright morphological *-i-* doubling of the kind seen in the Chichewa RAR case illustrated in (5b).

---

[2] Since Lusoga has a /L/ vs. Ø tone system (Hyman 2016), only L(ow) vowels are marked with a grave accent in underlying forms. Vowels without an accent receive their surface tones by specific rules. H(igh) tone is marked with an acute in output forms.

3.4 Reciprocal + Applicative

The CARIP template is complicated further by the behavior of the applicative, represented by "A" in CARIP. In all three of the following examples, the transitive verb *kùb-* 'beat' is both reciprocalized 'beat each other' and applicativized. Applicative *-ir-* licenses a locative argument, expressed by the enclitic *=wà* 'where'. Here again we observe alternative affix orders:

(13) 'where do they beat each other?'
    a. bà-[kùb-ír-ágán-á =wà   AR
    b. bà-[kùb-ágán-ír-á =wà   RA
    c. bà-[kùb-ír-ágán-ír-á =wà ARA

(13a) represents the expected AR order of CARIP, while the RA order of (13b) represents an order which is closer to the compositional interpretation of the resulting verb. In (13c) *-ir-agan-ir-* has both the AR and RA orders. The variation between AR, RA and ARA orders represents a competition between the demand of the CARIP template for one order and the requirement for affixes to appear in a surface order that reflects their relative scope. The AR order (13a) is templatic; the RA order in (13b) is a scope-based or compositional override. As suggested by Hyman (2003b), ABA affix doubling can thus be interpreted as a means of satisfying both template and compositionality considerations; if the template wants AR and scope wants RA, then ARA, in some manner, satisfies both.[3]

An illustrative pair of examples is presented in (14), based on the transitive verb *bal-* 'count', which is reciprocalized and applicativized. In this instance, applicative *-ir-* licenses a benefactive object:

(14) a. bà-bì-[bál-ír-ágán-á   AR 'they count them [inanimate class 8] for each other'
      b. bà-tù-[bál-ír-ágán-á   AR 'they [animate] count each other for us' ~ 'they count us for each other'

By varying the animacy of the object pronouns in (14), it is possible to bias the scope interpretation of reciprocal and applicative in opposite directions. In (14a) the object prefix *-bi-* 'them' (class 8) represents an inanimate object such as *èbitabo* 'books' or *èbikopò* 'cups', hence animate 'each other' (referring back to *bà-* 'they') claims the benefactive rôle over inanimate *-bì-* 'them'. In this sentence the AR order *-ir-agan-* satisfies both the CARIP template and scope: [[count them] for each other]. In (14b), animate first person object *-tù-* 'us' preferentially claims the benefactive role over third person *-agan-*, again

---

[3] The questions in (13) unambiguously ask where the action took place and could therefore be answered "in Jinga" or "in the house". The absence of the applicative in the corresponding question *bà-[kùb-agan-a =wà* 'where do they beat each other?' more narrowly asks what spot or area of the body was hit. An appropriate answer would therefore be "on the head". Finally, the double reflex of applicative *-ir-* of ARA *-ir-agan-ir-* in (13c) is reminiscent of the double reflex of RAR *-an-ir-an-* in Chichewa in (5c): the sequence *-ir-agan-* is licensed by CARIP, while *-agan-ir-* represents the scope override. Concerning ABA suffix ordering, one might note that Lusoga (13c) violates Hyman's 2003 generalization, observable in Chichewa (5c), that AB always reflects the scope, while BA is templatic.

referring back to *bà-* 'they'. The *-ir-agan-* order in this sentence is also templatic, but this time need not reflect scope: Although the preferred interpretation is [[count each other] for us], the other scope ([[count us] for each other]) is also possible, though pragmatically less likely. It is thus not surprising that the two alternatives are also possible in (15) with the same meaning:

(15) 'they [animate] count each other for us'
    a. bà-tù-[bál-ágán-ír-a   RA
    b. bà-tù-[bál-ír-ágán-ír-á   ARA

Parallel to (12b,c), (15a) is a scope override, while *-ir-agan-ir-* satisfies both CARIP and scope in (15b). What is surprising is that the same possibilities are at least marginally acceptable in (16), both sentences having the same meaning.

(16) 'they count them [inanimate cl. 8] for each other'
    a. bà-bì-[bál-ágán-ír-á   RA
    b. ??bà-bì-[bál-ír-ágán-ír-á ARA

As in (15a,b), the RA sequence occurs perfectly well in (16a), while the doubled RAR sequence in (16b) was judged as sounding "Lugandish," perhaps OK to use, but seems a little funny, "like a foreigner learning Lusoga." While we have an explanation for the variation in (13b,c) and (15a,b), neither CARIP nor scope predicts that (16a,b) should be possible. We thus arrive at a major divergence from the template + scope approach that accounts for the variations considered above in Lusoga, as well as Chichewa, Chibemba, and other Bantu languages. We now address why this may be so in the next section.

4 Inflectional FV suffixes in Lusoga

In §3 we were largely able to account for surface variations in verb extension order in Lusoga by appealing to a tradeoff between the CARIP template and scope considerations: While the templatic CARIP is always available and represents the default order of affixes, conflicting orders may be licensed by scope, and template-scope interactions can even result in ABA sequences. The one major exception concerns cases of atemplatic (A)RA *-(ir)-agan-ir-*, in which a-templatic RA *-agan-ir-* cannot be said to be a compositional override. In this section we show that this unexpected ordering likely owes its existence to an optional restructuring of reciprocal *-agan-*.

To illuminate this hypothesis, we now turn to the interaction of reciprocal *-agan-* with the set of complementary inflectional "final vowel" (FV) suffixes. Every verb must end in one of these. While most verbs end in the default FV *-a*, specific TAM categories require one of two other finals, the FV *-e* or the FV complex *-ir-e*, which have the following distributions:

(17) a. "irrealis" -e : hortative/subjunctive, affirmative imperative singular with an object prefix, affirmative imperative plural, negative near future (F1)
b. "perfective" -ir-e : perfect/today past (P1), yesterday past (P2)
c. "default" -a : elsewhere

As summarized in (17a) and exemplified in (18), what unifies the uses of *-e* is its use in a subset of irrealis constructions:

(18) a. bì-[bál-è   'count them!'   (singular imperative with an object prefix; cf. bàl-à 'count!')
b. mù-[bál-è   'count (pl.)!'   (plural imperative)
c. tù-[bál-è   'let's count!'   (hortative/subjunctive)
d. tì-bá-á-[bál-è 'they will not count' (negative near future F1)

As per the general Bantu stem structure in (1), the FV follows the verb extensions, e.g. applicative *-ir-* in (19).

(19) a. bì-tù-[bàl-ír-è   'count them for us!'
b. mù-tù-[bàl-ír-è   'count (pl.) for us!'
c. tù-bà-[bàl-ír-è   'let's count for them!'
d. tì-bá-á-tú-[bál-ìr-é 'they will not count for us'

However, two options are attested when the extension is *-agan-*:

(20) a. mù-[bàl-ágàn-é   'count each other!'
tù-[bàl-ágàn-é   'let's count each other!'
tì-bá-á-[bál-àgàn-é 'they will not count each other'
b. mù-[bàl-é-gàn-é   'count (pl.) each other!'
tù-[bàl-é-gàn-é   'let's count each other!'
tì-bá-á-[bál-è-gàn-é 'they will not count each other'

The expected forms are in (20a), where reciprocal *-agan-* is followed by FV *-e*. Surprisingly, the alternatives in (20b) show the FV *-e* occurring both before and after the reciprocal. In these forms we have segmented off the first FV as *-e-*, which means that the reciprocal allomorph is *-gan-* in this context. The alternative would be to recognize a reciprocal allomorph *-egan-* which is used whenever there is an upcoming FV *-e*.[4] We will see in the discussion of perfective *-ir-e* below that the first *-e-* is correctly interpreted as a copy agreeing with the final *-e*.

The same variation obtains when the applicative suffix is present:

---

[4] It is important to note that *-e-gan-* cannot be used if the FV is *-a*: ò-kú-[bál-ágán-á 'to count each other', bà-[bàl-ágán-á 'they count each other' vs. *ò-kú-[bál-é-gán-á, *bà-[bàl-é-gán-á.

(21) a. mù-bì-[bál-ìr-àgàn-é   'count (pl.) them for each other!'
         tù-bì-[bál-ìr-àgàn-é   'let's count them for each other!'
         tì-bá-á-bí-[bál-ìr-àgàn-é 'they will not count them for each other'
    b.   mù-bì-[bál-ìr-è-gàn-é   'count (pl.) them for each other!'
         tù-bì-[bál-ìr-è-gàn-é   'let's count them for each other!'
         tì-bá-á-bí-[bál-ìr-è-gàn-é 'they will not count them for each other'

In (21), the applicative -ir- precedes the reciprocal, showing the AR order predicted by the CARIP template, but the presence of the FV between the two in the forms in (21b) is highly unusual from a Bantu point of view.

Exactly the same phenomenon of FV doubling occurs with the perfective -ir-e FV complex. As in Luganda, Lusoga -ir-e has several allomorphs. These are presented in (22) in the form they take prior to the application of phonological rules:[5]

(22) a. -ir-e   : after a CV- verb root
     b. -i- ... -e : when fused ("imbricated") into a longer verb base
     c. -i-e   : after a labial consonant and /n/
     d. -i-e   : after a fricated consonant [s] or [z], where -i- → y → Ø

The above four allomorphs are illustrated in the perfect/today past (P1) tense below:

(23) a. /tù-[tì-ir-e/   →   tù-[tì-ìr-é   'we feared'
     b. /tù-[tomer-i-e/   →   tù-[tómèir-é   'we ran into (s.o./sth.)'
     c. /tù-[tùm-i-e/   →   tù-[tùm-y-é   'we sent'
     d. /tù-[bal-i-e/   →   tù-[báz-è   'we counted'

In (23a), the /-ir-e/ allomorph is realized after the CV verb /-tì-/ 'fear'. In (23b), longer verb bases that end in a coronal consonant undergo imbrication whereby -i- metathesizes with the consonant. We will see in further examples that the reciprocal -agan- extension also undergoes imbrication to become -again-e. In (23c), the /-i-/ of /-i-e/ glides to [y].[6] In (23d), -i- fricates the preceding /l/ to [z], yielding the same derivation as in (??): /-bal-i-e/ → baz-i-e → baz-y-e → baz-e, the [y] being absorbed into the preceding fricative.

We will now illustrate each of the above allomorphs of -ir-e in (23) as they are realized with the reciprocal extension. We start with the reciprocalized version of (23b), which exhibits the imbricating -i-e perfective FV allomorph. The historically conservative variant, in which the root is followed directly by the reciprocal suffix and then the -i-e FV, is

---

[5] As was discussed at the end of §2 with respect to Proto-Bantu, we represent -ir-e as bimorphemic. In (22) we omit the passive and causative forms that occur with final -a, thereby providing even more allomorphs, e.g. the perfective of the lexicalized passive verb /-lùm-u-/ 'be in pain' is tù-[lùm-íír-w-à 's/he was in pain', while the perfect of the lexicalized causative verb /-tèm-i-/ 'blink' is tù-[tèm-ííz-à 'we blinked', where r → z is triggered by the causative suffix /-i-/. Both occur with a long -iir- morph followed by -a. As seen in these examples, the fact that -a is used with passive -u- and causative -i- provides additional evidence that -ir- is a separate morpheme from -e or -a.

[6] The following -e actually lengthens, but then is shortened by a rule of final vowel shortening (FVS), which converts à-lím-y-èè to à-lím-y-è. Thus compare the long vowel in à-[lím-y-↓éé =kò which is realized when an enclitic follows. (↓ indicates a downstepped high tone).

shown in (24a). However, the preferred alternative is (24b), in which the perfective -i-e appears, imbricated, both immediately following the root AND immediately following the reciprocal. URs showing both a single and a doubled FV complex are provided for each form:

(24) 'we ran into each other'
    a. /tù-[tomer-agan-i-e/   tù-[tómèr-àgàin-é
    b. /tù-[tomer-i-e-agan-i-e/ tù-[tómèir-è-gàin-é

A parallel situation obtains in (25), which corresponds to (23c):

(25) 'we sent each other'
    a. /tù-[tùm-agan-i-e/   tù-[tùm-àgàin-é
    b. /tù-[tùm-i-e-agan-i-e/   tù-[tùm-y-è-gàin-é

Example (26), based on (23d), shows similar facts, the main difference being the frication triggered by causative -i- on the verb root -bal- 'count':

(26) 'we counted each other'
    a. /tù-[bal-agan-i-e/   tù-[bál-àgàin-é
    b. /tù-[bal-i-e-gan-i-e/   tù-[báz-è-gàin-é

Finally, in (27), we see a reciprocalized version of the root in (23a), which, on its own, would take the -ir-e FV allomorph. The historical variant is shown in (27a), but the preferred variant, with doubled FV, is given in (27b):

(27) 'we feared each other'
    a. /tù-[tì-agan-i-e/   tù-ty-àgàin-é
    b. /tù-[tì-ir-e-gan-i-e/   tù-tì-ìr-è-gàin-é

As before there are two instances of the perfective in (27b), vs. one in (27a). In this case of doubling, however, the allomorphy of the perfective is different in the two copies. The first copy of the FV follows a CV root and assumes the expected -ir-e form; the second copy, following the longer -agan-, assumes the imbricating -i-e form. The fact that the allomorphs are different suggests that the two copies are generated independently.

In sum, both the irrealis -e FV and the perfective FV allomorphs can appear once in a reciprocalized verb, or twice, with the double spell-out being clearly preferred. We now turn to an analysis of these facts in §5.

5 Towards an analysis

From the perspective of familiar cross-linguistic principles of affix ordering (derivation closer to the root than inflection; prohibition on multiple exponence), Lusoga presents two interesting puzzles: (i) derivational and inflectional suffixes both double; (ii) when inflectional suffixes double, they do so on either side of derivation, violating the "split morphology" hypothesis. Thus, in a form like tù-[bàl-é-gàn-é 'let's count each other' from (20b), the irrealis FV -e occurs both before and after the derivational reciprocal suffix -gan-. While doubling of derivational suffixes has been previously discussed in the Bantu literature (Hyman 2003b), the doubling of inflection has not. This is the final focus of this study. Given that the doubling occurs in verbs containing the reciprocal suffix -agan-, the question we face is what it is about this suffix that triggers the phenomenon. Why is it only the reciprocal that does this?

Our hypothesis is that the phonological form of the reciprocal has led to a reanalysis of the internal morphological structure of the reciprocalized Lusoga verb stem. The reciprocal suffix -agan- is the only Lusoga derivational suffix which is both disyllabic and a-initial. Taken together, these phonological facts are consistent with a reanalysis of the verb stem in which the reciprocal suffix is bimorphemic, -a-gan. Because of its phonological identity, the -a- portion became identified with the default FV -a. At the same time this permitted the reanalyzed reciprocal suffix, -gan-, to conform to the default -CVC- verb root structure.

As a result of this reanalysis, the verb structure in (28a) became reinterpreted as in (28b), where we use # to indicate the internal stem boundary:

(28) a. *Expected (inherited)*   b. *Unexpected (innovated)*
      Root-Reciprocal-FV   Root-FV#Reciprocal-FV
      Root-agan-a   Root-a#gan-a

From this step, the following analogical reanalyses follow straightforwardly, with allomorph variation in (29b) conditioned by the phonological size and shape of the root:

(29) a. *Expected (inherited)*   b. *Unexpected (innovated)*
      Root-agan-e   Root-e#gan-e   (irrealis)
      Root-agan-ir-e   Root-ir-e#gan-ir-e   (perfective)

In (29a) inflectional -e and -ir-e are suffixed after derivational -agan-. (We show the perfective as -ir-e in the above, although its exact allomorph will vary, as pointed out in (22).) In (29b) we see the reanalysis brought on by analogy. As a result, from the simple right-branching suffixing construction in (29a), reciprocal verb stems became reanalyzed, optionally, as compounding, with two roots: the verb root, and -gan-. Both are inflectable (29b), though it is possible also to inflect only the verb stem as a whole (29a).

As indicated, the compounding account allows us to account for the apparent affixation of the inflectional suffixes -e and -ir-e inside of a derivational suffix, the restructured reciprocal -gan-. These suffixes also potentially precede the short causative -i-. The inflection of stems containing both -(a)gan- and the short causative is seen in the following six alternants, based on the causative verb -lùm-i- 'injure', where -i- glides to [y] before the following vowel:[7]

---

[7] Although the verb root -lùm- means 'bite', the semantics of the lexicalized causative verb -lùm-ì- 'injure, cause pain' is most clearly seen in the corresponding lexicalized passive verb -lùm-ù- 'to ache, be in pain'.

(30) 'let's injure each other'
    a.   tù-[lùm-y-ágàn-é
           tù-[lùm-ágàn-y-é
           tù-[lùm-y-ágàn-y-é
    b.   tù-[lùm-y-é-gàn-é
           tù-[lùm-é-gàn-y-é
           tù-[lùm-y-é-gàn-y-é

The options in (30a) all follow the expected parsing, with *-agan-* treated as a derivational suffix. Those in (30b) represent the claimed restructuring in which the FV *-e* occurs both before and after reciprocal *-gan-*. In each set, causative *-i-* appears immediately after the root in the first example, after the reciprocal in the second, and both before and after in the third. In the last two examples of (30b), the first (inflectional) *-e* occurs not only before *-gan-*, but also before the (derivational) causative *-i-* suffix. Parallel cases could be illustrated in which *-i-* combines with the various perfective allomorphs. Our analysis, which assumes a double or compound stem structure, each of which is independently inflected, thus nicely accounts for the above (and other) cases where the inflectional FV linearly precedes (restructured) reciprocal *-gan-* and potentially other derivational suffixes.

(31)

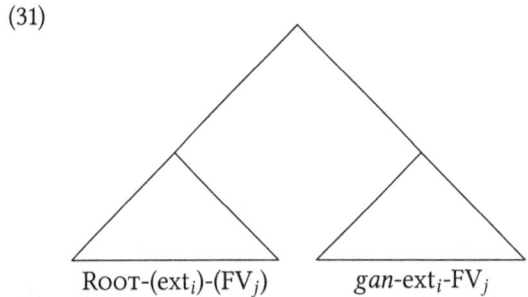

    Root-(ext$_i$)-(FV$_j$)   gan-ext$_i$-FV$_j$

Before moving on to our conclusion, we briefly cite phonological evidence for our analysis from closely related Lulamogi, which also optionally realizes the inflectional FV both before and after reciprocal *-gan-* (Hyman In press). In this language, there are two facts concerning vowel length and (pre-)penultimate position that are relevant to the analysis of the reciprocal. First, a word-initial V- prefix lengthens if it is followed by a monosyllabic stem (i.e. if it is in penultimate position). This is seen in (32a):

(32) a. /a-[ti-â/ → àà-[ty-â 's/he fears'
       b. /ba-[ti-â/ → bà-[ty-â 'they fear'
       c. /a-[sék-a/ → à-[sék-à 's/he laughs'

As seen in (32b), if the word-initial prefix has the shape CV-, its vowel doesn't lengthen, while in (32c) /a-/ fails to lengthen because it is in pre-penultimate position. The second length-related phenomenon is exemplified in (33):

(33) a. /tu-[á-ti-a/   →   tw-áá-[ty-à   'we will fear'
     b. /tu-á-[sek-a/ →   tw-á-[sèk-á   'we will laugh'

In (33a), the prefix sequence /tu-á-/ (1PL-FUT) undergoes gliding + compensatory lengthening to be realized [tw-áá-] in penultimate position. In (33b), on the other hand, the same gliding process applies, but the result is short [tw-á-], since prefixal vowel sequences are realized short in pre-penultimate position.

A systematic exception to both penultimate prefixal V-lengthening and pre-penultimate prefixal V+V shortening occurs when reciprocal -agan- is suffixed to a monosyllabic verb root:

(34) a. àà-[ty-ágán-à   's/he often fears'
     b. tw-áá-[ty-àgàn-á   'we will fear each other'

In (34a), where -agan- is used as a frequentative suffix, the initial subject prefix à- lengthens even though it is in pre-penultimate position. In (34b), the [tw-áá-] sequence remains long even though it too is in pre-penultimate position. Note also that the first vowel of the -ty-àgàn- sequence is short, i.e. compensatory lengthening appears not to apply. All of these observations can be accounted for if we assume the same analysis as in Lusoga:

(35) a. /a-ti-a#gan-a/   →   àà-ty-ágán-à   's/he often fears'
     b. /tu-á-ti-a#gan-a/   →   tw-áá-ty-àgàn-á   'we will fear each other'

In (35) the # symbol again represents the boundary between the two stems. The result in (35a) is that the initial /a-/ is now in penultimate position in the first stem and is thus free to lengthen. In (35b) the /tu-á-/ is now also in penultimate position, and so [tw-áá-] fails to shorten. Taken alone, either our Lusoga analysis or this Lulamogi analysis of Hyman (In press) might seem overly speculative—and especially surprising from a traditional Bantu perspective. However, taken together, the two sets of facts support each other. In fact, Lulamogi is the only other Bantu language we are aware of that allows the option of spelling out the FV both before and after the reciprocal extension. Thus compare the following with Lusoga (20a,b):

(36) 'let's count each other'
     a. tú-[bàl-àgàn-é
     b. tú-[bàl-è-gàn-é

As we stated earlier, we think this reconceptualization is due to the fact that -agan- is the only highly productive suffix that could be re-interpreted in the way we have suggested. It is significant that the historical Bantu reciprocal suffix *-an- often joins with other suffixes to make a -VCVC- conglomerate (cf. Bostoen & Nzang-Bie 2010: 1289–91 for further discussion). In Lusoga, Lulamogi, Luganda, and many other Bantu languages, *-an- has joined with an archaic *-ang- or *-ag- extension which likely had an original pluractional interpretation.[8] As we have suggested, the shape and "weightiness" of the resulting -agan- has led to multiple exponence and inflectional "entrapment" within the derivational morphology of the verb stem in Lusoga (and Lulamogi). We consider further implications in the next section.

6 Conclusion

In the preceding sections we have documented multiple exponence of derivational suffixes (§3) and inflectional suffixes (§4) in Lusoga, and have proposed a restructuring analysis of *-agan- > -a-gan- in §5 to account for the multiple copies of the inflectional FV in -e-gan- sequences. Harris & Faarlund (2006) discuss instances in which grammaticalization of an outer affix "traps" an inner one, with the result that the two affixes occur in an unexpected order. Loss of the trapped affix is an attested diachronic repair for this "entrapment" situation; doubling (by addition of an outer inflectional affix) is another. Lusoga, however, appears to illustrate reanalysis of a different kind, in which an existing affix is reanalyzed as a root, and doubling represents agreement in a compounding-like structure of the sort proposed by Inkelas & Zoll (2005) for reduplication, in which doubled morphemes can also show divergent allomorphy of the kind displayed by the perfective complex in Lusoga. If correct, the Lusoga facts are important both from a synchronic and diachronic point of view. An historical change of *affix > root would contradict the more broadly attested grammaticalization pattern *root > affix (but see Norde 2009). Synchronically, multiple exponence of the inflectional ending is quite different from the doubling of derivational suffixes. While the latter has been interpreted as the resolution of a template-scope mismatch, perhaps spelled out cyclically, this cannot work for inflectional doubling. In the examples in (30) above, it was seen that the derivational causative -i- can appear once or twice: It can appear either before the reciprocal (-i-agan-), after it (-agan-i-), or both before or after (-i-agan-i-). However, we have thus only shown two possibilities concerning inflectional FVs such as subjunctive -e. In (20), repeated as (37a,b), we saw that -e can appear either after -agan- or both before and after -agan-:

(37) a. mù-[bàl-ágàn-é   'count each other!'
         tù-[bàl-ágàn-é   'let's count each other!'
         tì-ba-a-[bál-àgàn-é 'they will not count each other'
     b. mù-[bàl-é-gàn-é   'count (pl.) each other!'
         tù-[bàl-é-gàn-é   'let's count each other!'
         tì-bá-á-[bál-è-gàn-á 'they will not count each other'
     c. *mù-[bàl-é-gàn-á   'count each other!'
         *tù-[bàl-é-gàn-á   'let's count each other!'
         *tì-bá-á-[bál-è-gàn-á 'they will not count each other'

---

[8] While the most general realization of the reciprocal is -agan- in Luganda, the form is regularly -aŋŋan- after CV verb roots, e.g. mw-aŋŋan- 'shave each other'. Since -aŋŋan- derives from *-angan- via Meinhof's Law (Katamba & Hyman 1991: 192–193), this provides evidence that the earlier bimorphemic form was likely *-ang-an- in all three closely related languages.

However, (37c) shows that it is not possible to express the inflection only on the first stem. These facts motivate the compounding structure we have offered for the Lusoga verb stem, and suggest that the second member, on which inflection is obligatory, is the head, and agreement in derivational and inflectional properties is optionally enforced, explaining the presence of duplicate morphology on the first constituent. The structures in (37) are not amenable to a cyclic analysis proceeding bottom-up from the verb root.

In Lusoga, compounding, derivation and inflection are intermingled in typologically unusual ways. The complexities of the system – and of multiple exponence in general (Anderson 2015: 21) – give credence to views in which morphology is a component of grammar with its own internal morphotactic organization; it does not mirror syntax directly and thus cannot be reduced to syntactic principles. This is a result of which we think Steve would approve.

References

Abasheikh, Mohammad. 1978. *The grammar of Chimwi:ni causatives*. University of Illinois PhD thesis.
Anderson, Stephen R. 1992. *A-morphous morphology*. Cambridge: Cambridge University Press.
Anderson, Stephen R. 2015. Dimensions of morphological complexity. In Matthew Baerman, Dunstan Brown & Greville G. Corbett (eds.), *Understanding and measuring morphological complexity*, 11–26. Oxford: Oxford University Press.
Bastin, Yvonne. 1983. *La finale -IDE et l'imbrication en bantou*. Annales, Série IN-8, Sciences Humaines 114. Tervuren: Musée Royal de l'Afrique Centrale.
Bastin, Yvonne. 1986. Les suffixes causatifs dans les langues bantoues. *Africana Linguistica* 10. Tervuren: Annales du Musée Royale de l'Afrique Centrale. Série IN-8, Sciences Humaines 121, 55–145.
Bostoen, Koen & Yolande Nzang-Bie. 2010. On how "middle" plus "associative/reciprocal" became "passive" in the Bantu A70 languages. *Linguistics* 48(6). 1255–1307.
Downing, Laura J. 2005. Jita causative doubling and paradigm uniformity. In Laura J. Downing, T. Alan Hall & Renate Raffelsiefen (eds.), *Paradigms in phonological theory*, 122–144. Oxford: Oxford University Press.
Good, Jeff. 2005. Reconstructing morpheme order in Bantu: the case of causativization and applicativization. *Diachronica* 22(1). 55–109.
Harris, Alice & Jan Terje Faarlund. 2006. Trapped morphology. *Journal of Linguistics* 42. 289–315.
Hyman, Larry M. 1994. Cyclic phonology and morphology in Cibemba. In Jennifer Cole & Charles Kisseberth (eds.), *Perspectives in phonology*, 81–112. Stanford: C.S.L.I.
Hyman, Larry M. 2003a. Sound change, misanalysis, and analogy in the Bantu causative. *Journal of African Languages and Linguistics* 24(1). 24–55.
Hyman, Larry M. 2003b. Suffix ordering in Bantu: A morphocentric approach. In Geert Booij & Jaap van Marle (eds.), *Yearbook of morphology 2002*, 245–281. Amsterdam: Springer.

Hyman, Larry M. 2016. *The autosegmental approach to tone in Lusoga*. Tech. rep. Ms. University of California, Berkeley.

Hyman, Larry M. In press. Prefixal vowel length in Lulamogi: a stratal account. *Journal of African Languages and Linguistics*.

Hyman, Larry M. & Sam Mchombo. 1992. Morphotactic constraints in the Chichewa verb stem. In *Proceedings of the Berkeley Linguistic Society*. Berkeley Linguistic Society.

Inkelas, Sharon & Cheryl Zoll. 2005. *Reduplication: Doubling in morphology*. Cambridge: Cambridge University Press.

Katamba, Francis & Larry M. Hyman. 1991. Nasality and morpheme structure constraints in Luganda. In Francis Katamba (ed.), *Lacustrine Bantu phonology* (Afrikanistiche Arbeitspapiere 25), 175–211. Cologne: Institut für Afrikanistik, Universität zu Köln.

Kiparsky, Paul. 1982. Lexical morphology and phonology. In Linguistic Society of Korea (ed.), *Linguistics in the morning calm: Selected papers from SICOL–1981*, 3–91. Seoul: Hanshin.

Meeussen, Achille E. 1967. Bantu grammatical reconstructions. *Africana Linguistica* 3(1). 79–121.

Muriungi, Peter Kinyua. 2003. *Phrasal movement inside Bantu verbs*. University of Tromsø PhD thesis.

Norde, Muriel. 2009. *Degrammaticalization*. Oxford: Oxford University Press.

Sibanda, Galen. 2004. *Verbal phonology and morphology of Ndebele*. University of California, Berkeley PhD thesis.

Chapter 10

Romansh allomorphy (Again!)

Martin Maiden
Oxford University

> This essay resumes a debate which has continued for some years between me and Stephen Anderson regarding the correct analysis of a complex set of data from the verb morphology of the Romansh dialect of Savognin. Anderson believes that the data are an example of "phonologically conditioned allomorphy", whilst I maintain that they exemplify "morphomic", or autonomously morphological, alternation patterns, whose only phonological motivation lies in diacrhrony. I reply below to Anderson's most recent analysis of the data, by discussing reasons in support of my "morphomic" account. I conclude, however, by considering the possibility that our two accounts may be too exclusivist in their respective "phonologizing" and "morphologizing" stances, and that they are not necessarily wholly incompatible.

1 Introduction

Some readers might regard this essay as an example of chutzpah, or downright impertinence, but it is a sincere mark of respect for Steve Anderson that I feel able to disagree with him even in a collection published in his honour. One would not do this with a less intellectually generous scholar. What follows is, in fact, a further instalment in an amicable difference of opinion I have had with him for some years (see Anderson 2008; Anderson 2011b; Maiden 2011b; Anderson 2013) concerning the analysis of a set of data from some Romansh dialects, and principally, the Surmiran variety spoken in Savognin. Readers, and not least the honorand himself, may be feeling that there is little left to say. That there is reason to continue the debate is suggested, for example, by Andrea Sims' deft review of the issues (Sims 2015: 202–206), to which I return in my conclusion.

Anderson's analysis displays not only his characteristically penetrating theoretical rigour, but also a quite formidable grasp of the data. Reasons of space, and the fact that the data are lucidly laid out by him in previous publications (e.g., Anderson 2008, 2011) permit me to do no more here than summarize them: Savognin has a recurrent pattern of vocalic alternations] in the verb root (or "stem"), such that one alternant occurs in the root of the singular and third person forms of the present indicative imperative, throughout the present subjunctive, and also in third conjugation infinitives, while another occurs in the root in the remainder of the paradigm. What is involved originates

Martin Maiden. 2017. Romansh allomorphy (Again!) In Claire Bowern, Laurence Horn & Raffaella Zanuttini (eds.), *On looking into words (and beyond)*, 189–211. Berlin: Language Science Press. DOI:10.5281/zenodo.495446

as alternation in vowel quality, phonologically conditioned by stress. The distinctions between stressed and unstressed positions may additionally manifest as differences in the number of syllables in the root, and in sundry consonantal alternations, including metathesis. In fact, what Savognin (and Romansh generally) exhibits is an unusually florid manifestation (in respect of the range of different alternation types involved) of a pattern of alternation recurrently attested across Romance languages, and I have argued extensively (e.g., Maiden 2005; 2011c) that it arose historically because of stress-related vowel differentiation, but then became "autonomously morphological" or "morphomic" in nature, being no longer determined by stress, but simply by the heterogeneous set of paradigm cells, one property of which is that they are "rhizotonic" (i.e., stressed on the lexical root). This set I label (for reasons that are here unimportant) the "N-pattern". Important diachronic proof that the N-pattern is independent of phonological causation is the rise in various Romance languages of alternation patterns whose phonological content cannot possibly ever have been determined by stress (including lexical suppletion), but which replicates the pattern originally "etched out" by the effects of stress. The distribution of alternation found in Savognin constitutes a widespread variant of this "N-pattern".[1] There is no space to recapitulate all the data and arguments, but crucially Anderson (e.g., 2010: 25;2011: 34f;2013: 10,16,23;2011: 173) accepts the "morphomic" nature of the "N-pattern" and its importance in determining morphological change in the Romance verb generally. He believes, however, that modern Savognin (and other Romansh varieties: cf. Anderson 2013) is, in effect, a "special case", indeed a prime example of 'phonologically conditioned allomorphy'. He convincingly shows that the alternation types involved have often become so disparate, and refractory to unique underlying representation, that they must be represented directly in the grammar, but he also argues that the alternant-pairs characteristically contain one member more suited to appear under stress, and another more suited to appear in unstressed position (Anderson 2011b: 18), and that the alternants are accordingly conditioned by the presence vs absence of stress. He also shows that the position of stress in Savognin is systematically predictable from the segmental content of the word-form. It follows that the alternations are fully predictable from the position of stress, and that appeal to the "N-pattern" is inappropriate. My response, *in nuce*, has been that there exist nonetheless within Savognin morphological phenomena that really are irreducibly "morphomic" and follow the N-pattern. Given this, I say that Anderson misses an important generalization by divorcing the vocalic alternations from clear-cut cases of the N-pattern. Anderson's response is, in effect, that my alleged N-pattern examples are secondary effects of the principle of stress-related allomorph selection, and that invocation of the morpheme risks missing another significant generalization, namely that the alleged stress-related alternations found in the verb are found across the grammar, outside the verb.

I need to comment briefly on a methodological assumption. Steve Anderson objected to me orally some years ago (cf. also Anderson 2011b: 13f.;17) that I could not draw in-

---

[1] Savognin is among a number of Romance dialects where the N-pattern alternant also appears in the first and second persons plural present subjunctive. The reasons are complex and not immediately relevant here (cf. Maiden 2012).

ferences about Savognin from apparently parallel developments in other Romance languages for which my "morphomic" analysis seemed correct, observing quite reasonably that the inhabitants of Savognin were "not Romance linguists" (and therefore could not know about what happens in other Romance languages). My very delayed response is, in effect: "Yes, but they are still Romance speakers". Let us suppose that in some other Romance variety, distant both historically and geographically (a real case is Romanian), virtually identical patterns of alternation are found, except that this time they are clearly morphomic; let us further assume that the analysis appropriate to, say, Romanian is perfectly *possible* for Romansh, even though rival possible accounts exist. Obviously native speakers of Romansh are not native speakers of Romanian, nor are they Romance linguists enjoying Olympian vistas over comparative Romance morphology: nothing we could say about Romanian could ever be definitively probative for Romansh. What does not follow, however, is that the comparative evidence can be ignored. Speakers of both languages obviously have the same mental endowment, and both languages have inherited much that is structurally common, particularly with regard to the organization of the inflexional morphology of the verb. What this means is that an analysis which is *justified* for Romanian deserves consideration as *plausible* for Romansh. The Romance languages ought not to be treated as hermetically isolated entities: rather, the analysis of one variety should always be allowed to inform that of another. That, in fact, is one of the reasons for doing Romance linguistics from a comparative perspective (in fact, there is no other way of doing it), and in the following pages the analysis will frequently be guided, with all due caution, by comparisons and inferences across cognate but separate varieties. I now examine the facts which seem to me to require acknowledgement of the morphomic N-pattern in Savognin.

2 Suppletion: dueir and deir

The verb *dueir* 'must, be obliged to (cf. German *sollen*)' (from Latin DEBERE) plays a central role in the debate, because it has a suppletive root allomorph in precisely that set of cells which, in other verbs, displays the "stressed" alternant (Table 1):

Table 1: *Dueir* in Savognin

INF	duéir					
PST.PART	duía					
GER	duónd					
	1SG	2SG	3SG	1PL	2PL	3PL
PRS.IND	stó	stóst	stó	duágn	duéz	stón
PRS.SBJV	stóptga	stóptgas	stóptga	stóptgan	stóptgas	stóptgan
IPF.IND	duéva	duévas	duéva	duévan	duévas	duévan
COND	duéss	duéssas	duéssa	duéssan	duéssas	duéssan

The suppletive forms are taken from another verb, *stueir* 'must, be necessarily the case (cf. German *müssen*)', which unlike *dueir* continues to have its own complete paradigm (Table 2):

Table 2: *Stueir* in Savognin

	1SG	2SG	3SG	1PL	2PL	3PL
INF	*stuéir*					
PST.PART	*stuía*					
GER	*stuónd*					
PRS. IND	stó	stóst	stó	stuágn	stuéz	stón
PRS. SBJV	stóptga	stóptgas	stóptga	stóptgan	stóptgas	stóptgan
IPF	stuéva	stuévas	stuéva	stuévan	stuévas	stuévan
COND	stuéss	stuéssas	stuéssa	stuéssan	stuéssas	stuéssan

For Anderson (2008; 2010) *dueir* is a defective verb and its pattern of alternation is a matter of phonologically conditioned allomorphy: he believes that the explanation of the suppletion is that *dueir* lacks a stressed stem-alternant, having only unstressed /dʊ/. Since /dʊ/ contains a vowel whose phonological characteristics debar it from occurring under stress, speakers in effect plug the resultant phonological gap by borrowing appropriate stressed forms from a near synonym of *dueir*, namely *stueir*. My view, from comparative and diachronic evidence, is that it is highly unlikely that *dueir* could ever have been, in any relevant sense, "defective", and that even if it were, the filling of the alleged gap could have nothing to do with phonology. Indeed, any explanation in terms of phonological conditioning crucially fails to account for the fine details of the allomorphy. If I am correct, and what we observe is a pattern of allomorphy identical in distribution to the vocalic alternations, yet independent of phonology, then in principle whatever explains the paradigmatic distribution of forms of *dueir* should also be available to explain the vocalic alternations. Indeed, considerations of economy would lead us to prefer that single explanation. This is a view that I have expounded before (e.g., Maiden 2011b: 46–49), while Anderson, in his latest discussion 2013: 8 states that there are no new facts, and that we simply disagree. I think that the facts remain very important, and I (re-)present them below in a slightly revised form.

The 'defectiveness' of *dueir* is the effect, not the cause, of the suppletion. All suppletive verbs whose morphology reflects the incursion of forms of the paradigm of one lexeme on the paradigm of another are, in one sense, "defective". If, for example, Grisch (1939: 89f.n5), *DRG* s.v. *dovair*, p.378, Decurtins (1958: 155;158), or Signorell, Wuethrich-Grisch & Simeon (1987: 165f), describe Romansh reflexes of DEBERE as "defective", this simply means that there are parts of the paradigm occupied by forms which are patently unconnected (diachronically or synchronically) with *dueir*, and which obviously are connected with *stueir*. This does not mean that the paradigm of the lexeme meaning 'must' somehow has "holes" in it.

One might object that the independent existence of *stueir* as a verb with its own full paradigm (and indeed with its own distinctive meaning, as I explain shortly) is grounds to view those forms of it which appear inside *dueir* as synchronic interlopers drafted in to occupy otherwise "empty territory". Such reasoning would force us into the highly counterintuitive position of claiming, for example, that Savognin *esser* 'to be' is "defective" in respect of its past participle, because the latter has the form *sto* which is also (and transparently) the past participle of a different verb, *star* 'to stand'. This is actually a case where there was, *historically*, defectiveness: the Latin ancestor of *esser* had no past participle, for semantic reasons. It is only with the rise in early Romance of verbal periphrases comprising auxiliary + past participle, that the verb 'be' needs to fill the past participle "slot", and it does so (in some regions) by supplying the missing form from the past participle of STARE 'stand'. But the idea that, in modern Romansh, the verb 'be' lacks a past participle and "borrows" it from *star* seems peculiar, given that the verb 'be' itself, and the use of forms of it involving its past participle, are utterly basic. Indeed, to the best of my knowledge no grammarian of the Romance languages has ever described the wholesale suppletion of 'be' in the Romance languages as involving "defectiveness". If one can analyse Savognin *esser* as suppletive but not defective, then surely the same analysis should be available for *dueir*.

My principal difficulty with Anderson's analysis of *dueir* is that I see absolutely no motivation to view this verb as defective, beyond the morphological facts which are the explanandum. All its cells are well and truly *filled* — and it is almost inconceivable that a subset of present-tense cells of a verb expressing such a basic meaning could ever be empty. Here, again, a comparative perspective is useful. Virtually all Romance languages conserve reflexes of DEBERE, with a full inflexional paradigm, and no Romance languages show any sign of defectiveness in the verb meaning 'must', whatever its origin: there is no reason for parts of its paradigm to be missing. Many Romansh dialects indeed have a full paradigm all of whose forms still continue DEBERE (see Decurtins 1958: 152f. *DRG* s.v. *dovair*), and the rhizotonic forms (usually *dé-*) are robustly attested from the earliest records, including in central dialects (of which Savognin is one); cf. also Anderson (2010: 30;32). There is simply nothing in the phonology of these dialects, either synchronically or diachronically, which could have determined *deletion* of such stressed forms, and the defectiveness certainly cannot be explained as a phonological effect of stress.[2]

Anderson (2010: 32) suggests that "the primary factor in the emergence of defectiveness in Surmiran *dueir*, as well as the complementary pattern in the Engadine languages, was the morphologization of the vowel alternations in Swiss Rumantsch. If we hypothesize that this was combined with reduced use of the verb due to competition with others such as *stueir*, it could well have led to the present situation with only one stem

---

[2] Could a stress-based account be salvaged if, unlike Anderson, one said that *any* kind of alternation, including an alternation where one of the alternants was zero, could be effected by stress? Given that the position of stress in Savognin is predictable on grounds of segmental phonological content, one can hardly invoke the case of zero alternants which would, by definition, lack any segmental content. The best one could say is that zero forms appear in those parts of the paradigm where stress *would normally be expected* to appear. But then one would have to ask: "Where would stress normally be expected to appear?", and the answer would be purely morphological: "the N-pattern".

conserved". I discuss later the nature of the "competition" from *stueir*, which involves overlap and replacement, not defectiveness. As for the alternation, regular sound change would indeed have given rise to a unique alternation between a stressed alternant /de/, and unstressed alternant /du/ (in the latter the back vowel is the result of an adjustment of the unstressed front vowel triggered in the environment of a following labial consonant: cf. Italian 3SG.PRS.IND *déve* vs INF *dovére*). But the notion that Romansh would eliminate an alternation type because it was "morphologized" (or, perhaps better, idiosyncratic and unpredictable), especially in such a high-frequency verb, seems unlikely, particularly given that Romansh is notable for retaining extreme and idiosyncratic patterns of vocalic alternation, even in isolated verbs which surely have a much lower frequency of use. Rogers (1972), in an analysis of Surselvan, lists no fewer than eleven sets of vocalic alternation each apparently limited to just one verb, with meanings such as 'vomit', 'scythe', 'drivel' - all without sign of resort to defectiveness; see also my discussion of Savognin *deir* 'say', below. One might add that the most natural response to any idiosyncratic type of alternation would surely be not to create a "gap", by jettisoning one alternant, but to attempt some kind of "repair" by analogically remodelling the alternants to be less different.[3] The last thing one expects is a reaction resulting in an alternation which, by virtue of being suppletive, is even stranger than the rejected original.

Viewed in a comparative-historical perspective, the notion that the Savognin reflexes of DEBERE could be in any significant sense "defective" seems most unlikely. And even if it were defective, the suppletive filling of the alleged gaps would take place because the *gaps* needed filling, not specifically because of the lack of a "stressed" alternant. What that perspective does suggest, however, is a different scenario (see also Maiden 2011b: 46–49), which involves not "gaps" but "overabundance" (cf. Thornton 2011), in which more than one realization became available for certain cells of the paradigm of *dueir*, and in which one of the alternative realizations ultimately prevails. This situation arises from particular discourse-related circumstances. The reflexes of DEBERE are subject in Romansh and beyond to intensive competition from other nearly synonymous alternatives.[4] I have no space to detail the facts or the mechanisms (see Maiden 2011b),[5] but essentially what appears to be involved is "face-saving": speakers avoid the charge of moral obligation inherent especially in present indicative forms of *dueir* by resorting to alternatives such as expressions equivalent to 'ought' (e.g., conditional forms of the verb), or expressions meaning "absolute" (rather then "moral") necessity, which is exactly expressed by *stueir*. This tendency created, I suggested, a situation in which the frequent use of *stueir* alongside *dueir* in the present tense led to effective synonymy between the two forms, eventually resolved by replacing *dueir* with *stueir* according to the familiar pattern of alternation (the "N-pattern") associated with vocalic allomorphy (a type of

---

[3] In any case, Savognin stems do sometimes have "inappropriate" forms. Thus Anderson (2011b: 32) discusses verbs such *baitár* 'babble' which has a stem suitable for stress only, but which is is nonetheless used throughout the paradigm in unstressed environments as well.

[4] See further Stürzinger (1879: 49); Tagliavini (1926: 84); Kramer (1976: 64); Maiden (2011a)

[5] In addition to the sources cited by Maiden (2011a), see also Pult (1897: 166f.) for the suppletive introduction of forms of the verb 'want' in the dialect of Sent.

reaction to synonymy attested elsewhere in Romance: cf.Maiden 2004; 2006). The same paradigmatic distribution, reflexes of DEBERE alternating this time with those of CONUENIRE (originally meaning 'be fitting'), emerges from *ALDII* (maps 829–833; 836–838), for Peio (point 54) and S. Michele all'Adige (point 66). The disappearance of reflexes of DEBERE from certain cells of the present indicative and the present subjunctive of *dueir* never involved "defectiveness", and has never had anything to do with phonology. The perception of "defectiveness" is a synchronic *effect* of the suppletion.

Crucially, the suppletive fusion of *dueir* and *stueir* in Savognin is of a significantly different kind from the alleged phonologically conditioned allomorphy of the vocalic alternations. The latter is a *binary* correspondence between alternants and stress: one alternant is selected under stress, the other elsewhere. The putative relation between the *dueir* - *stueir* alternation and stress can only be described as binary at a level which is in fact lacking any phonological content. For what, in the case of the suppletion, is allegedly selected by stress is not *a form* correlated with stress, but a whole array of phonologically and morphologically different forms. As Anderson himself points out 2008: 124,[6] "it is not just a single stem, but the full range of irregular forms of *stueir* (*ia stò, te stost, el stò, els ston*; Subjunctive *ia stoptga,* etc.) that replaces those of *dueir* where stress would fall on the stem".[7] More exactly: "the first and second person singular, and third person, forms of the indicative of *stueir* are mapped onto the first and second person singular, and third person, forms of the indicative of *dueir*, and the present subjunctive cells of *stueir* are mapped onto the corresponding cells of *dueir*". Only this way do we get the observed distribution. In effect, it is not "a stem", but an entire, morphomically defined, "slab", of the paradigm of *stueir*, a set of full word-forms replete with their own internal allomorphic idiosyncrasies, that has been mapped onto *dueir*. A rule of phonologically conditioned allomorphy involving stress could in principle select *a* stressed root allomorph of *stueir* and introduce it into *dueir*, but it could not necessarily insert the *right* root allomorph in the relevant cell. A rule that identifies a morphologically-defined portion of the paradigm as that in which the replacement of one lexeme by the other can do just that.

Dueir exemplifies lexical suppletion ("incursion", in the terminology of Corbett 2007), where one historically distinct lexeme obtrudes on the inflexional paradigm of another lexeme. Another diachronic route to suppletion is regular sound change so extreme in its effects that the synchronic result is allomorphy such that the alternants bear no phonological relation to each other. Savognin has at least one case of phonologically induced suppletion, namely *deir* 'say', which inflects as in Table 3:

---

[6] Anderson (2010: 29) even calls this verb "suppletive".

[7] As mentioned earlier, if we ask "where stress would fall on the stem", the answer is ineluctably morphological: in the cells of the singular and third person present and imperative and in the present subjunctive. It seems to me useless to say, instead, "wherever the endings would be unstressed" because the third person singular has no ending, and the distribution of the remaining, unstressed, endings turns out to be the morphomic N-pattern.

Table 3: *Deir* in Savognin

PST.PART	*détg*					
GER	*schónd*					
	1SG	2SG	3SG	1PL	2PL	3PL
PRS. IND	*déi*	*déist*	*déi*	*schágn*	*schéz*	*déian*
PRS. SBJV	*schéia*	*schéias*	*schéia*	*schéian*	*schéias*	*schéian*
IPF	*schéva*	*schévas*	*schéva*	*schévan*	*schévas*	*schévan*
COND	*schéss*	*schéssas*	*schéssa*	*schéssan*	*schéssas*	*schéssan*

I cannot here retrace the phonological history of this verb in detail. Suffice to say that the historically underlying root was **dik-*, and that sound changes involving, in particular, deletion of unstressed vowels and assimilation of resulting consonant clusters, created the modern situation. The rather unusual present subjunctive of this verb happens to show the effects of analogical levelling in favour of the originally arrhizotonic first and second person plural form stems togther with the associated stressed inflexional ending (cf. Decurtins 1958 for the reflexes of AMBULARE / IRE, DICERE, UENIRE, HABERE, or SAPERE in Samedan, Parsons, and Razen for other Romansh examples of this kind; further discussion also in Maiden, in progress). That aside (and there is every reason to believe that the *déi-* root originally occurred as expected in the present subjunctive), this verb shows N-pattern suppletion. Anderson (2011b: 17) acknowledges that it is "genuinely suppletive" and that "the choice of stem is determined by morphosyntactic features". He defines in the same way some other, less radically suppletive verbs, for which I give here just the present-tense forms, e.g, *(vu)léir* 'want', *néir* 'come' (Table 4):

Table 4: *(Vu)leir* and *neir* in Savognin

PRS. IND	*ví*	*vót*	*vót*	*léin*	*léz*	*vóttan*
PRS. SBJV	*víglia*	*víglias*	*víglia*	*víglian*	*víglias*	*víglian*

PRS. IND	*vígn*	*vígnst*	*vígna*	*nín*	*níz*	*vígnan*
PRS. SBJV	*vígna*	*vígnas*	*vígna*	*vígnan*	*vígnas*	*vígnan*

If we acknowledge that *deir* and some other verbs have (near-)suppletive patterns determined synchronically by morphosyntactic features, then we have to admit the presence of the morphomic N-pattern in Savognin. Yet if we say that the vocalic alternations are still a matter of "phonologically conditioned allomorphy", then the fact that they show exactly the same paradigmatic distribution becomes uncomfortably coincidental.

3 The "augment"

The "augment" is a functionally empty formative which, in certain cells of the inflexional paradigm of the verb, occurs between the lexical root and desinences denoting tense, mood, person, and number (for detailed discussions of its nature and origins, which lie in Latin and proto-Romance Aktionsart suffixes, see especially Maiden 2003;2011: 249–53;2016: 715f.). In Latin, the relevant affixes were restricted to imperfective-aspect forms, but had no restrictions for person, number, or tense. In most Romance languages, augments are associated with particular inflexion classes (in Romansh, usually the first and fourth conjugations), and have become restricted to certain cells of the inflexional paradigm defined by tense, mood, person, and number. In Savognin, the augment occurs solely in the singular and third person forms of the present indicative, and in all forms of the present subjunctive. That is to say, of course, that it has exactly the same paradigmatic distribution as the "stressed" vocalic alternants, a fact which clearly suggests a link between them. Thus first conjugation *luschardár* 'strut', and fourth conjugation *tradéir* 'betray' (Table 5):

Table 5: The augment in Savognin first and fourth conjugation verbs

	1SG	2SG	3SG	1PL	2PL	3PL
First conjugation						
PRS. IND	*luschardésch*	*luschardéschas*	*luschardéscha*	*luschardágn*	*luschardéz*	*luschardéschan*
PRS. SBJV	*luschardéscha*	*luschardéschas*	*luschardéscha*	*luschardéschan*	*luschardéschas*	*luschardéschan*
IPF.IND	*luschardéva*	*luschardévas*	*luschardéva*	*luschardévan*	*luschardévas*	*luschardévan*
Fourth conjugation						
PRS. IND	*tradésch*	*tradéschas*	*tradéscha*	*tradígn*	*tradíz*	*tradéschan*
PRS. SBJV	*tradéscha*	*tradéschas*	*tradéscha*	*tradéschan*	*tradéschas*	*tradéschan*
IPF.IND	*tradíva*	*tradívas*	*tradíva*	*tradívan*	*tradívas*	*tradívan*

It is undisputed that the distribution of the Romance augment cannot be explained, diachronically or in modern varieties, as the output of any kind of phonological process. The view that I have developed (see, e.g., Maiden 2005; 2011b,c) is that the redistribution of the alternant from Latin to Romance is *purely morphologically* determined, and reflects sensitivity to a paradigmatic pattern created, originally, as an effect of vocalic alternations between stressed and unstressed vowels: the same pattern can be shown to have provided a "template" for the suppletive merger of distinct lexical verbs in various Romance languages (notably, the verb 'go'). I see no reason why what we see in Savognin, and more generally in Romansh, should be viewed any differently: the distribution of the augment appears a matter of pure morphology, and given that the vocalic alternations have the same distribution as the augment, they too can be accounted for in the same, purely morphological, terms.

Anderson views the facts, in effect, in terms of a kind of "defectiveness": verbs showing the augment lack a stressed vocalic alternant, and the augment is inserted wherever this occurs. Since the augment is inherently stressed, the preceding root-form must be unstressed, and the lack of a stressed root allomorph is thereby resolved. My view is that this analysis inverts cause and effect: it is not the case that the augment is applied because there is no stressed root allomorph but, rather, that there is no stressed root allomorph because the relevant cells of the paradigm are specified as being filled by forms containing the augment. This latter analysis has the immediate advantage of avoiding the problem of arbitrary stipulation of defectiveness in one set of cells only. After all, if stressed alternants can be defective, why should not unstressed alternants too? Why do we not also find, that is, verbs with a stressed alternant but not an unstressed one? And if the distribution of the augment is dictated by the need to plug a phonological "gap", how is it that such gaps only occur in first and fourth conjugation verbs, precisely the inflexion classes to which the augments are historically restricted across the Romance?

Discussion of the Savognin augment has tended to focus on first conjugation verbs, where it is most productive, but where it still only constitutes a subset (and apparently a minority) of such verbs. We should not forget that the augment also appears in the great *majority* of fourth conjugation verbs (characterized by infinitives in *-eir*), a class comprising dozens of lexemes and endowed with some productivity. If we follow Anderson, this means that almost all of the fourth conjugation is characterized by lack of a stressed alternant. Nothing logically excludes this, but it seems counterintuitive to say that a major, semi-productive, inflexion class is, in effect, "defective" in most of its present tense. Nobody would countenance such an analysis for the cognate Romance varieties (Daco-Romance, Italo-Romance, Catalan) where the fourth conjugation behaves in this way.

Anderson (2011b: 22) points out that the augment frequently appears in neologisms, including where speakers feel doubt about the identity of the stressed allomorph. This does not mean, however, that the augment is *usually* a response to perceived lack of a stressed alternant. Using the Savognin first conjugation verb *luschardár* 'strut' (exemplified above), Anderson (2008: 122) observes that: "The use of this pattern [...] has the advantage that the speaker does not need to retrieve any information about the specific alternation pattern of the stem in order to produce all of the correct forms. Otherwise, it would be necessary to choose [...] among a variety of possibilities such as **luscharda*, **luscheirda*, **luschorda*, **laschurda*, **laschorda*, etc. Each of these patterns is more or less secure with reference to at least some verbs in the Surmiran lexicon, but the availability of the paradigm [given above] makes it possible to avoid the choice when positive evidence is not readily available." The problem here is that that there *is* unequivocal evidence for the stressed vowel. This verb is transparently and directly derived from the nominal *luschárd* 'dandy, fop, vain, proud', which actually contains, moreover, a highly frequent stressed pejorative suffix *-árd*. In this case, the identity of the "right" stressed alternant is patent. This is in fact true of a large number of other verbs that take *-esch*, all transparently derived from nouns or adjectives whose stressed vowel is known (examples from Signorell 2001), such as those give in Table 6:

Table 6: Nouns, adjectives, and derived verbs in Savognin

Basic noun/adjective	Infinitive	3SG.prs.ind	
cisél	*ciselár*	*ciseléscha*	'chisel'
dimóra[8]	*dimorár*	*dimoréscha*	'dwell (-ing)'
discrédit	*discreditár*	*discreditéscha*	'discredit'
fáx	*faxár*	*faxéscha*	'fax'
figúra	*figurár*	*figuréscha*	'figure'
fílm	*filmár*	*filméscha*	'film'
fírma	*firmár*	*firméscha*	'sign (-ature)'
guíd	*guidár*	*guidéscha*	'guide'
líber	*liberár*	*liberéscha*	'free'
nivél	*nivelár*	*niveléscha*	'level'
ódi	*odiiér*	*odiéscha*	'hate'
penél	*penelár*	*peneléscha*	'paint (-brush)'
schicána	*schicanár*	*schicanéscha*	'chicane'
teléfon	*telefonár*	*telefonéscha*	'telephone'
unifórm	*uniformár*	*uniforméscha*	'uniform'
vagabúnd	*vagabundár*	*vagabundéscha*	'bum'

What such derived forms lack is not a "stressed" alternant but an *unstressed* one: what appears in the verb is simply the root of the corresponding rhizotonic nominal form. Yet there is no sign of attempts to invent a predictable "unstressed" counterpart for the stressed vowel of the base-form (e.g., INF **udiiér from the noun *ódi* after the model of 3SG.PRS.IND *dórma* 'sleeps' vs INF *durméir*) and quite simply the derived verb-forms preserve the segmental identity of the base form. Many scholars have suggested that in Romance generally the augment serves to obviate root allomorphy that might otherwise occur in the lexical root. There are various reasons why this view does not account for the facts (cf. Maiden 2011c: 251f.), but note that in any case this kind of "solution" comports a paradox: one type of alternation is merely replaced by another, that between the augment and its absence, the augment itself retaining an irreducibly "N-pattern", morphomic, distribution.

Anderson (2013) broadens his survey beyond Savognin, arguing for a similar analysis for other Romansh varieties. In fact, in dialects where stress has a somewhat different distribution from Savognin, the augment duly follows that distribution. Thus Anderson (2013: 21f.), in Vaz (Valbella; data from Ebneter 1981) the first person plural present indicative, in addition to arrhizotonic forms, as in Savognin, also has rhizotonic forms with unstressed desinence *-an*, and the predicted "stressed" stem: e.g., INF *amblidár* 'forget', 1SG

---

[8] In fact, *dimóra* and *fírma* below may be derived from the corresponding verbs (cf. Thornton 2004: 517, and Cortelazzo & Paolo 1988 ss.vv. *dimorare, firmare* for this type in Italian). If this holds for Savognin, then these verbs do possess a 'stressed' alternant.

ambloid, 1PL *amblidáin*, but INF *amprastár* 'lend', 1SG *amprést*, 1PL *ampréstan*. Sometimes, the same verb has two possible first person plural present indicative forms, e.g.: INF *gudáir* 'enjoy', 1SG *giód*, 1PL *gudáin* / *giódan*. In verbs taking the augment, there are, correspondingly, forms in 1PL *-áin* without augment (e.g., INF *adorár* 'adore', 1SG *adorésch*, 1PL *adoráin*), and forms in 1PL unstressed *-an* duly showing it (e.g., INF *habitár* 'inhabit', 1SG *habitésch*, 1PL *habitéschan*). According to Anderson (2013: 23) such behaviour poses a "problem" for the morphomic account, because "it is fairly clear that the stem alternation and the appearance of *-esch* [...] are tied directly to the position of stress, even where this is potentially variable, and not to a fixed set of morphological categories". With respect to Anderson, I think that it poses no such problem: all it shows is that whatever principle governs the stressed root allomorph also governs the augment. In this particular case, in fact, we are not dealing with a change in position of stress at all: rather, we have a syncretism such that the first person plural form tends to be "taken over" by the third person plural. This is quite systematic in Vaz (and elsewhere), and occurs independently of stem stress (for example, in non-present forms).

More revealing is the case presented in Maiden (2011b: 45f.), of distributional *discrepancy* between augment and stressed vocalic alternant. The dialects of the Val Müstair (see Schorta 1938: 132) tend to place stress on the root of the infinitive in all conjugations.[9] Indeed, they are unique among Romance languages in generally having rhizotonic infinitives even in the first conjugation, as shown in Table 7:[10]

Table 7: Rhizotony in Val Müstair first conjugation infinitives

ARARE	>	ˈarər	'plough'
CAPTARE	>	ˈcatər	'find'
FILARE	>	ˈfilər	'spin'
IEIUNARE	>	jaˈynər	'fast'
LAETARE	>	ˈlai̯dər	'spread dung'
PESCARE	>	ˈpɛʃcər	'fish'
SCOPARE	>	ˈʃkuər	'sweep'
titˈtare	>	ˈtɛtər	'suckle'
IANTARE	>	ˈjai̯ntər (or janˈtar)	'breakfast'
telefonare	>	teleˈfonər	'telephone'

Schorta states, however, that root stress in first conjugation infinitives systematically fails to happen in that class of first conjugation verbs having the element *-aj-*, which I

---

[9] Some second conjugation verbs are exceptions.
[10] This phenomenon is mentioned by Stürzinger (1879: 35) and Huonder (1901: 518f.), and is amply confirmed by data from Val Müstair covered by *ALDI/II*. See also Grisch (1939: 222) for Vaz, Candrian (1900: 51) for Stalla, Solèr (1991: 135) for Schams.

identify as the augment.[11] Here, stress always remains on the ending of the infinitive: e.g., INF bɐˈtjar 'baptize', 3SG.PRS bɐˈtjaja; INF biˈar 'build', 3SG.PRS biˈaja; INF guˈjar 'dare', 3SG.PRS guˈjaja. The same holds of fourth conjugation infinitives, but apparently only if they belong to that minority of verbs that lack the augment: Schorta cites INF fiˈnir 'finish', a verb which takes the augment; compare this with, e.g., INF ˈbwɔʎər 'boil' a verb that does not show the augment). Now the most likely explanation of why the augment does not appear in the infinitive here is that, in Romance languages generally, root-stress in infinitives is limited to third conjugation verbs (cf. Maiden 2011c: 201f. 2016: 509), all other classes having non-rhizotonic infinitives. The augment, however, is characteristic solely of the fourth and first conjugations, not the third. The third, while a relatively small and unproductive class, contains some of the semantically most basic, and highest frequency, verbs, and the appearance of root stress in the Val Müstair fourth and first conjugations is almost certainly modelled, therefore, on the third conjugation. If no augment can appear in first conjugation infinitives, it is because the distribution of the augment is *morphologically* specified, and that specification happens to exclude infinitives.

In Maiden (2011b) I argued as follows: if the function of the augment is in effect to supplete the absence of a stressed root-alternant, and if infinitives in the Val Müstair are generally root-stressed, then we should expect verbs with the augment duly to show that augment in the infinitive, in lieu of root-stress (e.g., INF **bɐˈtjajər rather than the actually occurring bɐˈtjar). The fact that the augment never appears in the infinitive therefore also suggests that its distribution is independent of stress, and purely morphologically specified. The only way to "save" the stress-based account (and this is what Anderson 2013 does) is to claim that the augment is inherently limited to "tensed" forms, and is therefore not available for the infinitive. He observes, in support of his view, that it does not occur, either, in participles or in "related non-verbal forms". Since the augment also appears in second person singular imperatives, it is not clear that "tensed" is quite the right term: it might be more accurate to say that the domain of the augment involves cells with values for person and number. But now Anderson's claim must be that the augment is selected in those parts of the paradigm specified for person and number where stress would otherwise fall on the root, while my account can easily be reformulated, if we wish, as also applying to those parts of the paradigm specified for person and

---

[11] I must acknowledge here a different, and very careful, analysis of these facts by Kaye (2015: 291–310), for whom -*aj*- is not the 'augment' but part of the stressed lexical root of the verb, whose historically regular unstressed counterpart is -*j*- (*bateˈdjare > bɐˈtjar; *baˈtedja > *bɐˈtaja). In a form such as bɐˈtjaja, on Kaye's account, the unstressed element -j- has been analogically generalized into the root of the stressed alternant, originally of the type *bɐˈtaja < *baˈtedja (Kaye 2015: 307); resistance of bɐˈtjar (< *bateˈdjare) to stress retraction is then, Kaye suggests2015: 309, a function of the degree of phonological difference between stressed and unstressed root. I would observe that -*aj*- is exactly the expected reflex of the proto-form of the augment (although rarely attested in the rest of Romansh, where is has been supplanted by -*eʃ*-), and that it is not clear why the root found in the root-stressed present-tense forms of the verb would be phonologically disfavoured in root-stressed infinitives. In fact, even if -*aj*- turns not to be, in origin, an "augment", such an analysis suggests that speakers have effectively analysed bɐtj- as the lexical root, treating -*aj*- as a kind of excrescent element following it, and one that occurs just in the N-pattern cells. That is to say that its synchronic status is equivalent to that of the augment in other verbs.

number, except for the first and second persons plural present indicative. Both accounts acknowledge that the phenomenon is heavily *morphologized*, and applies over a domain whose definition corresponds to no natural phonological or morphosyntactic class. Even Anderson's account is, I submit, implicitly "morphomic".

4 The generality of the alternations: derivational morphology

Anderson's analysis gains support from the fact that the vocalic alternations that occur within the verb also occur outside it: nouns and adjectives with stressed derivational affixes show the corresponding "unstressed" vocalic alternants in the derived forms. The sensitivity of these alternations to stress is thereby argued to be a general property of the grammar, and not a peculiarity of verb morphology.morphology Take, for example, the behaviour of the vocalic alternants in derivational morphology (Table 8), as presented by Anderson (2011: 28–30;2013: 13–17):

Table 8: Vocalic alternants in Savognin derivational morphology

Verb			Basic noun	Derived nouns
Infinitive	3SG.PRS.	PST.PART		
guttár 'drip'	*gótta*		*gót* 'drop'	*gutélla* 'drip'
liiér 'bind'	*léia*		*léia* 'union'	*liadéira* 'binding'
néiver 'snow'	*néiva*	*navía*	*néiv* 'snow'	*naváglia* 'big snowfall'

In reality, this might be no more than the residual, and synchronically more or less accidental, effect of historical differentiation of vowel quality according to stress. This is suggested by the fact that there are derived forms with stressed suffixes (and therefore with unstressed roots) where, nonetheless, the *stressed* alternant occurs. Thus Table 9:

Table 9: Discrepancy between vowel alternation in verbs and derived forms

Verb	Derived forms
Infinitive	3SG.PRS.
satgér 'dry'	*sétga*
accumpagnér 'accompany'	*accumpógna*
durméir 'sleep'	*dórma*

Similar phenomena recur elsewhere in Romansh, as Anderson (2013: 20) points out: thus Vallader has *scóula* 'school', *scolár* 'to school' (3SG.PRS.IND *scóula*), *scolaziún* 'education', yet diminutives *scoulína* 'kindergarten', *scoulétta* 'craft school'. Anderson (2011b: 28) deals with such apparent counterexamples by assuming an architecture of the grammar in which morphology and phonology "interact cyclically (with some appropriate subsystem) of the phonology applying to adjust the results of each stage of morphological elaboration of a form". The selection of the stressed or unstressed stem alternant operates only during the "first cycle"; once the stem-shape is determined 'the decision is not revisited on subsequent cycles'. A "stressed" base will then persist through later cycles, even if it is itself no longer stressed: the derivational counterexamples can now be explained in terms of the cycle on which they occur.

One immediate objection is that saying that an apparently phonological phenomenon is confined to a particular "cycle" is in fact to concede that it is "morphologized" (the cycles being defined, precisely, as stages of "morphological elaboration of a form"), and restriction of a phonological rule to some morphologically defined domain is to introduce into the analysis a considerable degree of arbitrariness (precisely one of the things that for Anderson consitutes an objection to the purely "morphomic" analysis). Things look even more arbitrary, and "morphological", if we consider that we now have to say that the domain of the phonologically conditioned allomorphy is defined over two quite disparate sets of forms: "tensed" forms of the verb (at least in Vallader) and the "first cycle" in derivation. A more fundamental difficulty is that it is not always true that the "stressed" stem persists unchanged after the "first cycle": why do we have, say, derived forms *accumpagnedér* or *durmiglión* with "unstressed" alternants, yet *accumpognamáint* or *dormulént* with "stressed" alternants?[12] Actually, the predicted selection of the "unstressed" alternant usually occurs in words belonging to inherited vocabulary, but not in neologisms, which led me to conclude (Maiden 2011b: 41) that what we have is evidence of the "death" of phonological selection of the allomorphs, now reflected only in traditional vocabulary. This claim *tends* to be reflected in the behaviour of adjectives showing reflexes of Latin -ABILIS, -IBILIS (equivalents of English -*able*, -*ible*): the "popular" reflex by direct inheritance from Latin (-*evel*) displays the "unstressed" alternant (e.g., *ludével* 'praiseworthy'), while the "learned" -*ábel*/-*íbel* displays the "stressed" alternant (e.g., *accumodábel* 'accommodatable'). One might, perhaps, want to assign -*evel* to the "first cycle", and -*abel* to the second, but even this does not work too well, for we find occasional examples of the distinctive "unstressed" alternant with -*ábel*/-*íbel*: e.g., *schliíbel* 'soluble', *bavábel* 'drinkable', *purtábel* 'portable', *duvrabel* 'usable'.

Anderson (2013: 15) observes an "asymmetry", in that the counterexamples to his claim all involve the appearance of a "stressed" stem that does not bear stress, while no examples exist in which an "unstressed" stem appears under stress. But this is not proof that that the stem alternants are sensitive to stress. On such evidence as Anderson presents (and from Signorell 2001), the small inventory of possibly derived forms involving a stressed stem displays that stem simply because it is the phonologically regular result of their etyma (e.g., *preschaint* 'present' (adj.) < PRAESÉNTEM). In any case, it is perfectly

---

[12] For an inconclusive discussion of these data, see Wolf (2013: 171).

possible that some forms such as *preschánt* are not "derived", but are the base forms from which the corresponding verbs are derived. Anderson also observes 2013: 18 that in Surselvan (in fact, more widely) only "unstressed" root alternants appear in factive verbs formed with the suffix *-ent-* or *-ant-*,[13] where the lexical root is systematically unstressed (e.g., INF *béiber* 'drink', 1PL.PRS *buéin*, but factive INF *buentár* 'cause to drink', never **beibentár). He cites similar phenomena in Puter (Anderson 2013: 10), such as *stanglantér* from *stáungel* 'tired', but says that "[m]ore research is needed to establish the generality of the phenomenon". Here I concur: we need to be sure that selection of the "unstressed" stem is synchronically productive and therefore psychologically real. Otherwise, all we may have is the regular, lexicalized, outcome of old sound changes in the relevant derived forms. In any case, there do seem to be examples of factive verbs in *-entar* that bear the "stressed" root allomorph. Jaberg (1939: 291f.) lists Surselvan examples most of which indeed bear the "unstressed" allomorph, but also gives *dormentár* 'put to sleep' (cf. INF *durmír* 'sleep', 1SG.PRS.IND *dorm*), and a case in which the unstressed vowel of the derived form, while phonologically plausible, does not correspond to that of the base verb (*scumpentár* 'cause to be saved, heal', from INF *scampár* 'save', 3SG.PRS.IND *scómpa*).

Even leaving counterexamples aside (and I acknowledge that they are not many), it is not obviously necessary to invoke stress: given that the vast majority of cells of the inflexional paradigm of any Romansh verb are arrhizotonic, one might equally say that what we call the "unstressed" stem is the default, on which affixally derived forms are usually built. An apparent counterargument to such an approach might come (cf. Anderson 2013: 17) from the fact that, in cases of derivation where the stress falls on the root, it is always the "stressed" allomorph that appears: e.g., Surmiran *cumónd* 'order' (cf. INF *cumandár*, 1SG.PRS.IND *cumónd*), *clóm* 'call' (cf. INF *clamár*, 1SG.PRS.IND *clóm*), *gartétg* 'success' (cf. INF *gartagér*, 1SG.PRS.IND *gartétg*), *dórma* 'narcotic' (cf. INF *durmír*, 3SG.PRS.IND *dórma*), *stéma* 'esteem' (cf. INF *stimár*, 1SG.PRS.IND *stéma*). Significantly, however, Signorell, Wuethrich-Grisch & Simeon (1987: 51) describe such forms, pre-theoretically, as "deriving from a finite form": what we may have here is simply nominalization of first or third person singular verb-forms (which happen to contain stressed roots), not a derivational process which specifies a stressed root, and thereby must select the "stressed" alternant. In short, while it is indeed true that many patterns of root-alternation found in the verb recur across the grammar, this is largely a historical residue, not necessarily evidence of an active synchronic phonological principle.

5 Conclusion

Anderson (2013: 23) accepts that "morphological categories play a role (e.g. in constraining the appearance of *-esch* to tensed forms of first and fourth conjugation verbs)", but asserts that 'there is no warrant for invoking the further step of complete and arbitrary morphological categorization that would be implied by associating the variation with

---

[13] Cf. Signorell, Wuethrich-Grisch & Simeon (1987: 103f.).

a morphome'. I suggest that the data are in fact already inextricably permeated with "arbitrary" morphological specifications: in Savognin, and in Romansh at large, the morphomic N-pattern is really present. The need to specify that the alleged phonological principle only applies to "tensed" verb forms (for Val Müstair), or to certain levels of derivational morphology makes that principle itself "arbitrary". Given that the behaviour of suppletion in *dueir* and the distribution of *-esch* are, as I have argued, incompatible with the "phonological" account, attempts to account for the identically distributed vocalic alternations in phonological terms become superfluous. Finally, given that countless Romance varieties do have genuinely morphomic patterns of the kind attested in Savognin, treatment of Savognin as a special case is what may be "unwarranted". And yet....

I do not think that Savognin can be presented as the perfect example of "phonologically conditioned allomorphy" that Anderson claims, and yet one must ask whether Anderson's insight – that right across the grammar there is a close correlation between stress and the selection of alternants, might be at risk of being abandoned too lightly. My criticism has been that there exist some cases where such an analysis does not "work", and that since we need independently to invoke the N-pattern even for Savognin, we should do so for all types of alternation which follow that pattern. But there is an unspoken assumption here which may need to be challenged, and it involves what might be described as the "ghettoization of the morphomic". The classic examples of "morphomic" phenomena as adduced by Aronoff (1994) make the case for the existence of a "morphomic level" of linguistic analysis precisely because they are not plausibly explicable as effects of phonological, syntactic, or semantic conditioning: they are cases of "morphology by itself". In morphologists' enthusiasm to assert the existence of genuinely morphological phenomena, much weight has been placed on the notion of the "autonomy" of morphology (witness the titles of Maiden 2005, or Maiden et al. 2011). While there are very good reasons to proclaim loudly that "autonomously morphological" phenomena exist, the search for them should not become a reductivist obsession, nor is there any good reason to suppose that there cannot exist phenomena which contain a very high degree of purely morphological determination, while yet also possessing some degree of phonological or other conditioning.

The seeds of a possible compromise appear in Maiden (2013) (actually, in the same volume as, and immediately following, Anderson 2013). This deals with patterns of consonantal alternation in Italian verbs historically caused by two different kinds of palatalization. Synchronically, the result is that phonologically quite disparate types of alternant tend overwhelmingly to conform to a common distribution such that one alternant occurs in all (or most) forms of the present subjunctive, and in the first person singular and third person plural forms of the present indicative, but nowhere else in the paradigm. There are powerful arguments (see, e.g., Maiden 1992,20112011: 205–63) to say that this pattern has lost all phonological causation and is genuinely morphomic. In Maiden (2009) I had been extremely critical of attempts by Burzio (2004) to force a synchronic phonological analysis of the modern Italian facts, quite often by what is, in effect, the illegitimate resurrection of long dead phonological conditioning environments. For the most part, these are criticisms I stand by: it cannot be said too often that morphology suffers from a kind of "phonologizing bias" which too readily dismisses morphological analyses of the data, and is far too prone to give credence to phonologically-oriented accounts, even at the expense of postulating conditioning environments lacking plausible synchronic justification. Burzio's analysis appeared to me an example of this kind, but observation of some of the fine details of the diachrony of the alternations at issue later caused me to moderate my view.

One type of alternation involved an opposition between velar consonants and palatal affricates, the latter arising, historically, through palatalization and affrication of velars before front vowels. Now it is beyond reasonable doubt that there has existed no productive process of palatalization/affrication of velars before front vowels for over a millennium, such a putative process being massively counterexemplified by the existence of unmodified velars before front vowels from the time of the earliest documents, including within the paradigm of the verbs at issue. The principal fact[14] which made me revise (Maiden 2013) the "morphological exclusivism" of my earlier treatments of the subject, however, was the observation that in medieval Italian a certain type of analogical innovation affecting verbs displaying the relevant types of alternation, whereby the root of the present subjunctive was optionally extended into gerund forms with the ending -endo, was strikingly, and systematically, *blocked* just where the result would have been a velar consonant followed by a front vowel. Informally: "don't allow a velar alternant before a front vowel if an alternative (and more phonologically "natural") palatal alternant is also available". Thus Table 10 (where "**" means "not occurring"):

Table 10: Analogically reformed subjunctives in old Tuscan

subjunctive	inherited gerund	gerund analogically reformed on subjunctive
possa 'can'	*potendo*	*possendo*
ve/dʤ/a 'see'	*vedendo*	*ve/dʤ/endo*
te/ɲɲ/a 'hold'	*tenendo*	*te/ɲɲ/endo*
abbia 'have'	*avendo*	*abbiendo*
pia/tʃ/a 'please'	*pia/ʧ/endo*	*pia/tʃ/endo*
di/k/a 'say'	*di/ʧ/endo*	**di/k/endo*
pian/g/a 'weep'	*pian/ʤ/endo*	**pian/g/endo*

While it would have been impossible to explain the distribution of the alternants in *purely* phonological terms (for the reasons, see Maiden 2013: 25–31), this behaviour clearly suggests residual sensitivity to *phonologically plausible* environments for the distribution of certain alternants.

In short, while Anderson's analysis of the Savognin data seems to me too "phonologizing", it may be that my own approach, insisting on purely morphological aspects

---

[14] But see also Maiden (2013: 31–35).

of the phenomenon, has been too "morphologizing", and both approaches seem to be subject to the questionable assumption that redundancy must be eliminated from the analysis. I do not think that Savognin is as "pure" an example of "phonologically conditioned allomorphy" as Anderson believes, but the possibility that speakers are sensitive to the recurrent correlation between certain types of alternation and stress should not be sacrificed too hastily on the altar of formal economy. As Sims (2015: 205f.) observes, our two approaches need not in fact be mutually exclusive. We have probably reached the point where only appropriately devised psycholinguistic experimentation would be able to tell us more about the Savognin data. However that may be, morphologists and Romance linguists are truly in Steve Anderson's debt for having focused our attention so sharply on these fascinating data.

Abbreviations

AIS   Jaberg & Jud (1964)
ALDI   Goebl et al. (1998)
ALDII   Goebl et al. (2012)

Acknowledgements

I would like to thank Hans-Olav Enger for some very helpful remarks on an earlier draft of this chapter.

References

Anderson, Stephen R. 2008. Phonologically conditioned allomorphy in the morphology of Surmiran (Rumantsch). *Word Structure* 1(2).

Anderson, Stephen R. 2010. Failing one's obligations: Defectiveness in Rumantsch reflexes of DĒBĒRE. In Dunstan Brown Matthew Baerman Greville G. Corbett (ed.), *Defective paradigms: Missing forms and what they tell us*, 19–36. Oxford: British Academy & Oxford University Press.

Anderson, Stephen R. 2011a. Romansh (Rumantsch). In Adam Ledgeway & Martin Maiden (eds.), *The oxford guide to the Romance languages*, 169–184. Oxford: Oxford University Press.

Anderson, Stephen R. 2011b. Stress-conditioned allomorphy in Surmiran (Rumantsch). In Maria Goldbach, Marc-Olivier Hinzelin, Martin Maiden & John Charles Smith (eds.), *Morphological autonomy: Perspectives from Romance inflectional morphology*, 13–35. Oxford: Oxford University Press.

Anderson, Stephen R. 2013. Stem alternations in Swiss Rumantsch. In Silvio Cruschina, Martin Maiden & John Charles Smith (eds.), *The boundaries of pure morphology: Diachronic and synchronic perspectives (Oxford Studies in Diachronic and Historical Linguistics 4)*, 8–23. Oxford: Oxford University Press.

Aronoff, Mark. 1994. *Morphology by itself: Stems and inflectional classes.* Cambridge, MA: MIT Press.

Burzio, Luigi. 2004. Paradigmatic and syntagmatic relations in Italian verbal inflection. Julie Auger, Clancy Clements & Barbara Vance (eds.). 17–44.

Candrian, Johann Paul. 1900. *Der Dialekt von Bivio-Stalla.* Zürich: Halle.

Corbett, Greville. 2007. Canonical typology, suppletion, and possible words. *Language* 83(1). 8–42.

Cortelazzo, Manlio & Zolli Paolo. 1988. *Dizionario etimologico della lingua italiana.* Bologna: Zanichelli.

Decurtins, Alexi. 1958. *Zur Morphologie der unregelmässigen Verben im Bündnerromanischen.* Bern: Francke.

Ebneter, Theodor. 1981. *Vocabulari dil rumantsch da Vaz.* Tübingen: Niemeyer.

Goebl, Hans, Hans Böhmer, S. Gislimberti, D. Kattenbusch, E. Perini, T. Szekely, I. Dautermann, S. Heissmann, U. Hofmann, A. Kozak, H. Pamminger, H.-M. Rössler, R. Bauer & E. Haimerl. 1998. *Atlant linguistich dl ladin dolomitich y di dialec vejins, 1a pert.* Wiesbaden: Dr. L. Reichert Verlag.

Goebl, Hans, Ilaria Adami, Helga Böhmer, Axel Heinemann, Frank Jodl, Liza Klinger, Daniele Rando, Brigitte Rührlinger, Walter Strauß, Tino Szekely, Paul Videsott, Heidemarie Beer, Gertraud Klingler, Agnes Staudinger, Edgar Haimerl, Bernhard Schauer, Fabio Tosques & Andreas Wagner. 2012. *Atlant linguistich dl ladin dolomitich y di dialec vejins, 2a pert.* Strasbourg: Éditions de Linguistique et de Philologie.

Grisch, Mena. 1939. *Die Mundart von Surmeir: Ober-und Unterhalbstein.* Paris/Zurich: Droz/Niehans.

Huonder, Josef. 1901. Der Vokalismus der Mundart von Disentis. *Romanische Forschungen* 11. 430–566.

Jaberg, Karl. 1939. Considérations sur quelques caractères généraux du romanche. In Université de Généve Faculté des lettres (ed.), *Mélanges de linguistique offerts à Charles Bally*, 283–292. Geneva: Georg.

Jaberg, Karl & Jakob Jud. 1964. *Sprach- und Sachatlas Italiens und der Südschweiz.* Zofingen: Ringier.

Kaye, Steven. 2015. *Conjugation class from Latin to Romance: Heteroclisis in diachrony and synchrony.* University of Oxford PhD thesis.

Kramer, Johannes. 1976. *Historische Grammatik des Dolomitenladinischen. Formenlehre.* Gebrunn bei Würzburg: Lehmann.

Maiden, Martin. 1992. Irregularity as a determinant of morphological change. *Journal of Linguistics* 28(2). 285–312.

Maiden, Martin. 2003. Verb augments and meaninglessness in Romance morphology. *Studi di grammatica italiana* 22. 1–61.

Maiden, Martin. 2004. When lexemes become allomorphs: On the genesis of suppletion. *Folia Linguistica* 38. 227–256.

Maiden, Martin. 2005. Morphological autonomy and diachrony. In Geert Booij & Jaap van Marle (eds.), *Yearbook of morphology 2004*, 137–175. Dordrecht: Springer.

Maiden, Martin. 2006. Accommodating synonymy: How some Italo-Romance verbs react to lexical and morphological borrowings. In Arturo Tosi & Anna Laura Lepschy (eds.), *Rethinking languages in contact: The case of Italian*, 87–98. Oxford: Legenda.

Maiden, Martin. 2009. From pure phonology to pure morphology: The reshaping of the Romance verb. *Recherches delinguistique de Vincennes* 38. 45–82.

Maiden, Martin. 2011a. Instabilità e variazione dialettale nella storia di un verbo trascurato: Dovere nelle varietà italoromanze e "retoromanze". In Marcato Gianna (ed.), *Le nuove forme del dialetto*, 97–104. Padua: Unipress.

Maiden, Martin. 2011b. Morphomes and 'stress-conditioned allomorphy' in Romansh. In Maria Goldbach, Marc-Olivier Hinzelin, Martin Maiden & John Charles Smith (eds.), *Morphological autonomy: Perspectives from Romance inflectional morphology*, 36–50. Oxford: Oxford University Press.

Maiden, Martin. 2011c. Morphophonological innovation. In John Charles Smith Anna Laura Ledgeway Martin Maiden (ed.), *The Cambridge history of the Romance Languages*, 216–267. Cambridge: Cambridge University Press.

Maiden, Martin. 2012. A paradox? The morphological history of the Romance present subjunctive. In Sascha Gaglia & Marc-Olivier Hinzelin (eds.), *Inflection and word formation in Romance languages*, 27–54. Amsterdam.

Maiden, Martin. 2013. Semi-autonomous morphology: A problem in the history of the Italian (and Romanian) verb. In Silvio Cruschina, Martin Maiden & John Charles Smith (eds.), *The boundaries of pure morphology*, 216–267. Cambridge: Oxford University Press.

Maiden, Martin. 2016. Inflectional morphology. In Adam Ledgeway & Martin Maiden (eds.), *The Oxford guide to the Romance languages*, 497–512. Oxford: Oxford University Press.

Maiden, Martin, John Smith, Maria Goldbach & Marc-Olivier Hinzelin (eds.). 2011. Oxford: Oxford University Press.

Pult, Caspar. 1897. *Le parler de sent*. University of Lausanne PhD thesis.

Rogers, Kenneth. 1972. Vocalic alternation in the Sursilvan Romansh verb. In Fisher John & Gaeng Paul (eds.), *Studies in honor of Mario A. Pei*, 173–181. Chapel Hill: University of North Carolina Press.

Schorta, Andrea. 1938. *Lautlehre der Mundart von Müstair*. Paris: Droz.

Signorell, Faust. 2001. *Vocabulari surmiran-tudestg*. Chur: Departamaint d'educaziun digl Grischun.

Signorell, Faust, Mena Wuethrich-Grisch & Gion Pol Simeon. 1987. *Normas surmiranas*. Chur: Tgesa editoura cantunala per stampats e meds d'instrucziun.

Sims, Andrea. 2015. *Inflectional defectiveness*. Cambridge: Cambridge University Press.

Solèr, Clau. 1991. *Romanisch im Schams*. Züurich: Phonogrammarchiv der Universität Zürich.

Stürzinger, Jakob. 1879. *Über die Conjugation im Rätoromanischen*. Zurich: Winterthur, Buchdr. von Bleuler-Hausheer & cie.

Tagliavini, Carlo. 1926. Il dialetto del Comelico. *Archivum Romanicum* 10. 1–200.

Thornton, Anna. 2004. Conversione V > N. In Maria Grossmann & Franz Rainer (eds.), *La formazione delle parole in italiano*, 517–525. Tübingen: Niemeyer.

Thornton, Anna. 2011. Overabundance (multiple cells realizing the same cell): A non-canonical phenomenon in Italian verb morphology. In Martin Maiden, John Smith, Maria Goldbach & Marc-Olivier Hinzelin (eds.), *Morphological autonomy: Perspectives from Romance inflectional morphology*, 358–381. Oxford: Oxford University Press.

Wolf, Matthew. 2013. Candidate chains, unfaithful spell-out, and outwards-looking phonologically-conditioned allomorphy. *Morphology* 23(2). 145–178.

Chapter 11

How to wake up irregular (and speechless)

Charles Yang
University of Pennsylvania

> I suggest that morphological defectiveness arises when the learner fails to discover a productive/default process in a morphological category. The detection of productivity, or lack thereof, can be accomplished by the Tolerance Principle, a simple mathematical model of language learning and generalization. In this paper, I show that the absence of *amn't, the negative contracted form of *am*, in most English dialects can be predicted on purely numerical basis. Implications for language acquisition, variation, and change are also discussed.

1 From Irregular Verbs to Productivity

In my first linguistics talk, which was also my job interview at Yale, I proposed that English irregular past tense is not learned by forming associations between the stem and the inflected form, contrary to the dominant view in the psychological study of language (Rumelhart & McClelland 1986; Pinker 1999). Rather, irregular past tense is generated by *morpholexical* rules. These rules do not generalize beyond a fixed list but are rules nevertheless, in the sense that they take the stem (e.g., *think*) as the input and generate an output (e.g., *thought*), the inflection, via a computational process of structural change (e.g., "Rime → /ɔt/"). I was approaching the problem as a computer scientist: rules are most naturally realized as a list of if-then statements, for regulars and irregulars alike, which turns out to be the approach taken throughout the history of linguistics (Bloch 1947; Chomsky & Halle 1968; Halle & Marantz 1993) including Steve's own work (1973; 1992). There is in fact developmental evidence for the rule-based approach when I reanalyzed the past tense acquisition data purportedly confirming the associationist account (Yang 2002b).

I supposed Steve was at least somewhat persuaded by the argument; a few months later I got the job. But he did wonder aloud after the talk, with a quizzical frown-cum-smile that only he can manage: "But how does a rule wake up in the morning and decide to be irregular?"

Charles Yang. 2017. How to wake up irregular (and speechless). In Claire Bowern, Laurence Horn & Raffaella Zanuttini (eds.), *On looking into words (and beyond)*, 211–233. Berlin: Language Science Press. DOI:10.5281/zenodo.495447

Indeed. Since words do not wear tags of (ir)regularity, any morphological theory that recognizes regularity and irregularity, which is pretty much everything on the market, must say something about how a rule or process wakes up to be irregular. In fact, theories that reject such a categorical distinction (e.g., Hay & Baayen 2003; McClelland & Patterson 2002) ought to be off market. Children's morphological productivity is strongly discrete; see Yang 2016: Chapter 2 for a cross-linguistic review. Their errors are almost exclusively over-regularizations of productive rules. This is quite well known thanks to the past tense debate: for example, the past tense of *hold* sometimes surfaces as *holded*, with the "-d" rule (Marcus et al. 1992). What is not widely known and even less appreciated is the near total absence of over-*irregularization* errors, despite frequent anecdotes to the contrary (e.g., *bite-bote, wipe-wope, think-thunk*, etc.; Bowerman 1982; Bybee 1985; Pinker 1999). These errors are sufficiently rare, occurring in about 0.2% of English-learning children's past tense use, that Xu & Pinker (1995) dub them "weird past tense errors". Not a single instance of *bote, wope, thunk*, or many conceivable analogical patterns can be found in the millions of child English words in the public domain (MacWhinney 2000). The distinction between regular and irregular rules was in fact observed in Berko's (1958) original Wug test. While children were quite happy to add "-d" to novel verbs such as *rick* and *spow*, only one out of eighty six subjects irregularized *bing* and *gling*, although adults are often prone to form irregular analogies in an experimental setting.[1]

So Steve's question sent me on a long quest. To maintain that both regulars and irregulars are computed by rules, I needed a story of how children separate out productive and unproductive rules so precisely and effortlessly. Although a solution was worked out shortly after (Yang 2002a), it took me many years to fully recognize the scope of the productivity problem – one of the "central mysteries" in morphology (Aronoff 1976: 35) – and the challenges it poses.

At a first glance, it doesn't seem difficult to give an answer for English past tense. The rule "add -d" covers most verb types in the language and can thus be deemed regular, as "statistical predominance" has always been regarded as the hallmark of the default (e.g., Nida 1949: 14). But this is surely too simplistic when crosslinguistic and psychological factors are taken into account. More concretely, at least four empirical problems, each of which is illustrated with a familiar example in (1), fall under the productivity problem.

(1) a. English past tense: That a default rule is learned abruptly and results in over-regularization, after a protracted stage of rote memorization (Marcus et al. 1992; Yang 2002b).

b. English stress: That the grammar of English stress (Chomsky & Halle 1968; Hayes 1982; Halle & Vergnaud 1987) is not trochaic with a list of lexical exceptions despite an overwhelming majority of English words bearing stress on the first syllable (Cutler & Carter 1987; Legate & Yang 2013).

---

[1] This suggests that the Wug test and similar methods such as rating have task-specific complications and should not be taken as a direct reflection of an individual's morphological knowledge; see Schütze 2005 and Yang 2016 for discussion.

c. German noun plurals: That a suffix ("-s") can be the productive default despite coverage of fewer nouns than any of its four competitors (Clahsen et al. 1992; Wiese 1996).

d. Russian gaps: That morphological categories needn't and sometimes do not have a default, as illustrated by the missing inflections of certain Russian verbs in the 1st person singular non-past (Halle 1973).

In Yang (2016), I propose a model of productivity, the Tolerance Principle, which provides a unified solution for the problems in (1), as well as similar problems that involve inductive learning in phonology, syntax, and language change. In this paper, I revisit Steve's question which, in a significant way, drove this project forward. My focus is on a topic that has featured prominently in Steve's recent research: morphological gaps and the nature of defectiveness in word formation (e.g., Anderson 2008; 2010b).

2 The Tolerance Principle

The development of the Tolerance Principle started as a purely formal conjecture: How would one represent a rule (R) and the exceptions of that rule (e.g., a set of words w_1, w_2, ..., w_n)? If one is committed to a mechanistic account of the matter – like a computer programmer, for instance – perhaps the only way to encode rules and exceptions is through a set of conditional statements:

(2) If $w = w_1$ Then ...
 If $w = w_2$ Then ...
 ...
 If $w = w_e$ Then ...
 Apply R

This of course immediately recalls the Elsewhere Condition, ever present in linguistics since Pāṇini (Anderson 1969; Aronoff 1976; Kiparsky 1973; Halle & Marantz 1993). In particular, the data structure in (2) entails that in order for a (productive) rule to apply to a word, the system must scan through a list to ensure that it is *not* one of the exceptions (w_1, w_2, ..., w_e).

There is something perverse about (2). For example, to produce *walked*, one must scan through the irregular verbs to make sure that *walk* is not found on the list. But a moment of reflection suggests that the Elsewhere Condition makes perfect sense. The alternative to listing the irregulars would have to be listing the regulars. One can imagine assigning each regular verb a flag, which immediately triggers the application of the "add -d" rule. But that would imply that the morphological status of *every* word must be committed to special memory; the irregulars as well, since they are by definition unpredictable. Perhaps even more surprisingly, there is broad behavioral support for the irregulars-first-regulars-later representation of rules; see Yang 2016: Chapter 3 for review. The psycholinguistic evidence comes from real-time processing of words and morphology. When irregulars and regulars are suitably matched for various factors (e.g., stem and surface frequency) that affect the speed of processing, irregulars are recognized and produced significantly *faster* than regulars – which is consistent with the algorithmic interpretation of the Elsewhere Condition as a computational model of language processing.

From (2), then, we can develop an empirically motivated cost-benefit calculus for the price of exceptions. Specifically, words that fall under a productive rule must "wait" for the exceptions to be processed first: the more exceptions there are, the longer the rule will have to wait. Under very general assumptions about word frequencies, we can prove:

(3) *Tolerance Principle*
Suppose a rule R is applicable to N items in a learner's vocabulary, of which e are exceptions that do not follow R. The sufficient and necessary condition for the productivity of R is:

$$e \leq \theta_N \text{ where } \theta_N := \frac{N}{\ln N}$$

The Tolerance Principle requires two input values, N and e, and returns the productivity status of a rule. Its application requires a well-defined rule such that N and e can be measured, by the child learner during language acquisition and by the researcher when studying linguistic productivity. To learn the structural description of a rule, typically in the form of "X $\longrightarrow$ Y", one will need to invoke inductive learning models such as those studied in artificial intelligence, cognitive science, and indeed linguistics (e.g., Chomsky 1955). Almost all inductive models form generalizations over specific learning instances and try to discover the shared characteristics of individual elements associated with a shared pattern. For example, suppose two good baseball hitters can be described with feature bundles [+red cap, +black shirt, +long socks] and [+red cap, +black shirt, +short socks]. The rule "[+red cap, +black shirt] $\longrightarrow$ good hitter" will follow, as the shared features (cap, shirt) are retained and the conflicting feature (sock) is neutralized. Obviously, the application of inductive learning must encode the structural constraints on the human language faculty and other cognitive systems implicated in language acquisition (Chomsky 1965). While it is clear that the properties of human language are far from arbitrary, it remains an open question to what extent they reflect a unique system of Universal Grammar (e.g., Merge; Berwick & Chomsky 2016) or general principles of cognition and learning that show continuities with other domains and species; see Yang 2004; Chomsky 2005; Yang et al. 2017 for general discussions.

Table 1 provides some sample values of N and the associate threshold value θ_N.

The apparently, and perhaps surprisingly, low threshold has interesting implications for language acquisition. Most importantly, it suggests that all things being equal, smaller vocabulary (smaller values of N) can tolerate relatively more exceptions. That is, productive rules are *more* detectable when learners have *less* experience with a language, especially when they have a small lexicon that only consists of relatively high frequency words. This may explain children's remarkably early command of the main ingredients

Table 1: The tolerance threshold for rules of varying sizes

N	θ_N	%
10	4	40.0
20	7	35.0
50	13	26.0
100	22	22.0
200	38	19.0
500	80	16.0
1,000	145	14.5
5,000	587	11.7

of language (Yang 2013), as well as the reason why maturational constraints may aid rather than hamper language acquisition (Newport 1990); see Yang 2016: Chapter 7 for extensive discussion.

The Tolerance Principle has proved highly effective. In Yang (2016), it was applied almost 100 times, making accurate productivity predictions across many languages and domains using only corpus statistics. Furthermore, experimental studies in collaboration with Kathryn Schuler and Elissa Newport have found near categorical confirmation for the Tolerance Principle in artificial language studies with young children (Schuler, Yang & Newport 2016). Some of these robust results are unexpected. This is because the derivation in (3) makes use of numerical approximations that only hold when N is large. In the empirical case studies, however, the value of N is often very modest (e.g., 8 or 9 in the artificial language studies) as it refers to the number distinct lexical items in a morphological category. For the moment, I put these questions aside and return to the problems in (1): the low threshold of exceptions provides just the right approach to the productivity problem across languages.

Consider first the acquisition of English past tense. Through an inductive process illustrated earlier, the phonological diversity of the regulars will quickly establish that any verb can take the "-d" suffix. Its productivity will be determined by the total number of verbs (N) and the irregulars (e) in the learner's vocabulary. The same consideration applies to the irregular rules. For instance, the seven irregular verbs *bring, buy, catch, fight, seek, teach,* and *think* all follow the stem change "ought". Such a mixed bag of phonological shapes will also yield an all-inclusive rule, as shown by computational implementations (Yip & Sussman 1998). But the "ought" rule will fare terribly. It only works for seven items, with hundreds and thousands of exceptions, far exceeding the tolerance threshold. As a result, the rule will be relegated to lexicalization. Other irregular patterns can be analyzed similarly: as I show elsewhere (Yang 2016: Chapter 4), they all wake up nonproductive in the morning, thereby accounting for the near total absence of over-irregularization errors (Xu & Pinker 1995).

Following the same logic, we can see that the emergence of the "-d" rule will require a long period of gestation. Although children can quickly induce its structural description – using no more than a few dozen verbs (again Yip & Sussman 1998) – their early verbs will contain many irregulars. Of the top 200 verbs inflected in the past tense (MacWhinney 2000), 76 are irregulars. Because θ_{200} is only 37, it follows that children who know some 200 most frequent verbs cannot recognize the productivity of "-d" despite its "statistical predominance". During this period of time, even though verbs may be produced with the "-d" suffix, they are in effect irregular: the suffix has no productivity and does not extend beyond a fixed list rote-learned from the input. The telltale evidence for productivity comes from the first attested overregularization errors (Marcus et al. 1992). For individual learners with reasonably complete records of language development, the Tolerance Principle can help us understand why the regular rule becomes productive at that exact moment it did. For example, "Adam", the poster child of English past tense research (Pinker 1999), produced his first over-regularization error at 2;11: "What dat feeled like?" In the transcript of almost a year prior to that point, not a single irregular verb past tense was used incorrectly. It must be that by 2;11, Adam had acquired a sufficiently large number of regulars to overwhelm the irregulars. To test this prediction, I extracted every verb stem in Adam's speech until 2;11. There are $N = 300$ verbs in all, out of which $e = 57$ are irregulars. This is very close to the predicted $\theta_{300} = 53$, and the small discrepancy may be due to the under-sampling of the regulars, which tend to be less frequent and thus more likely missing from the corpus. The critical point to note here is that Adam apparently needed a filibuster-proof majority of regular verbs to acquire the "-d" rule: this is strongly consistent with the predictions of the Tolerance Principle as illustrated in Table 1.

The problems of English stress and German plurals in (1) are similar. In the English case, the assignment of stress to the first syllable may be transiently productive when the child has a very small vocabulary (Kehoe & Stoel-Gammon 1997; Legate & Yang 2013). But it will fail to clear the tolerance threshold when the vocabulary reaches a modest size: even 85% of coverage is not sufficient for larger values of N (e.g., 5000; Table 1). In the German case, none of the five plural suffixes can tolerate the other four as exceptions, not least the "-s" suffix, which covers the smallest set. In both cases, the learner will carry out *recursive* applications of the Tolerance Principle. When no rule emerges as productive over the totality of a lexical set, the learner will subdivide it along some linguistic dimension, presumably making use of constraints on language and other cognitive systems, and attempt to discover productive rules within. Such a move, while more complex, is always more likely to yield productive rules: again, smaller N's that result from subdividing the lexicon tolerate a relatively higher proportion of exceptions than larger N's. For the acquisition of stress, dividing words into nouns and verbs and taking the syllabic weight into account, as prescribed by all modern metrical theories, lead to productive rules of stress assignment, an outcome that accords well with both structural and behavioral findings (Ladefoged & Fromkin 1968; Baker & Smith 1976; Kelly 1992; Guion et al. 2003). The study by Legate & Yang (2013) also reveals important differences between theories of stress in their statistical coverage of the English lexicon: while all theories handle a great majority of English words, only the theory of Halle 1998 clears the tolerance threshold of exceptions. For the acquisition of German plurals, the move is to subdivide the nouns by grammatical gender as well as phonological conditions, similar to certain theoretical approaches to German morphology (e.g., Wiese 1996). The -s suffix indeed survives as the default because the other suffixes are productive with more restrictive domains of nouns.

The emergence of morphological gaps is a logical outcome of the Tolerance Principle, which constitutes the topic of the present study. When a rule wakes up irregular, the learner must learn, from positive evidence, the inflected form for each word. Failing to hear a particular inflected form will render the speaker speechless when that form is needed.

3 Why Am+Not ≠ Amn't?

3.1 Conditions on Gaps

Many current theories of morphology, including Distributed Morphology (for which see Halle & Marantz 1993), Optimality Theory (Prince & Smolensky 2004), Dual-Route Morphology (Pinker 1999; Clahsen 1999), Network Morphology (Brown & Hippisley 2012), Paradigm Function Morphology (Stump 2001) and others, invoke the notion of competition, which by design results in a default or winning form (at least in the inflectional domain). This architectural feature of the theories is inherently incompatible with the existence of morphological gaps, which are quite widespread across languages (Baerman, Corbett & Brown 2010). The Tolerance based approach, while also competition based (through the Elsewhere Condition), does not stipulate a default or productive rule as a primitive in the theoretical machinery. Rather, the presence or absence of a productive rule is the outcome of language acquisition, to be determined by children through the composition of the linguistic data. More specifically, the Tolerance Principle provides the following corollary (Yang 2016: 142):

(4) *Conditions on gaps*
Consider a morphological category C with S alternations, each affecting N_i lexical items ($1 \leq i \leq S$), and $\sum_i N_i = N$. Gaps arise in C only if:

$$\forall i, 1 \leq i \leq S, \sum_{j \neq i} N_j > \theta_N$$

That is, none of the alternations (S_i) in N are sufficiently numerous to tolerate all the rest ($\sum_{j \neq i} N_j$) as exceptions: no productive alternation will be identified. The speaker must hear the morphological realization of every word in C; if any is to slip through the cracks, a defective gap appears. I should note that in the conception and application of the Tolerance Principle, the terms such as "category" and "alternation" are meant to be general and not restricted to morphology per se. For instance, "category" can be interpreted as any well-defined structural class with a finite number of elements (phonemes, words, morphosyntactic structures, the directionality of a finite number of functional heads, etc.), and "alternation" can be understood as any outcome of a computational process defined over such a class. The Tolerance Principle asserts that in order for a productive pattern to emerge, one of the alternations must be statistically dominant. Elsewhere I have studied several well-known gaps in English, Polish, Spanish, and Russian (Yang 2016: Chapter 5). Their presence is predictable entirely on numerical ground, requiring nothing more than tallying up the counts of the lexical items subject to each alternation. In what follows, I provide a Tolerance Principle account of another much-studied instance of a defective paradigm.

3.2 The Statistics of N't Gaps

In many dialects of English, *n't* is not permitted to contract onto auxiliary verbs such as *am* and *may*, as seen in the unavailability of, for example, "*I amn't tired" and "*You mayn't do that" (e.g., Anderwald 2003a; Bresnan 2001; Broadbent 2009; Frampton 2001; Hudson 2000; Zwicky & Pullum 1983). Following Zwicky & Pullum (1983), I will assume that the contracted negative *n't* is an inflectional affix. The question is why *n't* cannot attach to all auxiliary verbs residing in the Tense node. From the perspective of the Tolerance Principle, the emergence of gaps must result from a critical mass of exceptions to the contraction process.

Let us consider the behavior of the auxiliary hosts for *n't*. Zwicky & Pullum (1983: p508) provide a near comprehensive list, which I revise with some additional information in Table 2.

Table 2 provides the frequencies of the auxiliary verbs and their negation in both uncontracted and contracted forms in the 520-million-word Corpus of Contemporary American English (COCA; Davies 2008). Given the heterogeneity of the textual sources, a handful tokens of *amn't* and *mayn't* can be found albeit at very low frequencies. The *n't*-contracted forms of *shall* and *dare* – *shan't* and *daren't* – are also impossible for most American English speakers but are included here for completeness. Although *shan't* is often perceived as a stereotypically British English feature, it seems to be vanishing across the pond as well. In a 6.6-million-word corpus of British English (MacWhinney 2000), not a single instance of *shan't* is found. And its frequency of usage has been in a steady decline since 1800, the beginning date of the Google Books Corpus. As of *daren't*, the OED does not provide any citation and it has always been very rare throughout the period of the Google Books Corpus. These gapped forms are marked by ∅.

The prescriptively maligned *ain't* ([eɪnt]), however, is robustly attested for *am*, *are*, *is*, *have*, and *has* in COCA as well as a six-million-word corpus of child-directed American English (MacWhinney 2000). Since the phonological form of [eɪnt] is unpredictable from the auxiliary host, it is boldfaced in Table 2 to mark its idiosyncrasy, along with a few other exceptions to which I return later. Note that the frequency estimates of the *ain't* forms are approximate. First, I only counted strings where *ain't* is immediately preceded by a pronoun – the majority case, but sentences with a lexical subject (e.g., "Kids ain't ready") are not included. Second, because both *be* and *have* can take on *ain't*, the counts

11 How to wake up irregular (and speechless)

Table 2: The morphophonological alternation of n't contraction

aux+not			n't contraction		(%)
could [kud]	45,256	[kudn̩t]		106,123	70.104
did [dɪd]	128,432	[dɪdn̩t]		342,202	72.711
does [dʌz]	72,194	[dʌzn̩t]		164,922	69.553
had [hæd]	27,410	[hædn̩t]		46,987	63.157
has [hæz]	28,529	[hæzn̩t]		29,578	50.255
has [hæz]	28,529	**[eɪnt]**		749	1.273
have [hæv]	24,957	[hævn̩t]		45,849	63.868
have [hæv]	24,957	**[eɪnt]**		981	1.367
is [ɪz]	189,538	[ɪzn̩t]		100,164	34.275
is [ɪz]	189,538	**[eɪnt]**		2,537	0.868
might [maɪt]	14,780	[maɪtn̩t]		78	0.525
must [mʌst]	4,156	**[mʌsnt]**		917	18.076
need [nid]	3,705	[nidn̩t]		1,235	25.000
ought [ɔt]	1,031	[ɔtn̩t]		66	6.016
should [ʃud]	20,577	[ʃudn̩t]		25,576	55.416
was [wʌz]	97,457	[wʌzn̩t]		141,384	59.196
would [wud]	46,205	[wudn̩t]		85,853	65.012
am [æm]	10,258	∅		5	0.041
am [æm]	10,258	**[eɪnt]**		2,046	16.622
are [ar]	89,083	[arnt]		50,137	35.602
are [ar]	89,083	**[eɪnt]**		1,073	0.765
can [kæn]	75,531	[kænt]		201,060	72.692
dare [dɛər]	320	∅		25	7.246
do [du]	81,074	**[dont]**		654,576	88.979
may [meɪ]	36,195	∅		12	0.033
shall [ʃæl]	1,271	∅		123	8.824
were [wr̩]	41,224	[wr̩nt]		35,120	46.002
will [wɪl]	39,068	**[wont]**		86,158	68.802

for the auxiliaries are parceled out by extrapolating from the frequencies of the regularly contracted *n't* forms.[2] For instance, there are 2,054 instances of "you/they ain't": the "share" for *are* is based on the count of "aren't" (50,137) relative to "haven't" (45,849).

---

[2] Here I gloss over the fact that there are English dialects in which *ain't* is also an alternative form of negative contraction for *do*, *does*, and *did* (e.g., Labov et al. 1968; Weldon 1994). It would be difficult to estimate their frequencies but formally, this use of *ain't* serves to create additional (unpredictable) exceptions to the contraction process which, as we discuss below, contributes to the breakdown of productivity and the emergence of gaps.

This amounts to 52.2% of 2,054, or 1,073, as recorded in the Table. Finally, the estimate of *ain't* as the contraction of *am + n't* cannot follow a similar process because, of course, *amn't* is gapped. I thus allocated roughly 75% of the "I ain't" counts, which is the share of "I am not" out of the total of "I am not" and "I have not", to the contraction of *am not*. For these five auxiliaries that can be realized as *ain't*, the percentage of the contracted forms are based on the sum of uncontracted, *n't*-contracted, and *ain't*-contracted forms. More precise estimates are certainly possible but as we will see, the exact frequencies are not especially important for our purposes: it is more pertinent to approximate a "typical" English speaker's experience with these forms. Roughly, we would like to know whether an English speaker will have encountered a specific phonological word at all, by using some independently motivated frequency threshold (e.g., once per million; Nagy & Anderson 1984): it is evident that the frequency of *ain't* is sufficiently high for this threshold despite our rough estimates.

A tempting approach to gaps is to appeal to indirect negative evidence (Chomsky 1981; Pinker 1989). A strong version takes the shape of *lexical conservatism*: do not use a form unless it is explicitly attested. This recalls Halle's [-Lexical Insertion] treatment of gaps in his classic paper (1973) and can be found in recent works as well (e.g., Pertsova 2005; Steriade 1997; Rice 2005; Wolf & McCarthy 2009). A weak version makes use of frequency information. For instance, if *amn't* were possible, language learners would have surely heard it in the input, especially since *am* is highly frequent and would have had plenty of opportunities to undergo *n't* contraction. Its conspicuous absence, then, would provide evidence for its ungrammaticality (e.g., Daland, Sims & Pierrehumbert 2007; Sims 2006; Baerman 2008; Albright 2009).

Traditional acquisition research has always viewed indirect negative evidence with strong suspicion (Berwick 1985; Osherson, Stob & Weinstein 1986; Pinker 1989). Research on the *amn't* gap (e.g. Hudson 2000) has also questioned its usefulness. However, with the recent rise of probabilistic approaches to language acquisition especially Bayesian models of inference, the field has seen a revival of indirect negative evidence. If the conception of learning is a zero-sum – or more precisely, one-sum – game which assigns a probabilistic distribution over all linguistic forms, the unattested will necessarily lose out to the attested, at least in most probabilistic models of language learning. A thorough assessment of indirect negative evidence within a probabilistic framework is beyond the scope of the present paper; see Niyogi 2006; Yang 2015; Yang et al. 2017. But a careful statistical examination of gaps serves to reveal its deficiencies. Note that the question is not whether indirect negative evidence can account for *some* missing forms: the absence of *amn't* is indeed unexpected under any reasonable formulation. The real challenge is to ensure that indirect negative evidence will pick out *only* the gapped forms but nothing else, while keeping in mind that morphological inflection is generally not gapped but fully productive, readily extending to novel items.

Two observations can be made about the frequency statistics in Table 2, which suggest that indirect negative evidence is unlikely to succeed. First the *n't* forms of several auxiliaries such as *might* and *need* are in fact quite rare. They appear considerably less frequently than once per million, which is generally regarded as the minimum threshold to guarantee exposure for most English speakers (Nagy & Anderson 1984). In the six-million-word corpus of child-directed American English (MacWhinney 2000), *mightn't* appears only once, *needn't* appears only twice, and *mustn't* does not appear at all. In the other words, these *n't* forms may be so rare that they are in effect absent for many children (Hart & Risley 1995). Lexical conservatism thus will not distinguish them from the truly gapped *amn't, mayn't, daren't*, and *shan't,* the last of which is in fact more frequently attested in COCA. Second, consider a statistical interpretation of indirect negative evidence. The last column of Table 2 provides the percentage of the *n't* contraction out of all negated forms. An auxiliary with an unusually low ratio may mean that it has performed below expectation and could be a clue for its defectiveness. However, the statistics in Table 1 suggest otherwise. It is true that *amn't* and *mayn't* have very low ratios: this fact alone is not remarkable because these are indeed gaps. But exactly how low should a ratio be for the learner to regard a contracted form to be defective? On the one hand, we have *mightn't* and *oughtn't* at 0.525% and 6.016%, and these are not defective. On the other hand, we have *daren't* and *shan't* at 7.246% and 8.824%, but these in fact are defective. There doesn't appear to be a threshold of frequency or probability that can unambiguously distinguish gapped from ungapped items.

3.3 N't Contraction in Language Development and Change

Let's see how the Tolerance Principle provides an account of the *amn't* gaps. The simplest approach is to consider all the auxiliary verbs and their *n't* contractions collectively as a homogeneous set. Using the once-per-million threshold as a reasonable approximation of a typical American English speaker's vocabulary, and taking the size of the Corpus of Contemporary American English (520 million words) into account, there are 18 auxiliaries with reliably attested *n't* forms. The four gapped forms are all below this threshold and are thus excluded from consideration. It is important to clarify that, unlike various forms of lexical conservatism and indirect negative evidence discussed earlier, we do not regard the absence of these forms as evidence for their defectiveness. Rather, the learner's task is to deduce, on the basis of the 18 well-attested forms, including *am~ain't,* that *n't* contraction is not a productive pattern in the English auxiliary system.

This is quite easily accomplished. Of the 18 auxiliaries, *n't* is realized as follows:

(5) a. [n̩t]: could, did, does, had, need, should, was, would (8)
 b. [ent] in variation with either [nt] or [n̩t]: have, has, is, are (4)
 c. [nt]: can, were (2)
 d. idiosyncratic vowel change: do, will (2)
 e. [ent]: am (1)
 f. [n̩t] but idiosyncratically deletes [t] in the auxiliary (see Zwicky & Pullum 1983: 508–509 for discussion): must (1)

For any of these alternations to be productive, it must have no more than $\theta_{18} = 6$ exceptions. The most promising [n̩t], which applies to 8 auxiliaries and thus has 10 exceptions, is a long way off. Even if we are to include the [ņt]-taking *have*, *has*, and *is* and ignore the unpredictable variant [eɪnt] form, the rule "nt ⟶ ņt" still falls short of productivity. Thus, the learner will be able to conclude, from the Conditions on Gaps (4), that *n't* contraction is not a productive process for English auxiliaries and must be learned lexically. If *amn't* fails to appear in the input, it will be absent. Only after the learner has already concluded that a category does not have a productive rule can they start to regard the absence of evidence as evidence of absence.

The preceding analysis, while correctly identifies the *n't* gaps, has some inadequacies. For one thing, based on the 18 contracted forms, the primary evidence for language acquisition, learners would also identify *mustn't* and *oughtn't* as gapped as they fall below the minimum frequency of once per million. This is not necessarily a fatal shortcoming: *mustn't* and *oughtn't* are still considerably more frequent than *amn't* and *mayn't*, the two genuinely gapped forms, and children may acquire them in later stages of acquisition. But more significantly, as Steve pointed out to me in a personal communication (unrelated to the current celebratory volume), the preceding brute-force approach misses an important structural generalization. Table 2 is divided into two halves on Steve's advice. As he insightfully observes, none of the auxiliaries that ends in an obstruent is gapped; these are listed in the top portion of the Table. By contrast, gaps are only found in the auxiliaries that do not end in an obstruent, which are listed in the bottom portion of the Table.

If we carry out a Tolerance analysis along the feature [±obstruent], a much more elegant and interesting pattern emerges. For the 12 [+obstruent] auxiliaries, only four have exceptions – *has*, *have*, *is*, and *must* – just below $\theta_{12} = 4$. Thus, English learners can identify a productive rule:

(6) nt ⟶ ņt / [+obstruent] # ___

This immediately accounts for the fact that speakers generally accept the forms *mightn't* and *oughtn't* despite their very low frequencies (well below once per million): these two auxiliaries, of course, follow the structural description of (6). By contrast, *amn't*, *mayn't*, *daren't*, and *shan't*, some of which appear more frequently than *mightn't* and *oughtn't*, are generally rejected because they fail to meet the structural descriptions of the productive rule in (6).

Consider now the six [-obstruent] auxiliaries in the bottom portion of Table 2. Here *am* and *are* have [eɪnt], *can* and *were* add [nt], and *do* and *will* have idiosyncratic vowel changes. Since the Tolerance threshold $\theta_6 = 3$, no distinct pattern will be identified as productive: lexicalization is required and gaps are predicted for *mayn't*, *daren't*, *shalln't*, and of course *amn't*.

The calculation here is very delicate but it is interesting to push the Tolerance Principle to the limit. What if the child has not learned *ain't* as the *n't*-contracted form for *am* and *are*? Although *ain't* forms are quite robustly attested in COCA as well as in child-directed English, they are still strongly dialectal and are, at least in the input to some children, less frequent than the "regular" forms such as *aren't*, *isn't*, *haven't*, and *hasn't*. If so, a child during an early stage of acquisition may in effect have only five [-obstruent] auxiliaries and their contracted forms to learn from: namely, *are, can, do, were,* and *will.* Here the statistically dominant pattern of "nt $\longrightarrow$ [nt] / [-obstruent] # ___" does reach productivity: the two idiosyncratic exceptions of *do* and *will* fall below the threshold of $\theta_5 = 3$, and *n't* contraction is predicted to be transiently productive!

Bill Labov (personal communication) distinctly recalls being a young *amn't* speaker only to exit that stage at a later time. Indeed, we can find attested examples in American English-learning children's speech. The three examples in (7) are taken from the CHILDES database (MacWhinney 2000):

(7) a. I amn't a dad. (Kate/Kim, 3;6: Sawyer Corpus 3-12-92.cha)
    b. I'm doing this puzzle well, amn't I? (Mark, 3;11: MacWhinney Corpus 67b1.cha)
    c. Amn't I clever? (Mark, 3;11: MacWhinney Corpus 67b2.cha)

The reader is encouraged to listen the audio recordings of the examples in (7) in the CHILDES database. The first child's identity is unclear due to discrepancies in transcription. The examples from Mark can be heard as the investigator's exact revoicing (Brian MacWhinney, personal communication). Although three examples seem quite rare, it is worth noting that almost all *am*'s are contracted onto the pronoun (i.e., *I'm not*). Of the one million American English child utterances, there are only 42 full forms of *am* followed by negation (i.e., *I am not*), which makes the three *amn't* errors not so negligible. Of course, everyone eventually hears 'I ain't': from pop songs on radio if not from the immediate family and friends. Thus, *amn't* will disappear according to the Tolerance-based analysis, for *ain't* introduces an additional exception which leads to the breakdown of productivity for the [-obstruent] class.

Corroborative evidence for the (transient) productivity of *n't* contraction can also be found in other auxiliaries. To my great surprise, there are numerous instances of *willn't* as the negative contracted form of *will* and *whyn't* for 'why don't/didn't' in the speech of many parent-child dyads, apparently all from the New England region. Other than enriching the empirical data on contraction, *willn't* and *whyn't* do not tell us much about the productivity of *n't* contraction or its acquisition: if parents use them frequently, and they do, children will follow. Nevertheless, *willn't* can also be found in the spontaneous speech of children who are not from the New England region:[3]

(8) a. No we willn't. (Ross 2;9, Colorado, MacWhinney Corpus 26b2.cha)
    b. Oh it willn't fit in there (Marie 6;6, Ontario, Evans Corpus dyad07.cha)
    c. He willn't be a good boy (Jared 6;7, Ontario, Evans Corpus dyad19.cha)

Perhaps most strikingly is an utterance produced by Sarah, a child from the Harvard studies (Brown 1973):[4]

(9) And the reindeer saidn't.

---

[3] Brain MacWhinney (personal communication) confirmed that the only time he or his wife ever used *willn't* was when transcribing Ross's speech.

[4] The contraction of *n't* onto the main verb as in (9) was attested in the history of English: see Brainerd 1989 for *caren't* ('don't care') and Jespersen 1917 for *bettern't, usen't,* and indeed *whyn't*.

Taken together, the examples in (7), (8), and (9) suggest that *n't* contraction is at least transiently productive for some English-learning children.

Ross's *willn't* presents an especially interesting opportunity for studying the productivity of *n't* contraction. The CHILDES corpus contains a relatively extensive record of Ross's longitudinal language development. We can then study his auxiliaries and contractions, and subject his individual grammar to the kind of fine-grained analysis of Adam's past tense (§2). By the time Ross produced *No we willn't*, he had used 9 *n't*-contracted auxiliaries:

(10)   a. couldn't, didn't, haven't, isn't, wouldn't
         b. aren't, can't, don't, won't

If Ross had not started partitioning the auxiliaries by the [±obstruent] feature, the $N = 9$ examples in (10) supports the productive use of *n't* contraction because the four examples in (10b) are below the number of tolerable exceptions ($\theta_9 = 4.2$). The 5/4 split between rule-governed and exceptional items is exactly the stimuli used in the artificial language study (Schuler, Yang & Newport 2016) where children nearly categorically generalized the rule. If he failed to distinguish the syllabic [n̩] in (10a) and the nonsyllabic [n] in *aren't* and *can't* in (10b), it would have been even easier for *n't* contraction to reach productivity. Thus, Ross's productive use of *n't* contraction in (8) is predicted by the Tolerance Principle.

The naturalistic evidence from child language is admittedly thin, but it suggests that the emergence of the *amn't* and other gaps in the auxiliary system may be due to the use of *ain't*. Again, the gaps would not be the result of mutual exclusivity: there are doublets such as *haven't~ain't* etc. so *amn't* and *ain't* could have coexisted side by side. Gaps arise/arose because the form of *ain't* weakens the numerical advantage of *n't* contraction, pushing it below the Tolerance threshold.

Finally, a little historical detective work bolsters our treatment of the *amn't* gap.[5] According to Jespersen (1917: 117), "the contracted forms seem to have come into use in speech, though not yet in writing, about the year 1600." The change appears to have originated in non-standard speech before spreading to mainstream usage. Subsequent scholarship, however, places the date to a somewhat later time (e.g., 1630, Brainerd 1989: 181; see also Warner 1993: 208–209). Pursuing the results from the Tolerance-based analysis, we can make two observations.

First, it is likely that *n't*-contraction was at one point productive, which seems especially effective for the [+obstruent] auxiliaries; see also (9) and fn 4. Brainerd's study finds that *didn't, hadn't, shouldn't*, and *wouldn't* appeared from 1670s, soon after the *n't* contraction appeared in the English language. These were followed by *couldn't, mightn't, needn't*, and *mustn't* in the 18th century, and the last to join the group was *oughtn't* in the 19th century, first attested in Dicken's 1836 *The Village Coquette*. Thus speakers at that time must have formed a productive contraction rule for [+obstruent] auxiliaries, perhaps like the one given in (6). Following this line of reasoning, we make the pre-

---

[5] I am grateful to Anthony Warner for pointing out the important study of Brainerd 1989.

11 How to wake up irregular (and speechless)

diction, admittedly one that is difficult to test, that if a new [+obstruent] auxiliary is to appear in the language, it will be immediately eligible for *n't* contraction.

Second, and in contrast to the [+obstruent] class that had been expanding the number of *n't* contractible auxiliaries, the [-obstruent] class has been steadily losing members. Interestingly, the [-obstruent] auxiliaries were quite systematically available for *n't* contraction by the end of the 17th century (Brainerd 1989). Of special interest are of course those that were *n't* contracted in the past but are presently gapped. According to Brainerd's study, the first instance of *shan't* appeared in 1631, *mayn't* in 1674, *daren't* in 1701: all three are now gapped. The very fact that they fall out of usage points to the non-productivity of *n't* contraction for these [-obstruent] auxiliaries: in general, a productive rule would have gained rather than lost members.

How, we wonder, did the [-obstruent] class lose its productivity? Much more detailed historical investigation will be needed but an interesting hypothesis can be offered as follows. The historical development of *n't* contraction may mirror the trajectory of language acquisition by children; that is, ontogeny may recapitulate phylogeny. Our discussion of children's *n't* contraction in modern American English suggests that the use of *ain't* for *am not*, which children probably acquire later during acquisition, increases the number of exceptions for the contraction process. It is conceivable that the emergence of *ain't*, an unpredictably contracted form of *am not*, was also the culprit for the breakdown of productivity.

Historically, *an't/a'nt* surfaced as the contracted form of *am not* between 1673 and 1690. But by the early 1700s, *an't/a'nt* began to be used for both *am not* and *are not* (Brainerd 1989: 186). Whatever the phonological cause for this convergence, or how/when *ain't* joined the fray, the effect is that *am not* no longer had a predictable form of contraction. If our analysis of children's *amn't* and *willn't* is correct, then we would find *amn't* and *ain't* to be in complementary distribution: If a dialect does not allow *ain't* for *am not*, *amn't* would be possible; otherwise *amn't* would be gapped.

The most direct evidence for this suggestion comes from the dialectal distribution of *amn't*, and its correlation with *ain't*. The OED notes that *amn't* is present in "nonstandard" American English and various northern parts of the UK. There is little to suggest that *amn't* is possible in American English at all; all the five occurrences in COCA come from Scottish and Irish writers.[6] It is remarkable, then, that Scotland and Ireland have "traditionally completely *ain't*-free dialects" (Anderwald 2003b: 520): it is precisely in these regions where *amn't* is robustly attested, both in the century-old *The English Dialect Dictionary* (Wright 1898) and in recent dialect surveys of English (Anderwald 2003a).[7]

Before I conclude this section, it is important to clarify the scope of the present analysis. The Tolerance Principle, through Conditions on Gaps (4), can identify defective morphological category where gaps *may* emerge. Such categories are defined by the

---

[6] The corpus of child-directed American-English, surprisingly, contains one instance of *amn't*: "I am stirring, amn't I?" It was produced by Colin Fraser, on staff in Roger Brown's Harvard study of language acquisition (1973). A little Internet research reveals that Fraser, later a Cambridge scholar with a few psychology textbooks to his credit, is a native of Aberdeen.

[7] I would like to thank Gary Thoms for discussion for the distribution of *amn't* in Scottish English.

structural descriptions of rules. It does not predict, at least synchronically, which items within these categories will be gapped. That issue, in my view, is completely a matter of usage frequency: if the inflected form of an item in a defective category is used very rarely or not at all, it will be gapped. Of course, it is also possible that no gaps are found in a defective morphological category, if all items happen to be inflected sufficiently frequently. In that case, however, we do predict that if a novel item matches the structural description of a defective category, the speaker will be at a loss to produce an inflected form. Thus, the emergence of gaps, just as the calibration of productivity, is determined by the composition of the input data. Finally, the preliminary work on the history of *n't* contraction suggests that the Tolerance Principle can be applied to the study of language change. It makes concrete predictions about productivity – the rules that could gain new members, and the rules that could only lose existing members – as long as the relevant values of N and e from historical data can be reliably estimated. The reader is referred to Yang 2016 for a case study of the so-called dative sickness in Icelandic morphosyntax.

4 Gaps in I-language

Halle's classic paper (1973) contains the much criticized proposal that gaps are caused by the [+Lexical Insertion] feature associated with certain forms. As noted earlier, this kind of lexical conservatism is difficult to reconcile with the unbounded generativity of word formation, and similar approaches using indirect negative evidence are also unlikely to succeed. But in a footnote of that very paper, Halle proposes an alternative approach which he himself regards as equivalent but has almost never been discussed by other researchers:

> The proposal just sketched might be modified somewhat as regards the treatment of words formed by rules that traditionally have been called "nonproductive". One might propose that all words formed by non-productive rules are marked by these rules as [-Lexical Insertion]. The smaller subset of actually occurring words formed by such rules would then be listed in the filter with the feature [+Lexical Insertion]. … In other words, it is assumed that words generated by a productive process are all actually occurring and that only exceptionally may a word of this type be ruled out of the language. On the other hand, words generated by a nonproductive rule are assumed not to be occurring except under special circumstances. In this fashion we might capture the difference between productive and nonproductive formations (5).

Hetzron (1975), while arguing against Halle's [+Lexical Insertion] proposal, makes essentially the same suggestion. Rules are either productive or lexicalized, and gaps arise in the unproductive corners of the grammar. His conception of gaps can be strongly identified with the Elsewhere Condition, a critical component of the present theory:

> The speaker must use ready-made material only for "exceptional" forms, while everywhere else he could very well "invoke the word formation component". Technically, this can be represented by a disjunctive set of rules where idiosyncratic or

"exceptional" formations are listed with as much explicitness as necessary, while the general word formation rules would appear afterward, with the power to apply "to the rest" (871).

That is, gaps arise when productivity fails. The problem of gaps thus reduces to the problem of productivity. Some subsequent proposals have adopted a similar approach (Albright 2009; Baronian 2005; Hudson 2000; Maiden & O'Neill 2010; Pullum & Wilson 1977; Sims 2006), including Steve's own account (2010): gaps result from conflicting forces in word formation such that the output form becomes unpredictable and thus unrealized. The Tolerance Principle provides a precise solution of what makes a rule productive, and its application to gaps reinforces the general position that gaps and productivity are two sides of the same coin.

The Tolerance Principle is a provable consequence of the Elsewhere Condition and follows from the general principle of efficient computation: the child prefers *faster* grammars, a "third factor" in language design par excellence (Chomsky 2005). In fact, a stronger claim can be made in favor of such an analytical approach. I submit that a descriptive analysis of languages, however typologically complete or methodologically sophisticated, cannot in principle provide the right solution for productivity. First, as noted earlier, the categorical nature of children's morphological acquisition suggests that productivity must be demarcated by a discrete threshold (see also Aronoff 1976: 36). But note that such a threshold is empirically *undiscoverable*. Productive processes will lie above the threshold and unproductive processes will lie below, but with arbitrary "distance" from it in both cases. Thus, the threshold cannot be regressed out of the data. Second, while linguists now have an ever expanding arsenal of investigative tools to study productivity, ranging from the Wug test to fMRI to Big Data, the psychological grammar is developed without supervision in a matter of few years; these new empirical methods presently are at best a description of the speaker's grammatical knowledge and not yet learning models that account for how such knowledge is acquired. Finally, even if we were to discover the threshold of productivity through a statistical analysis – e.g., a productive rule must hold for at least 85% of eligible words – it would still remain mysterious why the critical value is exactly what it is, rather than 80% or 90%.

In other words, an I-language approach to productivity is needed, one which builds exclusively on the inherent constraints on language and cognition that all children have access to, with deductively established properties that must hold universally across languages. The study of language as a part of human biology, I believe, is an approach that Steve endorses and pursues (Anderson & Lightfoot 2002), which can be seen in his writings on morphology and related issues (Anderson 2010a; 2015).

Finally, a personal note. It is no exaggeration to say that I owe my professional career to Steve. He managed to create a position for me at Yale, which kept me close to my young family and thus linguistics, and further away from the seductive fortunes in the tech sector. It was also Steve who taught me, more effectively than anyone, the difference between linguistic evidence and rhetoric. It has been a privilege to learn from him. To figure out how to wake up irregular took over 15 years; the answer, I hope, is to his satisfaction. It may once again win me a spot, this time in the Linguistic Club of Ashville, North Carolina.

Acknowledgements

I would like to thank Steve Anderson, Bill Labov, Brian MacWhinney, Gary Thoms, Anthony Warner, and an anonymous reviewer for helpful discussions and comments.

References

Albright, Adam. 2009. Lexical and morphological conditioning of paradigm gaps. In Curt Rice & Sylvia Blaho (eds.), *Modeling ungrammaticality in Optimality Theory*, 117–164. London: Equinox.

Anderson, Stephen R. 1969. *West Scandinavian vowel systems and the ordering of phonological rules*. Cambridge, MA: Massachusetts Institute of Technology PhD thesis.

Anderson, Stephen R. 1973. Remarks on the phonology of English inflection. *Language and Literature* 1(4). 33–52.

Anderson, Stephen R. 1992. *A-morphous morphology*. Cambridge: Cambridge University Press.

Anderson, Stephen R. 2008. Phonologically conditioned allomorphy in the morphology of Surmiran (Rumantsch). *Word Structure* 1(2). 109–134.

Anderson, Stephen R. 2010a. An I-language view of morphological 'exceptionality': Comments on Corbett's paper. In Horst J. Simon & Heike Wiese (eds.), *Expecting the unexpected: Exceptions in grammar*, 127–134. Berlin: Mouton de Gruyter.

Anderson, Stephen R. 2010b. Failing one's obligations: Defectiveness in Rumantsch reflexes of DĒBĒRE. In Matthew Baerman, Greville G. Corbett & Dunstan Brown (eds.), *Defective paradigms: Missing forms and what they tell us*, 19–34. Oxford: British Academy & Oxford University Press.

Anderson, Stephen R. 2015. Morphological change. In Claire Bowern & Bethwyn Evans (eds.), *The Routledge handbook of historical linguistics*, 264–285. New York: Routledge.

Anderson, Stephen R. & David W. Lightfoot. 2002. *The language organ: Linguistics as cognitive physiology*. Cambridge: Cambridge University Press.

Anderwald, Lieselotte. 2003a. *Negation in non-standard British English: Gaps, regularizations and asymmetries*. London: Routledge.

Anderwald, Lieselotte. 2003b. Non-standard English and typological principles: The case of negation. In Günter Rohdenburg & Britta Mondorf (eds.), *Determinants of grammatical variation in English*, 507–530. Berlin/New York: Mouton de Gruyter.

Aronoff, Mark. 1976. *Word formation in generative grammar*. Cambridge, MA: MIT Press.

Baerman, Matthew. 2008. Historical observations on defectiveness: The first singular non-past. *Russian Linguistics* 32(1). 81–97.

Baerman, Matthew, Greville G. Corbett & Dunstan Brown (eds.). 2010. *Defective paradigms: Missing forms and what they tell us*. Oxford: British Academy & Oxford University Press.

Baker, Robert & Philip Smith. 1976. A psycholinguistic study of English stress assignment rules. *Language and Speech* 19(1). 9–27.

Baronian, Luc. 2005. *North of phonology*. Stanford University PhD thesis.

Berko, Jean. 1958. The child's learning of English morphology. *Word* 14(2–3). 150–177.

Berwick, Robert. 1985. *The acquisition of syntactic knowledge*. Cambridge, MA: MIT Press.

Berwick, Robert C & Noam Chomsky. 2016. *Why only us: Language and evolution*. Cambridge, MA: MIT Press.

Bloch, Bernard. 1947. English verb inflection. *Language* 23(4). 399–418.

Bowerman, Melissa. 1982. Reorganizational process in lexical and syntactic development. In Eric Wanner & Lila R. Gleitman (eds.), *Language acquisition: The state of the art*, 319–346. Cambridge/New York: Cambridge University Press.

Brainerd, Barron. 1989. The contractions of not: A historical note. *Journal of English Linguistics* 22(2). 176–196.

Bresnan, Joan. 2001. Explaining morphosyntactic competition. In Mark Baltin & Chris Collins (eds.), *Handbook of contemporary syntactic theory*, 1–44. Malden, MA & Oxford: Blackwell Publishing.

Broadbent, Judith M. 2009. The *amn't gap: The view from West Yorkshire. *Journal of Linguistics* 45(2). 251–284.

Brown, Dunstan & Andrew Hippisley. 2012. *Network morphology: A defaults-based theory of word structure*. Vol. 133. Cambridge: Cambridge University Press.

Brown, Roger. 1973. *A first language: The early stages*. Cambridge, MA: Harvard University Press.

Brown, Roger, Courtney B. Cazden & Ursula Bellugi. 1973. The child's grammar from I to III. In Charles A. Ferguson & Daniel I. Slobin (eds.), *Studies of child language development*, 295–333. New York: Holt, Rinehart & Winston.

Bybee, Joan. 1985. *Morphology: A study of the relation between meaning and form*. Philadelphia: John Benjamins.

Chomsky, Noam. 1955. The logical structure of linguistic theory. Ms., Harvard University and MIT. Revised version published by Plenum, New York, 1975.

Chomsky, Noam. 1965. *Aspects of the theory of syntax*. Cambridge, MA: MIT Press.

Chomsky, Noam. 1981. *Lectures in government and binding*. Dordrecht: Foris.

Chomsky, Noam. 2005. Three factors in language design. *Linguistic Inquiry* 36. 1–22.

Chomsky, Noam & Morris Halle. 1968. *The sound pattern of English*. Cambridge, MA: MIT Press.

Clahsen, Harald. 1999. Lexical entries and rules of language: A multidisciplinary study of German inflection. *Behavioral and Brain Sciences* 22. 991–1069.

Clahsen, Harald, Monika Rothweiler, Andreas Woest & Gary Marcus. 1992. Regular and irregular inflection in the acquisition of German noun plurals. *Cognition* 45. 225–255.

Cutler, Anne & David M. Carter. 1987. The predominance of strong initial syllables in the English vocabulary. *Computer Speech and Language* 2(3–4). 133–142.

Daland, Robert T., Andrea D. Sims & Janet Pierrehumbert. 2007. Much ado about nothing: A social network model of Russian paradigmatic gaps. In *Proceedings of the 45th annual meeting of the Association for Computational Linguistics*, 936–943. Somerset, NJ: Association for Computational Linguistics.

Davies, Mark. 2008. Corpus of Contemporary American English (COCA): 410+ million words, 1990-present. Available at http://www.americancorpus.org/.

Frampton, John. 2001. The *amn't* gap, ineffability, and anomalous *aren't*: Against morphosyntactic competition. In Mary Andronis, Christopher Ball, Heidi Elston & Sylvain Neuvel (eds.), *Papers from the 37th meeting of the Chicago Linguistic Society*, 399–412. Chicago: Chicago Linguistic Society.

Guion, Susan, J.J. Clark, Tetsuo Harada & Ratree Wayland. 2003. Factors affecting stress placement for English nonwords include syllabic structure, lexical class, and stress patterns of phonologically similar words. *Language and Speech* 46(4). 403–427.

Halle, Morris. 1973. Prolegomena to a theory of word formation. *Linguistic Inquiry* 4(1). 3–16.

Halle, Morris. 1998. The stress of English words 1968-1998. *Linguistic Inquiry* 29(4). 539–568.

Halle, Morris & Alec Marantz. 1993. Distributed morphology and the pieces of inflection. In Kenneth Hale & Samuel Jay Keyser (eds.), *The view from Building 20: Essays in linguistics in honor of Sylvain Bromberger*, 111–176. Cambridge, MA: MIT Press.

Halle, Morris & Jean-Roger Vergnaud. 1987. *An essay on stress*. Cambridge, MA: MIT Press.

Hart, Betty & Todd R Risley. 1995. *Meaningful differences in the everyday experience of young American children*. Baltimore, MD: Paul H. Brookes Publishing.

Hay, Jennifer & R. Harald Baayen. 2003. Phonotactics, parsing, and productivity. *Italian Journal of Linguistics* 1. 99–130.

Hayes, Bruce. 1982. Extrametricality and English stress. *Linguistic Inquiry* 13(2). 227–276.

Hetzron, Robert. 1975. Where the grammar fails. *Language* 51(4). 859–872.

Hudson, Richard. 2000. *I amn't. *Language* 76(2). 297–323.

Jespersen, Otto. 1917. *Negation in English and other languages* (Historisk-filologiske Meddelelser 1). Copenhagen: A.F. Høst.

Kehoe, Margaret & Carol Stoel-Gammon. 1997. The acquisition of prosodic structure: An investigation of current accounts of children's prosodic development. *Language* 73. 113–144.

Kelly, Michael H. 1992. Using sound to solve syntactic problems: The role of phonology in grammatical category assignments. *Psychological Review* 99(2). 349–364.

Kiparsky, Paul. 1973. Elsewhere in phonology. In Stephen R. Anderson & Paul Kiparsky (eds.), *A festschrift for Morris Halle*, 93–106. New York: Holt, Rinehart & Winston.

Labov, William, Paul Cohen, Clarence Robins & John Lewis. 1968. *A study of the non-standard English of Negro and Puerto Rican speakers in New York City. Volume 1: Phonological and grammatical analysis*. Cooperative Research Project No. 3288, Columbia University, New York.

Ladefoged, Peter & Victoria Fromkin. 1968. Experiments on competence and performance. *IEEE Transactions on Audio and Electroacoustics* 16(1). 130–136.

Legate, Julie A. & Charles Yang. 2013. Assessing child and adult grammar. In Robert Berwick & Massimo Piattelli-Palmarini (eds.), *Rich languages from poor inputs: In honor of Carol Chomsky*, 168–182. Oxford: Oxford University Press.

MacWhinney, Brian. 2000. *The CHILDES project: Tools for analyzing talk*. 3rd. Mahwah, NJ: Lawrence Erlbaum.

Maiden, Martin & Paul O'Neill. 2010. On morphomic defectiveness: Evidence from the Romance languages of the Iberian Peninsula. In Matthew Baerman, Greville G. Corbett & Dunstan Brown (eds.), *Defective paradigms: Missing forms and what they tell us*, 103–124. Oxford: British Academy & Oxford University Press.

Marcus, Gary, Steven Pinker, Michael T. Ullman, Michelle Hollander, John Rosen & Fei Xu. 1992. *Overregularization in language acquisition.* Vol. 57 (Monographs of the Society for Research in Child Development 4). Chicago: University of Chicago Press.

McClelland, James L. & Karalyn Patterson. 2002. Rules or connections in past-tense inflections: What does the evidence rule out? *Trends in Cognitive Sciences* 6(11). 465–472.

Nagy, William E. & Richard C. Anderson. 1984. How many words are there in printed school English? *Reading Research Quarterly* 19(3). 304–330.

Newport, Elissa. 1990. Maturational constraints on language learning. *Cognitive Science* 14(1). 11–28.

Nida, Eugene A. 1949. *Morphology: The descriptive analysis of words.* 2nd. Ann Arbor: University of Michigan Press.

Niyogi, Partha. 2006. *The computational nature of language learning and evolution.* Cambridge, MA: MIT Press.

Osherson, Daniel N., Michael Stob & Scott Weinstein. 1986. *Systems that learn: An introduction to learning theory for cognitive and computer scientists.* Cambridge, MA: MIT Press.

Pertsova, Katya. 2005. How lexical conservatism can lead to paradigm gaps. In Jeffrey Heinz, Andrew Martin & Katya Pertsova (eds.), *UCLA working papers in linguistics 11: Papers in phonology 6*, 13–30. Los Angeles: UCLA Linguistics Department.

Pinker, Steven. 1989. *Learnability and cognition: The acquisition of argument structure.* Cambridge, MA: MIT Press.

Pinker, Steven. 1999. *Words and rules: The ingredients of language.* New York: Basic Books.

Prince, Alan & Paul Smolensky. 2004. *Optimality Theory: Constraint interaction in generative grammar.* Cambridge, MA: MIT Press.

Pullum, Geoffrey K. & Deidre Wilson. 1977. Autonomous syntax and the analysis of auxiliaries. *Language* 53(4). 741–788.

Rice, Curt. 2005. Optimal gaps in optimal paradigms. *Catalan Journal of Linguistics* 4. 155–170.

Rumelhart, David E. & James L. McClelland. 1986. On learning the past tenses of English verbs. In James L. McClelland, David E. Rumelhart & the PDP Research Group (eds.), *Parallel distributed processing: Explorations into the microstructure of cognition. Volume 2: Psychological and biological models*, 216–271. Cambridge, MA: MIT Press.

Schuler, Kathryn, Charles Yang & Elissa Newport. 2016. Testing the Tolerance Principle: Children form productive rules when it is more computationally efficient to do so. In *The 38th Cognitive Society Annual Meeting*. Philadelphia, PA.

Schütze, Carson T. 2005. Thinking about what we are asking speakers to do. In Stephan Kepser & Marga Reis (eds.), *Linguistic evidence: Empirical, theoretical, and computational perspectives*, 457–485. Berlin: Mouton de Gruyter.

Sims, Andrea D. 2006. *Minding the gap: Inflectional defectiveness in a paradigmatic theory.* Ohio State University PhD thesis.

Steriade, Donca. 1997. Lexical conservatism. In Linguistic Society of Korea (ed.), *Linguistics in the morning calm 4: Selected papers from SICOL–1997*, 157–179. Seoul: Hanshin.

Stump, Gregory. 2001. *Inflectional morphology: A theory of paradigm structure.* Cambridge: Cambridge University Press.

Warner, Anthony. 1993. *English auxiliaries: Structure and history.* Cambridge University Press.

Weldon, Tracey. 1994. Variability in negation in African American Vernacular English. *Language Variation and Change* 6(3). 359–397.

Wiese, Richard. 1996. *The phonology of German.* Oxford: Clarendon Press.

Wolf, Matthew & John J. McCarthy. 2009. Less than zero: Correspondence and the null output. In Curt Rice & Sylvia Blaho (eds.), *Modeling ungrammaticality in Optimality Theory*, 17–66. London: Equinox.

Wright, Joseph. 1898. *The English dialect dictionary.* London: Henry Frowde.

Xu, Fei & Steven Pinker. 1995. Weird past tense forms. *Journal of Child Language* 22(3). 531–556.

Yang, Charles. 2002a. A principle of word storage. Manuscript: Yale University.

Yang, Charles. 2002b. *Knowledge and learning in natural language.* Oxford: Oxford University Press.

Yang, Charles. 2004. Universal grammar, statistics or both? *Trends in Cognitive Sciences* 8(10). 451–456.

Yang, Charles. 2013. Ontogeny and phylogeny of language. *Proceedings of the National Academy of Sciences* 110(16). 6324–6327.

Yang, Charles. 2015. Negative knowledge from positive evidence. *Language* 91(4). 938–953.

Yang, Charles. 2016. *The price of linguistic productivity: How children learn to break rules of language.* Cambridge, MA: MIT Press.

Yang, Charles, Stephen Crain, Robert C. Berwick, Noam Chomsky & Johan J. Bolhuis. 2017. The growth of language: Universal Grammar, experience, and principles of efficient computation. *Neuroscience and Biobehavioral Review.*

Yip, Kenneth & Gerald J. Sussman. 1998. *Sparse representations for fast, one-shot learning.* Tech. rep. 1633. MIT Artificial Intelligence Laboratory.

Zwicky, Arnold M. & Geoffrey K. Pullum. 1983. Cliticization vs. inflection: English N'T. *Language* 59(3). 502–513.

Part III

Syntax and Morphosyntax

Chapter 12

Special clitics and the right periphery in Tsotsil

Judith Aissen

University of California, Santa Cruz

> This paper documents the distribution of the definite enclitic =e in Tsotsil (Mayan), a clitic which occurs on the right periphery of utterances. On the basis of this distribution, it is argued (contra some restrictive theories of clitic placement) that =e cannot reach its surface position in the syntax, but must be positioned by the phonology. The property of =e which determines its placement is its obligatory association with the prosodic peak of the intonational phrase, a peak which is located at the right edge of that phrase. The relation of =e to several other elements which likewise occur at or near the right periphery of the intonational phrase in Tsotsil is considered, and a possible historical scenario which can account for the properties of =e is suggested.

1 Introduction

This paper has two goals. The first is to document more fully than has been done previously the distribution of the definite enclitic =e in Tsotsil (Mayan), a clitic which is restricted to the right periphery of utterances, (§2-§3).[1] The second is to suggest that =e is a special clitic in the sense of Anderson (2005) (following Zwicky 1977): "a linguistic element whose position with respect to the other elements of the phrase or clause follows a distinct set of principles, separate from those of the independently motivated syntax of free elements in the language" (31–32). The property of =e which makes it "special" is the extent to which it may be separated from the phrase in which it is licensed (§4).[2] In the analysis proposed here, this separation results from the requirement that =e function as the prosodic peak of the intonational phrase in which it occurs (§5), a requirement which can place it at a significant remove from its syntactically-motivated position. The requirement of prosodic prominence is unusual for a clitic. Anderson (2005) emphasizes the fact that clitics cannot be defined by the absence of "accent", as a clitic can bear an

---

[1] The distribution of this enclitic is noted in Aissen (1992: 61) but without much supporting data or discussion. It is also discussed in Skopeteas (2010) as part of a broader treatment of terminal clitics in Mayan languages.
[2] This property is emphasized in Skopeteas (2010).

Judith Aissen. 2017. Special clitics and the right periphery in Tsotsil. In Claire Bowern, Laurence Horn & Raffaella Zanuttini (eds.), *On looking into words (and beyond)*, 235–262. Berlin: Language Science Press. DOI:10.5281/zenodo.495449

accent if it happens to fall in an accented position within a larger prosodic constituent. But cases in which a clitic is *required* to occupy such a position – and will reorder in order to reach it – have not, to my knowledge, been documented. §6 speculates on how =*e* might have come to be associated with the phonological properties that force it to its surface position.

The fact that =*e* can occur outside the syntactic domain in which it is syntactically licensed poses a challenge to theories which hold that clitics reach their surface positions through syntactic operations, e.g., Bošković (2000) and Bermúdez-Otero & Payne (2011). For them, even clitics which are pronounced in prosodically determined positions nonetheless reach those positions in the syntax, with the role of phonology limited to filtering the outputs of a possibly overgenerating syntax. §4 suggests that this view is difficult to maintain in the case of =*e*. It thus adds to a body of work which has argued that phonology can determine word order, especially in the case of weak elements (Halpern 1995; Chung 2003; Agbayani & Golston 2010; Agbayani, Golston & Ishii 2015; Bennett, Elfner & McCloskey 2015).

2 The definite enclitic in Tsotsil

2.1 The basics

All dialects of Tsotsil have at least one enclitic which is associated with definite determiners, as well as with several other elements. The dialects differ with respect to how many such clitics they have, how many determiners they have, and what other elements the clitics associate with. Under discussion here is the dialect of Zinacantec Tsotsil (Z Tsotsil). Z Tsotsil has one such clitic, =*e*.[3] Among other elements, =*e* is associated with both of the definite determiners, *li* (PROXIMATE) and *ti* (REMOTE) (this association is indicated in examples by an overbar).[4]

(1)   a.   I-bat la ti̅ ̅ ̅v̅i̅n̅i̅k̅=e.
           CP-go CL DET man-DEF
           'The man went (they say).' (Laughlin 1977: 28)

---

[3] Tsotsil is spoken in Chiapas, Mexico by some 400,000 people. Claims made here about Zinacantec Tsotsil are based on a large body of text material and work with five native speakers over a number of years. Texts include naturally occurring speech, texts originally written in Tsotsil, and texts translated from Spanish to Tsotsil (the New Testament, cited as NT). Grammatical examples are almost all taken from texts; unpublished sources are cited as AUTHOR. Examples cited as ungrammatical have been checked with several speakers and their impossibility is consistent with the patterns seen in the text material.

[4] Like other Mayan languages, Tsotsil is verb-initial, usually V(O)S. It is also a head-marking language with ergative alignment. Affixes glossed ERG, ABS, GEN express φ features of arguments on agreeing nouns and verbs. Absolutive 3rd singular has no exponent and is not indicated in examples. Orthographic symbols have the expected values except for *x* = [ʃ], *j* = [x], *ch* = [tʃ], and ' = [ʔ] (except in symbols for ejectives, *p', t', ts', ch', k'*).

b. Buy li j-ve'el=e?
   where DET GEN.1-meal-DEF

   'Where is my meal?' (Laughlin 1977: 57)

(Note: "Buy" and "li j-ve'el=e" are bracketed together above.)

The deictic distinctions made by determiner+enclitic are fairly subtle and both determiners can be translated by English 'the'. More salient distinctions are made by incorporating deictic adverbs into the DP. As these examples suggest, =e occurs in a "final" position and I sometimes refer to it as a TERMINAL CLITIC. This distinguishes it both from second position clitics (e.g., the reportative clitic *la* in (1a)) and from terminal elements which are not clitics (e.g., those discussed in §5.2).

2.1.1 Licensing

There is a dependency between the definite determiners and =e: the determiners almost always co-occur with =e. Written texts rarely omit it, and speakers judge sentences without it to be "incomplete". In spoken language, =e is sometimes omitted, perhaps due to performance factors, to register, to individual speaker style, or to some other factor. The claims made here hold for relatively careful speech and for written texts. Other elements which license =e include a set of deictics which function as demonstratives and adverbs, as well as certain subordinators. The lexical elements which license =e in Z Tsotsil are shown in Table 1. The determiners *li* and *ti* figure in many of the temporal adverbs and

Table 1: =e licensors in Zinacantec Tsotsil

Category	Items
Definite determiner	*li* (PROX)
	ti (DISTAL)
Spatial demonstrative/adverb	*li'* '(this) here'
	le' '(that) there'
	taj '(that) over there'
Temporal adverb	*lavi* 'today'
Subordinators	*ti* (complementizer)
	ti mi 'if'
	(ti) k'alal 'when'
	(ti) yo' 'place where'

subordinators listed in Table 1: in the third category, *lavi* 'today' is derived from *li avi*; in the fourth, the complementizer *ti* may *be* the determiner, serving to nominalize a clause; *mi* is the polar question particle, but always occurs with *ti* when it introduces the protasis to a conditional; *k'alal* 'when, the time when' frequently occurs in collocation with

237

ti, as does *yo'* ('place where'). I assume then that =*e* realizes the feature [+DEF] in this dialect.[5] Examples (2a,b) show =*e* licensed by elements other than determiners:

(2) a. Och-an ech'el li' ta ch'en=e!
    enter-IMP DIR here in cave-DEF
    'Enter the cave here!' (Laughlin 1977: 71)

   b. K'alal i-k'ot ta s-ch'en=e...
    when CP-arrive P ERG.3-cave-DEF
    'When he arrived at his cave...' (Laughlin 1977: 72)

Aside from the qualification noted in fn. 5, elements which are not [+DEF] do not license =*e* in Tsotsil. This includes lexical categories (nouns, verbs, adjectives), related semi-functional categories like auxiliaries, and functional categories like the indefinite article, prepositions, negation, focus markers, coordinators, etc. Thus, =*e* does not occur in the position marked by the asterisk in any of the following examples as none of them contains an appropriate licensor.

(3) a. S-nup la ta be jun tseb un *.
    ERG.3-meet CL on path INDF girl PAR
    'He met a girl on the path.' (Laughlin 1977: 306)

   b. I-k'opoj la tal ta vinajel *.
    CP-speak CL coming P heaven
    'He spoke on arriving in heaven.' (NT: Mark 1,11)

   c. Ta xa x-'och k'ok' ok'ob *.
    ICP CL ASP-enter fire tomorrow.
    'The war will start tomorrow.' (Laughlin 1977: 119)

2.1.2 Terminal position: 1st approximation

Examples (1)-(2) suggest that =*e* occurs at the right edge of the phrase headed by its licensor. We will need to revise this, but it is true that =*e* in DP's, for example, must follow all post-head material in the phrase, including modifiers (4a,b) and possessors (4c). There are no other possible positions for =*e* in these examples – in particular, it

---

[5] =*e* sometimes occurs without an overt licensor, but still associated with a definite interpretation. Nominal cases include 1st and 2nd person pronouns (in certain syntactic positions), proper names (occasionally), and headless relatives with definite interpretations (frequently). These are all clearly definite, so association with a [+DEF] head seems unproblematic. Certain semantically dependent clauses can also end in =*e* without an overt licensor being present (e.g., a determiner or subordinator). These usually present background (given) information and correspond, for example, to English *when* or *since* clauses. Whether =*e* in these cases should be viewed as the realization of a [+DEF] feature or some other related feature is unclear. The clausal cases are not directly relevant to present concerns since =*e* is never separated in these from the domain in which it is licensed (the entire clause). Hence I leave them aside.

absolutely cannot attach to the head noun nor to the first prosodic word in the phrase (these positions are marked with asterisks).

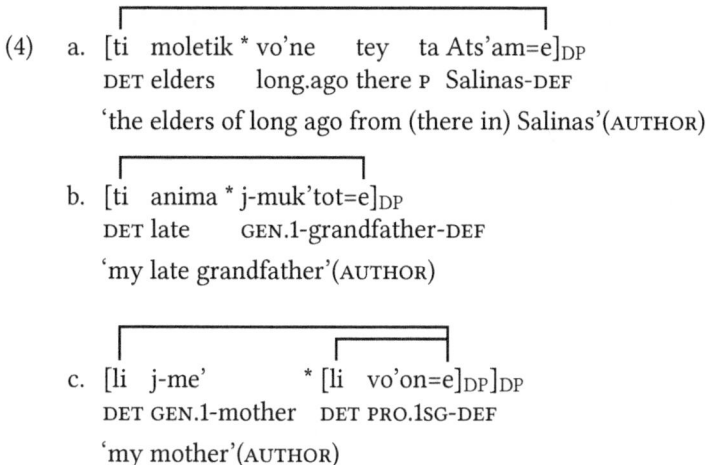

(4) a. [ti moletik * vo'ne tey ta Ats'am=e]_DP
    DET elders   long.ago there P Salinas-DEF
    'the elders of long ago from (there in) Salinas' (AUTHOR)

b. [ti anima * j-muk'tot=e]_DP
    DET late   GEN.1-grandfather-DEF
    'my late grandfather' (AUTHOR)

c. [li j-me'   * [li vo'on=e]_DP]_DP
    DET GEN.1-mother DET PRO.1SG-DEF
    'my mother' (AUTHOR)

(4a-c) come from texts in which the DP is a topic. These occur "external" to the clause and are thus isolated from the effects of other elements which (as we will see below) interact with the position of =e.

2.1.3 Coalescence

An important property of =e is COALESCENCE. In (4c), the larger DP contains two licensors, each of which should be matched by =e. One (the first *li*) is the head of the larger DP (the possessum), the other (the second *li*) is the head of the embedded DP (the possessor). The right edge of the two DP's coincide and only a single clitic is possible at this edge. This is a general property of terminal clitic systems in Mayan; even when multiply licensed, only a single such clitic occurs (within the relevant domain) (Skopeteas 2010).

2.1.4 Clitic vs. affix

Though it is generally accepted that "clitic" is a cover term for a diverse set of elements and not a formal grammatical category, the term is still used descriptively. To motivate the use of the term "clitic" to refer to Tsotsil =e, I survey some of the criteria that have been used in the past to distinguish clitics from (ordinary) affixes (Zwicky & Pullum 1983). All of these align =e more closely with "clitics" than with inflectional affixes. [1] it imposes no selectional restrictions on the host, but may attach to members of any lexical category that falls in the appropriate right-edge position. In addition to nouns, these include verbs, as in (5c), adjectives, particles (see §5.2), and even second position clitics like the reportative clitic *la* in (5a); [2] there are no arbitrary gaps in the possible X=e combinations; [3] the form of the host is not sensitive to the presence of the clitic (the clitic triggers no allomorphy and does not participate in lexical phonology); [4] there are no semantic idiosyncracies associated with =e; and [5] =e attaches outside all other suffixes, e.g., noun plurals, (5b), and agreement suffixes, (5c).

(5) a. a ti vo'ne la=e ...
    TOP DET long.ago CL-DEF
    'as for long ago (they say)'

  b. ti jeneral-etik=e
     DET general-PL-DEF
     'the generals'

  c. li tak'in ta j-ta-tikotik=e
     DET money ICP ERG.1-find-1PL.EXCL-DEF
     'the money that we could find'

At the same time, =e is prosodically more like an affix than other clitics in the language. Tsotsil has various "simple" clitics, i.e., syntactic words which are prosodically weak. Like other words in the language, all of these have an onset, e.g., the interrogative polarity particle *mi*, the definite determiners *ti, li*, negation *mu*, second position modal and aspectual clitics (*xa, to, me, la*). In contrast though, =e, like many inflectional affixes, lacks an onset. Further, except for the second position clitics, the simple clitics all precede their complements, while =e follows everything in its phrase.

If "clitic" is not a formal grammatical category, then the properties of =e must follow from its analysis as a word or affix. There are a number of possible analyses that could be considered. We could analyze it as a prosodically deficient word which heads its own phrase within the DP, as shown in (6).

(6)

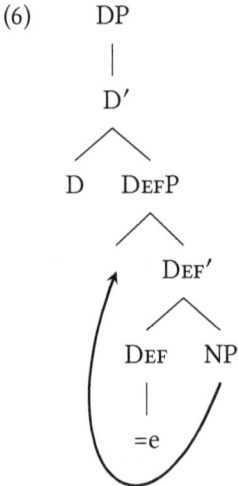

Here, =e heads a DEFP which is selected by D and which itself takes a NP complement. We could account for the phrase-final position of =e by assuming that =e requires that its specifier be filled, and that the NP complement raises to its left to satisfy this requirement (this would follow proposals of Cinque 2005 and Simpson 2005, who account for the phrase-final position of demonstratives in various languages via leftward movement of NP within DP).[6] Another possibility would be to analyze =e as inflectional morphology which spells out a definiteness feature associated with the noun phrase on the rightmost terminal of that phrase, much as Miller (1991) analyzes the French deictic clitics -ci and -là. A third possibility is to analyze =e as a phrasal affix, analogous to the treatment that Anderson (2005) proposes for the English genitive marker 's and somewhat tentatively for definitive accent in Tongan. In this approach, =e would be introduced post-syntactically by the phrasal morphology as spell-out of the feature [+DEF] on DP and its surface position would be determined by a constraint operating within an OT constraint system. Any of these approaches will have to confront the issues discussed in the next section; how well each would fare is not a question I address here. Going forward, I will assume the analysis sketched in (6), according to which =e is a prosodically deficient word which is introduced in the syntax.

Under any of these analyses, =e is licensed within the phrase headed by its licensor, usually DP, and I take this phrase to be the "syntactic domain" of the clitic. The puzzle that gives rise to this paper is the fact that =e does not in fact always close the phrase in which it is licensed but often occurs considerably further to the right. I argue below that this is because =e can occur only at the right edge of an intonational phrase (ιP), an edge which is often located further to the right than the right edge of the phrase in which =e is licensed. The evidence for this is presented in §3; in §5, I consider why =e is constrained in this way.

3 Prosodic constraints on =e

Although =e frequently appears at the right edge of the phrase in which it is licensed, the larger descriptive generalization about its position is not syntactic, but prosodic (Aissen 1992; Skopeteas 2010):

(7) =e occurs at the right edge of the ιP which contains its licensor.

Descriptions of Z Tsotsil characterize prosodic prominence at two levels – the word and the phrase. At the word level, stress falls on the initial syllable of the root; at the phrase level, it falls on the final syllable of the ιP (Laughlin 1975,23; Haviland 1981,14) (stress being predictable, it is not marked in the orthography). I assume then that the final syllable of the ιP is its prosodic peak.[7] A detailed phonetic study of intonational

---

[6] Note that this movement would violate the anti-locality constraints proposed in Pesetsky & Torrego (2001) and Abels (2003) which preclude movement of the complement of a head (a phase head in Abels' account) to the specifier of that head.

[7] The association of prosodic prominence with the final syllable of the ιP is reported for other Tsotsil dialects (Cowan 1969: 4; Delgaty & Sánchez 1978: 11) as well as for the sister language Tseltal (Shklovsky 2011; Polian 2013); see Bennett (2016: §6.1) for an overview of lexical and phrasal stress in Mayan.

phrasing in Tsotsil does not yet exist, but some preliminary observations are possible. The final syllable is associated with characteristic boundary tones. The most common pattern involves a rise in pitch on the vowel of the final syllable, with the larger context determining whether that rise is sustained throughout the syllable or followed by a fall (relevant factors include whether the ɩP is final in the utterance or not (as in the case of topics, for example, §3.2)). The final syllable of the ɩP is sometimes followed by a significant pause and when it is, the vowel of that syllable is often lengthened.

Some of these properties are evident in Figure 1, taken from a naturally-produced narrative by a Z Tsotsil speaker; this example occurs utterance-finally and shows a final fall.

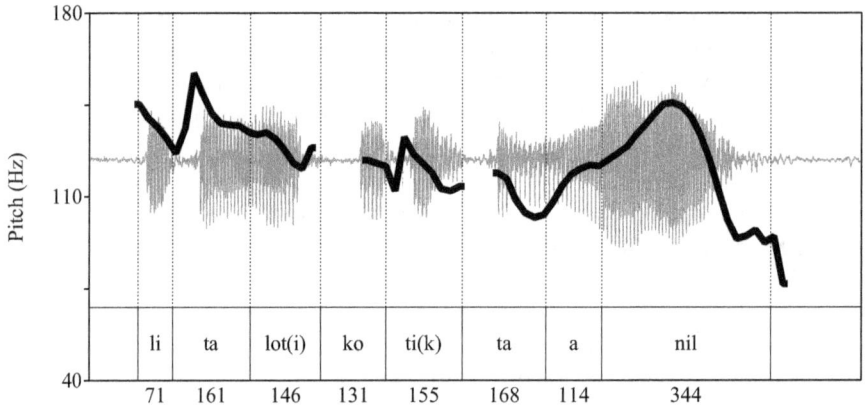

Figure 1: Pitch track and waveform for (8).

(8) L-i-tal-otkotik   ta anil.
    CP-ABS.1-come-1PL.EXCL in hurry
    'We came in a hurry.' (AUTHOR)

A key observation is that because =e aligns with the right edge of the ɩP, then, whatever else it is, it is the final syllable of the ɩP. It thus carries the boundary tone, and is often followed by significant pause and lengthened. This is illustrated in Figure 2, which is based on (9), from the same narrative as Figure 1; this phrase is also utterance-final.

(9) ... te   ta s-na   li Maryan Papyan=e.
        there P GEN.3-house DET Mariano Papyan-DEF
    '...there in the house of Mariano Papyan.' (AUTHOR)

The analysis proposed in §5 hinges on the obligatory association between =e and the prosodic peak of ɩP.

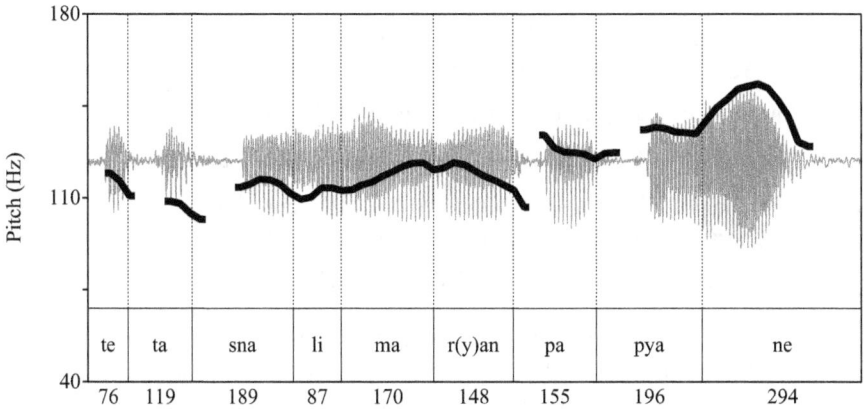

Figure 2: Pitch track and waveform for (9).

As in other languages, utterances consisting of a simple clause are parsed as a single ɩP. There are also two structures in Z Tsotsil which are associated with obligatory ɩP breaks, resulting in utterances with multiple ɩP's, and therefore multiple positions for =e under (7): an external topic is parsed as an ɩP separate from that of the following comment clause and an extraposed CP is parsed as a ɩP separate from that the preceding matrix clause.[8] Other complements, as well as relative clauses, are usually not extraposed and they are prosodically integrated into the ɩP of the matrix clause. In this section we provide support for (7), starting with simple clauses (§3.1), then considering structures with multiple ɩP's (§3.2-§3.3), and finally syntactically complex structures which map to a single ɩP (§3.4). §3.5 suggests an algorithm for mapping syntactic structure to prosodic structure.

3.1 Simple clauses

In utterances consisting of a single clause, regardless of where =e is licensed, it appears at the right edge of the ɩP corresponding to the clause. When the licensing phrase itself is clause-final, as in (1)-(2), that phrase has the appearance of being closed by =e. But if a clause contains several phrases which are headed by licensors, no phrase which occurs medially can end in =e. Adding it in in the positions of the asterisks in (10) and (11) is impossible.

---

[8] Some adverbial clauses are obligatorily parsed as separate ɩP's and some only optionally. These are not discussed here, but see Aissen (1992: 59).

(10) S-jipan la ta=ora [ti ok'il *] [ti t'ul] un=e.
ERG.3-tie CL right.away DET coyote DET rabbit PAR-DEF

'The rabbit tied Coyote up right away.' (Laughlin 1977: 160)

(11) I-s-ta la tal [li aniyo *] ta yut=vo' [li choy] un=e.
CP-ERG.3-find CL DIR DET ring P inside.water DET fish PAR-DEF

'The fish found the ring in the water.' (Laughlin 1977: 354)

One might think that =e is simply omitted when the licensing phrase does not occur clause-finally. But examples like (12)-(14) show otherwise. Here (and generally), the clause-medial DP *does* license =e but the clitic is delayed to the end of the clause.

(12) L-i-'abtej-otikotik xchi'uk [li Kumpa Lol]_{dp} ta museo-e.
CP-ABS.1-work-1PL.EXCL with DET Compadre Lol P museum-DEF

We worked with Compadre Lol at the museum. (Laughlin 1980: 25)

(13) Ch-'och xa [li k'ok']_{dp} [ok'ob]_{adv} [ta Nibak]_{pp}=e.
ICP-enter CL DET fire tomorrow P Ixtapa-DEF

'The war will begin tomorrow in Ixtapa.' (Laughlin 1977: 119)

(14) Ta=x-[y]-ak'-ik [ti kantela]_{dp} [noxtok]_{adv}=e.
ICP-ERG.3-give-PL DET candle too-DEF.

'They too were offering the candles.'(AUTHOR)

There are two properties to note in these examples. First, =e must be licensed by the determiner since there is no other licensor present; and second, the intervening PP's and adverbs are not part of the DP headed by the licensor. In (12)-(14), they modify the entire sentence (or the predicate), not the head noun. In (14), the adverb *noxtok* 'too, also' is associated with additive focus on the subject 'they' (= shamans in the town under discussion) not the object ('the candles') – the preceding discourse describes shamans from a neighboring town offering candles; the current utterance asserts that the ones in this town too were offering candles. =e attaches then outside its syntactic domain, assuming that domain to be the DP headed by its licensor.

Going back to (10)-(11), the right conclusion, I think, is that both determiners require =e, but that that requirement is satisfied by the single, clause-final enclitic (see also Skopeteas 2010). These cases too then involve coalescence, but in a configuration different from the one illustrated by (4c). In (4c), the right edges of the two DP's which

12 Special clitics and the right periphery in Tsotsil

license =e coincide, but here they do not. (10)-(11) actually provide another kind of evidence that =e does not always close its syntactic domain: the particle *un* which occurs in both examples (and in many subsequent ones) is not part of the preceding DP, yet whenever it occurs, it separates =e from its licensing phrase, (see §5.2 on *un*).

Examples like (15) and (16) provide further evidence that =e can occur outside its syntactic domain: they show that when the phrase that licenses =e is preposed, =e still surfaces in post-verbal position, at the right edge of the clause. (15) is from a narrative in which a mother gives advice to her son, (16) from one about the Kennedy assassination.

(15) [Ta sba me l-av-ajnil]_{PP}   ch-a-muy=e,
      on top CL DET-GEN.2-wife   ICP-ABS.2-climb-DEF
      'It's on top of your wife that you should climb [not onto the rafters].' (Laughlin 1977: 56)

(16) Ja' nox [li viniketik]_{DP} i-laj-ik   ta bala=e.
      FOC only DET men   CP-end-PL P bullet-DEF
      '[The women weren't hit by the bullets], it was only the men that were wounded by bullets.' (Laughlin 1980: 15)

In (15), a PP has been fronted into focus position, as sketched in (17) (the larger context makes clear that we are dealing with contrastive focus in both (15-16)). Note that a fronted focus does *not* occasion an ιP break (Aissen 1992).

(17) = structure of (15)

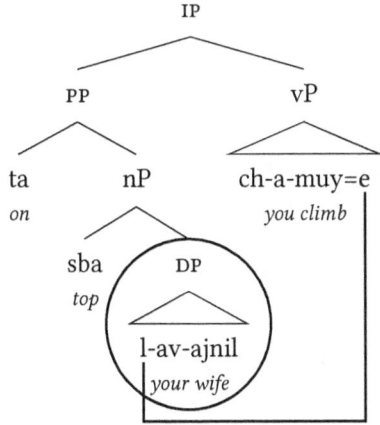

The licensor for =e in (17) is the head of the circled DP, which is embedded quite deeply within the fronted PP, but the enclitic does not close that DP. Instead it surfaces clause-finally. (16) is a cleft construction where the focus occurs preverbally. Again =e is licensed

245

by the head of that DP but occurs clause-finally (the verb phrase which follows the focus does not modify the focus and is presumably not embedded in it).

With respect then to simple, monoclausal structures, examples (12)-(16) show (in various ways) that in Z Tsotsil, =e does not in general close the *phrase* headed by its licensor. A closer approximation is that it closes the *clause* containing the licensor (though we will see shortly that this is not the whole story either). This holds whether the licensor is a determiner or some other element, e.g., a deictic adverb. (18)-(19) show that an =e licensed by a deictic adverb also occurs clause-finally, again separated from the phrase containing the licensor by intervening material (in (19), the adverb functions as the clausal predicate).

(18) J-tsak-tik   [lavi] [ta k'in]-e.
      ERG.1-grab-1PL.INC today P fiesta

      'Let's arrest him today at the festival.' (NT: Matthew 26:5)

(19) Muk' li'   s-malal=e.
      NEG here GEN-husband-DEF

      'Their husbands weren't around here [they had gone to the lowlands].' (Laughlin 1977: 101)

3.2 Topics

As in many other languages, external topics in Tsotsil are parsed as separate ιP's (by "external topic", I mean one which is attached outside the sentence, often entering into an anaphoric relation with a pronoun inside the sentence) (Aissen 1992). Topics are usually definite in Tsotsil and therefore are almost always closed by =e (the ιP break is indicated by "‖"):

(20) Ti moletik vo'ne   tey ta Ats'am=e, ‖ i-s-tsob   la s-ba-ik
      DET elders long.ago there P Salinas-DEF CP-ERG.3-gather CL GEN.3-RR-PL

      ta snuts-el   li biyaetik=e.
      P chase-NOMZL DET Villistas-DEF

      'The elders of long ago (from) there in Salinas gathered to chase the Villistas.' (AUTHOR)

(21) Ti anima j-muk'tot=e   ‖ x-'ok' xa la sutel   tal.
      DET late GEN.1-grandfather-DEF   ASP-cry CL CL returning here

      'My late grandfather returned crying.' (AUTHOR)

3.3 Complex clauses with CP complements

CP complements obligatorily extrapose in Tsotsil. While normal order in transitive clauses is VOS, when O is a CP complement, it occurs utterance-finally (Aissen 1992).

(22) I-y-il   ti s-me'   un=e ‖
     CP-ERG.3-see DET GEN.3-mother PAR-DEF
     ti   muk'=bu ta s-sa'   y-ajnil   ti s-krem   un=e   .
     COMP NEG   ICP ERG.3-seek GEN.3-wife DET GEN.3-son PAR-DEF
     'His mother saw that her son was never going to find a wife.' (Laughlin 1977: 55)

Extraposition is associated with an obligatory ιP break and, as expected, the matrix and CP complements form separate domains for clitic placement: the =e licensed by the first determiner closes the first ιP and the one licensed by the second closes the second ιP.

Extraposition of CP complements also occurs in ditransitive clauses. While the THEME precedes the GOAL when both are nominal, the THEME follows the GOAL when it is a CP:

(23) Ikalbe li kumpa   Lol un=e ‖ ti   yu'un   chicham xa un=e.
     I.told DET compadre Bob PAR-DEF COMP because I.was.dying CL PAR-DEF
     'I told Compadre Bob that I was feeling awful.' (Laughlin 1980: 30)

Again, extraposition forces an ιP break between the matrix clause and its extraposed complement. And as above, the two clauses form separate domains for clitic placement.

3.4 Prosodically integrated subordinate clauses

While CP complements extrapose, there are other embedded clauses which do not and thus remain in their base position. These include IP complements (selected by verbs of perception and some other higher predicates) as well as relative clauses. Prosodically these do not form separate ιP's, but are integrated into the ιP of the matrix clause (see An 2007 on languages in which restrictive relatives do not form separate ιP's).

Consider the IP complement in (24). It remains in its internal position and is followed by the matrix subject:

(24) Mi ja'uk o=bu y-a'i   [lok' ti y-ajnil   *]_{ip} ti vinik un=e.
     NEG even ever ERG.3-feel leave DEF GEN.3-wife   DET man PAR-DEF
     'The man didn't even feel his wife slipping out.' (Laughlin 1977: 49)

There is no extraposition here and the entire utterance is pronounced as a single ιP. If =e closed the (smallest) *clause* in which was licensed, we would expect one to surface in the position of the asterisk. But =e is not possible there. Instead, it appears that the enclitic licensed within the complement is delayed until the end of the entire utterance, where it coalesces with the one licensed by the subject. Consistent with (7), the enclitic licensed within the complement clause is pronounced at the right edge of the ɩP which contains its licensor.

Relative clauses (RC) also generally do not extrapose. Relative clauses with external heads do not occur utterance-internally (if necessary, the sentence is restructured so that they occur utterance-finally or sentence-initially as part of the topic), but headless relatives (or better, "light-headed" relatives involving a determiner + CP) can.[9] In (25) and (26), the RC is sandwiched between the matrix verb and the matrix subject.

(25) Y-il-oj   [ti [bu   k'ot ti j'ik'al *]RC] ti vinik un=e.
     ERG.3-see-PRF DET where arrive DET Spook   DET man PAR-DEF

'The man saw (the place) where the Spook landed.' (Laughlin 1977: 63)

(26) I-y-a'i   la [taj [k'alal ch-lok' tal taj
     CP-ERG.3-feel CL DET when   ICP-leave DIR DET

     chon   *]RC] taj ants   un=e,
     serpent   DET woman PAR-DEF

'That woman felt (the moment) when that snake left.' (Laughlin 1977: 371)

Like ɩP complements, RC's do not constitute separate ɩP's, but are parsed together with the matrix clause. Examples (25)-(26) show that an =e licensed in such a relative clause is realized not at the edge of the relative clause (marked here by an asterisk), but again at the right edge of the entire utterance where it coalesces with the clitic licensed by the matrix subject.

3.5 Summary

The position in which =e is pronounced in Z Tsotsil does not coincide with the edge of the phrase in which is licensed, nor even with the edge of the (minimal) clause in which it is licensed. Rather, it coincides with the right edge of ɩP containing its licensor.

While it is not necessary for our purposes to provide an algorithm for mapping syntactic structure to prosodic structure (what is important is that ɩP breaks fall in certain positions, not why they fall there), there is a simple principle which determines this mapping if we assume that external topics and extraposed clauses are both adjoined at the root of the sentence (Aissen 1992). Assuming that an element X which adjoins to Y is not dominated by Y, then neither topics nor extraposed clauses are dominated by any node. Hence, like simple clauses, the nodes which define these constituents are "undominated". In this respect they are like root nodes and, following Frank, Hagstrom & Vijay-Shanker

---

[9] I take the RC to be a CP since it contains a fronted WH expression in (25) and a complementizer in (26).

(2002), I will refer to them as such. With this understanding, the mapping from syntax to ɩP can be characterized as a *match* between a certain syntactic constituent (one dominated by a root node) and a corresponding prosodic constituent (an ɩP) (on MATCH constraints, see Selkirk 2009 and Elfner 2012; on the relevance of the *root* to defining ɩP, see Downing 1970; Nespor & Vogel 1986; Selkirk 2009). The formulation in (27) is based on Bennett, Elfner & McCloskey (2015) and Elfner (2012),

(27) MATCH ROOT
If a root node R in a syntactic representation S dominates all and only the set of terminal elements $\{a,b,c, ..., n\}$, then there must be in the phonological representation P corresponding to S an ɩP which dominates all and only the phonological exponents of $a,b,c, ..., n$.

When MATCH ROOT is satisfied in Tsotsil (as it appears always to be), simple clauses and some complex structures are parsed as single ɩP's; extraposed CP's and topics are parsed into their own ɩP's.

In §5, I develop an account of clitic placement in Tsotsil in which the syntax positions =e at the edge of the phrase in which it is licensed, per (6), and the phonology accounts for its subsequent dislocation to the right edge of ɩP. This attributes a more significant role to the phonology than some theories of clitic placement permit. Hence before turning to the phonological account, I consider the prospects for accounts in which phonology plays at most a filtering role in the placement of =e in Tsotsil.

4 A syntactic account?

While recognizing that the positioning of some clitics is sensitive to prosodic constituency, some recent theories of clitic placement propose that the role of phonology is limited to filtering outputs from the syntax. Consider, for example, Bošković (2000)'s account of second-position clitics in Serbo-Croatian. Bošković argues that these clitics attach to the first prosodic word within an ɩP. This is a prosodic generalization, but in his account, the prosody does not directly determine the position of second-position clitics. Rather, clitics reach their surface positions through syntactic mechanisms. Since syntactic mechanisms sometimes place clitics in other than "second" position, PF filters out derivations in which the clitics do not suffix to the initial prosodic constituent in the ɩP. Bermúdez-Otero & Payne (2011) propose that all cases of prosodic conditioning of clitic placement can be handled in the same way, i.e., clitics are positioned by a possibly over-generating syntax, with ill-formed configurations filtered out at PF.

The problem posed by =e is clear. If its syntactic domain is the phrase headed by its licensor (typically, DP), then the syntax should place =e somewhere within that domain. However, we have seen that =e can occur outside the phrase in which it is licensed, indeed outside the clause in which it is licensed. In fact, it *must* occur outside that phrase (or clause) when it is not ɩP-final. The only option for an account of clitic placement in which phonology does no more than filter outputs from the syntax is to extend the syntactic domain of =e (or the [+DEF] feature which it realizes) beyond the phrase in which it is licensed.

Conceived syntactically, the dependency between the position in which =e is licensed and the position in which it is pronounced can span a significant amount of syntactic structure – it crosses clause-boundaries including ones which define relative clauses. There are various ways that apparent long-distance dependencies are handled, depending both on the nature of the dependency and on the particular syntactic model – long-distance movement (Transformational Grammar), a sequence of local movements (Minimalism), feature percolation (GPSG/HPSG) and others (Alexiadou, Kiss & Müller 2012). It is beyond the scope of this article to develop a syntactic analysis of =e placement, but we can point out two properties of the phenomenon that any such analysis must account for. One is that the top of the dependency is limited to root (undominated) nodes: =e can spell out only at the right edge of an undominated node, and not at the right edge of any other node. If movement or percolation are involved, they must therefore be to the root, whether that node corresponds to a simple clause, a topic, or an extraposed complement. The other is that the bottom of the dependency can be located *anywhere* within the structure dominated by the root. In particular, it can be located within a constituent which is otherwise an island for extraction, for example within a PP, as in (15/17) (see Aissen 1996 for evidence that PP's are islands for extraction), or a relative clause, (25)-(26) (see Aissen 1992).

It is instructive to consider a particular analysis which would position =e in its low, syntactically-licensed position and account for its appearance at the right edge of ɩP's through late, prosodically-conditioned linearization. Bermúdez-Otero & Payne (2011) mention this as a possible analysis for cases in which a clitic attaches to a prosodically defined domain, like the second position clitics in Chamorro (Chung 2003). They point to Linear Syntax (Kathol 2004), a theory of linearization embedded in HPSG, as a possible framework for implementation. Linear Syntax imposes precedence relations on sisters but, in order to handle discontinuities, permits those relations to be "passed up" the tree and then "shuffled" with relations among higher elements. In this way, elements from an embedded domain may be separated from one another by elements that belong to higher syntactic domains. In the case at hand, =e, linearized, for example at the right edge of the phrase in which it is licensed, could be separated from that phrase at higher levels, extending its syntactic domain to a higher constituent.

The question for this account is just what constraints it imposes on the upward "percolation" of precedence relations. In a language which does not in general permit scrambling, which nodes pass precedence relations upwards and which do not? The most obvious challenge is posed by the fact that an =e licensed somewhere within a relative clause or a PP cannot surface within those phrases if they are not utterance-final, but must surface in the matrix. In the shuffling account of examples like (15/17) and (25)-(26), the precedence relation between =e and the rest of the licensing phrase (its specifier, under (6)) would be obligatorily passed up through the relative clause or PP and then shuffled with precedence relations among elements in the matrix clause. Since PP's and relative clauses are otherwise impermeable in Tsotsil, one must wonder why Shuffling, but not other syntactic operations, can access elements within them.

On the other hand, it is a prosodic fact, independent of anything about =e, that PP's and relative clauses in Tsotsil do not form separate ιP's. Hence the fact that an =e licensed within them surfaces outside them when they are not utterance-final follows from the prosodic generalization in (7). In short, if the relation between =e and the phrase in which it is licensed is conceived as a syntactic dependency, its properties are unexpected. But if the relation is instead phonological and holds within an ιP at a point when syntactic structure is no longer relevant, the distribution of =e and its relation to the licensing phrase begin to make sense.

5 A prosodic account

5.1 Association with prosodic prominence

I outline here an account of =e in Z Tsotsil. This account shares with Anderson's 2005 approach to clitic placement the assumption that the surface position of =e is determined post-syntactically through an optimization that evaluates alternative positions of the clitic against a set of ranked constraints (Prince & Smolensky 1993/2004). It differs from Anderson in that =e is not itself subject to a constraint which aligns it with the edge of a constituent. Rather the position of =e is motivated by an inherent lexical property, namely its association with the prosodic prominence that characterizes the right edge of ιP's in the language. In this, I closely follow Henderson (2012)'s account of certain "status" suffixes in K'iche' (also Mayan),[10] which surface only at the right edge of ιP. These suffixes attach only to verbs and surface only when the verb occurs ιP-finally, (28a). Otherwise, the suffix is suppressed, (28b) (accent marks here represent the prosodic peak of the utterance):

(28)   a.   X-in-tij-ó.
           CP-ERG.1SG-eat-SS
           'I ate it.'

   b.   X-in-tij   le   súb'.
           CP-ERG.1SG-eat DET tamalito
           'I ate the tamalito.' (Henderson 2012: 775–776)

Henderson notes that status suffixes are simply omitted from phrase-medial verbs, rather than being displaced to ιP-final position (see 28b) and attributes this to the fact that the suffix is an affix (not a clitic) and attaches only to verbs. He raises the issue of what would happen if the element in question were a clitic. The distribution of Tsotsil =e instantiates exactly this case: =e is not tied to any particular word class and thus faithful realization carries it away from the position in which it is licensed.

The lexical entry for =e is shown in (29), where the asterisk indicates association with the prosodic peak of ιP:

---

[10] These suffixes mark the transitivity status of the predicate and make other distinctions related to mood and dependency.

(29) *
      |
      e

I also adopt Henderson's constraint set, it being as well-suited to Tsotsil =e as it is to the K'iche' status suffixes. The constraints fall into three groups. The first two concern the location of prosodic prominence in the ιP and are independent of the distribution of =e. An alignment constraint (McCarthy & Prince 1993) locates the peak of prosodic prominence at the right edge of the ιP, (30). CULMINATIVITY (31) limits such peaks to one per ιP (Hayes 1995).

(30) ALIGN$_\iota$: A peak of prominence lies at the right edge of the ιP.

(31) CULM(INATIVITY): Every prosodic domain has exactly one peak of prominence.

The second two are faithfulness constraints on the morphology-to-phonology correspondence (Prince & Smolensky 1993/2004; McCarthy & Prince 1995). REALIZEMORPH (32), a general constraint, calls for faithful parsing of morphemes in the phonology (Kurisu 2001). IDENTPROM (33) is the key constraint here: it requires that the lexical association of =e with prosodic prominence be preserved in the output (Henderson 2012).[11]

(32) REALIZEM(ORPH): Every morpheme in the input has a phonological exponent in the output.

(33) IDENTPROM: if morpheme M has prominence P in the input, then M', the phonological correspondent of M, has prominence P in the output.

Tableau (34) shows the effect of these constraints on the evaluation of an input, that of (12), in which the syntactically determined position for =e does not correspond to the right edge of an ιP. The input in Tableau (34) is a morphophonological representation in which syntactic terminals have been spelled-out and in which the hierarchical structure of syntax has been replaced by precedence relations and prosodic structure. =e is a morphophonological element. Its position is syntactically determined per (6) and its association with the prosodic peak is indicated in the input by the asterisk, a morphological diacritic. Candidates for the output are fully linearized phonological representations, parsed into prosodic constituents. Prosodic prominence in the ιP is marked by an acute accent.

The optimal candidate is [b], which violates none of the constraints shown. However, it does violate one which is not shown, LINEARITY, which penalizes outputs which diverge from the precedence relations of the input (McCarthy & Prince 1995).[12] LINEARITY must be lower ranked than any of the four constraints shown in Tableau (34).

---

[11] I have slightly reworded IDENTPROM from Henderson to emphasize the distinction between M in the input and its correspondent M' in the output.

[12] The high-ranked constraint MATCH ROOT (27) prevents =e from moving "too far", by requiring that it be realized within the same ιP as its licensor.

(34) Tableau for (12)

[... li Kumpa Lol=e* ta museo]$_\iota$ ... DET compadre L-DEF P museum	ALIGN$_\iota$	CULM	IDENT PROM	REALIZE MORPH
a. [...li kumpa lol=é ta museo]$_\iota$	*!			
b. ☞ [...li kumpa lol ta museo=é]$_\iota$				
c. [...li kumpa lol=e ta museó]$_\iota$			*!	
d. [...li kumpa lol-é ta museó]$_\iota$		*!		
e. [...li kumpa lol ta museo]$_\iota$				*!

(35) LIN(EARITY): The precedence structure of the input is consistent with that of the output and vice versa.

When the input has two enclitics, they coalesce in the output.

(36) S-jipan la ta=ora [ti ok'il [ti t'ul] un=e.
    ERG.3-tie CL right.away DET coyote DET rabbit PAR-DEF
    'The rabbit tied Coyote up right away.' (Laughlin 1977: 160)

Taking the input to (36) to be [...ti ok'il=e* ti t'ul=e*], we can see that the optimal output, [b] in (38), violates none of the four constraints (30)-(33): the prosodic peak is aligned with the right edge of the ιP, there is only a single prosodic peak, the prosodic prominence associated with =e in the input is preserved in the output, and every morpheme in the input has a phonological exponent in the output. The association of input morphemes to phonological exponents, however, is many-to-one, as indicated by the subscripts on =e in input and output. Hence the optimal candidate, [b] (=36), violates the Anti-Coalescence constraint, UNIFORMITY (McCarthy & Prince 1995), as well as LINEARITY. Like LINEARITY, UNIFORMITY is ranked below the other constraints shown.

(37) UNIF(ORMITY): No element in the output has multiple correspondents in the input.

(38) Tableau for (36)

[...ti ok'il=e*$_1$ ti t'ul=e*$_2$]$_\iota$ ...DET coyote-DEF DET rabbit-DEF	ALIGN$_\iota$	CULM	IDENT PROM	REALIZE MORPH	LIN	UNIF
a. [...ti ok'il=é$_1$ ti t'ul=é$_2$]$_\iota$	*	*				
b. ☞ [...ti ok'il ti t'ul=é$_{1,2}$]$_\iota$					*	*
c. [...ti ok'il ti t'ul=é$_2$]$_\iota$				*		
d. [...ti ok'il=e$_1$ ti t'ul=é$_2$]$_\iota$			*			
e. [...ti ok'il=é$_{1,2}$ ti t'ul]$_\iota$	*				*	*
f. [...ti ok'il ti t'ul]$_\iota$				**		
g. [...ti ok'il ti t'ul=é$_1$=é$_2$]$_\iota$		*			*	

Candidates not shown include variations on [g] in which one =e or the other does not realize the prosodic prominence of the ιP, i.e., [...ti t'ul=e$_1$-é$_2$] and [...ti t'ul-é$_1$=e$_2$]. Both violate IDENTPROM and the second one violates ALIGN$_\iota$ as well.

Some additional facts, not yet presented, show that REALIZEMORPH must be indexed for particular morphemes and that the one which indexes =e is ranked below ALIGN₁, CULMINATIVITY and IDENTPROM. The definite enclitic =e is not the only morpheme in Zinacantec Tsotsil which is lexically associated with the prosodic peak of ιP. The other is an epistemic particle, *a'a*, which Laughlin (1975) classifies as an "exclamation" and translates *indeed!, surely! certainly! of course!*. *a'a* does not require licensing, though statistically, it tends to occur in utterances with 1st and/or 2nd person arguments and is likely cognate with a reduplicated form of the terminal clitic *a'* 'PROXIMATE' in Yucatec. Relevant here is that *a'a* occurs in the same position as =e, i.e., at the right edge of ιP, with its second syllable functioning as the prosodic peak of ιP.

(39) a. Ta'ajebal   li   j-ve'el-tik   a'a.
       almost.cooked DET GEN.1-meal-1PL.INC EXCLAM

   'Our meal certainly is about cooked.' (Laughlin 1977: 285)

   b. Ta j-ti'   lavi   a'a.
      ICP ERG.1-eat today EXCLAM

   'Of course I'll eat it today.' (Laughlin 1977: 283)

   c. Ik'-o   le'   a'a!
      take-IMP DEM EXCLAM

   'Take her!' (Laughlin 1977: 126)

   d. A li Pineda=e   mas mas ts'akal   a'a.
      TOP DET Pineda-DEF more more afterwards EXCLAM

   'Pineda was later, of course.' (Laughlin 1977: 116)

=e and *a'a* compete with one another, with priority given to realization of *a'a*. Thus =e must be omitted when *a'a* occurs. (39a-c) contain various elements (underlined) that otherwise require =e (see Table 1). Here though, *a'a* entirely precludes realization of =e.

As an epistemic operator, I assume that *a'a* occupies a position in the syntax; its exact location cannot be determined since it is pronounced only at the right edge of ιP. Assuming that e^* and $a'a^*$ can both be present in the input, one or the other must "disappear". Which is preserved is determined by the ranking of morpheme-specific REALIZEM constraints. In Zinacantec Tsotsil, REALIZE($a'a^*$) ≫ REALIZE($=e^*$). The overall ranking of the constraints under discussion then is shown in Figure 3.

5.2 Notes on the right periphery

I close this section by discussing the relation between the terminal elements =e and *a'a*, and two other elements which "pile up" at the right periphery. The ordering of the four is shown in (40):

(40)

un	=e/a'a	che'e
PAR	DEF/EXCLAM	'then'

12 Special clitics and the right periphery in Tsotsil

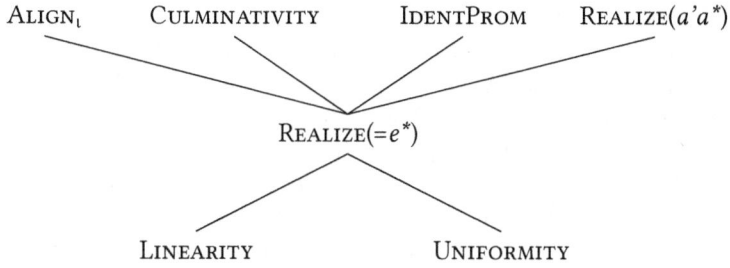

Figure 3: Constraint ranking

The particle *un* occurs in many of the examples cited above. No meaning (propositional or otherwise) has yet been identified for it. Some speakers have the intuition that it contributes some nuance of meaning to the sentence; others say that the sentence just "sounds better" with it. *un* has a distribution similar to that of =*e* and *a'a*: like them, *un* occurs at the right periphery of root sentences and of topics, and it can separate a matrix clause from its extraposed complement. Also like them, it occurs in no other positions. Unlike =*e*, it is not lexically licensed.

Aissen (1992) analyzed *un* as an enclitic which aligns with the right edge of ιP. While it is true that *un* always occurs very near the right edge of ιP, it does not occur rightmost when any of the other elements in (40) is present. While it is not yet clear what is responsible for its appearance and position, I assume that it is not lexically associated with the prosodic peak in ιP and that its position is therefore not determined by IDENT-PROM. For one thing, as observed in Skopeteas (2010), it does not coalesce with =*e* (nor with *a'a*). One possibility is that it is present already at Spell-Out at the right edge of ιP. It would then be present in the *input* to evaluations like those in (34) and (38), and the constraint ranking in Figure 3 would position *e* and *a'a* to its right. Another possibility is that *un* is introduced by the phonology for eurhythmic reasons, e.g., to improve the prosodic structure of the utterance, perhaps at lower levels of the prosodic hierarchy. I leave further development of these ideas for a later time.

The other element in (40) is *che'e*, which occurs only in the absolute final position. *che'e* is a discourse particle which Laughlin (1975) translates as 'then' (roughly Spanish *pues*):

(41) L-i-bat   xa li   vo'on=e   che'e,
     CP-ABS.1-go CL DET PRO.1SG-DEF then

  'Me, I went, then.' (Laughlin 1977: 131)

che'e can co-occur with =*e* and when it does, the high boundary tone appears to be realized on the last syllable of *che'e*, not on =*e*. It seems then to be a counterexample to the descriptive generalization that =*e* is always the prosodic peak of the ιP in which it occurs.

255

A plausible scenario is that *che'e* is incorporated into the ιP which ends in =*e* after the point at which the constraints discussed above have had an effect. Fleshing this out a little, *che'e* might be syntactically adjoined to the root and mapped into its own ιP (like topics and extraposed clauses). This ιP being however subminimal (two syllables, one word), *che'e* is incorporated into the preceding ιP (on the tendency to avoid short ιP's or sequences of ιP's of different length, see Nespor & Vogel 1986 and Dehé 2009). The result here is to push =*e* back from the edge, and for the boundary tone to fall on the final syllable of *che'e*. An account along these lines assumes that the constraints in Figure 3 apply within the domain of ιP's that result from the initial prosodic parsing and do not reapply at a later stage when prosodic restructuring of multiple ιP's occurs. If they did, =*e* would be reordered again, to the right of *che'e*. How such an account with its implied serial optimization fits into the larger theory of the syntax-phonology interface remains to be seen.

6 An historical scenario

Definite markers which close the phrase in which they are licensed are not uncommon (Dryer 2013).[13] It is plausible then that the definite enclitic =*e* in Z Tsotsil might, at an earlier stage, have been the final element in the noun phrase, a position in which it would not necessarily have functioned as the prosodic peak of ιP. Here I offer a suggestion for how =*e* might have come to be associated with that peak, an association which now sometimes forces it out of its licensing phrase.

The basic idea is simple: the syntax usually determines an utterance-final position for the *phrase which licenses* =e. Hence even without intervention from the phonology, =*e* would have found itself in most cases at the right edge of the utterance. As such, it would become statistically associated with the prosodic peak of the ιP and this could have been reanalyzed as a lexical property.

There are several reasons why the syntax usually puts the *phrase* which licenses =*e* in utterance-final position. A number of them come down to the fact that certain grammatical relations in Tsotsil are almost always instantiated by definite noun phrases and the syntax determines a position for these relations at the right edge of the utterance anyway. These include especially subjects, possessors, and topics. The usual ordering of these elements is shown in (42). Starting with topics, as we have already seen, the topic precedes its associated clause and always constitutes its own ιP. As the final element in the topic then, =*e* automatically falls at the right edge of ιP.

(42)
- Topic X
- V-O-S
- Possessum - Possessor

Basic word order in Tsotsil is usually described as VOS, with the subject in clause-final position. Transitive subjects (as well as active intransitive ones) are almost always defi-

---

[13] Languages with such markers include Wolof (Niger-Congo, Torrence 2013), Basque (Laka 1996), Angami (Tibeto-Burman, Giridhar 1980, cited in Dryer 2013), and Gaahmg (Nilo-Saharan, Stirtz 2012).

nite, so generally license =e. Unless the subject is followed by some other element (e.g., an adverb, a PP, an element in a matrix clause), =e again finds itself at the right edge of ιP. Finally, Tsotsil being a head-initial language, the possessor follows its possessum, as in (43).

(43) L-i-bat ta [s-na [li Xun=e]].
CP-ABS.1-go P GEN.3-house DET Juan-DEF
'I went to Juan's house.'

Possessors too are almost always definite, and often end up as the final phrase in an utterance. Here too, =e's position at the right edge of ιP is determined by the syntax. In all these cases then, =e is the last syllable in ιP, the position associated with the prosodic peak.

Of course, the phrase which licenses =e does not always occur utterance-finally – if it did, there would be no motivation for this paper. But in a fragment of written text containing 156 instances of =e, there were only three in which that phrase did *not* occur utterance-finally. In these cases, =e was separated from its licensing phrase, as in (12)-(17) above. Thus, if it is true that the position of =e was originally determined syntactically, it would nonetheless have had a statistical association with the phonological properties that characterize the prosodic peak of ιP and reanalysis of this association as a lexical property would have resulted in the situation we see today.

7 Conclusion

This paper has attempted to lay out the case for Z Tsotsil =e as a special clitic – one whose surface position is not always a position it could have reached syntactically. If this is correct, the phonology does something here *other* than select the prosodically optimal position for =e from among the syntactically possible ones. It must achieve the effect of moving =e within a prosodically-defined domain. In the analysis proposed here, =e is not subject to an alignment constraint; rather, it ends up at the right edge of ιP because it must function as the prosodic peak of ιP, and that peak is located at the right edge of ιP. Complying with this requirement sometimes involves reordering the enclitic over a fairly large distance. Since the reordering occurs in the phonology, it is not subject to syntactic locality. It is, though, subject to prosodic locality, as =e always remains within the ιP that contains its licensor (fn. 12).

Tsotsil =e thus appears to be different from the the second position clitics discussed in Bošković (2000) and Bermúdez-Otero & Payne (2011), clitics which can reach their surface positions by syntactic means. The difference might be understood in terms of the property which determines their surface position. The position of the second-position clitics of Chamorro and Serbo-Croatian is determined by a prosodic alignment condition. But prosodic constituency is introduced in the interface between syntax and phonology and is therefore present before the phonology proper. The placement of second-position clitics can therefore be determined prior to the phonology and without any involvement of the phonology. On the other hand, if the analysis of Z Tsotsil =e suggested here is on the right track, its position cannot be determined until the phonology proper, since it is only in the phonology that the location of prosodic prominence within the ιP is fixed at the right edge. In this light, the special clitic status of =e arises because the condition which makes it "special" – which forces it out of its licensing phrase – references a purely phonological property and not a prosodic edge.

Abbreviations

ASP	aspect	ICP	incompletive aspect
CL	clitic	P	preposition
CP	completive aspect	PRO	pronoun
DEF	definite terminal clitic	PAR	particle
DIR	directional	RR	reflexive/reciprocal
∃	existential predicate	SS	status suffix
EXCLAM	exclamatory particle		

Acknowledgements

Earlier versions of this paper were presented at UCSC, UC Berkeley, and at *Exploring the Interfaces III*, McGill University. I would like to thank all those who have given me feedback on this material, especially a number of anonymous reviewers – their comments were extremely helpful. I owe special thanks to Ryan Bennett, both for his comments on an earlier version and for sustained discussion of various issues relevant to this material. Ryan also prepared the pitch tracks included here. Needless to say I alone am responsible for the content of the paper.

I am delighted to contribute a paper on clitics to a festschrift which honors Steve Anderson. Steve's work in this area, as in others, has been foundational. But on a more personal note, it was at his suggestion in 1972 that I went to Mexico for the first time to work on Tsotsil. Steve was thus directly responsible for the direction my career took and I am glad to be able to thank him for that here.

References

Abels, Klaus. 2003. *Successive cyclicity, anti-locality, and adposition stranding*. University of Connecticut PhD thesis.
Agbayani, Brian & Chris Golston. 2010. Phonological movement in Classical Greek. *Language* 86(1). 133–167.
Agbayani, Brian, Chris Golston & Toru Ishii. 2015. Syntactic and prosodic scrambling in Japanese. *Natural Language & Linguistic Theory* 33. 47–77.
Aissen, Judith. 1992. Topic and focus in Mayan. *Language* 63(1). 43–80.

Aissen, Judith. 1996. Pied piping, abstract agreement, and functional projections in Tzotzil. *Natural Language & Linguistic Theory* 14. 447–491.

Alexiadou, Artemis, Tibor Kiss & Gereon Müller. 2012. Introduction. In Artemis Alexiadou, Tibor Kiss & Gereon Müller (eds.), *Local modelling of non-local dependencies in syntax*, 1–48. Berlin: Walter de Gruyter.

An, Duk-Ho. 2007. Clauses in noncanonical positions at the syntax-phonology interface. *Syntax* 10. 38–79.

Anderson, Stephen R. 2005. *Aspects of the theory of clitics*. Oxford: Oxford University Press.

Bennett, Ryan. 2016. Mayan phonology. *Language and Linguistics Compass* 10(10). 469–514.

Bennett, Ryan, Emily Elfner & Jim McCloskey. 2015. Lightest to the right: An apparently anomalous displacement in Irish. *Linguistic Inquiry* 47(2). 169–234.

Bermúdez-Otero, Ricardo & John Payne. 2011. There are no special clitics. In Alexandra Galani, Glyn Hicks & George Tsoulas (eds.), *Morphology and its interfaces*, 57–96. Amsterdam: John Benjamins.

Bošković, Željko. 2000. Second position cliticization: Syntax and/or phonology? In *Clitic phenomena in European languages*, 71–119. Amsterdam: John Benjamins.

Chung, Sandra. 2003. The syntax and prosody of weak pronouns in Chamorro. *Linguistic Inquiry* 34(4). 547–599.

Cinque, Guglielmo. 2005. Deriving Greenberg's universal 20 and its exceptions. *Linguistic Inquiry* 36(3). 315–332.

Cowan, Marion. 1969. *Tzotzil grammar*. Norman: Summer Institute of Linguistics of the University of Oklahoma.

Dehé, Nicole. 2009. Clausal parentheticals, intonational phrasing, and prosodic theory. *Journal of Linguistics* 45(3). 569–615.

Delgaty, Alfa Hurley & Agustín Ruíz Sánchez. 1978. *Diccionario tzotzil de San Andrés con variaciones dialectales*. Mexico, D.F.: Instituto Lingüístico de Verano.

Downing, Bruce. 1970. *Syntactic structure and phonological phrasing in English*. University of Texas at Austin PhD thesis.

Dryer, Matthew S. 2013. Definite articles. In Matthew S. Dryer & Martin Haspelmath (eds.), *The world atlas of language structures online*. Leipzig: Max Planck Institute for Evolutionary Anthropology. http://wals.info/chapter/37.

Elfner, Emily. 2012. *Syntax-prosody interactions in Irish*. University of Massachusetts, Amherst PhD thesis.

Frank, Robert, Paul Hagstrom & K. Vijay-Shanker. 2002. Roots, constituents and c-command. In Artemis Alexiadou (ed.), *Theoretical approaches to universals*, 109–137. Amsterdam: John Benjamins.

Giridhar, Puttushetra Puttuswamy. 1980. *Angami grammar*. Manasagangotri, Mysore: Central Institute of Indian Languages.

Halpern, Aaron. 1995. *On the placement and morphology of clitics*. Stanford: Center for the Study of Language (CSLI).

Haviland, John. 1981. *Sk'op sotz'leb: el tzotzil de San Lorenzo Zinacantán*. Mexico, D.F.: UNAM.
Hayes, Bruce. 1995. *Metrical stress theory: Principles and case studies*. Chicago: University of Chicago Press.
Henderson, Robert. 2012. Morphological alternations at the intonational phrase edge: The case of K'ichee. *Natural Language & Linguistic Theory* 30. 741–787.
Kathol, Andreas. 2004. *Linear syntax*. Oxford University Press.
Kurisu, Kazutaka. 2001. *The phonology of morpheme realization*. University of California, Santa Cruz PhD thesis.
Laka, Itziar. 1996. *A brief grammar of Euskara, the Basque language*. Leioa-Donostia: University of the Basque Country.
Laughlin, Robert. 1975. *The great Tzotzil dictionary of San Lorenzo Zinacantán*. Washington, D.C.: Smithsonian Institution Press.
Laughlin, Robert. 1977. *Of cabbages and kings*. Washington, D.C.: Smithsonian Institution Press.
Laughlin, Robert. 1980. *Of shoes and ships and sealing wax*. Washington, D.C.: Smithsonian Institution Press.
McCarthy, John & Alan Prince. 1993. Generalized alignment. In Geert Booij & Jaap van Marle (eds.), *The yearbook of morphology 1993*, 79–153. Dordrecht: Kluwer Academic Press.
McCarthy, John J. & Alan Prince. 1995. Faithfulness and reduplicative identity. In Jill Beckman, Laura Walsh Dickey & Suzanne Urbancyzk (eds.), *University of Massachusetts occasional papers 18: Papers in Optimality Theory*, 249–384. Amherst, MA: Graduate Linguistic Student Association, UMass.
Miller, Philip. 1991. *Clitics and constituents in phrase structure grammar*. University of Utrecht PhD dissertation.
Nespor, Marina & Irene Vogel. 1986. *Prosodic phonology*. Dordrecht: Foris.
Pesetsky, David & Esther Torrego. 2001. T-to-C movement: Causes and consequences. In Michael Kenstowicz (ed.), *Ken Hale: A life in language*, 355–426. Cambridge, MA: MIT Press.
Polian, Gilles. 2013. *Gramática del tseltal de Oxchuc*. México, D.F: CIESAS.
Prince, Alan & Paul Smolensky. 1993/2004. *Optimality Theory: Constraint interaction in generative grammar*. Oxford: Blackwell Publishing.
Selkirk, Elisabeth. 2009. On clause and intonational phrase in Japanese: The syntactic grounding of prosodic constituent structure. *Gengo Kenkyu* 136. 35–73.
Shklovsky, Kirill. 2011. Petalcingo Tseltal intonational prosody. In Kirill Shklovsky, Pedro Mateo Pedro & Jessica Coon (eds.), *Proceedings of Formal Approaches to Mayan Linguistics I*, 209–220. Cambridge, MA: MITWPL.
Simpson, Andrew. 2005. Classifiers and DP structure in Southeast Asian languages. In R. Kayne & G. Cinque (eds.), *The Oxford handbook of comparative syntax*, 806–838. Oxford: Oxford University Press.

Skopeteas, Stavros. 2010. Syntax-phonology interface and clitic placement in Mayan languages. In Vicenç Torrens, Linda Escobar, Anna Gavarró & Juncal Gutiérrez (eds.), *Movement and clitics*, 307–331. Newcastle: Cambridge Scholars Publishing.

Stirtz, Timothy. 2012. *A grammar of Gaahmg*. University of Leiden PhD thesis.

Torrence, Harold. 2013. *The clause structure of Wolof: Insights into the left periphery*. Amsterdam: John Benjamins.

Zwicky, Arnold. 1977. Hierarchies of person. In *Papers from the 13th regional meeting of the Chicago Linguistic Society*, 712–733. Chicago: Chicago Linguistic Society.

Zwicky, Arnold M. & Geoffrey K. Pullum. 1983. Cliticization vs. inflection: English N'T. *Language* 59(3). 502–513.

Chapter 13

Another way around causatives in Chamorro

Sandra Chung
University of California, Santa Cruz

> In Anderson's (1992) theory of a-morphous morphology, the traditional observation that inflection occurs "outside of" derivation follows from the assumption that only lexically complete stems can instantiate morphosyntactic representations. Anderson discusses an apparent counterexample to the traditional observation that involves causative verbs and number agreement in the Austronesian language Chamorro. Anderson defuses the apparent counterexample by proposing, following Durie 1986, that Chamorro number agreement is a derivational, rather than inflectional, process. I show that there is a different way of finessing the issue that preserves the intuition that Chamorro number agreement is inflectional. This alternative takes the causative 'prefix' to be a prosodically deficient verb, in the overall spirit of Anderson 2005.

1 Introduction

In Anderson's theory of a-morphous morphology, the traditional observation that inflection occurs "outside of" derivation follows from the assumption that only lexically complete stems can instantiate morphosyntactic representations. Anderson (1992: 127–128) discusses an apparent counterexample to the traditional observation from Chamorro, an Austronesian language of the Mariana Islands. Chamorro has causative verbs which, according to previous accounts, are formed by attaching the prefix *na'-* to a verb or adjective (see e.g. Baker 1985; Gibson 1980, Safford 1904: 108, and Topping & Dungca 1973: 247–249). The point of interest is that *na'-* can attach to a verb or adjective that already shows number agreement. Assuming that *na'-* is derivational but number agreement is inflectional, the fact that *na'-* can occur "outside of" number agreement is problematic. Anderson defuses the apparent counterexample by proposing, following Durie (1986: 364–365), that Chamorro number agreement is a derivational, rather than inflectional, process.

Here I explore a different way of finessing the issue, one that preserves the intuition that Chamorro number agreement is inflectional. The key to this alternative is to take

Sandra Chung. 2017. Another way around causatives in Chamorro. In Claire Bowern, Laurence Horn & Raffaella Zanuttini (eds.), *On looking into words (and beyond)*, 263–288. Berlin: Language Science Press. DOI:10.5281/zenodo.495450

the causative "prefix" to be a prosodically deficient verb, in the spirit of Anderson's 2005 approach to clitics as phrasal affixes. Chamorro has a small class of prosodically deficient verbs that are instances of Zwicky's 1977 bound words. These forms have the morphosyntax of verbs, but cannot serve as phonological words on their own. Instead, they must remedy their prosodic deficiency by undergoing stray adjunction to the phonological word to their immediate right, which is always the first phonological word of their complement.

I show that much of the distinctive profile of Chamorro causatives is accounted for if the causative *na'* is treated as a prosodically deficient verb that selects a vP complement. Moreover, once this route is taken, Chamorro causatives no longer pose a threat to the "outside-inside" order of inflection and derivation, even if number agreement is inflectional. This is because the causative *na'* that can appear "outside of" number agreement is not, in fact, derivational morphology, but rather the prosodically deficient content of a syntactic verb.

§2 of this paper gives a mini-introduction to the morphosyntax of Chamorro clauses. §3 presents the basics of causatives and their interaction with the language's two types of subject-verb agreement. §4 looks closely at Durie's 1986 evidence that Chamorro number agreement is derivational and concludes that it is not decisive. Then, §5 gives an overview of Chamorro's prosodically deficient verbs. §6 proposes that the causative *na'* is a prosodically deficient verb and explores some positive consequences of this proposal. §7 handles some challenges, and §8 concludes.

2 Chamorro Morphosyntax in Brief

Chamorro is a head-initial language that allows predicates of all major category types and a range of null arguments. When the predicate is a verb or adjective, the default word order of the clause is Predicate Subject Object Other, but the order of arguments and adjuncts after the predicate is flexible (see Chung 1998 and the references cited there).[1]

(1) a. Ha baba si Antonio i petta.
P.AGR open UNM Antonio the door.
'Antonio opened the door.'

b. Kumåti i neni sa' ma'å'ñao ni sanye'yi'.
N.AGR.cry the baby because N.AGR.afraid OBL spider
'The child cried because she's afraid of the spider.' (CD, entry for *sanye'yi'*)

DPs are case-marked with a proclitic that occurs to their immediate left. There are three morphological cases: unmarked, local, and oblique. Subjects, direct objects, possessors, predicate nominals, the objects of most overt prepositions, and DPs that occupy

---

[1] Most of the Chamorro examples cited here are from the CD database, which consists of some 30,000 sentences constructed by Chamorros in the CNMI as illustrative examples for the revised Chamorro-English dictionary. Other examples are from published sources listed in the references; unattributed examples are from my fieldwork.

topic or focus position occur in the unmarked case, which is overtly realized only when the DP is a proper name. Otherwise, DPs that denote locations or goals occur in the local case; most other types of DPs occur in the oblique case.

(2) Ma rikuknisa si Esthera ni finatton-ña gi hunta.
P.AGR recognize UNM Esther OBL arrival-POSS LOC meeting

'They acknowledged Esther for her coming to the meeting.' (CD, entry for *rikuknisa*)

Predicates that are verbs or adjectives show subject-verb agreement via forms that also indicate mood (realis vs. irrealis) and are sensitive to transitivity. There are two types of subject-verb agreement. *Person-and-number agreement* (glossed P.AGR in the examples) is realized via forms that could be analyzed as proclitics or prefixes, but are written as separate words in the Chamorro orthography; see the paradigm in (3).[2] In the realis mood, this type of agreement is found only on transitive verbs; in the irrealis mood, it is found on all verbs and adjectives.

(3) Person-and-Number Agreement

	Realis	Irrealis
1SG	hu	(bai) hu / bai
2SG	un	un
3SG	ha	u
1INCL.DU/PL	ta	(u)ta
1EXCL.DU/PL	in	(bai) in
2DU/PL	en	en
3DU/PL	ma	u (INTR) / uma (TR)

Number agreement (glossed N.AGR) is realized via a prefix or infix; see the paradigm in (4). This type of agreement is found only on intransitive verbs and adjectives.[3]

(4) Number Agreement

	Realis	Irrealis
SG/DU	-um- / —	—
PL	man-	fan-

---

[2] Chamorro has various standard and nonstandard orthographies (see Chung 1998: Appendix A). The orthography used here, which was officially adopted by the CNMI legislature in 2010, differs in small ways from the transcription used in Chung 1998, and more substantially from earlier spelling systems, including the official orthography on Guam.

[3] The choice between the two realizations of realis singular number agreement is determined lexically. Generally, -*um*- is used for event predicates, as well as for state predicates in the inchoative aspect; otherwise, the agreement is generally unrealized for state predicates. But there are exceptions. The realizations of plural number agreement have a final /n/ that undergoes the alternation known as nasal substitution.

Notice that dual is aligned with plural for the purposes of person-and-number agreement, but with singular for the purposes of number agreement. This will become important later.

Both types of agreement are the default realizations of subject-verb agreement for predicates of the relevant type, and fully productive; e.g. they can be added to recently borrowed words (as in 5a), even when the borrowings are creative or innovative (as in 5b).

(5) a. Man-meeting   ham gi Lunis.
       N.AGR-have.meeting we LOC Monday
       'We had a meeting on Monday.' (CNMI Senate session SJ 17–22: 20)

   b. Bai hu "love-mark" i kurason-mu.
      P.AGR love-mark the heart-POSS
      'I will "love-mark" your heart.' (EM 60)

Finally, the two types of agreement have overlapping distributions. Transitive verbs show only person-and-number agreement (see 1a, 2, 5b and 6a); intransitive predicates in the realis mood show only number agreement (see 1b, 5a, and 6b); but intransitive predicates in the irrealis mood show both. Note that when the two types of agreement co-occur, person-and-number agreement occurs "outside of" – i.e. to the left of – number agreement (see 6c).

(6) a. Hu   afuetsas gui' para u   atan   yu'.
       P.AGR compel her FUT P.AGR look.at me
       'I compelled her to (lit. that she would) look at me.' (CD, entry for *afuetsas*)

   b. Duränti-n i tinaitai, bula mang-åti.
      during-L the prayer many N.AGR-cry.
      'During the prayer, many cried.' (CD, entry for *duränti*)

   c. Ti para u   fang-åti i famalåo'an.
      not FUT P.AGR N.AGR-cry the women
      'The women are not going to cry.'

With this much in place, let us now zero in on causatives.

3 Causatives

Previous accounts describe Chamorro causatives as formed by adding the prefix *na'-* to a verb or adjective (see e.g. Baker 1985; Gibson 1980; Safford 1904; Topping & Dungca 1973). This process creates a derived transitive verb with an additional argument, which denotes the causer. The causer argument is realized as the subject of the causative; the subject of the original predicate (henceforth the *inner* predicate) is realized as the direct object of the causative; and the direct object of the inner predicate, if any, is realized as an oblique (see Gibson 1980). To illustrate, the causatives *na'baba* 'make open', *na'kåti* 'make cry', and *na'ma'å'ñao* 'make afraid, frighten' are derived, respectively, from the transitive verb *baba* 'open' (cf. 1a), the intransitive verb *kåti* 'cry' (cf. the first clause of 1b), and the adjective *ma'å'ñao* 'afraid' (cf. the second clause of 1b).

(7) a. In na'-baba si Antonio ni petta.
P.AGR CAUS-open UNM Antonio OBL door
'We made Antonio open the door.'

b. Ha na'-kåti si Gene i lahi-ña anai ha lalåtdi.
P.AGR CAUS-cry UNM Gene the son-POSS when P.AGR scold
'Gene made his son cry when he scolded him.' (CD, entry for *kåti*)

c. Un na'-ma'å'ñao yu' ni taklalo'-mu.
P.AGR CAUS-afraid me OBL great.anger-POSS
'You made me afraid with your great anger.'

Gibson's 1980 investigation of the syntax of Chamorro causatives established three points that will be in the spotlight here. First, causatives have the morphosyntax of the language's transitive verbs (Gibson 1980: 86–91). Like other transitive verbs, they can occur in the passive.[4]

(8) a. Ma-na'-gimin i patgun åmut ni ti dinanchi.
N.AGR.PASS-CAUS-drink the child medicine COMP not N.AGR.right
'The child was made to drink medicine that was not right.' (CD, entry for *tumaiguihi*)

b. Kulan n*in*a'-ma'å'ñao i biha nu esti na klåsi-n tinanum.
sort.of N.AGR.PASS.CAUS-afraid the old.lady OBL this L type-L plant
'The old lady was kind of made afraid by this type of plant.' (MAK 2)

They can also occur in the antipassive.[5]

(9) Mu-nana'-gupu papaloti si Juanito gi kantu-n tåsi.
N.AGR-AP.CAUS-fly.PROG kite UNM Juanito LOC edge-L ocean
'Juanito is flying a kite (lit. making a kite fly) by the seashore.' (CD, entry for *na'gupu*)

And they can be used to create reciprocals – derived intransitive verbs, formed with the stressed prefix *á-*, which are Chamorro's primary means of expressing reciprocal meaning.

---

[4] Passive verbs are formed with the infix *-in-* or the prefix *ma-*. The choice between *-in-* and *ma-* is determined primarily by the number of the passive agent: *-in-* appears when the agent is singular, *ma-* when the agent is dual/plural or implicit (see Chung 1998: 38, note 8).

[5] Antipassive verbs are usually formed with the prefix *man-/fan-*. However, some transitive verbs have suppletive antipassive forms (e.g. the antipassive of *kånnu'* 'eat' is *chotchu*); others have antipassive forms identical to their transitive forms (e.g. *gimin* 'drink'). The antipassive of a causative is formed by shifting primary stress to the causative prefix.

(10) Kao um-á-na'-patcha hamyu ni feggun?
    Q N.AGR-RECIP-CAUS-touch you.PL OBL stove
    'Did you two make each other touch the stove?'

Second, causatives can be derived from verbs that are morphologically complex (see Gibson 1980: 114–121). The causatives in the examples in (11) are derived from verbs – surrounded by brackets – that are passive (11a–11b), antipassive (11c), and reciprocal (11d).

(11) a. In na'-[ma-baba] as Antonio.
        P.AGR CAUS-PASS-open OBL Antonio
        'We made it be opened by Antonio.'
    b. Bai na'-[sinaolak] hao nu i ma'estra.
        P.AGR CAUS-PASS.spank you OBL the teacher
        'I will let you be spanked by the teacher.' (CD, entry for sinaolak)
    c. I bakulu-hu ha-na'-[fang-gånna] yu'.
        the shooter.marble-POSS P.AGR-CAUS-AP-win me
        'My shooter marble made me win.' (CD, entry for båkulu)
    d. Ma na'-[á-dispatta] i dos tåotao ni mumu.
        P.AGR CAUS-RECIP-separate the two person COMP N.AGR.fight
        'They separated (lit. caused to separate from each other) the two people who were fighting.' (CD, entry for na'ádispatta)

As these observations might lead one to expect, causatives derived from morphologically complex verbs can themselves occur in the passive, antipassive, or reciprocal.[6] The verbs in boldface in (12) are the passive of a causative derived from a passive verb (in 12a) and the passive of a causative derived from an antipassive verb (in 12b).

(12) a. ... yan maseha håyi malago'-ña i Lahi-ña para u
        and ever who WH.want-POSS the son-POSS FUT P.AGR
        n*ina*'-[ma-tungu'] Gui'.
        PASS.CAUS-PASS-know he
        '...and whoever his Son wants to cause Him (lit. that He be caused) to be known by.' (NT 124)
    b. **N*ina*'-[fañ-otsut]** anai ma-nå'i måolik na kunseha.
        N.AGR.PASS.CAUS-AP-repent when N.AGR.PASS-give good L advice
        'She repented (lit. was caused to repent) when she was given good advice.' (CD, entry for na'fañotsut)

---

[6] Although it is possible in principle for causatives formed from a verb in any voice to occur in any voice, the naturally occurring data suggest that some combinations are more frequent than others. When the causative is active transitive or passive, the inner predicate can be active (transitive or intransitive), passive, antipassive, or reciprocal. When the causative is antipassive or reciprocal, the inner predicate is most often active (transitive or intransitive).

A causative can even be derived from the passive of a causative, as (13) shows.

(13) Si   Josephine ha   **na'-[ma-na'-[suha]]**   i   atgoya   gi   gui'eng-ña.
      UNM Josephine P.AGR   CAUS-PASS-CAUS-go.away   the nose.ring LOC nose-POSS

'Josephine had her nose ring removed (lit. caused the nose ring to be caused to go away).' (CD, entry for *atgoya*)

Third, the inner predicate – the verb or adjective from which a causative is derived – does not show person-number agreement. But, surprisingly, the inner predicate *does* show number agreement (see Gibson 1980: 112–114). Inner predicates that are intransitive agree with the DP that would have been their subject via irrealis number agreement, which is unrealized in the singular/dual, but spelled out as the prefix *fan-* in the plural. This number agreement is not realized on the inner predicates in (11–13), because the DPs that would have been their subjects are singular/dual (e.g. the null pronoun 'it' in (11a), *hao* 'you (sg.)' in (11b), *yu'* 'me' in (11c)), but it is overt on the inner predicates in (14), because the DPs that would have been their subjects are plural. (Note that the inner predicates in (14) are clearly not agreeing with the subject of the causative, which is singular.)

(14)   a. Hu   na'-[fang-gupu] i   petbus.
           P.AGR CAUS-N.AGR-fly   the dust

       'I made the (particles of) dust fly around.' (CD, entry for *na'gupu*)

       b. Ha   na'-[fan-luhan]   ham.
           P.AGR CAUS-N.AGR-afraid us

       '[The wind] scared us (lit. made us afraid).' (CD, entry for *diripenti*)

       c. Ha   na'-[fan-ma-kotti]   i   guåtdia, ya ha   na'-[fan-ma-punu'].
           P.AGR CAUS-N.AGR-PASS-try   the guard   and P.AGR CAUS-N.AGR-PASS-kill

       'He had the guards brought to trial, and had them killed.' (NT 235)

       d. I   abisu ha   na'-[fan-man-unungu']   i   taotao na ...
           the alarm   P.AGR CAUS-N.AGR-AP-know.PROG   the person that

       'The alarm is letting the people know that…[the typhoon is close].' (CD, entry for *abisu*)

Baker (1985) used the relative order of the plural *fan-* with respect to the causative and passive affixes to argue for the Mirror Principle. As he observed, "clear examples of agreement morphemes that can appear intermixed with GF-rule morphemes seem quite unusual" (Baker 1985: 386). What matters here is that the plural *fan-* in the examples in (14) occurs "inside of" – i.e. to the right of – the causative *na'-*. Assuming that *fan-* is inflectional but *na'-* is derivational, this ordering appears to counterexemplify the traditional claim that inflection always occurs "outside of" derivation.

Sandra Chung

4 Number agreement revisited

A natural question to raise at this point is whether Chamorro number agreement might be derivational as well.

4.1 Is it derivational?

As Anderson (1992: 127–128) observes, this question is answered in the affirmative by Durie (1986), who contends that across languages, verbal number – whether realized by stem suppletion or productive affixation – is "selectional concord" (i.e. derivational) as opposed to "agreement". Durie's evidence for this claim comes from various languages, including Chamorro. In the suppletion cases he examines (in e.g. Huichol), verbal number is sensitive to semantic roles like patient or affected participant, not to syntactic relations like subject. Chamorro number agreement does not conform to this pattern, but instead cross-references the (surface) subject regardless of semantic role; this is one way that it behaves like a paradigmatic case of agreement. Still, Durie argues that number agreement in Chamorro is "inherent verbal Number morphology" (Durie 1986: 364) whereas person-and-number agreement is inflectional, on the basis of the following:

- Number agreement distinguishes plural from nonplural (i.e. plural from singular/dual), but the number feature on nouns and pronouns distinguishes singular from nonsingular (i.e. singular from dual/plural), so "[t]here is no [±plural] feature for the verb to agree with" (Durie 1986: 364).

- Number agreement can have an overt pronoun as antecedent, whereas person-and-number agreement cannot.

- Number agreement appears in infinitives, imperatives, and attributive modifiers, whereas person-and-number agreement does not.

- Number agreement is preserved in lexical derivations, such as causatives (see above), whereas person-and-number agreement is not.

These may look like good reasons for classifying number agreement as derivational – a move that would make it unsurprising in the extreme that the plural *fan-* can occur "inside of" the causative *na'-*. But further examination suggests a more equivocal picture.

4.2 A second look

Consider, to begin with, the claim that Chamorro nouns and pronouns have a different number feature than what is registered by number agreement. The specific claim is that nouns and pronouns employ the feature [±singular] – they distinguish singular from dual/plural – whereas number agreement employs the feature [±plural] – it distinguishes singular/dual from plural (see the paradigm in (4)). Assuming that inflectional morphology is the spell-out of syntactic features, the disconnect between these features might seem to pose an insuperable problem for the view that number agreement is inflectional (but see below).

Overt pronouns in Chamorro do indeed employ the feature [±singular] – they distinguish singular from dual/plural, as observed explicitly by e.g. Safford (1903: 308). The second person independent pronouns *hågu* and *hamyu*, for instance, differ in that *hågu* refers to just one addressee, while *hamyu* refers to two or more addressees. The other overt pronouns are similar. It is less obvious how number is handled in nouns, because most Chamorro nouns do not show obligatory number inflection. Just a handful of nouns, listed in (15), are inflected obligatorily, and somewhat irregularly, for number.

(15) a.

Singular	Dual	Plural	
che'lu	chume'lu	mañe'lu	'sibling'

b.

Singular	Plural	
låhi	lalåhi	'man, son'
palåo'an	famalåo'an	'woman'
påli'	mamåli'	'priest'
påtgun	famagu'un	'child'
saina	mañaina	'parent'

The noun *che'lu* has separate forms for singular, dual, and plural. The other nouns have forms which are usually termed "singular" and "plural" (e.g. Safford 1903: 302–304, Topping & Dungca 1973: 325), but actually distinguish singular/dual from plural. That is, they employ the feature [±plural]. The examples in (16) reveal that when these nouns refer to just two individuals, they are realized in the singular/dual form, not the plural form.

(16) a. Um-iskuekuela   i   dos påtgun sanlagu.
       N.AGR-attend.school.PROG the two child   continental.US

   'The two children are attending school in the continental U.S.' (CD, entry for *sanlagu*)

   b. Dos na palåo'an u   fang-gugulik   trigu.
      two L woman P.AGR N.AGR.AP-grind.PROG grain

   'Two women will be grinding grain.' (NT 48)

The claim that the nouns in (15b) align dual with singular is supported by naturally occurring data.[7] There are 30 instances in the CD database, and 23 instances in the first 150 pages of the Chamorro New Testament (NT), of these nouns occurring in explicitly dual DPs – DPs whose noun is preceded by the numeral *dos* 'two'. In 51 out of the combined 53 instances, the noun occurs in the singular/dual form.

It is now clear that Chamorro pronouns employ the feature [±singular], but obligatorily inflected nouns employ the feature [±plural] or – in the case of *che'lu* – both features.

---

[7] Native speakers' judgements trend in the same direction, but are more forgiving. For instance, when asked which of the following two forms she would use to refer to two children, one speaker commented that *i dos påtgun* 'the two children' (with the singular/dual form of the noun) was better for her, but that *i dos famagu'un* (with the plural form of the noun) "will be understood in most circumstances".

This makes it reasonable to suppose that Chamorro DPs are specified for [±singular] *and* [±plural], even though in the vast majority of cases, these features have no DP-internal realization. But then the way that number is handled by the agreement system is compatible with the idea that both types of agreement are inflectional. Person-and-number agreement simply registers one of the number features (namely, [±singular]), while number agreement registers the other ([±plural])

I now turn to Durie's other evidence that number agreement is derivational. It consists of the following:

- Number agreement can have an overt pronoun as antecedent, but person-and-number agreement cannot. (The only pronouns that can antecede person-and-number agreement are null pronouns; see also Chung 1998: 30–31.) Durie takes these facts, which are illustrated in (17), to show that person-and-number agreement is "anaphoric", but number agreement is not.

(17) a. Yayas (gui').
N.AGR.tired s/he
'S/he is tired.'

b. Ha fåhan (*gui') i lepblu.
P.AGR buy s/he the book
'S/he bought the book.'

Now, the contrast in (17) *could* ultimately reflect a difference between derivation and inflection. But it is equally likely that it flows from some linguistic notion of "efficiency" or "brevity" (cf. Grice) plus the featural content of the two types of agreement. Person-and-number agreement encodes exactly the same features as Chamorro pronouns – namely, person features and [±singular] – so a ban that prevents this type of agreement from being anteceded by an overt pronoun contributes to the goal of minimizing redundancy. A comparable ban on number agreement would have no rationale, because number agreement encodes a different feature – [±plural].

- Number agreement appears in infinitives, imperatives, and attributive modifiers, but person-and-number agreement does not. Consider the imperative in (18).

(18) (*En) Fan-man-hokka' sa' bula pineddung månmga gi egga'an.
P.AGR N.AGR-AP-pick because N.AGR.many fallen.L mango LOC morning
'Go and do some picking, because there were many fallen mangos in the morning.' (CD, entry for *poddung*)

To the extent that this observation is valid,[8] it *could* bear on the contrast between derivation and inflection, but other explanations are possible. Suppose, for instance, that number agreement realizes a feature of small v, whereas person-and-number agreement

---

[8] In conjoined imperatives, the leftmost imperative verb does not show person-and-number agreement, but verbs in subsequent conjuncts generally show irrealis person-and-number agreement as well as number agreement (if applicable). The embedded "clause" in restructuring constructions can either be inflected like an infinitive or show realis person-and-number agreement; see 6.2.

realizes features of T. Then number agreement would be expected to appear in infinitives and imperatives, because these constructions are at least vPs; there might be no similar expectations for person-and-number agreement. I will adopt a version of this approach below. As for attributive modifiers, it should be noted that Chamorro allows relative clauses to precede or follow the head NP; it also allows relative clauses whose head NP is null (see Borja, Chung & Wagers 2015). The attributive modifiers that show number agreement can straightforwardly be analyzed as predicates of one or another of these relative clause types.

- Finally, number agreement is claimed to be preserved in lexical derivations, such as causatives and what Durie calls "nominal derivatives". Causatives are, of course, the focus of investigation here. The "nominal derivatives" are not, in fact, derived nouns but rather relative clauses whose head NP is null. Two of Durie's examples are given below, with the spelling normalized. In these constructions, the word that shows number agreement is the verb of the relative clause, which happens to be intransitive.

(19) a. i humånao
 the N.AGR.go
 'the (one) who went' (translated by Durie as 'the goer')

 b. i man-hånao
 i N.AGR-go
 'the (ones) who went' (translated by Durie as 'the goers (> 2)')

Notice that when the verb of the relative clause is transitive, it can show person-and-number agreement; see the relative clauses in brackets below.[9] This too is expected if these constructions are relative clauses.

(20) a. Abånsa [i un chochogui].
 advance the P.AGR do.PROG
 'Go forward with the (thing) which you are doing.' (CD, entry for *abånsa*)

 b. Hu angokku na para un cho'gui [i hu faisin hao].
 P.AGR trust COMP FUT P.AGR do the P.AGR ask you
 'I trust that you will do the (thing) which I ask you.' (CD, entry for *angokku*)

In the end, the evidence cited by Durie provides no firm basis for classifying number agreement as derivational *or* inflectional. But then we are back to the original conundrum: why can the plural *fan-* occur "inside of" the causative *na'*-? I propose to answer this question by analyzing the causative *na'* not as a derivational prefix, but as a prosodically deficient verb.

5 Prosodically deficient verbs

The proposal to analyze the causative *na'* as a prosodically deficient verb assimilates it to a very small class of frequently used Chamorro verbs. This class contains the intransitive

---
[9] The verb of the relative clause can also show wh-agreement, but that is irrelevant here.

verb *malak/falak* 'go to, head to, depart for' and the transitive verb *fa'* 'pretend'.[10] Both verbs are clearly the content of lexical categories; they are not derivational prefixes. Like other verbs, they serve as the predicates of clauses, show subject-verb agreement, are inflected for mood and aspect, and so on. More significantly for our purposes, they select a functional projection as their complement.

Malak/falak 'go to' selects a DP that is linked to its goal argument. This DP, which is bracketed in (21), can include determiners (see 21a) and modifiers (21a–21b); it can also consist of a place name (21c) or an interrogative pronoun (21d). This range of expansions reveals that syntactic incorporation, however analyzed, is not involved.

(21) a. Man-malak [i Pala na kasinu] ham.
  N.AGR-go.to the Pala L casino we
  'We went to the Pala casino.' (CD, entry for *kasinu*)

  b. Ti ya-hu malak [ottru tånu'].
  not like-POSS N.AGR.INFIN.go.to other land
  'I don't like to go to other places.' (CD, entry for *gåstu*)

  c. Yanggin gaigi hao Saipan ya para un falak [Tinian], siempri
  if N.AGR.be.at you Saipan and FUT P.AGR N.AGR.go.to Tinian indeed
  humånao hao luchan.
  N.AGR.go you south
  'If you are on Saipan and traveling to Tinian, you will have to go south.' (CD, entry for *luchan*)

  d. Malak [månu] hao nigap?
  N.AGR.go.to where? you yesterday
  'Where did you go yesterday?' (CD, entry for *malak*)

Fa' 'pretend' selects a finite realis TP complement. This embedded TP can have a predicate of any major category type, and when the predicate is a verb or adjective, it shows subject-verb agreement, as expected.

(22) a. In fa' [in tingu' i ti un tungu'].
  P.AGR pretend P.AGR know the not P.AGR know
  'We (excl.) pretend we know what you don't know.' (from a conference speech)

---

[10] I represent these verbs without dashes in order to highlight the fact that they are not prefixes. Note that *malak/falak* is an *m/f* verb; its initial consonant is realized as /m/ in the realis mood or when preceded by plural number agreement, but as /f/ otherwise. *Fa'* is, confusingly, homophonous with a prefix *fa'-* that creates derived verbs meaning 'make (into, with)'. This prefix attaches productively to nouns (e.g. *fa'hånum* 'liquefy', from *hånum* 'water, liquid'; *fa'denni'* 'prepare with hot sauce', from *donni'* 'hot pepper'), and less productively to adjectives (e.g. *fa'baba* 'deceive', from *båba* 'bad'; *fa'tinas* 'make', from *tunas* 'straight'). The verb *fa'* 'pretend' and the derivational prefix *fa'-* are treated as the same affix by Topping & Dungca (1973: 176–77).

b. Ma tutuhun ma fa' [man-kubåtdi siha].
   P.AGR begin P.AGR pretend N.AGR-cowardly they

   'They began to pretend that they were afraid.' (NT 343)

c. Ha fa' [sen-metgut gui'].
   P.AGR pretend N.AGR.extremely-strong he

   'He pretended to be extremely strong.'

d. Ha fa' [i anghit gui'] si Juan sa' gaigi i
   P.AGR pretend the angel he UNM Juan because N.AGR.be.at the
   nobiå-ña.
   girlfriend-POSS

   John is acting like an angel (lit. pretending he is the angel) because his girlfriend is here' (CD, entry for ånghit)

The distinctive property of these verbs is that they are prosodically deficient; they are not phonological words and cannot bear primary stress. They remedy this deficiency by undergoing stray adjunction to the phonological word to their immediate right, which (in Chamorro) is always the first phonological word of their complement.[11] In (21c), for instance, stray adjunction attaches *falak* to the phonological word *Tinian* (as shown in (23a)); in (22a), it attaches *fa'* to the phonological word *in tingu'*, which itself consists of an agreement proclitic adjoined to the phonological word *tingu'* 'know' (as shown in (23b)).

(23)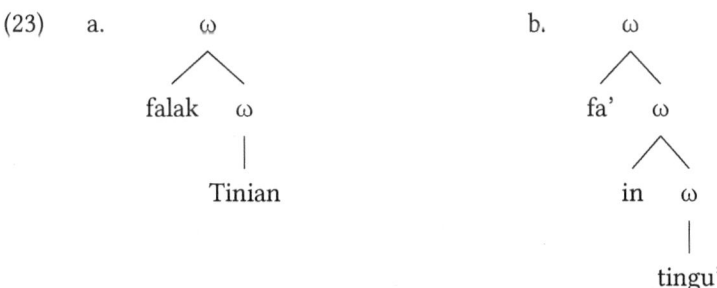

Morphophonological processes which affect verbs, but whose domain is the phonological word, cannot affect a prosodically deficient verb directly. Instead, they must target the phonological word that immediately dominates it. In Chamorro, for instance, the progressive aspect is realized via reduplication of the primarily stressed CV of the predicate. When *malak/falak* or *fa'* occurs in the progressive, the CV that is reduplicated is the primarily stressed CV of the phonological word that immediately dominates them

---

[11] In prosodic theory, stray adjunction is the operation that incorporates elements that are not parsed as prosodic units at a given level of prosodic structure into an adjacent prosodic unit at that level; see e.g. Anderson 2005: 13. The text assumes that in the cases under discussion, stray adjunction literally produces an adjunction structure. As Nick Kalivoda observes, another possibility is that a prosodically deficient verb simply becomes a daughter of the phonological word to its immediate right.

(which is also the primarily stressed CV of the phonological word to which they are adjoined). See (24).

(24) a. Siempri [malak i tetenda] yu'.
    indeed N.AGR.go.to the store.PROG I
    'I will definitely be going to the store.'

  b. Ha [fa' mudodoru] ha' gui'.
    P.AGR pretend N.AGR.stupid.PROG EMP he
    'He is just pretending that he is stupid.' (CD, entry for *mudoru*)

The same holds true for other processes that are sensitive to prosodic structure. Among the overt pronouns of Chamorro are a set of weak pronouns which are second position clitics (e.g. *yu'* 'I', *hao* 'you (sg.)'). These weak pronouns occur right after the first phonological phrase of the intonational phrase corresponding to their clause (see Chung 2003). Because most Chamorro clauses have predicates that are verbs or adjectives, and most verbs or adjectives are phonological words that project a phonological phrase of their own, a weak pronoun is usually positioned right after them (see e.g. 21c). But when the verb is prosodically deficient, a weak pronoun is – as expected – positioned right after the phonological word (and phonological phrase) dominating it. The relevant phonological word is enclosed in brackets below.

(25) a. Tåtnai [malak Luta] yu'.
    never N.AGR.go.to Luta I
    'I've never been to Rota.' (CD, entry for *tåtnai*)

  b. [Ha fa' gof-maolik] gui' na tåotao.
    P.AGR pretend N.AGR.very-good he L person
    'He pretended to be a very good person.' (CD, entry for *fa'*)

6 Causative na' as a prosodically deficient verb

The preceding should be enough to suggest why it would be helpful to reanalyze the causative *na'-* as a prosodically deficient verb. Then the exuberance of its interplay with voice, agreement, and the like can be attributed to the fact that it combines morphosyntactically with the material on its left, but merely prosodically with the material on its right.

6.1 Proposal

I propose to flesh out the details of this reanalysis as follows. Suppose that instead of a causative prefix *na'-*, Chamorro has a prosodically deficient verb *na'* 'make, let, cause', which selects a small clause complement – specifically, a vP complement. In Chamorro, small v selects a complement that is VP or AP, so the verb *na'* will occur in syntactic structures of the type shown in (26) (with specifiers omitted for convenience).

13 Another way around causatives in Chamorro

(26)

The V or A that heads the embedded VP or AP in (26) corresponds to what was referred to earlier as the inner predicate. Because the inner predicate has small v in its functional layer, and small v is responsible for voice, the inner predicate can be a verb that is passive, antipassive, or reciprocal. At the same time, when the verb *na'* occurs as the predicate of a finite clause, it will project its own small v (not represented in (26)), so it can independently be passive, antipassive, or reciprocal. This will account for much of the exuberant interplay that causatives exhibit.

What about subject-verb agreement? In Chamorro, person-and-number agreement is always realized to the left of number agreement. This makes it reasonable to suppose that the two types of agreement spell out features of different functional heads, where the head whose features are spelled out by person-and-number agreement is the higher of the two. Now, word order aside, finite clauses in Chamorro have a familiar architecture in which the functional layer of the clause contains (at least) T and small v (see Chung 1998; 2004). Let us assume, then, that T is specified for finiteness, mood, aspect, and the person and number of the DP in its specifier (= the subject). The relevant number feature here is, of course, [±singular]. These features of T are spelled out by person-and-number agreement when the predicate is transitive or the mood is irrealis; see (3). Let us make the further, more interesting assumption that small v is specified for the number of the DP in *its* specifier via the feature [±plural]. This feature of v is spelled out by number agreement when the predicate is intransitive; see (4).[12] In the finite clauses of interest here, T has a vP complement, the DP in vP's specifier raises to the specifier of T, and number agreement spells out some features of T (finiteness and mood) as well as the number feature of small v. The mechanisms responsible for the multiple exponence of finiteness and mood are irrelevant here. What matters is that in structures in which vP is the complement of the verb *na'*, number agreement is spelled out with "irrealis" forms: as the prefix *fan-* when the DP in small v's specifier is [+plural], and with no realization otherwise.

Let us now turn to the prosody. The verb *na'* is prosodically deficient, so in the prosodic structure corresponding to (26) it will undergo stray adjunction to the phonological word to its immediate right, which is always the first phonological word of its complement. Assuming – crucially – that the word order of the small clause complement has already been determined, this phonological word will be the content of a verb or adjective. The verb or adjective may be morphologically complex and may begin with the

---

[12] A reviewer asks how transitivity is folded into the picture. I assume that T's features are spelled out as person-and-number agreement when T shares features with transitive small v – a small v that assigns abstract Case. Small v's number feature is spelled out as number agreement when small v does not assign abstract Case. See 7.2.

277

plural *fan-*. In other words, stray adjunction will lead to one of the outcomes schematized in (27).

(27)

Overall, this proposal gives a remarkably successful account of the morphosyntactic profile of Chamorro causatives presented in §3. Causatives have the morphosyntax of transitive verbs (see (8–10)) because *na'* is, in fact, a transitive verb. The prosodic deficiency of this verb makes it appear to be a prefix – and therefore derivational morphology – but the appearance is illusory. Like other prosodically deficient verbs, the verb *na'* selects a complement that is a functional projection – namely, vP – and undergoes stray adjunction to the phonological word to its immediate right, which is always the first phonological word of its complement. For independent reasons, this word is always the content of a verb or adjective (see (7)). The verb or adjective projects a vP in the syntax, so it is inflected for number agreement (see (14)) and can be morphologically complex (see (11–12)). Moreover, the claim that *na'* is a verb, as opposed to derivational morphology, makes it unsurprising that it can be the content of both the main verb and an embedded verb in recursive structures like (13).

Note, finally, that the proposal is consistent with the way that *na'* interacts with morphophonological processes whose domain is the phonological word or phonological phrase. When *na'* occurs in the progressive aspect, the CV that is reduplicated is the primarily stressed CV of the phonological word that immediately dominates it (see Gibson 1980: 79–81).[13] (For consistency, I continue to use the parsing and glossing conventions adopted earlier for causatives, even though *na'* is now analyzed as a prosodically deficient verb.)

(28) a. Esta [ni*na*'-chachatkuentus] ni malangu-ña.
already N.AGR.PASS.CAUS-speak.incoherently.PROG OBL sickness-POSS
'Her sickness is making her speak incoherently.' (CD, entry for *chátkuentus*)

b. Hu ripåra na un [na'-malilisia] mampus i palabråk-ku.
P.AGR notice COMP P.AGR CAUS-malicious.PROG too.much the word-POSS
'I noticed that you really are making my words malicious.' (CD, entry for *malisia*)

Further, weak pronouns are positioned not immediately after *na'*, but right after the phonological word (and phonological phrase) that dominates it.

---

[13] The progressive aspect in these examples must be interpreted as affecting the causative *na'*; it cannot be interpreted as affecting the inner predicate of the causative. See especially (28b).

(29) [Man-na'-hanao] ham åbiu para i man-disgrasiåo.
　　　N.AGR-AP.CAUS-go we support for the N.AGR-in.accident
　　　'We sent help for those involved in that accident.' (CD, entry for *åbiu*)

This is what we expect from a prosodically deficient verb; see §4.

6.2 Consequences

If this new approach turns out to be correct, Chamorro causatives no longer provide a counterexample to the traditional observation that inflection is "outside of" derivation. Instead, the causative *na'* is a prosodically deficient verb, and its relative order with respect to morphology which it happens to be prosodically attached to, but which belongs morphosyntactically with a different predicate, is immaterial. The result stands even if Chamorro number agreement is taken to be inflectional, as in 6.1. This is why we embarked on the investigation in the first place.

Further, and interestingly, the small clause complement of the verb *na'* turns out to fill a gap in the paradigm of Chamorro complementation. As might be expected, the language has various types of clausal complements, including finite clauses, infinitive clauses, and the embedded "clause" of restructuring constructions. Finite clauses and infinitive clauses are clearly TPs. They differ in that finite clauses are specified for mood and can have an overt subject, whereas infinitive clauses are mood-invariant and cannot have an overt subject (see Chung 1998: 64–68). Embedded "clauses" of restructuring constructions are similar to infinitive clauses in these respects, but smaller (see Chung 2004). Given the claim in 6.1 that person-and-number agreement realizes features of T, these embedded "clauses" are best analyzed as defective TPs, as proposed by Bhatt 2005 for Hindi-Urdu – TPs whose head is parasitic on the T of the clause under which they are embedded.

The three types of clausal complements just described show number agreement and *some* person-and-number agreement. Finite clauses make full use of the agreement paradigms in (3–4). Infinitive clauses show realis number agreement when their predicate is intransitive and the invariant infix *-um-* when it is transitive. Embedded "clauses" of restructuring constructions show realis number agreement when their predicate is intransitive and either realis person-and-number agreement, or the infix *-um-*, when it is transitive.

If *na'* truly is a verb, then its small clause complement differs from the other types of clausal complements just mentioned along all of these dimensions. The small clause complement of the verb *na'* is merely a vP – even smaller than the embedded "clause" of restructuring constructions – but it can have an overt subject. And, because it is merely a vP, it shows (irrealis) number agreement but no person-and-number agreement at all.[14]

---

[14] Interestingly, Chamorro has at least one other verb that can select a vP complement: the imperative verb *cha'*- 'don't, shouldn't, better not'. As expected, the vP complement of *cha'*- (a) does not show person-and-number agreement, but (b) when intransitive, does show irrealis number agreement. Less expectedly, the specifier of this vP is always controlled PRO, and the verb or adjective from which vP is projected must be inflected for progressive aspect. Thanks to Pranav Anand for questions that uncovered this.

None of this language-particular fine detail is theoretically necessary or even expected, of course. But it is reassuring that the vP complement posited by our alternative approach to causatives can be integrated smoothly into the overall picture of complementation in Chamorro.

7 Other aspects of the morphosyntax of causatives

Other aspects of the profile of causatives present more of a challenge to the proposal just outlined. I discuss two such aspects below, with the aim of showing that they can be handled relatively straightforwardly once the right infrastructure is installed. One set of facts involves wh-agreement; the other involves morphological case.

7.1 Wh-agreement

When a constituent undergoes wh-movement in Chamorro, the verb or adjective on which it depends shows a special morphological agreement called wh-agreement (see Chung 1998 and the references cited there). This special agreement, which supersedes the normal forms of normal subject-verb agreement, signals the grammatical relation of the wh-trace – whether it is a subject, direct object, or oblique. For instance, when the wh-trace is a direct object, wh-agreement is realized by the infix -*in*- and nominalization of the verb. Nominalization is indicated, among other things, by the fact that the subject is cross-referenced by (suffixal) possessor agreement (glossed POSS) rather than subject-verb agreement. Compare the sentence in (30a), in which the verb shows person-and-number agreement, with the constituent question in (30b), in which the verb shows wh-agreement.

(30) a. Hu   kåkannu' i   gollai.
         P.AGR eat.PROG the vegetable
    'I'm eating vegetables.' (CD, entry for *nos*)

   b. Håfa k*in*annono'-mu?
      what? WH.eat-POSS.PROG
    'What have you been eating?' (from a tape-recorded narrative)

In earlier work I analyzed wh-agreement as the result of feature sharing in abstract Case between a wh-trace and the T that most immediately commands it. The shared Case feature is then spelled out on the verb or adjective that projects T's complement. I will adopt this analysis here, noting that in minimalist syntax, abstract Case is often reconfigured in terms of the syntactic head that licenses the relevant DP via Agree.

Let us now turn to causative sentences and consider the DP described at the beginning of §3 as the subject of the inner predicate. The proposal we are exploring treats this DP as the subject of the small clause complement of *na'* – in other words, as the specifier of the embedded vP in the schematic diagram below. (This specifier is represented to the right for convenience; see Chung 1998 on the derivation of predicate-first word order in Chamorro.)

(31)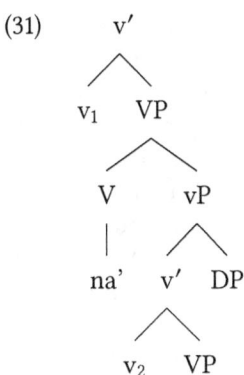

The small clause subject is in an ECM configuration, so it is licensed by Agree with the small v that immediately commands *na'* (= v_1 in the diagram in (31)) in essentially the same way as if it were the direct object of *na'*. This licensing is confirmed by wh-agreement: when the small clause subject undergoes wh-movement, wh-agreement signals that the wh-trace is a direct object (see Gibson 1980: 82, 164).[15]

(32) a. Håyi na pilotu n*ina*'-baståm-mu?
      who? L pilot WH.CAUS-quit-POSS
      'Which pilot did you fire (lit. make quit)?'

  b. Ha na'-moderåtu si Lillian i [n*ina*'-maipen-ña] hånum.
     P.AGR CAUS-moderate UNM Lillian the WH.CAUS-hot-POSS water
     'Lillian moderated (the temperature of) the water that she was making hot.'
     (CD, entry for *moderåtu*)

Next, consider structures in which the inner predicate is transitive and so the small clause complement of *na'* contains a direct object. This embedded direct object is licensed by Agree with the small v that immediately commands the inner predicate (= v_2 in (31)). Therefore, when it undergoes wh-movement, wh-agreement signals that the wh-trace is a direct object (see Gibson 1980: 197).

(33) Håfa n*ina*'-li'e'-ña si Maria nu hågu?
     what? WH.CAUS-see-POSS UNM Maria OBL you
     'What did Maria show you (lit. cause you to see)?'

Not only does wh-agreement register the same Case feature for both types of wh-traces, but in both constructions the verb on which the agreement is realized is the

---

[15] In (32b), the construction of interest is a prenominal relative clause (in brackets), and what has undergone wh-movement is – depending on one's assumptions – either a null relative operator or else the head NP *hånum* 'water'.

higher verb, namely, the causative *na'*. It is this verb that is infixed with *-in-* and undergoes nominalization, as can be seen from the fact that its subject (the causer) is the DP cross-referenced by possessor agreement. It may seem surprising that wh-agreement is realized on the higher verb, given that the wh-traces in (32) and (33) are arguments of the inner predicate. But the pattern follows from the syntactic structure proposed for causatives in §6.1, plus the independently motivated assumption that wh-agreement involves feature sharing between the wh-trace and T. Because small clauses do not contain T, a wh-trace in the small clause complement of a causative must share its abstract Case feature with the matrix T. As usual, the shared Case feature is spelled out on the verb or adjective that projects T's complement, which in this case is the causative *na'*.

It may seem even more surprising that the possessor agreement that ought to be realized on the nominalized verb is spelled out on what is apparently the inner predicate. I contend that what lies behind this unusual spell-out is the prosodic deficiency of *na'*. In Chamorro, affixes must attach to phonological words. This point emerges most clearly for suffixes, perhaps because suffixation invariably causes primary stress to shift to the penultimate syllable of the suffixed word. Since *na'* is not a phonological word, but rather prosodically deficient, the suffix that realizes possessor agreement must attach instead to the phonological word immediately dominating it – the phonological word formed by stray adjunction of *na'* to the inner predicate. This, I claim, is responsible for the unusual location of possessor agreement in (32–33).[16]

One might wonder how the same facts would be handled by a more traditional analysis of Chamorro causatives that treats *na'*- as a derivational prefix. Such an analysis could deal straightforwardly with the spell-out facts just described, because it takes the combination of *na'*- plus the inner predicate to be a complex word (and therefore a phonological word). It would, however, have more trouble with the evidence provided by wh-agreement that both the subject and direct object of the inner predicate are licensed by (different instances of) small v. This is because the more traditional analysis assumes that there is just one verb, and therefore just one small v, in the structure.

It should be noted that Chamorro has no double object verbs – no verbs whose small v licenses more than one DP as a direct object. Verbs of transfer, for instance, have just one DP that activates the object form of wh-agreement when it undergoes wh-movement – namely, the DP that realizes the theme (not the DP that realizes the goal; see Gibson 1980: 161–163). What this means is that a more traditional analysis of Chamorro causatives will have to stipulate that the derived causative verb, exceptionally, has *two* arguments that activate this form of wh-agreement. But no such stipulation is needed in the small clause analysis of this construction, as we have just seen.

---

[16] A reviewer asks if *-in-* infixation might target the phonological word containing the relevant verb. It might indeed. However, what matters here is that infixation does not target the phonological word consisting only of the inner predicate (which, recall, is distinct from the phonological word consisting of the inner predicate plus *na'*). This can be seen from the ill-formedness of **na'-lini'e'-ña* as opposed to *nina'-li'e'-ña* 'she caused to see'. More generally, it is hard to locate Chamorro evidence that prefixes and infixes must attach specifically to phonological words (as opposed to just any phonological material).

7.2 Morphological case

I mentioned in §2 that Chamorro has three morphological cases – unmarked, oblique, and local – and that subjects and direct objects occur in the unmarked case. We must now confront the fact that a causative sentence has just two DPs in the unmarked case: the subject of *na'* and the subject of the inner predicate. The direct object of the inner predicate, if there is one, occurs in the oblique case. See the examples below.

(34) a. Hu na'-ayao si Isidro ni kareta.
 P.AGR CAUS-borrow UNM Isidro OBL car
 'I let Isidro borrow the car.' (CD, entry for *ayao*)

 b. Maila' ya bai hu na'-li'i' hao ni cha'ka gi kodu-mu.
 come and P.AGR CAUS-see you OBL rat LOC arm.muscle-POSS
 'Come and let me show you (lit. I will make you see) the rat in your arm muscle.' (CD, entry for *chå'ka*)

This pattern raises a question. Given the wh-agreement evidence that the subject and direct object of the inner predicate are licensed in the same way (by a small v), why do these DPs occur in different morphological cases?

In minimalist syntax, one way of resolving disconnects between morphological case and morphological agreement is to take case to reflect some mechanism other than licensing by a syntactic head. The mechanism usually invoked is case competition (also known as dependent case assignment; see Marantz 1991 and many others since). The leading idea behind case competition is that if two DPs are in the same local domain, independent of each other, and not already case-marked, the presence of one DP will cause the other DP to be assigned case.

Baker (2015) develops a theory of structural case in which various aspects of case competition are parameterized, including the local domain in which the DPs occur and the specifics of the c-command relation holding between them. In his theory, dependent case can be assigned in two local domains, VP and TP, which are the spell-out domains of phases. Significantly for our purposes, the evidence that VP is a local domain comes, in part, from causative sentences in Chamorro. Baker (2015: 137–139) assumes that Chamorro causatives are morphologically complex verbs, and therefore causative sentences have a single VP that contains the complex verb's direct object (= the subject of the inner predicate) and can contain another DP (= the direct object of the inner predicate). The dependent case assignment that he proposes for Chamorro is essentially as follows.

(35) Baker (2015) on dependent case assignment in Chamorro
 a. Suppose DP_1 has not been marked for case. If DP_1 is c-commanded by DP_2 and both are in the VP domain, assign DP_1 oblique case;
 b. Otherwise, assign DP_1 unmarked case.

As he observes, this case assignment handles the distribution of oblique versus unmarked case in causative sentences as well as other clause types (e.g. clauses constructed from verbs of transfer).[17]

Obviously, this proposal does not mesh well with the analysis of Chamorro causatives being explored here. The small clause structure I proposed in §6.1 for causatives locates the subject and the direct object of the inner predicate in different VP domains (see (31)); this will prevent dependent case assignment from occurring. However, Baker's theory of case allows structural case to be assigned under Agree or through case competition, and this suggests other options.

Baker takes unmarked case to be the default case in Chamorro. Suppose we take the opposite position and declare oblique case to be the default case. Then the task becomes to assign unmarked case to the various types of Chamorro DPs that exhibit it.[18] Among the DPs that occur in the unmarked case are subjects, possessors, and DPs in topic/focus position. These DPs are the specifiers of the functional heads T, D, and C, which license them via Agree (see Chung 1998). Moreover, each licensing relation gives rise to some type of morphological agreement: person-and-number agreement (for subjects), possessor-noun agreement (for possessors), or operator-C agreement (for DPs in topic/focus position). All this suggests that unmarked case is assigned to these DPs under Agree.

Direct objects also occur in the unmarked case, where the "direct object" of a causative sentence is the inner predicate's subject but not the inner predicate's object. Since direct objects – including the inner predicate's object – are licensed by transitive small v via Agree, the obvious move is to try to get their case to follow from a more limited version of that relation. I claim that unmarked case is assigned to these DPs under Agree, but *only when transitive small v is selected by T*. The italicized extra requirement may look stipulative. But there is evidence from several areas of Chamorro grammar that feature sharing occurs between small v and the T that selects it. Number agreement spells out not only the number feature of small v but the finiteness and mood features of the T that selects it (see §6.1). Further, the morphological operations responsible for person-animacy effects in Chamorro require that this feature sharing extend to person and other features of the DPs licensed by these heads (see Chung 1998; 2014). This feature sharing can be achieved in multiple ways which, frankly, are not of particular interest. What is relevant is that case assignment to direct objects can now be understood as follows: unmarked case is assigned by transitive small v under Agree, but only when it shares features with T.

This achieves the desired outcome. In causative sentences, the subject of the inner predicate will be assigned unmarked case, because it is licensed in an ECM configuration by a small v (= v_1 in (31)) that shares features with T. But the direct object of the inner

---

[17] The local case does not enter into the picture, because it is not a structural case.
[18] The unmarked case is also used for predicate nominals and the objects of most overt prepositions. The oblique case is also used for various DPs treated in Chung 1998 as objects of null prepositions: passive agents, instruments, and DPs that realize the complements of antipassive verbs, other intransitive predicates, and nominalized verbs. It is unclear whether the proposals for case assignment in the text can, or should, be extended to these other uses.

predicate will *not* be assigned unmarked case, because it is licensed by the embedded small v (= v_2 in (31)), which does not enter into a feature sharing relation with T. This DP will instead be assigned oblique case by default.

The Agree-based case assignment that I have just proposed is summarized below.

(36) Agree-based case assignment in Chamorro
 a. Assign unmarked case to DP if it is licensed by T, D, C, or by a transitive small v that shares features with T;
 b. Otherwise, if DP has not been marked for case, assign oblique case.

This case assignment handles the distribution of unmarked versus oblique case in causative sentences as well as clauses constructed from verbs of transfer and various other clause types. In other words, it has the same empirical coverage as Baker's dependent case assignment for Chamorro, but does not require causatives to be analyzed as complex verbs.[19] A more sustained comparison of the two approaches to Chamorro case assignment is better left for another time. My goal here is merely to show that it is possible to give a coherent description of morphological case in causative sentences within the small clause analysis I propose.

8 Conclusion

Chamorro has many types of inflectional material that could perfectly well be analyzed as affixes or clitics; for instance, the material that realizes person-and-number agreement (and – conceivably – even the material that realizes number agreement). I hope to have shown here that the same freedom of analysis, when extended to material that is apparently derivational, can have thought-provoking theoretical consequences.

Abbreviations

AP	antipassive	P.AGR	person-and-number agreement
CAUS	causative		
COMP	complementizer	PASS	passive
EMP	emphatic	POSS	possessor agreement
FUT	future	PROG	progressive
INFIN	infinitive	Q	question
LOC	local	RECIP	reciprocal
N.AGR	number agreement	UNM	unmarked
OBL	oblique	WH	wh-agreement

---

[19] Mark Baker (personal communication) observes that a dependent case account of Chamorro morphological case can be maintained if the VP embedded under *na'* is what he calls a 'soft phase'. For reasons of space, the details are not spelled out here.

Sources for the Examples:
- CD   CD database: The database for the revised Chamorro-English dictionary. Saipan, CNMI and University of California, Santa Cruz
- EM   Borja, Joaquin F., Manuel F. Borja, and Sandra Chung. 2006. *Estreyas Marianas: Chamorro*. Saipan, CNMI: Estreyas Marianas Publications.
- MAK Marciano, Dolores. n.d. *Månnge' na Aråguan Kalamåsa*. National Dissemination and Assessment Center, CSULA
- NT   2007. *Nuebo Testamento* [The Chamorro New Testament]. Diocese of Chalan Kanoa, CNMI

Acknowledgements

This paper is for Steve, who for many years has been my teacher, mentor, intellectual role model, and friend.

References

Anderson, Stephen R. 1992. *A-morphous morphology*. Cambridge: Cambridge University Press.
Anderson, Stephen R. 2005. *Aspects of the theory of clitics*. Oxford: Oxford University Press.
Baker, Mark C. 1985. The mirror principle and morphosyntactic explanation. *Linguistic Inquiry* 16(3). 373–415.
Baker, Mark C. 2015. *Case: Its principles and parameters*. Cambridge: Cambridge University Press.
Bhatt, Rajesh. 2005. Long distance agreement in Hindi-Urdu. *Natural Language and Linguistic Theory* 23. 757–807.
Borja, Manuel F., Sandra Chung & Matthew Wagers. 2015. Constituent order and parser control processes in Chamorro. In Amber Camp, Yuko Otsuka, Claire Stabile & Nozomi Tanaka (eds.), *Proceedings of AFLA 21*, vol. 25, 15–32. Asia-Pacific Linguistics.
Chung, Sandra. 1998. *The design of agreement: Evidence from Chamorro*. Chicago: University of Chicago Press.
Chung, Sandra. 2003. The syntax and prosody of weak pronouns in Chamorro. *Linguistic Inquiry* 34(4). 547–599.
Chung, Sandra. 2004. Restructuring and verb-initial order in Chamorro. *Syntax* 7. 199–233.
Chung, Sandra. 2014. On reaching agreement late. In Andrea Beltrama, Tasos Chatzikonstantinou, Jackson L. Lee, Mike Pham, & Diane Rak (eds.), *Cls 48*, vol. 1, 169–190. Chicago: Chicago Linguistic Society.
Durie, Mark. 1986. The grammaticization of number as a verbal category. In *Proceedings of the twelfth annual meeting of the Berkeley Linguistics Society*, 355–368. Berkeley Linguistics Society.

Gibson, Jeanne D. 1980. *Clause union in Chamorro and in universal grammar.* University of California, San Diego PhD thesis.

Marantz, Alec. 1991. Case and licensing. In German Westphal, Benjamin Ao & Hee-Rahk Chae (eds.), *Proceedings of the 8th Eastern States Conference on Linguistics (ESCOL 8)*, 234–253. Ithaca: CLC Publications.

Safford, William Edwin. 1903. The Chamorro language of Guam. *American Anthropologist* 5(2). 289–311.

Safford, William Edwin. 1904. The Chamorro language of Guam – III. *American Anthropologist* 6. 95–117.

Topping, Donald M. & Bernadita C. Dungca. 1973. *Chamorro reference grammar.* reprinted in 1980. Honolulu: University of Hawaii Press.

Zwicky, Arnold. 1977. *On clitics.* Bloomington: Indiana University Linguistics Club.

Chapter 14

Preliminaries to the investigation of clitic sequencing in Greek and Indo-Iranian

Mark Hale
Concordia University, Montréal

> Beginning with Wackernagel (1892), scholars have dedicated a great deal of attention to the question of the placement of enclitic elements within their clause, particularly those which (tend to) appear in so-called "Second Position". Anderson (2005) summarizes the honorand's long-standing interest in and contribution to the critical "interface" issues which arise for linguistic theory from these elements. As has been well known, again since at least the time of Wackernagel's writings on the matter, several archaic Indo-European languages enjoy particularly rich inventories of relevant elements. Greek, in particular, has a set of toneless ("enclitic") and tonic ("postpositive") so-called "second position" lexemes. Since only one entity can technically occupy "second position" in any given string, an obvious empirical issue arises regarding clauses which contains multiple "second position" elements. This matter has received significantly less careful attention than has "second position clisis" generally in the past 125 years. In this paper I present a detailed analysis of what happens when multiple elements seem to have a demand on "second position" in the Attic Greek clause (focussing on the Plato and Euripides corpora), and demonstrate that in developing an account for why the ordering is the observed one, a richer understanding of the actual mechanisms behind our (ultimately epiphenomenal) Wackernagel's Law can be developed.

1 Introduction

In Anderson (2005) the honorand of this volume presented a detailed analysis of clitic placement, including the positioning of so-called "second position" (henceforth, 2P) clitics. I have neither the competence nor the space to fully engage with his insightful and intriguing proposals in this venue. However, given that his analysis was developed against the backdrop of a consideration of empirical data from a broad set of languages, we can all recognize that it is necessary for such cross-linguistic approaches to abstract away from a certain number of seemingly low-level technical matters which arise in individual linguistic systems so as to not impede the development of a general theory. In

Mark Hale. 2017. Preliminaries to the investigation of clitic sequencing in Greek and Indo-Iranian. In Claire Bowern, Laurence Horn & Raffaella Zanuttini (eds.), *On looking into words (and beyond)*, 289–310. Berlin: Language Science Press. DOI:10.5281/zenodo.495451

some cases, one is leaving to one side matters which are both well described and well understood in the specialist literature on the language in question. However, in the case of what is perhaps the most famous data on 2P clitics – the Greek and Indo-Iranian data made use of by Wackernagel (1892) in the grounding document for so-called "Wackernagel's Law" – this is not the case. Surprisingly, the empirical data for these languages is relatively poorly understood, in my view, even in the specialist literature.

It should be clear that building a general theory of clitic behavior in human linguistic systems is only going to be as successful as the quality of the empirical data on individual languages used as input to the theory construction process allows. The more poorly such data is described, or understood, the potentially weaker the resulting general theory. In this paper I focus on one aspect of clitic behavior in systems of the Greek/Indo-Iranian type:[1] the sequencing of 2P clitics. I argue that the weakness in our capacity to insightfully account for observed sequencing of 2P clitics highlights the shortcoming of our understanding of the phenomenon in these languages generally, and point toward some ways we might, in my opinion, approach these issues so as to improve our understanding. This would allow the Greek and Indo-Iranian data to play their rightful role in the evaluation of more broadly-based theories such as that of Anderson (2005).

2 Wackernagel's so-called Law

The literature on so-called "second-position" clitics goes back at least to Bartholomae (1886). Wackernagel's Law universally recognizes a *tendency* for certain types of prosodically deficient element to occupy "second position" in the clause in Ancient Greek and Indo-Iranian (at least). A very clear statement of Wackernagel's own version of his "law" can be seen at the beginning of his famous *Vorlesungen über Syntax* (Wackernagel 1920: 7).

> Z. B. im ältesten Griechisch, in sehr hohem Masse bei Homer, auch noch bei Herodot, ist das Gesetz lebendig, dass schwach betonte Wörtchen, welches immer ihre syntaktische Beziehung sei, unmittelbar hinter das erste Wort des Satzes gestellt werden.[2]

In spite of the 130 years which has passed since Bartholomae first posited the tendency, and the heaps of follow-up scholarly literature, work which addresses the specific issue we will concern ourselves with today – the sequencing of 2P clitics – in any serious way is quite sparse. Early work was impeded by the descriptive goals of traditional Indo-European studies: after all, if you only need to catalogue observed sequences of 2P clitics, the task simply involves gathering and reporting on the data provided by one's corpus.

---

[1] I think it is widely recognized that these two systems are very similar to one another, in an Indo-European context, both in terms of the richness and diversity of their clitic inventory and in the syntax of these elements.

[2] "For example, in the earliest Greek the law is active – to a very large extent in the case of Homer, also still in the case of Herodotus – which holds that weakly stressed 'little words', whatever their syntactic relationship might be, are placed directly after the first word of the clause."

However, when we try not to describe the superficial properties of a string, but to view that string as the epiphenomenal *output* of a computational device (the grammar), the system needs to be imbued with powers which will enable it to bring the linear order of the output string into existence, rather than just describe that order after the fact (the way the researcher does).

3 The "clitic cluster"

The various modern Indo-Europeanist approaches to Wackernagel phenomena in Greek and/or Indo-Iranian reference different methods for dealing with the sequencing problem. One approach, commonly seen in work that takes a "prosody-centric" view of things, posits a "second position" clitic "cluster" (or "chain") into which the clitics are placed, and assumes some kind of (usually stipulative) ordering algorithm which arranges the clitics within this cluster. This is my understanding of the general approach (though, of course, they differ in detail) of Keydana (2011), Lowe (2014) and Goldstein (2016). A rough graphical representation of such approaches is presented in Figure 1.

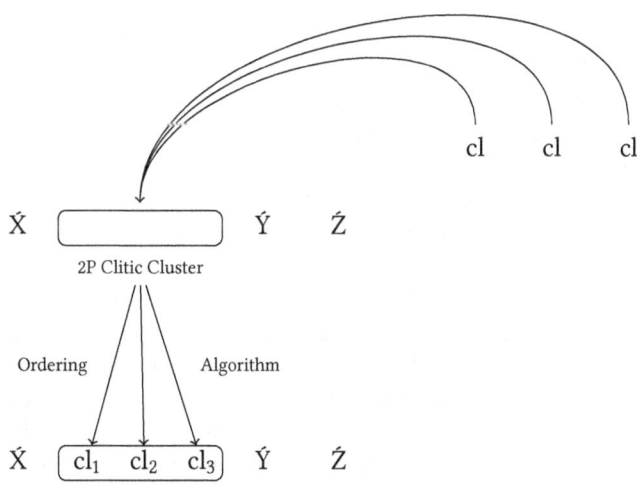

Figure 1: The "Clitic Cluster"

Typically, the domain within which 2P is defined is taken in these approaches to be prosodically defined, and the entities which undergo 2P placement (the clitics) are taken to be a prosodic class, but I have never seen an empirically-grounded proposal claiming that the observed ordering *within the clitic cluster* is determined by prosodic considerations alone. I imagine that this is because it is pretty hard to see any trace of the domination of such a factor in the observed clitic sequences in these languages.

But in general these authors have not yet ventured a systematic hypothesis about the sequencing, so it is hard to determine in any detail the nature of the envisioned system. For example, Keydana (2011: 108, fn. 3) says "[a]nother issue not to be addressed in this paper is the internal structure of clitic clusters." Goldstein (2016: 88) says that because the matter is a "difficult issue", he will "leave it for future research, and for the moment assume templatic ordering..."[3] Lowe (2014: 28) writes that "there are regular (though not inviolable) orders when more than one element from any one of those categories occurs...It is beyond the scope of this paper to account for those patterns."

Interestingly, each of the authors does seem to feel that the observed ordering is related to "classes" into which the clitics fall. Thirty years ago (Hale 1987: 73), I argued that there were three distinct classes of 2P clitics, taking distinct 2Ps for distinct reasons. Although these are not the labels I would use if I were creating them today, and the mechanisms described in 1986 for *how* the categorization of the clitic relates to its placement are woefully antiquated, the classes were: (1) "emphatic" clitics, (2) "sentence connective" clitics, and (3) "sentential" (usually pronominal) clitics. The first I took to involve word-level attachment and the second clause-level. The third were constrained to appearing in a very low position in what we would now call the CP domain, or, indeed, at the top of the IP domain.

I wrote then that "[t]he position of these elements relative to one another follows naturally from this account of their origins: the regular sequence is emphatic + sentence connective + sentential..." It is hard to see this statement as anything more than either wishful thinking or blissful ignorance, both of which I possessed in spades back in those days. From my crankier contemporary perspective, it is pretty easy to see that no explicit characterization of the membership in these classes was provided (though I gave isolated examples of each), nor was any mechanism even hinted at for what might trigger any specific ordering in cases of multiple instantiations of one of these categories in a single clause. In these matters, unfortunately, I have been largely followed by more recent work.

I think it is clear enough, however, what we would all like to see. Overt stipulation is in essence an admission of explanatory failure, and all principles of the scientific pursuit demand of us that we attempt to minimize the role of stipulation in our models. So, our hope must be that the clitics fall into non-arbitrarily-defined classes, and that these clitic classes occupy well-motivated positions (relative to the functions the clitics instantiate) in the linguistic representation. Since it is safe to assume that no two clitics do exactly the same work and co-occur in a single clause, if order falls out in some way from function, we should always be able to generate a predicted ordering for any pair of clitics. It is the "in some way" that I want to explore today. As a step in that direction, though, I must dwell a little longer on previous work.

---

[3] No explicit template is provided which accounts for the cited data.

4 The Hock template

Around the same time as I was writing the account discussed above, Hans Hock was working out the details of an overtly "templatic" approach to clitic sequencing in Vedic Sanskrit (e.g., Hock 1996, with earlier literature). The Hock system was not a model of internal consistency. In this system, the 2P clitics fall into three classes, P, Ṕ, and D:

(1) P: atonic non-"deictic" (i.e., non-pronominal) clitics
Ṕ: tonic non-"deictic" clitics (sometimes called "postpositives")
D: atonic "deictics" (i.e., pronominal clitics)

Clearly, the classification is based on *both* prosodic (tonic vs. atonic) and functional considerations (deictic vs. non-deictic). The template is basically stipulative, but in its most common instantiation, shown in (2), it is supposed to be partially motivated: non-deictics precede deictics (thus P, Ṕ before D, D́) and atonic elements from each class precede the corresponding tonic elements (thus P before Ṕ, D before D́).

(2) X́ P Ṕ D D́ ...

The template is often described as "phonological" or "prosodic" (including by Hock himself), but that, of course, is not accurate. It is important to note that no motivation is cited for either of the two ordering principles: no reason for why non-deictics should come earlier in the clause than the deictics is given, nor for why the atonic element of each category should precede the tonic one.[4]

The graphical representation of the template in (2), especially when coupled with the claim that the template is "prosodic", invites the inference that the "goal" of the system is have an alternating strong vs. weak tonicity sequence. But since P, Ṕ and D can all double, and since any of those elements can be absent in any given clause, no such alternating pattern is observed in the vast majority of utterances in the actual corpus. The prosodic motivation for the template is thus highly abstract (not that that determines whether it is accurate or not).

My actual point in discussing the Hock system, however, is to point out that the mechanisms involved are quite distinct from that which we saw in our discussion of "clitic cluster" approaches to clitic sequencing. We can visualize the system as seen in Figure 2 below.

There is no "second position" in this conception of things, but a variety of ordered positions into which clitics are placed based on their properties (prosodic and functional). We can see the differences between the two general models if we imagine a clause with only a single 2P clitic in it. In the "clitic cluster" approach that clitic will be "in 2P", plain and simple. The ordering algorithm will have no work to do. In an approach such as that found in the Hock template, we can (and must) still ask the question: where is the clitic?

---

[4] In fact, D́ elements may appear in the X́ position and, for Hock's version of the Rigvedic template, also in the Ṕ position, and thus come earlier in the clause than D elements, indicating that there isn't much content to this latter principle in any event.

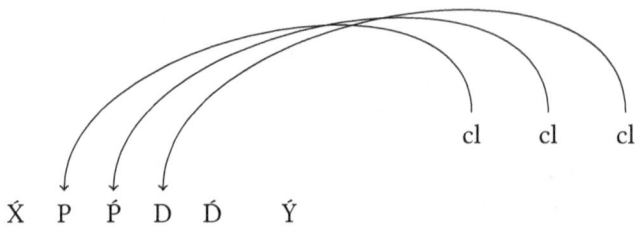

Figure 2: The "Hock template"

It could be in P (with Ṕ and D empty), or in Ṕ (with P and D empty), or in D (with P and Ṕ empty).

There is, of course, an inherent advantage, given that we are seeking to develop a non-stipulative account of ordering, if we assume that specific clitics map consistently to specific positions in the string, and that whether that position ends up being "second" or "third" or "fourth" is simply the epiphenomenal by-product of the mapping algorithm. A model which, by contrast, dumps the clitics unordered into a 2P cluster and then must impose an order on them has, in some sense, missed a chance to impose that ordering earlier in the initial mapping. Particularly if that mapping is prosody-driven, only a general slackening of constraints on the relationship between position (at the point of insertion) and interpretation – constraints which seem to hold of the linguistic representation generally – can allow a set of unordered elements, placed by a prosodic algorithm, to be realigned in an interpretationally-relevant manner (i.e., on the basis of the "functional class" of the clitic).

Hale (1996) represents an attempt to link the "positions" in the Hock template to specific structural elements within the clause (a similar orientation is found in other syntax-centric but prosody-sensitive approaches). I will not dwell on that reinterpretation of Hock here, but instead turn to one more modern model of 2P placement.

5 Wackernagel's optimality-theoretic approach

Wackernagel himself pretty clearly conceived of the 2P phenomenon as a kind of a compromise between a clitic element representing the kind of information which should come early in the clause (generally because of its "linking" function to the preceding context) and that same element being atonic, and thus not particularly suitable for initial position. This traditional conception is very closely followed by modern Optimality Theoretic approaches to 2P placement, as reflected, for example, in Anderson (2005).

The basic idea of such approaches, as with Wackernagel's, is that there is a drive for 2P clitics to be initial (captured by an ALIGNLEFT constraint, which incurs one violation for each step away from the left edge a clitic is) and a prohibition against the clitic appearing in initial position (captured by a NONINITIAL constraint). Obviously, both of these constraints cannot be satisfied in the same string. As always in OT, the conflicting demands are resolved via a ranking of the constraints. As long as NONINITIAL outranks ALIGNLEFT, the clitic will appear *as close as possible* to string-initial position, but not *in* initial position – hence the 2P effect.

We can see this with a tableau fragment concerning the positioning of Greek *gár* 'because, since' relative to two tonic lexical items, which I designate simply as X́ and Ý. Greek *gár* is a standard example of a "Wackernagel's Law" element in the language.[5]

(3)
			NONINITIAL	ALIGNLEFT(gár)
	a.	X́, Ý, gár		
	b.	X́ Ý gár		*!*
	c.	X́ gár Ý		*
	d.	gár X́ Ý	*!	
	e.	gár Ý X́	*!	
	f.	Ý gár X́		*
	g.	Ý X́ gár		*!*

Wackernagel believed that the drive towards initial position was of different strength for different enclitic objects. As long as we make the ALIGNLEFT constraints clitic (or clitic class) specific, a strict ranking version of OT will require us to decide for each clitic just how strong the demand is that it be aligned left. For example, if we take the Greek focus-marking enclitic *mén*, we are *compelled by the model* to ask: is it more important for *mén* to be on the left, or for *gár* to be on the left? (In Wackernagel's terms, is the "drive for initial position" stronger for *mén* or for *gár*?)

The tableau in (4) below shows how such a system generates – again by necessity – a sequencing of clitics. We should always be attentive, I think, when our modern models seem to converge on the ideas of important scholars like Wackernagel, who could not have envisioned the workings of OT, and thus independently had a similar conception of a certain class of linguistic phenomena. If Wackernagel and Anderson agree, it would be wise to not dissent too quickly! But is OT the happy confirmation of Wackernagel's less formal and more intuitive analysis?

The model in some sense combines properties of the two earlier approaches I sketched: there is a sense of a "fixed stipulative order" (as seen in the Hock Template) in the relative rankings of the ALIGNLEFT(x) constraints, but there is no sense of fixed stipulative positions in the resulting representation (as that model implies), thus making it more like the "clitic cluster" analysis. It has the advantage, over the "clitic cluster" analysis, of not adding a new object to our model of the grammar (the "clitic cluster"), nor requiring a distinct computational process which is responsible for explicitly ordering the elements within the cluster (the "ordering algorithm" mentioned above).

---

[5] The reader will notice that this tableau fragment does not select between two "winning" outputs: X́ *gár* Ý and Ý *gár* X́. Obviously other constraints will determine the ultimate optimal output form with respect to the relative ordering of the tonic elements to one another.

(4)

	X́, Ý, gár, mén	NonInitial (CL)	AlignLeft (mén)	AlignLeft (gár)
a.	X́ Ý gár mén		**!*	**
b.	X́ Ý mén gár		**!	***
c.	X́ mén Ý gár		*	***!
d.	mén X́ Ý gár	*!		***
e.	X́ gár Ý mén		**!*	*
f.	X́ gár mén Ý		**!	*
g. ☞	X́ mén gár Ý		*	**
h.	mén X́ gár Ý	*!		**
i.	gár X́ Ý mén	*!	***	
j.	gár X́ mén Ý	*!	**	
k.	gár mén X́ Ý	*!	*	
l.	mén gár X́ Ý	*!		*
m.	gár Ý X́ mén	*!	***	
n.	gár Ý mén X́	*!	**	
o.	gár mén Ý X́	*!	*	
p.	mén gár Ý X́	*!		*
q.	Ý gár X́ mén		**!*	*
r.	Ý gár mén X́		**!	*
s. ☞	Ý mén gár X́		*	**
t.	mén Ý gár X́	*!		**
u.	Ý X́ gár mén		**!*	**
v.	Ý X́ mén gár		**!	***
w.	Ý mén X́ gár		*	***!
x.	mén Ý X́ gár	*!		***

I have both conceptual and empirical concerns about the model. At the conceptual level, stipulation is built into the model pretty deeply: the so-called "factorial typology" argument says that we could just as easily have AlignLeft(gár) outrank AlignLeft(mén), and indeed that every ordering of every available AlignLeft(x) constraint should be, in principle, observed. This does not seem to me to be very consistent with the data I have seen from archaic Indo-European languages (which often involves etymologically unconnected, but functionally similar enclitics showing the same ordering principles).

Empirically, one of the great challenges to this model holds, in my view, for all of the other models we have treated to this point as well. The domain over which the AlignLeft(x) constraint must be assessed is, in the model, a pure stipulation (i.e., there are no principles regulating what a given enclitic might be "aligned" to). The same problem, in my view, plagues the so-called "prosody-centric" approaches which have become popular: the clitic is said to move into the "clitic cluster" in second position of some domain, but none of the approaches I have seen (Keydana 2011; Lowe 2014; Goldstein 2016) present a non-stipulative characterization of how the appropriate domain is established.

A clitic is said to take 2P within (some) Intonational Phrase, but the question of which one (when there are multiple IPs in the string) is left unclear. It also seems like the "Intonational Phrase" portion of the specification (and, in non-OT approaches, the 2P part as well) is purely stipulative: could one place a clause-conjoining clitic in 2P of (some) Utterance Group or (some) Phonological Word? How about in 3P in the Intonational Phrase? The models proposed are so inexplicit it is difficult to determine precisely what their allowable elements and operations are – the models are thus both highly stipulative and poorly constrained.

As mentioned above, my concerns about the Hock Template have been spelt out in considerable detail in Hale (1996), where I attempt to reduce the empirically valid aspects of the template to the interaction of (1) normal syntactic placement of the relevant entities and (2) Halpern's (1995) "prosodic inversion". I won't go through these details here, except to note that in this conception of things enclitic elements can be in a variety of structural positions (in the syntax) and may (or may not) undergo "prosodic movement" in the phonology (depending on whether they are "properly hosted" without such movement).

It is obvious that a system which leverages both syntax and phonology to account for observed clitic placement is in some sense more complex than either a purely syntactic or a purely phonological one. But the evidence that the process is not *purely syntactic* is, as far as I can tell, universally accepted. The 2P clitics often interrupt manifest syntactic constituents (in a manner the syntax does not allow) and are quite regularly placed in positions in the string from which appropriate scope relations could not possibly be established. "Prosodic" rearrangement allows the syntax to be mundane rather than strikingly bizarre (with all of the implications such bizarreness would have, if allowed, for our theories of grammar).

That the syntax is involved is, in my view, absolutely required if we are to solve the "domain" problem. Sanskrit *ca* and Attic *te* are 2P clitics, but they appear in clause-second position only when their domain is the clause. They appear in "DP-second" position when their domain is the DP, and in VP-second position when their domain is the VP. Their domain simply cannot be defined with respect to *prosody* alone.

6 Sample application: Enclitic subordination

Both of these observations can be seen to be at work in a set of examples involving enclitic subordinators. Before examining this data, which will also display the mechanisms I believe are at work in clitic placement (and thus what we might use to explain clitic sequencing), I will remind the reader that Hale (1987) showed that there was a process manifest in the language of the Rigveda, in Avestan, and in Greek, whereby a single constituent could be fronted to the left of a WH-element. Obviously, this analysis extends (though the matter was not overtly discussed – but rather implicitly assumed – in that earlier work) to other subordinators present in C ('if', 'when', 'because'). I will call that fronting process "topicalization" (and the position into which the fronting takes place Top), with no particular commitment to the discourse functions involved.

Familiar examples of this fronting looks like this:

(5) a. [áśmānam cid] yé bibhidúr vácobhiḥ
rock-Asg Emph.*cl* Rel-NPlM smashed-IIIPl words-ISgN
'who smashed even rock with (mere) words...' RV 4.16.6c

b. [idhmáṃ] yás te jabhārac
kindling-ASg Rel-NSg you-DSg.*cl* would bear-IIISg
chaśramāṇáḥ
exerting himself-NSg
'who, exerting himself, would bear the kindling to you...' RV 4.12.2a

Armed with the following assumptions, then, let us see what some structures look like, and how they might impact the development of a theory of clitic sequencing:

- enclitic elements are placed in "expected" syntactic position
- "prosodic inversion" is triggered when they are not properly hosted on their left edge

Wackernagel proposed long ago that there were traces in the Rigveda of a reflex of IE *k^we which (like OLat. *absque me esset* 'if it were without me', some uses of Gothic *nih*, and, although not known to Wackernagel, Hittite *takku*) is subordinating in function, generally rendered 'if, when.' As might be expected, the verb in such clauses, as in subordinate clauses in Vedic generally, is accented. This has given rise to some anxiety that the true subordination marker is the verbal accent, and that *ca* is simply (weakly) coordinating. Typical examples are:

(6) a. níuptāś ca babhrávo vácam ákrataṃ
scattered-down **ca** brown-NPl voice-ASg they made
émíd eṣāṃ niṣkṛtám jāríṇīva
I go=PTCL their$_{cl}$ appointed place-ASg paramour-NSg=like
'And as soon as, scattered down, the brown (dice) have raised their voice, I just go to their appointed place, like a girl with a lover.' (SJ/JB) 10.34.5cd

b. tuvám ca soma no váśo
you-NSg **ca** Soma-VSg us$_{cl}$ you should wish
jīvátum ná marāmahe
to live Neg we will die
'And if you will wish us to live, Soma, we will not die.' (SJ/JB) RV 1.91.6ab

I have provided the translation of Jamison & Brereton (2014) because it reflects directly the unease that some Vedicists feel about "subordinating" *ca*: they have translated 'and as soon as (=when)' and 'and if', leaving it unclear whether they believe that *ca* is coordinating ('and') and the verbal accent subordinating ('as soon as', 'if'), or whether perhaps they believe that this *ca* actually means 'and as soon as/if'.

14 *Preliminaries to the investigation of clitic sequencing in Greek and Indo-Iranian*

As one can imagine, determining whether or not such clauses are weakly connected to the preceding discourse – i.e., whether the 'and' should be in the English translation – is no easy task. And from this example, and other widely accepted ones (such as RV 8.21.6ab below), in which *ca* occupies second position, it doesn't seem likely that our approach to clitics is going to be much help in this task.

(7) áchā ca tvainá   námasā   vádāmasi
    PV ca you$_{cl}$=this-ISg homage-ISg we address
    kím   múhuś   cid   ví   dīdhayaḥ
    Q-marker for a moment even$_{cl}$ PV you will think
    'When we address you with this homage, will you hesitate even for a moment?'
                                                                RV 8.21.6ab

Hettrich (1988: 252) notes overtly on subordinating *ca* that *ca* stands "wie nach Wackernagels Enklisengesetz[fn deleted] zu erwarten, überwiegend an zweiter Stelle im Satz."[6]

It is somewhat striking to see the *überwiegend* in this statement, because coordinating *ca* is extremely regular in its "second position" behavior, being postponed only in cases in which there is a "phonological word" at the start of the conjoined domain. Are there actually cases of "late *ca*" in subordinating function? The following examples seem to answer this question "yes".

(8) a. asyá śloko   divíyate   pṛthivyám
       his call-NSg heaven-LSg=speeds earth-LSg
       átyo   ná yaṃsad   yakṣabhṛ́d
       steed-NSg like will control bringing-wondrous-apparitions-NSg
         vícetāḥ
         discriminating-NSg
       mṛgáṇām   ná hetáyo   yánti   cemá   bṛ́haspáter
       wild beasts-GPl like charges-NPl they go **ca**=these-NPl Brhaspati-GSg
       áhimāyām̐   abhí dyū́n
       having-snake-wiles-APl to heavens-APl
       'The discriminating one [=Bṛhaspati?], like a steed, bringing wondrous apparitions, will control it when these (words) of Brhaspati, like the charges of wild beasts, go to the snake-wiles-possessing heavens.'   RV 1.190.4
    b. ubháyaṃ   śṛṇávac ca na
       twofold-ASg will hear ca us$_{cl}$
       índro   arvā́g idám   vácaḥ
       Indra-NSg nearby this-ASg speech-ASg
       satrā́ciyā   maghávā   sómapītaye
       fully-focussed-ISg benefactor-NSg soma-drinking-DSg

---

[6] '...as would be expected according to Wackernagel's Law, overwhelmingly in the second position in the clause.'

dhiyā́ śáviṣṭha ā́ gamat
thinking-ISg most-powerful-NSg PV will come

'When Indra nearby will hear this twofold speech of ours, the most powerful benefactor will come here to the soma-drinking by reason of our fully focussed insight.' RV 8.61.1

To understand this data (and there are one or two more examples), we need to ask the following question: how does conjunctive *ca* end up in "second position" when it conjoins clauses, and how would we expect a "subordinating *ca*" to behave given the assumptions outlined above?

The behavior of coordinating *ca* is fairly straightforward. No matter what kind of syntactic (or prosodic!) entity *ca* is coordinating, it appears in this configuration:

(9)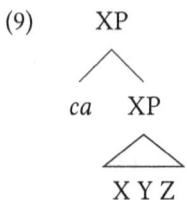

[X Y Z] can be a clause, as in the case under discussion, or an DP or VP or PP or whatever. Obviously, *ca* sits at the left edge of the XP-domain and thus does not have a proper prosodic host to its left. It therefore must undergo the "prosodic flip", and, assuming X is a "phonological word", the resulting operation will give rise to this string:

(10) *ca* X *ca* Y Z

It should be clear that one thing that *ca* can bring into a coordination relationship with what precedes it is a clause introduced by a *topicalized* phrase. Here's an example.

(11) yád agna eṣā́ sámitir bhávāti
when Agni-VSg this-NSg assembly-NSg will become
devī́ devéṣu yajatā́ yajatra
godly-NSg gods-LPl sacrifical-NSg sacrificial one
rátnā ca yád vibhájāsi
treasures-APl and$_{cl}$ when you will share out
svadhāvo
having-independent-will-VSg
bhāgáṃ no átra vásumantaṃ vītāt
share-ASg us$_{cl}$ then rich-in-goods-ASg pursue

'When, o Agni, this assembly will become godly among the gods, a sacrificial one, o sacrificial one, and when you will share out treasures, o you of independent will, then pursue a share for us rich in goods.' (SJ/JB)

RV 10.11.8

14 Preliminaries to the investigation of clitic sequencing in Greek and Indo-Iranian

The c-pada of this verse arises from a *syntactic* structure of the form:

(12)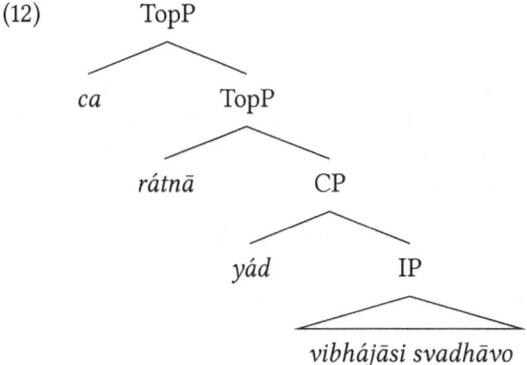

So where do we expect **subordinating** *ca* to be *syntactically*? Well, it is *isofunctional* with *yád* in the clause above. So the structure of the subordinate clause in (6a) at the end of *syntactic* computation would presumably be:

(13)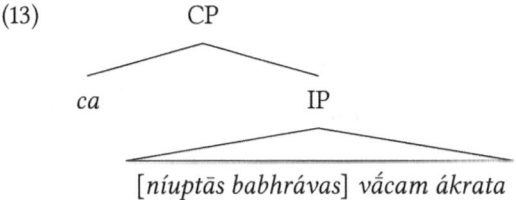

Since *ca* is alone up there in the left periphery, it must undergo the "prosodic flip" in the phonology to be properly hosted.

What would happen if we were to have a Top element in such a clause? In the case of coordination, it of course is the entire clause, including its initial Topic-phrase, which gets coordinated to a preceding (or following) clause, and *ca* thus dominates TopP. But topicalized material appears to the *left* of the subordinator (relative pronouns, *yádi* 'if', etc.), so if *ca* is a subordinator, we predict a structure such as (contrast coordinating *ca* in (12)):

(14)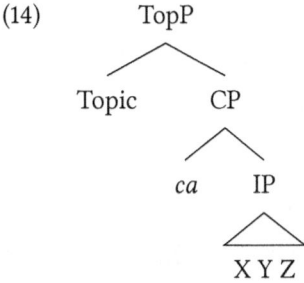

If the proper "hosting domain" for *ca* is the CP, then it is unhosted on its left, and we predict the *phonology* to restructure this to:

(15) Topic [*ca* X *ca* Y Z]

Note that, if there are such examples, since coordinating *ca* won't act this way, but subordinating *ca* should, we would have clear and unambiguous evidence for the *syntactic separation* of *ca* into two distinct types of grammatical element. And of course there are such examples. We saw them above in (8ab), whose structures are:

(16) a. [Top *mṛgáṇāṃ ná hetáyo*] [CP *ca* [*yánti ca imā́ bŕ̥haspáter áhimāyāṁ abhí dyū́n*]]

     b. [Top *ubháyaṃ*] [CP *ca* [*śṛṇávac ca na índro arvā́g idáṃ vácaḥ*]]

The construction as a whole is rare, but confirmation for this analysis is provided by the reflex of subordinating *ca* in later Vedic texts (and, rarely, already in the Rigveda) – the subordinating particle *céd* (etymologically from *ca* + *íd*). The "normal" position for this particle is, of course, in second position.

(17) a. ná vā́ araṇyānír hanti
       Neg PTCL Lady of the Wilderness-NSg slays
       anyáś cén nā́bhigáchati
       another-NSg **céd** Neg=attacks
       'In truth, the Lady of the Wilderness does no slaughter, if someone else does not attack.' (SJ/JB) RV 10.146.5ab

     b. yó asyā ū́dho ná veda-
       who-NSg her-GSg$_{cl}$ udder-ASg Neg knows
       -atho asyā stánān utá
       thereto=PTCL her-GSg$_{cl}$ teats-APl as well
       ubháyenaivā́smai duhe
       both-ISg=PTCL=him-DSg$_{cl}$ she yields milk
       dā́tuṃ céd áśakad vaśā́m
       to give **céd** he was able cow-ASg
       'Whoever knows not the udder of her, and likewise the teats of her, to him she yields milk with both, if he has been able to give the cow.' (Whitney) AVŚ 12.4.18

But, as with subordinating *ca*, we find unexpectedly "late" instances of *céd* as well.

(18) a. [arthíno] yánti céd ártham
       having-a-task-NPl proceed **céd** task-ASg
       gáchān íd dadúṣo rātím
       they will go to PTCL giver-GSg generosity-ASg
       'If those having a task proceed to their task, they will attain the generosity of the giver.' RV 8.79.5ab

b. [abandhv éke dádataḥ prayáchanto]
   kinless-NPl some-NPl giving-NPl bestowing-NPl
   dátuṃ céc chíkṣānt sá svargá evá
   to give **céd** they are able this-NSg heaven-NSg indeed

   'If some, without kin, giving, bestowing, are able to give, this is truly heaven.'
   AVŚ 6.122.2cd

c. hédaṃ paśūnáṃ ny èti
   wrath-ASg cattle-GPl PV comes
   brāhmaṇébhyó 'dadad vaśā́m
   Brahmans-DPl not-giving-NSg cow-ASg
   [devā́nāṃ níhitaṃ bhāgáṃ]
   gods-GPl deposited-ASg portion-ASg
   mártyaś cén nipriyāyáte
   mortal-NSg **céd** keeps (for himself)

   'The mortal not giving a cow to the Brahmans goes down to the wrath of the cattle, if he keeps to himself the deposited portion of the gods.'
   AVŚ 12.4.21

And note that we can use our analysis of these "late" instances to make our interpretations of certain Vedic passages more precise. Look at the AB passage (from the Śunaḥśepa legend) in (19).

(19) ṛnam asmin saṃnayaty
   debt-ASg him-LSg$_{cl}$ he pays
   amṛtatvaṃ ca gachati
   immortality-ASg and$_{cl}$ he goes to
   pitā putrasya jātasya
   father-NSg son-GSg born-GSg
   paśyec cej jīvato mukham
   he should see **ced** living-GSg face-ASg

   'A debt he payeth in him, and immortality he attaineth, that father who seeth the face of a son born living.' (Keith)   AB 7.13.4

Keith, whose translation I have provided, takes [putrasya jātasya... jīvato mukham] '(the) face of a son born living' as a (discontinuous) constituent, the direct object of the verb *paśyet*. That is, his analysis (ignoring for a moment the *ced*, to which we will turn momentarily) is that the subject and predicate divide like this:

(20) [pitā] [putrasya jātasya paśyet jīvato mukham]

There are two possibilities for where *pitā* could be under Keith's interpretation: it could have been fronted into the Topic position, or, of course, it could be in some position lower than C (in Focus, or in IP, e.g.). If it were below C, the output of the syntax (now with *ced* reintroduced) would have been as below, with the "prosodic flip" indicated:

(21) [_CP_ ced [pitā ced putrasya jātasya paśyet jīvataḥ mukham]]

If *pitā* were in Topic, we would have instead expected:

(22) [_Topic_ pitā] [_CP_ ced [putrasya ced jātasya paśyet jīvataḥ mukham]]

Neither of these is the sentence in the text. It is clear what the structure must be if the placement of *ced* is to fit with all the other evidence for the use of this particle in early Vedic:

(23) [_Topic_ pitā putrasya jātasya] [_CP_ ced [paśyet ced jīvataḥ mukham]]
'when the father of a (just) born son*ᵢ* sees the face of (him*ᵢ*) living'

7 *hí*, *gár*, and clitic sequencing

In my dissertation (Hale 1987), I dealt fairly extensively with the data from Vedic *hí* 'because, since'. I noted that while the vast majority of instances of *hí* are in "second position" (appropriately defined), there were a number of counterexamples. Note that *hí* occupies, at the end of the syntactic computation, the very same position ("C") as subordinating *ca* and *céd*.

I won't bother citing second position instances of *hí* – as I said, the vast majority of the approx. 630 attestations of the particle are in that slot, properly defined. Some of the not terribly numerous exceptions are given in (24) below. Several interesting issues arise, so I cite a healthy number of the exceptions.

(24) a. urukramásya   sá   hí bándhur itthā́
       wide-striding-GSg this-NSg **hí** bond-NSg thus
       'for exactly that is the bond to the wide-striding one' (SJ/JB)

       RV 1.154.5c

   b. asmā́ñ ca   tā́ṃś   ca   prá hí néṣi vásya   ā́
      us-APl and_cl them-APl and_cl PV **hí** lead better-ASg PostP
      'lead both us and them forth to a better state.' (SJ/JB)   RV 2.1.16c

   c. tribhíḥ   pavítrair   ápupod   dhí arkám
      three-IPl purifiers-IPl he purified **hí** chant-ASg
      'Since he [=Agni?] purified the chant with three purifying filters,' (SJ/JB)

      RV 3.26.8a

   d. ákṣetravit   kṣetravídaṃ   hí áprāṭ
      not-knowing-the-field-NSg knowing-the-field-ASg **hí** asked
      'Because the one not knowing the field asked the field-knower,' (SJ/JB)

      RV 10.32.7a

14 Preliminaries to the investigation of clitic sequencing in Greek and Indo-Iranian

In all of the "exceptions" I will cite here, we can analyze the data just as we did in the case of *ca* and *céd*: the first constituent of the clause is in the Topic position above the CP, *hí* is in C itself, and is not "properly hosted" by a tonic element *within its domain* on its left, and thus undergoes inversion. Thus we have [$_{Top}$ *urukramásya*] in (24a), [$_{Top}$ *asmáñ ca táṃś ca*] in (24b), [$_{Top}$ *tribhíḥ pavítrair*] in (24c), and [$_{Top}$ *ákṣetravit*] in (24d).

In my dissertation, I rather unwisely said, regarding examples such as these, that the poets were able to treat the *caesura* as equivalent to a clause-boundary, and thus place *hí* in second position after the caesura, rather than after the actual start of the clause. This is a not a particularly good idea, giving the meter far too much power to determine the data – certainly far more than I would be willing to concede at this stage of my research on the matter.

We can give a much more sensible assessment of this data if we instead note that the boundary between the element in Topic and the start of the CP-domain is marked by an intonational reset (or pause), and that the natural place to align this pause within the rhythmic structure of the verse line is at the caesura. In all of the examples above, the Topic ends at the caesura of a trimeter line (this will be true of the examples I cite below as well).

As usual, there are many other interesting things going on with these examples as well. For example, in support of the topicalization analysis, we see in an example such as (24a) a discontinuity (*urukramásya...bándhur*). We need to account for this discontinuity, and movement is the way to do it in our model – topicalization provides the relevant explanation for that movement. We will see additional examples of this type below.

Finally, and returning to the matter of clitic sequencing, we may be able to learn something important about how exactly the "prosodic flip" works to trigger specific orderings from examples such as those in (25).

(25) a. índro vidváṁ ánu hí tvā cacákṣa
Indra-NSg knowing-NSg PV **hí** you-ASg$_{cl}$ kept an eye on
ténāhám agne ánuśiṣṭa ā́gām
this-ISg=I-NSg Agni-VSg instructed-NSg have come hither
'Because the knowing Indra has kept you in his sights, instructed by him have I come here, o Agni.' (SJ/JB) RV 5.2.8cd

b. sadyó jajñānó ví hím iddhó ákhyat
at once being-born-NSg PV **hí**=them$_{cl}$ kindled-NSg he observed
'for immediately upon being born, he, kindled, observed them'
RV 10.45.5c

Recall that pronominal clitics occupy the lowest position in the C-domain (or the highest in IP), so one possible structure for what the *syntax* would have sent to the prosody for (25a) would be:

(26) [$_{Top}$ *índro vidvā́ṁ*] [$_{CP}$ *hí* [*tvā* [*ánu cacákṣa*]]]

In this structure, neither *hí* nor *tvā* can be properly hosted on their left, with the expected "prosodic inversion" being thus triggered:

(27) [$_{\text{Top}}$ *índro vidvā́m̐*] [$_{\text{CP}}$ *hí* [*tvā* [*ánu hí tvā cacákṣa*]]]

However, as we all also know, there are many "exceptions" to the syntactic "weak pronoun fronting" that seems to be responsible for making pronominal clitics targets for Wackernagel's Law-type effects in archaic IE languages. If the *tvā* of (25a) were to represent one of these exceptions, and thus be unfronted, the most likely input structure for the prosody would have been:

(28) [$_{\text{Top}}$ *índro vidvā́m̐*] [$_{\text{CP}}$ *hí* [*ánu tvā cacákṣa*]]

Which would have been operated on by the prosody so as to create:

(29) [$_{\text{Top}}$ *índro vidvā́m̐*] [$_{\text{CP}}$ *hí* [*ánu hí tvā cacákṣa*]]

These two possible analyses have quite different implications for how the system I have assumed gives rise to clitic sequencing. In the analysis in (26) we would be looking at the effects of *iterative prosodic inversion* events, and the examples would reveal an (as far as I can see somewhat unexpectedly) "outside-in" processing (*hí* flips in first, then *tvā*).

Under the analysis in (28), we are looking at the relationship between the resolution of the hosting needs of an unmoved *tvā* relative to the ability of an inverting *hí* to "slip in" between *tvā* and *tvā*'s potential (and ultimate) host *ánu*. The details of the processes involved under the latter set of assumptions are too complex for me to deal with in this context, but there is evidence that that approach does represent the correct analysis of examples such as (25ab).

Recall our earlier discussion of the Attic Greek *mén gár* clitic sequence. *gár* is of course essentially isofunctional with Rigvedic *hí*. In addition, Thomson's (1939) well-known paper on the "postponement of interrogatives" in Attic drama supports the idea that one could still front into a high Top position in this language. This has a specific entailment, since the WH-elements Thomson talks about are in CP, and the topics he deals with are higher, and since *gár* is in C, there should be Attic drama cases exactly like the "postponed" subordinating *ca*, *céd*, and *hí* examples we walked through earlier. And there are.[7]

(30) a. pròs taũta mè̄ psaúsēi tis Argeíōn
in light of these-APl NEG should touch any-NSg$_{cl}$ Greek-GPl
emoũ·
me-GSg

---

[7] Note that in (30c) the articular infinitive construction has a proclitic article, and the first prosodic word after which *gár* 'flips' is thus tõi=ploutẽin.

    [spʰagĕi paréksō gàr dérēn eukardíōs.
    knife-DSg I submit to **gár** neck-ASg bravely

    'In light of these things, no one of the Greeks need touch me, because I will bravely submit my neck to the knife.' Eur. IphA 1559–1560

b. hȭn   g'   oúte métron   oút' aritʰmós estí moi·
    which-GPl PTCL Neg measure-NSg Neg number is me-DSg_cl

    [kakȭi   kakòn   gàr eis hámillan   érkʰetai.
    trouble-DSg trouble-NSg **gár** to competition-ASg comes

    'Of which (woes) there is neither measure nor number for me, because woe comes into competition with woe.' Eur. Tro 620–621

c. kaì nề dí'   eí tí   g'   ésti lampròn   kaì
    and by Zeus-ASg if something-NSg PTCL is splendid-NSg and

    kalòn
    beautiful-NSg

    ề kʰaríen   antʰrṓpoisi, dià   sè   gígnetai·
    or elegant-NSg men-DPl through you-ASg it comes about

    [hápanta]   tȭi=ploutein   gár estʰ' hupékoa.
    everything-NPl Art-DSg=being rich-INF **gár** is subservient-NPl

    'and, by Zeus, if something is splendid and beautiful, or elegant for men, it comes about through you (=Wealth), because everything is subservient to being rich.' Ar. Plutus 144–146

In cases involving both *mén*, which marks focus,[8] and *gár*, meaning 'because', the interpretation of scope within the clauses indicates that we are dealing with a structure such as 'BECAUSE (*gár*) *one the one hand* (*mén*) ... *on the other hand* (*dé*) ...' When there is nothing for the *gár* to lean leftwards on, we get the surface order *mén gár*. This indicates sequential "prosodic inversion" of the form:

(31) [_CP_ gár [mén [X̂ mén gár Ý Ź]]]

But this is an "inside-out" (*mén* first, then *gár*) resolution of the hosting needs of these elements. If the Vedic mechanisms are the same – and all indications are that they are – then this is clear evidence against the analysis in (26), favoring the (28) analysis. The implications of this prosodic "tucking in" have not been explored in any significant detail.

8 Conclusions

If we tie the domain of a clitic like *hí* or *gár* to its semantic scope – which we can easily do by positioning it via the syntax, whose job, after all, is to create precisely these kinds

---

[8] The particle *mén* normally has a contrasting element, marked by the particle *dé*. I translate the contrastive relationship between these two elements as 'on the one hand X, on the other hand Y' below.

of scope relations – we need not worry about finding the structure for it to be in "second position" in. If the clitic cannot be hosted on its left *in situ*, that structure will be the one which provides the nearest prosodic host to the right of the *syntactic position* of the clitic, regardless of what entity that is.

As with other syntactic entities that take arguments, we sometimes do have to specify the nature of those arguments. But it doesn't follow from that that we need to do it *stipulatively* – it isn't chance that there is no word-level *hí* or *gár* 'because' clitic. A word doesn't express the kind of things 'because' needs to take as an argument to generate a coherent semantics.[9] But that same word would work fine as an argument of 'and'.

Given a sufficiently rich understanding of the semantics of a particular enclitic or postpositive, we should be able to deduce the nature of the kinds of syntactic entities it can take as an argument. No stipulation should be needed. Of course we are far from having this kind of understanding of the meaning of many Vedic and Attic Greek enclitics.

To the extent we can determine with some degree of confidence the *syntactic* position of the enclitic elements we are interested in, we are in an excellent position to examine their *surface position* (which may be the same as their syntactic position, but may be perturbed by the "prosodic inversion" process) with a view to determining the detailed mechanics of the interactions involved when multiple 2P elements are present in a string. The more explicit a conception we have of the relevant algorithms, the easier this task will be. One of the strengths, in my view, of the model assumed here is that its parts are all clearly enough defined that it should be easy to discover those instances, if any, in which stipulation may be, unfortunately, required.

By contrast, approaches which leave vague the processes that give rise to clitic sequencing are revealing in that shortcoming their general inadequacy. Getting prosodic positioning to interact in the required way with, on the one hand, syntactic positioning (which all grammatical theories require) and, on the other, with semantic interpretation (ditto), is a very non-trivial problem: it goes to the core architecture of the grammar. Working out the details of one's assumptions in this domain cannot be left as an exercise to future work – one needs to be formulate a clear notion about such things going in. When there are multiple clitics we see overtly the failure of inexplicit models (such as Hale 1987, and a lot of subsequent work), but those same problems are present, if obscured, in the case of simple clitics as well.

---

[9] Yes, I know about the prepositional 'because' phenomenon. If you think about what such strings *mean*, and assume that their meaning is representationally present (but not all pronounced), as in

Q: Who slew Vrtra?

A: Indra.

in which 'Indra' *means* 'Indra slew Vrtra' (because it can be a lie, and only propositions can be false, not nouns), then you'll see why I don't think this is a problem. Anyway, there's no evidence that the speakers of Rigvedic Sanskrit could say: 'Indra slew Vrtra. Because, the waters.'

References

Anderson, Stephen R. 2005. *Aspects of the theory of clitics*. Oxford: Oxford University Press.

Bartholomae, Christian. 1886. *Arische Forschungen, Bd. II*. Halle.

Goldstein, David M. 2016. *Classical Greek syntax: Wackernagel's Law in Herodotus*. Leiden: Brill.

Hale, Mark. 1987. *Studies in the comparative syntax of the oldest Indo-Iranian languages*. Harvard University PhD thesis.

Hale, Mark. 1996. Deriving Wackernagel's Law: Prosodic and syntactic factors determining clitic placement, in the language of the Rigveda. In Aaron L. Halpern & Arnold M. Zwicky (eds.), *Approaching second: Second position clitics and related phenomena*, 165–197. Stanford: CSLI.

Halpern, Aaron. 1995. *On the placement and morphology of clitics*. Stanford: Center for the Study of Language (CSLI).

Hettrich, Heinrich. 1988. *Untersuchungen zur Hypotaxe im Vedischen*. Berlin: de Gruyter.

Hock, Hans Henrich. 1996. Who's on first? Toward a prosodic account of P2 clitics. In Aaron L. Halpern & Arnold M. Zwicky (eds.), *Approaching second: Second position clitics and related phenomena*, 199–270. Stanford: CSLI.

Jamison, Stephanie & Joel Brereton (eds.). 2014. *The Rigveda*. Oxford: Oxford University Press.

Keydana, Götz. 2011. Wackernagel in the language of the Rigveda: a reassessment. *Historische Sprachforschung* 124. 80–107.

Lowe, John J. 2014. Transitive nominals in Old Avestan. *Journal of the American Oriental Society* 134(4). 553–577.

Thomson, George. 1939. The postponement of interrogatives in Attic drama. *CQ* 33(3/4). 147–152.

Wackernagel, Jacob. 1892. Über ein Gesetz der indogermanischen Wortstellung. *Indogermanische Forschungen* 1. 333–436.

Wackernagel, Jacob. 1920. *Vorlesungen über syntax: mit besonderer berücksichtigung von griechisch, lateinisch und deutsch*. Birkhäuser.

Chapter 15

Nominal verbs and transitive nouns: Vindicating lexicalism

Paul Kiparsky
Stanford University

> Event nominalizations and agent nominalizations provide evidence that all affixation is morphological, and that phrasal categories are projected from words in the syntax. Departing from both transformational and earlier lexicalist approaches to nominalizations, I first argue on the basis of English and Finnish evidence that gerunds are not DPs built on heads that embed an extended verbal projection (Baker & Vinokurova 2009; Kornfilt & Whitman 2011), but IPs that need Case. They are categorially verbal at all levels of the syntax, including having structural subjects rather than possessor specifiers. Their nominal behavior is entirely due to the unvalued Case feature borne by their Infl head, which they share with all participial verb forms. I then argue that agent nominalizations are categorially nominal at all levels of the syntax, and that the verb-like case assignment of transitive agent nominalizations is due to the verbal Aspect feature borne by their nominalizing head. Vedic Sanskrit, Northern Paiute, and Sakha evidence is shown to favor this analysis over B&V's analysis of intransitive agent nominalizations as nominal equivalents of Voice heads and transitive agent nominalizations as Aspect heads. The two "mixed" categories – gerunds and transitive nominalizations – thus prove to be formally duals: respectively verbs with Case and nouns with Aspect.

1 Nominalizations

The earliest generative work derived all nominalizations syntactically (Chomsky 1955; Lees 1960). Chomsky (1970) then argued that only *-ing* gerunds are derived syntactically, while all other types of event nominals, such as *refutation, acceptance, refusal*, are derived morphologically in the lexicon from bases that are unspecified between nouns and verbs. The suffix *-ing* was shown to serve both as the gerund formative and as one of the formatives that derive lexical event nominals. Chomsky's main argument was based on the fact that gerund phrases have the structure of verb phrases whereas other event nominals have the structure of noun phrases.[1] The differences are completely systematic. Unlike derived event nominals, gerunds are modifiable by adverbs, assign structural case to their complements (Table 1a,b), disallow articles and other determiners (Table 1c) and plurals (Table 1d), allow aspect (Table 1e) and negation (Table 1f), and they have a grammatical subject which is assigned a Th-role as in finite clauses (Table 1g), and which may be an expletive (Table 1h). In (Table 1g), *reading* refers to an event and *her* to its agent, the reader. In the derived nominal, *her* could also be a sponsor, organizer, or some other participant of a reading event not necessarily identical with the reader (Kratzer 1996; 2004), and *reading* could also mean 'manner of reading', 'interpretation'. Without an *of* complement, derived nominals are also interpretable in a passive sense: in *Mary's confirmation*, Mary could be the confirmer or the confirmee.

Table 1: Gerunds vs. Nominals.

		Gerunds ($-ing^V$)	Nominals ($-ing^N$, -ion, -al, -ance...)
a.	Adjectives	*her quick signing the document	her quick signing of the document
b.	Adverbs	her immediately reciting it	*her immediately recital of it
c.	Determiners	*the/a/this/each performing it	the/a/this/each performance of it
d.	Plural	*her readings it / *her reading its	her readings of it
e.	Aspect	by her having sung it	*by her having sung of it
f.	Negation	by her not approving it	*by her not approval of it
g.	Subject	we remembered her reading it	we remembered her reading of it
h.	Expletives	it(s) seeming to me that I exist[2]	*it(s) appearance to me that I exist

The lexicalist line of analysis continues to be developed in different ways (Malouf 2000; Blevins 2003; Kim 2016). But many recent treatments have reverted to a uniformly syntactic derivation of nominalizations, in which nominalizing heads project a nominal structure and have a verbal complement whose type determines the nominalization's properties. The differences between the two types in Table 1 is captured by introducing

---

[1] Chomsky also contrasted the uniformity, regularity and full productivity of gerunds with the morphological and semantic diversity, idiosyncrasies, and limited productivity of derived event nominals. As Anderson 2016 notes, these points played a subsidiary role in Chomsky's argument. Indeed, they are not compelling criteria by themselves, for there is no shortage of productivity and regularity in the lexicon, and syntax has its share of idiosyncrasy.

[2] *I can't help but feel a little despondant **due to it seeming to me** that the TIE/fo and the T-70 make the original TIE and T-65 somewhat redundant* (Internet), *evidence that "explains away" **its seeming to me** that p is the case* (James Pryor, The Skeptic and the Dogmatist, *Noûs* 34: 534, 2000). The variation between Poss-*ing* and Acc-*ing* gerunds seen here is briefly addressed in 2.3 below.

them at different levels in the functional structure. The gerund $-ing^V$ is structurally high, and derived nominals in $-ing^N$, $-ion$, $-al$, $-ance$ are structurally low.

Kornfilt & Whitman (2011) dub this the FUNCTIONAL NOMINALIZATION THESIS (FNT), and propose a typology of four levels of nominalization, CP, TP, vP and VP. In this typology, English gerunds are TP nominalizations, while derived nominals are VP nominalizations.[3] This paper vindicates a uniform treatment of nominalizations in a different way: all true nominalizations are derived lexically; gerunds are not nominalizations at all – they are neither DPs nor NPs but IPs that need Case.

As my point of departure I take Baker & Vinokurova's (2009) theory, which extends the FNT from event nominalizations to agent nominalizations. For gerunds, B&V posit the structure (1a), based on the version of the DP analysis originated (along with the DP itself) by Abney 1987. The DP's complement here is an NP headed by the gerund nominalizer $-ing^V$, below which the structure is entirely verbal: an AspP which hosts aspectual material and certain adverbs, and which has a vP complement whose v (v=Voice) head assigns structural case and introduces an external agent argument. This external agent argument shows up as a genitive in D head. B&V do not say exactly how it gets there in (1a); perhaps it is base-generated in D and bears a control relation to the PRO in the Spec-vP position where the agent role is assigned.

For derived nominals B&V propose the structure (1b), where the head ($-ing^N$, $-ion$, etc.) takes a bare VP complement. Because it has no Asp or v projection, it contains neither adverbs, agents, nor structural case.[4]

The structures in (1) take care of the contrasting properties Table 1b, e, f, and g, but leave the remaining four properties (Table 1a, c, d, and h) to fend for themselves. On the one hand, the DP in (1a) provides too little structure: expletive *it*-subjects are believed to occupy Spec-IP or Spec-TP, but (1)a provides no Spec-IP or Spec-TP for them.[5] On the other hand, the DP, needed in the analysis as a site for the gerund's subject, generates unwanted structure. Since DPs can have plural heads, adjective modifiers, determiners, and quantifiers, the DP analysis wrongly predicts that Table 1a, c, and d should be grammatical. To maintain it one must somehow prevent functional projections like AP, QP, and NumP from appearing in DPs that have NP complements that have AspP complements, while allowing them in other kinds of DPs, and one must prevent the head of a

---

[3] A syntactic derivation of gerunds from TP/IP is also developed by Pires 2006. The aspectual content of the gerund is treated in Pustejovsky 1995; Alexiadou 2001, and Alexiadou, Soare & Iordăchioaia 2010. Alexiadou and her co-workers conclude that gerunds are imperfective Aspect heads that dominate VoiceP and vP, while nominalizers are n heads that also dominate VoiceP and vP, but under NumberP and ClassifierP, housing adjective modifiers, determiners, and plural.

[4] All analyses have to contend with the fact that certain adverbs can occur as postmodifiers with derived nominals, and even with some underived ones (Payne, Pullum & Huddleston 2010); they cite examples such as *the opinion generally of the doctors*, *a timber shortage nationally*, *the people locally*, and *the intervention again of Moscow*. We shall see similar Finnish data in §3 below.

[5] Expletive *there*, which likewise appears in gerunds, may sit in a lower subject position, since it is sensitive to the argument structure of the predicate – the absence of Cause according to Deal 2009, who puts it in the specifier of v. Like expletive *it*, *there* does not appear in derived nominals (**there's appearance to be a problem*). On Deal's analysis, the distribution of expletive *there* is consistent with my IP analysis of gerunds, but adds no further support to it.

Paul Kiparsky

DP whose complement is an NP whose complement is an AspP from being an article or a demonstrative pronoun.[6]

(1) a. his reading the book (high)   b. the reading of the book (low)

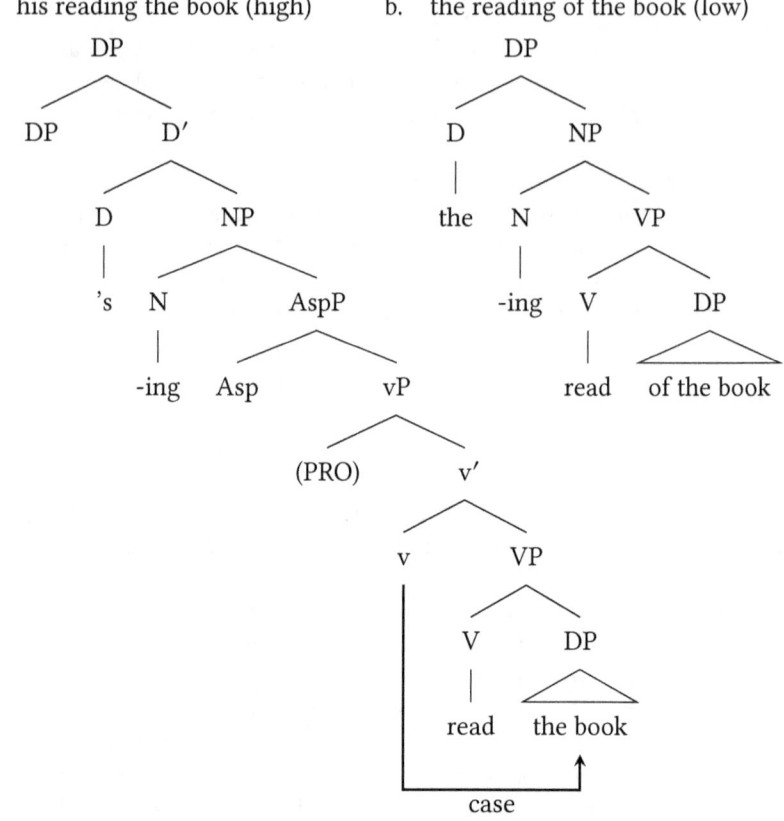

Contrary to what the FNT seems to promise, then, the morphosyntactic properties of a nominalization cannot be fixed just by locating its nominal head in a universal hierarchy of verbal functional categories, or even in a language-specific one. In that approach to mixed categories, it seems that the functional content that a given nominalizing head may combine with must be specified on an item-specific basis. But not just any arbitrary mixed category is possible. Consider the awesome unused power unleashed by the FNT. If functional N heads can convert AspPs into NPs in the syntax, as in (1a), why aren't there such things as Q heads with vP complements (*[some [he read it]$_{vP}$]$_{QP}$), let alone multiple verbalizing and nominalizing syntactic heads interspersed to generate phrases in which layers of verbal and nominal structure alternate in various combinations?

---

[6] Some of the overgeneration could be curbed by by eliminating the DP layer, or by eliminating the NP layer and having D select for AspP directly. But these projections cannot be struck from (1) because their heads are essential to the analysis. The D head serves as the site of the structural subject, and the N head houses the nominalizer *-ing*. Neither of these elements can be accommodated in the Asp head, for that is required for the aspectual auxiliary *have*.

15 Nominal verbs and transitive nouns: Vindicating lexicalism

The empirical problem of overgeneration is a direct result of the theoretical approach behind the FNT-style analysis. The derivation of gerunds in (1a) involves syntactic affixation of *-ing* to the phrasal projection AspP.[7] A lexicalist perspective rules out affixation to phrases. It dictates an entirely different kind of derivation, in which the gerund suffix *-ing* is added to verbs in the morphology to build words (e.g. *reading*), which are then inserted in terminal nodes in the syntax. On this view, a gerund phrase is the syntactic projection of a gerund, not of a determiner as in (1a). On that basis we can build a simple and restrictive theory of nominalizations that explains *all* the data in Table 1.

The key idea is that gerunds are participles, and that participial suffixes, *-ing* included, are Infl heads that differ from finite and infinitive Infl heads in that they bear a Case feature. The extended projection of a gerund is then an IP with a Case feature, which needs to be checked (or, from a non-lexicalist perpective, valued) in the syntax. The Case feature restricts participial phrases to two syntactic functions: arguments – gerunds – in positions where their value for Case can be checked by a predicate, and participial modifiers in positions where their value for Case can be checked by head-modifier agreement.

Lexicalism excludes not only FNT-style analyses of gerunds, but every kind of syntactic affixation to phrasal categories. This means that no syntactic process can have the effect of changing the category of a word. That holds for all types of nominalization: event nominalizations, result nominalizations, and agent nominalizations. All "mixed categories" must then arise from morphological specifications of lexical heads, rather than from syntactic embedding as in (1). In §3 I support this more general prediction by showing that transitive agent nouns do not have an embedded vP projection and that their verbal properties come from a Tense/Aspect feature on the agent suffix.

I assume that a phrasal constituent is a projection of its head, which inherits its category (Noun, Verb, etc.), its inflectional features (such as Aspect and Case), and its thematic roles (Agent, Patient, Instrument, Event, etc.).[8] Mixed categories are verbs, nouns, and adjectives that have an extra phi-feature. Their extended projections behave like extended projections of ordinary verbs, nouns, and adjectives, modulo the properties enforced by that feature content. The language-specific syntax of gerunds is determined by their Case feature. A gerund that can bear any Case projects a phrase with the distribution of a DP. A gerund that has a partially specified Case feature projects a phrase that is restricted to positions compatible with the specified values of the feature. For example, Finnish gerunds are restricted to internal argument positions (section 2.2). Similarly, the verbal properties of transitive agent nouns are due to a Tense/Aspect feature assigned to these nouns by the agent affix that forms them. This feature may likewise be lexically unvalued and specified by additional aspectual morphology (as in Northern Paiute), or inherently specified on the agent noun affix itself (as in Sanskrit and Sakha, see 3.3. Since the mixed categories under lexicalist assumptions are projected from a single head, we correctly predict the absence of mixed categories in which verbal and nominal structure

---

[7] A similar earlier proposal is Yoon (1996).
[8] E.g. $[\![\text{-er}]\!] = \lambda P \lambda x \lambda e [P(e) \wedge \text{Agent}(e,x)]$ (the set of human individuals that are the Agent of some event), $[\![\text{-ee}]\!] = \lambda P \lambda x \lambda e [P(e) \wedge \text{human}(x) \wedge \text{Undergoer}(e,x)]$ (the set of human individuals that are the Undergoer of some event).

is alternately layered in weird combinations, of vPs that function as DPs, and of the other abovementioned monstrosities.

A theoretical gain is that we need not divide nominalizations into a syntactic type and a lexical type, as in standard lexicalist analyses. Once gerunds are recognized as IPs, we can maintain that all nominalizations are derived morphologically in the lexicon. This can be done either in a realizational morphology of the type pioneered by Anderson (1992), or in a morpheme-based one such as the minimalist morphology of Wunderlich (1996a). It remains to be seen whether the analysis can be recast in a DM-friendly syntax-based format. What is clear is that it does not *follow* from any theory that countenances structures like (1). To that extent at least, its empirical success constitutes new empirical support for lexicalism.

I begin in §2 with "high" event nominalizations. I show that the lexicalist approach correctly predicts the syntax of English and Finnish gerund phrases, including aspects that go unexplained in FNT analyses, and that it curbs the typology in a good way. In §3 I apply the same idea to agent nominals, and support the resulting analyses with data from Vedic Sanskrit and Finnish that is new to the theoretical literature.

2 Gerunds

2.1 English gerunds

Gerunds and participles are formally identical in English (Pullum 1991; Yoon 1996; Huddleston & Pullum 2002; Blevins 2003). For example, they are the only verb forms that overtly distinguish perfect aspect but not progressive or past tense. Given the modest morphology of English this identity might be dismissed as an accident, but the testimony of richly inflected languages, such as Finnish (2b), Classical Greek (2c), Sanskrit (2d), and Latin (2e) leaves no doubt that participles are systematically used in two functions: adjectivally as modifiers and nominally as arguments.

(2)   a.   English *-ing* participle
       i.   *Modifier:* I saw Bill reading the book. (⇒ I saw Bill.)
       ii.   *Argument:* I hated Bill's reading the book. (⇏ I hated Bill.)
   b.   Finnish participles
       i.   *Modifier:*
          Muist-i-n   hunaja-a   syö-vä-n   karhu-n.
          remember-PST-1SG honey-PRTC eat-PTC-GEN bear-ACC
          'I remembered the/a bear (that was) eating honey.'
       ii.   *Argument:*
          Muist-i-n   karhu-n syö-vä-n   hunaja-a.
          remember-PRTC-1SG bear-GEN eat-PTC-GEN honey-PRTC
          'I remembered that the/a bear ate honey.'

15 Nominal verbs and transitive nouns: Vindicating lexicalism

c. Classical Greek participles

   i. *Modifier:*

     tòn   adikoũ-nt-a   Phílippo-n apéktein-a
     the-ACC act-unjustly-PRTC-ACC Philip-ACC kill-AOR-1SG

     'I killed the unjustly acting Philip.'

   ii. *Argument:*

     adikoũ-nt-a   Phílippo-n eksélenk-s-a
     act-unjustly-PRTC-ACC Philip-ACC prove-AOR-1SG

     'I proved that Philip acted unjustly.'

d. Sanskrit participles

   i. *Modifier:*

     rājān-am ā-ga-ta-m   śṛ-ṇo-mi
     king-ACC to-go-PRTC-ACC hear-PRES-1SG

     'I hear the king (who has) arrived.'

   ii. *Argument:*

     rājān-am ā-ga-ta-m   śṛ-ṇo-mi
     king-ACC to-go-PRTC-ACC hear-PRES-1SG

     'I hear that the king has arrived.'

e. Latin participles

   i. *Modifier:*

     Hannibal   vic-tu-s   ad Antiochu m   confug-i-t
     Hannibal.NOM defeat-PRTC.MASC-NOM to Antiochus-ACC flee-PERF-3SG

     'Defeated, Hannibal took refuge with Antiochus.'

   ii. *Argument:*

     Hannibal   vic-tu-s   Romano-s   metu
     Hannibal.NOM defeat-PRTC.MASC-NOM Roman.ACC.PL fear.ABL
     libera-vi-t
     free-PERF-3SG

     'Hannibal's being defeated freed the Romans from fear.'

Traditional grammars of these languages treat participles as verb forms which are inflected for Case, for good reasons. Participles distinguish the verbal categories of voice and tense/aspect, and they are formed off the same tense/aspect stems as the finite verbs. They supply the periphrastic forms that complete gaps in inflectional paradigms. They assign the same cases to their objects as the corresponding finite verbs and infinitives do. They are modified by adverbs, not by adjectives. They select for the same prefixes as the corresponding finite verbs and infinitives, with the same (often idiosyncratic) meanings. Those languages that disallow noun+verb compounds (such as classical Greek and Sanskrit) also disallow noun+participle compounds. As I show below, participles have structural subjects.

So there must be some property that distinguishes participles from finite verbs and infinitives, and which supports the double function of participles as nominal arguments and adjectival modifiers. The obvious candidate is Case. Suppose then that participial formatives are Infl heads that need Case. On lexicalist assumptions, they are affixed in the morphology to a verb to make a participle, which is then inflected for case if the language has case morphology, and enters the syntax with a specified Case feature that – like any Case feature – must be checked in the syntax. In a language that lacks case morphology, such as English, the participle remains unvalued for Case, and projects an IP with a Case feature that must be valued in the syntax. Both "checking" and "valuing" can be formalized as identical operations of feature unification, or as optimal matching in OT Correspondence Theory.

As an illustration consider first the derivation of gerunds in English. Prescinding from vP, AspP, VoiceP, and other possible functional projections, their syntactic structure is as in (3).

(3)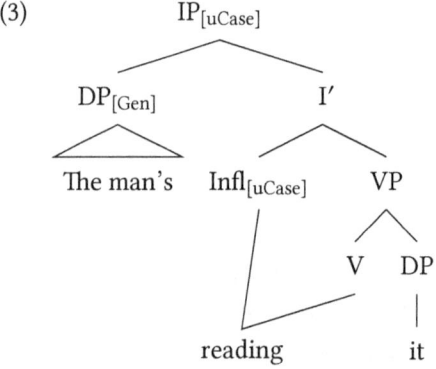

Infl$_{[uCase]}$ combines with V in the same way as Tensed Infl does. How this happens depends on the model of grammar. If we assume both lexicalist syntax and lexicalist morphology, the case-needing Infl *-ing* is suffixed to V in the morphology to form a participle, and the participle then projects a case-needing IP in the syntax, where the Case feature is valued. In argumental participles (gerunds), it is valued by the governing Case-assigner, and in participial modifiers it is valued by agreement with the nominal they modify.

If we assume minimalist syntax, we can comply with lexical morphology by using spanning (Svenonius 2016), which allows the lexically generated participle to be inserted under the two corresponding syntactic terminal nodes. In DM, *-ing* would be a syntactic terminal that is postsyntactically Lowered onto V. Thus, the idea that gerunds are case-needing IPs can probably be implemented in any grammatical architecture. However, in non-lexicalist frameworks this analysis is merely motivated on empirical grounds. In lexicalist frameworks that prohibit affixation to phrases it is required on principled grounds as well.

In languages where participles are morphologically inflected for Case, such as (2b-e), participles project an IP that bears a specified Case value that must be checked in the

15 Nominal verbs and transitive nouns: Vindicating lexicalism

syntax. The lexicalist approach now makes an interesting prediction: in such languages, gerunds may be morphologically restricted to particular Case features, which restrict their syntactic distribution to contexts compatible with those features. This prediction is confirmed in Finnish. Finnish gerunds bear an oblique Case – glossed as Genitive in (2b.ii) – which confines them to internal argument positions (section 2.2).[9]

(4)

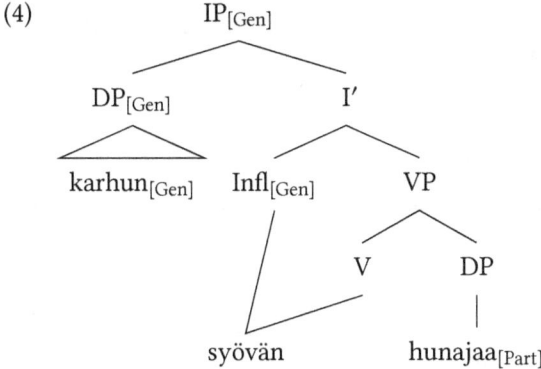

Returning to English, the analysis of participial clauses as IPs that have the single special property of needing structural Case explains at a stroke which clausal and nominal properties they have and which ones they lack. To start with the latter, it explains why gerund phrases, unlike DPs, have no articles, quantifiers, or numerals, why they cannot be modified by adjectives and relative clauses, why their head cannot be genitive or plural.

(5) a. * The/a/each compiling the corpus took over a year.
 b. * Both/every compiling corporas took over a year.
 c. * His two compilings corpora each took over a year.
 d. * His careful compiling the corpus was a turning point.
 e. * His editing texts that is funded will take a year.
 f. * His compiling corpora's results were dramatic.

The missing categories are just the ones that would originate in a DP.

As for the nominal properties that gerunds do have, they are accurately covered by the generalization that gerunds appear in Case positions. They function as subjects, objects, and predicates, as objects of prepositions (6e,f,g), and as objects of a small set of transitive adjectives (6f,g), all diagnosed as Case positions by the fact that full-fledged DPs occur in them.

(6) a. [Bill's leaving Paris] was unexpected.
 b. I regret [Bill's leaving Paris].
 c. The problem is [Bill's leaving Paris].

---

[9] There is no agreement relation between the genitive subject and the gerund in (4).

d. Because of Bill's leaving Paris we'll be hiring new personnel.
   e. We are worried about Bill's leaving Paris.
   f. This event is worth my visiting Paris.
   g. It's no good my playing this sort of game.[10]

This does not mean that all transitive verbs take gerund complements. Particular verbs can select for whether they take gerunds, *that*-clauses, or infinitive complements, just as they can select for whether they take DPs:

(7) a. *I said Bill's leaving Paris.
    b. I said it/something/several things.

What the analysis correctly predicts is that gerunds, unlike *that*-clauses and infinitives, appear *only* in Case positions:

(8) a. i. *I hope Bill's leaving Paris.
       ii. *I hope it.
       iii. I hope that Bill is leaving Paris.
       iv. I hope to leave Paris.
    b. i. *It is rumored Bill's leaving Paris.
       ii. *The proposal is rumored.
       iii. It is rumored that Bill is leaving Paris.
       iv. It is rumored to be happening.
    c. i. *It seemed / was expected Bill's leaving Paris.
       ii. *It seemed / was expected this event.
       iii. It seemed / was expected that Bill would leave Paris.
       iv. It seemed / was expected to happen.

A further consequence is that the subjects of gerunds are IP specifiers. If overt, they are Genitive or Accusative,[11] just as the subject of a finite IP is Nominative, and the overt subject of an infinitive requires a Case-assigning *for*. Crucially, they are true structural subjects analogous to subjects of finite clauses, not necessarily "agents" as in B&V's Table 1a, nor "possessors" with their varied functions as in derived nominals. This prediction is confirmed by three generalizations. Unlike genitive specifiers of nouns (including derived nominals), but like structural subjects of finite clauses, the specifiers of gerunds can be expletives:

(9) a. It(s) seeming to you that you dreamt is not evidence of it(s) being the case that you dreamt.
    b. *It(s) appearance to you that you dreamt is not evidence of it(s) truth that you dreamt.

---

[10] Cf. *It's no good this sort of game.* (Dickens, *Our Mutual Friend*)
[11] On Acc+*ing* gerunds see the brief and inconclusive remarks in §2.3 below.

15 Nominal verbs and transitive nouns: Vindicating lexicalism

Like structural subjects of finite clauses, they are subject to control (Huddleston & Pullum 2002: 1190):

(10)   a. Mary remembered locking the door. [the rememberer is the locker]
       b. Mary remembered the/a locking of the door. [the rememberer might not be the locker]

like structural subjects of finite clauses, and unlike genitive agents of nominals, they cannot be paraphrased with *of* or *by*:

(11)   a. the Persians' quick run = the quick run of/by the Persians
       b. the Persians' quick running = the quick running of/by the Persians
       c. the Persians' quickly running ≠ *quickly running of/by the Persians
       d. the Persians' quickly attacking the Greeks ≠ *quickly attacking the Greeks of/by the Persians
       e. the Persians quickly attacked the Greeks ≠ *of/by the Persians quickly attacked the Greeks

To summarize: the analysis of gerunds as IPs with Case explains the cross-linguistically common convergence of nominal and adjectival functions in a single morphological class of verbal forms. By not positing any DP or NP structure over the IP it avoids the overgeneration problem that FNT-type analyses face. It excludes the possibility of multiple alternating verbalizing and nominalizing syntactic heads to which the FNT opens the theoretical door, and gets rid of the constraint that heads of DPs whose complements are NPs whose complements are verbal projections may not be articles or demonstrative pronouns. It provides the basis for a uniform structure for all DPs, and for a uniform lexical derivation of all nominalizations. It correctly predicts that gerunds and participles have subjects – specifiers of Infl that are structural counterparts to the subjects of finite clauses. What is important is that the analysis is not motivated merely by these empirical arguments; it is a consequence of lexicalism, and, if correct, supports the lexicalist organization of grammar.

The question arises whether there might be a CP layer above the IP, headed by a null complementizer. This additional structure is not justifiable for English, because the distribution of gerunds differs from that of any type of CP. First, gerunds need Case, whereas CPs do not (Vergnaud 1977). Secondly, gerunds are permitted in clause-medial position, while *that*-clauses and other CP clauses must extrapose.[12]

That gerund phrases are full IPs with a structural subject, that they bear Case, and that, unlike derived nominals, they have no DP or NP projection, and in particular no possessor-type Specifier, makes many additional predictions that are testable in morphologically richer languages. They turns out to be abundantly supported, as demonstrated for Finnish in the next section.

---

[12] However, the case marking of participles in inflected languages could be considered as a kind of complementizer, as conjectured for the inherent case affix *-n* on Finnish gerunds in §2.2.

2.2 Finnish gerunds are IPs

Finnish participial propositional complement clauses are the closest functional counterparts of English gerunds, and I will call them gerunds here. They are not DPs with possessors but IPs with true structural subjects. Their Case is inherently marked by the oblique suffix *-n*, arguably functioning as a complementizer, which restricts them to internal argument positions. This illustrates how the typology of gerunds emerges from variation in what cases they can bear.[13]

Unlike English gerunds, Finnish gerunds are never external arguments. Thus they can be objects of transitive verbs such as *say, think, want, prove, remember* and *hear*, and subjects of presentational intransitives like *appear* and *become evident*, but they cannot be subjects of such predicates as *be obvious, prove,* and *mean*.[14]

(12) a. Selvis-i   Mati-n   ampu-nee-n   karhu-n.
         become-clear-PST.3SG Matti-GEN shoot-PERF.PRTC-GEN bear-ACC$_{GEN}$

         'It became clear that Matti had shot the/a bear.'

    b. * Mati-n   ampu-nee-n   karhu-n   suututt-i
         Matti-GEN shoot-PERF.PRTC-GEN bear-ACC$_{GEN}$ anger-PST.3SG

         Liisa-a.
         Liisa-PART

         'That Matti had shot the/a bear angered Liisa.'

This distribution suggests that the ending *-n* that participles bear in their gerundial function, glossed "GEN" in (12), marks an object Case that is compatible with internal arguments but not with external arguments. Historically, it is probably the old dative ending, which has fallen together phonologically with the genitive, but persists as a morphosyntactically distinct type of genitive which (unlike the structural genitive) cannot function as a subject (Kiparsky In press).

As shown in (13), Finnish gerunds behave more like bare finite CP clauses with *että-* (*that-*) than like DPs, whether nominal DPs (13c) or pronoun-headed finite clauses with *se että-* (*it that-*) (13d).

(13) a. Huomas-i-n / ymmärrä-n   / luule-n   / otaksu-n   tilante-en
         notice-1SG   / understand-1SG / think-1SG / assume-1SG situation-GEN
         ole-va-n   hankala-n.
         be-PRTC-GEN difficult-GEN

         'I noticed / understand / think / assume that the situation is difficult.' [lit. 'the situation's being difficult.']

---

[13] The data and analysis of Finnish gerunds presented in this section is condensed from my treatment of Finnish nonfinite complementation in Kiparsky (In press), to which I refer the reader for the details.

[14] In the glosses, ACC$_{GEN}$ and ACC$_{NOM}$ both refer to morphosyntactic Accusative structural case. The subscripts show three different morphological case realizations of this morphosyntactic Case. They will become important shortly, but for now the reader may ignore them.

b. Se-n huomat-tiin / ymmärre-tään / luul-laan / otaksu-taan
It-GEN notice-PASS-PST / understand-PASS / think-PASS / assume-PASS
ole-va-n hankala-n.
be-PRTC-GEN difficult-GEN

'It is noticed / understood / thought / assumed to be difficult.'

c. Huomas-i-n / ymmärrä-n / *luule-n / *otaksu-n häne-t /
notice-PST-1SG / understand-1SG / think-1SG / assume-1SG him-ACC_{ACC} /
se-n seika-n.
that-ACC_{GEN} thing-ACC_{GEN}

'I noticed / understand / think / assume him / this point (fact).'

d. Huomas-i-n / ymmärrä-n / *luule-n / *otaksu-n se-n, että
notice-PST-1SG / understand-1SG / think-1SG / assume-1SG it-ACC_{GEN} that
tilanne on hankala.
situation.NOM is difficult

'I noticed / understand / think / assume that the situation is difficult.'

The distinction between verbs that allow DP objects (*huomat-* 'notice' and *ymmärtä-* in (13)) and verbs that do not allow DP objects (*luule-* 'think' and *otaksu-* 'assume' in (13)) is correlated with factivity, but the correlation is not exact and my argument does not depend on it.

Since gerunds are not DPs but case-marked IPs, their genitive subjects behave like structural subjects and not like genitive specifiers of DPs. This is shown by five arguments.

The first argument that the genitive specifier of gerunds is a grammatical subject is that it gets assigned exactly the same Th-roles as the subjects of the corresponding finite clause, not the diverse range of interpretations that "possessors" of derived nominals receive (see above under Table 1). So *Matin* in (12a) picks out the agent of the shooting event, whereas the specifier *Matin* of the derived nominal (14) could be, among other things, the organizer or theme of the rescue.

(14) Muista-n Mati-n pelastukse-n.
remember.PRES-1SG Matti-GEN rescue-NOM-ACC

'I remember Matti's rescue.'

The second argument comes from extraction. The subjects of gerunds can be extracted as readily as objects:

(15) a. Kene-n väit-i-t ampu-nee-n hän-tä?
who-GEN claim-PST-2SG shoot-PFP-GEN he-PART

'who did you claim shot at him?'

b. Ke-tä väit-i-t häne-n ampu-nee-n?
who-PART claim-PST-2SG he-GEN shoot-PFP-GEN

'who did you claim he shot at?'

But possessors cannot be extracted (16a), and neither can genitive specifiers of tenseless nonfinite complements such as the third infinitive (16b) and the second infinitive (16c) (the Left Branch Condition, Ross 1967: 127).

(16) a. *Kene-n$_i$ väit-i-t ammu-tu-n t_i karhu-n / että
who-GEN claim-PST-2SG shoot-PERF.PRTC-GEN bear-GEN / that
ammu-ttin t_i karhu?
shoot-PASS.PST bear.ACC$_{NOM}$
'Whose bear did you claim (that) was shot?'

b. *Kene-n$_i$ väit-i-t e_i ampu-ma-n karhu-n paina-nee-n
who-GEN claim-PST-2SG shoot-3INF-GEN bear-GEN weigh-PERF.PRTC-GEN
500 kilo-a?
500 kg-PART
'The bear shot by whom did you claim weighed 500 kg?'

c. *Kene-n$_i$ itk-i-t e_i ampu-e-ssa karhu-n?
who-GEN claim–PST-2SG shoot-2INF-INESS bear-ACC$_{GEN}$
'Who did you weep while he shot the/a bear?'

A third diagnostic which shows that gerunds have structural subjects and not possessors is that they do not undergo possessor agreement. Nouns and infinitives agree with their genitive specifiers, as exemplified for nouns in (17a), for the second infinitive in (17b), and for the third infinitive in (17c).

(17) a. (Minu-n$_i$) karhu-ni$_i$ paino-i 500 kilo-a
(My-GEN) bear.NOM-1SG weigh-PST-3SG 500.ACC kg-PART
'My bear weighed 500 kilograms.'

b. Matti itk-i (minu-n$_i$) ampu-e-ssa-ni$_i$ karhu-n
Matti.NOM weep-PST.3SG (my-GEN) shoot-2INF-1SG bear-ACC$_{GEN}$
'Matti wept as I shot the/a bear.'

c. (minu-n$_i$) ampu-ma-ni$_i$ karhu
(my-GEN) shoot-3INF-1SG bear.NOM
'the/a bear I shot.'

But gerunds do not possessor-agree with their subjects, as we can see in (18a,b) and (with a raised subject) in (18c).

(18) a. Matti ties-i minu-n$_i$ ampu-nee-n
Matti.NOM know-PST.3SG me-GEN shoot-PRF.PRT-GEN
(*ampu-nee-ni$_i$) karhu-n
(shoot-PRF.PRT(-GEN)-1SG) bear-ACC$_{GEN}$
'Matti knows that I've shot the/a bear.'

b. Selvis-i hāne-n$_i$ ampu-nee-n
become clear-PST-3SG he-GEN (shoot-PRF.PRT(-GEN))
(*ampu-nee-nsa$_i$) karhu-n
(shoot-PERF.PRTC(-GEN)-3P) bear-ACC$_{GEN}$
'it became clear that he had shot the/a bear.'

c. Näytä-t$_i$ ampu-nee-n (*ampu-nee-si$_i$) karhu-n
seem-2SG shoot-PRF.PRT-GEN (shoot-PERF.PRTC-(GEN)-2SG) bear-ACC$_{GEN}$
'you seem to have shot the/a bear.'

Of course the subjects of gerunds cannot subject-predicate agree with the gerunds like nominative subjects of finite clauses agree with the finite verb, for genitive subjects never subject-predicate agree in Finnish.

The fourth argument that gerunds have structural subjects comes from the distribution of accusative Case morphology. Descriptively, Finnish morphosyntactic Case is realized as morphological case as follows.[15]

(19) a. The subject of a participial clause is always Genitive.

b. The object of a participial clause can be morphosyntactic Accusative or Partitive. Partitive is assigned to objects under the same conditions as in finite clauses:

   i. Objects under overt or implicit negation are Partitive.
   ii. Objects of certain predicates (such as *love* and *touch*) are Partitive.[16]
   iii. Otherwise objects are Accusative.

Morphosyntactic Partitive is always realized as morphological partitive. And now comes the essential and trickiest part. Morphosyntactic Accusative is realized by three morphological cases:

(20) a. as morphological accusative on personal pronouns,

b. otherwise as morphological genitive if the object is plural, or if the clause has a subject with structural case (this last condition is called JAHNSSON'S RULE),

c. otherwise as morphological nominative.

Clause types that lack subjects with structural case for purposes of Jahnsson's Rule include imperatives, bare infinitives ("to see Naples and to die"), passives (which in Finnish do not involve "promotion" of the object), and clauses with "quirky case" subjects.

Since the argument to be presented below uses Jahnsson's Rule as a diagnostic for the presence or absence of a structural subject, I will gloss the examples in such a way that the reader can see whether Jahnsson's Rule has taken effect in them. This means glossing not only morphosyntactic Accusative Case, but whether morphosyntactic Accusative

---

[15] For details see Kiparsky 2001; a sophisticated OT treatment of the variation is developed by Anttila & Kim (2016).

[16] The class of partitive-assigning predicates is often called "telic" (e.g. Kratzer 2002). This is not quite correct; for an attempt at a more accurate formulation see Kiparsky 2005a.

Case is realized as morphological accusative case or nominative case. So I will mark morphosyntactic Case by the main gloss and morphological case with a subscript on it. For example, in (21) both objects bear morphosyntactic Accusative Case, realized in (21a) as morphological genitive case and in (21b) as morphological nominative case.

(21) a. Matti   ampu-i   karhu-n
       Matti.NOM shoot-PST(3SG) bear-ACC$_{GEN}$
       'Matti shot the/a bear.'

   b. ammu   karhu!
      shoot-IMPER bear-ACC$_{NOM}$
      'shoot the bear!'

Through the rest of the text in this section I use capitalization to distinguish morphosyntactic Case (such as Accusative) from morphological case (nominative, accusative, etc.).

At last we are ready for the argument. Nonfinite complement clauses are translucent to the triggering of Accusative and Partitive Case and to the realization of Accusative case as genitive or nominative, in the sense that (19) and (20) can be conditioned either within the gerund clause or in the larger domain of the higher clause with its gerund complement. So in (22a) the object of the lower clause, which contains no negation, can have either Accusative Case (realized as morphological genitive case by (20a)), or Partitive Case from the negated main clause by (19b.ii). In (22b) the morphosyntactic Accusative Case on the object of the gerund is realized either as morphological genitive case because the main clause has a subject, or as morphological nominative case, because the participle, being passive, is subjectless (Jahnsson's Rule, (20b)).[17] In (22c) the morphosyntactic Accusative Case on the object can only be realized as morphological nominative case because both the matrix verb and the participle are subjectless.

(22) a. En   tien-nyt   heidä-n   ampu-nee-n   /
       Not-1SG know-PERF.PTC they-GEN shoot-PERF.PRTC-GEN /
       ampu-va-n   karhu-n   / karhu-a
       shoot-PRS.PRTC-GEN bear-ACC$_{GEN}$ / bear-PART
       'I didn't know that they had shot / were (would be) shooting the/a bear.'

   b. Ties-i-n   metsä-ssä   ammu-tu-n   karhu-n   / karhu
      know-PST-1SG forest-ILLAT shoot-PASS.PRTC-ACC$_{GEN}$ bear-ACC$_{GEN}$ / bear.ACC$_{NOM}$
      'I knew a bear to have been shot in the forest.'

   c. Eilen   ilmen-i   ammu-tu-n   *karhu-n   / karhu
      Yesterday turn.out-PST.3SG shoot-PASS.PRTC-GEN bear-ACC$_{GEN}$ / bear.ACC$_{NOM}$
      'It turned out yesterday that a bear was shot.'

---

[17] The variation between case governed locally within the subordinate clause and in the larger domain that includes the main clause is sensitive to as yet poorly understood semantic, stylistic and discourse factors. The distribution of the Partitive in particular is affected by factivity and the scope of negation ("Lausetyyppien käsittely transformaatioteoriassa [The treatment of sentence Types in Transformational grammar]" 1970: 31, Hakulinen & Karlsson 1979: 365). For example, in (22a), the Partitive registers surprise or skepticism, and in (22b) the Accusative (realized as nominative) is likely to be interpreted factively.

15 Nominal verbs and transitive nouns: Vindicating lexicalism

The crucial case is (23), where the morphosyntactic Accusative Case of the object may be realized as morphological genitive case. Since the matrix verb is subjectless, the object's realization as morphological genitive case must be licensed by the subject of the gerund, *Matin*. Therefore the subject has structural Case.

(23) Ilmen-i   Mati-n   ampu-nee-n   karhu-n   / karhu.
     turn.out-PST.3SG Matti-GEN shoot-PERF.PRTC-GEN bear-ACC$_{GEN}$ / bear.ACC$_{NOM}$
     'It turned out that Matti shot the/a bear.'

This completes the fourth argument that the genitive subject of gerunds is a structural subject.

In contrast, the fact that "quirky" genitive subjects induce the nominative form of the object tells us, by Jahnsson's Rule, that they are non-structural:

(24) a. Hänen pitää   osta-a   auto.
        He-GEN must-3SG buy-1INF car.ACC$_{NOM}$
        'He has to buy the/a car.'
     b. Hänen on   helppo nosta-a tämä   säkki.
        He-GEN be-3SG easy   lift-1INF this.ACC$_{NOM}$ sack.ACC$_{NOM}$
        'It is easy for him to lift this sack.'

This is as expected, since they are not assigned structurally but idiosyncratically by particular predicates.

A fifth argument that gerunds have structural subjects is that they can have a generic null subject *pro$_{arb}$*. In Finnish *pro$_{arb}$* can be a subject (Hakulinen & Karttunen 1973) but it cannot be a possessor: contrast (25a) and (25b). So, the fact that gerunds can have a generic *pro$_{arb}$* subject, as seen in (25c), is another datum in support of the claim that gerunds have structural subjects and not possessors. Moreover, gerunds can be subjectless under the same conditions as subjects of finite clauses. For example, gerunds can have the impersonal passive form, see (25d).

(25) a. Siellä ∅ voi   tanssi-a.
        there *pro* can-3SG dance-1INF
        'One can dance there.'
     b. *On   mukava katsel-la   ∅ valokuv-i-a.
        be-3SG nice   look.at-1INF *pro* photo-PL.PART
        *'It's nice to to look at one's photos.' (OK without ∅: 'It's nice to look at photos.'
     c. Siellä väite-t-ään   ∅ voi-va-n   tanssi-a.
        there claim-PST.PASS *pro* can-PRES.PRTC-GEN dance-1INF
        'It is claimed that one can dance there.'
     d. Siellä väite-tt-iin   voi-ta-va-n   tanssi-a.
        there claim-PST.PASS can-PASS-PRES.PRTC-GEN dance-1INF
        'It was claimed that there is dancing there.'

I conclude that Finnish gerunds are IPs like English gerunds, albeit with a different syntactic distribution due to their oblique Case specification.

2.3 Desultory remarks on Acc-*ing*

The English "Acc-*ing*" construction differs in many ways from the "Poss-*ing*" gerund considered here so far. I have no serious analysis of it to offer. Its behavior resembles Acc-Inf ("ECM") constructions in some ways. First, unlike gerunds with genitive subjects, it is degraded by intervening adverbs, extraposition, and fronting, under roughly the same conditions as nominal objects ("Quantification, Events, and Gerunds"; Pires 2006):

(26) a. We anticipated (*?eagerly) him leaving Paris.
  b. (We anticipated his resignation, but) *?him/his leaving Paris we did not anticipate.

This is the same pattern as:

(27) a. We believe (*?strongly) him to have told the truth.
  b. (We believed him to have been mistreated, but) *?him to be telling the truth we did not believe.

Acc-Inf gerunds allow extraction, like Acc-Inf complements and unlike Poss-*ing* gerunds:

(28) a. Which city do you remember him/*his describing? (Portner 1995: 637, citing L. Horn)
  b. Who do you resent Bill/*Bill's hitting? (Williams 1975: 263)
  c. Who/*whose do you resent hitting Bill? (cf. *Who do you resent (it) that hit Bill?)
  d. Who do you believe to be telling the truth?
  e. What do you believe him to be saying?

Another frequently noted difference between the constructions is that the genitive subject of gerunds is preferentially human, and cannot be expletive *there* at all, whereas the accusative is unrestricted in this respect, again like Acc-Inf subjects.

(29) a. There (*there's) being no objection, the proposal is approved.
  b. ? I imagined the water's being 30 feet deep.

Accusative subjects of gerunds do not seem to be getting their case from the main verb, since they can appear in gerunds that function as subjects. Possibly the accusative case assigner is a null preposition or complementizer, an analog of the overt *for* of *for-to* infinitives.

3 Agent nominals, transitive and intransitive

Like the FNT, my alternative theory of nominalizations is in principle applicable to every type of nominalization, including agent nominalizations and result nominalizations. The mixed category that most gravely challenges analyses of agent nominals is transitive agent nouns, which function as nominals except for assigning structural case to their objects and allowing some adverbial modifiers. I will make a case that, just as gerunds are categorially verbal at all levels of the syntax and their noun-like behavior is entirely due to a nominal Case feature borne by their Infl head, such transitive agent nominalizations are categorially nominal at all levels of the syntax and their verb-like behavior is entirely due to a verbal feature borne by their nominalizing head, namely Aspect. Gerunds and transitive nominalizations thus prove to be duals in a sense – respectively verbs with Case and nouns with Aspect.

I show that this idea predicts the distinction between transitive and intransitive agent nouns, whereas the functional properties of nominalizations neither correlate with each other as the FNT predicts, nor match the height of their nominalizing heads in syntax or word structure. In Vedic Sanskrit (sections 3.1-3.3) and in Finnish (2.2), high agent nominalizations *do not* assign structural case if they lack Tense/Aspect features, and even low agent nominalizations *do* assign structural case if they have Tense/Aspect features.

3.1 Agent nominals and subject nominals

In their illuminating study based on the FNT approach, Baker & Vinokurova (2009) propose an analysis and typology of agent nominalizations similar to the one I have called into question for event nominalizations. They begin by noting an asymmetry between agent and event nominals. "High" event nominals like (1a) have no agent noun counterpart such as (30).

B&V claim that this is a systematic gap, and propose to explain it on the basis of two key assumptions. First, agentive nominalizing morphology is added by a nominal head immediately above VP.[18] Secondly, in some languages, such as English, structural case is assigned to objects by an active Voice/v head, whereas in other languages, structural case is assigned configurationally (dependent case).[19] Together, these assumptions rule out transitive agent-denoting nominalizations, such as (30) *the reader the book*. Instead, they require the structure (31). Here the agent nominalizer pre-empts the case-assigning active Voice morpheme in v that assigns structural case to objects in English, but (by hypothesis) has no case-assigning force itself.

---

[18] It is fair to ask why it is added there and not in a higher position. B&V hint that this is "a position apparently forced on it by the natural (iconic) semantic composition of the clause" (Baker & Vinokurova 2009: 521), but this remains to be justified.

[19] B&V equate Voice with v, following Kratzer (2004), but contra Alexiadou (2001); Alexiadou, Soare & Iordăchioaia (2010); Harley (2012), among others.

(30) * the reader of the book

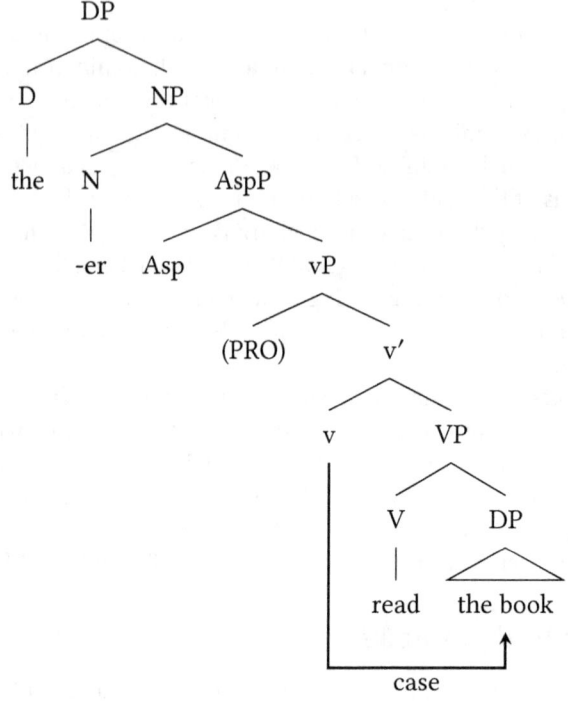

(31)

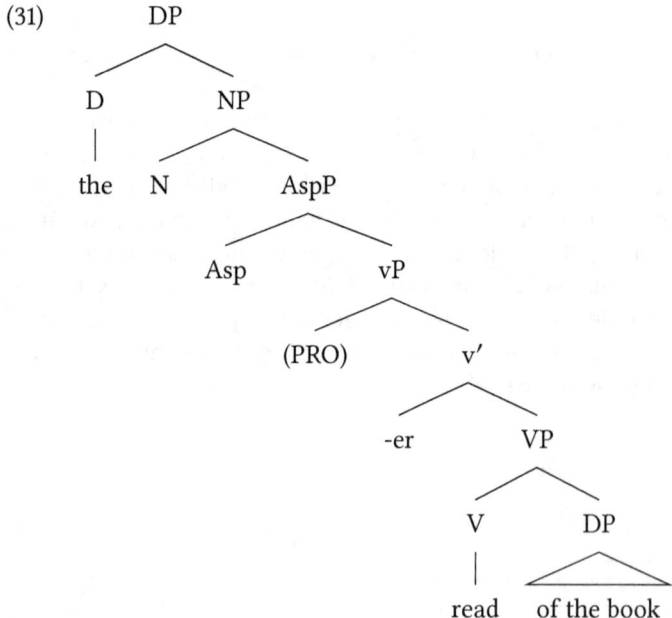

15 Nominal verbs and transitive nouns: Vindicating lexicalism

The analysis further predicts that, since voice markers cannot attach to unaccusatives,[20] such agent nouns cannot attach to unaccusative verbs.

B&V then draw a distinction between agentive and non-agentive "agent" nominalizers – let's call the latter SUBJECT NOMINALIZERS. Subject nominalizers do assign structural case, and can be attached to unaccusative verbs. B&V (p. 547) analyze them as "nominal equivalents of an ASPECT head", in the sense in which agentive nominalizers like -*er* are nominal equivalents of a VOICE head. Their example is Gĩkũyũ -*i*, another example is Northern Paiute -*dɨ* (Toosarvandani 2014). B&V propose the structure (32):

(32) Subject nominalizers (high)

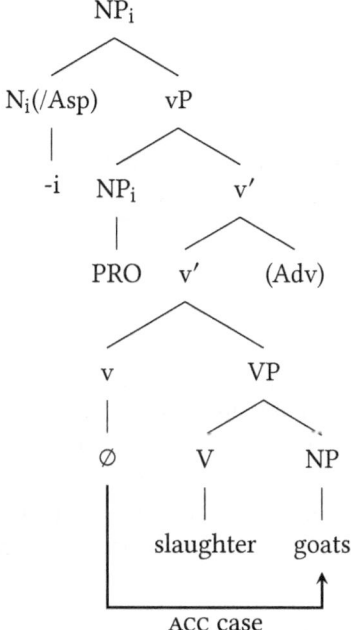

As an immediate challenge to the FNT in the domain of agent nominalizations, B&V note that otherwise low agent nominalizations unexpectedly assign structural case in some languages. For B&V, these languages must be special in that they assign structural case by a dependent case mechanism, whereas languages in which low agent nouns have oblique complements assign structural case by little v. The need to maintain two entirely distinct mechanisms of structural case assignment on the basis of evidence that cannot loom large in the learner's experience would be another disappointing consequence of the FNT.[21] We'll also see that B&V's analysis of agent nominals imposes a functional

---

[20] In fact an incorrect premise: unaccusative verbs passivize in numerous languages, including Finnish and Sanskrit (Kiparsky 2013).

[21] Levin, Preminger & Omer (2015) propose that *all* structural case can be assigned by dependent case, provided that the algorithm is parametrized in certain ways. However, they do not touch on the case variation in objects of agent nominalizations, and the parametrization of structural case assignment that they propose does not account for it, as far as I can tell.

overload on little v that makes the FNT's various criteria for syntactic height mutually irreconcilable.

In summary, B&V's proposal generates the typology of agent nouns shown in Table 2. In the remainder of this section I show that the predicted correlations do not hold for agent nouns of Vedic Sanskrit and Finnish, and propose a much simpler alternative that does justice to the data.

Table 2: Typology of agent nouns predicted by Baker & Vinokurova (2009).

Agent Nominalizers (low, v)	Subject Nominalizers (high, Asp)
always agentive	non-agentives OK
no unaccusatives	unaccusatives OK
structural case only if dependent case	structural case
no adverbs	adverbs OK
no Aspect	compatible with Aspect
no Voice	compatible with Voice

3.2 Vedic agent nouns

Vedic and Pāṇinian Sanskrit has a large number of agent noun suffixes, which fall into two clearly demarcated types. A minimal pair that highlights the contrast are the two agent noun types in accented *-tár-^{N}* and preaccenting *'-tar-^{V}*.[22] Agent nouns in accented *-tár-^{N}* have genitive objects and get only adjective modifiers, never adverbs, e.g. (33a). Agent nouns in preaccenting *'-tar-^{V}* (boldfaced in (33)) regularly assign structural case to their objects and, can get certain aspectual adverb modifiers, such as *punaḥ* 'again' in (33b).[23]

(33) a. tvā́-m hí satyá-m ... vid-má **dātár-am** iṣ-ā́m
you-ACC PRT true-ACC ... know-1PL **giver-ACC** good.thing-PL.GEN
'we know you as the true giver of good things.' (RV. 8.46.2)

b. **iṣ-kar-tā́** víhruta-m púnaḥ
fixer-NOM wrong-ACC again
'the maker right again (of) what has gone wrong.' (RV 8.1.12)

Both suffixes are true nominalizers: they form nouns, not verbs. They have a complete nominal case and number inflection paradigm, take denominal derivational suffixes, such

---

[22] Their Indo-European provenance is guaranteed by Greek and Avestan cognates (Lowe 2014). The following exposition of their contrasting semantics, morphophology, and syntax draws on the generalizations and evidence in Kiparsky 2016, to which the reader is referred for details.

[23] Other agent nouns with verbal properties are attested in early Vedic include *-i-^{V}* RV 9.61.20 *jághnir vṛtrám* 'killer of Vtra', *-(i)ṣṇu-^{V}* RV 1.63.3 *dhṛṣṇúr etā́n* 'bold against them', *-u-^{V}* AV 12.1.48 *nidhanáṃ titikṣuḥ* 'enduring poverty', *-∅-^{V}* RV 1.1.4 *yáṃ yajñám ... paribhū́r ási* 'the sacrifice that you embrace'.

as derived feminines, and can be compounded.[24] They allow adjectival modification (in addition to adverbial modification, in the case of *'-tar-^{V}*). These nominal properties are unsurprising for the noun-like *-tár-^{N}* formations; that they hold also for the more verb-like *'-tar-^{V}* is documented in (34).

(34) a. āśúṃ   jétāram
       āśú-m   jé-tār-am
       quick-ACC   win-er-ACC
       'the quick (Acc.) winner (Acc.)'   (RV 8.99.7)

    b. tásṭeva   pṣṭyāmayí
       tákṣ-tar   iva   pṛṣṭya-āmay-ín
       carve-er.NOM like   back-ache-ed.NOM
       'like a notalgic (Nom.) carpenter (Nom.)'   (RV 1.105.18)

Semantically both *-tár-^{N}* and *'-tar-^{V}* are *agent* nominalizers, not *subject* nominalizers: they are never added to non-agentive verbs or unaccusatives of any kind, and the meaning of the nominalization is canonically agentive.[25] So by these criteria both nominalizations are "low" in the sense of B&V, not Gikũyũ-type "high" nominalizations.

The agent nominalizers *'-tar-^{V}* and *-tár-^{N}* form a *privative* semantic opposition, missed in the modern philological literature but correctly delineated already by Pāṇini, whose description turns out to tally perfectly with the Vedic data. The unmarked member of the opposition is *-tár-^{N}*, which simply denotes agency (like English *-er*). The marked member *'-tar-^{V}* has two additional meaning components:

(35) a. *'-tar ^{V}* denotes agency in ONGOING TIME.
     b. *'-tar-^{V}* denotes HABITUAL, PROFESSIONAL, or EXPERT agency.

The criteria of the FNT make contradictory predictions. Since both nominalizations are agentive, both should be structurally low "little v" heads. On the other hand, *'-tar-^{V}* nominalizations, which have the verbal properties of assigning structural case and allowing adverbial modification, should be structurally high, while *-tár-^{N}* nominalizations, which have strictly nominal properties, should be structurally low. Neither of these is the case. In fact, as far as the case and adverb properties are concerned, the structure is just the opposite of what is predicted: verbal *'-tar-^{V}* is low and nominal *-tár-^{N}* is high. This is shown by four arguments (details in Kiparsky 2016).

The first argument that verbal *'-tar-^{V}* is low and nominal *-tár-^{N}* is high is their morphological position in the word. *'-tar-^{V}* always follows the bare verbal root directly, without

---

[24] E.g. *kṣirá-hotar-* 'milk-offerer' (ŚBr.), and *neṣṭā-potā́rau* 'leader and purifier' (TS.), co-compounds (Kiparsky 2010b) denoting pairs of priests.

[25] Thus, the following roots do *not* take either *-tár-^{N}* and *'-tar-^{V}* or any other agent suffixes for that matter: *as* 'be', *ā́s* 'sit', *śī* 'lie', *sru* 'flow', *plu* 'float', *tras* 'tremble', *vyath* 'sway', *bhraṃś* 'fall', *svap* 'sleep', *kṣudh* 'be hungry', *tṛṣ* 'be thirsty', *svid* 'sweat', *ṛdh* 'flourish', *ru(d)h* 'grow', *pyā* 'swell', *riṣ* 'sustain damage', *mṛ* 'die', *śam* 'become calm', *mad* 'get drunk', *mud* 'rejoice', *hṛṣ* 'get excited', *dhṛṣ* 'dare', *bhī* 'fear', *hīḍ* 'be angry', *krudh* 'become angry', *gṛdh* 'be greedy', *ruc* 'shine', *śubh* 'shine, be beautiful', *bhā* 'shine' *bhās* 'gleam', *dyut* 'to strike' (of lightning), *pat* 'to fall'.

any other intervening suffix; it cannot be added to compound or prefixed bases. -tár-^{N}, on the contrary, can be separated from the root by verb-to-verb suffixes commonly analyzed as Voice/v heads (causative, denominative, intensive, desiderative). It is affixed to the whole verb base, including the extended root plus any prefix that combines with it:

(36)   a.   RV *cod-ay-i-tr-í-* 'impeller (fem.)' (caus. *cod-áy-a-ti* 'impels')
         b.   TS *pra-dāp-ay-i-tár-* 'bestower' (caus. *prá-dāp-ay-a-ti* 'bestows'),
         c.   *ni-dhā-tár-* 'one who sets down' (*ní-dadhā-ti* 'sets down')

The morphological data point to the respective constituent structures in (37):

(37)   a.   *Low:* [Prefix [Root '-tar-^{V}]]
         b.   *High:* [[Prefix [Root (Caus)...]] -tár-^{N}]

The second argument that verbal '-tar-^{V} is low and nominal -tár-^{N} is high comes from word accentuation. The morphological conditioning of accent placement provides a convenient probe into the constituent structure of words. In Vedic and Pāṇinian Sanskrit, the accentuation of words is computed cyclically from the accentual properties of the morphemes from which they are composed. Morphemes may be accented or unaccented, and at the word level, all accents but the first in a word are erased (Kiparsky 2010a). Both of our agent suffixes (like the majority of derivational suffixes) belong to the accentually DOMINANT type: they erase the accent off the bases to which they are added. The crucial fact for present purposes is that dominant affixes exercise this erasing effect exactly on the stems to which they are added, no more and no less. Thanks to this property we can use accentuation to diagnose constituent structure in morphologically complex words.

The empirical generalization is that prefixes always prevail over low (bare-root) suffixes, including '-tar-^{V}, whereas high suffixes always prevail over prefixes, dictating the place of the word accent. The reason is that prefixes are added after the low suffix '-tar-^{V}:

(38)   Prefixation to nouns with the the low suffix '-tar-^{V}:
         bhar-   Root
         bhár-tar^V add dominant preaccenting '-tar-^{V}
         prá-[bhár-tar]   add accented prefix
         prábhartar-   erase all accents but the first

On the other hand, -tár-^{N} is accentually dominant, causing all accents on its base to be deleted, and attracting accent to itself. This shows that it is added to the entire stem including the prefix, causing the resulting word to be accented on the suffix.

(39)   Suffixation of high -tár-^{N} to prefixed verbs:
         bhar-   Root
         ápa-bhar   add accented prefix
         [apa-bhar]-tár^N add dominant accented -tár-^{N}
         apabhartár-

The third argument that verbal '-tar-^{V} is low and nominal -tár-^{N} is high comes from tmesis, the splitting of prefixes from stems. Prefixes can be separated from verbs and from nominals formed with low suffixes like verbal '-tar-^{V}.

15 Nominal verbs and transitive nouns: Vindicating lexicalism

(40) a. *sáttā ní yónā* (= *nísattā yónā*) 'a sitter down in the womb' (RV 9.86.6)

b. *úpa sū́re ná dhā́tā* (= *sū́re nópadhātā*) 'like the Placer of the Sun' (RV 9.97.38).

Prefixes are never separated from nominals formed with high suffixes such as nominal -*tár*-^{N}.

The explanation comes from the same constituent structure that accounts for the accentual difference: low suffixes such as the agent suffix '-*tar*-^{V} are added directly to the root to form a noun, which can then be composed with a prefix (see (41a)), while high suffixes such as the agent suffix -*tár*-^{N} are added to the entire verb, which may already bear a prefix and/or another suffix (41b,c).

(41)

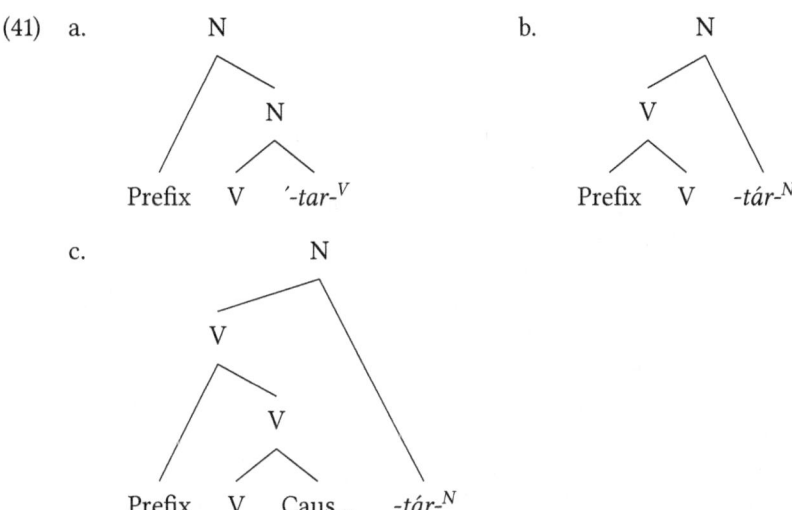

It will be seen the prefix is an immediate constituent of the word in (41a), but not in (41b) or in (41c). The natural generalization is that a prefix can only be split if it is an immediate constituent of the word.

The fourth argument that verbal '-*tar*-^{V} is low and nominal -*tár*-^{N} is high comes from selectional properties of prefixes. Prefixes that only combine with verb roots require high -*tár*-^{N}, because the right-branching constituent structure (41a) would require them to combine with nouns.[26] Conversely, prefixes and other elements that cannot be combined with roots, only with nouns, require the right-branching constituent structure (41a), which is available either with -*tár*-^{N} or with '-*tar*-^{V}.[27]

---

[26] Many examples are given in Kiparsky 2016. One will have to suffice here. The interjection *hiṁ* 'the sound hmm' cannot be compounded with nouns. It can only combine with the root *kr̥* 'do', 'make'. The agent noun from *hiṁ-kr̥*- 'to make the sound hmm' must therefore have the high suffix -*tár*-^{N}, viz. *hiṁkartár*-.

[27] Again we must make do with a couple of examples. There is no compound verb such as **para-apara-i-* 'to go far and near' from which *párāpara-etar*- 'one who goes far and near' might be derived. In fact *párāpara*- 'far and near' is never compounded with verbs. Instead, the agent noun is a nominal compound formed from *para-apara*- 'far and near' plus *e-tár*- 'goer' (← *i-tár*-^{N}). Another illustration of this generalization is that the negation *a*- combines only with nouns. From *hótar* 'priest' (← *hu-'tar*-^{V}) we get *á-hotar*- 'a non-priest'.

The above arguments establish the morphological constituency displayed in (37) and (41). But Distributed Morphology is a resourceful theory that makes available various movement operations that cause mismatches between morphology and syntax. So could the morphologically low nominalizing morphemes be spelled out high where B&V predict they should be, and then undergo Lowering to their actual position? And conversely, could the high nominalizing morphemes be spelled out low as predicted, and then undergo Raising to their actual position? The answer is negative on both counts.

The way morphologically low suffixes such as the agent suffix *'-tar-*^{V} could be syntactically high for purposes of the FNT is by DM's LOWERING operation, which applies before Vocabulary insertion to adjoin a head to the head of its complement (Embick & Noyer 2001):

(42) X_0 lowers to Y_0:
 $[_{XP} X_0 ...[_{YP} ...Y_0 ...]] \rightarrow [_{XP} ...[_{YP} ...[Y_0\ Y_0+X_0]...]]$

In English, Lowering of T is assumed to adjoin T to v (Embick & Marantz 2008). But if *'-tar-*^{V} is generated in the N head of (32) and is lowered from there into the v, it would, on B&V's assumptions, have the properties of a subject nominalizer, forming nouns from unaccusative and non-agentive verbs. But it does *not* have any properties of a subject nominalizer – it is a true agent nominalizer, as we showed above.

The other thing required to maintain the FNT is to generate *-tár-*^{N} low in v (as in (31)) and then raise it to its actual high position. This is not going to work in the DM model either, for morphological head-raising can only adjoin a head to the next head above it (Harizanov & Gribanova 2016), and in this case it would have to skip intervening heads, including the v head that may be occupied by causative and other V→V suffixes, which must not raise. Moreover, in more recent DM (Embick 2010), phonology is cyclically interleaved with morphology, and this would cause problems with the abovementioned accent erasure and tmesis phenomena.

It should also be noted that *'-tar-*^{V} is overwhelmingly preferred when its special meaning and morphological restrictions allow its use, and *-tár-*^{N} is used elsewhere. Moreover, other agent suffixes supersede each of them with particular roots and/or in particula special meanings. Since competition in DM obtains only between morphemes that have the same meaning and are realized in the same slot (such as English plural *-s* and *-en*), all these competing suffixes would have to be generated in the same syntactic position.

The conclusion from the Vedic data is that the nominalizations' verbal vs. nominal properties do not correlate with structural height of their heads in the word or in the syntax. In fact, the majority of morphologically high nominalizers in Vedic have nominal properties, and the majority of morphologically low nominalizers have verbal properties – the opposite of what the FNT predicts.

3.3 Aspect in Vedic agent nouns

A preliminary survey of nominalizations suggests that the Aspect feature of a nominalizer is the best predictor of verbal properties. Consider the following alternative to the FNT.

(43) The Aspect hypothesis
Nominalizations assign structural case if and only if they have Aspect, either as an inherent feature of the nominalization, or in virtue of combining with overt Aspect morphology.

By aspect features I mean outer aspect features such as imperfective and habitual, not inner aspect (Aktionsart), such as telicity. Sanskrit agent nouns in *'-tar-^{V}* are inherently present/imperfective and habitual. Those in *-tár-^{N}*, English agent nouns made with *-er*, and Finnish agent nouns made with *-ja* have no inherent aspect: a *driver* can be a habitual or professional driver, or just someone who happens to be at the wheel on a particular occasion.[28]

The Aspect hypothesis is not implausible a priori because Aspect features are cross-linguistically known to affect case assignment – think of split ergativity based on imperfect vs. perfect aspect, and accusative vs. partitive objects in Finnish depending on gradability (Kiparsky 2005a). It looks promising for Vedic Sanskrit in particular because nominalizing endings with verbal properties, such as *'-tar-^{V}*, are added to the bare root, in the same morphological position as the Aorist and Perfect Tense/Aspect suffixes. It is also consistent with the fact that Northern Paiute deverbal nominalizations, which assign structural accusative case, can have overt aspectual morphology below them (Toosarvandani 2014: 793, fn. 6).

The Aspect hypothesis is compatible with a lexicalist treatment of morphology. A Distributed Morphology analysis of Vedic agent nouns is problematic because of the conflicting criteria for structural height. In addition, they show a type of competition between morphemes that DM rejects. The semantically nondescript *tár-^{N}*, structurally low by B&V's criteria but high in word structure, is the default (elsewhere) case. The semantically restricted *'-tar-^{V}* suffix, structurally high by B&V's syntactic criteria but low in the word morphology, is strongly preferred whenever it is applicable, namely to denote habitual agency in ongoing time with morphologically simple verbs. Elsewhere the default is *-tár-^{N}*, structurally low by B&V's syntactic criteria but high in the word morphology – for past or future agency, or occasional agency, *or* when the verb is morphologically complex (causative, intensive, desiderative, denominative, or prefixed). Suppose then that a structurally low agent is added in a syntactic derivation. The derivation must crash if and only if a structurally high agent can be successfully added in a competing derivation. But DM does not allow rules that spell out syntactico/semantic features in different positions to compete with each other. Moreover, if we assume bottom-up morphological spellout of the syntax (by cycles or phases), the syntactically low agent would have to "know" about the upstairs high agent in order to be blocked by it. On the other hand, in a *morphological* theory of word-formation, morphologically low items naturally block morphologically high items. Besides, blocking of affixes with general meanings by affixes with special meanings regardless of the locus of affixation is straighforward in lexicalist approaches such as those of Wunderlich (1996b; 2001) and Kiparsky (2005b).

---

[28] Gerunds are arguably inherently imperfective (Alexiadou 2001; Alexiadou, Soare & Iordăchioaia 2010).

3.4 The Finnish subject nominalizer *-ja*

B&V's formulation of the FNT entails that agent nominalizations don't assign case and subject nominalizations do (§2). We have seen that Vedic falsifies the first of these claims. Finnish (among many other languages) falsifies the second. The fully productive Finnish suffix *-ja* is not an agent nominalizer, but a subject nominalizer, which is to say a high nominalizer in B&V's typology. It can go on non-agentive/unaccusative verbs, and freely attaches to causatives, often assumed to be under v, as well as denominatives, reflexives, inchoatives, and inner aspect morphemes such as frequentatives and semelfactives, thus testing positively for high position by several diagnostics.

(44) a. *kuolija* 'one who dies', 'dier', *eläjä* 'one who lives', 'liver', *toipuja* 'one who gets well', 'convalescent', *olija* 'one who is', *osaaja* 'one who is able to', *syntyjä* 'one who is born', *hikoilija* 'one who sweats', *putoaja* 'one who falls', *turpoaja* 'one who swells', *pelkääjä* 'one who fears', *luulija* 'one who supposes', *tuntija* 'one who knows, expert', *muistaja* 'one who remembers', *jääjä* 'one who remains', *palelija* 'one who feels cold', *tarvitsija* 'one who needs', *hukkuja* 'one who drowns'

   b. i. Frequentative *-ele-*: *kys-eli-jä* 'inquirer', from *kys-ele-* 'to make inquiries' (cf. *kysy-jä* 'asker', from *kysy-* 'ask'). Similarly *ryypiskelijä* 'tippler', *lähentelijä* 'harasser', *myyskentelijä* 'peddler', *rehentelijä* 'bragger', *riitelijä* 'quarreler'.

   ii. Causative: *laula-tta-ja* 'one who makes sing', from *laula-tta-* 'to make sing', cf. *lauja-ja* 'singer', from *laula-* 'to sing'.

   iii. Inchoative + causative: *selv-en-tä-jä* 'clarifier', ← *selv-en-tä-* 'make clear, clarify' (← *selv-en-* 'become clear' ← *selvä* 'clear').

   iv. Causative + frequentative: *sopi-ja* 'agreer', *sovi-tta-ja* 'fitter, arranger', *sovi-tt-el-ija* 'reconciler, negotiator'

   v. Reflexive: *puolusta-ja* 'defender' *puolusta-utu-ja* '(self-)defender'

   vi. Denominative: *testamentt-aa-ja* 'bequeather' (← *testamentt-at-* 'to bequeath' ← *testamentti* 'testament')

However, nominals in the suffix *-ja* do not assign structural case, whether they have any of these suffixes below them or not. Their object complement (unlike that of passive verbs) can only receive genitive case.

(45) a. palkinto-j-en (*palkinno-t) saa-ja
       prize-PL-GEN (prize-PL.ACC) get-er.(NOM)
       'the/a winner of the prizes'

   b. minu-n (*minu-t) käv-el-ytt-eli-jä-ni
      me-GEN (*me-ACC) walk-FREQ-CAUS-FREQ-er.(NOM)-1SG.POSS
      '(the) one who frequently takes me around for walks'

Nominals in *-ja* do take oblique nominal modifiers, as do all nominalizations, including action nominalizations, and even to some extent ordinary basic nouns.

(46) a. Saksa-sta   voitta-ja-na   palaa-ja   / pal-uu
       Germany-ELAT win-er-ESSIVE return-er.(NOM) / return-ing.(NOM)

   '(the) one who returns / a return from Germany as a winner'

   b. hallitse-va-ssa   asema-ssa   oli-ja   / ol-o
      govern-in-INESS position-INESS be-er.(NOM) / be-ing.(NOM)

   '(the) one who is in a governing position'

   c. palatsi Cannesi-ssa
      palace Cannes-INESS

   'the/a palace in Cannes'

They generally do not take adverbs, except for certain perfectivizing adverbs (47d,e):

(47) a. * nopea-sti juoksi-ja
        quick-ly run-er.(NOM)

   '(the) one who runs/ran/will run quickly'

   b. * kilpailu-n   taas voitta-ja
        competition-GEN again win-er.(NOM)

   '(the) one who wins/won/will win the/a competition again'

   c. * aina   matkusta-ja
        always travel-er.(NOM)

   '(the) one who always travels'

   d. kilpailu-sta   pois jää-jä
      competition-ELAT away remain-er.(NOM)

   'one who does not join the competition', 'eliminee'

   e. viime-ksi   tuli-ja
      lat-TRANSL come-er.(NOM)

   'the last to arrive'

In (48) (an example adapted from the internet) the adverb *jälleen* 'again' appears with an agent noun.

(48) Cannesi-ssa   jälleen palkinno-tta jää-jä
     Cannes-INESS again   prize-ABESS remain-er.(NOM)

   'one who ended up prizeless again in Cannes' (lit. 'a remainer prizeless again...')

Possibly it modifies not the nominalization but the abessive modifier *palkinno-tta* 'prizeless'.

Since Finnish *-ja* must be high in order to get a non-agentive interpretation and to scope over every kind of verb-to-verb suffix, it should assign structural case, which it doesn't. So it does not fit into B&V's syntactic typology, and constitutes a problem for the FNT generalization. In this case, morphological raising or lowering, even if they were available and motivated, would not help to resolve the contradiction.

The lexicalist alternative, however, holds up. Like English *-er*, nouns in *-ja* are morphologically incompatible with overt Aspect or Voice morphology, and they refer indifferently to prospective, present, or past events, hence have no inherent Aspect features.

(49) *maksaja* 'payer' (one who has paid, is paying, or will pay), similarly *ostaja* 'buyer', *vuokraaja* 'renter', *maahanmuuttaja* 'immigrant', *lähtijä* 'goer', *siittäjä* 'inseminator'

Since *-ja* has no Aspect features and no verbal properties, the fact that it doesn't assign structural case is consistent with the Aspect hypothesis but inconsistent with the FNT. I conclude that Finnish *-ja* supports the lexicalist analysis of nominalizations.

3.5 The Sakha agent nominalizer -AAccY

Baker & Vinokurova (2009: 536) note that the correlation predicted by the FNT breaks down for Sakha agent nominalizations, which have structural accusative objects but otherwise conform to the low type, in that they have no Aspect morphology or adverbs. Their solution is that Sakha accusative case is not assigned by Voice/v but by a different mechanism, DEPENDENT CASE assigment.

(50) Dependent case assignment (Marantz 1991; Baker 2015)

  a. If there are two distinct NPs in the same spellout domain such that NP_1 c-commands NP_2, then value the case feature of NP_2 as accusative unless NP_1 has already been marked for case.

  b. If there are two distinct NPs in the same spellout domain such that NP_1 c-commands NP_2, then value the case feature of NP_1 as ergative unless NP_2 has already been marked for case.

Their main argument that Sakha accusative is dependent case is that objects of passives receive accusative case. This argument depends on the fragile assumption that the implicit agent of Sakha passives is a syntactically visible but phonologically null NP, which receives nominative case and serves as the NP_1 that triggers the assignment of accusative case to the object of the passive by (50a).

I am skeptical of this solution for both theoretical and empirical reasons. It would be strange for UG to offer two entirely different methods of structural case assignment, since their empirical differences are rather obscure, and offer learners of most languages little core data to choose between them. Secondly, the analysis of impersonal passives as having an invisible nominative agent subject is excluded on general grounds by any kind of demotion analysis of passive, including the typologically grounded theory proposed in Kiparsky 2013. Finnish provides empirical evidence against the idea that objects of passives receive dependent structural case because of a syntactically visible but phonologically null nominative implicit agent. The object of passives in Finnish is assigned structural case as in Sakha, but the case cannot possibly be assigned by the dependent case algorithm (50), for the implicit agent of passives in Finnish is *invisible* to case assignment, as clearly demonstrated by Jahnsson's Rule (20b), see e.g. (22c,d).

Our approach predicts the transitivity of Sakha agent nouns in -*aaccy* out of the box. The reason is that they have an aspect feature. Agent nouns in Sakha -*aaccy* denote specifically habitual or generic agents. B&V (p. 531) illustrate this generalization with the following examples:[29]

(51) a. ynaq-y ölör-ööccü
 cow-ACC kill-AG.NOM
 'a killer of cows, a butcher'

 b. *Misha-ny ölör-ööccü
 Misha-ACC kill-AG.NOM
 'the killer of Misha'

The habitual aspect feature of the Sakha agent nouns licenses its structural case assignment just as the habitual aspect feature of agent nouns formed by the Sanskrit agent suffix *'-tar-^{V}* does, as opposed to aspectually void agent nouns in *-tár-^{N}*, Finnish *-ja*, and English *-er*. This accounts fully for the case data without resorting to the unsupported syntactic height distinctions demanded by the FNT.

Summing up our conclusions about agent nominalizations so far: the syntactic FNT is falsified by Vedic agent nominalizations in one direction, and by Finnish subject nominalizations in the other, and it requires an otherwise unsupported parametric choice between two heterogeneous structural case assignment algorithms. The analysis reveals that little v can't do *all* of the following things: (1) introduce Agents, (2) host voice heads or agent nominalizer heads, (3) host causative V affixes, (4) host aspectual material, and (5) assign structural case. In agent nominals it is not possible to place nominalizing heads above or below little v in a consistent way that satisfies all of (1)-(5). (1) and (5) cannot be reconciled with an agent nominalizer that assigns structural case such as Sanskrit *'-tar-^{V}*, or with a subject nominalizer that does not assign structural case such as Finnish *-ja*. The Sakha nominalizer *-AAccY* can dominate causatives (high) but not aspectual adverbs – a conflict between (3) and (4) – and introduces agents (low) but assigns structural case (high) – a conflict between (2) and (5).

These difficulties fall away if we assume that that agent nominals are nouns, and that nouns assign structural case if and only if they have Aspect features.

4 Conclusion

The Functional Nominalization Thesis claims that so-called "mixed categories" arise when a nominal head is affixed to an extended verbal projection that is its syntactic complement. My findings instead support a lexicalist approach, in which mixed categories are projections of a nominal or verbal heads with an extra phi-feature. Their extended projections behave like normal extended projections modulo the properties enforced by that feature.

---

[29] This component is foregrounded in the related habitual participle function of the same suffix: e.g. *salaj-aaccy* means both 'manager' (agent noun) and 'habitually managing' (participle), see Vinokurova (2005: 123).

In §2 I argued that gerund phrases are not DPs/NPs with AspP complements. They are not even nominalizations. They are participial phrases – IPs with a Case feature that is checked or valued in an argument position. In all other respects their syntax is entirely clausal: they lack DP material such as articles, demonstratives, quantifiers, and adjectives, and they are formally built like IPs, complete with structural subjects. The lexicalist analysis explains these properties.

In §3 I argued that agent nominalizations that assign structural case to their objects are not nouns with vP complements (or with any other phrasal complements), but deverbal nouns derived by agent suffixes that have an Aspect feature. The Aspect feature makes the nouns transitive, and modifiable by aspectual adverbs. Otherwise their syntax is entirely nominal. The merit of this analysis is that it tightly correlates the transitivity of agent nouns with their aspectual meaning. Also, by relieving the burden on little v, it eliminates the mismatches between word structure and syntax that we found in Vedic and Finnish agent nouns under the FNT analysis.

The lexicalist approach retains the key idea of the FNT without the typologically unwarranted overgeneration caused by allowing syntactic affixation. It preserves a uniform mechanism of structural case assigment, a unified analysis of true nominalizations, and the insights that originally led Chomsky to lexicalism.

Acknowledgements

I am grateful to Vera Gribanova and to an anonymous reviewer for their very helpful comments and queries.

References

Abney, Steven. 1987. *The English noun phrase in its sentential aspect*. Massachusetts Institute of Technology PhD dissertation.
Alexiadou, Artemis. 2001. *Functional structure in nominals: nominalization, and ergativity*. Amsterdam: John Benjamins.
Alexiadou, Artemis, Elena Soare & Gianina Iordăchioaia. 2010. Number/aspect interactions in the syntax of nominalizations: a distributed approach. *JL* 46. 537–574.
Anderson, Stephen R. 1992. *A-morphous morphology*. Cambridge: Cambridge University Press.
Anderson, Stephen R. 2016. The role of morphology in transformational grammar. In Andrew Hippisley & Gregory T. Stump (eds.), *The Cambridge handbook of morphology*, 587–608. Cambridge: Cambridge University Press.
Anttila, Arto & Jong-Bok Kim. 2016. Locality and variation in Finnish structural case. *Natural Language and Linguistic Theory*. DOI:doi:10.1007/s11049-016-9352-x
Baker, Mark & Nadya Vinokurova. 2009. On agent nominalizations and why they are not like event nominalizations. *Language* 85. 517–556.

Baker, Mark C. 2015. *Case: Its principles and parameters*. Cambridge: Cambridge University Press.
Blevins, James P. 2003. Remarks on gerunds. In Peter Sells & C. Orhan Orgun (eds.), *English morphology and the web of grammar*. Stanford: CSLI Publications.
Chomsky, Noam. 1955. *The logical structure of linguistic theory. ms. published 1985*. Chicago: University of Chicago Press.
Chomsky, Noam. 1970. Remarks on nominalization. In R. Jacobs & P. Rosenbaum (eds.), *Readings in English transformational grammar*, 184–221. Waltham, MA: Ginn.
Deal, Amy Rose. 2009. The origin and content of expletives: evidence from "selection". *Syntax* 12. 285–323.
Embick, David. 2010. *Localism versus globalism in morphology and phonology*. Cambridge: MIT Press.
Embick, David & Alec Marantz. 2008. Architecture and blocking. *Linguistic Inquiry* 39(1). 1–53.
Embick, David & Rolf Noyer. 2001. Movement operations after syntax. *Linguistic Inquiry* 32(4). 555–595.
Hakulinen, Auli & Fred Karlsson. 1979. *Nykysuomen lauseoppia*. Vol. 350. Suomalaisen kirjallisuuden seura.
Hakulinen, Auli & Lauri Karttunen. 1973. Missing persons: on generic sentences in Finnish. In *Cls9: papers from the ninth regional meeting*, 157–71. Chicago Linguistic Society, Chicago.
Harizanov, Boris & Vera Gribanova. 2016. *Whither head movement?* Workshop on the Status of Head Movement in Linguistic Theory. Stanford.
Harley, Heidi. 2012. External arguments and the mirror principle: on the distinctness of voice and v. *Lingua* 125. 34–57.
Huddleston, Rodney & Geoffrey Pullum. 2002. *The cambridge grammar of the English language*. Cambridge: Cambridge University Press.
Kim, Jong-Bok. 2016. *The syntactic structures of Korean: a construction grammar perspective*. Cambridge: Cambridge University Press.
Kiparsky, Paul. 2001. Structural case in Finnish. *Lingua* 111. 315–376.
Kiparsky, Paul. 2005a. *Absolutely a matter of degree: The Semantics of Structural Case in Finnish*. https://web.stanford.edu/.
Kiparsky, Paul. 2005b. Blocking and periphrasis in inflectional paradigms. In Geert Booij & Jaap van Marle (eds.), *Yearbook of morphology 2004*, 113–135. Dordrecht: Springer.
Kiparsky, Paul. 2010a. Compositional vs. paradigmatic approaches to accent and ablaut. In Stephanie W. Jamison, H. Craig Melchert & Brent Vine (eds.), *Proceedings of the 21st annual UCLA Indo-European conference*. Bremen: Hempen.
Kiparsky, Paul. 2010b. Dvandvas, blocking, and the associative: The bumpy ride from phrase to word. *Language* 86. 302–331.
Kiparsky, Paul. 2013. Towards a null theory of the passive. *Lingua* 125. 7–33.
Kiparsky, Paul. 2016. The agent suffixes as a window into Vedic grammar. In Joshua Katz Dieter Gunkel Brent Vine & Michael Weiss (edd (eds.), *Sahasram ati srajas: Indo-Iranian and Indo-European studies in honor of Stephanie W. Jamison*.

http://web.stanford.edu/ kiparsky/Papers/agentnouns.final.pdf. Ann Arbor: Beech Stave Press.

Kiparsky, Paul. In press. *Paradigm effects and opacity*. Stanford: CSLI.

Kornfilt, Jaklin & John Whitman. 2011. Afterword: nominalizations in syntactic theory. *Lingua* 121. 1297–1313.

Kratzer, Angelika. 1996. Severing the external argument from its verb. In J. Rooryck & L. Zaring (eds.), *Phrase structure and the lexicon*. Dordrecht: Kluwer Academic Press.

Kratzer, Angelika. 2002. *The event argument and the semantics of verbs*. Manuscript, University of Massachusetts, Amherst.

Kratzer, Angelika. 2004. Telicity and the meaning of objective case. In Jacqueline Lecarme & Jacqueline Guéron (eds.), *The syntax of time*. Cambridge, MA: MIT Press.

Lausetyyppien käsittely transformaatioteoriassa [The treatment of sentence Types in Transformational grammar]. 1970. *Ajatus (Journal of the Finnish philosophical society]* XXXII. 150–159.

Lees, Robert B. 1960. The grammar of English nominalizations. *International Journal of American Linguistics* 26(3).

Levin, Theodore, Preminger & Omer. 2015. Case in Sakha: are two modalities really necessary? *Natural Language and Linguistic Theory* 33. 231–250.

Lowe, John J. 2014. Transitive nominals in Old Avestan. *Journal of the American Oriental Society* 134(4). 553–577.

Malouf, Robert. 2000. *Mixed categories in the hierarchical lexicon*. Stanford: CSLI Publications.

Marantz, Alec. 1991. Case and licensing. In German Westphal, Benjamin Ao & Hee-Rahk Chae (eds.), *Proceedings of the 8th Eastern States Conference on Linguistics (ESCOL 8)*, 234–253. Ithaca: CLC Publications.

Payne, John, Geoffrey K. Pullum & Rodney Huddleston. 2010. The distribution and category status of adjectives and adverbs. *Word Structure*. 31–81.

Pires, Acrisio. 2006. The derivation of clausal gerunds. *Syntax* 10. 165–203.

Portner, Paul. Quantification, events, and gerunds. In Emmon Bach, Eloise Jelinek, Angelika Kratzer & Barbara Partee (eds.), *Quantification in natural language*, 619–659. Dordrecht & Boston: Kluwer Academic Publishers.

Pullum, Geoffrey. 1991. English nominal gerund phrases as noun phrases with verb-phrase heads. *Linguistics* 29. 763–799.

Pustejovsky, James. 1995. *The generative lexicon*. Cambridge, MA: MIT Press.

Ross, John. 1967. *Constraints on variables in syntax*. Massachusetts Institute of Technology Ph.D. dissertation.

Svenonius, Peter. 2016. Spans and words. In Daniel Siddiqi & Heidi Harley (eds.), *Morphological metatheory*. Amsterdam & Philadelphia: John Benjamins.

Toosarvandani, Maziar. 2014. Two types of deverbal nominalization in Northern Paiute. *Language* 90. 786–833.

Vergnaud, Jean-Roger. 1977. Open letter to chomsky and lasnik. *LingBuzz* 461. http://ling.auf.net/lingbuzz/000461.

Vinokurova, Nadezhda. 2005. *Lexical categories and argument structure.* Utrecht: LOT Publications. http://www.lotpublications.nl/Documents/103_fulltext.pdf.
Williams, Edwin S. 1975. Small clauses in English. In John Kimball (ed.), *Syntax and semantics*, vol. 4, 249–273. New York: Academic Press.
Wunderlich, Dieter. 1996a. A minimalist model of inflectional morphology. In Chris Wilder, Hans-Martin Gärtner & Manfred Bierwisch (eds.), *The role of economy principles in linguistic theory*, 267–298. Berlin: Akademie Verlag.
Wunderlich, Dieter. 1996b. Minimalist morphology: the role of paradigms. *Yearbook of Morphology.* 93–114.
Wunderlich, Dieter. 2001. How gaps and substitutions can become optimal: the pronominal affix paradigms of Yimas. *Transactions of the Philological Society* 99. 315–366.
Yoon, James Hye Suk. 1996. Nominal gerund phrases in English as phrasal zero derivations. *Linguistics* 34. 329–356.

Chapter 16

On mechanisms by which languages become [nominative-]accusative

Ashwini Deo
The Ohio State University

New Indo-Aryan languages are characterized by accusative (DOM) objects in ergative, perfective clauses. This paper traces the emergence of this ergative–accusative marking pattern with the goal of determining whether it is to be considered part of a single "de-ergativization" trajectory, in which languages gradually lose aspects of their ergative orientation in analogy to the non-ergative portion of the grammar. Data from Middle Indo-Aryan suggests that accusative marked objects — a deviation from the classic ergatively-oriented sub-system — cannot be analyzed in terms of the analogical extension of any existing nominative-accusative model or as a reduction of markedness. In contrast, the empirical facts of Indo-Aryan diachrony align better with the possibility that such deviations have to do with independent changes in the broader argument realization options for the language. This is consistent with Anderson's (1977; 2004) claim that a significant part of the explanation for ergativity-related patterns lies in patterns of diachronic change rather than abstract structural considerations of Universal Grammar.

1 Introduction

The term *ergative* is used to refer to a grammatical relation marking pattern in which the object of a transitive verb patterns with the single argument of an intransitive verb (surfacing with absolutive case), while the transitive subject patterns distinctly (surfacing with ergative case) (Dixon 1979; 1994; Comrie 1978; Plank 1979). It has sometimes been claimed that there is a clear asymmetry between the pervasiveness of ergative–absolutive vs. nominative–accusative marking systems across sub-domains of grammars in languages.

> No ergative language is fully consistent in carrying through the ergative principle throughout its entire morphology, syntax, and lexicon: all languages that exhibit ergative patterning in their commonest case-marking system also exhibit some accusative pattern somewhere in the rest of their grammar. (Moravcsik 1978, p.237)

Ashwini Deo. 2017. On mechanisms by which languages become [nominative-]accusative. In Claire Bowern, Laurence Horn & Raffaella Zanuttini (eds.), *On looking into words (and beyond)*, 347–369. Berlin: Language Science Press. DOI:10.5281/zenodo.495453

A possible way of interpreting this stated generalization is to take it to refer to the presence of accusative case-marking in ergative languages – that is, that every language with an ergative-nominative case marking or agreement pattern also exhibits a nominative–accusative pattern in some subsystem of the grammar. However, this interpretation is clearly not borne out since several languages exist that have ergative case but lack accusative case marking altogether.[1] Coon & Preminger (to appear) interpret the above claim to mean that even in languages which show a high number of ergative characteristics, there can generally be found some portion of the grammar in which the ergative pattern is lost, and transitive and intransitive subjects are treated alike. In this case, the term "ergative pattern" seems to refer, not to surface morphological properties, but more broadly to syntactic properties like control and binding with respect to which the highest arguments of a clause may pattern alike. Split-ergativity is a term reserved specifically for morphological marking patterns and refers to the systematized occurrence of a mixed indexing system, which is ergatively organized in well-defined syntactic-semantic configurations with nominative–accusative marking elsewhere in the language. The question of how such systems arise in natural languages and change (or persist) through time, as well as the possible diachronic reasons for the parameters on which the split is based, can only be answered by an investigation of split-ergative languages for which we have some clear diachronic record available.

Anderson (1977, and later in 2004)has suggested that to the extent we have such information, changes involving ergative orientation seem to be "consequences of relatively superficial phenomena." According to him, ergative patterning is not a deep syntactic property of linguistic systems but rather an emergent effect arising from several distinct trajectories in the morphological systems of languages. In effect, there is no principle that determines an "ergative" or "accusative" pattern; rather languages may innovate or lose specific cases such as ergative or accusative, with such patterns arising more as emergent effects of the change and not as abstractly determined invariant objects. This paper examines one such emergent effect in trajectories associated with systems containing ergative case – the emergence of overt accusative (object) marking in ergative clauses. New data from Late Middle Indo-Aryan (MIA) and Early New Indo-Aryan (NIA) suggests that transitions resulting in deviations from the classic ergatively-oriented sub-system in a split ergative language cannot be analyzed uniformly in terms of the analogical extension of any existing nominative-accusative model or as a reduction of markedness. In contrast, the empirical facts of Indo-Aryan diachrony align better with the possibility that such deviations have to do with independent changes in the broader argument realization options for the language. This is consistent with Anderson's claim that a significant part of the explanation for ergativity-related patterns lies in patterns of diachronic change rather than abstract structural considerations of Universal Grammar (contra Delancey 1981; Dixon 1994; Tsunoda 1981).

---

[1] An anonymous reviewer points to languages like Chukchi, Tabassaran, Chamalal, Tzutujil, Central Yupik Eskimo, and Burushaski that lack an accusative case, and therefore lack nominative-accusative "patterning" in terms of case marking.

2 Morphosyntactic changes in Middle Indo-Aryan

2.1 The emergence of ergativity

One well-discussed source for ergative marking in natural languages is a passive clausal structure that gets reanalyzed as active. Oblique marking on the optionally surfacing agent is reanalyzed as ergative case while the unmarked subject of the passive clause surfaces as absolutive object, identical to the subjects of intransitive clauses. Indo-Aryan languages bear the most concrete diachronic record for such a passive–to-ergative shift scenario. In the history of these languages, a passive construction with resultative semantics was reanalyzed as an active, ergative clause with perfective aspectual reference at least by the time of Epic Sanskrit (Old Indo-Aryan (OIA)) and Early MIA (Andersen 1986; Peterson 1998; Condoravdi & Deo 2014 a.o.).[2] In the oldest Vedic texts, the -*ta*-affixed form of the verb serves to describe a result-state brought about by a preceding event when it is used predicatively in an adjectival passive construction. The -*ta* forms (bold-faced) in (1a) agree with the nominative patient while the agent remains unexpressed. In (1b), the agents and instruments are overtly expressed in the instrumental case.

(1) a. stīr-ṇám   te   barhíḥ   su-tá
       strew-PERF.N.SG you.DAT.SG Barhis.NOM.N.SG press-PERF.M.SG

       indra   sóma-ḥ   kr̥-tá   dhānā́   át-tave
       Indra.VOC.SG Soma-NOM.M.SG do-PERF.M.PL barley.NOM.M.PL eat-INF

       te   hári-bhyāṃ
       you.GEN.SG horse-DAT.SG

   'The Barhis has been strewn for thee, O Indra; the Soma has been pressed (into an extract). The barley grains have been prepared for thy two bay-horses to eat.' (Rgveda 3.35.7)

   b. nr̥-bhir   dhū-táḥ   su-tó   áśna-iḥ   áv-yo
      man-INST.PL wash-PERF.M.SG press-PERF.M.SG stone-INST.PL wool-GEN.SG

      vā́ra-iḥ   páripū-taḥ
      filter-INST.PL strain-PERF.M.SG

   'It (the Soma) has been washed by men, pressed with the help of stones, strained with wool-filters.' (Rgveda 8.2.2)

As shown in (2), the -*ta* form agrees with the sole (nominative) argument of intransitive verbs. This results in a difference in the marking of the subject arguments of transitive and intransitive verbs. In (1) the verb does not agree with the instrumental agentive arguments. In (2), in contrast, the verb *śri-taḥ* has a nominative subject *soma* and agrees with it in number and gender.

---

[2] The Indo-Aryan branch of Indo-European inherits the deverbal result stative form with the affix -*ta* (allomorph -*na*) (reconstructed for Indo-European as *-*to*/-*no*). -*ta*, attested at all stages of OIA and MIA, attaches directly to the root, and the resulting stem is adjectival, inflecting for number and gender like any other adjectival forms.

(2) div-i somo adhi śri-taḥ
heaven-LOC.SG soma.NOM.M.SG on rest-PERF.M.SG

'Soma rests (is supported) in the heaven.' (Ṛgveda 10.85.1)

This resultative -*ta* construction (sometimes in periphrasis with tense auxiliaries) is the source of the ergative pattern observed in the perfective aspect in the later languages. In later stages of OIA, the construction was extended to marking the perfect aspect and it exhibited existential as well as universal perfect readings (Condoravdi & Deo 2014). By the time of Epic Sanskrit (late stage of OIA), the -*ta* construction became a frequently used device for marking past perfective reference. The agent argument in these cases is most frequently overt and marked with instrumental case. Past eventive reference is indicated by the presence of past referring frame adverbials like *purā* 'formerly' and *tadā* 'then'. Perfective clauses containing intransitive verbs occur with nominative subjects (3c). All the examples below are from the *Mahābhārata*, one of two epics that constitute the record for this stage of the language.

(3) a. purā devayug-e ca eva dṛṣ-ṭam sarvam mayā
formerly god.age-LOC.SG and PTCL see-PERF.N.SG everything I-INST.SG
vibho
lord-VOC.SG

'Lord, formerly, in the age of the Deva (Gods), I *saw* everything.' (*Mahābhārata* 3.92.6a; Deo 2012)

b. hṛ-tā gau-ḥ sā tadā t-ena
steal-PERF.F.SG cow-NOM.F.SG that-NOM.F.SG then he-INST.3.SG
prapāta-s tu na tark-itaḥ
fall-NOM.M.SG PTCL NEG consider-PERF.M.SG

'Then he *stole* that cow, but *did* not *consider* the fall (consequences).' (*Mahābhārata* 1.93.27e; Deo 2012)

c. jaratkāruḥ ga-taḥ svarga-m sahitaḥ
Jaratkāru.NOM.M.SG go-PERF.M.SG heaven-ACC.SG accompanied
sva-iḥ pitāmaha-iḥ
self-INST.M.PL ancestor-INST.M.PL

'Jaratkāru went to heaven accompanied by his ancestors.' (*Mahābhārata* 1.130.43c)

The main change between Epic Sanskrit (OIA) and the later MIA stage of the language concerns the erosion and simplification of the rich tense-aspect system (Pischel 1900; Bloch 1965). Inflectional past referring forms such as the aorist, the inflectional perfect, and the imperfect disappeared from the language, leaving the -*ta* construction as the only past referring device.[3] This loss of the inflectional system has often been cited as a reason for the increase in the frequency and scope of the participial construction, which

---

[3] Traditional grammarians do provide instances of the inflectional perfect and the aorist during this period, but they only occur as isolated, unanalyzed forms for a few verbs like *āha-*'say-AOR' and *akāshi -*'do-AOR'.

in turn led to the unmarking of the stative nature of the construction. The change to an ergative alignment was certainly complete at the Mid to Late MIA stage (Hock 1986; Bubenik 1998). The examples below from an archaic MIA Mahāraṣṭrī text *Vasudevahiṃḍī* (ca. 500 AD) shows this ergative alignment. The verb agrees with the nominative subject in (4a). In (4b) the verb agrees with the nominative marked object while the agentive argument ('that running one') appears in the instrumental.

(4) a. **pat-to** ya seṇiyo rāyā ta-m
   reach-PERF.M.SG and Seṇiya.NOM.M.SG king.NOM.M.SG that-ACC.SG
   paesa-m
   place-ACC.SG
   'And King Seṇiya *reached* that place.' (*Vasudevahiṃḍī* KH. 17.1)

b. t-eṇa palāyamāṇ-eṇa purāṇakuv-o
   that-INST.SG running-INST.SG old.well-NOM.M.SG
   taṇadabbhaparichinn-o diṭ-ṭho
   grass.covered-NOM.M.SG notice-PERF.M.SG
   'That running one *noticed* an old well covered with grass.' (*Vasudevahiṃḍī* KH. 8.6)

Indo-Aryan diachrony after the MIA stage has often been characterized as involving a progressive loss of ergative alignment and gradual drift towards a nominative-accusative marking in perfective clauses. There are three observed ways in which the descendent systems deviate from the proto-ergative system of MIA: (a) Loss of ergative morphology in pronominal and nominal paradigms[4]; (b) Subject agreement (replacing or in addition to object agreement); (c) Accusative marking on a privileged class of objects, i.e. the spread of differential object marking.

It is logical to think of the implementation of any of these changes independently or together as the "de-ergativization" of an ergative system in analogy to the non-ergative portion of the grammar. Indeed, the patterns seen in individual NIA languages, such as suppression of overt ergative case (e.g. in Old Hindi and Marathi); nominative subjects (e.g. in Bangla) and agreement with overt ergative subject (e.g. in Nepali) are all analogizable to existing marking patterns in the language such as unmarked subjects, nominative subjects, and subject agreement. However, the emergence of accusative marking on objects of transitive, perfective clauses poses a puzzle for a straightforward analogical

---

[4] In fact, data from some Early NIA languages, e.g. Hindi, reveals that the original instrumental marking observed on transitive subjects for the MIA ergative system is entirely lost for *all* nominal and pronominal expressions in some stages of Indo-Aryan. The ergative pattern of agreement is nevertheless retained. The example in (i) is from the work of Kabir, a poet from the 15th century CE. There is no overt ergative marking on the 3rd person subject but the agreement on the verb is with the feminine object argument (explicit or unpronounced) *chādar* 'sheet'.

(i) jo **chādar** sura-nara-muni oḍh-i
   which sheet.NOM.F.SG gods-men-sages.∅ERG wrap-PERF.F.SG
   'Which sheet the Gods, men, and sages, all wore, (that sheet)...'

extension narrative for de-ergativization. The puzzle arises from the evolution of case marking in MIA, to which we now turn.

2.2 Syncretism in nominal case marking

A critical change between the OIA and MIA stages, particularly in the Late MIA period, is the restructuring of the nominal case system. Notable here is the loss of morphological contrast between nominative and accusative as well as between the genitive and the dative cases. The syncretized set of case-endings for full nouns are given in Table 1.

Table 1: Case-endings for full nouns.

	Singular	Plural
Nominative/Accusative	-u, a, aṃ	-a, aĩ
Instrumental/Ergative	-eṃ, iṃ, he, hi	-e(h)ĩ, ehi, ahĩ
Ablative	-hu, ahu, aho	-hũ, ahũ
Genitive/Dative	-ho, aho, ha, su, ssu	-na, hã
Locative	-i, hi, hiṃ	-hĩ

Table 2 contains an example of inflected -a stems with the noun *putta* 'son'.

Table 2: Inflected a-stems with *putta* 'son'.

Stem	Case	Singular	Plural
a-stems	Nominative/Accusative	putt-u	putt-a
	Instrumental/Ergative	putt-eṃ	putta-hiṃ/ehiṃ
	Genitive/Dative	putt-aho/ahu	putta-haṃ

The pronominal system retains more contrasts and syncretism between the nominative and accusative is observed only in the plural sub-part of most pronominal paradigms. Table 3 (culled from Clercq 2010) provides inflectional forms for some pronominal expressions to illustrate.

The loss of contrast between the nominative and accusative cases in most paradigms in a relatively free-word order language leads to heavy reliance on semantic cues from the linguistic material to determine grammatical relations. Consider the following examples from the *Paumacariu*, an 8th century text in verse, to illustrate the syncretic nominative-accusative marking (glossed NOM).[5] In (5), a sequence of parallel clauses,

---

[5] This is a Jaina rendition of the Epic Sanskrit text *Rāmāyana*. The edition used is the H.C. Bhayani edition published by the Bharatiya Vidya Bhavan between 1953 and 1960. The text is available in searchable electronic format, input by Eva De Clercq at Ghent University. The reason for using a late MIA text is to identify properties of the system that is as close to the grammars of the Early NIA system as possible.

Table 3: Inflectional forms for pronominals.

Stem	Case	Singular	Plural
1st pronoun	Nominative	hauṃ	amhẽ, amhaiṃ
	Accusative	mai(ṃ)	amhẽ, amhaiṃ
	Genitive/Dative	mahu, majjhu	amha, amhaha
2nd pronoun	Nominative	tuhuṃ	tumhẽ
	Accusative	paiṃ, taiṃ	tumhẽ
	Genitive/Dative	tahu, tujjha	tumha, tumhaha
3rd pronoun MASC;FEM	Nominative	so, su; sā	te, tāu
	Accusative	taṃ; sā	te; tāu
	Genitive/Dative	taho, tahu; tāhe	tāhaṃ; tāhaṃ

whether the first-occurring nominative expression realizes the grammatical subject or the grammatical object is determined by the meaning of the clause.[6] In (6), the relative pronoun, which refers to a human participant, disambiguates the grammatical structure.

(5) #kiṃ **tamu**   han-ai   na vālu **ravi**#
    QUES darkness.NOM.SG destroy-IMPF.3.SG NEG young sun.NOM.SG
    #kiṃ vālu **davaggi**   na dah-ai   **vanu**#
    QUES young fire.NOM.SG NEG burn-IMPF.3.SG forest.NOM.SG
    #kiṃ **kari**   dal-ai   na vālu **hari**#
    QUES elephant.NOM.SG shatter-IMPF.3.SG NEG young lion.NOM.SG
    #kiṃ vālu na daïk-ai   **uragamanu**#
    QUES young NEG bite-IMPF.3.SG snake.NOM.SG

   'Does the young (rising) sun not destroy darkness? Does the young fire (spark) not burn down the forest? Does a young lion (cub) not shatter the elephant? Does the young snake not bite?' (*Paumacariu* 2.21.6.9)

(6) **jo**   ghañ **ṇisi-bhoyaṇu**   ummah-ai
    who.REL.NOM.M.SG PTCL night.LOC-meal.NOM.M.SG give.up-IMPF.3.SG
    vimalattaṇu   **vimala-gottu**   lah-ai
    spotless.body.NOM.M.SG spotless.name.NOM.M.SG attain-IMPF.3.SG

   'One who gives up eating in the evening (he) attains a spotless body and name.' (*Paumacariu* 2.34.8.8)

Accusative marking is clearly visible only on first and second person singular pronouns in imperfective clauses as shown in the examples in (7).

---

[6] The #...# marks clause boundaries in the sequence.

(7) a. suggīu deva **paiṃ** sambhar-ai
Suggiu.NOM.M.SG deva.NOM.M.SG you.ACC.SG remember-IMPF.3.SG

'Lord Suggiu remembers you.' (*Paumacariu* 3.45.10.8)

b. jai ṇa vihāṇa-e **paiṃ** vandhāv-ami
if NEG tomorrow.LOC.SG you.ACC.SG bind-IMPF.1.SG

'If I do not capture you tomorrow...' (*Paumacariu* 3.49.20.3)

c. jo **maiṃ** muevi aṇṇu
who.REL.NOM.M.SG I.ACC.SG besides another.NOM.M.SG

jayakār-ai
adore-IMPF.3.SG

'(The one) who adores another one besides me...' (*Paumacariu* 2.25.1.9)

Syncretism rooted in sound change is also observed between the nominative and instrumental forms (the case form that gets re-interpreted as ergative when appearing with agentive arguments in perfective clauses) of the first and second person plural pronouns as in Table 4.

Table 4: Nominative and instrumental pronominal forms.

Aspect	Person	Number	
		Singular	Plural
Non-perf	1	hauṃ	amhaĭ/amhẽ
Perf	1	maiṃ	amhaĭ/amhẽ/amhe-hiṃ
Non-perf	2	tuhuṃ	tumhaĭ/tumhẽ
Perf	2	taiṃ	tumhaĭ/tumhẽ/tumhehiṃ
Non-perf	3	so	te
Perf	3	teṃ, teṇẽ	tehĭ/tāhaṃ

Despite this syncretism, agreement is uniformly with the nominative argument – with the nominative object in constructions based on the *-ta* form and with the nominative subject elsewhere. The examples in (8) illustrate this pattern with the first and second person plural pronouns *amhẽ* and *tumhẽ*. (8a) contains the syncretized pronoun *amhẽ* which triggers agreement in the imperfective aspect while the same form fails to trigger agreement in (8b). In (8c) the second person plural syncretic form used in an imperative clause triggers agreement while it fails to trigger verb agreement in the perfective (8d).

(8) a. **amhẽ** jāe-va vaṇavāsa-ho
we.SYNCR go-IMPF.1.PL forest.dwelling-DAT.SG

'We are going to our forest-exile.' (*Paumacariu* 2.23.14.3)

b. ki-u **amhĕ** ko avarāh-o
do-PERF.M.SG we.SYNCR what crime-NOM.M.SG

'What crime have we done?' (*Paumacariu* 1.2.13.9)

c. jiha sakk-aho tiha utthar-aho **tumhĕ** 'Save
in.which.way can-IMP.2.PL in.that.way save-IMP.2.PL you.SYNCR.PL
yourselves in the way that you can.' (*Paumacariu* 5.82.12.4)

d. **tumhĕ** jaṃ cint-iu taṃ
you.SYNCR.SG what.REL.M.SG think-PERF.M.SG that.CORREL.M.SG
hū-a
happen-PERF.M.SG

'That, which you thought (would happen), happened.' (*Paumacariu* 3.47.9.6)

These patterns of syncretization within the nominal inflectional system of MIA are difficult to reconcile with a story in which there is a straightforward extension of an existing alignment pattern in the language to a marked sub-system of the grammar. Although there is a contrast between the nominative and accusative cases in MIA, it is exhibited only in selected parts of the pronominal system (a subset of the singular pronouns) and therefore seems to be rather weak evidence for extending the accusative marking pattern to ergative clauses. A reviewer argues that the regular presence of such a case-marking pattern in imperfective clauses, however limited in terms of its application, should not be seen as "weak" evidence for a nominative accusative pattern. I concede that it is indeed theoretically possible that the pattern observed in a small subset of imperfective non-ergative clauses gets extended to perfective, ergative clauses. However, neither existing grammars of MIA (Pischel 1900; Vale 1948; Clercq 2010) nor an examination of the textual data indicate any presence of accusative marked object arguments in perfective transitive clauses at this stage in the language. Even pronominal objects (9a)–(9b) and human-denoting full noun phrase objects (9c)–(9d) of canonical transitive verbs, which obligatorily appear with overt accusative marking in the NIA languages, are uniformly marked nominative at this stage.[7]

(9) a. **hauṃ** ṇikkāraṇe ghall-iya rām-eṃ
I.NOM.SG without.reason drive.out-PERF.F.SG Rām-ERG.SG

'Rām drove me out (of Ayodhya) without any reason.' (*Paumacariu* 5.81.13.8)

b. cakkesar-eṇa kema **tuhũ** di-ṭṭhī
Cakkesara-ERG.M.SG how you.NOM.SG see-PERF.F.SG

'How were you noticed by Cakkesara (Rāvaṇa)?' (*Paumacariu* 2.4.2.1.5)

c. viṇivār-iu **rāvaṇu** rāhav-eṇa
dissuade-PERF.M.SG rāvaṇa.NOM.M.SG rāhava-ERG.M.SG

'Rāhava (Rāma) dissuaded Rāvaṇa' (*Paumacariu* 4.66.14.6)

---

[7] Thus, there are no positive instances with pronominal forms *maiṃ, taiṃ, taṃ* etc. being used instead of *hauṃ, tuhuṃ,* or *so/su* etc. in ergative clauses with pronominal objects at even the latest stages of Middle Indo-Aryan.

d. di-ṭṭhu   jaṇaddaṇu   rāhavacand-eṃ
   see-PERF.M.SG jaṇaddaṇa.NOM.M.SG rāhavacanda-INS.SG
   'Rāhavacanda saw Jaṇaddaṇa.' (*Paumacariu* 2.29.8.1)

Moreover, no language of the later stage (Early NIA) has an ergative-accusative marking pattern which uses the pronominal forms of late MIA in ergative clauses that accusative marking on objects. While the issue needs to be more closely investigated, it seems reasonable to look for an alternative source for accusative marking in ergative clauses than the template offered by MIA.

3 Differential object marking: A New Indo-Aryan innovation

The previous subsection established that accusative marking of the MIA variety is both weakly present and shows no evidence of being extended to perfective ergative clauses at later stages of Indo-Aryan. This leaves the possibility that the incidence of object marking in ergative clauses – a pervasive phenomenon in the Modern NIA languages – begins with the Differential Object Marking pattern – which is considered to be an NIA innovation. Differential Object Marking (henceforth DOM) in Indo-Aryan languages is sensitive to animacy and referentiality features of arguments. It is obligatory on 1st and 2nd pronominal objects, and on 3rd person animate-denoting pronominals. It is optional with animate-denoting full NPs where the absence of object marking correlates with a non-referential interpretation of the NP. In the Modern NIA languages, this semantically driven pattern of object marking does not distinguish between ergative and non-ergative clauses; i.e. the case marking on objects is entirely independent of any overt or covert presence of case on the subject.

Logically, one can imagine two ways in which an ergativity-insensitive object marking pattern can emerge in a system. It could be that the DOM pattern first emerges in Late MIA or Early NIA in non-ergative clauses. Such a pattern is then later extended analogically to ergative clauses as part of the de-ergativization trajectory characterizing Indo-Aryan diachrony. The second possibility is for the DOM pattern to emerge simultaneously in both ergative and non-ergative clauses and gradually extend to different classes of verbs. On this latter scenario, the presence of DOM in ergative clauses is not part of the larger de-ergativization trajectory that characterizes NIA diachrony, but rather attributable to independent developments that introduce overt marking on direct objects into the case system.[8] The empirical facts of Late MIA and Early NIA texts support the second scenario. In what follows, I will suggest that the emergence of DOM in both ergative and non-ergative clause types of MIA amounts to the extension of an inherited OIA marking pattern observed with the class of so-called "double object" verbs.

---

[8] The effects on agreement in languages which exhibit such a changed case-marking pattern may be different. In Modern NIA we see both default agreement in ergative clauses when both subject and object are case-marked (e.g. in Hindi, Marathi) or continued object agreement despite overt accusative marking on the object (e.g. in Gujarati, Marwari).

3.1 Double object verbs in Old Indo-Aryan

A class of verbs in OIA exhibits a double object pattern in which the theme or goal and another participant of the denoted event are marked in the accusative case. Semantically, this is a diverse class and includes at least the subclasses in Table 5.

Table 5: Double object verbs in Old Indo-Aryan.

Class	Verbs
Verbs of speaking	*brū* 'speak', *vac* 'say', *kath* 'tell'
Verbs of asking	*pṛcch* 'ask', *yāc* 'request, solicit', *bhikṣ* 'beg', *prārth* 'plead'
Verbs of teaching	*upa-diś* 'teach', *anu-śās"* 'teach', *ā-diś* 'direct'
Causatives of some transitives	*khād-aya* 'cause to eat', *pā-yaya* 'cause to drink', *darś-aya* 'cause to see', *śrāv-aya* 'cause to hear'
Miscellaneous ditransitives	*jī* 'win', *duh* 'milk', *daṇḍ* 'punish', *nī* 'lead'

(10) contains examples from OIA (Epic Sanskrit) involving verbs of speaking in imperfective, non-ergative clauses. In (10a), the pronominal denoting the addressee if the verb of speaking event *tvāṃ* is accusative as is the information communicated, *nidurśunam* 'the teaching'. (10b), from a proximal location in the text, is similar.

(10) a. atas tvā-m kathay-e karṇa nidarśan-am
 hence you-ACC.SG tell-IMPF.1.SG karṇa.VOC.SG teaching-ACC.N.SG
 idam punaḥ
 this.ACC.N.SG again
 'Hence, O Karṇa, I tell you this teaching (advice) again.' (*Mahābhārata* 8.28.8e)

b. śalyo 'brav-īt punaḥ karṇ-am
 śalya.NOM.M.SG speak-IMPFCT.3.SG again karṇa-ACC.M.SG
 nidarśan-am udāhar-an
 teaching-ACC.N.SG announce-PART.NOM.M.SG
 'Śalya again spoke out his advice to Karṇa' (*Mahābhārata* 8.28.1c)

An alternative realization for pronominal animate-denoting higher arguments of double object verbs is as DAT/GEN clitics.

(11) a. hanta **te** kathay-iṣy-āmi nām-āni iha
 PTCL you.DAT/GEN.CL tell-FUT-1.SG name-ACC.N.PL here

manīṣi-ṇām
wise-one-GEN.M.PL

'Ah, I will tell you the names of the wise ones.' (*Mahābhārata* 1.48.4a)

b. ... īś-ate bhagavān ekaḥ saty-am
reign-IMPF.3.SG Lord.NOM.M.SG alone.NOM.M.SG truth.ACC.N.SG
etad brav-īmi te
this.ACC.N.SG speak-IMPF.1.SG you.DAT/GEN.CL

'The Lord alone reigns [over time and death and this universe of mobile and immobile objects], this truth I tell you.' (*Mahābhārata* 5.66.13c)[9]

In ergative, perfective clauses, this higher argument may surface variably: either as the nominative subject of the passivized verb form (examples in (12)) or as a DAT/GEN marked clitic pronoun (examples in (13)).[10]

(12) a. uk-to rātr-au mṛg-air as-mi
speak-PERF.M.SG night-LOC.SG animal-INST.PL be-IMPF.1.SG

'I was spoken to by the beasts at night.' (*Mahābhārata* 3.244.11a)

b. ta-yā... śr-āv-ito vacan-āni **saḥ**
she-INS.SG hear-CAUS-PERF.M.SG word-ACC.N.SG he.NOM.SG

'He was made to hear (these) words by her.' (*Mahābhārata* 2.2.6a)

c. **sa** mayā varadaḥ kām-am
he.NOM.M.SG I.INS.SG boon.granting.NOM.M.SG desire-ACC.M.SG
yāc-ito dharmasaṃhit-am
solicit-PERF.M.SG virtue.bound-ACC.M.SG

'He, the boon-granting one, was solicited by me for (fulfilling my) virtuous desire.' (*Mahābhārata* 1.78.3c)

(13) a. sāṃkhyadarśan-am etāvad uk-taṃ **te**
sāṃkhyadarśan-NOM.N.SG so far speak-PERF.N.SG you.DAT/GEN.SG
nṛpasattama
best.king.VOC.SG

'Thus far, the Sāṃkhyadarśana was spoken to you, O best of kings.' (*Mahābhārata* 12.295.1a)

b. tad etat kath-itaṃ sarv-aṃ mayā **vo**
thus, this.NOM.N.SG tell-PERF.N.SG all-NOM.N.SG I.INS.SG you.DAT/GEN.PL
munisattamāḥ
great.sage.VOC.PL

'Thus, I have told you all this, O great sages.' (*Mahābhārata* 1.20.12a)

---

[9] The previous line of verse completes the translation: *kālasya ca hi mṛtyoś ca jaṅgamasthāvarasya ca* (*Mahābhārata* 5.66.13a)

[10] In (12a), the passivized subject is covert and the nominative case marking of the pro-dropped subject is inferred from the agreement on the auxiliary verb *asmi.*

c. upadiṣ-ṭo   hi **me**   pitr-ā   yogo
   teach-PERF.M.SG PTCL I.DAT/GEN.CL father-INST.3.SG method.NOM.M.SG
   'nīka-sya   bhedan-e
   array-GEN.M.SG penetration-LOC.N.SG

   'The method of penetrating into this (military) array has been taught to me by my father.' (*Mahābhārata* 7.34.19a)

d. brahmacary-am   idaṃ bhadr-e   **mama**
   celibacy-NOM.N.SG this good.lady-VOC.SG I.GEN.SG
   dvādaśavārṣik-am   dharmarāj-ena   ca ādiṣ-ṭam
   twelve.years-NOM.N.SG Dharmarāja-INS.SG and command-PERF.N.SG

   'Good lady, this twelve-year celibacy has been commanded of me by Dharmarāja.' (*Mahābhārata* 1.206.21a-c)

The argument realization pattern illustrated in (11) and (13), where the higher argument of a double object verb surfaces with dative or genitive marking in both ergative and non-ergative clauses, is fairly robust in OIA. The alterations to the nominal case system in MIA described in Section 2.2, have no effect on this pattern, since the syncretized DAT/GEN remains available for overt marking throughout the period. Crucially, given the organization of the MIA case system, this dative/genitive marking is the only reliably present overt marking on non-subject arguments in both ergative and non-ergative clauses at this later stage. Based on the data from MIA, it seems most reasonable to conjecture that this template triggers the reanalysis of DAT/GEN as accusative marking on a subset of direct objects.

3.2 Double object verbs in Middle Indo-Aryan

In (14) are given examples of the OIA double object verbs in their MIA incarnations. Notice that themes surface with the syncretized nominative–accusative case (glossed NOM) while the non-theme higher argument (the addressee of the speech verb in (14a)–(14b) and the causee in (14c)) appear with the syncretized DAT/GEN marking.[11]

(14) a. sabbhāv-eṃ   **rāma-ho**   kah-ai   ema
       goodwill-INS.SG rāma-DAT/GEN.SG tell-IMPF.3.SG this.NOM.N.SG

       'He said this to Rāma with goodwill.' (*Paumacariu* 2.40.13.7)

   b. mārui   kah-ai   vatta   **valadeva-ho**
      Mārui.NOM.SG tell-IMPF.3.SG news.NOM.SG valadeva-DAT/GEN.SG

      'Māruti told the news to Valadeva.' (*Paumacariu* 3.55.9.1)

   c. **ta-ho**   daris-āv-ami   ajju jamattaṇu
      he-DAT/GEN.SG see-CAUS.IMPF.1.SG now yama.prowess.NOM.N.SG

      'Now, I will show him the prowess of Yama (the god of death).' (*Paumacariu* 1.11.10.6)

---

[11] (14a) and (14c) have subject pro-drop.

A look at perfective, ergative clauses in MIA containing double object verbs reveals overt DAT/GEN marking on the non-theme argument and unmarked themes. (15a) contains the causative of a perception verb, while (15b)–(15c) contain verbs of speaking. Just like OIA, there is no difference between ergative and non-ergative clauses vis-à-vis the realization of non-subject arguments.

(15) a. paḍ-e   paḍima...   sīya-he...   daris-āv-iya
screen-LOC.SG image.NOM.F.SG Sita-DAT/GEN.SG see-CAUS-PERF.F.SG
bhāmaṇḍala-ho
Bhāmaṇḍala-DAT/GEN.SG

'(He) showed the image of Sita on a screen (painting) to Bhāmaṇḍala.' (*Paumacariu* 2.21.8.9)

b. kah-iu   āsi   **ma-hu**   parama-jiṇind-eṃ
tell-PERF.M.SG be.PST.3.SG I.DAT/GEN.SG great-Jinendra-ERG.M.SG

'The great Jinendra told (this) to me.' (*Paumacariu* 1.1.12.8)

c. **ta-ho**   maiṃ   parama-bheu   ehu
you.DAT/GEN.SG I.ERG.SG great.secret.NOM.SG this.NOM.SG
akkh-iya
tell-PERF.N.SG

'I have told you this great secret.' (*Paumacariu* 1.16.8.9)

In addition to the non-theme arguments of double object verbs, the syncretized DAT/GEN marking also appears on possessor and goal arguments of standard ditransitives (examples in (16)) and on themes of verbs that describe a reciprocal experience (examples in (17)).

(16) a. **kikkindha-ho**   ghall-iya   māla   tāe
kikkindha-DAT/GEN.SG put-PERF.F.SG garland.F.SG she.ERG.SG

'She garlanded Kikkindha (lit. put a garland on)' (*Paumacariu* 1.7.4.1)

b. paripes-iu   lehu   **pahāṇā-ho**   aṇaraṇṇa-ho
send-PERF.M.SG letter.NOM.M.SG chief-DAT/GEN.SG Anaraṇya-DAT/GEN.SG
ujjha-he   rāṇā-ho
Ayodhyā-DAT/GEN.SG king-DAT/GEN.SG

'(He) sent a letter to Anaraṇya, the king of Ayodhya' (*Paumacariu* 1.15.8.4)

c. aṅgutthala   ṇav-evi   samapp-iu   tāvahñ **mahu**
finger.ring.NOM.M.SG bow-GER hand-PERF.M.SG then I.DAT/GEN.SG
cūḍāmaṇi   app-iu
precious.gem.NOM.M.SG give-PERF.M.SG

'(After) I handed her the finger ring, having bowed to her, (she) gave me this precious gem.' (*Paumacariu* 3.55.9.7)

d. diṇṇa   kaṇṇa   maiṃ   dasaraha-taṇay-aho
   give-PERF.F.SG daughter.NOM.F.SG I.ERG.SG dasaraha-son-DAT/GEN.SG

   'I have given my daughter to the son of Dasaraha (Daśaratha).' (*Paumacariu* 2.21.11.4)

(17) a. salil-u   samudd-aho   jiha milai
        water-NOM.SG ocean-DAT/GEN.SG as meet-IMPF.3.SG

        'Just as the water meets the ocean' (*Paumacariu* 3.56.1.12)

     b. tāvehñ gayaṇa-ho oar-evi   añjaṇā-he   vasantamāla
        then, sky-ABL   descend-GER Añjanā-DAT/GEN.SG Vasantamāla.NOM
        mil-iya
        meet-PERF.F.SG

        'Then, having descended from the sky, Vasantamālā met Añjanā.' (*Paumacariu* 1.19.8.10)

Critically, the syncretized DAT/GEN marking is the only reliable signal of non-subject arguments in MIA and it appears without discernible difference in distribution in both ergative and non-ergative clauses. It does not however appear, for the most part, on theme/patient arguments of canonical transitive or ditransitive verbs – animate or otherwise. (18a)–(18b) are examples of ergative clauses with animate-denoting subjects while (18c) contains a non-ergative clause.

(18) a. hā vahue-vahue mañ   bhantiy-ae   tuhũ
        alas bride.VOC I.ERG.SG unthinking-INST.SG you.NOM.SG
        ghall-iya   aparikkhantiy-ae
        drive.out-PERF.F.SG without.testing-ERG.F.SG

        'Alas, O bride, I drove you out without testing you in any way.' (*Paumacariu* 1.19.15.7)

     b. ṇi-u   tihuaṇa-paramesaru   tettahe sapparivāru
        take-PERF.M.SG three.worlds.lord.NOM.M.SG there with.family.NOM.M.SG
        purandaru   jettahe
        purandara.NOM.M.SG where

        '(She) took the lord of the three worlds there where Purandara was with his family.' (*Paumacariu* 1.2.2.8)

     c. muṇivara   ghall-es-ai   rajjesar-u
        sage.NOM.M.PL drive.out-FUT-3.SG king-NOM.SG

        'The king will drive out the sages.' (*Paumacariu* 2.35.9.1)

3.3 The emergence of DOM

The key suggestion I make here is that the Indo-Aryan differential object marking pattern emerging between late MIA and Early NIA amounts to the generalizing reanalysis of syncretic DAT/GEN marking on non-subject non-theme arguments as accusative marking on (a privileged class of) objects. The data that provide evidence to enable such a reanalysis are clauses containing double object and other ditransitive verbs which either have implicit (non-overt) theme arguments or where the arguments (in the case of verbs of speech) are propositional. Such clauses are not very frequent but they do occur quite reliably in MIA. Examples of non-ergative clauses are given in (19) and ergative clauses are in (20).

(19) a. akkh-ai sīya **samīraṇa-putt-aho**
tell-IMPF.3.SG Sita.NOM.SG Samīraṇaputta-DAT/GEN.SG
'Sita told Samīraṇa-putta (this).' (*Paumacariu* 3.50.10.7)

b. kahai mahārisi gayaṇa-gai
say-IMPF.3.SG great.sage.NOM.M.SG sky.traveling.NOM.M.SG
taho lavaṇ-aho samar-e **samatth-aho**
that.DAT/GEN.SG Lavaṇa-DAT/GEN.SG battle-LOC.M.SG capable-DAT/GEN.SG
'The great sage said to that Lavaṇa, who was capable in battle (thus).' (*Paumacariu* 5.82.8.9)

(20) a. **aṭṭhāvaya-giri-kampāvaṇ-aho** paḍihār-eṃ akkh-iu
eight.regions.trembling-DAT/GEN.SG messenger-ERG.SG tell-PERF.M.SG
rāvaṇ-aho
rāvaṇa-DAT/GEN.SG
'The messenger told (this) to Ravana, who was capable of causing the eight territories (*aṣṭapada*) to tremble.' (*Paumacariu* 1.15.4.1)

b. to **pamiṇipura-paramesar-aho** daris-āv-iya
then pamiṇipura-lord-DAT/GEN.SG see-CAUS-PERF.M.PL
vijaya-mahīhar-aho
vijaya-king-DAT/GEN.SG
'They showed (the boys) to the lord of Pamiṇipura (Padminipura), the king Vijayaparvata.' (*Paumacariu* 2.33.2.1)

c. **añjaṇ-ahe** samapp-iu jāya dih-i
Añjanā-DAT/GEN.SG hand-PERF.M.SG birth day-LOC.SG
'They handed him (the baby Hanumān) to Añjanā on the day of his birth.' (*Paumacariu* 1.19.11.6)

In clauses such as those in (19) and (20), the only overt non-subject argument carries DAT/GEN marking. Moreover, this pattern of marking does not differentiate between whether the subject carries ergative marking or is unmarked (nominative).

Consider a learner that must arrive upon the case inventory of a language based on the observable input. The MIA system provides reliably present morphological evidence for nominative, ergative, and dative/genitive case but no reliable evidence for accusative case. It also provides robust data in which the only non-subject argument overtly expressed in a clause carries case marking (the syncretic DAT/GEN marking). It is possible that the learner takes this subset of data as evidence for extending the DAT/GEN marking, reserved for non-theme arguments, to theme and patient arguments as well. The Differential Object Marking pattern evidenced in Early NIA emerges because the analogical extension of the overt DAT/GEN marking is constrained by the semantic properties associated with the original class of arguments marked by it – animacy and referentiality. If this hypothesis is correct, then we expect that there may be early data supporting this extension of DAT/GEN case marking to direct objects – in effect, the reanalysis of dative marking as accusative case, restricted to arguments meeting the criteria of high animacy and referentiality.

In the previous subsection, it was claimed that as far as the MIA stage is concerned, direct arguments of canonical transitive verbs do not, *for the most part*, surface with DAT/GEN marking (examples in (18)). The caveat was provided precisely because the MIA stage itself seems to exhibit some data which is possibly analyzable as emergent DOM. The tentativeness with which this claim can be made emerges from three uncertainties about the data: (a) Although the lexical verbs appearing with the DAT/GEN marked objects arguably have an argument structure corresponding to transitive verbs and their translational equivalents in English are realized as canonical transitives, given the semantics of these verbs, it seems possible that they pattern either with ditransitives or with "reciprocal" verbs" or with intransitives having accusative goal arguments in Sanskrit. Thus, it is necessary to investigate more closely whether these cases are early DOM-instances or whether they should be reclassified as exhibiting previously occurring patterns (b) The object-marking pattern is very infrequent outside of the class of double-object verbs, other ditransitives, and "reciprocal verbs". (c) There is absolutely no example of perfective clauses with ergative subjects in which the object appears with DAT/GEN marking.

It is possible therefore that the human-denoting DAT/GEN marked NPs in the data below are not the theme/patient arguments in a standard transitive template as they appear to be; they may be better analyzed as recipient or goal arguments. I will leave the adjudication of this issue for further research. But regardless of their status, they provide further surface evidence to the language acquirer for an object marking case "accusative" in the language.

In (21) and (22), we see that the human-denoting non-subject arguments of the transitive verbs *khama* 'forgive', *pekkha* 'look at', *garaha* 'denounce, curse', *abhiṭṭa* 'attack', *ḍhukka* 'approach' and *bhiḍ* 'battle' appear with DAT/GEN marking. The examples in (21) contain non-perfective clauses ((21b) is an imperative) while those in (22) illustrate the argument realization pattern in perfective clauses.

(21) a. ekkavāra **ma-hu**   khama-hi   bhaḍār-ā
       one.time I-DAT/GEN.SG forgive-IMP.2.G warrior-VOC.SG
       'O warrior (Lakshmana), please forgive me one time' (*Paumacariu* 3.44.4.7)

   b. sundari   pekkhu   pekkhu   jujjh-ant-aho
      beautiful.one.VOC.SG see.IMP.2.SG see.IMP.2.SG fight-PART.DAT/GEN.SG
      'O beautiful one, look at the battle.' (*Paumacariu* 2.31.12.3)

c. ema jāma garah-anti **jiṇind-aho** āsaṇu
thus when denounce-IMPF.3.PL jiṇinda-DAT/GEN.SG seat.NOM.M.SG
cal-iu tāma dharaṇind-aho
shake-PERF.M.SG then dharaṇinda-DAT/GEN.SG

'When they were denouncing Jiṇinda thus, the seat of Dharaṇinda started to shake.' (*Paumacariu* 1.2.14.5)

d. ham abbhiṭṭ-ami **dūsaṇ-aho**
I.NOM.SG attack-IMPF.1.SG Dūsaṇa-DAT/GEN.SG

'I will attack Dūsaṇa' (*Paumacariu* 2.40.4.10)

(22) a. dhā-iu aṅkusu lakkhaṇ-aho abbhi-ṭṭu
run-PERF.M.SG aṅkusu.NOM.M.SG lakṣmaṇa-DAT/GEN.SG attack-PERF.M.SG
lavaṇu raṇ-e **rām-aho**
lavaṇa.NOM.M.SG battlefield-LOC.SG rāma-DAT/GEN.SG

'Aṅkuṣa ran to Lakshmaṇa (while) Lavaṇa attacked Rāma' (*Paumacariu* 5.82.14.13)

b. kattha vi **bhaḍ-aho** sivaṅgaṇa
some.place PTCL warrior-DAT/GEN.SG she-jackal-group.NOM.M.PL
ḍhukk-iya
approach-PERF.M.PL

'At some places (on the battlefield), she-jackals approached the (dead) warriors.' (*Paumacariu* 1.17.13.8)

c. indai bhiḍ-iu samar-e
battle-PERF.M.SG battlefield-LOC.SG
haṇuvant-aho
Indai.NOM.M.SG haṇuvant-DAT/GEN.SG

'Indai (Indrajit) battled with Haṇuvanta in the battlefield.' (*Paumacariu* 3.53.10.9)

3.4 The DOM pattern in Early New Indo-Aryan

Turning to the Early New Indo-Aryan stage (illustrated here with Old Marathi), we see a clearly established animacy- and referentiality-sensitive DOM pattern in both ergative and non-ergative clauses from the earliest period.[12] The syncretic DAT/GEN marking of MIA appears as a generalized oblique case and it is augmented with innovated postpositions that correspond to accusative and dative case markers. This trajectory, in which the MIA case-system reduces to a nominative/oblique contrast and new postpositions are innovated to convey the semantic and structural information associated with the older cases, is shared across Indo-Aryan languages (Masica 1991; Bubenik 1996; 1998 a.o).

---

[12] This period is represented here by two texts – Līḷācharitra (ca. 1286 CE, prose) and the Dnyāneśvarī (ca. 1287 CE, verse).

16 On mechanisms by which languages become [nominative-]accusative

Direct objects in Old Marathi surface with an innovated postpositional accusative clitic, *-tem*, attached to the oblique stem (the reflex of the MIA DAT/GEN marker). The examples selected for presentation here contain transitive verbs whose animate-denoting theme arguments in both ergative and non-ergative clauses appear with overt accusative marking in (23)–(25).

(23) a. āmhīṃ **tuma=teṃ** ne-unuṃ
I.NOM.PL you.PL-ACC take-FUT.1.PL

'We will take you (to Varanasi).' (*Līḷācaritra* 1.25)

b. aiseṃ mhaṇ-auni **yā=teṃ** śrīkarī-ṃ dhar-ūni āpuleyā
thus speak-GER this.OBL=ACC hand-INS.SG hold-GER self.OBL

gharā=si ne-leṃ
house.OBL=DAT take-PERF.N.SG

'Having spoken thus, taking him by the hand, she took him to her house.' (*Līḷācaritra* 1.34)

(24) a. mhaṇoni prakāśā=ce=ni=hi dehabaḷ-eṃ na dekh-atī
therefore light.OBL=OF=BY=PTCL strength-INS.SG NEG see-IMPF.3.PL

mā=teṃ
I.OBL=ACC

'Therefore, even by the strength of light, they do not see me.' (*Dnyāneśvarī* 7.25.158)

b. tehīṃ **yāṃ=teṃ** uparīye-varauni dekh-ileṃ
he-ERG.SG this.M.SG-ACC upper.storey.OBL-from.top see-PERF.N.SG

'He saw this one from the upper story (of the house).' (*Līḷācaritra* 1.6)

(25) a. āṇi te **āma=teṃ** dhari-tī
And they.NOM.PL we-ACC catch-IMPF.3.PL

'And they (honorific) would catch us.' (*Līḷācaritra* 1.18)

b. ekī-ṃ ākāś-īṃ **sūryā=teṃ** dhar-ileṃ
one-ERG.SG sky-LOC.SG sun.OBL=ACC catch-PERF.N.SG

'Someone (might) catch the sun in the sky.' (*Dnyāneśvarī* 10.0.37)

The examples in (26) contain the same non-animate denoting but referential argument *jaga* 'world' that also receives accusative marking in both imperfective and perfective, ergative clauses ((26a) and (26b) respectively).

(26) a. maga āpu-leṃ keleṃ phokār-itī āṇi **jagā=teṃ**
then self-GEN.N.SG deed.NOM.N.SG proclaim-IMPF.3.PL and world-ACC

dhikkār-itī
denounce-IMPF.3.PL

'Then they proclaim their own deeds and denounce the world.' (*Dnyāneśvarī* 16.10.328)

b. prabaṃdhavyāj-eṃ jagā=teṃ rakṣ-ileṃ   jāṇa
   literary.work.INST.SG world-ACC save-PERF.3.N.SG know.IMP.2.SG

'Know that (the Guru) has saved the world through this literary work.'
(*Dnyāneśvarī* 18.78.1765)

It is necessary to take a much closer look at the pattern of DOM seen in Old Marathi languages and compare it on a verb-by-verb and argument-type by argument-type basis with the MIA pattern. It is only such an investigation that can accurately establish the nuanced differences between the impoverished accusative marking of Late MIA and the innovated accusative marking of Old Marathi. Noteworthy is the fact that no reflexes of the MIA accusative marking survive in the pronominal system of Old Marathi; only traces of the syncretized GEN/DAT marking remain.

4 Conclusion

At first glance, the presence of accusative marking (DOM) in NIA ergative clauses could be considered to be a case in which an existing template from the imperfective domain is extended by analogy to the perfective ergative domain. However, a closer study of the case-marking patterns of Late MIA reveals that there is no evidence for any direct extension of the MIA accusative marking to ergative clauses. It is more likely the case that the DOM pattern emerges in NIA languages as a reanalysis of the MIA DAT/GEN marking that appears systematically on a specific subset of non-subject arguments into a marker of accusative case. This reanalyzed accusative case is attested in both ergative and non-ergative clauses in the earliest texts of Old Marathi, supporting the hypothesis that accusative marking in ergative clauses is not part of any "de-ergativization" trajectory in the history of Indo-Aryan but rather an emergent effect of across-the-board changes in argument realization options for the languages.

Abbreviations

Glosses are as follows. "-" stands for a morpheme boundary, "=" for a clitic boundary.

ABL	ablative		IMPF	imperfective
ACC	accusative			(Old Indo-Aryan Present)
AOR	aorist		IMPFCT	Old Indo-Aryan Imperfect
DAT	dative		INF	infinitive
ERG	ergative		INST	instrumental
F	feminine		LOC	locative
FUT	future		M	masculine
GEN	genitive		N	neuter
GER	gerund		NEG	negation
IMP	imperative		NOM	nominative

PASS	passive		PROG	progressive
PERF	perfective		PV	verb particle
PFCT	perfect		SG	singular
PL	plural		SYNCR	syncretic (NOM/INST)
PTCL	discourse particle		VOC	vocative
PTCPL	participle			

Acknowledgements

Support from the National Science Foundation (NSF BCS-1255547/BCS-1660959.) is gratefully acknowledged.

References

Andersen, Paul Kent. 1986. Die *ta*-Partizipialkonstruktion bei Aśoka: Passiv oder ergativ? *Zeitschrift für vergleichende Sprachforschung* 99. 75–95.

Anderson, Stephen R. 1977. On mechanisms by which languages become ergative. In Charles Li (ed.), *Mechanisms of language change*, 317–363. Austin: University of Texas Press.

Anderson, Stephen R. 2004. Morphological universals and diachrony. In Geert Booij & Jaap van Marle (eds.), *Yearbook of morphology 2004*, 1–17. Dordrecht: Springer.

Bloch, Jules. 1965. *Indo-Aryan from the Vedas to Modern Times*. Translated by Alfred Master. Paris: Adrien-Maisonneuve.

Bubenik, Vit. 1996. *The structure and development of Middle Indo-Aryan dialects*. Delhi: Motilal Banarsidass.

Bubenik, Vit. 1998. *Historical Syntax of Late Middle Indo Aryan (Apabhramsa)*. Amsterdam: John Bejamins Publishing Co.

Clercq, Eva de. 2010. *The Apabhraṃśa of Svayambhūdeva's Paumacariu*. Delhi: Motilal Banarsidass.

Comrie, Bernard. 1978. Ergativity. In Winfred P. Lehmann (ed.), *Syntactic typology: Studies in the phenomenology of language*, 329–394. Austin: University of Texas Press.

Condoravdi, Cleo & Ashwini Deo. 2014. Aspect shifts in Indo-Aryan and trajectories of semantic change. In Chiara Gianollo, Agnes Jäger & Doris Penka (eds.), *Language change at the syntax-semantics interface*, 261–292. Berlin: Mouton de Gruyter.

Coon, Jessica & Omer Preminger. To appear. Split ergativity is not about ergativity. In Jessica Coon, Diane Massam & Lisa Travis (eds.), *Oxford Handbook of Ergativity*. Oxford: Oxford University Press.

Delancey, Scott. 1981. An interpretation of split ergativity and related patterns. *Language* 57(3). 626–657.

Deo, Ashwini. 2012. The imperfective–perfective contrast in Middle Indic. *Journal of South Asian Linguistics* 5. 3–33.

Dixon, Robert M. W. 1979. Ergativity. *Language* 55. 59–138.

Dixon, Robert M. W. 1994. *Ergativity*. Cambridge: Cambridge University Press.
Hock, Hans Henrich. 1986. *Principles of historical linguistics*. Berlin: Mouton de Gruyter.
Masica, Colin. 1991. *The Indo-Aryan languages*. Cambridge: Cambridge University Press.
Moravcsik, Edith. 1978. On the distribution of ergative and accusative patterns. *Lingua* 45. 233–279.
Peterson, John M. 1998. *Grammatical relations in Pāli and the emergence of ergativity in Indo-Aryan*. München: Lincom Europa.
Pischel, Richard. 1900. *Grammatik der Prākrit-Sprachen*. Translated from German by Subhadra Jha, 1981. Delhi, India: Motilal Banarsidass.
Plank, Frans (ed.). 1979. *Ergativity: Towards a theory of grammatical relations*. New York, NY: Academic Press.
Tsunoda, Takasu. 1981. Split case-marking patterns in verb types and tense/aspect/mood. *Linguistics* 21. 385–396.
Vale, Ramchandra N. 1948. *Verbal Composition in Indo Aryan*. Poona, India: Deccan College Postgraduate & Research Institute.

Chapter 17

OF as a phrasal affix in the English determiner system

Randall Hendrick

University of North Carolina at Chapel Hill

> This paper examines the distribution of *of* in the complex determiner system of English nominal expressions. The hypothesis is advanced that *of* in degree phrase inversion constructions (expressions like *more influential of a book*) is a phrasal affix in the sense of Anderson's classic work asserting the autonomy of morphological theory. The phrasal affix analysis can be distinguished from syntactic accounts that treat *of* as a syntactic head of phrase. It is argued that the phrasal affix account can capture *of*'s sensitivity to morphological sub-category features and to second position more naturally than the syntactic head of phrase analysis. In contrast to the syntactic head analysis, the phrasal affix analysis also has the advantage of explaining why *of* fails to exhibit typical syntactic properties such as selection, dislocation, conjunction, and adjunction of focus particles. The analysis extends neatly to the use of *of* in complex determiners involving fractions.

1 Introduction

Anderson (1992) has argued that the classical distinction between words and affixes can be profitably extended to the phrasal domain, a line of argumentation that is extended in Anderson (2005). On this view, some properties of constructions might be better understood if analyzed as involving affixes attached to phrases, parallel to the attachment of affixes to words. Anderson identifies the possessive *'s* as the prototype of such a phrasal affix, but (special) clitics more generally are identified as phrasal affixes in this sense. In the same spirit of enlarging the explanatory work of morphological theory into the domain of phrasal syntax, Anderson (2005) argues carefully that some verb second phenomena should be given a morphological explanation parallel to second position clitics. Both claims have proven provocative because they seem to compete with other rather popular analyses that make use of syntactic movement.[1] In this paper I will argue that *of*

---

[1] The true difference between these types of analyses may be less than meets the eye if one assumes a syntactic engine like that advocated in Chomsky (1995). There is a real substantive difference in the embrace of optimality theoretic explanations in Anderson (2005), but I will ignore that issue here in the belief that

Randall Hendrick. 2017. OF as a phrasal affix in the English determiner system. In Claire Bowern, Laurence Horn & Raffaella Zanuttini (eds.), *On looking into words (and beyond)*, 369–384. Berlin: Language Science Press. DOI:10.5281/zenodo.495454

as it occurs in the pre-determiner system of English provides compelling corroboration for the attempt to extend the range of morphological analysis into at least some areas of phrasal syntax because alternative syntactic explanations for these instances of *of* are relatively weak.

The center of our attention is on the formative *of* as it occurs in sentences like (1)-(2). These sentences appear to have some string before the indefinite D *a(n)* as part of the bracketed nominal constituent. They have been the focus of attention in a number of works, including Bolinger (1972), Bresnan (1973), Hendrick (1990), and Kennedy & Merchant (2000), among others. Kim & Sells (2011) present a wide variety of naturally occurring examples of the construction. A range of proposals have been offered to provide syntactic accounts of such sentences. Such sentences seem closely related to (4), in which the adjective abuts *a* directly without the cushioning of *of*, and (3), in which the adjectival constituent appears to the right of *a* rather than to its left. Kennedy & Merchant (2000) label (4) and (1) as *inverted DegP* (i.e., inverted degree phrases), suggesting that they originate as (3) and subsequently move to a higher position.

(1) It is difficult to find [more influential of a book]

(2) [How long of a vacation] did she take?

(3) It is difficult to find [a more influential book]

(4) It is difficult to find [more influential a book]

The degree phrases that are implicated in this inversion are semantically fairly heterogenous: a great many, like (1), appear to be evaluative in the sense of Keenan & Faltz (1985), but others, like (2), are extensional and amenable to a model theoretic interpretation.

There is another family of constructions that exhibit *of* preceding indefinite [$_D$ *a(n)*]. These are the complex determiners that have figured prominently in the study of the semantics of determiners and general quantifiers. Keenan & Stavi (1986) noted a range of complex determiners as part of their attempt to establish the semantic conservativity of a large set of determiners. Many of those determiners include *of* to the left of *a*, and denote proportions or frequencies, as noted in Peters & Westerståhl (2006). The examples in (5) list some of the complex determiners involving *of*.[2]

(5) a. They sang for half of an hour.
    b. She ate two thirds of an orange.
    c. The tornado damaged one quarter of an entire neighborhood.

---

the existence of phrasal affixes is conceptually independent of any commitment to optimality theoretic explanations.

[2] Peters & Westerståhl (2006) observe sentences like *two of ten interviewed persons have not answered the question*. The analysis in the text does not generalize to such an example because it does not exhibit [$_D$ *a(n)*]. Unlike the examples examined in the text, a plural NP is involved here as well. The *of* in this example would have to be accounted for separately. The fact that such examples can occur with *out* before *of* in contrast to (1) could be evidence supporting this inference.

17 OF as a phrasal affix in the English determiner system

My principal claim is that *of* is inserted in (6) as an affix to D̄, formally marking the relation between the head D and its specifier when α is phonologically non-null.

(6)
```
            DP
          /    \
       DegP     D̄
        |     /   \
        α    D    NP
             |    |
             a    β
```

This affixed *of* is evinced in all of (1), 2 and (5). As a marker of a formal relation, it itself is not semantically evaluated, and in this sense, it is not meaningful. As an adjunct, It is also syntactically inert for movement processes that target specifiers, heads or complements.[3]

I have framed my claim in terms of the DP hypothesis in (6), where D is the head of the entire nominal phrase. If one were instead to assume the NP hypothesis, where N is the head of the nominal phrase, we would have structures like (7). In this case we would say that *of* is adjoined as an affix of D̄, formally marking the relation between D̄ and the phrase α to its left when α is non-null.

(7)
```
              NP
            /    \
          DP      N̄
        /   \     |
      DegP   D̄    N
       |    / \   |
       α   D   β
           |
           a
```

2 OF as a phrasal affix

There is a prima facie case to be made that *of* in examples like (1) and (5) are phrasal affixes. The insertion of *of* is sensitive to morphological properties and shows second position effects common to other putative examples of phrasal clitics that Anderson identifies.

2.1 OF as sensitive to morphological properties

The inversion of degree phrases in examples like (1) does not apply generally. It is unnatural if the degree phrases are an instance of unmodified synthetic comparatives, as illustrated in (8).

---

[3] See Kaufman (2010) for a broadly similar analysis of Tagalog and other Austronesian clitic systems. In lexical theories of the sort that Anderson has generally favored, the syntactic inertness of the phrasal clitic will follow from the post-syntactic affixation of the phrasal clitic.

(8) a. We are shopping for a better/prettier/finer vase.
b. *We are shopping for better/prettier/finer a vase.
c. *We are shopping for better/prettier/finer of a vase.

When synthetic comparatives are modified, inversion of degree phrases, as in (9), is acceptable for some speakers, although others reject the inversion of degree phrases even when modified.

(9) a. *We have never seen a any better/prettier/finer vase.
b. We have never seen any better/prettier/finer a vase.
c. We have never seen any better/prettier/finer of a vase.

Speakers who reject all synthetic comparatives in (8)–(9) treat inversion of degree phrases as sensitive to that morphological class. Speakers who accept (9) in contrast to (7) appear to treat the inversion of degree phrases as sensitive to the prosodic contour of the phrase. Degree phrases composed of a single prosodic word, as in (8), are excluded. When more prosodic material is added, the same synthetic comparatives appear acceptable once again, as in (9).

The inversion is also sensitive to the morphological properties of the D to its right. The D cannot be definite, as shown by (10b) and (11b). Of the indefinite D's, it is only able to employ *a(n)*, and resists co-occurring with *some* or *no*.

(10) a. How long a novel did she write?
b. *How long the novel did she write?
c. *How long some novels did she write?
d. *How long no novel did she write?

(11) a. She wrote more fascinating a novel this time.
b. *She wrote more fascinating the novel this time.
c. *She wrote more fascinating some novels.
d. *She wrote more fascinating no novel.

If *a(n)* has the features [+INDEF, -PLURAL] while *some* is [+INDEF, +PLURAL] and *no* is [+INDEF] but lacks a feature specification for plurality, we can stipulate for the explicitness of description that degree inversion is restricted to D's that carry the feature specification +INDEF, -PLURAL.[4]

---

[4] It is worth noting that there is another formative *some* that is stressed and is definite. In addition, the table is offered only to make explicit the morphological use of *indefinite* in the text. It is not a theoretical claim. If we were to decide that we needed to specify *no* as PLURAL we could appeal to a feature CARD for cardinality and stipulate that degree phrase inversion could only occur with D's specified as -CARD. By the same token, we might have reason for adopting a morphological theory that avoided features altogether. In any scenario we need to restrict Degree Inversion to the D *a(n)* and not other members of the D class, much as /n/ is added to /a/ and not other indefinites.

17 OF as a phrasal affix in the English determiner system

Table 1: Co-occurrence of indefinite D's with count nouns

Indefinite D	Singular N	Plural N
a	a novel	*a novels
some	*some novel	some novels
no	no novel	no novels

2.2 OF as sensitive to second position

The *of* described in the preceding subsection is not capable of bearing stress. Nor is it able to appear initially in a nominal domain. When it surfaces, it always occupies second position in the nominal expression. To see this point, consider sentences like (12) that contain two pre-nominal adjectives. If *long* is part of a wh-phrase, it preposes (as in (12b)), and if *romantic* is part of a degree phrase, it may prepose, as in (12c). However, if both are before *a*, the result is the unacceptable (12d).

(12) a. *Jane Eyre* is a long romantic novel.
 b. How long of a romantic novel is *Jane Eyre*?
 c. *Jane Eyre* is more romantic of a long novel (than *Middlemarch*).
 d. * How long more romantic of a novel is *Jane Eyre*?

We begin to capture these facts if we assume that the preposed wh-phrase in (12b) and degree phrase in (12c) target a (unique) specifier position for movement (i.e. specifier of DP). We might accomplish this by way of (13a) that gives *a(n)* an EPP feature, parallel to what is often assumed for T. We could then posit a spell out rule that prefixes *of*.

(13) a. There is an optional feature on [$_D$ *a*] that requires a filled specifier.
 b. This feature is optionally spelled out as the phrasal prefix *of*.

3 Could *OF* be a syntactic head of phrase?

Some researchers have suggested that the *of* that occurs in the Degree Inversion structures is a syntactic head of phrase.[5] On this view we should assign *how long of a vacation* the structure in (14), whereas the proposal I have suggested in (13) is (15), if we assign *of* to the category F and adopt an item and arrangement approach to affixation in order to facilitate the comparison of the two theoretical viewpoints.[6]

---

[5] This structure is advocated in Kennedy & Merchant (2000) and is assumed in other work, for example, Borroff (2006). The labels of constituents differ in other analyses, in particular Matushansky (2002) and Kim & Sells (2011), but the constituency is broadly the same. The crucial point is to contrast analyses that treat *of* as a head of phrase from the analysis defended in the text where *of* is a phrasal affix.

[6] In a word-and-paradigm approach *of* might not be given a structural position at all but simply spelled out at the left bracket D̂. This point of view is probably closer to Anderson's. I believe that the structure in (15) gives some insight into why *of* occurs between the D and its specifier, as I explain at the end of this paper.

(14)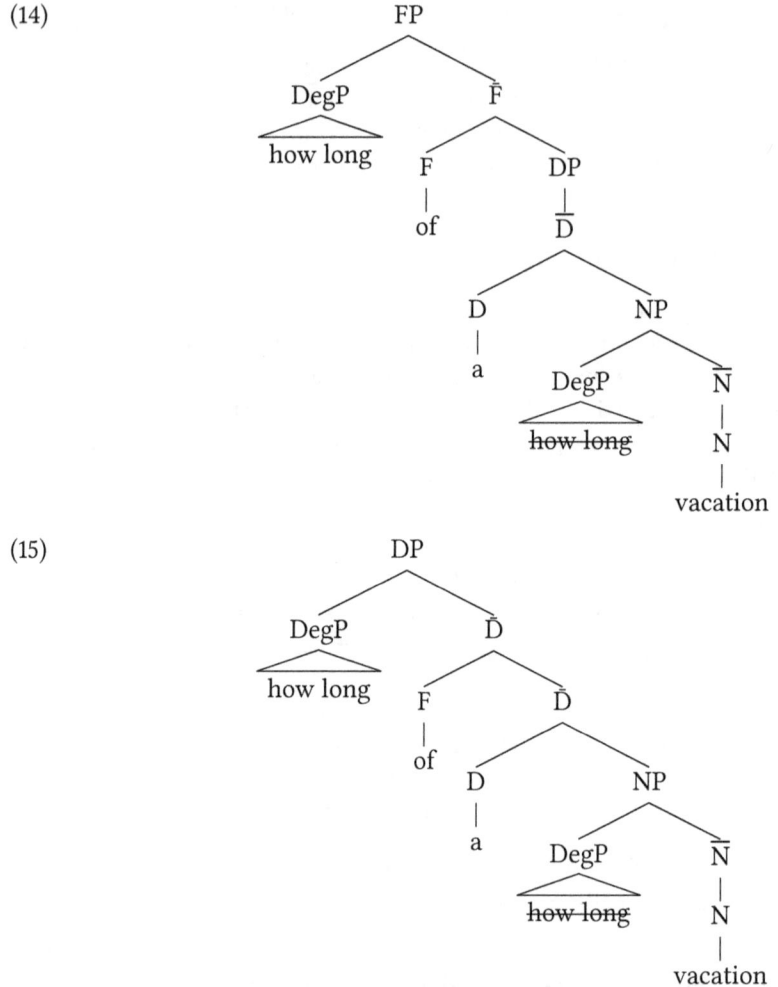

(15)

Some authors, following the lead of Bennis, Dikken & Carver (1998), have tried to treat *of* as parallel to a copular construction in which predicates have been claimed to invert in (16).

(16)   a. Jill was a much better friend.
        b. A much better friend was Jill.

Den Dikken (2006) offers an extended analysis in this vein over a range of languages. However, I find compelling the argumentation in Heycock & Kroch (1999) that rejects the inversion analysis in (16) in favor of viewing these as identity statements. On this view there is no basis for the parallel between (16) and (14), as Heycock and Kroch note.

Four reasons lead us to avoid a structure like (14).⁷ First, heads of phrases are able to stand in a selection relation with other heads of phrases. Yet, there is no lexical head that ever selects the FP of (14). This fact is accidental if *of* is a head of phrase, but it is a necessary consequence if it is not actually a head, as in (15).⁸ Second, the *of* phrase in (14) is immune to syntactic dislocation. Other *of* phrases are able to prepose or postpose, as shown in (17) and (18). It is also possible to strand *of* in examples parallel to (19). In this sense, they are syntactically active.

(17) a. Three of these books have been reviewed.
b. Of these books three have been reviewed.

(18) a. The announcement of the Nobel Prize in Chemistry was delayed.
b. The announcement was delayed of the Nobel Prize in Chemistry.

(19) What book did the newspaper publish a review of?

Yet (14) stands in contrast to examples like (17) in being unable to be preposed, postposed, or stranded. They appear to be syntactically inert.⁹

(20) a. More extensive of an experiment was in the planning stages.
b. *Of an experiment more extensive was in the planning stages.

(21) a. More extensive of an experiment was delayed
b. *More extensive was delayed of an experiment

(22) *What (kind of) experiment did the journal report more extensive of?

However, if *of* is not a head of phrase with its own phrasal projection as in (15), the lack of syntactic dislocation is expected.

A third challenge to the analysis in (14) involves conjunction. Locative prepositions like *on* can be repeated members of a conjunction with *only*, presumably for pragmatic reasons related to defeasing conversational implicatures that would otherwise obtain. The same seems true of *of* that introduces the complement of derived nominals like *destruction*.

---

⁷ Some work has suggested that the fronted *how long* must originate as a predicate adjective. See, for example, Wood & Vikner (2011) and Troseth (2009). This seems unlikely, at least for English. Expressions like *a beautiful dancer* are ambiguous between a predicative reading in which the dancer is beautiful and a non-predicative reading in which the dancer dances beautifully. The ambiguity is preserved in *how beautiful (of) a dancer*. This fact is surprising if the preposed degree phrase could only arise from a predicate adjective. These facts are general and can be reproduced with *a skillful manager*.

⁸ This challenge can be given a sharper formulation if we accept the stipulation that the complement of V is reserved for selected arguments of V. This stipulation requires that V select *of*, if *of* is a head of phrase. To the extent that every V that selects DP also selects this *of* we miss a regularity in the system of selection, a cost that is not incurred if *of* is provided as a phrasal affix. One can imagine mechanisms that allow *of*, if it were a head of phrase, to inherit argument properties of its complement DP, but such mechanisms would obscure the generalization that *of* is syntactically inert generally.

⁹ A reviewer observes that this second challenge can be met by stipulating that only maximal phrasal projections are available for movement. While this defense of the head of phrase analysis will side step the second challenge, it does not generalize to meet the other challenges. For this reason the phrasal affix account seems to me to offer a more straight forward explanation, all other things being equal.

(23) a. You may place the notebook on, and only on, the desk.
  b. The tornado caused the destruction of, and only of, one residence.
  c. You may place the notebook only on the desk.
  d. The tornado caused the destruction only of one residence.

In contrast, the *of* that appears with degree phrase inversion is unable to appear in similar conjunctions. If *of* is syntactically and semantically inert, as the phrasal affix analysis contends, it could not conjoin and co-occur with *only* to defease any conversational implicatures.

(24) a. You can't find more valuable of a proposal.
  b. * You can't find more valuable only of a proposal.
  c. * You can't find more valuable of, and only of, a proposal.
  d. How long of a vacation did they take?
  e. * How long of, and only of, a vacation did they take?

A fourth reason to be skeptical of the analysis in (14) is that it is unable to generalize to explain the appearance of *of* in fractions. Fractions have been treated as complex determiners since the classic work of Keenan & Stavi (1986) on the conservativity of determiners. Fractions exhibit this semantic property, a fact that is easy to explain if they are (complex) determiners, but that looks accidental if they are assimilated to constructions that take *of* to be a head of phrase, like the partitive constructions discussed in the next section. The use of *of* in the fraction in (25) parallels its use in degree phrase inversion. In both cases *of* is adjacent to the indefinite D *a(n)*, in both cases *of* is optional, and in both cases *of* lacks the ability to be lexically selected, or syntactically preposed or stranded as illustrated in (25). The phrasal affix analysis in (15) can provide a unified analysis, on the assumption that fractions occur in specifier of DP.[10]

(25) a. The recipe called for one half of a cup.
  b. * Of a cup the recipe called for one half.
  c. * A cup the recipe called for one half of.
  d. * The recipe called for one half of, and only of, a cup.

4 Partitive *OF* is a syntactic head of phrase

There is a second construction involving *of* which should be distinguished from *of* as a phrasal affix in Degree Inversion structures. This second type of construction is exemplified in (26) and has traditionally been labeled a partitive.

---

[10] It is tempting to extend this analysis of fractions to proportions like *six of ten adults don't vote*. Proportions like this do not make use of the D *a(n)* and are plural rather than singular. Without a more detailed analysis of the proper structural analysis of cardinals like *ten*, and an understanding of why proportions admit some form of dislocation (e.g. *(out) of (every) ten adults six don't vote*) the extension of the analysis will have to remain incomplete.

(26) a. She invited ten of the students to the party.
   b. Jack offered to buy any three of her paintings.
   c. Sandy knows the answer to the last (one) of those questions.

(27)
```
              DP
             /  \
            D    NP
                /  \
               N    PP
               |   /  \
               α  P    DP
                  |    |
                  of   β
```

The *of* in these partitives is a syntactic head of phrase, appearing in structures like (27), where *of* heads a PP. With the exception of *half (of) the*, partitive *of* appears obligatorily, like other heads of phrases and in contrast to the pattern of *of* with Degree Phrase Inversion. In addition, the *of* phrase can be topicalized as a syntactic constituent. In this respect it differs from *of* in Degree Inversion constructions like (20).

(28) a. Of the students, she invited ten to the party.
   b. Of her new paintings, Jack offered to buy any three.
   c. Of those questions, Sandy knows the answer to the last (one).

The *of* phrase can also be co-ordinated, a standard test for constituency. Examples are somewhat limited, presumably because of semantic restrictions on partitives. However, naturally occurring examples are not difficult to find.[11]

(29) a. If you accept it to be a part of you and of your life, you gain control of the illness.
   b. I try to be very aware of all of the students and of their strengths and weaknesses.

In contrast, Degree Inversion structures do not show the same support for co-ordination.

(30) a. *More expensive of a house or of a car would be hard to find.
   b. *How good of a novel or of a play did she write?

It is also possible to use expressions like *only* with partitive *of*, in contrast to the *of* in Degree Inversion structures.

(31) a. She invited ten of the linguistics students, and only of the linguistics students, to the party.
   b. *How good of a novel, and only of a novel, did she write?

---

[11] (29a) occurs at https://www.sicknotweak.com/2016/08/its-a-piece-of-you-make-it-yours/ as accessed September 24, 2016. (29b) occurs at http://www.ballet-dance.com/200505/articles/GloriaGovrin20041200.htm and was accessed September 24, 2016.

My claim that *of* in Degree Inversion structures is structurally distinct from *of* in partitives can be better appreciated if it is contrasted with the classic analysis presented in Bresnan (1973).[12] Bresnan suggests that *of* should be inserted in examples like (33) by an elegant rule like (32).[13]

(32) ∅ → *of* / Q_D N

(33) She has enough of a problem as it is.

(34) more of an egg

(35) more of the egg

(32) is similar to the phrasal clitic analysis I suggested earlier in that *of* is inserted rather than being treated as a syntactic head of phrase. It differs from the phrasal clitic analysis in two ways: (i) it does not require Q to be complex, and (ii) it does not require D to be *a(n)*.

The first of these differences is more apparent than real. I say this because Bresnan argues that *more* originates as a syntactically complex constituent *-er much*, and that this complex constituent is replaced in the course of the derivation with *more*. Bresnan analyzes *enough* in a parallel complex structure, with the difference that *enough* necessarily co-occurs with a null specifier. If this complex structure is correct, there is a point in the derivation where (34) is not a counter-example to our phrasal affix account of *of*; we only need to insure that the phrasal clitic *of* is inserted prior to *-er much* suppletion.

Consider now the second way in which rule (32) differs from the phrasal clitic analysis that I suggested in §2. By inserting *of* before any D, the rule in (32) loses the important empirical generalizations about the way in which *of* in (35) patterns like a syntactic head of a phrase in terms of conjunction, the distribution of *only*, and the possibility of movement. It does not code naturally the way in which the *of* in Degree Inversion constructions patterns differently along these dimensions. In the absence of other evidence, considerations of simplicity would make (32) quite attractive, but in this case, that very simplicity obscures important ways in which *of* patterns in distinct, rather than haphazard, ways. Moreover these distinct patterns have a semantic reflex. Peters & Westerståhl (2006) argue that semantic definiteness is a necessary characteristic of partitives. From this perspective the distinction between (34) and (35) that the phrasal affix analysis encodes is a natural one.

5 *OF* in complements of nominalization and syntactic Case theory

Since Chomsky (1981) it has been popular to say that the presence of *of* after nominalizations like *picture* in (36) is required to provide the nominalization's complement (*Mary*

---

[12] Stockwell, Schachter & Partee (1973) also distinguished partitives with *of* from other constructions where *of* surfaces. Selkirk (1977) distinguishes true partitives from pseudo-partitives like *two pounds of turkey* in part by pointing to differences in the distribution of *of* in the two types of constructions.

[13] Q in (32) is intended to denote quantified expressions like *more* and *enough*.

in this example) with Case. The details of the required derivation have rarely been made precise.[14] This imprecision is remedied in an interesting way in Kayne (2002). There, Kayne gives a careful description of the insertion of *of* in (36) and links it to an explanation for why the *of* in derived nominals like (36) can show stranding effects like (37), superficially in violation of subjacency requirements.

(36) John was admiring a picture of Mary.

(37) Who was John admiring a picture of?

(38) John was [$_{VP}$ admiring [$_{DP}$ a [$_{NP}$ picture of Mary]]]]

(39) John was [of [$_{KP}$ K − of [$_{VP}$ admiring [$_{DP}$ a [$_{NP}$ picture Mary]]]]]

If one thought that the structure of (36) was like (38) where *of* formed a constituent with the logical complement of picture, *Mary*, and was internal to the VP, one has trouble explaining in a non-stipulative fashion why (37) is not a subjacency violation (hence the debate between Bach & Horn 1976 and Chomsky 1977). Kayne's suggestion is that there is an abstract functional head K-*of* that is merged into the syntactic structure outside of the VP. On his assumption (defended in Emonds 2000) that every lexical noun requires Case valuation from an appropriate head, *Mary* will be unable to be so valued by the verb *admiring*. Instead it will be forced to move to specifier of K-*of*. The formative *of* is merged above KP and provides another specifier position for the remnant VP to move to. This derivation will provide the linear order observed in (36) without treating *a picture of Mary* as a constituent. In this way the challenge of (37) to subjacency is side-stepped.

Kayne sees a fundamental unity between the presence of *of* in nominalizations like (36) and its appearance in constructions like (40) and (41).[15]

(40) He has lots of money.

(41) They bought too big of a house.

Kayne suggests that *lots* in (40) and *big* in (41) have a nominal property and, for that reason, have a Case feature that needs valuation. Because they intervene between the verbs *has* and *bought* and *money* and *house* respectively, they prevent the verbs from valuing the Case feature on those nouns. This intervention forces the need for *of*. The derivation of (40) and (41) parallels (39). A functional head *of* (and K-*of*) is merged above VP. The nominals *money* and *house* raise to specifier of K-*of* where their Case features can be valued. The remnant VP subsequently moves to a specifier position on the left in order to get the appropriate left to right linear order.

Kayne's analysis of (36) makes *of* deeply syntactic in the sense that it takes *of* to be a head of phrase that enters into selection relations and that also provides a landing site for other putative syntactic operations. It is also syntactic in the sense that, whether it is ultimately judged to be true or not, it ultimately aims to resolve a syntactic problem (regarding the ability of (37) to avoid subjacency like island effects). The extension

---

[14] Harley & Noyer (1998) is a notable exception to this trend.
[15] Examples like (40) are the *pseudo-partitives* of Selkirk (1977).

of the analysis to the Degree Inversion construction in (41) is not deeply syntactic in the same sense: the *of* in (41) does not enter into other independently required syntactic operations. For example, it is unable to feed topicalization or clefting to strand the preposition:

(42)   a.   (It is) Mary John was admiring a picture of.
          b.   (It is) Money he has lots of.
          c.   * (It is) a house John bought too big of.

Further, the *of* in (41) is optional, while it is obligatory in (40) and (36). This fact leads Kayne to posit that in some situations we should stipulate that multiple Case evaluation is available, allowing both *big* and *house* to be Case valued by the verb, thereby circumventing the intervention effect. We should also note that unlike (36), there is no syntactic problem that the Case-intervention account of (41) provides a resolution to.

My claim is that there is no deeply syntactic foundation for the putative structure (14), and in this sense there is a fundamental asymmetry between the Case licensing *of* in (36) and the *of* that appears in Degree Inversion structures like (41). This lack of a deeply syntactic account of *of* in Degree Inversion constructions is what opens the door for the phrasal affix account.[16] Parity of reasoning prompts the question of whether the analysis of *of* in degree inversion structures like (41) is deeply morphological in any comparable sense. I would like to suggest that, rather than simply being a competing analysis, the phrasal affix analysis of *of* is deeply morphological, offering a response to a fundamental morphological puzzle. From this vantage, the contention that there are phrasal affixes poses the puzzle of how these affixes interact with the syntax of phrases and whether that interaction is principled in any morphological sense. Of course, Anderson's perspective on this puzzle is to say that phrasal affixes are syntactically inert because such morphological operations are ordered as a block after syntactic operations by virtue of the architecture of grammars. This paper has offered a different view that does not necessarily assume a late, or even a block, ordering of phrasal affixation. The analysis of *of* as a phrasal affix advanced here treats phrasal affixes as structural adjuncts, and by virtue of that structural relation, as inert to canonically syntactic operations such as movement.

6 Envoi

This paper has provided an analysis of *of* as it appears in Degree Inversion constructions and in fractions. It has been suggested that *of* in these constructions marks a formal relation between the indefinite D *a(n)* and its specifier, and that structurally it is

---

[16] It is possible to posit a syntactic feature, say +EPP, on some instances of *a(n)* and stipulate that the feature triggers *of* as its spell out phonologically. While I think this style of analysis could be descriptively successful, it would not be either deeply syntactic or deeply morphological as I have been using these terms. It would stipulate that *of* appears to the left of *a(n)*, for example, rather than linking its appearance to a second position effect.

a D̂ adjunct. This occurrence of *of* is distinct from its presence after derived nominals, which has been attributed by a number of researchers to Case theoretic requirements, and the *of* that appears in partitive constructions. This paper has defended the spirit of Anderson's claim that phrases can be provided with inflectional affixes by showing that the claim can offer an explanation for phenomena that are, from the syntactic point of view, unprincipled. In the process it draws attention to the kind of phenomena a morphological analysis is well suited for: formatives that are syntactically inert but sensitive to morphological class features, prosody, and to linear position (second position). I have also suggested that phrasal affixes should have the syntax of structural adjuncts. Whether this last point is valuable depends on a substantive theory of adjuncts and a comparison of other putative instances of phrasal affixes. For example, it has been suggested in Chomsky (1986), and argued for in some empirical detail in McCloskey (1996), that adjunction to lexically selected phrasal projections is prohibited. If this adjunction prohibition is correct, and if phrasal affixes must enter a derivation as adjuncts, we expect them to avoid adjunction to lexically selected phrasal projections. In effect, they must enter the derivation adjoined to a lower phrasal projection. I draw attention to this implication because it can provide some foundation for the second position effect that the phrasal affix *of* exhibits. The intuition here is that if *of* were adjoined to the DP, it would violate the prohibition on adjunction to a lexically selected phrase. It can only appear on the lower phrase, D̂ in (6), in effect producing a type of second positioning. Alternatively, one could stipulate that the phrasal affix *of* carries a constraint against appearing on the left edge of a phrase. A similar tension between syntactic and morphophonemic edge effects is present in explanations of verb second phenomena in various languages, as Anderson (2005) has observed, especially in regard to the description of Swiss Rumantsch. The choice between these explanatory crossroads will have to remain undetermined for the moment since it will inevitably depend on assumptions about the relationship between hierarchical order (i.e. c-command) and linear order. In forthcoming work on linking elements in Austronesian compounding, I hope to produce some reason for preferring the explanation in terms of adjunction that I sketched here.

References

Anderson, Stephen R. 1992. *A-morphous morphology*. Cambridge: Cambridge University Press.
Anderson, Stephen R. 2005. *Aspects of the theory of clitics*. Oxford: Oxford University Press.
Bach, Emmon & George M. Horn. 1976. Remarks on 'Conditions on transformations'. *Linguistic Inquiry* 7(2). 265–299.
Bennis, Hans, Marcel den Dikken & Norbert Carver. 1998. Predication in nominal phrases. *Journal of Comparative Germanic Syntax* 1. 85–117.
Bolinger, Dwight. 1972. *Degree words*. Vol. 53. Berlin: Walter de Gruyter.
Borroff, Marianne L. 2006. Degree phrase inversion in the scope of negation. *Linguistic Inquiry* 37 (3). 514–521.

Bresnan, Joan W. 1973. Syntax of the comparative clause construction in English. *Linguistic Inquiry* 4(3). 275–343.
Chomsky, Noam. 1977. On wh-movement. In Adrian Akmajian, Peter Culicover & Thomas Wasow (eds.), *Formal syntax*, 71–132. New York: Academic Press.
Chomsky, Noam. 1981. *Lectures on government and binding*. Dordrecht: Foris.
Chomsky, Noam. 1986. *Barriers*. Cambridge, MA: MIT Press.
Chomsky, Noam. 1995. *The minimalist program*. Cambridge: MIT Press.
den Dikken, Marcel. 2006. *Relators and linkers: The syntax of predication, predicate inversion, and copulas*. Cambridge, MA: MIT Press.
Emonds, Joseph E. 2000. *Lexicon and grammar: The English syntacticon*. Berlin: Mouton de Gruyter.
Harley, Heidi & Rolf Noyer. 1998. Mixed nominalizations, short verb movement and object shift in English. In Pius N. Tamanji & Kiyomi Kusumoto (eds.), *Proceedings of NELS 28*, 143–157. Amherst, MA: GLSA University of Massachusetts.
Hendrick, Randall. 1990. Operator movement within NP. In *The Proceedings of the Ninth West Coast Conference on Formal Linguistics*, 249–261.
Heycock, Caroline & Anthony Kroch. 1999. Pseudocleft connectedness: Implications for the LF interface level. *Linguistic Inquiry* 30(3). 365–397.
Kaufman, Daniel. 2010. *The morphosyntax of Tagalog clitics: A typologically driven approach*. Cornell PhD thesis.
Kayne, Richard S. 2002. On some prepositions that look DP-internal: English *of* and French *de*. *Catalan Journal of Linguistics* 1. 71–115.
Keenan, Edward L & Leonard M Faltz. 1985. *Boolean semantics for natural language*. Dordrecht, Netherlands: Reidel.
Keenan, Edward L & Jonathan Stavi. 1986. A semantic characterization of natural language determiners. *Linguistics and Philosophy* 9(3). 253–326.
Kennedy, Christopher & Jason Merchant. 2000. Attributive comparative deletion. *Natural Language & Linguistic Theory* 18(1). 89–146.
Kim, Jong-Bok & Peter Sells. 2011. The big mess construction: Interactions between the lexicon and constructions. *English Language and Linguistics* 15(2). 335–362.
Matushansky, Ora. 2002. *Movement of degree/degree of movement*. Massachusetts Institute of Technology PhD thesis.
McCloskey, James. 1996. The scope of verb movement in Irish. *Natural Language & Linguistic Theory* 14(1). 47–104.
Peters, Stanley & Dag Westerståhl. 2006. *Quantifiers in language and logic*. Oxford: Oxford University Press.
Selkirk, Elisabeth O. 1977. Some remarks on noun phrase structure. In Adrian Akmajian, Peter Culicover & Thomas Wasow (eds.), *Formal syntax*, 285–316. New York: Academic Press.
Stockwell, Robert, Paul Schachter & Barbara H. Partee. 1973. *The major syntactic structures of English*. New York: Holt, Rinehart & Winston.
Troseth, Erika. 2009. Degree inversion and negative intensifier inversion in the English DP. *The Linguistic Review* 26 (1). 37–65.

Wood, Johanna L. & Sten Vikner. 2011. Noun phrase structure and movement. In Petra Sleeman & Harry Parridon (eds.), *The Noun Phrase in Romance and Germanic: Structure, variation and change*, 89–109. Amsterdam: John Benjamins.

Chapter 18

Split-morphology and lexicalist morphosyntax: The case of transpositions

Andrew Spencer
University of Essex

> One of Anderson's many contributions to morphological theory is the claim that morphology is split between syntactically mediated inflection and lexically mediated derivation. In Minimalist morphosyntax all morphology is syntax. This means that the split morphology proposal is not meaningful for that model. In lexicalist models, however, the split morphology hypothesis manifests itself as a distinction between direct accessibility to syntactic representations (inflection proper) and lack of accessibility. However, there are construction types which bring the inflection-derivation distinction into question. One of these is the transposition, as illustrated by the ubiquitous deverbal participle. This is a mixed category, being at once a form of a verb yet having the external syntax of an adjective. It is thus unclear which side of the split participles fall. Similarly, participles seem to be an embarrassment for the Word-and-Paradigm models of inflection which have become dominant since Anderson first introduced them to contemporary theorizing. This is because they seem to require us to define a "paradigm-within-a-paradigm" (or "quasi-lexeme-within-a-lexeme").
>
> I provide an analysis of Russian participles within Stump's PFM2 model, deploying the model of lexical representation developed in Spencer (2013), which fractionates representations into more finely grained subcategories than is usual. I take a participle to be the adjectival representation of a verb, coded directly by means of a set-valued feature, REPR. I show how a set of rules can be written which will define the adjectival paradigm as a set of forms belonging to the overall paradigm of the original verb lexeme. The rules define a partially underspecified lexical entry for the participle ("quasi-lexeme"), which has essentially the same shape as the lexical entry for an (uninflected) simplex adjective. Thus, the participle's lexical entry is that of an adjective, just as though we were dealing with derivation, but it realizes the verbal properties of voice/aspect and it shares its semantics and lexemic index with its base verb, just as in the case of verb inflection. The participle thus straddles the split, but in a principled fashion.

Andrew Spencer. 2017. Split-morphology and lexicalist morphosyntax: The case of transpositions. In Claire Bowern, Laurence Horn & Raffaella Zanuttini (eds.), *On looking into words (and beyond)*, 385–421. Berlin: Language Science Press. DOI:10.5281/zenodo.495456

Andrew Spencer

1 Introduction: Morphological architecture

Since Anderson (1977) (re-)introduced to generative grammar the traditional notion of "word-and-paradigm", and particularly the ground-breaking work of Matthews (1972) on Latin inflection, morphologists have been grappling with the challenge of providing an adequate characterization of the key notions "word" and "paradigm".

Central to this debate has been the fate of the Bloomfield/Harris interpretation of the morpheme concept (Anderson 2015) and the notion of "Separationism" (Beard 1995). The "word" notion presupposes (at least) a word/phrase distinction. (In morpheme-based approaches no such distinction is necessary and all morphology and syntax can be subsumed under a model of morphotactics.) There are very well known problems with any attempt to find necessary and sufficient conditions for the 'concrete' instantiations of word – the phonological word, (inflected) word form, syntactic word, even. This is generally on account of incomplete grammaticalization, which strands constructions and formatives in a limbo between the status of function word – clitic – affix, compound element– affix, analytical syntactic construction – periphrasis and so on. However, the 'abstract' notions of word are no less problematic, specifically the lexeme and the morphosyntactic word (i.e. an inflected word form together with the morphosyntactic property array that it realizes). Defining the set of morphosyntactic words often requires us to make decisions about what constitutes a word form, which brings us back to the issue of clitics, periphrasis and so on. It also requires us to make sometimes arbitrary decisions about morphosyntactic property sets (MPSs) in the light of form-content mismatches such as (some types of) syncretism (Baerman, Brown & Corbett 2005), overabundance (Thornton 2012), defectiveness (Sims 2015), and deponency (Baerman et al. 2007), as summarized in Stump (2016a).

Inflectional properties, and word-oriented functional categories generally, such as definiteness (for nouns) or modality (for verbs) in English, seem to presuppose an inflection ~ derivation dichotomy that is notoriously hard to pin down. Broadly speaking it distinguishes the creation of new lexical items/units (generally, Saussurean signs pairing a cognitive meaning with a set of forms) from forms of a lexical item/unit. The component of grammar that defines new lexical units or lexemes is derivational morphology. However, as Spencer (2013) itemizes in some detail, such a (canonical) inflection/derivation dichotomy represents just two poles of a scale of types of lexical relatedness. Some of the intermediate types of relatedness pose problems for any clean characterization of the lexeme concept (part of the problem of "lexemic individuation", Spencer 2016b).

One way of characterizing the core of the inflection/derivation distinction is the notion of split morphology (Anderson 1982: and subsequent references). The essence of the distinction can be thought of as an interface claim: inflection interfaces directly with syntax ('inflection is what is relevant to syntax'). The obverse to this claim is that derivation interfaces with the lexicon, in the sense that derivation is what gives rise to expansion of the lexical stock (as well as defining relatedness between already fixed lexical entries), in other words derivation is 'what is relevant for the lexicon'. Anderson implements this architectural claim by saying that it is the rules of syntax themselves which define inflectional morphology.

18 Split-morphology and lexicalist morphosyntax: The case of transpositions

This move raises the important question of what model of syntax we are presupposing. Most versions of the Minimalist Program presuppose something very close to the model of morphotactics proposed by the American Structuralists: the atoms of representation are morphemes, morphology and syntax are identical (it is therefore a terminological choice whether we think of sentence construction as morphotactics or syntax), and the notions lexeme, word form, inflection, derivation, inflectional paradigm are at best heuristic descriptive terms which cannot be given a coherent definition within the model. The natural syntactic framework for investigating a word-and-paradigm, or rather, lexeme-and-paradigm approach to inflection is, perhaps, a lexicalist, or constraints-based, model (Miller & Sag 1997; Sadler & Spencer 2001; Sadler & Nordlinger 2006). In that case the question of split morphology takes on a somewhat different aspect. Rather than claiming that syntactic rules *construct* inflected forms as such, we must say that inflected forms, compared with derived lexemes, are permitted to interact in specific ways with syntactic representations, or equally that inflected forms bear properties which are visible to syntactic representations and principles.

The obvious way to implement this idea is to say that the abstract characterization of an inflected word includes a morphosyntactic description which overlaps with that of a corresponding syntactic representation. A concrete version of this type of overlap is seen in the form-content mapping, as defined in Stump's notion of paradigm linkage (Spencer & Stump 2013; Stewart & Stump 2007; Stump 2002; 2006; 2016a,b). Stump distinguishes morphological properties, the FORM paradigm, from syntactic properties, the CONTENT paradigm. By default these are homologous, but there are many instances of mismatch. For example, Latin syntax distinguishes singular and plural number and a variety of cases, including dative and ablative, but those two cases are never distinguished morphologically for any lexeme in the plural. On the other hand, Spanish verbs have two distinct subparadigms for the imperfect subjunctive but that distinction is nowhere reflected in the syntax. Other mismatches include deponency and periphrasis. To a limited extent we can say that the form-content paradigm distinction is a reflex of covert split morphology: such a distinction is not definable for derivational morphology.

In lexicalist models, the derivational morphology ~ lexicon interface operates over property sets which don't play a direct role in syntax. The hedge "direct" is important: typically, derivation *is* relevant to syntax, in the sense that it changes a lexeme's morphosyntactic class. More subtly, derivation may make appeal to argument structure realization (witness English Subject Nominalizations, *able*-Adjective formation and so on). But if it is assumed that lexemes have a representation of their word class argument structure and other relevant properties, then such syntactically expressed relations can be defined over lexical representations, as extensively argued in the constraints-based literature (see Wechsler 2014: for a review). This is effectively a statement of the doctrine of lexical integrity, at the abstract level of representation as defined by Ackerman & LeSourd (1997).

The conclusion to be drawn is that morphology interfaced with a constraints-based syntax needs to be split in essentially the way proposed by Anderson, but as an abstract architectural property, which sometimes bears a rather complex relation to concrete morphophonological expression. Inflectional morphology maps to syntactic representations in a way in which derivational morphology is unable to, while derivational morphology serves to define (specific kinds of) lexical relatedness. However, there remain interesting cases of violations of lexical integrity with derivational relations, in which syntax appears to have access to the internal structure of the derived word. This paper will argue that such phenomena require us to extend the scope of the split in morphology in a way that takes the notion of "lexeme" as syntactic atom seriously, and which ultimately provides conceptual motivation for a lexicalist interpretation of split morphology.

A case in point is the class of denominal (relational) adjectives in many languages, which allow one noun to modify another by taking on the morphosyntax of an adjective. In European languages, including English and Russian, such adjectives respect lexical integrity, in the sense that the base noun is opaque to syntax. For example, the base noun *kniga* 'book' in the Russian relational adjective *knižnyj* 'pertaining to a book/books' is opaque to agreement, government or any other syntactic process, just as in English the noun *tide* in *tidal* is opaque. For instance, the phrases *poderžannaja kniga* 'second-hand book' and *knižnyj magazin* 'book shop' do not gives us *poderžannaja/poderžannyj knižnyj magazin*, and although we can say *high tide* and *tidal barrier* we can't say **high tidal barrier*. The importance of these observations is that there are languages in which just such attributive modification into a derived adjective is possible (see the discussion of Tungusic and Samoyedic examples in Nikolaeva (2008), and also the detailed discussion of the Samoyedic language Selkup in Spencer 2013: Chapter 10).

The relational adjectives of Russian and English, however, share one important property with the Tungusic and Samoyedic pure relational adjectives, namely, they have precisely the same lexical semantics (cognitive content) as the base noun. This leaves us with the question of how to explain why in some languages relational adjectives are opaque and in others they are transparent to attributive modification.

Spencer (2013) argues that the crucial difference between true transpositional relational adjectives of, say, Selkup, and the "fake" transpositions of English/Russian is that true transpositions are effectively forms of the base noun lexeme, while the English and Russian relational adjectives are distinct lexemes, though ones which have a semantic representation identical to that of their base, what Spencer (2013: 275) calls a transpositional lexeme. Other types of transpositional lexeme include English property nominalizations (*kindness, sincerity, ...*), deverbal nominalizations such as *destruction*, and participial forms which have been converted into qualitative adjectives such as *(very) boring/bored, charming, excited, ...* A relational adjective which is a true transposition permits inbound attributive modification because it is, in an important sense, still a noun, just as a noun stem marked for number, case, possession or definiteness is still a noun.

One consequence of this reappraisal of the morphology~syntax interface is that the crucial divide can no longer be straightforwardly equated with a traditional distinction between inflection and derivation. It is not appropriate to think of a deverbal participle or a relational adjective as merely an inflected form of a verb or noun, because that participle or adjective will in general inflect like an adjective, not like a verb/noun. However, following Haspelmath (1996), Spencer (2013: Chapter 10) argues for an enrichment of the traditional notion of the inflection paradigm to include an attribute REPRESENTATION (taken from Russian descriptive practice). Thus, a participle is the adjectival representation of the verb, and as such it can have its own adjectival inflectional paradigm. It thus has the outward appearance of an autonomous lexeme, but appearances are deceptive. Rather, the transposition is a "quasi-lexeme", and the transpositional relationship therefore represents a particularly striking instance of a deviation from inflectional canonicity.[1] Like transpositions, these are not usually described under the heading of morphology-syntax mismatches, and like transpositions they are not discussed in Stump's (2016a) otherwise very detailed survey.

In the model of lexical representation argued for in Spencer (2013) the notion "form of a lexeme" in this somewhat extended sense is reflected very simply: all forms of a lexeme share their Lexemic Index. This leads us to propose a (no doubt too strong) hypothesis about the nature of the split in morphology:

Principle of Lexemic Transparency
Let D be a word derived by some regular morphological process from a word B, possibly of different morphosyntactic category. If morphosyntactic processes treat D in the same manner as they would treat the base word, B, even where the category of D is such that we would not otherwise expect it to be subject to such processes, then D is a form of the lexeme B (shares B's Lexemic Index).

I shall argue that the architectural equivalent of splitting inflectional from derivational morphology is this modification of the notion of lexical integrity: if morphology defines a set of forms of a lexeme, rather than defining a new, autonomous lexeme, then those forms will show lexical transparency. Derived lexemes, however, show lexical opacity (one reflex of which is the more familiar property of lexical integrity). This paper will illustrate that proposal on the basis of the behaviour of Russian deverbal participles. These are particularly useful. First, Russian adjectival morphosyntax is very clearly distinguished from noun or verb morphosyntax, so it is easy to show that the participles behave like adjectives. Second, the Russian past tense and conditional mood are expressed by a form which is historically a participle and which show participle-like agreement, but which has been reanalysed as a verb form (the l-participle). This contrasts in important ways with the true participles. Third, like many languages, Russian often converts its participles into true qualitative adjectives. These have (almost) exactly the same set of forms as the participles but their syntax is no different from that of a simplex adjective. The true participles are like the l-participle in showing lexical transparency with respect to the base verb. They therefore both appear on the inflectional side of the split morphology. This is because they are forms of the verb's paradigm, and do not constitute independent lexemes in their own right. They contrast with the converted participles,

---

[1] Other such deviations are certain forms of evaluative morphology (cf "the diminutive *form of* a noun") and grammaticalized argument structure alternations (cf "the passive/anti-passive/applied/causative *form of* a verb").

which are autonomous lexemes and hence opaque with respect to the verb properties of their (etymological) base lexeme.

2 Lexical representations and lexical relatedness

2.1 Introduction

Our discussion will require us to be explicit about a number of aspects of lexical representation and the way that words, in the broadest senses of the term, are related to each other. I shall adopt a generalized form of Stump's (2001) Paradigm Function Morphology, which I have called *Generalized Paradigm Function Morphology*, GPFM (Spencer 2013). The GPFM model is designed to permit us to use the machinery of PFM to describe types of lexical relatedness which go beyond normal inflectional morphology. It thus extends the lexical representations that morphology has access to by incorporating representations of syntactic properties and the lexical semantic representation of words. In GPFM lexemes have to be individuated by means of an arbitrary index, the Lexemic Index (defining something like the key field in a database). One of the reasons for this is because it is arguably not possible in the general case to individuate lexical representations of lexemes in terms of any of the linguistically relevant properties that can be ascribed to a lexical representation. In addition, however, the index serves an important role in distinguishing certain types of morphological relatedness.

2.2 Lexical representations

I begin with the descriptive representational apparatus required to characterize an inflected word form, taking inflection to be an uncontroversial category for the sake of exposition. I then generalize the representational format to provide a characterization of the lexemic entry.

A word has a minimum of three contentive attributes (together with a fourth, its Lexemic Index, LI): FORM, SYN(TAX), SEM(ANTICS). The SYN attribute records idiosyncratic selectional or collocation properties, but its main component is the argument structure attribute, ARG-STR. This records thematic argument arrays in the standard fashion (notated here as x, y, ... variables). However, it also includes a semantic function (sf) role.

For nouns and verbs the sf roles are the "R" and "E" roles respectively, familiar from the literature. The "R" (for "referential") argument is canonically associated with lexical entries whose SEM value belongs to the ontological class of *Thing*. It thus identifies those predicates that typically denote (concrete or abstract) objects and that can serve as the lexical head of a referring expression, i.e. a canonical noun. Thus, the "R" argument of TREE[2] corresponds to the "x" variable in the semantic representation $\lambda x.\text{TREE}(x)$. It is the argument that is the target of attributive modifiers: *(tall) tree* (Spencer 1999). See Lieber (2004: 16; 55–59) for concrete examples of the R role being deployed in morphology. The

---

[2] Where relevant, I adopt the standard convention of putting the name of a lexeme in SMALL CAPS.

18 Split-morphology and lexicalist morphosyntax: The case of transpositions

"E" (for 'event(uality)') argument (sometimes written as "e" or "s" (for "situation")) is canonically associated with lexical entries whose SEM value belongs to the ontological class of *Event*. It thus identifies those predicates that typically denote states or events (eventualities) and that can serve as the lexical head of a clause, i.e. a canonical verb. Thus, the "E" argument of FALL corresponds to the "e" variable in the (neo-Davidsonian) semantic representation $\lambda e,x.FALL(e,x)$. For attributive modification (principal role of the traditional adjective class) I assume a semantic function role labelled "A". This is coindexed to a noun's R sf role to represent attributive modification. All adjectives which function as attributive modifiers, including relational adjectives and participles, have an "A" semantic function role.

I assume the SEM attribute is essentially a formula in predicate calculus defined over the ontological types *Thing, Event, Property* (Jackendoff 1990), and perhaps others, corresponding loosely to the morphosyntactic categories of Noun, Verb, Adjective. I remain here agnostic as to whether the categories N, V, A are universal and if so, in what sense. I assume that some languages also have a category of Adverb, and also transpositional morphosyntax, adjective-to-adverb (as in English *ly*-suffixation), verb-to-adverb (gerund) and noun-to-adverb (found in Selkup, for example), but I will not have much to say about that category here.

Adpositions may mandate a further ontological category of, say, *Relation*, but I ignore that too. The SEM attribute can be thought of as a label for an encyclopaedic representation, such as $\lambda x.CAT(x)$ or $\lambda x,y.WRITE(x,y)$, but sometimes including linguistically encoded information relevant to semantic interpretation that cannot simply be consigned to an undifferentiated encyclopedia, for instance, $\lambda x,y,\delta.SIMILAR\_TO(x,y,\delta) \wedge CAT(y) \wedge DIMENSION(\delta)$, 'similar to the property of "cat" in some dimension, δ', or $\lambda x,y.AGAIN(WRITE(x,y))$ 'to re-write something'.

The FORM attribute is essentially a record of the word's morphology. Assuming an articulated inflectional system, complete with arbitrary inflectional classes and possibly other purely morphological, paradigm-based properties, the FORM attribute needs to specify all the information needed to locate the word form in the appropriate inflectional paradigm. The first property is the morpholexical category, MORCAT. This will typically be derived by default from the syntactic category of the representation (the SYN|CAT attribute),[3] but that default mapping is not infrequently overridden, sometimes in rather complex ways.

The next property is largely defined by reference to the syntactic category of the word form/lexeme, namely, the morpholexical signature, MORSIG. This specifies all those morphosyntactic properties for which an element of that MORCAT is obligatorily inflected. An inflected word has to have a specification of the morphosyntactic property set (or sets), MPSs, that it realizes. In the case of syncretism this may be a (natural or unnatural) class of MPSs. For example, a Russian adjective is obligatorily inflected for at least

---

[3] Given the complexities of category mixing it is better to dispense entirely with morphological or syntactic category labels such as "verb", "adjective". The required lexical classes can be defined over other aspects of representation much more efficiently and it is not difficult in constraints-based models to ensure that those aspects of representation are accessible to rules of morphosyntax. However, for convenience of exposition I will continue to talk of (morphological or syntactic) verbs, adjectives and so on.

the properties of number, gender and case, and these features are therefore listed in the MORSIG (a gradable adjective is also inflected for comparative and superlative forms). We will see in §5 that the conception of MORSIG assumed in Spencer (2013) can be enriched and extended to include the FORM-CONTENT paradigm distinction introduced in Stump (2006) and subsequent work.

Finally, the representation has to specify a phonological form for the word, through an attribute FORM|PHON. The precise characterization of the PHON entry, in general, will be given by the rules of inflectional morphology. I will assume that one aspect of the PHON representation will be a specification of the STEM on which the inflected form is based, but I ignore this refinement because it will not be relevant to the question of split morphology.

The actual inflected word forms of the lexeme are defined by inflectional rules, which apply to the pairing $\langle £, \sigma \rangle$, where σ is a complete, permissible feature set for the lexeme with Lexemic Index £. The lexemic representation has to include all the idiosyncratic morphological information relevant to a lexeme's realized paradigm. In the next subsection I summarize the way that the Paradigm Function can be generalized to define not only inflection but all the systematic forms of relatedness.

One aspect of these representations is worth noting. In keeping with the inferential-realizational assumptions underlying our model of inflection the SEM attribute remains constant for all inflected forms. In particular, there is no characterization at the level of the lexical representation of a word form (much less the level of lexemic representation) of the semantics of, say, tense or number. What this means is that in the syntax the VP which is headed by a past tense form verb may, ceteris paribus, be interpreted as referring to an event situated prior to speech time. However, since 'past tense' forms are also used in sequence of tense constructions, irrealis conditionals and so on, 'past time' is only the default interpretation.

2.3 Lexical relatedness

We can now ask what types of systematic relatedness lexemic entries (i.e. lexemes) can exhibit. Spencer (2013) argues extensively that we can find pretty well all the logically possible types as defined by the very crude but simple artifice of defining non-trivial differences in the four principal attributes, FORM, SYN, SEM, LI. For instance, if we consider pairs of representations of distinct lexemic entries, $£_1, £_2$, i.e. those with distinct LIs, then we can identify several different types of relatedness (usually all treated as derivation).

Suppose that the lexemes $£_1, £_2$ are distinct in FORM, SYN, SEM representations. Suppose also that the FORM/SEM representations of $£_2$ subsume or properly include (in some sense) those of $£_1$. Then we have standard (canonical) derivational morphology, DRIVE ⇒ DRIVER. Languages sometimes define derived lexemes without changing the FORM attribute at all, however. A case in point is that of adjectives which are converted wholesale to nouns without any change in morphology (Spencer 2002; see also the discussion of *Angestellte(r)* nouns in Spencer 2013). We will later see examples of derivation in which FORM/SYN/LI attributes are changed but without changing the meaning (transpositional lexeme).

Now let's consider what happens if we keep the LI constant, that is, we consider intralexemic relatedness. To begin with, let us assume that only the FORM attribute can change. In the canonical case this is the same as inflectional morphology. Ignoring for the present the transpositional interpretation of the participles as a verbal noun or as verbal adjectives, we can say that all inflected forms of SING are forms of a verb. We have to be a little cautious when referring to syntactic properties: the syntactic distribution of any given inflected form is, in general, distinct from that of other forms. The 3sg subject agreement form of a verb does not occur in the same syntactic positions as the 3pl form. The properties that give rise to these differences, however, are precisely the MPSs which bifurcate into FORM/CONTENT paradigms. This means that we must enrich lexical representations in the obvious way: FORM paradigms are defined over features typed as FORM features, and CONTENT paradigms are defined over features typed as SYN features, with the proviso that the two sets of features are identical by default. Modulo the CONTENT paradigm, then, in canonical inflection the SYN value of a given word form is identical to that of the other forms of that lexeme. This means that most inflection is what Booij (1994) would call contextual inflection.[4]

Likewise, the lexeme SING denotes the same event type in all of its inflected forms, and in that sense all word forms share the same SEM representation. In Spencer (2013) I argue that there are certain types of inflection that enrich the semantic representation of the base lexeme, whilst remaining inflectional. Certain kinds of Aktionsart marking, as well as semantic case marking often have this characteristic, as do causative argument structure alternations. In traditional descriptions of languages with such inflection we often find terminological vacillation, as linguists are unsure whether to label, say, the iterative form or the causative of a verb inflectional or derivational (and similar problems afflict evaluative morphology).

The GPFM descriptive framework proposed in Spencer (2013) generalizes the PFM model so that all forms of lexical relatedness, from contextual inflection to derivation, are defined over four principal attributes of a lexical representation. This requires us to generalize the notion of the Paradigm Function to that of a Generalized Paradigm Function (GPF), which is like the Paradigm Function except that it consists of four component functions, $f_{form}, f_{syn}, f_{sem}, f_{li}$. For canonical derivation the GPF introduces non-trivial changes to all four components (including the LI). For the converted adjectives and *Angestellte(r)* nouns the f_{form} function has no effect (it can be thought of as a kind of identity function). For most inflection, the $f_{syn,sem,li}$ functions are the identity function, because the GPF simply realizes inflectional properties of the lexeme at the FORM level.

In the GPFM model the lexemic representation is defined in terms of the Lexemic Index and a completely underspecified (empty) feature set, u, for example, $\langle \text{PUT}, u \rangle$, a special case of the GPF. This maximally underspecified GPF defines just those properties of a

---

[4] This includes Booij's parade examples of inherent inflection, past tense and plural number. See Spencer (2013: 77–82) for critical discussion of Booij's distinction.

lexeme (identified by its Lexemic Index) that are completely idiosyncratic and completely unpredictable. However, although such a representation reflects the traditional notion of a maximally compact, non-redundant dictionary entry, it is not a representation that can serve as the direct input to rules of inflection. This is because the lexemic entry has to be specified for those inflectional properties that it can and must inflect for. This set is defined by the morphological signature, MORSIG. In Spencer (2013: 199) I make this rather obvious point explicit in the *Inflectional Specifiability Principle*. In the current context this can be stated as follows: a lexeme is inflected for a given MPS, iff that MPS is defined in its MORSIG.

In Spencer (2013) I treat the MORSIG attribute as part of the FORM paradigm of a lexeme. However, we know that the FORM and CONTENT paradigms of a lexeme can differ substantially. For this reason, it is necessary to enrich the SYN attribute of a lexemic entry with a (possibly distinct) MORSIG attribute. The values of the (FORM and CONTENT) MORSIG attribute are for the most part predictable from other aspects of the lexical representation. First, the FORM MORSIG attribute is generally projected from the CONTENT MORSIG and by default the two attributes are identical. Second, to some extent the meaning of the lexeme can determine the content of the MORSIG attribute. Most importantly, however, the MORSIG (which, recall, is essentially a record of the properties for which a lexeme inflects) is largely projectable from various aspects of the SYN attribute, notably the ARG-STR attribute. Thus, a lexeme with the SYN|ARG-STR value $\langle E \langle x, ...\rangle\rangle$ (i.e. a verb) will by default have the syntax and morphology of a verb. The lexemic representation needs to be enriched to include purely idiosyncratic information, such as irregular stem forms, irregular inflections, defective cells or subparadigms, and so on. Technically, this can easily be achieved in GPFM by defining very specific functions for particular properties over the LIs of the lexemes concerned. For instance, the irregular past tense of PUT can be defined by a function defining the $STEM_{pst}$ form for the pairing $\langle PUT, u\rangle$: GPF($\langle PUT, \{STEM_{pst}|PHON\}\rangle$) = /pʊt/ or similar. This will override any less specific (in practice, any other) statement of past tense morphology. Similarly, a defective lexeme such as FORGO (lacking a past tense form) will have a tense-specific GPF($\langle FORGO, \{tense:pst \}\rangle$) = undefined. This again will override any other statement, including the GPF($\langle GO, \{tense:pst \}\rangle$) = /wɛnt/, which applies to one other verb based on GO (cf *underwent*) and hence is less specific.

The role of the MORSIG attribute can be simply illustrated by the English plural. Any lexeme with the SYN|ARG-STR|$\langle R \rangle$ value licenses MORSIG|num:{sg, pl}, provided that its SEM attribute specifies it as a count noun. For a mass noun the MORSIG value will be just num:{sg}, while for a plurale tantum noun it will be num:{pl}. The {pl}, resp. {sg} values for such nouns are therefore undefined, so that a GPF($\langle SINCERITY, \{num:pl\}\rangle$) or GPF($\langle SCISSORS, \{num:sg\}\rangle$) will not correspond to any legal output.

In summary, I assume a representation for a dictionary entry of a very traditional kind: it is minimally redundant, specifying just the unpredictable phonological and semantic information, together with any morphosyntactic information that cannot be projected from the phonological and semantic specifications. For an entirely well-behaved lexeme belonging to the default inflection class for that word category, this is all the information that is required, but that is only because the morphological signature can be projected from that entry too.

To all intents and purposes GPF collapses with PFM for most cases of inflectional morphology. However, the model is designed to cover all types of lexical relatedness, up to regular derivation, but using essentially the same machinery as PFM. For instance, for the derivation of a Subject Nominal such as DRIVER from DRIVE we would have the partial GPF shown in (1), where $\mathcal{V}$ is the Lexemic Index of a verb lexeme and δ is the derivational feature which defines the Subject Nominal formation process.

(1)   a. $f_{li}(\langle \mathcal{V}, \delta \rangle) = \Delta(\mathcal{V})$, where Δ is a function over LIs corresponding to the derivational feature δ

      b. $f_{sem}(\langle \mathcal{V}, \delta \rangle) = [\text{Thing } \lambda x, \text{PERSON}(x) \wedge \mathcal{P}'(x)]$, where $\mathcal{P}'$ is a suitable form of the semantic representation of the lexeme $\mathcal{V}$

      c. $f_{syn}(\langle \mathcal{V}, \delta \rangle) = u$

      d. $f_{form}(\langle \mathcal{V}, \delta \rangle) = Z \oplus er$, where Z is the δ-selected stem form of $\mathcal{V}$

This corresponds to a novel lexemic entry which is exactly like that in (1) except that it is defined over the pairing $\langle \Delta(\mathcal{V}), u \rangle$. If DRIVE is the LI of the verb DRIVE, then $\Delta(\mathcal{V})$ is the LI of the derived lexeme DRIVER and $\langle \Delta(\mathcal{V}), u \rangle$ defines its lexemic entry.

The representation in (1) lacks any syntactic specification. This is because that specification can be given by a default mapping from the SEM attribute, by virtue of the Default Cascade (Spencer 2013: 191–194). Under that principle, regularly derived lexemes have their principal morphosyntactic properties projected from their semantic representations, in accordance with the notional model of parts of speech. Thus, DRIVER is of ontological category *Thing* and therefore by default has the semantic function role R. I assume that the SEM attribute includes an indication that the lexeme denotes a countable *Thing* so that the lexeme licenses the full MORSIG|NUM:{sg, pl}. However, the lexeme in (1) is derived, not simplex. In Spencer (2013) I propose a Category Erasure Principle, under which the morphosyntactic properties of a base lexeme in derivation are deleted so that they can be overwritten by the Default Cascade. However, given maximally underspecified lexemic entries to start with this is probably not necessary: the word formation rule interpretation of the GPF takes the only information it has available in a lexical entry, that is the phonology of the root and the meaning, and modifies it, say, by adding an affix, and by enriching the SEM representation systematically, for instance, by adding a predicate. The Default Cascade then specifies the underspecified properties, including the two MORSIG representations. If the base lexeme's entry includes non-default specifications such as irregular inflected forms or non-standard argument realization, these will override the Default Cascade. Illustrative examples of simple inflection and derivation are provided in the Appendix.

I have sketched the GPFM approach to inflection on the one hand, and standard derivation on the other hand. Non-standard types of derivation are handled by overriding some of the defaults in the GPF. However, this still leaves us with the somewhat intriguing, but very widespread set of relatedness types in which FORM/SYN attributes are altered, much as in derivation, but without changing either the SEM representation or, crucially, the LI attribute, one of the class of relatedness types often called a "transposition". The parade example of this type is, perhaps, the deverbal participle, the 'adjectival representation' of a verb.

Transpositions pose particular difficulties for a simple interpretation of the inflection-derivation divide (and, indeed, for any architecture with the equivalent of split morphology): on the one hand, a participle is generally taken to be 'a form of' the base verb (regular participles are never given their own entry in a traditional dictionary, for instance). On the other hand, a participle is morphologically and syntactically a kind of adjective. If morphology is split, on which side do transpositions fall?

3 Paradigm Linkage: the problem of transpositions

Spencer & Stump (2013) (see also Bonami & Stump 2016; Stump 2016a) describe a variant of the Paradigm Function Morphology model, PFM2, which explicitly distinguishes two types of paradigm. FORM paradigms determine the mapping between MPS's and the word forms realizing them; CONTENT paradigms determine the set of grammatical distinctions a lexeme needs to make in a syntactic representation. The two paradigms are related by rules of paradigm linkage. In the default case the two paradigms align perfectly: a morphological plural noun is syntactically plural and vice versa. However, there are numerous mismatches. A simple case in point is provided by English perfect and passive participles. These have distinct syntax (they collocate with different auxiliaries, and only the passive participle can be used attributively), but they are never distinguished morphologically. Thus, the (single) FORM property (say, VFORM:en-ptcp, or the output of a function f_{en}, as in Aronoff 1994) has to map to two CONTENT properties. Stump (2016a) provides an extensive survey of the principal types of mismatch encountered in the world's inflectional systems.

I will argue that we can regard the FORM/CONTENT paradigm distinction as a reflex of split morphology for constraints-based lexicalist models of syntax. The reasoning is very simple — no corresponding FORM/CONTENT distinction can be mandated for derivation. Indeed, given standard PFM2 assumptions it is difficult to imagine what such a distinction could mean.

Incorporating the FORM-CONTENT paradigm distinction into GPFM has consequences for the way in which lexical representations are organized. We have seen that the FORM attribute of a lexical representation is defined in part in terms of its MORSIG, which determines precisely those properties a lexeme must inflect for. In the original GPFM model the MORSIG attribute is only defined at the level of FORM paradigms, therefore. Since CONTENT paradigms are not always congruent to FORM paradigms we will need to draw the appropriate distinction in lexical representations. The obvious way to do this is to assume that each lexeme is associated with *two* (at least) MORSIG attributes, one of which is a value of the FORM attribute and the other of which is a value of the SYN attribute. We can call these f-MORSIG, c-MORSIG respectively.[5]

Stump (2016a: 253) defines paradigm linkage in terms of the Paradigm Function and a ***Corr*** function. Given a lexemic index £, a set of MPSs σ, τ, and a stem form, Z, the function ***Corr***(⟨ £,σ⟩) delivers a form correspondent ⟨Z,τ⟩, such that if PF(⟨Z,τ⟩) = ⟨w,τ⟩, then PF(⟨£,σ⟩) = ⟨w,τ⟩. By default the FORM and CONTENT features are identical, that is the set σ = τ, as defined by a set of property mappings (***pm***), that is, ***pm***(σ) = σ. However, the function ***pm*** is called upon whenever there is a mismatch between FORM and CONTENT properties. This is the case, for instance, with deviations such as syncretism, deponency and so on. In the case of active~passive deponency the property mapping maps the morphological passive voice forms to the syntactic active paradigm and leaves the morphological active voice forms undefined.

We can ask how paradigm linkage would work for derivation, by taking the example of a derivational feature, δ, such as the privative denominal adjective feature, *privadj*, which derives *friendless* from *friend*, as described in Stump (2001:252–60).[6] Here, we are dealing with trivial (two-celled) paradigms, so that the featural mismatches of inflectional paradigms will not be found, and we can work with just a single derivational feature, δ.

(2) Let ***Corr***(⟨FRIEND, *privadj*⟩) be the correspondence function for *privadj* applied to the lexeme FRIEND.
Corr(⟨FRIEND, *privadj*⟩) = ⟨Z,δ⟩, where Z = |friend|, the stem of FRIEND, and δ = *privadj*. If PF(⟨Z,δ⟩) = ⟨w,δ⟩, then PF(⟨£,δ⟩) = ⟨w,δ⟩, hence, PF(⟨FRIEND, *privadj*⟩) = ⟨friendless, *privadj*⟩.

This seems very straightforward, but there is a hidden difficulty, not immediately apparent from a language like English, with limited inflection. Consider a hypothetical language just like English but in which nouns and adjectives have entirely different inflectional paradigms, or, indeed, consider a derivational process such as that of Subject Nominalization which derives DRIVER from DRIVE. What we have to ensure is that the output lexeme is (automatically, by default) inflected as a noun, as opposed to the base lexeme which is inflected as a verb. As it stands, the Paradigm Function applied to a pairing of Lexemic Index and derivational feature will not deliver what Stump calls the realized paradigm of the output lexeme. At best, it might define the (or an) uninflected stem form of the derived word. Moreover, without significantly altering the nature of the ***Corr*** function it will be impossible to define additional lexical information such as

---

[5] A number of authors have proposed that cells in a lexeme's paradigm can be realized by multiword, periphrastic, constructions (Sadler & Spencer 2001; Brown et al. 2012; Bonami 2015). Popova & Spencer (forthcoming), following suggestions by Bonami (2015), propose that such constructions demand additional CONTENT feature sets specifically to define the content of the periphrastic expression, which is often at odds with the default feature content of the words which make up that expression. Periphrasis therefore provides substantial motivation for a FORM/CONTENT or m-/s-feature (Sadler & Spencer 2001) distinction.

[6] Stump does not discuss derivation, or, indeed, transpositions in his works on paradigm linkage.

inflectional class membership, idiosyncratic stem forms or other deviations from default inflection, or indeed any non-default or purely morphological property of the output.[7]

A direct solution to this problem might be to enrich the content of the derivational feature, δ, so that it incorporates the full set of paradigmatic oppositions realizable by the derived lexeme. Thus, the Subject Nominal feature (say *subjnom*) could be defined as the complex [*subjnom*, NUMBER:α]. This would mean that we would have to define the Paradigm Function so that it defines each inflected form of the output lexeme, rather than defining an underspecified lexemic entry, which then gets inflected by the standard inflectional rules applying to words of that category. For instance, the Paradigm Function could take the form PF(⟨DRIVE,{*subjnom*, NUMBER:sg}⟩) = ⟨driver, {*subjnom*, NUMBER:sg}⟩, PF(⟨DRIVE,{*subjnom*, NUMBER:pl}⟩) = ⟨drivers, {*subjnom*, NUMBER:pl}⟩. We could call this approach the 'full-listing approach'.

Now, the full-listing approach would have the rather peculiar consequence that the word forms {*driver, drivers*} would be inflected forms of the verb DRIVE, and there would be no such thing as a DRIVER lexeme. Not only is this entirely counter-intuitive, and at variance with any sensible distinction between inflection and derivation, it becomes even more counter-intuitive when we see recursive derivation. It would entail that the noun *reprivatizability* was an inflected form of the adjective *private*. The problem is that the ***Corr*** function needs to be able to define not a cell in a realized paradigm (what syntacticians refer to, misleadingly, as the lexical entry of a word(form)), but it has to define a featurally underspecified lexemic entry (an autonomous dictionary entry in traditional terms). I therefore reject the full-listing approach in favour of that adopted in the GPFM model.

We are now in a position to examine the case of transpositions. The problem we must address is how to ensure that the transposition is assigned to its own inflectional paradigm, proper to its new morphosyntactic category, whilst still in some sense remaining part of the inflectional paradigm of the base lexeme. Recall that I have proposed adopting a class of features, [REPRESENTATION:{...}] to define the paradigm space of a transposition. I now consider the way this feature can be deployed to define the inflectional paradigm-within-a-paradigm of a transposition. Let ρ = [REPR:κ] for some transpositional relation κ, e.g. a verb-to-adjective (participle) transposition. I assume that the GPF applied to the pairing ⟨£,ρ⟩ defines a partially specified representation for the transposition. Normally, when the Paradigm Function applies to a pairing of LI and MPS the MPS has to represent a complete and coherent set of features sufficient to define the inflected form. However, this is not strictly speaking a property of the PFM system itself. In principle, we could define a partial paradigm for a lexeme by reference to just a proper subset of the features required to define any fully inflected word form. For instance, suppose that verbs in a language inflect for a variety of tense-aspect-mood-voice (TAMV) series, and that in addition they show subject agreement. We could, in principle, define the stem sets for the TAMV categories independently of the agreement morphology, by simply not specifying the subject agreement properties, effectively defining a set of "screeves" for the language (as in the Georgian descriptive tradition, Anderson

---

[7] It is also not clear how the additional semantic predicate of the output would be defined.

1992: 141–45). This makes use of the same notion of feature underspecification used in GPFM to define derivation, but relativized to a specific feature set.

The GPF for a transposition has to specify the derived morphosyntactic category, κ, and, by default, the f-/c-MORSIG attribute, associated with that category, together with additional morphological properties inherited from the base, such as TAMV properties. If the Paradigm Function were to apply in the same way for transpositions as for other inflected forms then the *Corr* function would have to provide the form correspondents for each inflected form, but it would not be able to provide a lexemic entry for the uninflected transposition. In other words, standard application of PFM2 principles would give rise to a full listing interpretation of the paradigm. It would not be possible to provide any characterization of the transposition as a quasi-lexeme (see p. 389). This generates many of the same conceptual and technical problems as the application of *Corr* to derivation. One additional consequence is that it would be difficult to describe the very common situation in diachronic change in which a participle is reanalysed as a qualitative adjective, often without significantly changing the lexical semantics of the original verb lexeme (transpositional lexeme). If we treat the participle as akin to a lexeme, then we can easily define the diachronic reanalysis over that representation, just as we would for ordinary derivational conversion. One of the problems with the full-listing approach is that it is not clear how we could permit the transposition to inherit MORSIG properties of the derived category (Adjective in the case of participles). We therefore need to define the GPF in such a way that it allows us to define a quasi-lexeme as part of the paradigm of the base.

First note that application of the Default Cascade to define derived categories is entirely excluded in the case of (pure) transpositions, since these preserve the meaning, and hence the ontological category, of their base; indeed, this is the whole point of a transposition. The most natural assumption is that the transpositional morphosyntax effects a shift in the syntactic categorization and that morphological recategorization falls out as a consequence. (In fact, the extent to which the transposition acquires derived categorial properties and loses those of its base is subject to a good deal of cross-linguistic variation, tempered by poorly understood typological tendencies. See Malchukov (2004) for discussion in the context of action nominal transpositions.) This is effectively a weaker instantiation of the Default Cascade. Following Spencer (1999; 2013), I will assume that the shift in syntactic representation is actually a modification of the argument structure representation; specifically, the definition of a complex sf role (see below). The crucial point is that the transpositional GPF changes the SYNCAT value of the base lexeme to that of a mixed category and this, ceteris paribus, will automatically entrain a shift in the morphological category and hence the MORSIG attributes.

The basic machinery is only hinted at in Spencer (2013: Chapter ten). In order to develop an explicit account we first need to refine the definition of the REPR(ESENTATION) attribute. I will therefore assume that the REPR feature takes an ordered pair as value, not a singleton element, [REPR:⟨κ,λ⟩], where κ, λ range over lexical categories. Thus, a participle represents a verb as an adjective and hence bears the specification [REPR:⟨V,A⟩], while a predicatively used noun will have the specification [REPR:⟨N,V⟩]. We then couple these feature values to syntactic category specifications in the obvious way, stated informally in (3).

(3) Given [REPR:⟨κ,λ⟩], for λ = N, V, A.
Then SYNCAT = λ,
and by default, MORCAT = λ

In the GPFM framework the [REPR] attribute will be associated with an appropriate enrichment of the semantic function role of the ARG-STR attribute. A verb base ARG-STR includes E, the event semantic function role, ⟨E, ⟨x,...⟩⟩. That of the participle is enriched by addition of the A semantic function role, to become (simplifying somewhat) ⟨A_i⟨E, ⟨x_i,...⟩⟩⟩, where the co-indexing indicates that the element of which the participle is predicated is an element of the argument array of the base verb lexeme (the highest such argument for Indo-European type participles, though not necessarily so in other languages). This representation reflects the mixed categorial nature of the participle. While its main external syntax (Haspelmath 1996) is now that of an adjective, it retains the eventive ARG-STR of the base verb, which permits it, on a language specific basis, to realize a number of verb properties. These typically include the realization of internal arguments as verb dependents (complete with quirky case marking). The E semantic function role also permits modification by adverbials targeting event semantics.

Exactly which adjectival properties are acquired and, more crucially for participles, which verb properties are lost or retained, differs cross-linguistically. The Indo-European participle, for instance, typically retains the active~passive alternation, but may also retain aspect (Slavic) or tense (Sanskrit; Lowe 2015). As attributive modifiers, the Indo-European participles can only modify a noun which expresses the participle's highest (subject) argument, effectively making them into heads of subject-oriented relative clauses, but in other languages there is much greater freedom in the choice of argument that can be relativized on by the participle (for discussion see Spencer 2016c).

In §5 'Paradigm linkage rules for Russian' I present a more detailed analysis of Russian participles in which this basic schema for transpositions is expanded upon.

4 Russian participles

In this section we look at the set of four participles that are regularly associated with Russian verbs. Before we can consider these, however, we need to understand Russian verb inflection and the place of the participles in that system. I begin with an overview of the grammatical distinctions as a whole made by verbs, in other words, the CONTENT paradigm, before considering the actual morphological forms themselves. We encounter the familiar problem that there is no consensus on just what the oppositions are and how they relate to each other, and so some of my descriptive decisions will be motivated in part by expositional convenience. I illustrate with the second conjugation transitive verb UDAR′IT′ 'hit', whose imperfective aspect series is formed by shifting to the first conjugation, UDAR′AT′.

18 Split-morphology and lexicalist morphosyntax: The case of transpositions

The simplest categories are the infinitive and imperfective ("present") and perfective ("past") gerunds. These are indeclinable. Telic verbs such as UDARʹITʹ/UDARʹATʹ, 'hit', require imperfective and perfective aspect forms for most of their paradigm. We can distinguish three moods, indicative, imperative, conditional. The imperative is straightforward and I will ignore it here. The indicative distinguishes three tenses, present (for imperfectives only), past, future. I return to the conditional below.

Transitive verbs show an active~passive voice opposition. However, the voice system is complicated by the fact that imperfective verbs are able to take the reflexive suffix -sʹa/sʹ. This has the basic function of giving a reflexive/reciprocal meaning (though similar meanings can also be expressed with fully-fledged reflexive/reciprocal pronouns). The reflexive form also has a wide variety of other uses, including the passive (Gerritsen 1990). This means that we should set up a reflexive voice category and define the imperfective passive in terms of this, but I set this task aside since it is not directly relevant. The perfective verbs express the passive alternation periphrastically, with BE + perfective passive participle. At the level of the CONTENT paradigm we need to be able to define [VOICE:{act,pass}] for both perfective and imperfective verbs, therefore.

Present tense is expressed morphologically, but only for imperfective verbs. There is no dedicated tense marker, and in effect, present tense is realized by the person/number subject agreement morphology. The future tense is expressed periphrastically by imperfective verbs, by means of BE + the infinitive form. For perfective verbs the future is expressed by a paradigm which is essentially the same as the present tense paradigm for imperfective verbs. Thus, the present tense of the imperfective verb PʹISATʹ 'write' is pʹišu, pʹišešʹ,... and the future tense of the prefixed perfective verb form NAPʹISATʹ is napʹišu, napʹišešʹ,....

One of the main challenges of the Russian verb system is the representation of the past tense. This is derived historically from a periphrastic perfect tense series formed by BE and a resultative participle expressed by a suffix -l, the l-participle. Syntactically, the l-participle behaved like a predicative adjective, agreeing with the subject in number and gender, but not in person. The auxiliary BE was lost, leaving the l-participle and its adjective-like agreement as the sole exponent of past tense. The agreement inflections on an l-participle such as (na)pʹisal 'wrote' are almost identical to those on a predicative (short-form) adjective such as MAL 'short': (na)pʹisal, (na)pʹisala, (na)pʹisalo, (na)pisalʹi vs mal, mala, malo, maly. The only real difference is that in the plural the l-participle stem is palatalized but not the predicative adjective stem: (na)pʹisalʹi vs maly.

The simple way of analysing the past tense construction would be to take the -l formative to be an exponent of past tense and define two distinct sets of subject agreement rules for present/future and past tenses. However, the l-participle has one other significant usage which precludes this direct analysis. The conditional mood is expressed by means of the invariable particle *by*, a kind of freely distributed enclitic (it can occur anywhere in the clause except absolute initial position). This can co-occur with the infinitive, (4).

(4) Esl'i by skazat' pravdu, ...
    if   BY say.INF truth
    'To be honest, ...'

However, it is much more often found with the l-participle, (5).

(5) Esl'i by ty skaza-l   pravdu, ...
    if   BY you say-L-PTCP truth
    'If you told/were to tell/had told the truth, ...'

As is indicated in the gloss, the conditional is tenseless, and serves as the translation equivalent of past or non-past conditional in English. The existence of the conditional construction means that we cannot regard the l-participle simply as the exponent of past tense. In fact, it is an instance of what, since Aronoff (1994) morphologists have called a "morphome", that is, a pure morphological form, which serves as a stem for building up inflected word forms, but which realizes no MPSs on its own and whose distribution is not mandated by any semantic, phonological or other non-morphological properties. The CONTENT paradigm for Russian is summarized in Table 1, but ignoring the true participles.

Table 1: Russian verb CONTENT paradigm for UDAR'IT'/UDAR'AT' 'hit'

ASPECT	imperfective	perfective
INFINITIVE	udar'a-t'	udar'i-t'
GERUND	udar'a-ja	udar'i-v(ši)
IMPERATIVE	udar'a-j(te)!	udar'(te)!
TENSE		
present	udar'a-ju, -eš, ...	<none>
future	bud-u, -eš, ...udar'at'	udar'-u, -iš
past	udar'a-l, -a, -o, -'i	udar'i-l, -a, -o, -'i
CONDITIONAL	udar'a-l, -a, -o, -'i + by	udar'i-l, -a, -o, -'i + by
PASSIVE	udar'at'-s'a, etc	(byl) udaren, -a, -o, -y

I turn now to the morphological or FORM paradigm. We can divide Russian verb forms into five groups. The first is the infinitive and the second the set of two indeclinable gerund forms. The third is the set of finite forms, including the imperative mood. In practice, these are limited to the present (non-past) forms showing subject agreement in person/number. The fourth is the l-participle. Finally, we have the set of (declinable) active and passive participles discussed earlier. These are tabulated in Table 2.

Summarizing Table 2, the verb can/must inflect for aspect. The verb system also shows voice alternations. However, these are effected either through reflexive morphology (imperfective verbs) or periphrastically (perfective verbs) so voice proper lacks a dedicated, purely morphological exponent, except for the true participles. The infinitive, gerunds

18 Split-morphology and lexicalist morphosyntax: The case of transpositions

Table 2: Russian verb FORM paradigm for UDAR'IT'/UDAR'AT' 'hit'

ASPECT	imperfective	perfective
INFINITIVE	udar'a-t'	udar'i-t'
GERUND	udar'a-ja	udar'i-v
IMPERATIVE	udar'a-j(te)!	udar'(te)!
TENSE		
present/future	udar'a-ju, -eš, …	udar'-u, -iš
L-PTCP	udar'a-l, -a, -o, -'i	udar'i-l, -a, -o, -'i
REFLEXIVE	udar'at'-s'a, etc	<none>

and the l-participle do not show any tense oppositions. The subject agreement shown by l-participles differs from that of finite verb forms in that it is defined in terms of MPSs proper to predicative adjectives, not those of finite verbs.

Table 3: CONTENT feature array

ASPECT	{ipfv,pfv}
VFORM	INFINITIVE
	TENSE:{prs, fut, pst}
	IMPERATIVE:{sg, pl}
	CONDITIONAL:{yes, no}
REFLEXIVE	{yes, no}
AGRSUBJ	PERSON:{1, 2, 3}
	NUMBER:{sg, pl}
	GENDER:{m, f, n}
VOICE	{ACTIVE, PASSIVE}
REPR	{⟨V,A⟩, ⟨V,Adv⟩}

In Tables 3, 4 I provide a summary list of the features which populate the CONTENT and FORM paradigms. I have provided only basic labels for the various MPSs. Ideally, we would want to know how they are grouped together, if at all, in the two paradigms. This is a difficult question, and I finesse it by just assuming what is effectively a list structure for the MPSs, with a number of dependency statements between them. Thus, I have not distinguished, say, a finite from a non-finite set of forms or constructions. However, for the purposes of giving a broad-brush characterization of the morphology~syntax mapping this is probably not a problem.

From this overview we can see that there is a very clear divide between the CONTENT paradigm MPSs required to describe the system as a whole and the FORM paradigm MPSs required to describe the individual word forms. These tables ignore the inflectional paradigms of the participles, of course, but adding them will just serve to emphasize the CONTENT~FORM disparity.

403

Table 4: FORM feature array

ASPECT	{ipfv,pfv}
VFORM	INFINITIVE
	TENSE:{prs-fut}
	IMPERATIVE:{sg, pl}
	L-PTCP
REFLEXIVE	{yes, no}
AGRSUBJ	PERSON:{1, 2, 3}
	NUMBER:{sg, pl}
	GENDER:{m, f, n}
REPR	{⟨V,A⟩, ⟨V,Adv⟩}

Russian has four participles, active~passive and perfective~imperfective, which are typical attributive modifiers with the agreement morphosyntax of standard adjectives. However, they retain a variety of verb properties, making them into typical examples of mixed categories. Thus, in (6a), the imperfective active participle *upravl'ajuščij* takes a temporal PP adjunct and assigns instrumental case to its complement, just like the finite verb (6b).

(6) a. (čelovek-a), upravl'a-jušč-ego v tečen'ie mnogo let
(the.person[M]-GEN.SG) run-PRSPTCP-M.GEN.SG in course many of.years
mestnoj školoj
local.INSTR school.INSTR

'of (the person) (who has been) running the local school for many years'

b. Ivanov upravl'aet v tečen'ie mnogo let mestnoj školoj
Ivanov runs in course many of.years local.INSTR school.INSTR

'Ivanov has been running the local primary school for many years'

The participles are often described as present/past tense forms, but their semantics is essentially aspectual and they fit somewhat better into the overall verb scheme if they are treated as perfective~imperfective pairs. They are summarized in Table 5 (cf Wade 1992: 361).

Table 5: Russian participles of the verb UPRAV'IT'/UPRAVL'AT' 'control'

Aspect	imperfective	perfective
Active	*upravl'aju-šč-*	*uprav'i-vš-*
Passive	*upravl'a-em-*	*upravl'-on(n)-*

Perfective aspect participles, for semantic reasons, usually only have past time reference.[8] The imperfective participles realize a time relative to the main verb of the clause, so that 'present tense' is a particularly misleading label for these forms (Wade 1992: 375).

(7) Ja v′idel/v′ižu sobak-u, bega-jušč-uju   po beregu
    I saw/see   dog[F]-ACC.SG run-ACTPRSPTCP-F.ACC.SG along the shore

   'I saw/see the dog running along the shore'

The participle differs from the finite form in this respect. Example (8) would only be possible with either the meaning '(dog) which usually runs along the shore' or as a somewhat marked form of the historic present (cf *Russkaja Grammatika I*: 665).

(8) Ja v′idel sobak-u,   kotor-aja   begaet po beregu
    I saw dog[F]-ACC.SG which-F.NOM.SG runs along the shore

   'I saw the dog which is running along the shore'

In this respect, Russian participles are just like their English counterparts, of course.

The participles have a number of properties aligning them with verbs. In addition to realizing the purely verbal (eventive) categories of tense-aspect-voice, the active participles can take reflexive forms, either as reflexive variants of non-reflexives, inheriting all the semantics of the reflexive forms, *upravl′at′(s′a)* 'manage, control' ~ *upravl′ajuščijs′a*, or as inherent reflexives (with no non-reflexive counterpart), *bojat′s′a* 'fear' ~ *bojaščijs′a*. As we have seen, syntactically, the participles retain the verb's argument structure, including quirky case assignment to complements, such as instrumental in the case of *upravl′ajuščijs′a* (see examples (6)) and genitive in the case of *bojaščijs′a*.

On the other hand, the participles have a number of adjectival properties. The most salient morphosyntactic property is that of attributive adjective agreement together with the morphological property of belonging to a well-defined adjectival inflectional class. (As attributive modifiers the participles can be restrictive or non-restrictive, like other attributive modifiers, including relative clauses.) However, they can also be used as predicates with the copula BYT′ 'be' or with "semi-copulas" such as STAT′ 'become', KAZAT′S′A 'seem', OSTAT′S′A 'remain', and others. Most commonly it is the perfective passive participles that can be used as predicates but active participles can also be found in this role (Švedova 1980b: 291, §2346). The passive (though not the active) participles can also appear as predicates, in the so-called short form, a typically adjectival property.[9]

(9) užin   uže   poda-n
    supper.M.SG already serve-PASSPTCP.M.SG

   'Supper has already been served'

---

[8] But see the counter-examples in the Academy of Sciences grammar *Russkaja Grammatika, I*: 667, *pred′javl′ajuščij* 'presenting', *vzvolnujuščij* 'exciting', *sdelajuščij* 'doing', *smoguščij* 'being able'.
[9] Present active participles can be used in the short form, however, when they are converted into true, qualitative, adjectives (Švedova 1980a: 666).

Given this brief descriptive summary of the basic facts of Russian participles we can turn to the central questions: how do we represent participles in a formal, constraints-based grammar with an inferential-realizational morphology? How do these representations relate to the inflection~derivation divide and the issue of split morphology?

5 Paradigm linkage rules for Russian

In the extension to GPFM presented here, the FORM paradigm and the CONTENT paradigm are modelled by the attributes f-MORSIG, c-MORSIG. However, those types of lexical relatedness which modify the MPSs of a representation, such as transpositions, will ipso facto modify the content of Stump's FORM/ CONTENT paradigms and the f-/c-MORSIG attributes. The GPF for such types of relatedness therefore has to specify that novel content, by stipulation, if necessary. In the rules I propose below I show how this can be achieved for Russian conjugation. The reference to MORSIG is taken to mean c-MORSIG by default and by default, this is identical to f-MORSIG.

I shall begin by specifying the CONTENT and FORM MORSIG attribute for non-participial verb categories. We need to define the f-MORSIG in part in terms of the c-MORSIG and in part independently. The default is the identity mapping from c-MORSIG to f-MORSIG. The c-MORSIG list shown earlier in Table 1 is defined for any lexical representation whose ARG-STR includes the E semantic function role. The MPSs that are shared across the CONTENT and FORM paradigms of Russian verbs are fairly limited (cf. Tables 1 and 2 above). They are (ignoring for the present the participles and gerunds): ASPECT:{ipfv, pfv}, VFORM:{INFINITIVE, IMPERATIVE:{sg, pl}}, VOICE:{act, pass}, and AGRSBJ:{PERSON/NUMBER/GENDER}.

The c-features ASPECT, VFORM:{INFINITIVE, IMPERATIVE:{sg, pl}} have relatively straightforward f-feature correspondents. I shall ignore INFINITIVE and IMPERATIVE for present purposes. AGRSUBJ is also a FORM property but with some complications and I return to it when I discuss the l-participle.

The status of the TENSE feature is a little unclear. At the CONTENT level there are clearly three values, *prs, fut, pst*, but only the *prs* and *fut* values have a FORM correspondent, and even then the value of the FORM correspondent is a composite *prs/fut*, and therefore not a direct correspondent of either c-[TENSE:prs] or c-[TENSE:fut]. The c-TENSE:{pst} property is realized by the morphomic l-participle, and not by any dedicated f-TENSE:{pst} property. I shall therefore assume a univalent FORM property, TNS, itself a value of VFORM, realizing c-TENSE:{prs, fut} depending on the value of ASPECT. This replaces the atom-valued TENSE:{present-future} shown in Table 2 above. The property VOICE:{act, pass} is intriguing. It is a CONTENT property of the verb system but it is not a FORM property of any part of the verb system proper, outside of the participle subsystem. However, the participles distinguish active and passive sets, and the perfective passive participle is actually part of the periphrastic exponence of the syntactic (CONTENT) VOICE property. Moreover, the two passive participles have the passive SYN|ARG-STR representation, namely, ...⟨E⟨(x), y, ...⟩, where (x) denotes the demoted active subject argument role. Therefore, VOICE is both part of the CONTENT and the

FORM paradigm, albeit with a somewhat complex realization, which will require the f-MORSIG attribute to be modified by a feature co-occurrence statement restricting f-VOICE to the participles. The other CONTENT paradigm features are represented by forms which are effectively periphrastic. It is for these reasons that the FORM MPSs have to be defined independently, as shown below.

One attribute that is shared across FORM/CONTENT paradigms is REPRESENTATION. The only reason for a language to define a true transpositional category is to allow a lexeme to assume the syntactic distribution of a word of a different class, so REPR clearly has to be a CONTENT feature. In languages such as Russian, in which participles are marked morphologically, this also means that REPR is a FORM feature. I shall assume that the REPR attribute as applied to verbs has three values. The first is *plain* (or ⟨V,V⟩), the 'identity representation', and the default value. Where no indication of REPR is given the default is to be understood. The second value of REPR is ⟨V, A⟩, defining the four participles. The third value is ⟨V,Adv⟩,[10] defining the imperfective and perfective gerunds. I shall ignore the gerunds for simplicity of exposition. This means that I shall only mark the participles explicitly.

We now define the content of the c-MORSIG attribute by reference to the verb's SYN value. The aspects, and voice are defined with the mapping shown informally in (10). This will apply to any representation whose ARG-STR contains the E sf role. In practice, this means verbs, participles, and gerunds.

(10)   ... E ... ⇒ ASPECT, VOICE ⊂ MORSIG

I return to the c-MORSIG|CONDITIONAL, TENSE:{pst} mappings below when I discuss the status of the l-participle.

The feature array defining participles is given in Fig. 1. This is the "derived" MORSIG attribute for any lexical representation defined by the feature REPR:⟨V,A⟩. The property sets labelled 1 in Fig. 1 come from the MORSIG attribute of the base verb by virtue of (10). The property sets 3, 4 are those which ensure that the participles are inflected like adjectives. I return to these when I have introduced adjective inflection.

The key to my analysis of transpositions is to incorporate part of the analysis of derivational morphology into the definition of the transposition's entry. Given a feature pairing ⟨£,ρ⟩, where £ is a lexemic index and ρ contains a value of REPR (for instance, [REPR:⟨V,A⟩] for participles), the GPF applied to this pairing leaves the LI and the SEM representations of the base unchanged, but enriches the SYN|ARG-STR attribute by creating a complex semantic function role $\langle A_i \langle E \langle x_i, ... \rangle \rangle \rangle$. The coindexation guarantees that the noun head modified by the participle is identified with the highest thematic argument of the base verb's argument array, i.e. its SUBJECT. The FORM function component of the GPF defines the stem set for the participle, but underspecifies all other FORM information, including the MORSIG (and the CONTENT paradigm MORSIG is also underspecified by the SYN function).

---

[10] The semantic function role label Adv stands proxy for whatever the appropriate way is of defining adverbs as distinct from adjectives.

$$\begin{bmatrix} & & \begin{bmatrix} \text{ASPECT} & \{\text{ipfv, pfv}\}\boxed{1} \\ \text{VOICE} & \{\text{act, pass}\}\boxed{2} \\ \text{CONCORD} & \begin{bmatrix} \text{NUMBER} & \{\text{sg, pl}\} \\ \text{GENDER} & \{\text{m, f, n}\} \\ \text{CASE} & \{\text{nom, ...}\} \end{bmatrix}\boxed{3} \\ \text{MORCLASS} & \text{adj}\boxed{4} \end{bmatrix} \end{bmatrix}$$

Figure 1: Feature structure for Russian participles

The lexemic entry for a typical transitive Russian verb such as UDAR′IT′/UDAR′AT′ is that shown in Fig. 2, where $\mathcal{V}$ stands for the verb's lexemic index. The lexemic entry's value for LI is just the LI of the lexeme, of course (the GPF here does not describe a process of derivational morphology). Note that for this lexeme the SYN attribute, too, is completely underspecified, lacking even the ARG-STR attribute. The value of that attribute is determined by default from the *Event* ontological type of the SEM representation. However, the REPR feature which defines transpositions introduces a realization rule which has to be defined over a specified ARG-STR representation. Therefore, the ARG-STR attribute has to be part of the lexeme's (SYN attribute's) morpholexical signature (inflection-like argument structure alternations such as passive or antipassive impose a similar requirement). In this respect, the transpositions are like inflection and not like derivation.

We can informally state the realization rule which defines adjectival representations of lexemes (transpositions-to-adjective) as a function α from ARG-STR representations to ARG-STR representations, as shown in (11), where (11a) defines a participle's ARG-STR and (11b) defines that of a relational adjective.

(11) a. $\alpha(\langle E\langle x,...\rangle\rangle) = \langle A_i \langle E\langle x_i,...\rangle\rangle\rangle$
      b. $\alpha(\langle R\rangle) = \langle A \langle R\rangle\rangle$

Given the lexemic entry in Fig. 2 and the realization rules for Russian morphology, the GPF for the imperfective active participle, *udar′ajušč-* will map to a partially underspecified lexical representation, as shown in Fig. 3. A representation such as this is the 'quasi-lexeme' discussed earlier. Like a simple lexemic entry, or an entry defined by a derivational GPF, it needs to have its MORSIG attributes specified in order to be inflectable. I turn now to how those MORSIG entries are defined.

The partially specified MORSIG we need to be able to define for participles is that shown in Fig. 4. The ASPECT/VOICE properties are shared with verbs. This can be achieved by writing the rules defining the MORSIG of verbs and participles in such as way as to refer either to the "outermost" E semantic function role of the ARG-STR at-

$$f_{form}(\langle \mathcal{V}, u \rangle) = \begin{bmatrix} \text{STEM0} & \begin{bmatrix} \text{PHON} & \text{udar}' \\ \text{MORCLASS} & \text{V} \mid \text{CONJ2} \end{bmatrix} \\ \text{STEM1} & \begin{bmatrix} \text{PHON} & \text{udar}'\text{aj} \\ \text{MORCLASS} & \text{V} \mid \text{CONJ1} \end{bmatrix} \end{bmatrix}$$

$$f_{syn}(\langle \mathcal{V}, u \rangle) = u$$

$$f_{sem}(\langle \mathcal{V}, u \rangle) = \lambda x,y[\text{HIT}(x,y)]$$

$$f_{li}(\langle \mathcal{V}, u \rangle) = u$$

Figure 2: Lexemic entry for UDAR′IT′/UDAR′AT′

$$\text{FORM}(\langle \mathcal{V}, \{\text{REPR}:\langle V,A\rangle\}\rangle) = \begin{bmatrix} \text{STEM0} \mid \text{PHON} & \text{udar}'\text{ajušč} \\ \text{MORSIG} & u \end{bmatrix}$$

$$\text{SYN}(\langle \mathcal{V}, \{\text{REPR}:\langle V,A\rangle\}\rangle) = \begin{bmatrix} \text{ARG-STR} & \langle A_i \langle E\langle x_i,y\rangle\rangle\rangle \\ \text{MORSIG} & u \end{bmatrix}$$

$$\text{SEM}(\langle \mathcal{V}, \{\text{REPR}:\langle V,A\rangle\}\rangle) = \text{identity function}$$

$$\text{LI}(\langle \mathcal{V}, \{\text{REPR}:\langle V,A\rangle\}\rangle) = \text{identity function}$$

Figure 3: Underspecified entry for *udar′ajušč(ij)*

$$\begin{bmatrix} \text{MORSIG} & \begin{bmatrix} \text{ASPECT:} \{u\} \\ \text{VOICE:} \{u\} \\ \text{CONCORD:} \{u\} \\ \text{MORCLASS: ADJ} \mid \text{DECL1/2} \end{bmatrix} \end{bmatrix}$$

Figure 4: MORSIG for Russian participles

tribute, or the "embedded" E role found with participles.[11] The CONCORD attribute, $\boxed{3}$, comes from the generic c-MORSIG of an adjective, shown in (12).[12]

(12)   ... A ... ⇒ [CONCORD:{NUMBER, GENDER, CASE}] ⊂ MORSIG

The [MORCLASS adj] specification, $\boxed{4}$, is strictly speaking a stipulation, except that in Russian (in contrast to, say, Latin) all participles belong to the default adjectival class, DECL1/2.

Given this machinery we can now account for the transpositional mixed category of participle by application of the (quasi-inflectional) generalized paradigm function applying to a verb and delivering its participial forms, triggered by the [REPR] feature. These representations will be underspecified for (adjectival) CONCORD features. For concreteness, consider the imperfective active participle, *udar'ajušč-*. Given ρ = {REPR:⟨V,A⟩, ASPECT:ipfv $\boxed{1}$, VOICE:act $\boxed{2}$}, then for $\mathcal{V}$ = UDAR′IT′/UDAR′AT′, the GPF(⟨$\mathcal{V}$,ρ⟩) will apply to a lexical representation which is derived from the lexemic entry for UDAR′IT′/UDAR′AT′ whose MORSIG attributes have been fully specified, allowing the lexeme to be inflected (in the broad sense of this term, including "inflection" for participle formation). This GPF will deliver a partially underspecified lexical representation for the participle. The GPF will specify the participle's stem form(s), the ASPECT, VOICE features which define that particular participle, and the enriched ARG-STR attribute with complex semantic function role.

The lexical representation which is input to the GPF is shown in Fig. 5 and the lexical representation of the participle is shown in (13). In Fig. 5, STEM0 denotes the perfective stem, which is effectively the lexeme's root. CONJ2 is second conjugation, and this means that most inflectional rules will be defined over another stem, *udar'i-*, derived by regular rules of stem formation. STEM1 denotes the imperfective stem, a member of CONJ1, the first conjugation, whose inflectional stem is therefore *udar'aj-*. Attributes which belong to both FORM and SYN (CONTENT) paradigms are tagged to make them more easily identifiable.

(13) f_{form} = STEM-iap ⊕ šč = udar'aju-šč-
       f_{syn} = ARG-STR:⟨A$_i$⟨E⟨x$_i$,y⟩⟩⟩

where STEM-iap denotes the imperfective active participle stem, derived from STEM1.

We have now achieved our goal of defining participles. In effect, we have defined the lexemic entry for a class of adjectives, whose peculiarity is that they are marked for verbal voice and aspect and they share their semantics and lexemic index with a parent verb.

It is instructive to compare the behaviour of the true participles with that of the l-participle. While the true participles are mixed categories, the l-participle is essentially a verb form with unusual agreement morphology. It is not entirely clear how best to

---

[11] Russian action nominals are transpositional lexemes and not true transpositions.
[12] Members of the semantically defined class of quality or scalar adjectives will also have the feature COMPARISON added to their MORSIG to define comparative/superlative morphology.

18 Split-morphology and lexicalist morphosyntax: The case of transpositions

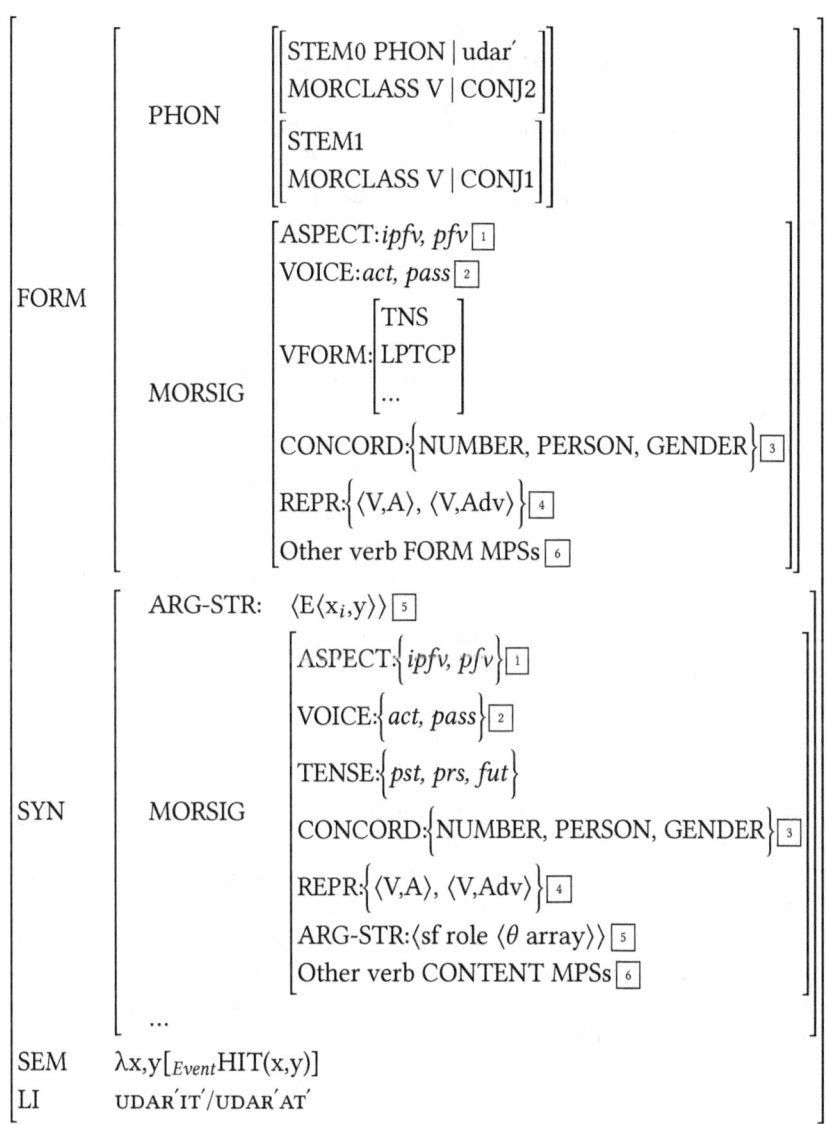

Figure 5: Lexical representation of the lexeme UDAR'IT'/UDAR'AT' 'to hit'

account for the peculiar agreement properties of the l-participle in the past tense and conditional constructions, but the simplest (if somewhat crude) way to do this is to assume that verbs in general agree with their subjects in person, number, gender features, but that in the past/conditional forms agreement is restricted to number, gender, while in the present tense forms it is restricted to person, number.[13]

I conclude, then, that the l-participle is a verb form that inflects just like a (subtype of) predicative (short-form) adjective. Assuming a feature ADJDECL covering adjectival morphology generally, we can distinguish several sub-types of declension, including that for the predicative adjectives, [ADJDECL:predadj]. The l-participles will belong to a subtype of this class, [ADJDECL:predadj:lptcpdecl]. The ADJDECL feature is part of the MORSIG attribute of ordinary adjectives, as defined by the paradigm linkage rule in (14).[14]

(14)   ... A ... ⇒ ADJDECL ⊂ MORSIG

We also compare true participles with qualitative adjectives derived by conversion from participles. These are a type of transpositional lexeme. The theoretical significance of this type of lexical relatedness for current morphological models was first identified, as far as I am aware in Spencer (2013: 275), where I discuss English words such as PREPOSITIONAL, from PREPOSITION. These look like relational adjectives (noun-to-adjective transpositions), because their lexical semantic content seems to be identical to that of their base noun (*prepositional phrase* means the same as the compound *preposition phrase*, for instance). However, the English adjectives are syntactically opaque: *monosyllabic prepositional phrase* does not mean 'phrase headed by a monosyllabic preposition' but only 'monosyllabic phrase headed by a preposition' (though that interpretation is possible for the compound, *monosyllabic preposition phrase*). In other words, the adjectival expression only has the structure *monosyllabic [prepositional phrase]*, not *[monosyllabic preposition]al phrase*.

English has a large number of qualitative adjectives derived by conversion from participles, which are also instances of transpositional lexemes (Spencer 2016a): *amazed/ amazing, bored/boring, challenged/challenging, interested/interesting, ...* In very many cases it is not possible to identify a meaning difference between the adjective and the etymological verb base: *This book bores me/This book is boring.* Russian participles likewise are often converted into qualitative adjectives: *potr'asajuščij* 'amazing', *vyzyvajuščij* 'provocative, defiant, challenging'. In Russian it is often possible to determine that a word with the shape of a participle is actually an independent adjective, since only true adjectives have the short predicative form: *uspexi potr'asajušči* (plural, from *potr'asajušč*)

---

[13] A more sophisticated approach might define agreement in a morphology-driven fashion by stating that the agreement features that the syntax can manipulate are restricted to those that can be expressed by a particular morphological form, so that it is the morphological MORSIG that determines which features trigger agreement, even in identical syntactic positions.

[14] As adjectives, we might expect the participles to have predicative forms, too. This is true, however, only for the passive participles, especially the perfective passive, which has a special stem form ending in a singleton /n/, *nap'isan* 'written', in contrast to the attributive form with geminated /nn/: *(v speške) nap'isannaja (zap'iska)* '(a hastily) written (note)'.

'the-progress is-amazing' (lit. 'the-successes are-amazing'), *ego poveden´ie vyzyvajušče* 'his behaviour is-defiant'. True participles do not have the predicative form (Russkaja Grammatika II, p.666). English converted participles fail to inherit the complementation properties of the base verb: *The obstacle course challenged the stamina of the athletes~The obstacle course was very challenging (*the stamina of the athletes)*. Russian transpositional adjective lexemes behave likewise. The transitive base verb POTR´ASAT´ 'to amaze' gives us *uspexi potr´asal'i nas* 'the-successes amazed us', but the (active) transpositional lexeme cannot take a direct object: **uspexi potr´asajušči nas*. The true participle remains transitive: *potr´asajuščie nas uspexi* 'progress (successes) which amaze us'.

We thus have a double dissociation of properties: on the one hand, we have the l-participle which has the form of a predicative adjective but which realizes finite (tense/mood) verb properties and retains the full complementation properties of the verb, and on the other hand we have participle-like adjectives which, while allowing predicative adjective forms, lack all the crucial morphosyntax of verbs. In between we have the true participles, with the external morphosyntax of an adjective but the complementation properties of the base verb.

6 Conclusions: Transpositions and split morphology

I have argued in this paper for a view of morphosyntax which recognizes a word/phrase distinction and, given that, a distinction between (abstract) lexemes and (concrete) inflected word forms of those lexemes, valid for very nearly all known languages. I have also assumed that languages can increase their stock of lexemes by means of derivational morphology, and that in some cases this is sufficiently regular to be regarded as paradigmatic, hence, part of the grammatical system proper. The inflection/derivation distinction is controversial, however, because it is often difficult to know where the boundary actually lies and where to place intermediate types of lexical relatedness. The transpositions, as exemplified by the Russian participial system discussed here, represent a particularly troublesome case-in-point.

Participles and other transpositions are often treated as a type of derivational morphology, because they involve a shift in word class, but this is a wrong characterization. Participles are part of a verb's paradigm, they are not a type of lexical stock expansion (Beard 1995). Nonetheless, participles inflect like adjectives, not like verbs and thus seem to straddle the inflection/derivation divide in a way that calls that very distinction into question, and, on the face of it, even provides support for models in which all morphology is just syntax by other means (Minimalism/Distributed Morphology) or in which all syntax is just morphology by other means (American morphemics). Here I have claimed that, on the contrary, we can only make sense of participles against a set of background assumptions that contradict monolithic models in which there is no autonomous morphology module (Aronoff's "morphology-by-itself"), so that morphology is no more than syntax by other means. The crucial observation is that derivational morphology induces a type of lexical opacity which is lacking in transpositions, which, by contrast, show the kind of lexical transparency associated with inflected forms.

In the GPFM model, canonical derivation is a relation between maximally underspecified (minimally redundant) lexical representations (lexemic entries), consisting of a specification of the basic root form (FORM|PHON) and the ontological/semantic representation (SEM). The morphosyntactic properties are then projected from these by default mappings. Canonically, derivation enriches the PHON and the SEM representations, and the Default Cascade then specifies the morphosyntactic properties of the derived lexeme. One consequence is that there will then be no "trace" left of the morphosyntactic properties of the base lexeme, such as its word class or its argument structure. This automatically guarantees most of the lexical opacity/lexical integrity effects familiar from the literature. In some (noncanonical) cases it may be necessary to stipluate overrides of lexical information as part of the derivational Generalized Paradigm Function. This might be true if, for instance, a base lexeme belongs to a lexical category which is not the default for its ontological class. For instance, a language with a distinct lexical category of (qualitative) adjective may also have non-derived stative verbs whose denotations are of the ontological type Property, and which by the Default Cascade should be adjectives, not verbs. Such a verb would have to have its ARG-STR|⟨E ...⟩ value prespecified. If such a lexeme were the input to a verb-to-noun derivational function (nominalization), then that ARG-STR would have to be overridden by the nominalization function, replacing it wholesale with the ARG-STR|⟨R⟩ value. Exactly how such cases are to be handled has to remain a matter for future research.

No such opacity is found with canonical inflection: in general, the syntax treats a noun as a noun no matter what its number, case, definiteness, ... value. Thus, although a locative case marked noun would normally be restricted to functioning as an adjunct or the complement of a class of adpositions, it can still be modified by an adjective, just like any other noun form, so that for a noun 'house', *new house-LOC* means 'at a new house'. In this respect, a locative case marked noun typically differs from a derived denominal lexeme denoting a location. Many languages have a denominal derivational marker meaning 'place where there is/are NOUN, place associated with NOUN': N-PLACE. Typically, the base noun, N, is not accessible to morphosyntax, so that an expression such as *new house-PLACE* could only mean 'new place where there is a house/are houses' and not 'place where there is/are a new house(s)'. Thus, inflection differs from derivation in being lexically transparent.

The significance of these rather obvious points about inflected forms is that we are far less able to make similarly categorical claims where transpositions are concerned. A participle behaves in the syntax *to some extent* as though it were an inflected verb form, but not entirely. In GPFM the lexical representation of a transposition exhibits transparency by virtue of being a member of the base lexeme's (extended) paradigm, that is, by bearing the same LI as the base. In this respect it is not an autonomous lexeme. On the other hand, the transposition exhibits the external syntax of a distinct (derived) lexical category. The extension to the GPF proposed here permits us to model this "inflectional-paradigm-within-a-paradigm" effect in a way that reflects the lexical transparency of the transposition while also allowing us to state restrictions on full transparency as a restriction on the MORSIG of the transposition.

A crucial aspect of the analysis is the distinction between FORM/CONTENT properties (m-/s-features). Without at least this level of differentiation we cannot make sense of Russian participles and we cannot distinguish them from the verbal l-participle form or the transpositional lexemes. A second crucial aspect of the analysis of any type of transposition is the Lexemic Index (LI). In the general case, there is no combination of lexical properties that will uniquely serve to individuate lexemes, but it is nonetheless essential to impose such an individuation to account for the patterns of lexical relatedness that are found across languages, specifically, to distinguish true participles from departicipial converted adjectives (transpositional lexemes).

The combination of the FORM/CONTENT paradigm distinction (or its equivalent) and the Lexemic Index allow us to define not just canonical inflection but also non-canonical intra-lexemic types of relatedness such as that shown by transpositions. That combination also serves to reconstruct the split in the morphology argued for originally by Anderson. Indeed, split morphology is entailed by this set of assumptions, except that in a constraints-based model the split is defined in terms of access: inflectional morphology is that which permits syntax to retain access to the properties of the base lexeme (lexical transparency), while derivational morphology permits no such access (lexical opacity/integrity).

The more articulated view of morphosyntax proposed here allows us to pose a question which was not at the forefront of debate over the question of split morphology, as far as I am aware: which side of the split do transpositions fall on? The answer, given the foregoing, is "both". The transposition is inflectional by virtue of preserving the base's LI and by virtue of the, at least partial, transparency of the base's properties. It is derivational by virtue of the fact that it defines the paradigm of a quasi-lexeme, within the paradigm of the base. But it would be difficult to make sense of this conclusion without assuming the basic split in the first place.

Appendix: Illustration of the lexical representations assumed

To specify, say, the 3sg form *drives*, the GPF($\langle$DRIVE,{3sg}$\rangle$) applies to the output of Figure 6 to specify the FORM value |STEM0⊕z|, leaving other aspects of the representation unchanged. This is equivalent to the operation of the paradigm function in PFM1 and the output of the *Corr* function in PFM2.

$$\begin{bmatrix} \text{FORM} & \text{STEM0} \mid \text{draɪv} \mid \\ \text{SYN} & - \\ \text{SEM} & [_{Event}\ \lambda x,y.\textbf{drive}(x,y)] \\ \text{LI} & \text{DRIVE} \end{bmatrix} \Rightarrow$$

$$\begin{bmatrix} \text{FORM} & \begin{bmatrix} \text{STEM0} & \mid \text{draɪv} \mid \\ \text{MORSIG} & \begin{bmatrix} \text{TNS} & \{\text{prs, pst}\} \\ \text{VFORM} & \{\text{ing-form, ed-form, base}\} \\ \text{AGR} & \{\text{3sg, none}\} \end{bmatrix} \end{bmatrix} \\ \text{SYN} & \begin{bmatrix} \text{SYNCAT} & \text{V} \\ \text{ARG-ST} & \langle E\langle x,y\rangle\rangle \\ \text{MORSIG} & \begin{bmatrix} \text{TNS} & \{\text{prs, pst}\} \\ \text{ASP} & \{\text{simple, prog, perf}\} \\ \text{AGR} & \{\text{3sg, none}\} \\ \ldots \end{bmatrix} \end{bmatrix} \\ \text{SEM} & [_{Event}\ \lambda x,y.\textbf{drive}(x,y)] \\ \text{LI} & \text{DRIVE} \end{bmatrix}$$

Figure 6: Illustration of the application of the GPF for standard inflection.

(15) DRIVE ⇒ DRIVER
   Where δ = SubjNom, Σ = [$_{Event}$ λx,y.**drive**(x,y)], GPF(⟨DRIVE,δ⟩) =

$$\begin{bmatrix} \text{FORM} & \text{STEM0} \mid \text{draɪv} \mid \\ \text{SYN} & - \\ \text{SEM} & \Sigma \\ \text{LI} & \text{DRIVE} \end{bmatrix} \Rightarrow$$

$$\begin{bmatrix} \text{FORM} & [\text{STEM0} \quad\quad\quad \text{STEM0}(\text{DRIVE})\oplus \mid \text{ə} \mid \\ \text{SYN} & - \\ \text{SEM} & [_{Thing}\ \lambda\text{x.PERSON(x)} \land \Sigma \\ \text{LI} & \delta(\text{DRIVE}) \end{bmatrix}$$

Figure 7: Illustration of the application of the GPF for standard derivation

The output of this GPF then undergoes specification of MORSIG by the Default Cascade, which defines the derived lexeme as a syntactic and morphological noun.

Abbreviations

AGRSUBJ	subject agreement	MORCAT	morpholexical category
act	active		
ARG-STR	argument structure	MORCLASS	morphological class
		MORSIG	morpholexical signature
CONJ	conjugation		
DECL	declension	MPS	morphosyntactic property set
GPF	Generalized Paradigm Function	pass	passive
		PF	Paradigm Function
GPFM	Generalized Paradigm Function Morphology	PFM	Paradigm Function Morphology
		pfv	perfective
		PHON	phonological form
ipfv	imperfective	REPR	REPRESENTATION
LI	lexemic index	SEM	semantics
L-PTCP, l-ptcp	l-participle	SYN	syntax

Acknowledgements

I am grateful to two anonymous referees and to Larry Horn for very helpful commentary and for correcting a number of typos and other errors. I would also like to express my gratitude to Steve Anderson for his pioneering work in getting morphology accepted as a legitimate subject for generative grammar, and also to thank him for his enlightening and entertaining contributions to the field, admirably limpid, often witty, and always thought-provoking.

References

Ackerman, Farrell & Phil LeSourd. 1997. Toward a lexical representation of phrasal predicates. In Alex Alsina, Joan Bresnan & Peter Sells (eds.), *Complex predicates*, 67–106. Stanford, CA: CSLI Publications.
Anderson, Stephen R. 1977. On the formal description of inflection. In Woodford A. Beach, Samuel E. Fox & Shulamith Philosoph (eds.), *Papers from the thirteenth regional meeting of the Chicago Linguistic Society*, 15–44. Chicago: Chicago Linguistic Society.
Anderson, Stephen R. 1982. Where's Morphology? *Linguistic Inquiry* 13(4). 571–612.
Anderson, Stephen R. 1992. *A-morphous morphology*. Cambridge: Cambridge University Press.
Anderson, Stephen R. 2015. The morpheme: Its nature and use. In Matthew Baerman (ed.), *The Oxford handbook of inflection*, 1–34. Oxford: Oxford University Press.
Aronoff, Mark. 1994. *Morphology by itself: Stems and inflectional classes*. Cambridge, MA: MIT Press.
Baerman, Matthew, Dunstan Brown & Greville G. Corbett. 2005. *The syntax-morphology interface: A study of syncretism*. Cambridge: Cambridge University Press.
Baerman, Matthew, Greville G. Corbett, Dunstan Brown & Andrew Hippisley (eds.). 2007. *Deponency and morphological mismatches*. Oxford: Oxford University Press.
Beard, Robert. 1995. *Lexeme-morpheme base morphology*. Stony Brook, NY: SUNY Press.
Bonami, Olivier. 2015. Periphrasis as collocation. *Morphology* 25. 63–110.
Bonami, Olivier & Gregory Stump. 2016. Paradigm Function Morphology. In Andrew Hippisley & Gregory T. Stump (eds.), *The Cambridge handbook of morphology*, 449–481. Cambridge: Cambridge University Press.
Booij, Geert. 1994. Against split morphology. In Geert Booij & Jaap van Marle (eds.), *Yearbook of Morphology 1993*, 27–49. Dordrecht: Kluwer Academic Publishers.
Brown, Dunstan P., Marina Chumakina, Greville G. Corbett, Gergana D. Popova & Andrew Spencer. 2012. Defining 'periphrasis': Key notions. *Morphology* 22(2). 233–275.
Gerritsen, Nellike. 1990. *Russian reflexive verbs: In search of unity in diversity*. Amsterdam: Rodopi.
Haspelmath, Martin. 1996. Word-class changing inflection and morphological theory. In Geert Booij & Jaap van Marle (eds.), *Yearbook of Morphology 1995*, 43–66. Dordrecht: Kluwer Academic Publishers.
Jackendoff, Ray S. 1990. *Semantic structures*. Cambridge, MA: MIT Press.

Lieber, Rochelle. 2004. *Morphology and lexical semantics*. Cambridge: Cambridge University Press.
Lowe, John. 2015. *Participles in Rigvedic Sanskrit: The syntax and semantics of adjectival verb forms*. Oxford: Oxford University Press.
Malchukov, Andrej L. 2004. *Nominalization/verbalization: Constraining a typology of transcategorial operations*. Munich: Lincom Europa.
Matthews, Peter H. 1972. *Inflectional morphology: A theoretical study based on aspects of Latin verb conjugation*. Cambridge: Cambridge University Press.
Miller, Philip H. & Ivan A. Sag. 1997. French clitic movement without clitics or movement. *Natural Language and Linguistic Theory* 15(3). 573–639.
Nikolaeva, Irina A. 2008. Between nouns and adjectives: A constructional view. *Lingua* 118(7). 969–996.
Popova, Gergana & Andrew Spencer. Forthcoming. Stacked periphrases. In *Proceedings of the 11th Formal Description of Slavic Languages conference*.
Sadler, Louisa & Rachel Nordlinger. 2006. Case stacking in Realizational Morphology. *Linguistics* 44(3). 459–488.
Sadler, Louisa & Andrew Spencer. 2001. Syntax as an exponent of morphological features. In Geert Booij & Jaap van Marle (eds.), *Yearbook of morphology 2000*, 71–96. Dordrecht: Kluwer Academic Publishers.
Sims, Andrea. 2015. *Inflectional defectiveness*. Cambridge: Cambridge University Press.
Spencer, Andrew. 1999. Transpositions and argument structure. In Geert Booij & Jaap van Marle (eds.), *Yearbook of morphology 1998*, 73–102. Dordrecht: Kluwer Academic Publishers.
Spencer, Andrew. 2002. Gender as an inflectional category. *Journal of Linguistics* 38(2). 279–312.
Spencer, Andrew. 2013. *Lexical relatedness: A paradigm-based model*. Oxford: Oxford University Press.
Spencer, Andrew. 2016a. How are words related? In Daniel Siddiqi & Heidi Harley (eds.), *Morphological metatheory*, 1–26. Amsterdam: John Benjamins.
Spencer, Andrew. 2016b. Individuating lexemes. In Miriam Butt & Tracy Holloway King (eds.), *Proceedings of LFG15*, 357–377. Stanford: CSLI Publications.
Spencer, Andrew. 2016c. Participial relatives in LFG. In Miriam Butt & Tracy Holloway King (eds.), *Proceedings of LFG15*, 378–398. Stanford: CSLI Publications.
Spencer, Andrew & Gregory Stump. 2013. Hungarian pronominal case and the dichotomy of content and form in inflectional morphology. *Natural Language and Linguistic Theory* 31. 1207–1248.
Stewart, Thomas & Gregory Stump. 2007. Paradigm Function Morphology and the morphology-syntax interface. In Gillian Ramchand & Charles Reiss (eds.), *The Oxford handbook of linguistic interfaces*, 383–421. Oxford: Oxford University Press.
Stump, Gregory. 2001. *Inflectional morphology: A theory of paradigm structure*. Cambridge: Cambridge University Press.

Stump, Gregory. 2002. Morphological and syntactic paradigms: Arguments for a theory of paradigm linkage. In Geert Booij & Jaap van Marle (eds.), *Yearbook of morphology 2001*, 147–180. Dordrecht: Kluwer Academic.

Stump, Gregory. 2006. A theory of heteroclite inflectional paradigms. *Language* 82. 279–322.

Stump, Gregory. 2016a. *Inflectional paradigms: Content and form at the syntax-morphology interface*. Cambridge: Cambridge University Press.

Stump, Gregory. 2016b. Paradigms at the interface of inflectional morphology. In Daniel Siddiqi & Heidi Harley (eds.), *Morphological metatheory*, 27–58. Amsterdam: John Benjamins.

Švedova, Natalija Ju. (ed.). 1980a. *Russkaja grammatika*. Vol. 1. Issued by the Academy of Sciences of USSR. Moskva: Izdatel'stvo nauka.

Thornton, Anna. 2012. Reduction and maintenance of overabundance. A case study on Italian verb paradigms. *Word Structure* 5. 183–207.

Wade, Terence. 1992. *A comprehensive Russian grammar*. Oxford: Blackwell Publishing.

Wechsler, Stephen. 2014. *Word meaning and syntax: Approaches to the interface*. Oxford: Oxford University Press.

Švedova, Natalija Ju. (ed.). 1980b. *Russkaja grammatika*. Vol. 2. Issued by the Academy of Sciences of USSR. Moskva: Izdatel'stvo nauka.

Chapter 19

Rules and blocks

Gregory Stump
University of Kentucky

> In a series of publications, Stephen Anderson developed the idea that the definition of a language's inflectional morphology involves blocks of realization rules such that (i) realization rules' order of application follows from the ordering of the blocks to which they belong and (ii) realization rules belonging to the same block stand in a relation of paradigmatic opposition. A question that naturally arises from this conception of rule interaction is whether it is possible for the same rule to figure in the application of more than one block. I discuss two systems of verb inflection exploiting exactly this possibility – those of Limbu and Southern Sotho. In order to account for the special properties of such systems, I argue that in the definition of a language's inflectional morphology, one rule may be dependent upon another, and that in such cases, the dependent rule may figure in the application of more than one block precisely because the "carrier" rules on which it is dependent differ in their block membership. In formal terms, this means that the definition of a language's inflectional morphology may draw upon principles of rule conflation by which a dependent realization rule combines with its carrier rule to form a single, more complex rule, typically occupying the same block as the carrier rule. I further show that there is considerable independent motivation for the postulation of these principles.

1 Introduction

In a series[1] of articles culminating in his 1992 monograph *A-morphous Morphology*, Stephen Anderson developed a model for the precise inferential-realizational definition of complex inflectional patterns.[2]

Two central principles of this model are (1) and (2). According to (1), the definition of the Latin word form *laudā-ba-nt-ur* 'they were being praised' involves the realization of a morphosyntactic property set through the interaction of ordered rule blocks. One of these houses a rule realizing the imperfect indicative through the suffixation of *-bā*;

---

[1] Key references include Anderson 1977; 1982; 1984a,b; 1986.
[2] In the typology of morphological theories proposed by Stump (2001), a theory is inferential if it employs rules to infer the form of a language's words and stems from that of less complex stems; a theory is realizational if its definition of a language's morphology takes a word's content as logically antecedent to its form.

Gregory Stump. 2017b. Rules and blocks. In Claire Bowern, Laurence Horn & Raffaella Zanuttini (eds.), *On looking into words (and beyond)*, 421–440. Berlin: Language Science Press. DOI:10.5281/zenodo.495457

this is followed by a block housing a rule realizing third-person plural subject agreement by the suffixation of -*nt*; this, in turn, is followed by a block containing a rule realizing passive voice through the suffixation of -*ur*. The successive application of these rule blocks infers the word form *laudābantur* from the stem *laudā*- as the realization of the property set {3 pl imperf ind pass} in the paradigm of the lexeme LAUDĀRE 'praise'.

(1) A language's inflectional rules are organized into ordered blocks such that two rules' order of application depends on the ordering of the blocks to which they belong.

(2) Rules belonging to the same block are disjunctive: at most one rule per block applies in the realization of a given word form. In general, competition between rules is resolved in favor of the rule with the narrower domain of application.

According to (2), the definition of a word form by a sequence of rule blocks involves the application of at most one rule per block. Two rules belonging to the same block may be defined so as to apply in disjoint contexts; for instance, the rule realizing third-person plural subject agreement through the suffixation of -*nt* realizes different property sets from the rule realizing first-person plural subject agreement throught the suffixation of -*mus*. But it can also happen that two rules belonging to the same block are both in principle applicable in the same context; for instance, -*ī* and -*ō* both realize first-person singlar subject agreement and might therefore be seen as entering into competition in the realization of certain forms. Given that the -*ī* rule applies only in the first-person singular perfect indicative active (e.g. *laudāvī* 'I have praised'), its domain of application is narrower than that of the -*ō* rule, which apparently applies as a default, surfacing in the present and future indicative active (*laudō* 'I praise', *laudābō* 'I will praise') and passive (*laudor* 'I am praised', *laudābor* 'I will be praised') as well as in the future perfect indicative active (*laudāverō* 'I will have praised'); accordingly, the -*ī* rule overrides the -*ō* rule in the realization of the first person singular perfect indicative active.

Anderson's model has afforded the most plausible existing accounts of a diverse range of inflectional systems (see, for example, the analyses of Potawatomi and Georgian in **Anderson1984a**; Anderson 1977; 1986 and that of German in Zwicky 1985), and it continues to raise important theoretical questions. One such question is whether the same rule[3] may figure in the application of more than one rule block. I argue here that in a particular class of cases, this is precisely what happens.

In the cases in question, there is always a relation of dependency among particular rules. Harris (2017) describes relations of this sort in affixal terms as involving a dependent affix that only appears in the presence of an available carrier affix. Adopting and extending her terminology, I describe such relations as involving a dependent rule that only applies in combination with an available carrier rule. As I show, a dependent rule may figure in the application of more than one block if the rules on which it is dependent differ in their block membership. Instances of this sort are of two kinds.

---

[3] Two rule applications are seen as involving the "same rule" if they realize the same morphosyntactic content by means of the same exponent even if they introduce that exponent into different positions.

First, there are instances of multiple exponence in which the same rule of affixation apparently applies in more than one block in a word form's inflectional realization; an example from the Limbu language [Kiranti; Nepal] is the multiple exponence of certain agent concord properties in the inflection of transitive verbs. Second, there are instances of polyfunctionality involving a rule of affixation whose function varies systematically according to the block in which it applies; an example is the polyfunctionality of concordial affixes in the verbal inflection of the Bantu languages. In order to account for cases of these two sorts, it is desirable to supplement (1) and (2) with principles (3) and (4).

(3) A dependent rule may be conflated with a carrier rule to produce a more complex rule. Where a dependent rule R_1 realizes property set σ by means of exponent x and its carrier rule R_2 realizes property set τ by means of exponent y, the conflation of R_1 with R_2 is intuitively a rule realizing the property set $\sigma \cup \tau$ by means of the combined exponents x and y.

(4) A rule block may contain both simple and conflated rules.

As I shall show, these principles afford economical accounts of multiple exponence in Limbu verbs and of polyfunctional verbal concord markers in Southern Sotho [Bantu; Lesotho]. After describing the expression of agent properties in Limbu verbs (§2) and the Southern Sotho system of verbal concord (§3), I propose a formal framework for rule conflation in inflectional morphology (§4). I then present explicit theories of the observed pattern of multiple exponence in Limbu (§5) and that of polyfunctional concordial morphology in Southern Sotho (§6). I conclude with some observations about the wider importance of rule conflation in an adequate theory of morphology (§7).

2 Multiple exponence in the expression of agent inflection in Limbu verbs

In Limbu, two agent concord suffixes participate in relations of multiple exponence: -*ŋ*, an expression of first-person singular agent concord, and -*m*, an expression of non-third-person plural agent concord. Table 1 exemplifies the distribution of these suffixes in positive forms of HUʔMAʔ 'teach'.[4] (In this table, parenthesized segments are superficially elided in prevocalic position by an ordinary phonological process.) Both suffixes

---

[4] The structure of Table 1 should be carefully noted. Each row in the table is occupied by a different word form in the paradigm of the Limbu verb HUʔMAʔ 'teach'. Each word is in exploded form, with its parts arranged in columns corresponding to the affix position classes postulated by van Driem. (I follow him in labeling these classes **pf1** and **sf1–sf10**.) Thus, the word form in the 1s → 3ns row of the nonpreterite part of the table is *huʔr-u-ŋ-si-ŋ* 'I teach them'. This table does not comprise the complete paradigm of HUʔMAʔ 'teach', but encompasses those forms that involve the agent suffixes -*ŋ* and -*m* (as well as a few other pertinent forms in which the appearance of these suffixes is overridden). The claim that these suffixes appear in two different positions means that they appear in two different columns, since each column defines an affix position class in the traditional sense.

423

appear in two different affix positions; van Driem (1987) labels these positions **sf5** and **sf9**.[5]

Table 1: The agent suffixes -ŋ and -m in positive forms of the Limbu verb HUʔMAʔ 'teach'

	agent → patient	pf1 a	pf1 b	stem[1]	sf 1	sf 2	sf 4	sf 5	sf 7	sf 8	sf 9	sf 10
Nonpreterite	1s → 2s			huʔ	nɛ							
	1s → 2d			huʔ	nɛ					ci³	ŋ	
	1s → 2p			huʔ	n(ɛ)					i	ŋ	
	1s → 3s			huʔr			u	ŋ				
	1s → 3ns			huʔr			u	ŋ		si	ŋ	
	1pi → 3s	a		huʔr			u	m				
	1pi → 3ns	a		huʔr			u	m		si	m	
	1pe → 2			huʔ	nɛ				ci			ge
	1pe → 3s			huʔr			u	m				be⁴
	1pe → 3ns			huʔr			u	m		si	m	be⁴
	2 → 1	a	gɛ²	huʔ								
	2p → 3s		kɛ	huʔr			u	m				
	2p → 3ns		kɛ	huʔr			u	m		si	m	
Preterite	1s → 2s			huʔ	n(ɛ)	ɛ						
	1s → 2d			huʔ	n(ɛ)	ɛ				ci³	ŋ	
	1s → 2p			huʔ	n(ɛ)	(ɛ)				i	ŋ	
	1s → 3s			huʔr		(ɛ)	u	ŋ				
	1s → 3ns			huʔr		(ɛ)	u	ŋ		si	ŋ	
	1pi → 3s	a		huʔr		(ɛ)	u	m				
	1pi → 3ns	a		huʔr		(ɛ)	u	m		si	m	
	1pe → 2			huʔ	n(ɛ)	ɛ			ci			ge
	1pe → 3s			huʔ					mʔna			
	1pe → 3ns			huʔ					mʔna	si		
	2 → 1	a	gɛ²	huʔr		ɛ						
	2p → 3s		kɛ	huʔr			u	m				
	2p → 3ns		kɛ	huʔr			u	m		si	m	

1. *huʔr* is a prevocalic alternant of *huʔ*.
2. *gɛ* is an alternant of *kɛ* (van Driem 1987: 2)
3. *s* becomes *c* after *ɛ* (van Driem 1987: 77)
4. *be* is a phonologically conditioned alternant of *ge* (van Driem 1987: 102)

---

[5] Affix positions **sf3** and **sf6** are missing from Table 1 because the affixes that appear in these positions don't occur in forms having a first-person singular agent or a nonthird-person plural agent.

The distribution of these suffixes is, in fact, doubly puzzling. Besides participating in relations of multiple exponence, they also exhibit gaps in their distribution. Consider first the suffix *-ŋ*. Because ten of the forms in Table 1 realize first-person singular agent properties, all ten would be compatible with the appearance of the *-ŋ* suffix in both the **sf5** and **sf9** positions. Yet, only two of the forms exhibit *-ŋ* in both positions; two exhibit it only in position **sf5**; four, only in postion **sf9**; and two lack *-ŋ* altogether. Consider likewise the distribution of the nonthird-person plural agent suffix *-m*. Among the fourteen forms in Table 1 that realize nonthird-person plural agent properties, only five exhibit *-m* in both the **sf5** and **sf9** positions; five have it in the **sf5** position only; and four lack *-m* altogether.

A cursory examination reveals the distributional generalization accounting for these results: *-ŋ* and *-m* appear in position **sf5** only if there is an overt affix in position **sf4**, and they appear in **sf9** only if there is an overt affix in **sf8**. In other words, the rules that introduce *-ŋ* and *-m* in Limbu are dependent rules whose application presumes that of a carrier rule filling position **sf4** or **sf8**. Because there are carrier rules in more than one rule block, the *-ŋ* and *-m* rules may both figure in the application of more than one block.

3 Polyfunctional concordial morphology in the verb inflection of Southern Sotho

Typically of Bantu languages, Southern Sotho has a rich noun-class system one of whose manifestations is the inflection of verbs for the noun class of their subject and object arguments. In the analysis proposed by Doke & Mofokeng (1985), this system exhibits seven noun classes; these have the effect of subclassifying the third person, so that like the first and second persons, each noun class subsumes both singular and plural forms. Table 2 presents the inventory of prefixes by which verbs inflect for the person, number and noun class of their subject. By a similar inventory of prefixes, transitive verbs may[6] inflect for the properties of their object; the examples in Table 3 illustrate. Table 4 presents the inventories of subject-coding and object-coding prefixes side by side; as this table shows, the two inventories are nearly identical; the only exceptions are in the singular of the first person and of class 1, where the exponents of subject properties differ from those of the corresponding object properties.

The principal difference between the two inventories is morphotactic: subject-coding prefixes occupy the position before that of tense prefixes (such as the future-tense prefix *tla-* in Tables 2 and 3) while object-coding prefixes occupy the position following that of tense prefixes. Thus, the general pattern is that the prefixes in Table 4 express properties of person, number and noun class, and that it is a prefix's position that determines whether the properties that it expresses are subject or object properties. Put another

---

[6] Unlike the subject concords, whose use is obligatory in finite forms, the object concords are optional, generally being use to express a pronominal object rather than to express agreement with an overt object phrase (Doke & Mofokeng 1985: 242).

Gregory Stump

Table 2: Future-tense forms of Southern Sotho BÒNA 'see': 'I / you / etc. will see' (Doke & Mofokeng 1985: 207ff.)

Subject person	Subject class			Subject number	
	Doke & Mofokeng	Meinhof		Singular	Plural
		sg	pl		
1				kē-tla-bòna	rē-tla-bòna
2				u-tla-bòna	lē-tla-bòna
3	1	1	2	ō-tla-bòna	ba-tla-bòna
	2	3	4	ō-tla-bòna	ē-tla-bòna
	3	5	6/10	lē-tla-bòna	a-tla-bòna, li-tla-bòna
	4	7	8	sē-tla-bòna	li-tla-bòna
	5	9	10	ē-tla-bòna	li-tla-bòna
	6	14	6	bō-tla-bòna	a-tla-bòna
	7	15/17		hō-tla-bòna	

Table 3: Future-tense forms of Southern Sotho BÒNA 'see': 'they will see me / you / etc.' (Doke & Mofokeng 1985: 242ff)

Object person	Object class			Object number	
	Doke & Mofokeng	Meinhof		Singular	Plural
		sg	pl		
1				ba-tla-m-pòna	ba-tla-rē-bòna
2				ba-tla-u-bòna	ba-tla-lē-bòna
3	1	1	2	ba-tla-mō-bòna	ba-tla-ba-bòna
	2	3	4	ba-tla-ō-bòna	ba-tla-ē-bòna
	3	5	6/10	ba-tla-lē-bòna	ba-tla-a-bòna, ba-tla-li-bòna
	4	7	8	ba-tla-sē-bòna	ba-tla-li-bòna
	5	9	10	ba-tla-ē-bòna	ba-tla-li-bòna
	6	14	6	ba-tla-bō-bòna	ba-tla-a-bòna
	7	15/17		ba-tla-hō-bòna	

way, the rules introducing the noun-class concords in Table 4 generally figure in the application of more than one rule block, expressing subject properties in one block and object properties in another.

4 Rule conflation

It is clear from the foregoing evidence that in the definition of a language's inflectional morphology, the same realization rule may figure in the application of more than one rule block. I propose that this is an effect of the phenomenon of rule conflation; in particular, I propose that when rule R figures in the application of both Blocks A and B,

Table 4: Indicative verbal concords in Southern Sotho (Doke & Mofokeng 1985: 197,243)

Person	Class				Subject		Object	
	Doke & Mofokeng	Meinhof			sg	pl	sg	pl
		sg	pl					
1					kē-	rē-	N-*	rē-
2					u-	lē-	u-	lē-
3	1	1	2		ō-	ba-	mō-	ba-
	2	3	4		ō-	ē-	ō-	ē-
	3	5	6/10		lē-	a-, li-	lē-	a-, li-
	4	7	8		sē-	li-	sē-	li-
	5	9	10		ē-	li-	ē-	li-
	6	14	6		bō-	a-	bō-	a-
	7	15/17			hō-		hō-	

*N represents a homorganic nasal

it is because R may conflate both with certain Block A rules and with certain Block B rules. I represent the conflation of R_1 with R_2 as $[R_1 © R_2]$.

I make six essential assumptions about the definition of rule conflation.

4.1 Rule-block membership

A conflated rule $[R_1 © R_2]$ belongs to the same rule block as its carrier rule R_2.

4.2 Forms defined by conflated rules

Where R_1 is a rule that affixes a by means of operation F and R_2 is a rule that affixes b by means of operation G, the conflated rule $[R_1 © R_2]$ affixes b' by means of operation G, where b' is the result of affixing a to b by means of operation F. According to this definition, there are four logically possible patterns of conflation for rules of affixation; these are represented schematically in part (A) of Table 5. The conflation of R_1 with R_2 is analogous to function composition when R_1 and R_2 both effect prefixation or when both effect suffixation. But when R_1 is prefixational and R_2 is suffixational, the application of $[R_1 © R_2]$ to stem X is Xab rather than aXb; and when R_1 is suffixational and R_2 is prefixational, the application of $[R_1 © R_2]$ to stem X is baX rather than bXa. In these latter cases, the conflation of R_1 with R_2 cannot be likened to the mathematical notion of function composition.

Gregory Stump

Table 5: Six logical possibilities for the conflation $[R_1 © R_2]$ of a dependent rule R_1 with a carrier rule R_2

	Dependent rule R_1	Carrier rule R_2	Conflated rule $[R_1 © R_2]$	$[R_1 © R_2]$ applied to stem X
(A)	*a*-prefixation	*b*-prefixation	*ab*-prefixation	*ab*X
	a-prefixation	*b*-suffixation	*ab*-suffixation	X*ab*
	a-suffixation	*b*-prefixation	*ba*-prefixation	*ba*X
	a-suffixation	*b*-suffixation	*ba*-suffixation	X*ba*
(B)	*a*-prefixation	identity function	*a*-prefixation	*a*X
	a-suffixation	identity function	*a*-suffixation	X*a*

4.3 A conflated rule's direction of affixation

Whether $[R_1 © R_2]$ is a rule of prefixation or suffixation is uniquely determined by the properties of R_1 and R_2. If R_2 is a rule of affixation, then the direction of affixation of $[R_1 © R_2]$ is that of R_2, as indicated in (ii) above; but if R_2 is a rule of significative absence,[7] then the direction of affixation of $[R_1 © R_2]$ is that of R_1, as in part (B) of Table 5.

4.4 Content realized by a conflated rule

If rule R_1 realizes the morphosyntactic property set α and rule R_2 realizes the property set β, then rule $[R_1 © R_2]$ realizes the combination of α and β. In the simplest cases, the relevant mode of combination can simply be seen as set union: α ∪ β. But in the general case, it is preferable to regard the mode of set combination as unification;[8] for instance, the combination of {fut, {sbj 3 sg}} with {{sbj fem}} should be the unification {fut {sbj 3 sg fem}} rather than the union {fut, {sbj 3 sg}, {sbj fem}}. That is, if R_1 realizes α and R_2 realizes β, then $[R_1 © R_2]$ realizes the unification α ⊔ β.

---

[7] A rule of significative absence realizes a particular property set by means of an identity function. In a realizational theory of morphology, a rule of significative absence realizing a property set σ overrides the overt morphology of a competing rule realizing some property set of which σ is an extension. (Cf. the analysis of Bulgarian verb inflection proposed by Stump 2001: 441ff).

[8] The assumed definition of unification is as in (i); this definition depends on the assumed definition of extension in (ii). (Cf. Gazdar et al. 1985: 27; Stump 2001: 41.)

(i) The **unification** of ρ and σ [i.e. ρ ⊔ σ] is the smallest well-formed extension of both ρ and σ.
  Example: {{sbj 3 sg}, {obj pl}} ⊔ {prs, {obj 1}} = {{sbj 3 sg}, prs, {obj 1 pl}}

(ii) Given two sets σ, τ: σ is an **extension** of τ [i.e. τ ⊑ σ] iff for each property x ∈ τ,
  either (i) x is simple property and x ∈ σ
  or (ii) x is a complex property (= a set of properties) such that y ∈ σ and y is an extension of x.
    Examples: {pl} ⊑ {1 pl}
         {prs {obj 1}} ⊑ {prs {obj 1 pl}}

4.5 Recursion

The definition of rule conflation does not exclude the possibility that a conflated rule might itself enter into the conflation of a still more complex rule; that is, rule conflation may be recursive.

4.6 Nonconcatenative rules and conflation

A priori, there is no reason why the morphological rules that enter into such conflations must necessarily be rules of affixation or of significative absence. The most convincing cases, however, do involve rules of these two sorts, and I shall focus exclusively on such cases here. Nevertheless, nothing that I say here should be seen as excluding the possibility that nonconcatenative rules might also enter into relations of rule conflation.

Rule conflation is an operation on rules rather than on affixes; nevertheless, if R_1 and R_2 are rules introducing the respective affixes *a* and *b*, one can, as a kind of shorthand, refer to the affix *ab* (or *ba*) introduced by the conflated rule $[R_1 \odot R_2]$ as a CONFLATED AFFIX.

As I now show, this conception of rule conflation affords a straightforward account of multiple exponence in the expression of Limbu agent inflection (§5) and of polyfunctional concordial morphology in Southern Sotho (§6).

5 Rule conflation and multiple exponence in Limbu

Consider again the inflection of Limbu verbs for the properties of their agent argument. As was seen in §2, the suffix *-ŋ* (expressing first-person singular agent properties) and the suffix *-m* (expressing nonthird-person plural agent properties) may appear in either of two positions—or in both—in a verb form's inflectional morphotactics; but their appearance in either position is dependent on that of a suffix in the immediately preceding position. The following analysis of this distributional pattern is based on two key assumptions:[9]

- the agent-coding suffixes *-ŋ* and *-m* are introduced by dependent rules that only apply in conflation with another, "carrier" rule, and
- carrier rules for the *-ŋ* and *-m* rules exist in more than one block.

This analysis employs independent realization rules that introduce the suffixes[10] in Table 1; these are organized into several rule blocks, each of which fills a particular affix position. These independent rules and their block membership are given in Table 6. There are also dependent realization rules; these introduce the agent-coding suffixes *-ŋ* and *-m*,

---

[9] The dependent rules at issue in the proposed analyses of Limbu and Southern Sotho are only manifested in conflation with a carrier rule. But one can also imagine that a rule might be able to function both as a dependent rule and as an independent rule; the rules introducing the Swahili relative affixes are argued to have this status in the analysis proposed by Stump (To appear).

[10] Concerning the person prefixes *a-* and *kɛ-* in Table 1, see van van Driem 1987: 77ff.

as in (5). Rule conflation is defined by the conflation rules in (6). Rule (??) conflates the dependent rules with the three carrier rules identified in Table 6: 4-a, 8-a and 8-b. The resulting conflated rules are listed (redundantly) in Table 7.

Because a conflated rule belongs to the same rule block as the carrier rule on which it is based, the conflated rule and the carrier rule compete to realize certain morphosyntactic property sets; in any such instance of competition, the conflated rule prevails by virtue of the fact that its domain of application is smaller than that of the carrier rule.[11]

Table 6: Some independent realization rules of Limbu verb inflection

Block	Rule label	Realization rules		Carrier rule?
		Properties realized	Operation	
sf1	1-a	{{agt 1} {pat 2}}	X → Xnɛ	no
sf2	2-a	{pret}	X → Xɛ	
sf4	4-a	{{pat 3}}	X → Xu	yes
sf7	7-a	{{agt 1 ns} {pat 2}}	X → Xci	no
sf8	8-a	{{pat ns}}	X → Xsi	yes
	8-b	{{pat −3 −incl pl}}	X → Xi	
sf10	10-a	{{excl}}	X → Xge	no
sf11	11-a	{{agt 1 pl excl} pret {pat 3}}	X → Xmʔna	yes, for 8-a

(5) Dependent realization rules
    Ŋ. {{agt1 sg}}   : X → Xŋ (van van Driem 1987: 99)
    M. {{agt −3 pl}} : X → Xm (van van Driem 1987: 99f)

(6) Conflation rules
    a. Where R is a rule in Block α (α ∈ {4, 8}),
       [Ŋ © R], [M © R] ∈ Block α.
    b. [8-a © 11-a] ∈ Block 11.[12]

---

[11] Concerning each rule in Table 6, see van Driem (1987): 1-a, pp.88f; 2-a, pp.89ff; 4-a, p.82; 7-a, p.100; 8-a, pp.101f; 8-b, pp.95f; 10-a, p.102f; 11-a, 100f.

[12] Conflation rule (??) helps to resolve a conundrum in Table 1. Notice first that the suffix -mʔna introduced by rule 11-a as an exponent of the property set {{agt 1 pl excl} pret {pat 3}} only combines with one other suffix, namely the suffix -si introduced by rule 8-a as an exponent of {{pat ns}}; yet, it is featurally compatible with the suffixes introduced by 4-a and 10-a. Moreover, the suffix -si in the form huʔ-mʔna-si 'we (excl) taught them' does not carry -m, even though (a) it is a carrier elsewhere and (b) -m would be featurally appropriate for this word form. I therefore depart from van Driem in postulating Block 11 as a portmanteau rule block (Stump 2001: 141) that is paradigmatically opposed to and defaults to the sequence of other suffixal blocks. It houses exactly two rules: the simple rule 11-a (which suffixes -mʔna) and the conflated rule [8-a © 11-a] (which suffixes -mʔna-si). Because Block 11 is paradigmatically opposed to the sequence of rule blocks to which Block 8 belongs, the application of rule [8-a © 11-a] excludes that of rule [M © 8-a], effectively blocking the appearance of -m in forms such as huʔ-mʔna-si 'we (excl) taught them'.

Table 7: Some conflated realization rules of Limbu verb inflection

Block	Rule label	Realization rules	
		Properties realized	Operation
4	[I] © 4-a]	{{agt 1 sg} {pat 3}}	X → Xuŋ
	[M © 4-a]	{{agt −3 pl} {pat 3}}	X → Xum
8	[I] © 8-a]	{{agt 1 sg} {pat ns}}:	X → Xsiŋ
	[I] © 8-b]	{{agt 1 sg} {pat−3 −incl pl}}	X → Xiŋ
	[M © 8-a]	{{agt −3 pl} {pat ns}}:	X → Xsim
11	[8-a © 11-a]	{{agt 1 pe} pret {pat 3 ns}}	X → Xmʔnasi

This analysis correctly defines all of the forms in Table 1. In particular, it accounts for the superficially erratic distribution of the agent concords *-ŋ* and *-m*. Thus, Table 8 presents the manner in which the rules in Tables 6 and 7 define four words:

- *huʔr-u-ŋ-si-ŋ* 'I teach them', in which *-ŋ* appears twice—after *-u* and after *-si*;
- *huʔr-u-ŋ* 'I teach him', in which *-ŋ* appears after *-u* only;
- *huʔ-nɛ-ci-ŋ* 'I teach you two', in which *-ŋ* appears after *-si* only; and
- *huʔ-nɛ* 'I teach you (sg.)', in which *-ŋ* fails to appear.

As Table 8 shows, *-ŋ* only appears in conflation with an immediately preceding carrier: in one case, it appears twice because there are two carriers to conflate with; in another, only the carrier *-u* is available; in yet another, only the carrier *-si* is available; and sometimes, there is no carrier at all to conflate with. The proposed analysis provides a similar account of the comparable behavior of the suffix *-m*.

6 Rule conflation and polyfunctional concord in Southern Sotho

Return now to the morphology of verbal concord in Southern Sotho. As we saw in §3, this morphology is largely polyfunctional. Typically, a verbal concord may appear in either of two positions in a verb's inflectional morphotactics; but unlike the agent-coding suffixes in Limbu, which express the same content no matter where they appear, the Southern Sotho verbal concords express subject properties in one position but object properties in another. The notion of rule conflation makes it possible to account for this difference by assuming that in Southern Sotho, the rules expressing noun-class concord conflate with a general rule of subject concord in one block and with a general rule of object concord in a different block. Because the two general rules are formulated as identity functions (realizing subject concord and object concord, respectively), the conflated subject concords have the same phonological form as the conflated object concords.

Thus, consider the following definition of the Southern Sotho inflectional markings in Tables 2 and 3. In this analysis, there are three blocks of independent realization rules,

Table 8: The definition of four Limbu verb forms in the proposed analysis

	Property set: Stem:	{{agt 1 s} {pat 3 ns}} huʔ 'teach' (prevocalically huʔr)	{{agt 1 s} {pat 3 s}} huʔ 'teach' (prevocalically huʔr)
Rule applying in			
Block:	sf1:	(none)	(none)
	sf2:	(none)	(none)
	sf4:	[I] © 4-a]: huʔr-u-ŋ	[I] © 4-a]: huʔr-u-ŋ
	sf7:	(none)	(none)
	sf8:	[I] © 8-a]: huʔr-u-ŋ-si-ŋ	(none)
	sf10:	(none)	(none)
	sf11:	(none)	(none)
		huʔr-u-ŋ-si-ŋ 'I teach them'	huʔr-u-ŋ 'I teach him'
	Property set: Stem:	{{agt 1 s} {pat 2 de}} huʔ 'teach'	{{agt 1 s} {pat 2 s}} huʔ 'teach'
Rule applying in			
Block:	sf1:	1-a: huʔ-nɛ	1-a: huʔ-nɛ
	sf2:	(none)	(none)
	sf4:	(none)	(none)
	sf7:	(none)	(none)
	sf8:	[I] © 8-a]: huʔ-nɛ-ci-ŋ	(none)
	sf10:	(none)	(none)
	sf11:	(none)	(none)
		huʔ-nɛ-ci-ŋ 'I teach you two'	huʔ-nɛ 'I teach you (sg.)'

as in Table 9. Block **a** houses the rules of object concord: these include the special object-concord rules for the first-person singular (a-i) and third singular class 1 (a-ii); in addition, it includes a default rule (a-iii) realizing object concord by means of an identity operation. Block **b** houses rules realizing tense properties, here exemplified by the future tense. Block **c** houses rules of subject concord, including the special rule (c-i) of first-person singular subject concord and a default rule (c-ii) realizing subject concord by means of an identity operation. In addition to the independent realization rules in Table 9, the analysis requires the large inventory of dependent rules in Table 10. The conflation rule in (6) conflates each dependent rule with the default object-concord rule (a-iii) and with the default subject-concord rule (c-ii). The resulting conflated rules are listed (redundantly) in Table 11.

Table 9: Three blocks of independent realization rules in Southern Sotho

Block	Rule label	Realization rules Properties realized	Operation	Carrier rule?
a	a-i	{{obj 1 sg}}	X → NX*	
	a-ii	{{obj 3 sg CL:1}}	X → mōX	
	a-iii	{{obj}}	X → X	yes
b	b-i	{fut}	X → tlaX	
c	c-i	{{sbj 1 sg}}	X → kēX	
	c-ii	{{sbj}}	X → X	yes

*N represents a homorganic nasal.

Table 10: Dependent realization rules for verbal concord in Southern Sotho

Rule label	Realization rules Properties realized	Operation
agr-i	{{2 sg}}	X → uX
agr-ii	{{3 sg}}	X → ōX
agr-iii	{{3 sg CL:3}}	X → lēX
agr-iv	{{3 sg CL:4}}	X → sēX
agr-v	{{3 sg CL:5}}	X → ēX
agr-vi	{{3 sg CL:6}}	X → bōX
agr-vii	{{3 CL:7}}	X → hōX
agr-viii	{{1 pl}}	X → rēX
agr-ix	{{2 pl}}	X → lēX
agr-x	{{3 pl CL:1}}	X → baX
agr-xi	{{3 pl CL:1|2}}	X → ēX
agr-xii	{{3 pl CL:3}}	X → aX | liX
agr-xiii	{{3 pl CL:4|5}}	X → liX
agr-xiv	{{3 pl CL:6}}	X → aX

(7) Conflation rule
Where **agr-n** is a dependent realization rule and R is a carrier rule in Block α, [agr-n © R] ∈ Block α.

Gregory Stump

Table 11: Some conflated realization rules of Southern Sotho verb inflection

Block	Rule label	Realization rules	
		Properties realized	Operation
a	[agr-i © a-iii]	{{obj 2 sg}}	X → uX
	[agr-ii © a-iii]	{{obj 3 sg CL:1|2}}	X → ōX
	[agr-iii © a-iii]	{{obj 3 sg CL:3}}	X → lēX
	[agr-iv © a-iii]	{{obj 3 sg CL:4}}	X → sēX
	[agr-v © a-iii]	{{obj 3 sg CL:5}}	X → ēX
	[agr-vi © a-iii]	{{obj 3 sg CL:6}}	X → bōX
	[agr-vii © a-iii]	{{obj 3 CL:7}}	X → hōX
	[agr-viii © a-iii]	{{obj 1 pl}}	X → rēX
	[agr-ix © a-iii]	{{obj 2 pl}}	X → lēX
	[agr-x © a-iii]	{{obj 3 pl CL:1}}	X → baX
	[agr-xi © a-iii]	{{obj 3 pl CL:1|2}}	X → ēX
	[agr-xii © a-iii]	{{obj 3 pl CL:3}}	X → aX | liX
	[agr-xiii © a-iii]	{{obj 3 pl CL:4|5}}	X → liX
	[agr-xiv © a-iii]	{{obj 3 pl CL:6}}	X → aX
c	[agr-i © c-ii]	{{sbj 2 sg}}	X → uX
	[agr-ii © c-ii]	{{sbj 3 sg CL:1|2}}	X → ōX
	[agr-iii © c-ii]	{{sbj 3 sg CL:3}}	X → lēX
	[agr-iv © c-ii]	{{sbj 3 sg CL:4}}	X → sēX
	[agr-v © c-ii]	{{sbj 3 sg CL:5}}	X → ēX
	[agr-vi © c-ii]	{{sbj 3 sg CL:6}}	X → bōX
	[agr-vii © c-ii]	{{sbj 3 CL:7}}	X → hōX
	[agr-viii © c-ii]	{{sbj 1 pl}}	X → rēX
	[agr-ix © c-ii]	{{sbj 2 pl}}	X → lēX
	[agr-x © c-ii]	{{sbj 3 pl CL:1}}	X → baX
	[agr-xi © c-ii]	{{sbj 3 pl CL:1|2}}	X → ēX
	[agr-xii © c-ii]	{{sbj 3 pl CL:3}}	X → aX | liX
	[agr-xiii © c-ii]	{{sbj 3 pl CL:4|5}}	X → liX
	[agr-xiv © c-ii]	{{sbj 3 pl CL:6}}	X → aX

Each of the conflated rules in Table 11 belongs to the same rule block as the carrier rule on which it is based. As in the Limbu analysis proposed above, a conflated rule and the carrier rule on which it is based compete to realize certain morphosyntactic property sets, and being the narrower rule, the conflated rule prevails in each such case.

This analysis correctly defines all of the forms in Tables 2 and 3. In particular, it accounts for the fact that in all but a handful of cases, each subject concord has a corresponding object concord that expresses the same person, number and noun class by means of the same prefix. Thus, Table 12 presents the manner in which the rules in Tables 10 and 11 define two words:

- *ba-tla-bō-bòna* 'they (CL:1) will see it (CL:6)', in which *ba-* is a third-person plural class 1 subject concord and *bō-* is a singular class 6 object concord; and

- *bō-tla-ba-bòna* 'it (CL:6) will see them (CL:1)', in which *bō-* is a singular class 6 subject concord and *ba-* is a third-person plural class 1 object concord.

Table 12: The definition of two Southern Sotho verb forms in the proposed analysis

	Property set:	{{sbj 3 pl CL:1} fut {obj 3 sg CL:6}}
	Stem:	*bòna* 'see'
Rule applying in		
Block a:	[agr-vi © a-iii]:	*bō-bòna*
b:	b-i:	*tla-bō-bòna*
c:	[agr-x © c-ii]:	*ba-tla-bō-bòna*
		ba-tla-bō-bòna
		'they (CL:1) will see it (CL:6)'
	Property set:	{{sbj 3 sg CL:6} fut {obj 3 pl CL:1}}
	Stem:	*bòna* 'see'
Rule applying in		
Block a:	[agr-x © a-iii]:	*ba-bòna*
b:	b-i:	*tla-ba-bòna*
c:	[agr-vi © c-ii]:	*bō-tla-ba-bòna*
		bō-tla-ba-bòna
		'it (CL:6) will see them (CL:1)'

As Table 12 shows, the dependent rules introducing *bō-* (**agr-vi** in Table 10) and *-ba* (**agr-x** in Table 10) both conflate with the carrier rule **a-iii** (Table 9) to produce rules of object concord in Block **a** and both conflate with the carrier rule **c-ii** (Table 9) to produce a rule of subject concord in Block **c**.

7 Wider evidence for rule conflation

The analyses proposed here for multiple exponence in Limbu agent concord and for polyfunctional verbal concords in Southern Sotho both depend on the notion that morphological rules may conflate to produce more complex rules (= principle (3)) and the notion that conflated rules may compete with simple rules as members of the same rule block (= principle (4)).

These principles of rule conflation are motivated independently of the need to account for multiple exponence and polyfunctionality. First, they make it possible to account for apparent anomalies in the interaction of inflectional rule applications. For example, a rule's order of application may seem to depend on whether or not another rule applies.

435

In Fula, a pronominal object suffix on a verb in the relative past tense ordinarily follows that verb's subject suffx, as in (8a,8b); but in the particular case in which a verb has both a singular personal object suffix (2sg -*mA* or 3sg -*mO*) and the first-person singular subject suffix -*mi*, the expected order is reversed, as in (8c,d). Principles (3) and (4) allow one to say that the rules realizing the subject and object suffixes in the relative past tense belong to a single rule block; that the object rules ordinarily conflate with the subject rules; but that the -*mi* rule instead conflates with the -*mA* and -*mO* rules.

(8)   a.   *mball-u-mi-ɓe-'*
  help-REL.PST.ACT-1SG.SBJ-3PL.CL.2.OBJ-FG
  'I helped them'
  b.   *mball-u-daa-mO-'*
  help-REL.PST.ACT-2SG.SBJ-3SG.CL.1.OBJ-FG
  'you (sg.) helped him'
  c.   *mball-u-mA-mi-'*
  help-REL.PST.ACT-2SG.OBJ-1SG.SBJ-FG
  'I helped you (sg.)'
  d.   *mball-u-mO-mi-'*
  help-REL.PST.ACT-3SG.CL.1.OBJ-1SG.SBJ-FG
  'I helped him'   (Arnott 1970, Appendix 15)

In another apparently anomalous interaction of inflectional rules, an affix either precedes the stem with which it joins or follows it, with the choice of position being conditioned by the presence or absence of some other affix. In Swahili, the verbal concord coding the properties of a relative verb form's relativized argument appears postverbally in tenseless affirmative forms, but preverbally in forms that are prefixally marked for tense or negation; thus, the class 8 relative concord *vyo* is postverbal in (9a) but preverbal in (9b). The principles of rule conflation make it possible to say that the relative affix is suffixed to the verb stem by default, but is suffixed to an overt prefixal exponent of tense or negation (Stump To appear).

(9)   a.   *a-vi-soma-vyo*
  SBJ:CL.1-OBJ:CL.8-read-REL:CL.8
  '(books) which he reads'
  b.   *a-si-vyo-vi-soma*
  SBJ:CL.1-NEG-REL:CL.8-OBJ:CL.8-read]
  '(books) which he doesn't read'

As Stump (2017a) shows, the principles of rule conflation afford simple solutions to a number of other apparent anomalies in the interaction of inflection rules. These include the incidence of variable affix order (Bickel et al. 2007) and of Wackernagel affixes (Nevis & Joseph 1992, Bonami & Samvelian 2008) as well as the superficially puzzling fact that affix sequences may preserve the same internal order whether the sequence as a whole is prefixal or suffixal, as in European Portuguese verb inflection (Luís & Spencer 2005).

Second, the principles of rule conflation in (3) and (4) make it possible to account for nonmonotonic interactions among inflectional rules. The usual expectation is that a realization rule possesses the same intrinsic properties whether it applies alone or in combination with other rules. But there are anomalous cases in which this expectation is not met. Once the definition of a language's morphology includes a conflated rule $[R_1 © R_2]$, this rule may evolve independently, taking on properties not directly stemming from either R_1 or R_2. In this way, the properties exhibited by a rule applying in isolation may not always be preserved when it is conflated with other rules. In view of this fact, the content attributed to conflated rules in §4.4 above should be seen as their *default* content, subject to modification by processes of grammaticalization. That is, the content expressed by rule $[R_1 © R_2]$ is, in the default case, a monotonic function of the content expressed by rules R_1 and R_2; but this default is subject to override.

There are at least three ways in which the resulting nonmonotonicity may be manifested. One reflection of this fact is the phenomenon of "potentiation" (Williams 1981), by which an unproductive rule becomes productive when applying in combination with another rule (as the unproductive *-ity* rule becomes productive in combination with the *-able* rule; cf. Aronoff 1976, Bochner 1992).

Another reflection is the fact that the domain of rule R_1 seems to depend on whether a particular rule R_2 applies subsequently. By principles (3) and (4), such cases arise when a conflated rule $[R_1 © R_2]$ evolves a domain application distinct from that of R_2. Thus, a stem may be in the domain of R_2 but not that of $[R_1 © R_2]$, as in the case of *base → basic, *basical*; at the same time, a stem may be in the domain of $[R_1 © R_2]$ but not that of R_2, as in the case of *whimsy → whimsical, *whimsic*. A third reflection arises in cases in which two rules apparently realize less content separately than they do together. In Latin *regēmus* 'we shall rule', the conflation of the rules that suffix *-ē* and *-mus* expresses the first-person plural future active even though neither rule by itself is an expression of future tense.[13] These nonmonotonic phenomena have never before been seen as manifestations of a single overarching principle; the principles of rule conflation, however, facilitate precisely such a perspective.

Third, the principles of rule conflation make it possible to account for parallelisms between the application of a single rule and that of a sequence of rules. A word form's inflectional morphology is sometimes informally conceived of as instantiating a sequence of "slots" each of which corresponds to a set of rules available to fill it. Andersonian rule blocks are a kind of formal reconstruction of this idea, whose simplest interpretation involves individual rules providing alternative ways of filling the same slot. There are, however, apparent deviations from this pattern, in which successive slots are ordinarily filled by successive rule applications but may in some instances be simultaneously filled by a single rule application introducing a "wide" affix that somehow straddles two or more slots. The Swahili portmanteau prefix *si-* is an example. In Swahili negative indicative verb forms, the usual pattern is for the negative *ha-* rule to fill slot 1 and a

---

[13] See Stump (2017a) for discussion of a similar case from Old English.

subject-concord rule to fill slot 2, e.g. *ha-tu-ta-taka* [NEG-1PL-FUT-want] 'we will not want'. But in first-person singular negative verb forms, the application of the negative first-person singular *si-* rule seems to straddle slots 1 and 2. The principles of rule conflation resolve this conundrum by allowing a rule block to contain both conflated rules (e.g. the first-person plural negative *ha-tu-* rule) and simple rules (e.g. the *si-* rule) in paradigmatic opposition; in this way, the behavior of portmanteau rules is reconciled with the natural assumption that paradigmatic opposition is a relation between two rules rather than a relation between a rule and a sequence of rules.

The principles of rule conflation in (3) and (4) are a simple and natural extension of the principles of realization-rule interaction developed by Anderson (see again 1 and 2). Rule conflation allows a variety of apparently recalcitrant phenomena to be reconciled with a general scheme of rule interaction based on ordered blocks of realization rules in which the members of a given block are mutually exclusive in their application.

Abbreviations

The following abbreviations are employed for the morphosyntactic properties.

AGT	agent
PAT	patient
PRET	preterite
1/2/3	first/second/third person
−3	nonthird person
EXCL	exclusive
−INCL	noninclusive
NS	nonsingular
SG	singular
PL	plural

References

Anderson, Stephen R. 1977. On the formal description of inflection. In Woodford A. Beach, Samuel E. Fox & Shulamith Philosoph (eds.), *Papers from the thirteenth regional meeting of the Chicago Linguistic Society*, 15–44. Chicago: Chicago Linguistic Society.
Anderson, Stephen R. 1982. Where's morphology? *Linguistic Inquiry* 13(4). 571–612.
Anderson, Stephen R. 1984a. On representations in morphology: Case marking, agreement and inversion in Georgian. *Natural Language and Linguistic Theory* 2. 157–218.
Anderson, Stephen R. 1984b. Rules as 'morphemes' in a theory of inflection. In D. Rood (ed.), *Mid-america linguistics conference papers*, 3–21. Boulder: University of Colorado.
Anderson, Stephen R. 1986. Disjunctive ordering in inflectional morphology. *Natural Language and Linguistic Theory* 4. 1–31.
Arnott, D.W. 1970. *The nominal and verbal systems of Fula*. Oxford University Press.
Aronoff, Mark. 1976. *Word formation in generative grammar*. Cambridge, MA: MIT Press.

Bickel, Balthasar, Goma Banjade, Martin Gaenzle, Elena Lieven, Netra Prasad Paudyal, Ichchha Purna Rai, Manoj Rai, Novel Kishore Rai & Sabine Stoll. 2007. Free prefix ordering in Chintang. *Language* 83. 43–73.

Bochner, Harry. 1992. *Simplicity in generative morphology*. Berlin: Mouton de Gruyter.

Bonami, Olivier & Pollet Samvelian. 2008. *Sorani Kurdish person markers and the typology of agreement*. Paper presented at the 13th International Morphology Meeting. Vienna.

Doke, C.M. & S.M. Mofokeng. 1985. In *Textbook of Southern Sotho Grammar*, 2nd edn. Cape Town: Maskew Miller Longman.

Gazdar, Gerald, Ewan Klein, Geoffrey Pullum & Ivan Sag. 1985. *Generalized phrase structure grammar*. Cambridge: Harvard University Press.

Harris, Alice C. 2017. *Multiple exponence*. Oxford: Oxford University Press.

Luís, Ana & Andrew Spencer. 2005. A paradigm function account of 'mesoclisis' in European Portuguese. In Geert Booij & Jaap van Marle (eds.), *Yearbook of morphology*, 177–228. Dordrecht: Springer.

Nevis, Joel A. & Brian D. Joseph. 1992. Wackernagel affixes: evidence from Balto Slavic. In Geert Booij & Jaap van Marle (eds.), *Yearbook of morphology 3*, 93–111. Dordrecht: Kluwer Academic Press.

Stump, Gregory. 2001. *Inflectional morphology: A theory of paradigm structure*. Cambridge: Cambridge University Press.

Stump, Gregory. 2017a. *Rule conflation in an adequate theory of morphotactics*. Vol. 64. Acta Linguistica Academica.

Stump, Gregory. To appear. Polyfunctionality and the variety of inflectional exponence relations. In Ferenc Kiefer, James P. Blevins & Huba Bartos (eds.), *Morphological paradigms and functions*. Leiden: Brill.

van Driem, George. 1987. *A grammar of Limbu*. Berlin: Mouton de Gruyter.

Williams, Edwin. 1981. On the notions "lexically related" and "head of a word". *Linguistic Inquiry* 12. 245–74.

Zwicky, Arnold M. 1985. How to describe inflection. In Mary Niepokuj, Mary Van Clay, Vassiliki Nikiforidou & Deborah Feder (eds.), *Proceedings of the eleventh annual meeting of the berkeley linguistics society*, 372–386. Berkeley: Berkeley Linguistics Society.

Part IV

Language and Linguistic Theory

Chapter 20

Darwinism tested by the science of language

Mark Aronoff
Stony Brook University

> Linguistics enjoyed great success in the last half of the 19th century. The use of tree diagrams to express the genetic relations between languages spread from linguistics to evolutionary biology. The achievements of the Neogrammarians in establishing sound laws, however, led to a realization that the exceptionless laws of language change bore no resemblance in kind to the laws of natural science. Language evolution had no principled basis akin to natural selection. Saussure solved this problem in the *Cours* by rooting linguistic theory in synchronic states of language rather than historical change, thus relegating diachronic linguistics to a minor position in the field. In recent decades, the field of cultural evolution has allowed for the application of well-established principles from evolutionary biology and ecology. The application of one of these, Gause's principle of competitive exclusion, to central problems of morphology has produced good results, suggesting prospects for the revival of evolutionary explanation in language along the lines of what linguists envisioned a century and a half ago.

1 Introduction

Steve Anderson refuses to forget the past. Along with Peter Matthews, throughout his career he has reminded the community of theoretical linguists, especially morphologists, of the continuity of our culture. His two most recent publications, one of them a tribute to Matthews (Anderson 2017; to appear b), deal with the history of morphology. The following brief essay is a small tribute to Steve's life-long effort to demonstrate that we can understand how we think and act today only to the extent that we also understand where our thinking comes from. In it, I trace the rise and fall of the relation between linguistics and evolutionary biology in the half century between the publications of the foundational work of modern biology, Darwin's *On the Origin of Species by Means of Natural Selection, or the Preservation of Favoured Races in the Struggle for Life*, in 1859, and the foundational work of modern linguistics, Saussure's *Cours de linguistique générale*, in 1916.

Mark Aronoff. 2017. Darwinism tested by the science of language. In Claire Bowern, Laurence Horn & Raffaella Zanuttini (eds.), *On looking into words (and beyond)*, 443–456. Berlin: Language Science Press. DOI:10.5281/zenodo.495459

In 1859, historical (also termed evolutionary at the time) linguistics was on a meteoric trajectory as one of the most successful of academic disciplines, having provided precise demonstrations that numerous modern languages were related in specific ways. In the next thirty years, it would produce even more remarkable results and Darwin himself would invoke its successes.

Saussure, author in 1878 of one of the most spectacular works in historical linguistics, did a complete *volte face* in his posthumous book forty years later, advocating that the field concentrate on description of single language states rather than historical relations. He rejected evolutionary accounts of language for one sweeping reason: the lack of an explanatory framework. Saussure's argument quickly turned the field away from diachrony to synchrony.

A century later, though, it has become clear that an evolutionary account of what Darwin himself was referring to when he wrote that "The survival or preservation of certain favoured words in the struggle for existence is natural selection" (Darwin 1871: 61) can provide just such a framework, allowing historical explanation of language to return to its rich relation with evolution and evolutionary theory.

2 Schleicher, Haeckel, and stem trees

They were friends, both professors at the University of Jena, who shared a love of botany and gardening. August Schleicher, the linguist, born in 1821, was 13 years older than Ernst Haeckel, the embryologist, and had been on the faculty since 1857. Haeckel had taken up his post as professor of comparative anatomy in 1862, soon after receiving his doctorate in zoology. Haeckel had been captivated by Darwin's landmark 1859 work and had recommended it to Schleicher. Schleicher opened his 1863 pamphlet, *Die Darwinsche Theorie und die Sprachwissenschaft – offenes Sendschreiben an Herrn Dr. Ernst Haeckel* [*Darwinian theory and language science – an open letter to Dr. Ernst Haeckel*] with an acknowledgement so notable that I repeat the passage here in its entirety.[1]

> You would leave me no peace until I began reading Bronn's [1860] translation of the much discussed work of Darwin *On the Origin of Species by Means of Natural Selection, or the Preservation of Favoured Races in the Struggle for Life.* I have complied with your request; I have waded through the whole of the book, in spite of its being rather clumsily arranged, and heavily written in a curious kind of German, and the greater part of the work I was tempted to read again and again. My first thanks are now offered to you for those repeated inducements of yours which ended in my study of this incontestably remarkable work. (Schleicher 1863/1869: 13–14)

Schleicher had very recently achieved academic renown as the author in 1861/2 of the two-volume *Compendium der vergleichenden Grammatik der indogermanischen Sprachen: Kurzer Abriss e. Laut–u. Formlehre d. Indogerm. Ursprache, d. Altindischen, Alteranischen,*

---

[1] All passages from Schleicher (1863) are quoted from Alex V. W. Bikkers's 1869 English translation.

Altgriechischen, Altitalischen, Altkeltischen, Altslavischen, Litauischen u. Altdeutschen [Compendium of the Comparative Grammar of the Indo–European languages. A brief outline of the Indo–European parent language, Old Indian, Old Iranian, Ancient Greek, Old Italian, Old Celtic, Old Slavic, Lithuanian and Old German]. He would die five years later in 1868 at the age of 47. Haeckel would outlive his friend by over a half century and become the greatest Continental disseminator of Darwinian thought through his best-selling book *Natürliche Schöpfungsgeschichte*, published in the year of Schleicher's death and translated into English as *The History of Creation*. Haeckel, as an embryologist, is perhaps most famous for the slogan "ontogeny recapitulates phylogeny" and the associated erroneous theory. Together, though, as described by Burrow (1972), O'Hara (1996), and Gontier (2011), the two friends are responsible for the use of tree diagrams in depicting evolutionary relations among languages first (Schleicher 1861/1862; 1863) and then species (Haeckel 1866). Haeckel (1874) presented *Stammbäume* lit. 'stem trees', of both the historical evolution of Indo-European languages and the 'pedigree of man' together in the same book. What Haeckel had learned from Schleicher during the few years that they were colleagues in a small university was that the evolution of languages and the evolution of species were sufficiently analogous to warrant the use of the same diagrammatic method to describe the two. The method survives to this day in both fields, but little else remains in common between the two. How did they move so far apart?

3 Darwinism tested by the science of language

Schleicher went further than analogy. The main point of his 1863 pamphlet, only 48 pages long in the original German edition, shorter than many academic journal articles today, was that the results of historical linguistics over the previous half century constituted a successful "test" of Darwin's theory of evolution. First, Schleicher asserted that languages were what he called "organisms of nature." He needed this to be true in order to directly test Darwin's theory, which deals with natural organisms, by applying it to languages.

> Languages are organisms of nature; they have never been directed by the will of man; they rose, and developed themselves according to definite laws; they grew old, and died out. They, too, are subject to that series of phenomena which we embrace under the name of "life." The science of language is consequently a natural science; its method is generally altogether the same as that of any other natural science. (Schleicher 1863: 20–21)

> The rules now, which Darwin lays down with regard to the species of animals and plants, are equally applicable to the organisms of languages, that is to say, as far as the main features are concerned. (Schleicher 1863: 30)

Here is where Schleicher understood that linguistics had a contribution to make. As is well known, Darwin acknowledged in his introduction that he had no direct evidence for the application of his theory to "the variability of species in a state of nature" (Darwin

1859: 4). The closest he could come was "a careful study of domesticated animals and of cultivated plants" (ibid.), which is why he devoted the first chapter of his book to "Variation under Domestication." Only in the last quarter century have we been able to observe evolution at work, most notably in Richard Lenski's Long Term Experimental Evolution Project (e.g, Tenaillon et al. 2016). Schleicher offered language evolution as the only tangible proof of evolution available at the time:

> Nobody doubts or denies any longer that the whole Indogermanic family of speech – Indic, Iranic, (old Armenian, Persic, & c.,) Hellenic, Italic, (Latin, Oscan, Umbrian, with the daughters of the former) Keltic, Slavonic, Lithuanian, Teutonic or German, that all these languages, consisting of numerous species, races and varieties, have taken their origin from one single primitive form of the Indo-Germanic family. (Schleicher 1863: 34)

> We are actually able to trace directly in many idioms that they have branched off into several languages, dialects & c., for we are in a position to follow the course of some, nay, of whole families of them during a period of more than two thousand years, since a faithful picture of them has been left us in writing. This, for instance, is the case with Latin. (Schleicher 1863: 41–42)

4 Max Müller

Darwin learned of Schleicher's work in an indirect way but in time to mention it in his second book, a dozen years after the publication of his first (Darwin 1871). The 1863 pamphlet received a very positive brief anonymous review in a short-lived British weekly, the *Reader*, in 1864 but appears to have attracted little attention in England, where German was not commonly read.[2] The English translation, though, published in 1869, caused a stir. Max Müller himself, the best-known linguist and popularizer of language study in the country, reviewed it at some length in the first volume of *Nature*, a successor to the *Reader* as a general science periodical for the public (Müller 1870). Darwin quoted from this review in his most famous passage on language. In the review, Müller acknowledged the power of Schleicher's analogy: "He thinks rightly that the genesis of species, as explained by Mr. Darwin, receives a striking illustration in the genealogical system of languages" (Müller 1870: 257); "No reader of Mr. Darwin's books can fail to see that an analogous process pervades the growth of a new species of language, and of new species of animal and vegetable life" (Müller 1870: 258).

Müller disagreed with Schleicher on a number of points. The least noticed but most insightful was his objection to Schleicher's claim that linguistics is a natural science. It is natural only in that "languages are not produced by the free-will of individuals . . . [T]he freedom of the individual is necessarily limited by the pressure exercised by all upon all. Speech in its very nature is mutual" (Müller 1870: 258), a point that presaged Saussure's

---

[2] Alter (1999) speculates that the writer of the *Reader* piece was Frederic William Farrar, who was later responsible, as Dean of Westminster Abbey, for Darwin's interment there.

observation on the social nature of *langue*. The second point was Müller's hobby-horse, his idiosyncratic idea that "In tracing the origin of species, whether among plants or animals, we do not begin with one perfect type of which all succeeding forms are simple modifications... It is the same with languages" (Müller 1870: 258). Müller here betrays his complete misunderstanding of Darwinism as well as of mainstream linguistics of his time, whose proponents – most prominently William Dwight Whitney – he sparred with throughout his career (Whitney 1875; Alter 1999). It is no wonder that Darwin had little use for Müller, with whom he also disagreed on a more fundamental issue: the continuity of humans with other creatures. This passage of Müller's is important enough to be cited in its entirety:

> A much more striking analogy, therefore, than the struggle for life among separate languages, is the struggle for life among words and grammatical forms which is constantly going on in each language. Here the better, the shorter, the easier forms are constantly gaining the upper hand, and they really owe their success to their own inherent virtue. Here, if anywhere, we can learn that what is called the process of natural selection, is at the same time, from a higher point of view, a process of rational elimination; for what seems at first sight mere accident at the dropping of old and the rising of new words, can be shown in most cases to be due to intelligible and generally valid reasons. Sometimes these reasons are purely phonetic, and those words and forms are seen to prevail which give the least trouble to the organs of pronunciation. At other times the causes are more remote. We see how certain forms of grammar which require little reflection, acquire for that very reason a decided numerical preponderance; become, in fact, what are called regular forms, while the other forms, generally the more primitive and more legitimate, dwindle away to a small minority, and are treated at last as exceptional and irregular. In the so-called dialectic growth of languages we see the struggle for life in full play, and though we cannot in every instance explain the causes of victory and defeat, we still perceive, as a general rule, that those forms and those words carry the day which for the time being seem best to answer their purpose. (Müller 1870: 258)

Darwin evidently approved of the argument, for he was generous enough to cite Müller's last point in *The descent of man, and selection in relation to sex* the following year:[3]

> We see variability in every tongue, and new words are continually cropping up; but as there is a limit to the powers of the memory, single words, like whole languages, gradually become extinct. As Max Müller has well remarked: – "A struggle for life is constantly going on amongst the words and grammatical forms in each language. The better, the shorter, the easier forms are constantly gaining the upper hand, and they owe their success to their own inherent virtue." To these more important

---

[3] Dingemanse (2013) is a fascinating blog-post about the evolution of the citation of this passage in the last decade. Most have attributed the observation to Darwin and neglect to note that Darwin had himself directly credited and cited Müller.

> causes of the survival of certain words, mere novelty may, I think, be added; for there is in the mind of man a strong love for slight changes in all things. The survival or preservation of certain favoured words in the struggle for existence is natural selection. (Darwin 1871: 60–61)

5 Darwinism and the laws of language

With Müller's approving review of Schleicher's pamphlet, and more importantly with Darwin's endorsement, linguistics had entered the mainstream of scientific discourse, a long-time goal of its practitioners that persists to this day. But not for long. In the end, the most important legacy of Darwinian thinking for 19th century linguistics was the clarification of the scope of the term *law* as it applies to language. As late as Müller's review, linguists could still see their ultimate goal as the formulation of general laws of language origin and structure on a par with the laws of physics and chemistry, perhaps based on Darwin's theory of evolution. What linguists discovered instead were the one-off contingent laws of sound change, from Grimm's law to Verner's law, startling but of no general significance beyond their purported exceptionlessness. Linguists could still call them laws, though, not on account of generality but because of their regularity. This was, however, small consolation. As Osthoff and Brugmann so memorably declared in their Neogrammarian credo:

> First, every sound change, inasmuch as it occurs mechanically, takes place according to laws that admit no exception. That is, the direction of the sound shift is always the same for all the members of a linguistic community except where a split into dialects occurs; and all words in which the sound subjected to the change appears in the same relationship are affected by the change without exception. (Osthoff & Brugmann 1878/1967: 204)

Hermann Paul stressed a couple of years later that sound laws in no way resemble those of physics and chemistry, but were statements of regular but contingent historical facts. To those who had aspired to gain for the science of language a place among the natural sciences, laws of this character would have been disappointing:

> Can we assert uniformity of sound-laws? In the first place, we must fully understand what we mean, generally speaking, by a sound-law. The word 'law' is itself used in very different senses, and this fact induces errors in its application. The idea of sound-law is not to be understood in the sense in which we speak of 'laws' in Physics or Chemistry, nor in the sense of which we were thinking when we contrasted exact sciences with historical sciences. Sound-law does not pretend to state what must always under certain general conditions regularly recur, but merely expresses the reign of uniformity within a group of definite historical phenomena. (Paul 1880/1889: 57)

6 Ferdinand de Saussure and the end of evolution

The greatest individual achievement of Neogrammarian historical linguistics was Saussure's *Mémoire sur le système primitif des voyelles dans les langues indo-européennes*. Written in a fury and printed in fascicles one by one in 1878 when Saussure was a 21-year-old student, it was the only sizable work of his lifetime. He published brief articles on scattered topics afterwards, apparently unable to find a unifying vision.

Saussure returned to his native Geneva in 1891 as Extraordinary Professor of Indo-European languages. He was not named Ordinary Professor of General Linguistics until December of 1906, an additional responsibility added to Sanskrit, comparative philology, and the occasional language course. Between 1906 and 1911, he gave three biennial series of lectures on general linguistics as required by his new position, all covering similar ground, to his devoted but few students and colleagues (Joseph 2012: 617). We will never know whether he intended to publish this work. Saussure died in February 1913. His students gathered their notes together and organized them, publishing the results in 1916 in tribute to their late master as the *Cours de linguistique générale*, whose reputation gradually grew, until it became justly regarded as the founding document of modern theoretical linguistics. The *Course in general linguistics* remains influential today across a broad range of disciplines.

The *Course in general linguistics* comprises for the most part an attempt to establish a new foundation for the science of language. The first chapter of the *Cours*, "A glance at the history of linguistics," is five pages long in Baskin's 1959 translation. Of traditional grammar, Saussure writes that "It lacked a scientific approach" (Saussure 1959: 1). He credits Bopp with "realiz[ing] that the comparison of related languages could become the subject matter of an independent science" (Saussure 1959: 2), noting that he could not have succeeded without Jones's 'discovery' of Sanskrit, which is "exceptionally well-fitted to the role of illuminating the comparison [with Greek and Latin]" (Saussure 1959: 2). Importantly for both Sausssure and us, "the comparative school . . . did not succeed in setting up the true science of linguistics. It failed to seek out the nature of its study" (Saussure 1959: 3). "Not until around 1870 did scholars begin to seek out the principles that govern the life of languages" (Saussure 1959: 4). He credits Whitney (1875) and the Neogrammarians with realizing that language is "a product of the collective mind of linguistic groups" (Saussure 1959: 5) and not "an organism that develops independently" (Saussure 1959: 5), as Schleicher had claimed in rhetorical support of his Darwinian argument. Saussure concludes the chapter by stating that "the fundamental problems of general linguistics still await solution," a solution that he proceeds to outline in the rest of the book.

One of the most important components of Saussure's solution was the observation that the science of language could be divided into the analysis of single states of a language, *états de langue* – synchronic linguistics – and the analysis of a succession of such states – diachronic linguistics. Tellingly, the chapter devoted to this fundamental distinction was entitled "Static and evolutionary linguistics," (Saussure 1959: 79), a title that echoes the earlier connection between linguistics and evolutionary biology. He used the term *diachronic* interchangeably with *evolutionary* but *diachronic* eventually won out, presumably because it lacked any suggestion of a connection to biological evolution; perhaps also because of the bad reputation that the term *evolution* had gained when applied to the study of the human language faculty since being banned by the Société de Linguistique de Paris in 1866. Saussure made clear that synchrony was more important in the last two paragraphs of the chapter:

> *Synchronic linguistics* will be concerned with the logical and psychological relations that bind together coexisting terms and form a system in the collective mind of speakers.
>
> *Diachronic linguistics*, on the contrary, will study relations that bind together successive terms not perceived by the collective mind but substituted for each other without forming a system.

It is fair to say that Saussure's distinction was the most important factor leading to a shift in the focus of linguistics in the century since. In the last chapter of the book, "Concerning retrospective linguistics," Saussure reduces diachrony to synchrony and thus dispenses with the former in a single argument. Diachrony, for Saussure, is simply "an infinite number of photographs, taken at different times" (Saussure 1959: 212).

The photographic analogy is striking. The Lumière brothers had perfected the *cinématographe* in 1895, only a decade before Saussure's first lectures on general linguistics and it had quickly grown in popularity in Saussure's French-speaking world. Cinematography allowed for the depiction of passage through time as a sequence of successive photographs or states: a moving picture is a succession of photographs shot and projected at regular very short intervals. The individual photographs matter much more than the interval, which is always the same. No single transition is of interest. The depiction of the passage of time is simply an illusion created by the sequence of static photographs. We cannot know if the cinema had any influence on Saussure's thought, but he was very clear in asserting that "From the speakers' point of view, diachrony does not exist; speakers deal only with a state." (Joseph 2012: 594).

Saussure had struggled through his life with the problem that the field to which he had devoted his career, evolutionary historical linguistics, had not been able find any principled theoretical basis. Once he sat down to provide a theory of language, the result was a theory of what we now call linguistic structure or grammar, not of historical linguistic evolution. He could come to terms with this conclusion only by killing the field that had borne him. His reduction of diachrony to synchrony and his double insistence that a linguistic system must be synchronic and that diachronic linguistics is not systematic in this sense was the most important factor leading to the radical shift that the field underwent in the next few decades. By 1945, the synchronic system and Saussure had won. Modern linguistics *was* synchronic linguistics and attempts to tie linguistics to evolution in any way had been abandoned.[4]

---

[4] As late as 1929, though, Edward Sapir could still proudly proclaim, in an article entitled "The status of linguistics as a science," that "Many of the formulations of comparative Indo-European linguistics have

7 Principles of cultural evolution

Historical or evolutionary linguistics had been one of the most successful academic enterprises of the nineteenth century, amassing concrete results such as the establishment of historical language families and the reconstruction of a number of proto-languages. Saussure's conjecture on the vowel system of Indo-European, for example, was confirmed by the decipherment of Hittite in the early 20th century and the observation made by Kuryłowicz (1935) that a number of consonants in the recently deciphered ancient Hittite language, not found in other Indo-European languages, lined up nicely in their distribution with the *coefficients sonantiques* that Saussure had proposed based solely on historical analysis. The problem that Saussure confronted in his theoretical work was that, unlike Darwinian evolutionary biology, which was grounded in the great insight of natural selection, the field had no explanatory basis. His solution was to dismiss the field.

All biologists agree that, in the memorable words of Theodosius Dobzhansky (2013), "nothing in biology makes sense except in the light of evolution." Darwin's theory of natural selection provides a satisfying sweeping explanation for the origin and evolution of all biological species, while the modern synthesis provides the genetic mechanism that underpins reproductive success. As the Neogrammarians noted themselves (see above), there are no equivalent principles in historical linguistics. All the 'laws', exceptionless though they may be, are contingent facts.

Can there be general principles of linguistic change?[5] Saussure certainly did not propose any, but there are reasons for optimism. William Labov, whom many consider to be the most important linguist of our time, published a massive work in three volumes (Labov 1994; 2001; 2010) entitled just that: *Principles of Linguistic Change*. Blevins (2004) has written an influential book entitled *Evolutionary phonology: The emergence of sound patterns*. Others, notably Boer (2001), Galantucci (2005), Simon Kirby (Verhoef, Kirby & Boer 2014), and Kenny Smith (Kirby et al. 2015) have looked at emergent systems of language based on evolutionary models. None of these have direct ties to Darwinian theory. Some, though, are firmly within the tradition of what has come to be called cultural evolution.

The founder of cultural anthropology, Edward B. Tylor, had embraced evolution from the start (Tylor 1871) but he entwined evolution with material progress, providing fodder for a long detour into social Darwinism, an idea also traceable in part to Ernst Haeckel, and to related eugenics movements around the globe. Franz Boas, the most prominent anthropologist of his time, took up the flag against all things evolutionary in culture (Boas 1928) and drove evolution from the field for close to a century in both anthropology and the closely related sociology. The idea that culture could and should be studied from an evolutionary point of view raised its head occasionally (e.g., Sahlins 1960), with Marvin Harris especially exploiting the notion of an ecological niche as an explanatory

---

a neatness and a regularity which recall the formulae, or the so-called laws, of natural science." (Sapir 1929: 160). One could write a book about this confusion of formulae with laws. Saussure understood the difference.

[5] Kuryłowicz (1935) set out a set of six laws of analogy, but these are far from general principles.

device in cultural adaptation (e.g., Harris 1979), but the most important development in anthropology was the anti-empirical direction of the field under the influence of Geertz (1973), which was profoundly anti-evolutionary and even anti-explanatory. This line of thought soon led to a great weakening of the scope of the field of cultural anthropology.

The disintegration of cultural anthropology left an opening for a more biologically oriented study of human behavior, often called behavioral ecology. A major thrust of this biological approach was the direct application of insights from evolutionary biology to cultural evolution. One of the most influential lines of work in this direction was led by a duo made up of a biologist (Peter Richerson) and an anthropologist (Robert Boyd), who, over a thirty-year collaboration, have written three influential books (Boyd & Richerson 1985; 2005; Richerson & Robert 2005) and many articles in which they directly and precisely apply principles from evolutionary theory to human culture, with many examples, works which have unfortunately had little influence in linguistics. Their framework provides a simple answer to Saussure's concern about the lack of principled explanation in evolutionary linguistics: cultural evolution can be explained using precise methods and we can start by exploiting principles taken quite directly from evolutionary biology. Applying these methods to language requires that we first step back from the position that has dominated our field for the last half century and accept Sapir's position: language is a product of the interaction of biology and culture and we cannot understand it by confining ourselves to one or the other. Once we adopt this position, we can look at how languages evolve culturally, on the basis of well-established principles.[6]

Taking direct inspiration from Richerson and Boyd, over the last half decade I have shown that a simple well-known principle from ecology, Gause's law of competitive exclusion (Lotka 1925; Volterra 1926; 1931; Gause 1934), provides very satisfying explanations for a variety of important long-standing problems in morphology and lexicology, including the absence of lexical synonyms, morphological productivity, allomorphy, the existence of inflectional classes, and the relation between morphology and writing (Lindsay & Aronoff 2013; Aronoff & Lindsay 2015; 2016; Berg & Aronoff 2017).

8 Conclusion

The moment I discovered Gause's principle, I was seized by an Andersonian impulse that I could not shake until I had satisfied myself that I understood what had had happened in the relationship between linguistics and evolutionary biology since Darwin and Schleicher. Why, as Morris Halle pronounced many years ago, did Saussure never publish the *Course in general linguistics* if it was so important? Why does mainstream academia pay lip service at best to Saussure's most accomplished work, the *Mémoire sur le système primitif des voyelles dans les langues indo-européennes*? Why did this greatest linguist of his time publish so little? Why did historical linguistics, the most successful human science of the 19th century, fall into the tenuous position that it holds today? And finally,

---

[6] This research has nothing to say about the evolution of the language faculty, only about the evolution of individual languages.

how should we approach the relation between evolutionary theory and linguistics today? In this piece, I have begun to answer these questions for myself, in the profound belief, which I share with Steve Anderson and Peter Matthews, that we cannot get lasting answers unless we understand the basis of the questions that drive our work and thought. Steve himself has recently written cogently about taking evolutionary biology seriously in any discussion of language. Notably, in Anderson (2013), he has reminded us that that the general properties of languages are not necessarily attributable solely to the language faculty. Many may have an external basis, and some may have been incorporated into the language faculty by natural selection itself.

References

Alter, Stephen G. 1999. *Darwinism and the linguistic image: Language, race, and natural theology in the nineteenth century.* Baltimore: Johns Hopkins University Press.

Anderson, Stephen R. 2013. What is special about the human language faculty, and how did it get that way? In Rudolf Botha & Martin Everaert (eds.), *The evolutionary emergence of language: Evidence and inference*, 18–41. Oxford: Oxford University Press.

Anderson, Stephen R. 2017. Words and paradigms: Peter H. Matthews and the development of morphological theory. *Transactions of the Philological Society* 115. 1–13.

Anderson, Stephen R. to appear b. A short history of morphological theory. In Jenny Audring & Francesca Masini (eds.), *The Oxford handbook of morphological theory*. Oxford: Oxford University Press.

Aronoff, Mark & Mark Lindsay. 2015. Partial organization in languages: La langue est un système où la plupart se tient. In Sandrea Augendre, Graziella Couasnon-Torlois, Déborah Lebon, Clément Michard, Gilles Boyé & Fabio Montermini (eds.), *Proceedings of Décembrettes 8*, 1–14. Toulouse: CNRS & Université Toulouse – Jean Jaurès.

Aronoff, Mark & Mark Lindsay. 2016. Competition and the lexicon. In Annibale Elia, Claudio Iacobino & Miriam Voghera (eds.), *Livelli di analisi e fenomeni di interfaccia. Atti del XLVII congresso internazionale della Società di Linguistica Italiana*, 39–52. Roma: Bulzoni Editore.

Berg, Kristian & Mark Aronoff. 2017. Spelling English suffixes. *Language* 93. 37–64.

Blevins, Juliette. 2004. *Evolutionary phonology: The emergence of sound patterns*. Cambridge: Cambridge University Press.

Boas, Franz. 1928. *Anthropology and modern life*. New York: Norton.

Boer, Bart de. 2001. *The origins of vowel systems*. Oxford: Oxford University Press.

Boyd, Robert & Peter J. Richerson. 1985. *Culture and the evolutionary process*. Chicago: University of Chicago Press.

Boyd, Robert & Peter J. Richerson. 2005. *The origin and evolution of cultures*. Oxford: Oxford University Press.

Burrow, John W. 1972. Editor's introduction. In John W. Burrow (ed.), *Charles Darwin: The origin of species*, 11–48. Harmondsworth: Penguin.

Darwin, Charles. 1859. *On the origin of species by means of natural selection, or the preservation of favoured races in the struggle for life*. London: John Murray.

Darwin, Charles. 1871. *The descent of man, and selection in relation to sex*. London: John Murray.

Dingemanse, Mark. 2013. *Evolving words: Darwin on Müller on Schleicher*. accessed 16 October, 2016. https://dlc.hypotheses.org/author/markdingemanse. https://dlc.hypotheses.org/author/markdingemanse.

Dobzhansky, Theodosius. 2013. Nothing in biology makes sense except in the light of evolution. *The american biology teacher* 75(2). 87–91.

Galantucci, Bruno. 2005. An experimental study of the emergence of human communication systems. *Cognitive science* 29(5). 737–767.

Gause, Georgy. 1934. *The struggle for existence*. Baltimore: Williams & Wilkins.

Geertz, Clifford. 1973. *The interpretation of culture*. New York: Basic Books.

Gontier, Nathalie. 2011. Depicting the tree of life: The philosophical and historical roots of evolutionary tree diagrams. *Evolution: Education and Outreach* 4(3). 515–538.

Haeckel, Ernst. 1866. *Generelle Morphologie der Organismen*. Berlin: Georg Reimer.

Haeckel, Ernst. 1868. *Natürliche Schöpfungsgeschichte*. Berlin: Georg Reimer.

Haeckel, Ernst. 1874. *Anthropogenie: oder, Entwickelungsgeschichte des Menschen, Keimes– und Stammesgeschichte [Anthropogeny: Or, the evolutionary history of man]*. Leipzig: W. Engelmann.

Harris, Marvin. 1979. *Cultural materialism: The struggle for a science of culture*. Walnut Creek, CA: AltaMira Press.

Joseph, John E. 2012. *Saussure*. Oxford: Oxford University Press.

Kirby, Simon, Monica Tamariz, Hannah Cornish & Kenny Smith. 2015. Compression and communication in the cultural evolution of linguistic structure. *Cognition* 141. 87–102.

Kuryłowicz, Jerzy. 1935. *Études indoeuropéennes I*. Cracow: Polska Akademia Umiejętności.

Labov, William. 1994. *Principles of linguistic change, Volume I: Internal factors*. Oxford: Wiley-Blackwell.

Labov, William. 2001. *Principles of linguistic change, Volume II: Social factors*. Oxford: Wiley-Blackwell.

Labov, William. 2010. *Principles of linguistic change, Volume III: Cognitive and cultural factors*. Oxford: Wiley-Blackwell.

Lindsay, Mark & Mark Aronoff. 2013. Natural selection in self–organizing morphological systems. In Fabio Montermini, Gilles Boyé & Jesse Tseng (eds.), *Morphology in Toulouse: Selected proceedings of Décembrettes 7*, 133–153. Munich: Lincom Europa.

Lotka, Alfred J. 1925. *Elements of physical biology*. Baltimore: Williams & Wilkins.

Müller, Max. 1870. Darwinism tested by the science of language (review). *Nature* 1. Translated from the German of Professor August Schleicher, 256–259.

O'Hara, Robert J. 1996. Trees of history in systematics and philology. *Memorie della Società Italiana di Scienze Naturali e del Museo Civico di Storia Naturale di Milano* 27(1). 81–88.

Osthoff, Hermann & Karl Brugmann. 1878/1967. Preface to morphological investigations in the sphere of the Indoeuropean languages, vol. I. English translation. In Winfred P. Lehmann (ed.), *A reader in nineteenth–century historical Indo-European linguistics (In-*

diana University studies in the history and theory of linguistics), 197–209. Bloomington, IN: Indiana University Press.

Paul, Hermann. 1880/1889. *Principien der Sprachgeschichte. [Principles of the history of language]*. Trans. by Herbert A. Strong. New York: Macmillan.

Richerson, Peter J. & Boyd Robert. 2005. *Not by genes alone: How culture transformed human evolution.* Chicago: University of Chicago Press.

Sahlins, Marshall D. 1960. *Evolution and culture.* Ann Arbor: University of Michigan Press.

Sapir, Edward. 1929. The status of linguistics as a science. *Language* 5(4). 207–214.

Saussure, Ferdinand de. 1878. *Mémoire sur le système primitif des voyelles dans les langues indo-européennes.* Leipzig: BG Teubner.

Saussure, Ferdinand de. 1916. *Cours de linguistique générale.* Paris: Payot.

Saussure, Ferdinand de. 1959. *Course in general linguistics.* Trans. by Wade Baskin. New York: Philosophical Library.

Schleicher, August. 1861/1862. *Compendium der vergleichenden Grammatik der indogermanischen Sprachen: Kurzer Abriss e. Laut–u. Formlehre d. Indogerm. Ursprache, d. Altindischen, Alteranischen, Altgriechischen, Altitalischen, Altkeltischen, Altslavischen, Litauischen u. Altdeutschen [Compendium of the comparative grammar of the Indo–European languages. A brief outline of the Indo–European parent language, Old Indian, Old Iranian, Ancient Greek, Old Italian, Old Celtic, Old Slavic, Lithuanian and Old German].* Weimar: Böhlau.

Schleicher, August. 1863. *Die Darwinsche Theorie und die Sprachwissenschaft – offenes Sendschreiben an Herrn Dr. Ernst Haeckel [Darwinian theory and language science – an open letter to Dr. Ernst Haeckel].* Weimar: Böhlau.

Schleicher, August. 1863/1869. *Darwinism tested by the science of language.* English translation of Schleicher 1863, translated by Alex V. W. Bikkers. London: John Camden Hotten.

Tenaillon, Olivier, Jeffrey E. Barrick, Noah Ribeck, Daniel E. Deatherage, Jeffrey L. Blanchard, Aurko Dasgupta, Gabriel C. Wu, Sebastien Wielgoss, Stephane Cruveiller, Claudine Médigue, Dominique Schneider & Richard E. Lenski. 2016. Tempo and mode of genome evolution in a 50,000-generation experiment. *Nature* 536(7615). 165–170.

Tylor, Edward B. 1871. *Primitive culture: Researches into the development of mythology, philosophy, religion, language, art, and custom.* London: John Murray.

Verhoef, Tessa, Simon Kirby & Bart de Boer. 2014. Emergence of combinatorial structure and economy through iterated learning with continuous acoustic signals. *Journal of Phonetics* 43. 57–68.

Volterra, Vito. 1926. *Variazioni e fluttuazioni del numero d'individui in specie animali conviventi. Memorie della Reale Accademia dei Lincei 2.* Rome: C. Ferrari.

Volterra, Vito. 1931. Variations and fluctuations of the number of individuals in animal species living together. In Royal N. Chapman (ed.), *Animal ecology*, 409–448. New York: McGraw-Hill.

Whitney, William Dwight. 1875. *The life and growth of language: An outline of linguistic sciences.* New York: D. Appleton.

Chapter 21

Temporal patterning in speech and birdsong

Louis Goldstein
Department of Linguistics, University of Southern California

> Speech and birdsong are complex motor behaviors in which patterning over time is itself informational. This is obvious in the case of speech, but in birdsong, too, the sequencing (and possibly timing) of syllables determines in part the well-formedness of the song. Despite gross differences in function, in the physical substrate (method of sound production), in brain structure, and in the scale of the animals, recent work has revealed a surprising degree of similarity in their solutions to the problem of controlling temporal patterning. There are differences, too, of course, and when we find them, it deepens our understanding about the (unique) structure of speech. Because Steve has had a lasting interest in birds and birdsong (Anderson 2006), this seemed to be an appropriate context to review these similarities. Two of them will be the focus of discussion here: decomposition of the behavior into a *sequence of discrete motor units* and the role of an *internal clock system*, partly independent of the units themselves.

1 Discrete decomposition

One of the foundational motivations for Articulatory Phonology (Browman & Goldstein 1992; 1995) is to address the apparent incompatibility between the discrete phonetic and phonological structure of speech, on the one hand, and the observation that the vocal tract articulators move in a continuous fashion, producing continuous modulation of the acoustics, on the other. AP hypothesizes that it is possible to model the continuous motion of the articulators as arising from discrete, context-independent dynamical control systems, called *gestures*, that govern the formation of phonologically-relevant constrictions within the vocal tract (for example bringing the tongue tip to the palate, with a particular degree of constriction). The control parameters of these dynamical systems (*target*, e.g., the phonologically-specified degree of constriction, and *stiffness*, the time constant that determines the amount of time required for the system to settle at its target value) remain fixed during the duration of the constriction action (roughly a consonant or a vowel), even though the articulators are moving. The decomposition of

 Louis Goldstein. 2017. Temporal patterning in speech and birdsong. In Claire Bowern, Laurence Horn & Raffaella Zanuttini (eds.), *On looking into words (and beyond)*, 457–471. Berlin: Language Science Press. DOI:10.5281/zenodo.495460

speech into a pattern of gesture activations over time (or *gestural score*), is an abstract analysis (as Steve argued in his earliest work (Anderson 1974) must be the case for a phonetic representation), and can only be discovered by use of explicit dynamical and acoustical models. We cannot observe it directly. Recently, Nam et al (2012) showed that with the use of the TaDA gestural production model, it is possible to parse an acoustic signal into the maximum likelihood gestural score that could have produced it.

A similar strategy is employed by Amador et al. (2013), to decompose zebra finch song into discrete gestures. The authors first developed a dynamical model of sound production in the syrinx, the sound production organ in songbirds. The syrinx is a vibratory system located at the base of the trachea. The trachea divides into two tubes at that point, each of which hosts a pair of vibrating membranes called labia. The two pairs of labia can vibrate together or separately, or can be sequenced (Riede & Goller 2010). The model developed in Amador et al. (2013) (for a single pair of labia) allowed them to generate sound from two dynamical control parameters: the average tension in the labia, and tracheal pressure. Then, using a table-lookup scheme, they were able to estimate the time functions of these two parameters from audio recordings of the sound. This representation was then validated by generating audio from those time functions and playing those sounds to zebra finches. Neural responses from the synthetic song were highly similar (nearly identical) to the responses obtained by playing the original song (BOS, Bird's Own Song). Next, they showed that the derived time functions are essentially discrete: they exhibit sequences of intervals of time during which the values of the control parameters remain essentially fixed (just as with speech gestures), and refer to these intervals as elemental gestures of the song. The key similarity to speech gestures is that the continuous song can be decomposed into discrete intervals of time, longer by an order of magnitude than the periodicity of the song, during which the dynamical parameters are essentially fixed.

There are also some salient differences between speech gestures and zebra finch song gestures. Most superficial is that the control parameters for the zebra finch gestures are different from those of speech gestures that control the constrictions of the suprlaryngeal structures (as expected, because forming constrictions is not generally thought to be part of the bird's song behavior), but they are similar to those control parameters involved in controlling tone and intonation in speech (McGowan & Saltzman 1995). A somewhat deeper difference is that the zebra finch gestures (as analyzed in Amador et al. 2013) are strictly sequential, while speech gestures exhibit various types of overlap in time. At first blush, this makes sense, as the mechanism of sound production in birds is generally thought to be limited to a single device, the syrinx, while the distinct vocal organs of the human vocal tract can each make their own contribution to the filtering action of sound generated at the larynx. There are, however, as noted above, two sets of labia comprising the syrinx (Trevisan et al. 2007), and some avian species employ primarily one set, while others (like zebra finches) use both sets, simultaneously or sequentially. Trevisian et al. (2007) have shown how such symmetry-breaking (different functioning of the two sides at the same time) arises in the species that employ either one side only or both sides, but not symmetrically. So there is the possibility that distinct patterns of gesture overlap may yet be uncovered.

Another obvious potential difference between speech gestures and birdsong is compositionality. A small set of discrete speech gestures are employed in different combinations to create the set of segments and syllables in a language. It is unknown whether gestures in birdsong are compositional in this sense. Zebra finch songs (on which a large bulk of the research on song birds has been done) have been described as having a hierarchical structure. Syllables are the most immediately identifiable units, as they consist of the vocalization intervals produced by the bird that are bounded by (silent) inspirations. The total number of distinct syllables in a given bird's inventory is relatively small, on the order of 20 or so. As described in Yu & Margoliash (1996), syllables can be composed of distinct notes, and in turn, sequences of syllables form *motifs*, that can be repeated as part of a song. It is unclear to what extent the elemental gestures identified in Amador et al. (2013) can form parts of more than one syllable in an individual's inventory. Yu and Margoliash (1996) do report instances of distinct syllables in a bird's inventory that begin with the same note (and end with different notes). To the extent that those shared notes are produced with the same gestures, this would be evidence for some limited compositionality.

2 Clocks

2.1 Clocks in speech?

A lively debate in the 1980's sparked by the work of Carol Fowler (Fowler 1980) considered whether speech units had their own intrinsic timing as dynamical systems (as argued by Fowler), or whether the timing is imposed externally by some kind of central clock. Gestures in Articulatory Phonology are units with intrinsic timing; the time required for a gesture to reach its goal state is determined by its dynamical stiffness parameter. But what of the time between gestures? For a sequence of two gestures, x_1 and x_2, we can ask how the system controls when to trigger x_2 with respect to x_1. A natural answer to this is that x_2 is triggered when some reference state value of x_1 is achieved $\{x_{1,1}\}$. Sequencing in motor systems is often modeled by a mechanism of "competitive selection" of the sequenced items (Bullock & Rhodes 2002; Grossberg 1978), where feedback from the completion of element x_1 (achievement of its target state) allows it to be deactivated and element x_2 to be selected and triggered. In the case of speech, this feedback could be kinesthetic, orosensory and/or acoustic. However, there is an argument that this cannot be the complete story for speech. Consider the gestural score for the word "spot" in the left panel of Figure 1. The boxes represent intervals in which the the supralaryngeal gestures would be active, in some token of this word. The onset of the lip closure for /p/ initiates at a moment when the tongue tip fricative gesture (for /s/) is at a particular state (close to its target and not moving much), as marked by the vertical line in the figure. A possible mechanism for sequencing the these gestures would be to learn that in producing the word "spot," the lip closure gesture "waits" until the system has feedback that the tongue tip is near the alveolar ridge and is moving with little velocity, and at that point it is triggered. But now consider the phrase "toss spot" shown on the right side of Figure 1. Here, the state that the lip closure is looking for, in order to trigger, occurs too early, because the tongue tip is already in position for /s/. And there is a interval of time (shaded in white) during which the state of the tongue tip does not change much, so there is no information in its state that can inform when the /p/ should be triggered. Nonetheless, its timing must show some regularity, as the [s] in "toss spot" systematically differs in duration from, for example "pa spot." Figure 2 shows the kinematics of the tongue tip in a sequence of identical supralaryngeal gestures ("had tied"). It is clear that there is indeed a considerable stretch (70 ms or so) marked with a yellow box where its state does not change, and so information about when to trigger a next gesture is lacking.

This case appears to argue that a simple state-based chain triggering will not work for speech, in the general case, and relative timing must be specified in some way separately from the actual gestural content of the units. It would also be possible to argue, in this case, that the lip gesture is triggered when the tongue tip gesture begins to release, but this just pushes the problem back onto the tongue tip release gesture. How does it know know when to trigger, without access to information about time? It can't just use the position and velocity of the tongue tip. Tilsen (2016) has recently proposed a theory that gestural sequencing based on feedback from the preceding gestures does indeed characterize the system at early stages of the child's development, gradually shifting to a different, coordination-based scheme as described below (for at least some syllable-contexts). It could also be countered that the cases presented here involve timing across words, and perhaps word-sequencing is controlled by a separate mechanism from within-word gesture sequencing. However, the same issue would arise within words in the case of geminate consonants (consonants that are maintained for a long temporal interval). And of course, the existence of geminates at all is itself *prima facie* evidence for some independence of timing and gestural content, as the same constrictions can be maintained for different durations, under linguistic control.

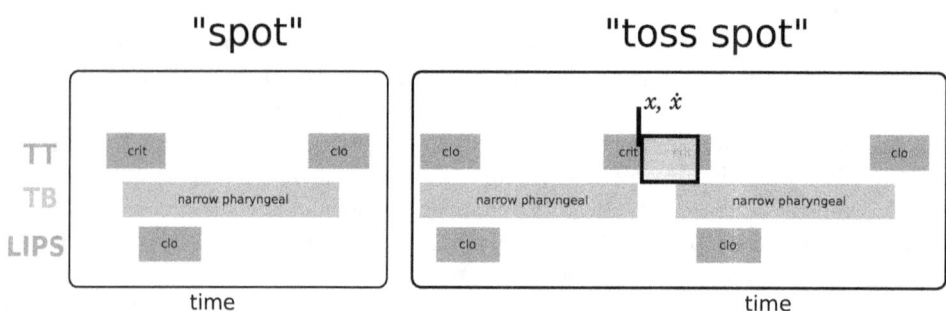

Figure 1: Gestural scores. On the left for the word "spot" and on the right for the phrase "toss spot." Rows represent (from the) top, gestures of the Tongue Tip, Tongue Body and Lips. See text. Shaded area represents interval of time during which state of tongue tip is not changing.

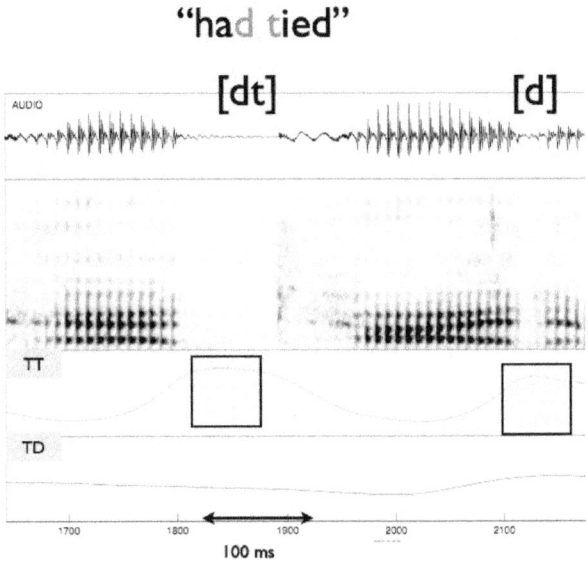

Figure 2: Time functions of the vertical position of the Tongue Tip (TT) and Tongue Dorsum (TD) in the phase "had tied." See text.

The coupled oscillator model of syllable structure (Goldstein, Byrd & Saltzman 2006) proposes a specific alternative to gesture sequencing, in which the clock machinery is separate from the particular gestures that form the syllable. In this model, the gestures composing a syllable are triggered by a system of planning oscillators (clocks) that are coupled to one another in distinct modes. Each planning oscillator triggers activation of a gesture. Specifically, clocks that trigger gestures comprising onset consonants (consonants preceding the vowel in a syllable) are coupled in-phase (the most stable mode) to the vowel gesture and clocks that trigger gestures comprising coda consonants (consonants following the vowel in a syllable) are coupled in anti-phase mode to the vowel. If every gesture is triggered at phase 0 degrees of its planning oscillator, then two gestures that are coupled in phase will be triggered synchronously. This synchronous triggering explains data that show that the onset of articulatory movement for an onset consonant and for the following vowel begin at roughly the same time (Goldstein, Byrd & Saltzman 2006). When two gestures are coupled in anti-phase mode, however, they will be triggered a half-period apart in time, which would be consistent with the observed time lag between the onset of the vowel gesture and the onset of a coda consonant gesture (Goldstein, Byrd & Saltzman 2006). The ensemble of oscillators can be formally represented as a (coupling) graph, and Figure 3 shows the coupling graph for the word "tab." Green edges represent in-phase coupling and the dashed red edge represents anti-phase coupling. Note that the same graph topology would underlie the timing of gestures in any CVC syllable, and in that sense, the clock is separate from, and independent of, the particular gestures that are deployed. The model has been used to explain patterns of syllable typology, acquisition (Nam, Goldstein & Saltzman 2009), asymmetric coordination patterns in onset vs coda (Marin & Pouplier 2010), and weight, and it has been used as a diagnostic for the syllable structure of complex pre-vocalic clusters (Hermes, Muecke & Grice 2013; Shaw et al. 2009).

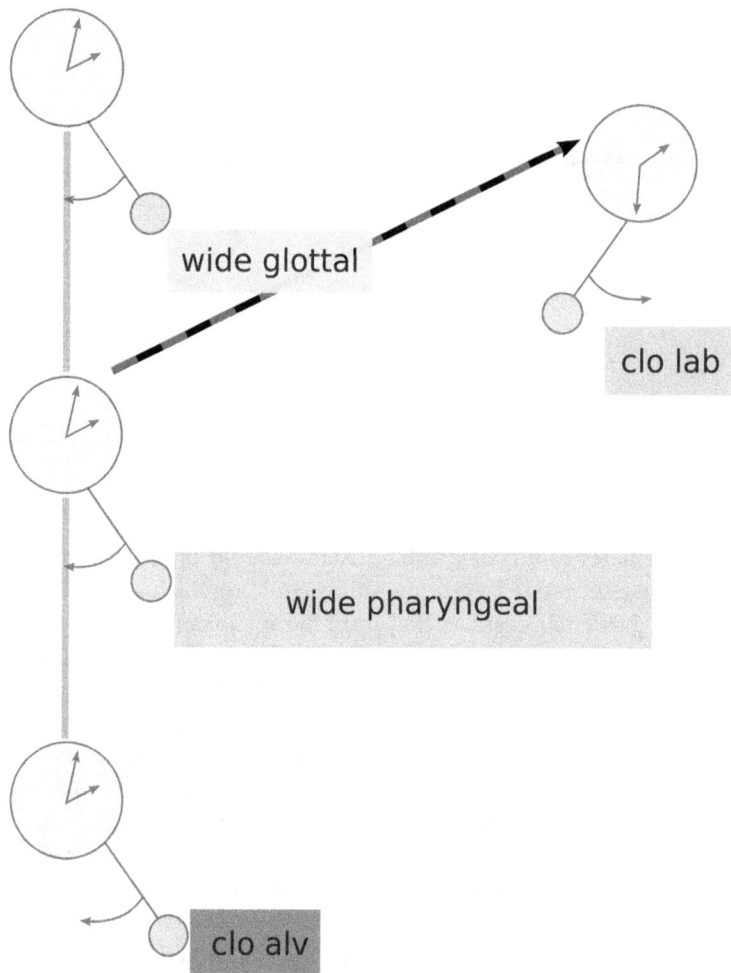

Figure 3: Coupling graph for the word "tab." Each clock represents one of the gestures in the word and they are the nodes of the coupling graph. From the top down the left, these are glottal abduction for the initial /t/, pharyngeal constriction (for the vowel), and tongue tip closure for the /t/. At the right is the lip closure for /b/. Green lines are graph edges that represent in-phase coupling and the red dashed line with arrowhead is the edge that represents anti-phase coupling. Boxes represent the gestural score for the the word (gesture activation over time) that results from running the coupled oscillator model.

The frequencies of the planning oscillator clocks are all defined with reference to the ticks of an overall speech rate clock. Prosodically-induced lengthening can thus be modeled as slowing of the rate of this overall clock, as has been proposed in the π-gesture model (Byrd & Saltzman 2003). Phrase edges are associated with local π-gestures, which function to slow the movements of all gestures that fall under the scope of the π-gesture. This model has been shown to account for the acoustic and kinematic correlates of boundary lengthening in a variety of languages (e.g. Greek; Katsika et al. 2014).

2.2 Clocks in birdsong?

Work on birdsong over the last 15 years has also revealed, within limits, separate control of timing and vocal organ activation patterns. Two areas of the avian cortex have been identified as significant for the production of the song: HVC, a pre-motor nucleus, and RA (robust nucleus of the arcopallium). HVC projects to RA, which in turn projects to the vocal motor neurons (and to midbrain vocal control areas). HVC was suspected to be a major site of timing control, and this was tested in a seminal study by Long and Fee (2008). Reasoning that cooling a brain region would result in a slowing of neural patterns, they used a miniature Peltier device to locally cool either HVC or RA. They found that cooling HVC resulted in slowing of the song, with the amount of slowing being proportional to the degree of cooling. Further, the slowing was fairly linear throughout the song. Syllable durations, onset lags, gap durations between motifs were all slowed to roughly the same degree, indicating that something like an overall clock (like the proposed speech clock) was being slowed. Consistent with the independence of timing account, there was very little change at all in the actual acoustics of the song, indicating that the control of the activation patterns at the level of the motor neurons remained intact, just spread out in time. (In other words, the rate at which the motor commands were issued was slowed down, but the commands were not changed, so the frequencies of the song were not altered by slowing). Conversely, even though spiking was decreased by cooling RA, the ability of (uncooled) HVC to drive RA and produce typical song speeds was not impaired, thus providing evidence for localizing timing control in HVC.

A more recent study of cooling from a different lab using canaries (Goldin et al. 2013) found that with more extreme cooling of HVC, the song begins to break down, exhibiting period-doubling of respiratory patterns, causing the emergence of additional syllables. The authors provide a formal model that predicts these transitions from the nonlinear interaction between the (hypothesized) neural pulse train (from HVC) and the dynamics of the respiratory cycle. Interestingly, this kind of period-doubling can also be observed in "gestural intrusions" human speakers produce when repeating phrases like "top cop", and a similar dynamical account has been proposed, less formally (Goldstein et al. 2007). That study found that when speakers produce such phrases repeatedly, they will begin to produce an "extra" copy of the tongue tip gesture of /t/ concurrently with the initial tongue dorsum gesture of "cop" (resulting in a co-produced /k͡t/) and conversely an extra tongue dorsum gesture during the initial tongue tip gesture of "top". These extra cycles of repeated tongue tip or tongue dorsum movement can be analyzed as a period doubling

– 2:1 to 1:1 transitions in frequency mode locking between the tongue tip (or tongue dorsum) oscillators and the lip oscillator of the syllable-final lip gesture (there is a lip gesture in every syllable, but a tongue tip or dorsum gesture only every other syllable; Goldstein et al. 2007). Since such period-doubling transitions in birdsong are analyzed by Goldin et al. (2013) as resulting from a presumed slowing of a clocking pulse in HVC, the results do not contradict the main finding and conclusion of the earlier work of Long and Fee. However, there is disagreement between the two research groups as to the nature of the temporal code in HVC and how it interacts (or not) with the rest of the system, as will be fleshed out a bit in the last section.

2.3 Brain-cooling in speech

The technique of focal brain cooling was recently employed with humans for the first time (Long et al. 2016) with patients undergoing brain surgery for either epilepsy or tumor resection. Cooling was applied in up to 4 locations in each subject, two in Broca's area within the left inferior frontal gyrus (IFG) and the others in the precentral gyrus (speech motor cortex). The hypothesis was that there would be a double dissociation with cooling in Broca's area causing changes in speech timing but not in articulatory quality, and that cooling the speech motor cortex would disrupt articulation, but not timing. Patients were recorded producing the digits from 1 to 20 or the names of the days of the week (one sequence per trial, with breaks between trials) while respective sites were being cooled, and also during control trials with no cooling. The utterances were judged for quality via crowd-sourcing on a scale from 0 (extremely degraded) to 1 (typical/normal). Timing was determined through durational measurements. Results supported the double dissociation. Cooling Broca's area resulted in changes to speech timing. Typically utterances were slowed down (both the actual articulation of words and the gaps between them were stretched), but some cases speeding up occurred. No effect was found on judged quality. When the speech motor cortex was cooled, ratings shifted to more degraded, with no effect on timing.

To examine the slowing more carefully, the authors generously made available the data from two of their subjects, one of which is analyzed here. Figure 4(a-b) shows boxplots for durations of the names of the days of the week (excluding pauses between names); on the left, control utterances are displayed and on the right, the trials with cooling of Broca's area. Results show fairly uniform slowing across the names of the days of week, except for "Friday," which shows less slowing. Somewhat surprising is that Friday is the shortest of all the words (even in the controls); there is certainly no tendency for list-final prosodic lengthening here. In terms of intonation, M-W generally appear to be produced with an extended High tone. Falling begins on "Thursday" and "Friday" is generally produced on a Low tone. So it is possible that the durations follow the prominence profile of the utterance. By itself, however, this does not explain the reduced percentage of slowing on "Friday." Another possibility is that cooling in Broca's area has a bigger effect on more complex syllable types (for example with coda consonants or clusters). The initial syllables of the days of the week all have closed syllables (with coda consonants) except "Friday". To test this, the durations of the initial syllables and final syllable ("day") were analyzed separately, and the magnitude of lengthening of initial (dark blue bars) vs. final (light yellow bars) syllables are shown in Figure 5. Magnitude of lengthening is calculated as the ratio of the median duration of that syllable when cooled divided by the median duration of controls. The lengthening of the (open) syllable "day" is approximately the same across all the days' names. The lengthening of the first syllable in "Friday" (an open syllable) is about the same as for "day", while the other first syllables (that are closed) lengthen more. The most lengthening is observed on the first syllable of "Wednesday", which is also the most complex syllable, closed with a coda cluster. This is consistent with the hypothesis that more complex syllables exhibit more slowing due to cooling in Broca's area.

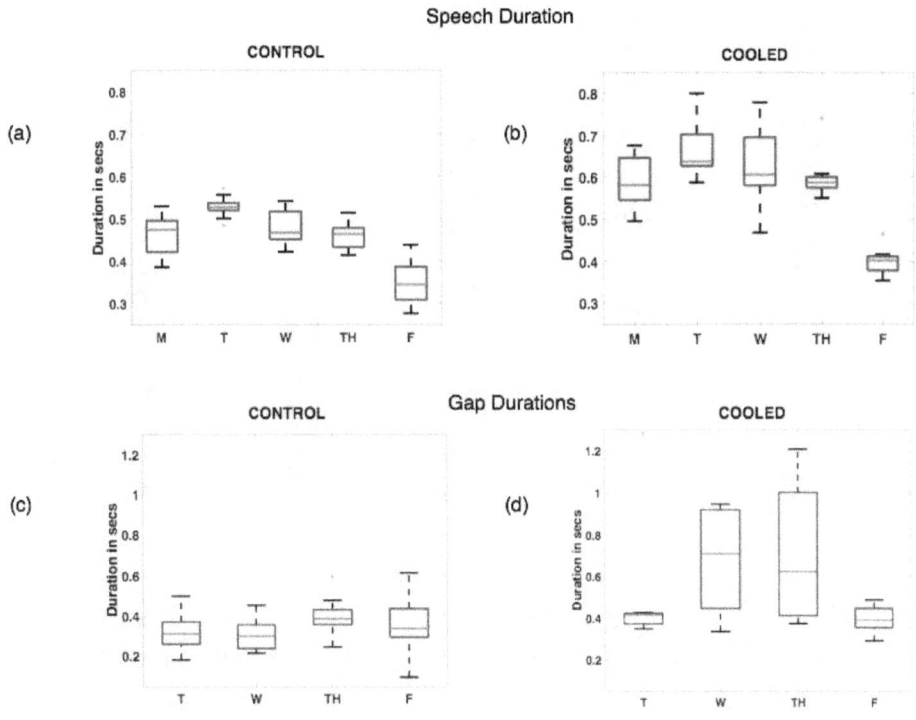

Figure 4: (a-b) Boxplots of duration of the names of days of the week from one patient. Control condition is shown in (a), cooling Broca's area is shown in (b). (c-d) Boxplots of silent gap durations before the production of the names of the week Tuesday-Friday. Control condition is shown in (c), cooling Broca's area is shown in (d).

Figure 4(c-d) shows the durations of the silent period before initiation of the words "Tuesday" to "Friday" from the time of completion of the preceding word. This shows a strikingly different pattern from that exhibited by the word durations. The silent gaps before "Tuesday" and "Friday" show very little effect, while the gaps before "Wednesday" and "Thursday" show almost 3:1 lengthening. The pattern is reminiscent of the classic pattern of recall in short-term memory (Deese & Kaufman 1957; Ebbinghaus 1885; Brown, Neath & Chater 2007). The items in the middle of the list have more competitors on either side and therefore more interference, although many other models have been proposed. Such results could be modeled by a competitive queuing model of sequence selection (Bullock & Rhodes 2002), depending on exactly how the parameters are set. In any case, it is clear that more is going on than just clock slowing when Broca's area is cooled, unlike what is observed in zebra finch, though clock slowing is also going on.

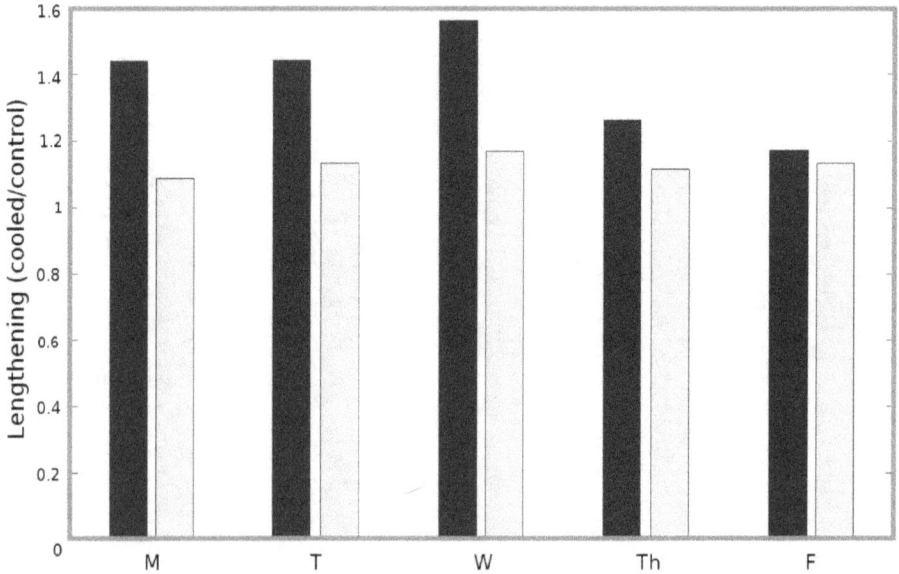

Figure 5: Magnitude of lengthening of initial (dark blue bars) vs. final (light yellow bars) syllables of the names of the days of the week. Magnitude of lengthening is calculated as the ratio of the median duration of that syllable when cooled divided by the median duration of that syllable in the uncooled control condition.

In summary, the results with humans generally confirm the dissociation of the timing clock from the articulatory gestural patterning that it paces. Differently from birds, however, where gaps between syllables and motifs were slowed in a roughly similar way to the actual song syllables, the gaps between the days of the week showed marked differences in response to cooling, depending on position in the list (for the one patient examined). This suggests that even for an over-learned list, mechanisms of selection of discrete individual words must still be in play, while for the bird, the entire song may just "run off" at different rates. This may be related to the relative lack of flexibility in the zebra finch song. Also the possible effect of syllable complexity on the magnitude of slowing also suggests that more is going on for humans when Broca's area is cooled than just uniform slowing of the clock.

2.4 Continuous vs discrete temporal representations

The last point brings up the nature of temporal coding that characterizes the representation in HVC of the bird (compared for example to the clock model proposed for speech discussed above). The work of Fee and collaborators has consistently supported the view that the representation is a continuous-time representation of the song (in 10 ms or so slices). This is based on the earlier discovery (Hahnloser, Kozhevnikov & Fee 2002) of individual cells that burst sparsely in the song at a fixed lag from song onset. Theoretically then, there could be such cells for each 10ms sample in the sound, and they jointly produce a continuous representation. Further, their hypothesis is that the continuous-time representation completely drives (or enslaves) the downstream activity in RA and the vocal muscles to reproduce the song (Long & Fee 2008), which is why the slowing does not result in distortions to the song (but cf. the results discussed earlier with extreme values of cooling). An alternative discrete view was proposed by the Margoliash and Mindlin group (Amador et al. 2013). After discovering that it was possible to decompose the dynamical parameters governing song production into discrete gestures, as discussed above, they found that burst times of HVC neurons projecting to RA tended to be synchronized with the gestural extrema, for 14 of the 15 sites they examined with recordings of single neurons. This is exactly what would be predicted by coupled oscillator model of syllable structure described above: the clock mechanism generates a sequence of bursts that trigger their corresponding gestures. However, attempts to replicate this finding with a substantially larger population of cells, in both Long's lab (Picardo et al. 2016) and Fee's (Lynch et al. 2016), failed to replicate this finding. It is unclear why this is, apart from possible differences in sites examined and the types of electrodes used. It would not be surprising to find that both continuous and discrete representations co-exist in different subpopulations of neurons. The discrete representation would be useful during learning to produce individual "pieces" of the song on the way to mastery (assuming a continuous representation of the target song in auditory areas is any case available to the system). Consistent with this, Lynch et al. (2016) did find evidence of 10-Hz rhythmicity locked to song syllables, which was significant for HVC projections to Area-X (basal ganglia loop employed in learning) but not for HVC projections to RA. Given the stereotypy of zebra finch song, it is not surprising that a continuous-time representation could work. Obviously in the case of speech, we are capable of producing novel forms, and for that a discrete representation like the coupled oscillator model is really the only viable candidate (or compatibly, models like that of Bohland and Guenther, e.g., Bohland, Bullock & Guenther 2010).

3 Summary

Speech and birdsong share the property that their production can be decomposed into a sequence of discrete motor actions. In addition, the control of those actions is governed by a separate timing representation. The nature of the timing representation appears to be substantially different however, possibly due to the essential combinatoriality and productivity of human speech, though there is a lot still unknown about both speech and birdsong in this regard. It is interesting to consider why they should be as similar they are. One functional similarity is that while they are both species-specific capabilities, in both cases the specific behavioral forms must be learned by individuals (in the bird species in which the song is learned from experience). There are other odd similarities as well, such as the compatible frequency of their syllable rates. This flies in the face of hypotheses that the duration of the syllables in speech is related to the natural frequency of the jaw (e.g., Davis & MacNeilage 2004). A more likely cause may be the similarity of their auditory systems. In any case, the existence of a model system that can be probed in ways that speech cannot provides the opportunity of deepening our understanding of speech, particularly when we observe the particular places in which the systems diverge.

Acknowledgements

Many thanks to Michael Long and Kalman Katlowitz for making their data available, and to Jelena Krivokapic, Mairym Llorens, Sarah Bottjer, and two anonymous reviewers for their comments on an earlier draft.

References

Amador, Ana, Yonatan S. Perl, Gabriel B. Mindlin & Daniel Margoliash. 2013. Elemental gesture dynamics are encoded by song premotor cortical neurons. *Nature* 495(7439). 59–64.
Anderson, Stephen R. 1974. *The organization of phonology.* New York: Academic Press.
Anderson, Stephen R. 2006. *Doctor Dolittle's delusion: Animals and the uniqueness of human language.* New Haven: Yale University Press.
Bohland, Jason W., Daniel Bullock & Frank H. Guenther. 2010. Neural representations and mechanisms for the performance of simple speech sequences. *Journal of Cognitive Neuroscience* 22(7). 1504–1529.
Browman, Catherine & Louis Goldstein. 1992. Articulatory phonology: An overview. *Phonetica* 49(3–4). 155–180.
Browman, Catherine & Louis Goldstein. 1995. Dynamics and articulatory phonology. In Timothy van Gelder & Robert F. Port (eds.), *Mind as motion*, 175–193. Cambridge, MA: MIT Press.
Brown, Gordon, Ian Neath & Nick Chater. 2007. A temporal ratio model of memory. *Psychological Review* 114(3). 539–576.

Bullock, Daniel & Bradley J. Rhodes. 2002. Competitive queuing for planning and serial performance. *CAS/CNS Technical Report Series* 3(3). 1–9.

Byrd, Dani & Elliot Saltzman. 2003. The elastic phrase: Modeling the dynamics of boundary-adjacent lengthening. *Journal of Phonetics* 31. 149–180.

Davis, Barbara L. & Peter F. MacNeilage. 2004. The frame/content theory of speech evolution: From lip smacks to syllables. *Primatologie* 6. 305–328.

Deese, James & Roger A. Kaufman. 1957. Serial effects in recall of unorganized and sequentially organized verbal material. *Journal of Experimental Psychology* 54(3). 180–187.

Ebbinghaus, Hermann. 1885. *Memory: A contribution to experimental psychology.* (Originally published 1885 in German. Translated by Henry A. Ruger and Clara E. Bussenius). New York: Teachers College, Columbia University.

Fowler, Carol A. 1980. Coarticulation and theories of extrinsic timing. *Journal of Phonetics* 8. 113–133.

Goldin, Matías A., Leandro M. Alonso, Jorge A. Alliende, Franz Goller & Gabriel B. Mindlin. 2013. Temperature induced syllable breaking unveils nonlinearly interacting timescales in birdsong motor pathway. *PLoS One* 8(6). e67814.

Goldstein, Louis, Dani Byrd & Elliot Saltzman. 2006. The role of vocal tract gestural action units in understanding the evolution of phonology. In Michael A. Arbib (ed.), *From action to language via the mirror neuron system*, 215–249. Cambridge: Cambridge University Press.

Goldstein, Louis, Marianne Pouplier, Larissa Chen, Elliot Saltzman & Dani Byrd. 2007. Dynamic action units slip in speech production errors. *Cognition* 103(3). 386–412.

Grossberg, Stephen. 1978. A theory of human memory: Self-organization and performance of sensory-motor codes, maps, and plans. *Progress in Theoretical Biology* 5. 233–374.

Hahnloser, Richard H. R., Alexay A. Kozhevnikov & Michale S. Fee. 2002. An ultra-sparse code underlies the generation of neural sequences in a songbird. *Nature* 419(6902). 65–70.

Hermes, Anne, Doris Muecke & Martine Grice. 2013. Gestural coordination of Italian word initial clusters – The case of 'impure s.' *Phonology* 30(1). 1–25.

Katsika, Argyro, Jelena Krivokapić, Christine Mooshammer, Mark Tiede & Louis Goldstein. 2014. The coordination of boundary tones and their interaction with prominence. *Journal of Phonetics* 44. 62–82.

Long, Michael A. & Michale S. Fee. 2008. Using temperature to analyse temporal dynamics in the songbird motor pathway. *Nature* 456(7219). 189–194.

Long, Michael A., Kalman A. Katlowitz, Mario A. Svirsky, Rachel C. Clary, Tara McAllister Byun, Najib Majaj, Hiroyuki Oya, Matthew A. Howard & Jeremy D.W. Greenlee. 2016. Functional segregation of cortical regions underlying speech timing and articulation. *Neuron* 89(6). 1187–1193.

Lynch, Galen F., Tatsuo S. Okubo, Alexander Hanuschkin, Richard H. R. Hahnloser & Michale S. Fee. 2016. Rhythmic continuous-time coding in the songbird analog of vocal motor cortex. *Neuron* 90(4). 877–892.

Marin, Stefania & Marianne Pouplier. 2010. Temporal organization of complex onsets and codas in American English: Testing the predictions of a gestural coupling model. *Motor Control* 14(3). 380–407.

McGowan, Richard S. & Elliot L. Saltzman. 1995. Incorporating aerodynamic and laryngeal components into task dynamics. *Journal of Phonetics* 23. 255–269.

Nam, Hosung, Louis Goldstein & Elliot Saltzman. 2009. Self-organization of syllable structure: A coupled oscillator model. In François Pellegrino, Egidio Marisco & Ioana Chitoran (eds.), *Approaches to phonological complexity*, 299–328. Berlin/New York: Mouton de Gruyter.

Nam, Hosung, Vikramjit Mitra, Mark Tiede, Mark Hasegawa-Johnson, Carol Espy-Wilson, Elliot Saltzman & Louis Goldstein. 2012. A procedure for estimating gestural scores from speech acoustics. *Journal of the Acoustical Society of America* 132(6). 3980–3989.

Picardo, Michel A., Josh Merel, Kalman A. Katlowitz, Daniela Vallentin, Daniel E. Okobi, Sam E. Benezra, Rachel C. Clary, Eftychios A. Pnevmatikakis, Liam Paninski & Michael A. Long. 2016. Population-level representation of a temporal sequence underlying song production in the zebra finch. *Neuron* 90(4). 866–876.

Riede, Tobias & Franz Goller. 2010. Functional morphology of the sound-generating labia in the syrinx of two songbird species. *Journal of Anatomy* 216. 23–36. DOI:doi:10.1111/j.1469-7580.2009.01161.x

Shaw, Jason, Adamantios I. Gafos, Philip Hoole & Chakir Zeroual. 2009. Syllabification in Moroccan Arabic: Evidence from temporal stability in articulation. *Phonology* 26. 187–215.

Tilsen, Sam. 2016. Selection and coordination: The articulatory basis for the emergence of phonological structure. *Journal of Phonetics* 55. 53–77. DOI:doi:10.1016/j.wocn.2015.11.005

Trevisan, Marcos A., Brenton Cooper, Franz Goller & Gabriel B. Mindlin. 2007. Lateralization as a symmetry breaking process in birdsong. *Physical Review E* 75(3 Pt 1). 031908.

Yu, Albert C. & Daniel Margoliash. 1996. Temporal hierarchical control of singing in birds. *Science* 273(5283). 1871–1875.

Chapter 22

"Constructions" and grammar: Evidence from idioms

Julia Horvath
Tel Aviv University

Tal Siloni
Tel Aviv University

> The paper presents results of our investigation of the distribution of idioms across diatheses (voice alternations) in English and Hebrew. We propose an account and discuss its consequences for idiom storage and its implications for alternative architectures of grammar. We provide evidence that idioms split into two distinct subtypes, which we label "phrasal" versus "clausal" idioms. Based on idiom surveys, we observe that phrasal idioms can be specific to the transitive, the unaccusative or the adjectival passive diathesis, but cannot be specific to the verbal passive. Clausal idioms, in contrast, do not discriminate between diatheses: they tend to be specific to a single diathesis. These findings, we argue, cannot be accommodated by a Construction Grammar approach, such as Goldberg (2006), which assumes knowledge of language consists merely of an inventory of stored 'constructions', and does not distinguish between a storage module versus a computational system, attributing all significant grammatical generalizations to inheritance networks relating stored entities, and general cognitive and functional constraints. An adequate theory of idioms must have recourse to a distinction between stored items and unstored derivational outputs, and to grammatical distinctions. We outline an account of the findings, distinguishing between diatheses according to where they are formed, and assigning different storage to idioms according to whether their head is lexical or functional.

1 Introduction

Theories of linguistic knowledge all assume a storage component, where the associations of form and meaning are stored. There is a controversy as to the nature of this component, call it the lexicon: How much does it list? What does it allow? What else is there beyond the lexicon? In contrast with Generative Grammar, which assumes a modular, multi-component model (Chomsky 1965 and subsequent work), Usage-based

Julia Horvath & Tal Siloni. 2017. "Constructions" and grammar: Evidence from idioms. In Claire Bowern, Laurence Horn & Raffaella Zanuttini (eds.), *On looking into words (and beyond)*, 471–489. Berlin: Language Science Press. DOI:10.5281/zenodo.495462

Construction Grammar (CxG) (e.g. Goldberg 2006) and similar work assume that human knowledge of language is nothing more than a network of stored constructions.[1] There is no faculty of language and no language specific mechanisms, no derivations, just a lexicon of constructions, labelled 'Construct-i-con', which includes morphemes, words, idioms, partially lexically filled as well as fully abstract phrasal patterns. Generalizations across languages are explained by general cognitive constraints together with the functions of the particular constructions. Language-specific generalizations across constructions arise via inheritance networks.

The rationale behind the assumption of a construct-i-con is as follows: (i) Idioms, for the most part, involve an internal makeup consisting of phrasal units. Since their meaning is unpredictable and associated with the whole construction, they are most plausibly stored as constructions. (ii) The distinction between idioms and 'other constructions' (involving argument realization) is hard to detect in many instances, because often the specific meaning of a sentence not involving an idiom (in the traditional sense) seems better specified as a property of the construction, not as properties of the verb and of its complements (e.g., the 'transfer of possession' meaning of 'He sliced Chris a piece of cake' vs. the 'caused motion' interpretation of 'He sliced carrots into the salad', although both sentences feature *sliced*). Hence, constructions in general should be stored as such.

Indeed, idioms exhibit an inherent duality. On the one hand, they are phrasal units with internal syntactic structure, and on the other, they are associated with an unpredictable, conventionalized meaning. Therefore, the question as to how they are stored is particularly intriguing. Given that they are grammatical constructs and interact with grammar (can be embedded, can allow passivization, etc.), they must be stored intra-grammatically, in the lexicon. This paper investigates the storage of idioms, aiming to shed light on the nature of the lexicon. Further, idioms are the archetypal construction to be stored à la CxG; therefore, they constitute a test case (for alternative conceptions of grammar and the lexicon) most favorable to CxG. So if our investigation of idioms finds that the storage they require is inconsistent with CxG's central tenet that grammar is comprised of nothing but networks of stored 'constructions', this must be all the more so for more productive, prima facie compositional kinds of 'constructions'.

Investigating the distribution of idioms across diatheses (transitive, unaccusative, adjectival passive, and verbal passive), we observe contrasts between the cross-diatheses distribution of distinct types of idioms. One type of idiom (which we will label 'phrasal') distributes differently in the verbal passive diathesis versus the transitive, unaccusative and adjectival passive diatheses: it cannot be specific to the verbal passive, but can be specific to the latter diatheses. Another type of idiom ('clausal'), in contrast, does not discriminate between diatheses in this way: Idioms of this type tend to be specific to a single diathesis. We then show that a construct-i-con type of theory cannot account for these findings. To account for these systematic distinctions, which idioms (the archetypal 'construction' à la CxG) exhibit, the theory requires more than cognitive principles, reference to functional needs, and inheritance of properties between stored entities ('constructions').

---

[1] This approach is also referred to as Cognitive Construction Grammar (CCxG); see Boas (2013) for an overview of this versus other varieties of construction grammar models.

The structure of the paper is as follows. Sections 2 and 3 draw a distinction between lexically headed idioms, which we label 'phrasal' idioms, and idioms headed by a sentential functional head, which we label 'clausal' idioms, and discuss each type (respectively), paying particular attention to their distinct distribution across diatheses. §4 offers additional evidence for the partition into phrasal and clausal idioms, and lays out the implications regarding a CxG-type model. §5 sketches an account for the findings in the framework of a derivational and modular architecture of grammar.

2 Phrasal idioms

It has sporadically been observed in the literature that the verbal (eventive) passive (e.g., *sold* in 'The first costumer was sold the car') and the adjectival (stative) passive (e.g., *shaven*) differ regarding the distribution of idioms. While there do not seem to be idioms specific to the verbal (eventive) passive (i.e., idioms in the verbal passive that have no transitive (active) alternant), there are idioms specific to the adjectival (stative) passive (see Ruwet 1991 for English and French, and Dubinsky & Simango 1996 for Chichewa). A first quantitative survey of idiom dictionaries examining these observations is reported in Horvath and Siloni's 2009 study of Hebrew idioms: Out of 60 predicates sampled for 4 diatheses – verbal passive, adjectival passive, transitive, and unaccusative– only the verbal passive exhibited no unique idioms. An idiom is considered 'unique' to a given diathesis α, if α does not share the idiom with its (existing) root-counterpart β, which α would most directly be related to by derivation. Specifically, verbal passives, adjectival passives, and unaccusatives are unique if there is no corresponding transitive idiom. Transitives are unique if there is no corresponding unaccusative idiom. Except for the verbal passive, all other three diatheses can head unique idioms.[2] This will be illustrated shortly with English examples in (4–6).

Two observations are in order. First, the idioms mentioned in the above studies are all phrasal idioms (VP and AP) involving no sentential functional categories such as auxiliaries, negation, etc. Second, verbal passives in Hebrew are known to be rarer in spoken language in comparison to say English (Berman 2008), which may affect the inventory of verbal passive idioms in the language.

In light of the above, we ran a parallel survey of English idiom dictionaries. We believe such surveys are necessary for the study of idiom distribution, as speakers may sometimes have a hard time distinguishing whether a certain idiom variant exists and is commonly used or only could exist, i.e., is a priori possible, but is not documented. This is so because the spontaneous formation and learning of novel idiomatic expressions is part of speakers' linguistic competence. Also, knowledge of idioms varies considerably among speakers (similar to vocabulary knowledge).

---

[2] The survey proceeded as follows. 60 predicates of each diathesis were sampled from a verb dictionary. The number of predicates out of the sample of 60 giving rise to unique phrasal idioms were counted. This was done by searches of idiom dictionaries, followed by Google searches to check occurrences of relevant root-mate idioms, and consultation of native speakers regarding the results. The number of unique idioms found: 0 verbal passive ones; 21 unaccusatives; 23 transitives; and 13 adjectival passives.

We have systematically distinguished between phrasal and clausal idioms, as defined in (1) and illustrated in (2).

(1) Phrasal vs. clausal idioms
   a. Phrasal Idioms are headed by a lexical head (e.g., 2a).
   b. Clausal Idioms are headed by a sentential functional head (a fixed tense or mood, a modal, obligatory (or impossible) sentential negation or CP-material); they are not necessarily full clauses (e.g., 2b)

Fixed sentential material is specified in parentheses. Non-idiomatic material within idioms is marked by italics.

(2) a. land on *one*'s feet
      'make a quick recovery'
   b. can't see the forest for the trees   (modal, negation)
      'doesn't perceive the whole situation clearly due to focusing on the details'

Given that 'idiom' is a pre-theoretic term referring to various types of fixed expressions, we defined a core set. The set consisted of conventionalized multilexemic expressions whose meaning is figurative (metaphoric) and unpredictable by semantic composition. A property often mistakenly conflated with the unpredictability of idioms' meaning is the level of opacity or transparency of their meaning. Idioms indeed differ from one another in the level of their transparency (opacity). For example, the phrasal and clausal idioms in 3a and 3b respectively may be felt more opaque than those in (2-??). However, the degree of opacity can be determined only once we know the meaning of the idioms; neither the former nor the latter meanings can be predicted based on the meaning of their building blocks. Hence, the meanings of the idioms in (2) just like those of the idioms in (3) are unpredictable (even if a posteriori, more transparent). Such idioms are therefore part of the core set we have defined and included in our study.

(3) a. cool *one*'s heels
      'wait'
   b. can't hold a candle to *someone/something*   (modal, negation)
      'be not as good as someone/something else'

We first concentrated only on phrasal idioms. This enabled us to examine a coherent set of idiomatic expressions.

The English survey we ran produced similar results to those of the Hebrew one. The transitive, unaccusative, and adjectival passive exhibited unique idioms, just like their Hebrew counterparts.[3] Examples of unique unaccusative (4), adjectival passive (5), and transitive (6) idioms are given below. Notice that the nonexistent idiomatic version is no less plausible than the existing idiom. (# means the relevant sequence of words has no idiomatic meaning.)

---

[3] The English survey was conducted following the guidelines in Horvath & Siloni (2009) (see note 2). The number of predicates out of the sample of 60 giving rise to unique phrasal idioms in English: 15 unaccusatives; 18 transitives; 10 adjectival passives.

(4) a. burst at the seams (unaccusative)
'filled (almost) beyond capacity'
b. #burst *something* at the seams (transitive)

(5) a. caught in the middle (adjectival passive)
'trapped between two opposing sides'
b. #catch *someone* in the middle (transitive)

(6) a. turn *something* on its ear (transitive)
'change something in a surprising and exciting way'
b. #turn on its ear (unaccusative)

However, unlike in Hebrew, the verbal passive in English turned out, prima facie, to present unique verbal passive idioms for 2 out of the 60 predicates, namely for *caught* and *bitten*. These idioms are given in (7).

(7) a. caught in the crossfire
'hurt by opposing groups in a disagreement'
b. bitten by the *x* bug (where *x* forms a compound with *bug*)
'having the need/desire/obsession for *x*'

These phrasal idioms can be suspected at first to constitute unique verbal passive idioms, due to their listing in idiom dictionaries in the passive form, and not in the active, in contrast to the norm of listing verb phrase idioms in dictionaries in the active form. Moreover, according to native speakers, these forms can be modified by adverbials of duration or appear in the progressive, suggesting that they have eventive, verbal occurrences.

However, on closer examination, both of these turned out not to constitute true counterexamples to the generalization that there are no idioms unique to the verbal passive. Starting with 7a, the idiom *caught in the crossfire*, which indeed appears in the verbal passive, in fact is attested – based on Google searches accompanied by native speakers' judgments – also in the transitive (active) form, as in (8), for instance; hence it is not a unique verbal passive idiom.

(8) a. This **caught him in the crossfire** between radical proponents of independence and French opponents of anti-colonialism.
(Scheck, 2014:282)[4]
b. ...the Israeli-Palestinian conflict, which has often **caught them in the crossfire**. https://goo.gl/f2FbbG

The idiom in 7b is instantiated by versions such as *bitten by the travel bug*, *bitten by the acting bug*, etc. These, just like 7a, can be true verbal passive forms; however, again,

---

[4] Scheck, Raffael. 2014. *French Colonial Soldiers in German Captivity during World War II*. Cambridge: Cambridge University Press. Available at https://goo.gl/QAGf9E. All online examples accessed 9 December 2016.

Google searches turn up a significant number of active transitive examples of the same idiom, e.g., (9–10).

(9) Before the **acting bug bit me** I had dreamed of being another Glenn Cunningham. (Halbrook 2001, 66)[5]

(10) It was during my time in the Army in the 1960s and 1970s that **the travel bug bit me**. (MacKrell 2006, Introduction)[6]

The listing of (7–??) in the passive participial form may well be due to the fact that in addition to occurring as a verbal (eventive) passive, they are also attested in the adjectival (stative) passive; the latter point is demonstrated by the idioms' occurrence as complements of verbs selecting APs but not VPs, such as *seem* and *remain* (Wasow 1977), as illustrated by (11–12).

(11) a. Everyone else seems **caught in the crossfire** between these two, I honestly feel bad about everyone involved. https://goo.gl/trJp5o

b. The Starbucks coffee chain remains **caught in the crossfire** of a dispute over "open carry" laws... https://goo.gl/PMCiMF

(12) a. ...and Kevin remains **bitten by the travel – and mapping – bug**. https://goo.gl/xC8kWp

b. It made an impression on Bowley, and he too seems **bitten by the renovation bug**... https://goo.gl/H04LWn

More generally, in the case of English in particular, it is important to keep in mind that there is the interfering factor of the common identity of form between verbal passives and adjectival passives, and only diagnostics can establish whether or not the particular idiom is indeed a verbal passive, and not (only) an adjectival passive one (see Wasow 1977 for diagnostics).

We can thus conclude that the idioms in (7) are not exceptions to the generalization that there is no unique idiom in the verbal passive.[7] The next question is what can explain this.

A priori, two alternative types of explanations for the above generalization come to mind: a derivation-based account in the spirit of derivational approaches of Generative Grammar or alternatively, an inheritance-based account, along the guidelines proposed by CxG. Abstracting away from details, a derivation-based account would have the verbal passive formed beyond the domain of special meanings, which would prevent verbal passives from having their own special/idiomatic meaning. An inheritance-based account would have the verbal passive inherit the inability to give rise to idioms that it

---

[5] Halbrook, Hal. 2011. Harold – The Boy Who Became Mark Twain. New York: Farrar, Straus and Giroux. Available at https://goo.gl/ivWkAQ.

[6] MacKrell, Thomas. 2006. One Orbit – Around the World in 63 Days. Victoria, Oxford: Trafford. Available at https://goo.gl/bRlHKA.

[7] Additional idioms (headed by predicates not included in our sample) that may be suspected to be unique verbal passive idioms are discussed by Horvath & Siloni (2016), and are shown to also conform to the generalization.

does not share with its transitive alternant from the inability of verbal passives to lack a transitive alternant.

A first indication that an inheritance-based account is not on the right track comes from inspection of the transitive-unaccusative alternation. This alternation manifests regularity at the verb level, but pervasive uniqueness at the idiom level. Intransitive unaccusative verbs have a transitive alternant (with a Cause external role) and vice versa (13), except for isolated instances (Härtl 2003, Reinhart 2002, among others).[8]

(13) a. Dan / The storm / The stone broke the window.
     b. The window broke.

In other words, there are sporadic, isolated gaps in the transitive-unaccusative verbal alternation but the paradigm is rather regular. Nonetheless, there is pervasive uniqueness, namely, unpredictable gaps are common, at the idiom level. If so, then, the distribution of phrasal idioms across diatheses is not determined by or inherited from the degree of productivity of their respective predicates.

In sum, an inheritance-based account does not seem to be able to account for the observation that the verbal passive, unlike the transitive, unaccusative and adjectival passive cannot head unique phrasal idioms. Additional evidence against an inheritance-based account comes from clausal idioms, which are discussed in the next section.

3 Clausal idioms

As defined in 1b, clausal idioms are not necessarily full clauses; they are headed by a sentential functional element: a fixed tense or mood, a modal, obligatory (or impossible) sentential negation or CP-material. Examples of clausal idioms are given below: 2b and 3b repeated as (14–??) and additional examples in (14–??).

(14) a. ...can't see the forest for the trees (modal, negation)
        'doesn't perceive the whole situation clearly due to focusing on the details'
     b. can't hold a candle to *someone/something* (modal, negation)
        'be not as good as someone/something else'

---

[8] For example, the transitive alternant may be missing idiosyncratically and sporadically in a given language for a few instances, but these instances have a transitive alternant with a Cause role at some other stage in the evolution of the same language (e.g., the recently developing transitive *faint* in Hebrew (i)) or in other languages at present (e.g., existence of the transitive *fall* in Hebrew (ii), but not in English).

(i) Barur še-hu xavat bo dey xazak im hu ilef oto.
    evident that-he hit in.him rather strong if he fainted.TRANSITIVE him
    'It is evident that he hit him rather strongly if he made him faint.'
    https://goo.gl/GK7MWR

(ii) Dan hipil šney sfarim.
     Dan fell.TRANSITIVE two books

  c. butter wouldn't melt in *someone*'s mouth   (modal, negation)
    'someone is acting innocent'
  d. The squeaky wheel gets the grease.   (tense)
    'The most noticeable (loudest) ones are the most likely to get attention.'
  e. not have a leg to stand on   (negation)
    'have no support (for your position)'
  f. Where does *someone* get off *doing something*?   (interrogative, wh-phrase)
    'Where does someone get the right to/how dare someone do something?'

  One may wonder at this point whether some of what we consider clausal idioms here would not be classified more appropriately as proverbs rather than (clausal) idioms. Indeed, the common though informal distinction between proverbs vs. idioms is worth some clarification.

  Proverbs have no precise linguistic definition. Just like our clausal idioms, they too are headed by some functional, rather than lexical, head. The definition we have given to delineate the core set of idioms, given the goals of our study, is aimed at obtaining evidence about lexical storage; therefore, our idioms all have properties that force them to be stored, and specifically stored in the grammar (not in extralinguistic storage in general memory). Consequently, the questions we need to ask regarding any clausal idiom suspected to be a proverb are: (a) Is the meaning of the expression unpredictable based on composition of its parts and does it involve figuration? If so it must be stored; (b) Is there evidence that it is stored in the storage component of the grammar, and not extragrammatically? The clausal idioms used in our study satisfy both of these criteria (on satisfaction of criterion (b), see our discussion of examples 19–22 below), thus they are properly falling within the set of relevant idiom data to be considered. As for whether some of them may be felt to be proverb-like (due to some additional, stylistic, aspectual or other properties) this is not a factor that effects the validity of the conclusions drawn based on them, as long as they meet the criteria for intra-grammatical (lexical) storage, as explained above.[9]

  Unlike phrasal idioms, clausal idioms do occur as unique to the verbal passive. Examples are given in (15–16) for English and (17–18) for Hebrew. As mentioned in §1, it is

---

[9] Observe that there is a difference between the various (fixed) clausal expressions in terms of the presence/absence of figuration they manifest. Expressions such as (i) are fixed in form and are felt to be proverbs (as pointed out by an anonymous referee), but involve no figuration and hence are not classified as idioms according to our criteria; in contrast the expressions in (ii) do manifest figuration and constitute idioms under our definition. At the same time, both (i) and (ii) may be felt to be proverbs. This intuitive notion does not seem to be associated with figuration. A property that does appear to play a role in the perception of a fixed clausal expression as a proverb is that it applies to a generic, rather than episodic, situation. (This property is orthogonal to qualifying as an idiom.)

 (i) a. *Two wrongs don't make a right.*
   b. *When the going gets tough, the tough get going.*
 (ii) a. *A stitch in time saves nine.*
   b. *A chain is only as strong as its weakest link.*

often difficult to decide whether a certain idiom variant exists or only could exist, but not documented, and constitutes an ad hoc "playful" intended distortion, alluding to an existing idiom. Our data therefore are based on idiom dictionaries and the diathesis/es that they list the idioms in. In addition, however, we have googled idioms to check their existence in root-mate variants. We did not consider isolated occurrences, including playful distortions, which mostly appear in specific styles, such as media language, as evidence of existence.

(15) a. might/may as well be hung/hanged for a sheep as (for) a lamb (modal)
'may as well commit a larger transgression, as the same punishment will result'

b. #(They) might/may as well hang *someone* for a sheep as (for) a lamb.[10]

(16) a. Gardens are not made by sitting in the shade. (negation, tense)
'Nothing is achieved without effort.'

b. #One doesn't make gardens by sitting in the shade.

(17) a. Nigzezu maxlafot-av. (tense)
sheared.VPASSIVE hair-his
'lost one's power/influence.'

b. #gazezu et maxlafot-av.
sheared.TRANSITIVE.IMPERSONAL ACCUSATIVE hair-his

(18) a. Hutla ha-kubiya. (tense)
cast.VPASSIVE the-die
'The process is past the point of return.'

b. #Hetilu et ha-kubiya.
cast.TRANSITIVE.IMPERSONAL ACCUSATIVE the-die

Thus, while there are no unique phrasal idioms in the verbal passive, there appear to exist clausal idioms unique to the verbal passive. This provides additional evidence against an inheritance-based account of the lack of phrasal idioms unique to the verbal passive, that is, against the proposal that it is the necessary existence of a transitive alternant for all verbal passives that is inherited by (or transmitted to) the corresponding phrasal idioms. Initial evidence that such an inheritance-type account is not on the right track was presented in §2 based on inspection of the transitive-unaccusative alternation. This alternation, as we noted, manifests regularity at the verb level, but pervasive uniqueness at the idiom level. Its behavior thus is incompatible with the idea that there is inheritance of properties from the verb level to the idiom level. Our findings regarding the existence of clausal idioms unique to the verbal passive, exemplified in (15)–(18), are also incompatible with such an inheritance-based account. If it was indeed merely inheritance by the verbal passive idiom of the non-uniqueness property of the verbal diathesis

---

[10] A reviewer called our attention to the existence of occurrences of the idiom in the unaccusative. One online dictionary (out of eight) listed the clausal idiom in the unaccusative form, not in the verbal passive: *One may/might as well hang for a sheep as a lamb.*

(i.e., necessary existence of a transitive alternant), then there does not seem to be any reason why phrasal idioms would inherit "non-uniqueness", while clausal idioms in the verbal passive would not do so. So not only is there no inheritance of distribution from the verb level to the idiom level, as shown by the transitive-unaccusative alternation, but in addition, an inheritance-based account could not explain the distributional distinction between phrasal versus clausal idioms regarding the verbal passive. Note also that the discrepancy between phrasal and clausal idioms with regard to uniqueness in the verbal passive seems to hold across languages, yet it certainly cannot be attributed to general cognitive constraints or functional needs of the constructions. If all the theory has at its disposal is inheritance networks, cognitive constraints, and functional needs to explain generalizations exhibited by members in the construct-i-con, the above findings cannot be accounted for.

One could perhaps suggest that unlike phrasal idioms, clausal idioms are stored extra-grammatically, outside the construct-i-con (similar to memorized language material such as lines of poems, etc.), and therefore they do not inherit the non-uniqueness property from the verbal passive. Such a line of explanation however does not seem to be tenable. Unlike memorized language material, clausal idioms interact with the grammar and it is thus hardly plausible that their storage is extra-grammatical. First, they can appear as embedded clauses within various matrix contexts (19–??). Further, they need not be full clauses and can include a non-idiomatic argument (20–??). Moreover, the non-idiomatic element can occur within a sub-constituent (21–??). Finally, they can include variable pronouns obligatorily bound by a non-idiomatic noun phrase (22–??), (the variable pronoun indicated by *one* has to be bound by the subject in 22a and 22b).

(19) a. One should take into account the fact that [the squeaky wheel gets the grease]. (tense)
'One should take into account the fact that [the most noticeable (loudest) ones are the most likely to get attention].'

b. They had to realize that [the leopard does not change his spots]. (negation)
'They had to realize that [one remains as one is even if one pretends otherwise/tries hard].'

(20) a. can't see the forest for the trees (modal, negation)
'doesn't perceive the whole situation clearly due to focusing on the details'

b. wouldn't touch *someone/something* with a ten-foot pole (modal, negation)
'wouldn't have anything to do with someone/something'

(21) a. wouldn't put it [past *someone*] (modal, negation)
'consider it possible that someone might do something wrong or unpleasant'

b. butter wouldn't melt in [*someone*'s mouth] (modal,negation)
'someone is acting innocent'

(22) a. can't fight *one's* way out of a paper bag (modal, negation)
'be an extremely inept'

b. would give *one's* right arm (for...) (modal)
'would like something very much'

Below we turn to an additional distinction between phrasal and clausal idioms in order to reinforce our conclusion thus far.

4 Diathesis sharing vs. rigidity

In both English and Hebrew, phrasal idioms can be common to, i.e., shared between, root-alternants. The verbal passive always shares its idiomatic meaning with the corresponding transitive (e.g., 23), as discussed in §2. Moreover, the other diatheses (the transitive, unaccusative, and adjectival passive), which appear in unique idioms, can also share their idiomatic meaning with their root-alternants (24–25).[11]

(23) a. spill the beans (transitive)
'divulge the secret'
b. The beans were spilled. (verbal passive)

(24) a. burst *someone*'s bubble (transitive)
'destroy someone's illusion'
b. someone's bubble burst (unaccusative)

(25) a. carve s*omething* in stone (transitive)
'fix some idea/agreement permanently'
b. carved in stone (adjectival passive)

In contrast, the clausal idioms in our preliminary investigation, unlike the phrasal ones, fail to exhibit sharing across diatheses. Clausal idioms seem to be unique, as illustrated by examples (26–29) below.

Transitive vs. verbal passive

(26) a. can't see the forest for the trees (modal, negation)
'doesn't perceive the whole situation clearly due to focusing on the details'
b. #The forest can't be seen for the trees.[12]

---

[11] We have conducted two surveys of shared idioms. The results are as follows. The number of English transitive predicates (out of the sample of 60) sharing phrasal idioms with the verbal passive: 35, with unaccusative: 17, and with adjectival passive: 21. The number of Hebrew transitive predicates (out of the sample of 60) sharing phrasal idioms with the verbal passive: 10, with unaccusative 16, and with adjectival passive: 5. Note that while phrasal idioms in the verbal passive always have a transitive version; it is not the case that any transitive idiom has a corresponding verbal passive idiom, as discussed in §5.

[12] This idiom does have occurrences in the verbal passive (found by Google searches). However, the idiom shows signs of being in the process of developing a phrasal version. This process is indicated by the existence of a large number of occurrences of this idiom in a phrasal version headed by a variety of lexical verbs, each yielding the same meaning as the original clausal idiom: *ignore the forest for the trees*, *miss the forest for the trees*, *neglect the forest for the trees*. The evolving use of this idiom in a phrasal form may be the reason for the occurrences of a verbal passive version. See also fn. 17.

Transitive vs. unaccusative (in the adjunct clause)

(27) a. You can't make an omelet without breaking a few eggs. (modal, negation)
'It is difficult to achieve something important without causing any unpleasant effects.'
b. #You can't make an omelet without a few eggs breaking.

Adjectival passive vs. transitive

(28) a. The road to hell is paved with good intentions. (tense)
'People often mean well but do bad things.'
b. #Good intentions pave the road to hell.

Unaccusative vs. transitive

(29) a. do(es) not grow on trees (auxiliary, negation)
'is not abundant, not to be wasted'
b. #do(es) not grow *something* on trees

One might think at this point that the emerging lack of cross-diathesis flexibility of clausal idioms could be due to the fact that in English the relevant diathesis alternations involve syntactic movements reordering subparts of the idiom. These movements might be suspected to be incompatible with the idiomatic reading for reasons of information structure, independent of the diathesis change itself. However, examining clausal idioms with regard to parallel diathesis alternations in Hebrew, a language in which diathesis alternations do not have to involve such potentially interfering factors, seems to point in the same direction. For instance, the Hebrew clausal idiom in 30a does not require reordering (nor addition of words), when undergoing the diathesis alternation in 30b; still the latter is impossible.

(30) a. kše-xotvim ecim, nitazim švavim.
when-chop.TRANSITIVE.IMPERSONAL trees, sprinkle.UNACCUSATIVE chips (tense)

'When you act, there are risks.' 'Where trees are felled chips will fly.'

b. #kše-xotvim ecim, metizim švavim.
when-chop.TRANSITIVE.IMPERSONAL trees, sprinkle.TRANSITIVE.IMPERSONAL chips

If knowledge of language were nothing more than an inventory of constructions whose properties derive from cognitive constraints, functional needs and inheritance hierarchies, there would be no way to explain why the clausal idioms we have examined (full and partial sentential structures) are unique to their diathesis, while phrasal idioms are commonly shared across diatheses.

In sum, an inheritance-based account cannot explain why idioms headed by members of the unaccusative alternation show pervasive uniqueness at the idiom level, although the verbal alternation is rather systematic. Moreover, under such an account, it is completely unclear why clausal idioms can be unique to the verbal passive as well as to other diatheses, and even seem to be unique generally, while phrasal idioms cannot be unique to the verbal passive, but can be unique to other diatheses.

Below we consider what an alternative approach, one that can provide a principled account for the above generalizations, should look like, and sketch our proposal in terms of idiom storage, which derives these findings.

5 Alternative, derivational accounts

CxG imposes no principled limitation on lexically stored syntactic objects and assumes no syntactic (online) derivation, only stored objects ("constructions"), whose interrelations are expressed via inheritance networks. The inability of CxG to capture the distributional asymmetries of diatheses in idioms established in the preceding sections is a direct consequence of these fundamental characteristics of the model. We believe that in contrast to the CxG model, modular derivation-based theories, namely theories incorporating a fundamental distinction between lexically stored entities versus syntactic objects derived by the computational system of grammar have the potential to provide an adequate account for the above findings. Before sketching the particular account that we propose, observe what assumptions are available in derivation-based modular architectures – and absent in non-derivational, construction-based models – that seem prerequisites for accounts aiming to capture the diathesis asymmetries discussed above.

What seems crucial for conceiving a syntactic account is the incremental building of structure in the syntactic derivation, yielding units in the course of the derivation ("phases") that impose locality limitations on the accessibility of special/idiomatic meanings. As for lexical accounts (involving the storage component of grammar) what is crucial would be principled constraints on what can be stored in the lexicon and in what manner, as will be explained in what follows.

In the remainder of this section, we sketch an account along the latter lines within our model of Type Sensitive Storage (TSS) (Horvath & Siloni 2016). The model derives the diathesis asymmetries discussed in the previous sections from a different storage technique motivated for phrasal versus clausal idioms. Under this proposal, the distinct storage technique of phrasal versus clausal idioms is a direct consequence of their having a lexical versus a functional head, respectively. Each storage strategy, in turn, results in a different pattern of distribution across diatheses. As summarized in (31), the Type-Sensitive Storage model suggests that phrasal idioms are stored as subentries of existing lexical entries, whereas clausal idioms constitute independent lexical entries on their own, that is, are not stored as subentries.

(31) The Type-Sensitive Storage (TSS) Model
    a. Idioms are stored as part of our linguistic knowledge (not as general, non-linguistic information).

b. Phrasal idioms – Subentry Storage: Phrasal idioms are stored as subentries of the lexical entry of their head (and possibly of their other constituents).[13]

c. Clausal Idioms – Independent Storage: Clausal idioms are stored as independent entries on their own.

Let us see how this would account for the findings. Subentry storage is contingent upon the listing, i.e., the existence, of the (mother) entry in the lexicon. The verbal passive is formed beyond the storage component, the lexicon (Baker, Johnson & Roberts 1989, Collins 2005, Horvath & Siloni 2008, Meltzer 2012, among others). It follows that the verbal passive is not stored; it is not a lexical entry. Hence, the verbal passive cannot have subentries. Thus, under 31b, phrasal idioms cannot be unique to the verbal passive because such idioms cannot be stored. Phrasal idioms in the verbal passive can only be formed by passivization of their transitive counterparts. Hence, they always share their idiomatic meanings with the corresponding transitive. The transitive, unaccusative and adjectival passive, in contrast, are formed in the lexicon (Horvath & Siloni 2008; 2011, Reinhart 2002), and stored there; therefore, they can have subentries.

It should be observed that unlike the existence of a transitive (active) version for every verbal passive phrasal idiom, we, correctly, do not predict the automatic existence of a verbal passive version for every transitive idiom. Since verbal passives are derived in the syntax, the question determining whether or not a transitive idiom will exist in the verbal passive depends on whether the idiom is able to undergo the syntactic operation of passivization resulting in a well-formed output. This in turn involves interpretive factors, such as whether the idiom chunk to become the derived subject of the passivized idiom has the appropriate semantic properties, e.g., referentiality, to be compatible with the information structure consequences of being in subject position. Hence, the contrast between *The beans were spilled* vs. **The bucket was kicked* (see for instance Nunberg, Wasow & Sag 1994, Ruwet 1991, Punske & Stone 2014 on what factors may determine whether or not a verbal passive version of a transitive idiom is possible).

Clausal idioms in contrast are stored as independent entries. Let us first motivate this claim. The head of clausal idioms is a functional, not a lexical, element. Functional elements unlike lexical ones are closed class items, have no descriptive content (Abney 1987), and bear no thematic relation to their complement. Functional elements have often been argued to be stored in a separate lexicon, e.g., Emonds' 2000 "Syntacticon", or as "f-morphemes" (Distributed Morphology). One storage option for clausal idioms would be storage as subentries of their functional head. This would, for instance, mean storage of the idiom *not have a leg to stand on* as a subentry of its functional head, Neg. This would be storage of entities that have descriptive content in the "functional lexicon", where entries do not have descriptive content. This seems to us incoherent. We therefore do not pursue this option.

Two additional options come to mind: (i) Clausal idioms are stored as subentries of the lexical head of the "extended projection" (in Grimshaw's 1991 terms) constituting

---

[13] The question as to whether they are also stored as subentries of the lexical entries of their other constituents is important but irrelevant for our purposes here. We therefore abstract away from it here.

the clausal idiom, namely, storage under the verb on a par with VP idioms. (ii) Clausal idioms are independent entries on their own; they are not stored as subentries of another lexical entry 31c. Subentry storage under the lexical head (option (i)) predicts the absence of unique clausal idioms in the verbal passive (just like in the case of phrasal idioms); this is contradicted by our findings (e.g. 15–18).

Independent storage 31c predicts occurrence of unique clausal idioms in the verbal passive, in concert with our findings. Under independent storage, clausal idioms get lexicalized in one piece (following consistent use of the expression in the relevant contexts). Clausal idioms thus do not require that their subconstituents be represented as entries in the lexicon. They get stored as a whole and can therefore include any diathesis (or any other syntactic output). Hence, there should be clausal idioms unique to the verbal passive. There are thus reasons to adopt the independent storage strategy for clausal idioms.[14]

If phrasal idioms were stored as independent constructions, on a par with clausal idioms, there would be no reason why they could not be unique to the verbal passive. Precisely because phrasal idioms are not stored constructions (contra CxG's assumptions), they cannot be unique to the verbal passive.

The difference in storage that the two types of idioms employ can also explain the second distinction revealed between them. While phrasal idioms commonly share idiomatic meanings across root-counterparts, clausal idioms tend not to be shared across diatheses (§4). As already discussed above, a verbal passive phrasal idiom must share its idiomatic meaning with the corresponding transitive because it is formed by syntactic passivization of the latter (it is not stored). Further, under the TSS model, sharing of phrasal idioms between the transitive and its (lexically derived) unaccusative or adjectival passive alternants is the result of the links between root-related entries in the lexicon, which can induce spread of special meanings and idiomatic expressions between the entries. Sharing is not automatic though, as it requires additional listing under the entry of the relevant alternant; hence there are also unique phrasal idioms in these diatheses, as discussed in §2.

In contrast, under 31c, clausal idioms are stored as independent entries, not as subentries of other entries that may be linked to root-mates. The model therefore predicts that nothing would induce sharing of idiomatic meaning between the transitive and its unaccusative or adjectival passive alternants; such sharing thus should be unattested or rare, as our preliminary results show.[15]

Verbal passives, unlike the transitive, unaccusative, and adjectival passive, are derived in the syntax. So there is no a priori reason not to expect the application of this operation to (some) transitive clausal idioms. If that occurred, at least some clausal idioms would

---

[14] Interesting questions arise with regard to the storage of idioms with no recognizable internal structure (e.g., *trip the light fantastic*), as well as idioms (arguably) headed by a non-sentential functional element (a light verb, a functional preposition, or a conjunction, as in *take a shower, in a rut,* and *cut and dried,* respectively). These important questions are beyond the scope of this paper and are not directly relevant for the issue of cross-diatheses distribution.

[15] A priori, nothing rules out the independent development and storage of a clausal idiom in a root-related diathesis. However, we predict this to be very rare (if at all attested) as nothing induces this.

be available in the verbal passive.[16] If no sharing occurs in the case of clausal idioms, it could be due to the inaccessibility of clausal idioms to internal syntactic operations, resulting from their being lexical entries inserted into the syntax as single one-piece units.[17]

6 Conclusion

We have distinguished between two different types of idioms – phrasal idioms vs. clausal idioms – and investigated their cross-diathesis distribution. Phrasal idioms distribute differently in the verbal passive vs. other diatheses: they cannot be specific (unique) to the former but can be specific to the latter. Clausal idioms do not seem to discriminate between diatheses in this way: They seem specific to a single diathesis. These systematic distinctions show that even the properties of idioms, the archetypal "construction" à la CxG, require more than cognitive principles, reference to functional needs, and inheritance networks of stored entities ('constructions') to be accounted for. An adequate theory of idioms must have recourse to a distinction between stored items and unstored derivational outputs, and to grammatical distinctions such as those between diatheses, and those between functional versus lexical elements. We sketched an account of the above findings, distinguishing between diatheses according to where they are formed, and storing idioms according to the type of element heading them (lexical or functional). Thus, the domain of idioms (surprisingly, from the CxG point of view) turns out to reinforce the conclusion that there must be more to knowledge of language than a hierarchical inventory of items and extra-grammatical constraints.

Acknowledgements

We are grateful to the editors for the opportunity to contribute to this Festschrift in honor of Steve Anderson, whose work in the field is incredibly rich, multifaceted and profound. Our paper addresses the choice between alternative architectures of grammar and examines an issue central to both syntactic and phonological/morphological

---

[16] Whether or not syntactic passivization would apply to a particular clausal idiom would depend on whether the idiom has the semantic properties compatible with the changes in information structure induced by passivization (as mentioned above concerning phrasal idioms).

[17] A Google search reveals that the verbal passive version of the idiom in (i) does have some occurrences, though substantially fewer than the transitive form.

(i) could've knocked me over with a feather
'I was extremely surprised, astonished'

(ii) (#)I could've been knocked over with a feather.

The question is whether or not these occurrences indeed are clausal idioms at all. This cannot be unequivocally determined because along with the clausal idiom (i), this idiom turns out to have also a phrasal transitive version: 'knock (someone) over with a feather' (listed in this form, with no fixed tense, no modal (and no fixed subject or object) (see the online Free Dictionary https://goo.gl/cv7RlT). See also fn. 12.

research: the nature of lexical representations and the division of labor between the lexicon and post-lexical derivation, a theme recurrent in Steve's work. More specifically, the paper has consequences with regard to the status of lexical vs. syntactic operations for capturing relations between diathesis alternants. Its empirical basis involves particular differences uncovered between diathesis alternations; our findings provide novel reinforcement for the distinction between lexically versus syntactically derived diatheses. This is a topic that Steve has directly contributed to in his paper *Comments on the paper by Wasow*, delivered in 1976 at the ground-breaking UC, Irvine Conference on the Formal Syntax of Natural Language, and published as Anderson (1977). We wish to thank two anonymous referees for their helpful comments.

References

Abney, Steven. 1987. *The English noun phrase in its sentential aspect*. Massachusetts Institute of Technology PhD dissertation.

Anderson, Stephen R. 1977. Comments on the paper by Wasow (The role of the theme in lexical rules). In Peter Culicover, Thomas Wasow & Joan Bresnan (eds.), *Formal Syntax*, 361–377. New York: Academic Press.

Baker, Mark, Kyle Johnson & Ian Roberts. 1989. Passive arguments raised. *Linguistic Inquiry* 20(2). 219–251.

Berman, Ruth. 2008. The psycholinguistics of developing text construction. *Journal of Child Language* 35. 735–771.

Boas, Hans C. 2013. Cognitive Construction Grammar. In G. Trousdale & T. Hoffmann (eds.), *The Oxford Handbook of Construction Grammar*, 233–254. Oxford: Oxford University Press.

Chomsky, Noam. 1965. *Aspects of the theory of syntax*. Cambridge, MA: MIT Press.

Collins, Christopher. 2005. A smuggling approach to the passive in English. *Syntax* (2). 81–120.

Dubinsky, Stanley & Silvester Ron Simango. 1996. Passive and stative in Chichewa: Evidence for modular distinctions in grammar'. *Language*, 72. 749–781.

Emonds, Joseph E. 2000. *Lexicon and grammar: The English syntacticon*. Berlin: Mouton de Gruyter.

Goldberg, Adele. 2006. *Constructions at work: The nature of generalization in language*. Oxford: Oxford University Press.

Grimshaw, Jane. 1991. Extended projection and locality. In Jane Grimshaw, Peter Coopmans & Martin Everaert (eds.), *Lexical specification and insertion*, 115–133. Amsterdam: John Benjamins.

Horvath, Julia & Tal Siloni. 2008. Active lexicon: Adjectival and verbal passives. In Sharon Armon-Lotem, Gabi Danon & Susan Rothstein (eds.), *Current issues in generative Hebrew Linguistics*, 105–134. Amsterdam: John Benjamins.

Horvath, Julia & Tal Siloni. 2009. Hebrew idioms: The organization of the lexical component. *Brill's Annual of Afroasiatic Languages and Linguistics* 1. 283–310.

Horvath, Julia & Tal Siloni. 2011. Causative across components. *Natural Language & Linguistic Theory* 29(3). 657–704.
Horvath, Julia & Tal Siloni. 2016. *Idioms: The Type-Sensitive Storage Model.* Manuscript. Tel Aviv University.
Härtl, Holden. 2003. Conceptual and grammatical characteristics of argument alternations: The case of decausative verbs. *Linguistics* 41(5). 883–916.
Meltzer, Aya. 2012. Verbal passives in Hebrew and English: A comparative study. In Martin Everaert, Tal Siloni & Marijana Marelj (eds.), *The Theta System: Argument structure at the interface*, 279–307. Oxford: Oxford University Press.
Nunberg, Geoffrey, Thomas Wasow & Ivan Sag. 1994. Idioms. *Language* 70(3). 491–538.
Punske, Jeffrey & Megan Stone. 2014. *Idiomatic Expressions, Passivization and Gerundivization.* Talk given at the annual meeting of the LSA. Minneapolis, Minnesota.
Reinhart, Tanya. 2002. The Theta System: An overview. *Theoretical Linguistics* 28(3). 229–290.
Ruwet, Nicolas. 1991. On the use and abuse of idioms. In John Goldsmith (ed.), *Syntax and human experience*, 171–251. Chicago: University of Chicago Press.
Wasow, Thomas. 1977. Transformations and the lexicon. In Peter Culicover, Thomas Wasow & Joan Bresnan (eds.), *Formal Syntax*, 327–360. New York: Academic Press.

Chapter 23

A-morphous iconicity

Ryan Lepic
University of California, San Diego

Carol Padden
University of California, San Diego

> A-morphous Morphology is a morpheme-less theory of word-internal structure (Anderson 1992). Under this approach, derivational patterns are analyzed using Word Formation (redundancy) Rules. By specifying systematic relations among the words of a language, Word Formation Rules generally describe, rather than derive, the structure of complex words. Here, on the basis of data from American Sign Language, we present a complementary view of lexical iconicity. We suggest that in the discussion of iconicity and of morphological structure alike, a distinction can be made between those signs whose internal structure has been eroded away, and those signs whose motivated internal structure is analyzable as part of a systematic pattern.

1 Introduction

Stephen R. Anderson's *A-morphous Morphology* characterizes morphology as a form of linguistic knowledge (Anderson 1992: 181). This characterization is a response to resilient misconceptions about word structure and the lexicon: morphology is traditionally thought to primarily involve an inventory of minimally meaningful forms and the general mechanisms through which these meaningful forms are combined to make complex words. This procedural view of morphology is in turn often justified by reference to de Saussure's definition of the linguistic sign. However, Anderson (1985; 1992; In press) has shown that, in contrast to the "exaggeratedly minimal" (Anderson 1992: 326) analysis of complex words as composed incrementally from independently meaningful pieces, the Saussurean sign is a holistic, conventional relation "between a possibly complex form and its possibly complex meaning" (Anderson 1992: 193).

Treating morphology as the knowledge that speakers have about holistic relationships between complex word forms and their complex meanings leads to a quite different conceptualization of the lexicon. Rather than merely a list of minimally meaningful forms, a speaker's lexical knowledge must also comprise systematic relations between and among

Ryan Lepic & Carol Padden. 2017. A-morphous iconicity. In Claire Bowern, Laurence Horn & Raffaella Zanuttini (eds.), *On looking into words (and beyond)*, 489–516. Berlin: Language Science Press. DOI:10.5281/zenodo.495463

the whole words of their language. Anderson proposes that these systematic relationships can be formalized using what are referred to as *Word Formation (redundancy) Rules* (after Jackendoff 1975). As a formal representation of patterns of similarity and difference among related words, Word Formation Rules are "only superficially" a process by which new words are actively created or procedurally derived; their primary job is to codify systematic correspondences between words as an aspect of any speaker's linguistic knowledge (Anderson 1992: 186). This perspective is motivated by the treatment of syntax as the knowledge that speakers have about how words are organized into sentences and of phonology as the knowledge that speakers have about how sounds are organized into words in linguistic theory.

In this chapter, we demonstrate that Anderson's "a-morphous" view of morphological structure provides a template for the study of iconic motivation in sign language structure, as well. Characterizing *morphology* as the knowledge that speakers have about the relationships between word forms and their meanings leads to a quite different conceptualization of *iconicity*, the perception of a motivated link between word forms and their meanings.

Iconicity has traditionally posed a challenge to the field of sign language linguistics. Because the linguistic sign relation is commonly characterized as an *arbitrary* pairing of a word form and its meaning, the obvious links between sign forms and their meanings originally presented an obstacle to the recognition of sign languages as natural human languages. A way around this obstacle was to argue that lexical signs are essentially arbitrary, despite their apparent iconicity, and moreover that signs can be shown to consist of smaller meaningless formative units. This view casts iconicity aside as etymological residue that is irrelevant for the understanding of recurring structural patterns in sign languages.

Our claim is that, like morphology, iconicity is an aspect of linguistic knowledge. Our perspective follows Anderson's (1992) key observation about the nature of synchronically analyzable morphological structure: While responsible for the formation and analysis of *new* words, derivational morphology is not typically actively engaged in the derivation of *established* words from smaller meaningful components. Instead, the perception of transparent word-internal morphological structure is a reflection of the knowledge that speakers have about the relationships between whole words and their analogous constituent parts. Here, we demonstrate that this approach can also account for several morphological patterns in American Sign Language (ASL) in which a *motivated, iconic link between meaning and form* serves as the organizing principle.

Our analysis of sign-internal structure in ASL builds from Anderson's treatment of Word Formation Rules as formal representations of patterns of similarity and difference among related whole words. When we consider whole words to be derivationally related to one another, partial relations among related words can be captured with a general rule, without expecting that whole words should exhibit incremental, semantically compositional morphological structure (see also Ackerman, Malouf & Blevins 2016, Aronoff 1976, Bochner 1993, Hay & Baayen 2005, Aronoff 2007, Blevins 2016, Anderson In press). Under this view, whole words are the primary unit of morphological organization. Related whole words with transparent, analyzable internal structure participate in morphological patterns that can be described by a structural rule. However, individual words can become quite reduced and opaque over time, such that they eventually lose their synchronic morphological connection to other words in the language. Taken seriously, Anderson's view leads to the conclusion that analyzable word-internal structure is most often a gradient reflection of etymological history, and only infrequently the derived output of a synchronic operation.

2 The erosion of transparency in lexical signs

The field of sign language linguistics has been compelled to demonstrate that, despite their apparent semantic and gestural transparency, signs are arbitrary linguistic symbols that are analyzable into smaller formal units (see Stokoe 1960, Klima & Bellugi 1979, and Supalla 1986 for examples). Underlying this work is the assumption that conventional linguistic symbols are, by definition, inherently arbitrary. Accordingly, if they are truly linguistic in nature, lexical signs should also be arbitrary symbols, even if they were once iconically motivated (however, see Wilcox & Wilcox 1995, Taub 2001, Perniss, Thompson & Vigliocco 2010, and Emmorey 2014 for critical reviews of this assumption). This perspective leads to the conclusion that iconicity is a secondary, etymological feature of individual signs, and ultimately erodes over time. For example, Frishberg (1975: 718) compares old (ca. 1918) and modern (ca. 1965) versions of several ASL signs, and argues that over time, "in general, signs have become less transparent, pantomimic, and iconic; they have become more arbitrary, conventionalized, and symbolic."

Accordingly, when comparing old and modern versions of signs like COW and HORSE, which are both articulated at the signer's head, and are motivated by an image of the animal's horns and ears, respectively, we can appreciate that the older forms are more faithful to their original motivating image, while the newer forms have lost some of their original iconicity: The older form of COW is signed with two hands, one for each of the paired horns to be represented Figure 1a, while the newer, more typical form is signed with only one hand Figure 1b. This change over time has an articulatory motivation. It requires less effort to move one hand than it does to move both hands, and, because the second hand is configured identically to the dominant hand in these cases, the absence of the second hand does not hinder recognition of the target sign. As a result, the involvement of the second, non-dominant hand has been deleted from these signs in the course of history (Battison 1974, Frishberg 1975).

As another example, Napoli, Sanders & Wright (2014: 437–438) demonstrate that synchronically, in casual signing, the form of the iconic sign HOUR is often altered to make the sign less difficult to articulate, which can result in the formation of a less iconic sign. In the citation form, the iconic sign HOUR is articulated with a dominant index finger tracing a full circle around the palm of the non-dominant hand. The iconic motivation for this sign is the movement of a minute hand around the face of a clock, with the non-dominant hand representing the face of a clock, and the dominant hand representing the angle and movement of the minute hand. In the citation form, the wrist serves as a

a. (beginning of sign)   (end of sign)

b. (beginning of sign)   (end of sign)

Figure 1: The ASL sign COW signed (a) with two hands and (b) with one hand.

hinge for the circular movement of the dominant hand (Figure 2a). However, in the more casual form of HOUR, the locus of the dominant hand's movement is transferred away from the wrist to the elbow and shoulder (Figure 2b). This change partially disrupts the iconic image of a clock hand tracing a journey around the clock face, as it is the whole hand, rather than the extended finger alone, which traces a circular movement. This change obscures the iconic representation of a clock's minute hand in the sign HOUR, and again, this change is favored for an articulatory reason, as it avoids "a physiologically awkward movement" (Napoli, Sanders & Wright 2014: 438). The logical conclusion, based on examples like COW and HOUR, is that in time, true, systematic processes work to erode the coincidental, iconic origins of any sign.

We contend that these discussions about erosion of iconicity require more nuance. The cases cited above are indeed instances of signs reducing in ways that partially obscure their original motivating visual image. In these examples, the iconic motivation for a single sign is overcome by articulatory considerations. We assume that the primary constraint on this phonetic reduction is that the overall form of the sign itself should nevertheless remain recognizable as "the same sign": Processes of phonetic reduction can erode the forms of signs only once they have been registered as conventional lexical items with conventional forms and agreed-upon meanings, to begin with. However, we note that even in the face of phonetic reduction, the reduced versions of the signs COW or HOUR actually remain quite faithful to their iconic motivations. Both signs still transparently represent the horn of an animal and the face and hand of a clock, respectively. In

23 A-morphous iconicity

a. (beginning of sign) (middle of sign) (end of sign)

b. (beginning of sign) (middle of sign) (end of sign)

Figure 2: The ASL sign HOUR signed (a) with the locus of rotation at the wrist and (b) with the locus of rotation at the elbow.

these cases, at least, the shift is not from "wholly iconic sign" to "wholly arbitrary sign," but rather from "more transparent conventional sign" to "less transparent conventional sign."

Here it is important to note that this sort of gradient phonetic erosion also affects *morphological* transparency in conventional signs. Like spoken words[1] and like iconic signs, morphologically complex signs, once registered as conventional pairings of meaning and form, may begin to drift in ways that obscure their original etymology. An example discussed by Frishberg (1975: 707) is the ASL sign HOME. The conventional sign HOME derives etymologically from the composition of the signs EAT and SLEEP (this combination can be glossed as EAT+SLEEP). These signs were almost certainly selected to represent the concept 'home' because a "home" is "where one eats and sleeps." However, as a function of its lexical entrenchment as a conventional sign, EAT+SLEEP has drifted both in form and in meaning. It has been reanalyzed as a semantically holistic sign meaning 'home', and has reduced in form so as to mask its former transparent relationship to its original constituent signs. As a result of this drift over time, the sign HOME no longer bears an

---

[1] A anonymous reviewer rightly comments that this erosion is likely also modulated by frequency. In English, the classic example *cupboard* has undergone assimilation and reduction that obscures its connection to its original constituent words, while other (newer/less frequent) words like *clipboard* retain their original compound pronunciation (see Zipf 1935, Bybee 2001). The same reviewer eloquently notes that written alphabetical systems have also developed through this type of "creeping opacity," in which the written symbols became streamlined and less connected to their "original causal denotata."

overt morphological relationship to its former constituent signs EAT and SLEEP in modern ASL.

A related, synchronic example is the sign STUDENT, which is etymologically derived from the composition of the signs LEARN (whose form is iconically motivated by the image of moving an object into the mind) and PERSON (whose form is iconically motivated by the silhouette of a human figure). While the citation form for STUDENT still retains much of its analyzable internal structure as a composite of LEARN+PERSON (Figure 3a), in casual signing, STUDENT is typically reduced to the point that its analyzable morphological structure is no longer identifiable (Figure 3b).

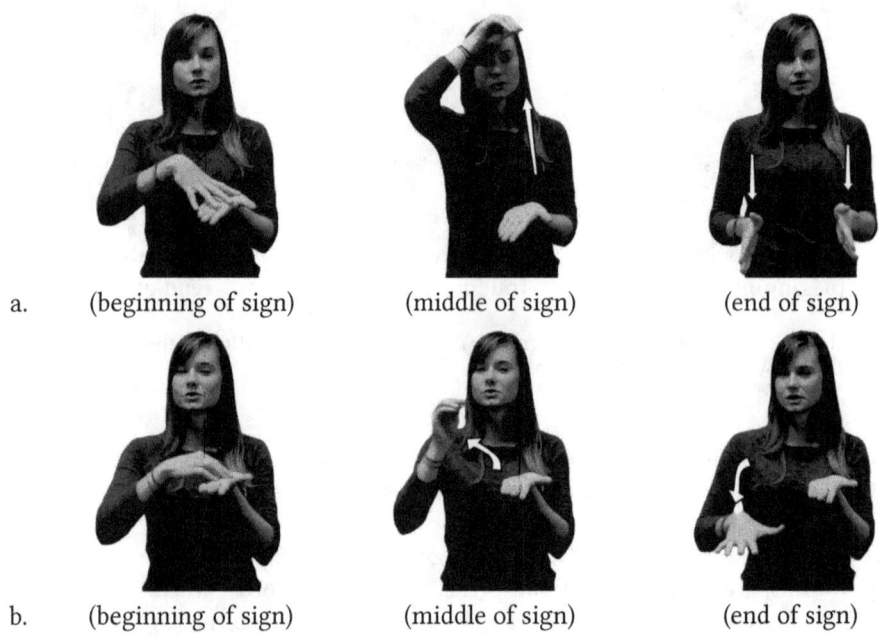

a.   (beginning of sign)   (middle of sign)   (end of sign)

b.   (beginning of sign)   (middle of sign)   (end of sign)

Figure 3: The ASL sign STUDENT (a) in a fuller, more transparent form ("LEARN+PERSON") and (b) in a reduced, more opaque form ("STUDENT").

Similar reduction can also be observed in the casual forms of the related signs INTERPRETER and TEACHER. Like the sign STUDENT, these signs are morphologically complex, and they can be analyzed as previously derived from INTERPRET+PERSON and TEACH+PERSON. These signs participate in a productive derivational pattern in ASL involving the addition of PERSON as an "agentive suffix." However, as frequently occurring signs, INTERPRETER, STUDENT, and TEACHER have all drifted in ways that render their morphological structure increasingly opaque in casual signing. We discuss some implications of this erosion (and possible reanalysis) of transparent morphological structure in §3.

As in (spoken and signed) morphology (see Bybee 2006), the gradual loss of iconicity is not an across-the-board phenomenon. Iconicity can also persist within signs when it becomes *morphologized*, or made systematic as a learned, language-internal pattern (see

Anderson 1992: 337). The loss of iconicity is therefore not as inevitable as is commonly believed. An example of a sign which might be considered to have lost its iconicity (an analysis that has been debunked by Wilcox & Wilcox 1995: 153, Taub 2001: 228, and Wilcox 2004: 123) is VERY-SLOW. The sign SLOW is articulated with the dominant hand sliding over the back of the non-dominant hand in a single movement (Figure 4a). The slow movement of the hand can be considered iconically motivated, as the friction resulting from the contact between the two hands causes the sign to be articulated somewhat slowly. In the derived sign VERY-SLOW, however, the movement pattern has changed: VERY-SLOW is articulated with a short initial hold, followed by a quick, larger burst of movement (Figure 4b). We will demonstrate that this change in movement is characteristic of an "intensive" derivational pattern in ASL, but these facts originally led Klima & Bellugi (1979: 30), for example, to conclude that the iconicity of SLOW has been "overridden and submerged" in the formation of the sign VERY-SLOW, as it is signed with a very *fast* movement.

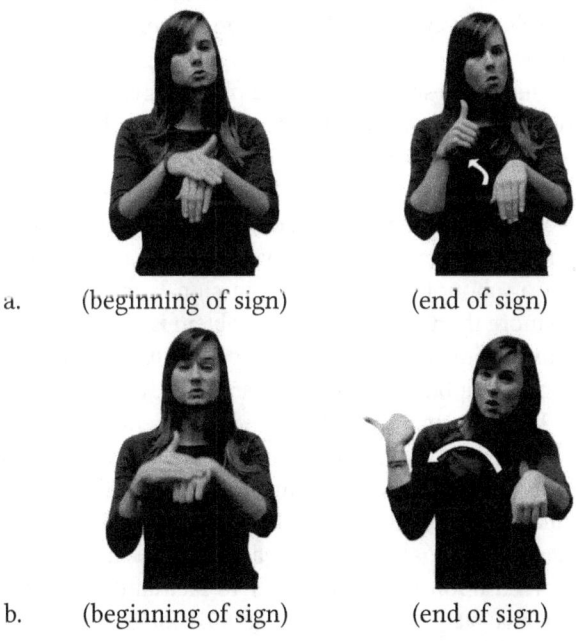

Figure 4: The forms of the ASL signs (a) SLOW and (b) VERY-SLOW differ primarily in their speed and size: VERY-SLOW is signed with a faster, larger movement.

While the movement of the sign VERY-SLOW is indeed quite fast, the process that derives the intensive version of SLOW by changing its original form to incorporate a quick burst of movement is at once iconically motivated *and* systemically motivated: it is also at work in the formation of a number of other ASL signs. These signs include predicate adjectives like VERY-CLEVER, VERY-EXPENSIVE, and VERY-STUBBORN, and they all have in common that they derive the intensive form of a sign by increasing the intensity of its conventional movement. Accordingly, it is not the case that VERY-SLOW has lost its iconicity. Instead, VERY-SLOW has taken on a different type of iconic motivation, one that happens to be at odds with the idea that the only way to represent "incredible slowness" is to use a very slow movement (Taub 2001: 229). In this intensive derivational pattern in ASL, the intensity of a sign's movement is increased, thereby iconically signaling an increase in the intensity of the sign's meaning (Wilcox & Wilcox 1995: 153).

This systematic iconic correspondence between whole words is precisely the kind of relationship that can be described using a Word Formation Rule. The fact that aspects of the pattern happen to be iconically motivated in no way precludes this rule from having been taken up and made systematic in ASL. Indeed, this discussion of the loss of iconicity in individual signs, and the preservation of iconicity when it is relevant for language-internal structure, is entirely compatible with Anderson's a-morphous view of morphology, in which conventional words are Saussurean signs, regardless of whether they contain transparent, analyzable structure. Though they are often referred to as "lexical entries," Saussurean signs cannot be considered entries on a structureless list. Instead, a language user's morphological knowledge also encompasses their knowledge of the relationships between the established words of their language.[2]

Word Formation Rules are descriptions of the phonological, syntactic, and semantic differences and correspondences between two or more morphologically related forms. For example, the rule that describes the relationship between pairs of English words like *breath* and *breathe*, *loss* and *lose*, and *grief* and *grieve* (minimally) specifies a change in word-final voicing, a change in syntactic category, and concomitant changes in meaning. However, as in the analysis of non-concatenative morphology in spoken languages, the formal representation of phonological changes in sign language morphology has the potential to obfuscate more than to clarify. This problem is also compounded by the fact that there is no dominant conventional system for describing sign forms on analogy to the International Phonetic Alphabet for spoken language research.

In order to discuss Word Formation Rules in ASL, we require a representational system that will allow us to recognize that signs are holistic pairings of complex form and complex meaning. The convention of labeling ASL signs with English metalinguistic glosses is, by itself, inadequate for this task. Labeling signs with English glosses illustrates that they have conventional, holistic meanings, and implies that they similarly have conventional, agreed-upon forms. In order to facilitate an analysis of the iconic structure within ASL signs, we will adopt Taub's (2001) convention of listing the aspects of form in a sign with their corresponding aspects of meaning. As Meir and colleagues (Meir 2010: 874; Meir et al. 2013: 316) have demonstrated, such *iconic mapping* diagrams

---

[2] An anonymous reviewer comments that Anderson (1992) presents a realizational theory of morphology, in which an inflected word's semantic content precedes and determines its phonological form. This is in opposition to concatenative theories in which a word's form determines its content. Our a-morphous analysis of iconicity in ASL word formation is meant to be consistent with a realizational theory of inflection. We do not discuss ASL inflectional morphology here because there are several competing perspectives as to what should even count as morphosyntactic inflection (namely agreement) in ASL. Reviewing these perspectives takes us beyond the scope of this chapter, but the reader is referred to Lillo-Martin & Meier (2011), Wilbur (2013), and Wilcox & Occhino (2016) for a sense of these different perspectives.

make it clear that iconicity is neither a deterministic nor a compositional property of signs: a sign may be a conventional pairing of form and meaning and *also* exhibit transparent and motivated aspects of structure. Crucially, the perception of iconicity arises as a consequence of the fact that signs are conventional pairings of a potentially complex form and potentially complex meaning, and not from a compositional analysis of the sign's parts.[3] The meaning of the whole facilitates the (re)analysis of its parts, rather than the other way around.

As an illustration of an iconic mapping in ASL, consider the sign SLOW, already described impressionistically above (and pictured in Figure 4a). This sign has a conventional form and meaning, and aspects of its form can be analyzed as transparently motivated by its meaning. These correspondences can be represented through an explicit pairing of aspects of the sign's form with aspects of its meaning, as in Table 1.

Table 1: Aspects of the iconic mapping for SLOW.

Form	Meaning
non-dominant hand	a stationary object
back of the non-dominant hand	a surface that creates friction
dominant hand	an object in motion
palm of the dominant hand	a surface that creates friction
contacting movement	contact between two surfaces
dragging movement	a movement slowed by friction

This representation illustrates that the conventional sign SLOW exhibits analyzable internal structure: formational aspects of this sign can be linked to aspects of the visual and kinesthetic images that provide the sign's iconic motivation. For example, in this case, it is possible to assign an iconic aspect of meaning to each of the two hands, as well as the manner in which the dominant hand contacts the non-dominant hand.

The benefit of the representation in Table 1 is that it allows us to discuss the relationship between the form and meaning of the whole sign as well as the relationship between the whole and its parts, including how these aspects of structure may change from sign to sign. For example, as discussed above, the Word Formation Rule for the "intensive" pattern alters the conventional mapping for SLOW by changing the character of the base sign's movement: the sign VERY-SLOW is formed with a movement pattern that is superimposed onto the form of the original sign SLOW, keeping the overall trajectory of the movement but adding a brief initial hold followed by a quicker and larger burst

---

[3] A reviewer notes, and it has been pointed out previously (e.g. Fernald & Napoli 2000), that there are also similarities between ASL morphology and iconic, sound-symbolic elements in spoken language such as phon(a)esthemes and ideophones. Phonaesthemes are recurring pairings of meaning and form occurring in words that cannot otherwise be analyzed as exhibiting compositional morphological structure (Anderson 1992: 49, Bergen 2004). Ideophones are depictive, sound-symbolic words that appear in a variety of languages (Dingemanse 2012). We expect that an "a-morphous" analysis of iconicity and morphology should also extend to these classes of words, but leave the details of this project for future work.

of motion. The resulting sign VERY-SLOW (pictured in Figure 4) can be represented as in Table 2. In this representation, the aspects of form and meaning that have been changed by the intensive Word Formation Rule are emphasized in bold.

Table 2: Aspects of the iconic mapping for VERY-SLOW.

Form	Meaning
non-dominant hand	a stationary object
back of the non-dominant hand	a surface that creates friction
dominant hand	an object in motion
flat palm of the dominant hand	a surface that creates friction
contacting movement	contact between two surfaces
brief initial hold	**buildup of pressure**
quick, large movement	**release of built-up pressure**

Following Anderson's (1992: 186) formulation of the *-able* Word Formation Rule, for example, we can think of this relationship between pairs of signs SLOW and VERY-SLOW in the following way: The form of the intensive Word Formation Rule specifies that the intensive form of a sign is made by changing its movement pattern. However, rather than a true "derivational" rule, the Word Formation Rule is regarded as a description of the systematic differences between the signs represented in Table 1 and Table 2.

3 The (re)analysis of lexical iconicity

Iconic mappings provide a way to represent the relationship between the form and meaning of a conventional complex sign. They also provide a way to specify how aspects of a sign's analyzable internal structure can be reanalyzed by speakers based on the meaning of the complex sign that they appear in. In this section, we explore this tradeoff between form and meaning. We begin with the ASL sign TIME, as an illustrative example of how a sign's relationship to its original iconic motivation can become obscured, and even how the form of the conventional sign can subsequently be reanalyzed by signers. We suggest that such reanalysis can only happen in a system where the sign relation between form and meaning takes precedence over the compositional structure that originally contributed to the sign's creation.[4]

The ASL sign TIME is formed with the crooked index finger of the dominant hand tapping the back of the non-dominant wrist (Figure ??). ASL signers and non-signers alike

---

[4] Of course, signers can, and often do, create new signs, as well. We analyze these new signs as repurposing the patterns and elements that recur among established signs. A popular (in both senses) article from 2015, for example, discusses some ASL candidates for internet slang like *selfie* and *photobomb*. These potential signs make creative new use of old sign parts, though we hesitate to analyze them as semantically "compositional" in the traditional sense. The article is accessible online (http://www.hopesandfears.com/hopes/now/internet/168477-internet-american-sign-language), as is some additional commentary from an ASL news "vlog" (https://www.youtube.com/watch?v=wI8o8zgEK88).

readily recognize the similarities between this sign and the act of tapping the face of a wristwatch, for example as part of a gesture of impatience. The sign TIME can therefore be considered to have a transparent iconic motivation, stemming from the cultural association of reading a wristwatch with the telling of time. For signers, this analysis of TIME's iconic motivation is also reinforced by the fact that the ASL sign WRISTWATCH is indeed articulated in the same location, at the back of the non-dominant wrist.

Figure 5: The ASL sign TIME.

However, this etymological description of the ASL sign TIME is in fact a folk reanalysis. As Shaw & Delaporte (2010: 177) explain, "the origin of TIME was identified long before the advent of the wristwatch in 1904." They demonstrate that as early as 1785, the French Sign Language sign TIME was recorded in a form similar to that of ASL, its daughter language, with the crooked index finger repeatedly contacting the back of the non-dominant hand. The image motivating the form of this historical sign is the design and function of an early mechanical clock that uses a hammer to strike a bell at the stroke of an hour. Historical texts documenting Old French Sign Language describe this sign's form as showing "the hammer which taps the bell" and using the index finger to "ring the hour on the back of the hand which is in the guise of a bell" (Ferrand 1896 and Lambert 1865, respectively, as cited by Shaw & Delaporte 2010: 177–178). Following Taub's (2001) conventions for analyzing iconic mappings, we can represent aspects of the mapping between the phonological and semantic elements of this historical sign TIME as in Table 3:

Table 3: Aspects of the historical iconic mapping for TIME.

Form	Meaning
non-dominant hand	the bell of a clock
back of the non-dominant hand	surface of the bell
dominant hand	a figure which rings the clock
crooked index finger	the hammer which strikes the bell
contacting movement	the hammer striking the bell
repeated movement	a repeated action

By the time the wristwatch became popular in the early 1900s, the sign TIME had been in use for well over a century. Having already been established as a conventional pairing of form and meaning, it was, presumably, no longer primarily analyzed as deriving its meaning from its constituent parts. Parallel to the examples of COW and HOUR mentioned above, the formational aspects of the sign TIME began to drift slightly, such that the index finger moved "a few centimeters from the back of the hand to the back of the wrist" (Shaw & Delaporte 2010: 178). The sign TIME was also no longer concretely linked to the image of a particular time-telling device. Accordingly, to the extent that they were associated with any meaning at all, the parts of the sign TIME must have derived their meanings by association with the meaningful whole sign. The sign's existing internal structure was thus open to reanalysis as motivated by the image of a wristwatch, as is represented in Table 4. Here we see that the aspects of form are the same across both Table 3 and Table 4, however the mapped *meanings* differ between the historical and modern versions of the sign TIME.

Table 4: Aspects of the modern iconic mapping for TIME.

Form	Meaning
non-dominant hand	a human hand
back of the wrist	the location of a wristwatch
dominant hand	a human hand
crooked index finger	a human finger
contacting movement	a human finger contacting a wristwatch
repeated movement	a repeated action

We re-emphasize that this iconic reanalysis could only happen because the holistic relation between TIME's form and meaning takes precedence over the aspects of structure that originally contributed to its creation. The sign TIME provides a very nice example, but it is not an exceptional case: all conventional signs in ASL are by definition registered as learned pairings of form and meaning, and many sign forms also remain open to iconic interpretation and reanalysis. Of course, conventional signs can serve as the input for productive derivational *morphological* processes as well. As a result, the motivating factors of language internal systematicity (morphology) and of analyzable visual imagery (iconicity) are inextricably interlinked as aspects of lexical motivation in ASL.

Another relevant example, a somewhat uncommon sign which we refer to here as HASH-THINGS-OUT, is ultimately a reduced derivative of the ASL verb DEBATE. As we will show, the sign DEBATE is both iconically and derivationally related to a number of other ASL signs that conventionally connote 'argumentation', including ARGUE, OPPOSE, STRUGGLE, DISCUSS, and DISCUSS-IN-DEPTH. These signs are all morphologically related in ASL, though their corresponding English translations are not. Rather than getting bogged down in a discussion of the nuances of meaning between the English meta-language glosses, we will focus primarily on the relationship between form and meaning among these morphologically-related iconic signs. We begin with the sign AR-GUE, which is formed with the index fingers of both hands pointing toward one another and simultaneously moving up and down several times (Figure 6).

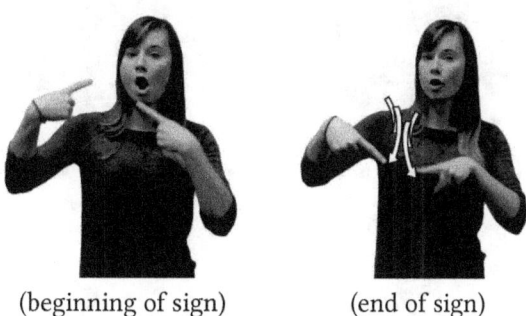

(beginning of sign)   (end of sign)

Figure 6: The ASL sign ARGUE.

The iconic motivation for the sign ARGUE is the visual image of two people engaged in heated conversation, with each hand representing a participant in the argument, and with the orientation of the two hands towards one another representing that each participant's communicative efforts are directed toward the other (see Lepic et al. 2016 regarding use of the two hands to represent paired referents in lexical signs). This sign's form also seems be motivated by the rhythmic properties of the beat gestures that often accompany continuous speech, and by the form of the finger-shaking gesture that often accompanies "scolding" or "telling somebody off." The association between form and meaning in the conventional sign ARGUE can thus be represented as in Table 5.

Table 5: Aspects of the iconic mapping for ARGUE.

Form	Meaning
dominant hand	one side of an argument
non-dominant hand	the other side of an argument
orientation of hands toward each other	two sides communicating with each other
index finger handshape	the direction of attention
coordinated movement of the hands	communicative interaction between sides
repeated movement	an on-going process

The signs OPPOSE (Figure 7) and STRUGGLE (Figure 8) are formed similarly to the sign ARGUE, with two index fingers pointed toward one another, however the movement patterns for these signs are different. While ARGUE is articulated with repeated up-and-down movements, OPPOSE is signed with the hands pulling away from one another in a single motion, and STRUGGLE is signed with both hands repeatedly moving back-and-forth together along the imagined line they form.

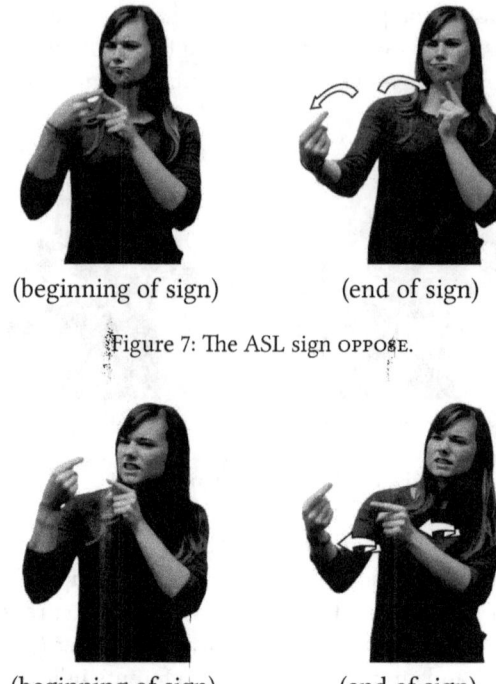

(beginning of sign) (end of sign)

Figure 7: The ASL sign OPPOSE.

(beginning of sign) (end of sign)

Figure 8: The ASL sign STRUGGLE.

In the sign OPPOSE, the movement of the hands away from one another can be analyzed as motivated by an image of two participants in an argument giving up and retreating from one another. In the sign STRUGGLE, the movement of the hands together can be analyzed as motivated by an image of two opposing forces retreating and advancing together in turn. These associations between form and meaning can be represented as in Tables 6 and 7, respectively. Note that the first several aspects of the iconic mapping, such as the use and relative orientation of the two hands, are shared between the signs ARGUE, OPPOSE, and STRUGGLE: the aspects that differ between these signs are again marked in bold. Here, again, the benefit of the iconic mapping notation is that it makes recurring configurations of form and meaning explicit among related and conventional iconic signs.

Turning now to the related signs DISCUSS, DISCUSS-IN-DEPTH, and DEBATE, we see that these signs similarly use the index finger of the dominant hand to represent one side of an argument, however, in each of these signs, the "opposing side" is represented quite differently. In the sign DISCUSS, the "other side" is actually not represented at all: This sign is conventionally formed with the index finger of the dominant hand repeatedly striking the flat palm of the non-dominant hand (Figure 9). The form of the sign DISCUSS is also partially motivated by the visual image of a list of written topics under discus-

Table 6: Aspects of the iconic mapping for OPPOSE.

Form	Meaning
dominant hand	one side of an argument
non-dominant hand	the other side of an argument
orientation of hands toward each other	two sides communicating with each other
index finger handshape	the direction of attention
movement of hands away from each other	retreating to opposite sides of an argument
single movement	a single event

Table 7: Aspects of the iconic mapping for STRUGGLE.

Form	Meaning
dominant hand	one side of an argument
non-dominant hand	the other side of an argument
orientation of hands toward each other	two sides communicating with each other
index finger handshape	the direction of attention
movement along the same plane	advancing and falling back in an argument
repeated movement	an on-going process

sion; in this sign, the non-dominant hand represents the message itself, serving as the primary target of communicative effort and as the place of articulation for the dominant hand. Note that the flat palm of the non-dominant hand similarly represents a surface for written material in signs like JOT-DOWN (Figure 10), LEARN (first two segments of Figure 3a above), and WRITE. We do not provide an in-depth analysis of these "written-upon surface" signs here, but see Frishberg & Gough (1973: 118) and Aronoff et al. (2003: 75) for additional discussion. The association of form and meaning in the sign DISCUSS can be represented as in Table 8, which again exhibits several aspects of structure that have been seen already in the iconic mappings for ARGUE, OPPOSE, and STRUGGLE.

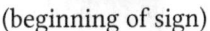
(beginning of sign)   (end of sign)

Figure 9: The ASL sign DISCUSS.

(beginning of sign)   (end of sign)

Figure 10: The ASL sign JOT-DOWN.

Table 8: Aspects of the iconic mapping for DISCUSS.

Form	Meaning
dominant hand	one side of an argument
index finger handshape	the direction of attention
non-dominant hand	topics under discussion
flat palm handshape	a written surface
repeated movement	an on-going process

The sign DISCUSS-IN-DEPTH is in turn formed similarly to the sign DISCUSS, with the index finger contacting the flat palm of the non-dominant hand. However, rather than remaining in a single, fixed location, the hands move together between two locations, signed at first in front of the signer's body, and then away from the body to represent a second interlocutor (Figure 11). The mapping for this sign is represented in Table 9. Like the signs OPPOSE and STRUGGLE, this movement between two locations represents the contributions of two participants to the discussion. However, unlike the sign OPPOSE, here there is not an implicit contrast between "sides of an argument." Instead, the addition of another's perspective to the discussion is collaborative, and the discussion takes on greater depth as a result.

When we move to consider the related sign DEBATE, we again find opposition between two sides, which are mapped onto each of the two hands. The sign DEBATE is formed similarly to the signs DISCUSS and DISCUSS-IN-DEPTH, with the index finger of the dominant hand repeatedly striking the flat palm of the non-dominant hand. However, DEBATE also exhibits what is known as "dominance reversal" (Frishberg 1985; Padden & Perlmutter 1987): in the formation of this sign, the index finger of the dominant hand first strikes the non-dominant hand, then the hands switch roles and configurations, and the index finger of the non-dominant hand strikes the flat palm of the dominant hand, with this

(beginning of sign)   (end of sign)

Figure 11: The ASL sign DISCUSS-IN-DEPTH.

Table 9: Aspects of the iconic mapping for DISCUSS-IN-DEPTH.

Form	Meaning
dominant hand	one side of an argument
index finger handshape	the direction of attention
non-dominant hand	topics under discussion
flat palm handshape	a written surface
movement along the same plane	two sides communicating with each other
repeated movement	an on-going process

reversal being articulated several times in succession (Figure 12).[5] The iconic image motivating the form of the sign DEBATE, then, is that one side discusses its case, then the other side discusses its own case, and these discussions continue back and forth. The iconic mapping for this sign is given in Table 10.

Coming finally to the sign HASH-THINGS-OUT, this sign's form is quite similar to the sign DEBATE, the two signs differing primarily in that HASH-THINGS-OUT has a faster and smaller series of movements. The form of the sign HASH-THINGS-OUT has undergone some restructuring that partially obscures the iconic role of the flat palm as representing a written surface, and of the alternation between two distinct points of view. Similarly, the sign's meaning is "softened," still denoting a discussion or negotiation, but with less emphasis on the the number and alignment of the participants in the discussion. The sign HASH-THINGS-OUT is articulated with the dominant index finger of one hand briefly striking the flat palm of the other hand, with this motion alternating between hands multiple times in quick succession (Figure 13). This sign is not as amenable to analysis in terms of its iconic structure as the preceding signs in this section, as it has undergone

---

[5] The direction of the movement in the sign DEBATE is also changed; the hands move right-and-left instead of forward-and-back as in the previous examples. We suspect that this is because a side-to-side movement is easier to articulate while also reversing the dominance of the hands, though this changed direction of movement may well have a semantic motivation (or lend itself to reanalysis based on a semantic motivation), as well.

(beginning of sign)   (end of sign)

Figure 12: The ASL sign DEBATE.

Table 10: Aspects of the iconic mapping for DEBATE.

Form	Meaning
dominant hand	one side of an argument
index finger handshape	the direction of attention
non-dominant hand	topics under discussion
flat palm handshape	a written surface
reversal of dominance	**yielding the floor to another perspective**
repeated movement	an on-going process

some degree of phonetic erosion: though we can identify, through comparison to the related signs DEBATE and DISCUSS, that the contacting motion between the dominant and non-dominant hands is not an arbitrary coincidence, the simplest account for this sign is that it is a phonetically reduced and semantically idiosyncratic derivative of the sign DEBATE. The sign HASH-THINGS-OUT has drifted both in meaning and in form from the sign DEBATE, yielding a new, related sign.

(beginning of sign)   (end of sign)

Figure 13: The ASL sign HASH-THINGS-OUT.

The point of this extended discussion is to demonstrate that there is no clear delineation between morphology and iconicity in these examples. As with morphological (re)analysis, the assessment of an iconic motivation necessarily follows from the primary association of a potentially complex form with a potentially complex meaning in a holistic sign. Each of the signs discussed in this section can be described both in terms of the relationship between the sign's form and its motivating visual image, and of the sign's conventional form and meaning relative to other conventional ASL signs. Similar to the discussion of the sign VERY-SLOW, here we see that aspects of iconic representation can also become systematic across groups of signs, and codified as a morphological pattern.

Importantly, an a-morphous theory of iconicity recognizes that lexical signs are the primary unit of morphological organization, and an analysis of the relationship between meaning and form necessarily proceeds from there. Aspects of form such as the flat hand or the extended index finger may come to be associated with aspects of meaning by virtue of their systematic re-use across formationally and semantically related signs. However, as in spoken language morphology, it is the identifiable parts that may gain their meanings by association with their complex wholes, rather than the other way around.

4 Iconicity in word formation

In this section, we discuss two additional patterns that are iconic and systematic in ASL. Both patterns relate to the distinction between morphologically-related pairs of nouns and verbs. These patterns are referred to in the literature as the "noun-verb pair" pattern and the "handling-instrument" pattern, respectively.

A quite widely-discussed morphological pattern in ASL concerns pairs of related verbs and nouns that differ only in their conventional movement pattern. Following Supalla and Newport's (1978: 100–102) original formulation, these verbs and nouns are related pairs of signs such that "the verb expresses the activity performed with or on the object named by the noun." Because they associate verbs and nouns through a non-concatenative phonological operation, these pairs of signs have been compared to verb-noun pairs in English that differ in terms of syllabic stress (*recórd/récord*) or vowel quality (*bleed/blood*), for example. The classic examples are the ASL verb SIT and the noun CHAIR: both signs are formed with the index and middle fingers extended and held together on each hand (a configuration typically referred to as the "U handshape"), and in the articulation of both signs, the hands have the same orientation and overall movement, with the dominant hand moving to contact the top of the non-dominant hand. However, the movement pattern differs between the two signs: SIT is signed with the dominant hand moving to rest on the top of the non-dominant hand (Figure 14a), while CHAIR is signed with a shorter, repeated movement (Figure 14b).

Across noun-verb pairs, nouns are signed with repeated, restrained movements, while verbs are signed with longer, continuous movements: Supalla and Newport identify a number of sub-patterns within this broader generalization, and across all pairs that they

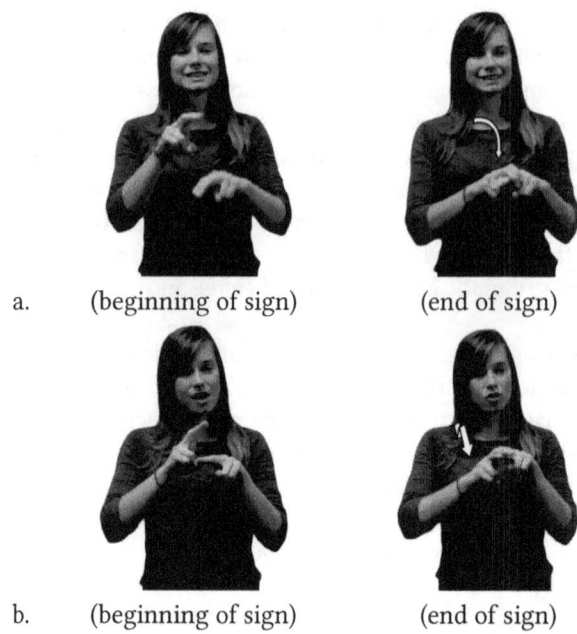

Figure 14: The ASL sign SIT (a) is articulated with a longer, single movement, and CHAIR (b) is articulated with a shorter, repeated movement.

identify, the nouns are all articulated with a constrained, repeated movement. However, several different movement patterns are observed among the verbs. These sub-patterns include a single unidirectional movement (as in FLY-AIRPLANE and AIRPLANE); a repeated unidirectional movement (as in SWEEP and BROOM); and a repeated bidirectional movement (as in ERASE-CHALKBOARD and ERASER).

Relevant for our purposes here is the fact that the forms of these signs remain quite iconic in synchronic ASL; not only does the configuration and orientation of the hand iconically profile aspects of the referent object, as we discuss below, but, similar to the discussion of the sign VERY-SLOW in §2, the contrasting movement patterns themselves have an underlying iconic motivation (and see Wilcox 2004 for additional discussion of this point). Regarding the multiple verbal movement sub-patterns found among noun-verb pairs, Supalla and Newport note that "in general, *single* movement in the sign corresponds to single, punctual or perfective action. *Repeated* movement, in contrast, refers to durative or iterative activity which is made of punctual actions" (Supalla & Newport 1978: 103–104). This description suggests that the perception of iconicity has not diminished from these signs. These verbs can be analyzed as transparently representing motion with motion, with, for example, the single phonological motion of the sign SIT motivated by the motion of a human body settling on a flat surface.

The movement pattern for nouns can similarly be analyzed as motivated by meaning (see also Wilcox 2004: 131–132). In ASL, repeated forms can represent repeated actions or, more abstractly, a general activity or the instrument canonically associated with an action. A derivational process discussed by Padden & Perlmutter (1987: 343), for example, is the "activity noun" rule, in which small repeated movements derive the noun ACTING from the verb ACT, and the noun SWIMMING from the verb SWIM. This is also consistent with the cross-linguistic use of reduplicated forms to derive nouns from verbs (e.g., Nivens 1993, Kouwenberg & LaCharité 2001, Adelaar & Himmelmann 2005): Kouwenberg & LaCharité (2015: 984), for example, provide *kriep-kriep* 'scrapings' as a noun derived through reduplication of the verb *kriep* 'to scrape' in Jamacian, and *doro-doro* 'sieve' as a noun derived through reduplication of the verb *doro* 'to sift' in Sranan. In noun-verb pairs in ASL, as well, the repetition of the verb's phonological movement is used to denote the instrument associated with the action by de-emphasizing the action inherent to the verb.

To make the relationship between related verbs and nouns concrete, in Tables 11 and 12 we provide the iconic mapping for the signs SIT and CHAIR, respectively. These iconic mappings are identical except for their phonological movements and the corresponding aspects of meaning. These differences in movement mark this pair of signs as participating in the "noun-verb" pattern in ASL.

Table 11: Aspects of the iconic mapping for SIT.

Form	Meaning
non-dominant hand	a surface to be sat on
dominant hand	an object in motion
U-handshape	paired human legs
contacting movement	human figure settles on the surface
single, continuous movement	**a single, perfective action**

Table 12: Aspects of the iconic mapping for CHAIR.

Form	Meaning
non-dominant hand	a surface to be sat on
dominant hand	an object in motion
U-handshape	paired human legs
contacting movement	human figure settles on the surface
repeated, constrained movement	**an object that is acted on**

In our recent work, we have discussed another pattern that distinguishes a subset of related verbs and nouns in ASL: the "handling and instrument" pattern (Padden et al. 2015). Unlike the noun-verb pairs described above, which are distinguished from one another based on properties of their movement, handling and instrument signs are distinguished from one another based primarily on their phonological handshapes. As an example, in ASL, the concept 'toothbrush' can be represented by either of two related forms, both of which involve a constrained, repeated movement near the mouth: the "handling" form has the hand configured in a variant of the fist handshape, shaped as though grasping an imagined toothbrush. The corresponding "instrument" form additionally has the index finger extended, representing the shape of the toothbrush, itself (see Padden et al. 2015: 82).

Another pair of signs fitting this pattern are two variant forms for the concept 'nail polish': Both 'nail polish' forms are articulated with the fingers of the dominant hand repeatedly brushing the fingers of the non-dominant hand. The handling form is signed with the dominant hand in what is known as the "F handshape", with the index finger contacting the thumb as though grasping a small, thin brush (Figure 15a), and the instrument form is signed with the "U handshape", with index and middle finger extended and closed, representing the bristles of a small brush (Figure 15b).

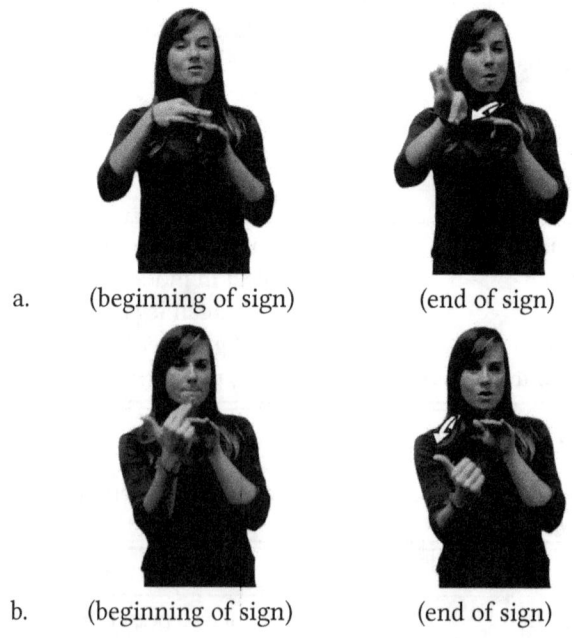

a.   (beginning of sign)   (end of sign)

b.   (beginning of sign)   (end of sign)

Figure 15: Two signs meaning 'nail polish'. The handling form (a) is signed with a "grasping" handshape, while the instrument form (b) is signed with a "brushing" handshape.

In ASL, handling and instrument forms can both also function as verbs, for example 'to brush one's teeth' or 'to paint one's nails', when signed with the appropriate longer movement pattern. However, analyzing elicited sentences in a vignette description task (Padden et al. 2015), we found previously that ASL signers are more likely to employ handling and instrument forms as verbs and nouns, respectively. Unlike the movement contrast that distinguishes noun-verb pairs, the association of handling forms with verbs and instrument forms with nouns is a statistically reliable preference, rather than a categorical rule. As an example of this preferred pattern, consider the sentence in (1). In this signed sentence, the signer used an instrument form to name the object, and a handling form to name the action associated with that object:

(1) NAIL-POLISH, WOMAN PAINT-NAILS
  'A woman paints her nails with nail polish.'

In this example, the topicalized sign NAIL-POLISH is identifiable as a noun because of the semantics of the sentence, as well as its participation in the movement-based noun-verb pattern described above: This sentence was uttered as a description of a short vignette in which a woman painted her nails, and in this sentence, the sign NAIL-POLISH is articulated with the short, restrained movement that is characteristic of derived nouns. In contrast, the sign PAINT-NAILS is identifiable as a verb: it is articulated with several longer, unidirectional movements to represent 'brushing' as an on-going process. In this sentence, the handshapes for the noun NAIL-POLISH and the verb PAINT-NAILS also differ: NAIL-POLISH is formed with the index and middle finger together representing the brush used to apply nail polish, while PAINT-NAILS is formed with the fingers configured as though handling the brush as a small object. These aspects of form and meaning for the signs NAIL-POLISH and PAINT-NAILS can be represented as in Tables 13 and 14, below.

Table 13: Aspects of the iconic mapping for NAIL-POLISH.

Form	Meaning
dominant hand	the hand of an agent
U-handshape	the bristles of a small brush
non-dominant hand	a human hand
repeated, constrained movement	an object that is manipulated

Table 14: Aspects of the iconic mapping for PAINT-NAILS.

Form	Meaning
dominant hand	the hand of an agent
F-handshape	grasping a small object
non-dominant hand	a human hand
repeated, unidirectional movement	the repeated action of a human agent

The preferential pairing of instrument forms with nouns and handling forms with verbs can be analyzed as motivated by the fact that in a handling form, the phonological structure profiles the action performed by a human agent (see also Brentari et al. 2012 and Hwang et al. 2016). The phonological structure of the instrument form additionally profiles the shape of the object used to perform the action.

In these "noun-verb pair" and "handling and instrument" examples, it is possible to associate an aspect of form (such as a handshape or movement pattern) with a syntactic category (such as noun or verb) and/or an aspect of meaning (such as agency or duration). But these consistent form-meaning pairings are identifiable only in comparison to other signs: There is no recurring "handling affix" or "derived noun affix" to mark these patterns. Instead, both noun-verb pairs and handling-instrument signs are distinctive patterns recognizable only through their iconicity. They are paradigmatic relationships that are identifiable on the basis of their iconic motivations.

5 Conclusion

In this chapter, we have taken inspiration from Anderson's a-morphous theory of morphology, which views Saussurean signs as holistic pairings of potentially complex form and potentially complex meaning. From this perspective, rather than complex words deriving their meanings from the meanings of their parts, it is instead the parts of a complex word that may derive their meanings from the whole words that they appear in. We have demonstrated that this "a-morphous" view provides a fresh perspective on sign-internal motivation, regardless of whether this motivation can be considered morphological or iconic. In sign languages, the perception of iconicity or morphological complexity arises from speaker (re)analysis of the relation between form and meaning among the words of a language. Any whole word may drift in form and meaning in a way that obscures its original, analyzable internal structure. However, signs also often receive analogical support from other, related signs. As the field of sign language linguistics continues to recognize the relationship between iconicity and morphology as related aspects of motivation in linguistic structure, Anderson's insights will continue to provide a useful framework for analysis for some time to come.

Acknowledgements

We wish to thank the editors and contributors to this volume, particularly Claire Bowern, for this opportunity to honor Steve Anderson. Ryan Bennett and two anonymous reviewers provided helpful feedback on this work. Thank you also to Mark Aronoff, Lynn Hou, Irit Meir, Hope Morgan, Corrine Occhino, Wendy Sandler, Amira Silver-Swartz, and Tessa Verhoef for additional discussion and comments.

References

Ackerman, Farrell, Robert Malouf & James P. Blevins. 2016. Patterns and discriminability in language analysis. *Word structure* 9(2). 132–155.

Adelaar, K.A. & Nikolaus Himmelmann. 2005. *The Austronesian languages of Asia and Madagascar*. Hove: Psychology Press.

Anderson, Stephen R. 1985. *Phonology in the twentieth century: theories of rules and theories of representations.* Chicago: University of Chicago Press.

Anderson, Stephen R. 1992. *A-morphous morphology.* Cambridge: Cambridge University Press.

Anderson, Stephen R. In press. A short history of morphological theory. In Jenny Audring & Francesca Masini (eds.), *The Oxford handbook of morphological theory.* Oxford: Oxford University Press.

Aronoff, Mark. 1976. *Word formation in generative grammar.* Cambridge, MA: MIT Press.

Aronoff, Mark. 2007. In the beginning was the word. *Language* 83(4). 803–830.

Aronoff, Mark, Irit Meir, Carol A. Padden & Wendy Sandler. 2003. Classifier constructions and morphology in two sign languages. In Karen Emmorey (ed.), *Perspectives on classifier constructions in sign languages,* 53–83. Mahurah, NJ: Lawrence Erlbaum Associates.

Battison, Robbin. 1974. Phonological deletion in American Sign Language. *Sign Language Studies* 5. 1–19.

Bergen, Benjamin K. 2004. The psychological reality of phonaesthemes. *Language* 80(2). 290–311.

Blevins, James P. 2016. *Word and paradigm morphology.* Oxford: Oxford University Press.

Bochner, Harry. 1993. *Simplicity in generative morphology.* Berlin: Mouton de Gruyter.

Brentari, Diane, Marie Coppola, Laura Mazzoni & Susan Goldin-Meadow. 2012. When does a system become phonological? handshape production in gesturers, signers, and homesigners. *Natural Language and Linguistic Theory* 30(1). 1–31.

Bybee, Joan. 2001. *Phonology and language use.* Cambridge: Cambridge University Press.

Bybee, Joan. 2006. From usage to grammar: the mind's response to repetition. *Language* 82(4). 711–733.

Dingemanse, Mark. 2012. Advances in the cross-linguistic study of ideophones. *Language and Linguistics Compass* 6(10). 654–672.

Emmorey, Karen. 2014. Iconicity as structure mapping. *Philosophical Transactions of the Royal Society B: Biological Sciences* 369(1651). 20130301. DOI:10.1098/rstb.2013.0301

Fernald, Theodore B. & Donna Jo Napoli. 2000. Exploitation of morphological possibilities in signed languages: Comparison of American Sign Language with English. *Sign Language and Linguistics* 3(1). 3–58.

Ferrand, J. 1896. *Dictionnaire des sourds-muets.* Manuscript, ca. 1785, ed. J. A. A. Rattel, "Collection ancienne et moderne d'otologie". Republished 2008: *Dictionnaire à l'usage des sourds et muets,* coll. "Archives de la langue des signes française." Limoges: Lambert-Lucas.

Frishberg, Nancy. 1975. Arbitrariness and iconicity: historical change in American Sign Language. *Language* 51(3). 696–719.

Frishberg, Nancy. 1985. Dominance relations and discourse structures. In William C. Stokoe & Virginia Volterra (eds.), *SLR '83. Proceedings of the Third International Symposium on Sign Language Research,* 79–90. Rome: CNR.

Frishberg, Nancy & Bonnie Gough. 1973. Morphology in American Sign Language. *Sign Language and Linguistics* 3(1). 103–131.

Hay, Jennifer & R. Harald Baayen. 2005. Shifting paradigms: gradient structure in morphology. *Trends in Cognitive Sciences* 9(7). 342–348.

Hwang, So-One, Nozomi Tomita, Hope Morgan, Rabia Ergin, Deniz İlkbaşaran, Sharon Seegers, Ryan Lepic & Carol A. Padden. 2016. Of the body and the hands: Patterned iconicity for semantic categories. *Language and Cognition*. 1–30. DOI:10.1017/langcog.2016.28

Jackendoff, Ray. 1975. Morphological and semantic regularities in the lexicon. *Language* 51(3). 639–671.

Klima, Edward & Ursula Bellugi. 1979. *The signs of language*. Cambridge: Harvard University Press.

Kouwenberg, Silvia & Darlene LaCharité. 2001. The iconic interpretations of reduplication: issues in the study of reduplication in Caribbean Creole languages. *European Journal of English Studies* 5(1). 59–80.

Kouwenberg, Silvia & Darlene LaCharité. 2015. Arbitrariness and iconicity in total reduplication: evidence from Caribbean Creoles. In D. Rossi (ed.), *The why and how of total reduplication: current issues and new perspectives*, 971–91. Amsterdam: John Benjamins.

Lambert, L. M. 1865. *Le langage de la physionomie et du geste mis à la portée de tous*. Republished 2005: *Dictionnaire de la langue des signes française d'autrefois*. Paris, Editions du CTHS. Paris: Lecoffre.

Lepic, Ryan, Carl Börstell, Gal Belsitzman & Wendy Sandler. 2016. Taking meaning in hand: Iconic motivations in two-handed signs. *Sign Language and Linguistics* 19(1). 37–81.

Lillo-Martin, Diane & Richard P. Meier. 2011. On the linguistic status of 'agreement' in sign languages. *Theoretical linguistics* 37(3/4). 95–141.

Meir, Irit. 2010. Iconicity and metaphor: Constraints on metaphorical extension of iconic forms. *Language* 86(4). 865–896.

Meir, Irit, Carol Padden, Mark Aronoff & Wendy Sandler. 2013. Competing iconicities in the structure of languages. *Cognitive Linguistics* 24(2). 309–343.

Napoli, Donna Jo, Nathan Sanders & Rebecca Wright. 2014. On the linguistic effects of articulatory ease, with a focus on sign languages. *Language* 90(2). 424–456.

Nivens, Richard. 1993. Reduplication in four dialects of West Tarangan. *Oceanic Linguistics* 32(2). 353–388.

Padden, Carol A. & David Perlmutter. 1987. American Sign Language and the architecture of phonological theory. *Natural Language and Linguistic Theory* 5. 335–375.

Padden, Carol A., So-One Hwang, Ryan Lepic & Sharon Seegers. 2015. Tools for language: patterned iconicity in sign language nouns and verbs. *Topics in Cognitive Science* 7(1). 81–94.

Perniss, Pamela, Robin L. Thompson & Gabriella Vigliocco. 2010. Iconicity as a general property of language: Evidence from spoken and signed languages. *Frontiers in Psychology* 1. 1–15.

Shaw, Emily & Yves Delaporte. 2010. New perspectives on the history of American Sign Language. *Sign Language Studies* 11(2). 158–204.

Stokoe, William C. 1960. Sign language structure: an outline of the visual communication systems of the American deaf. In *Studies in linguistics: occasional paper 8*. University of Buffalo.

Supalla, Ted. 1986. The classifier system in American Sign Language. In Collette Craig (ed.), *Noun classes and categorization*, 181–214. John Benjamins.

Supalla, Ted & Elissa L. Newport. 1978. How many seats in chair? the derivation of nouns and verbs in American Sign Language. In Patricia Siple (ed.), *Understanding language through Sign Language research*, 91–132. Academic Press.

Taub, Sarah F. 2001. *Language from the body: Iconicity and metaphor in American Sign Language*. Cambridge: Cambridge University Press.

Wilbur, Ronnie B. 2013. The point of agreement: changing how we think about sign language, gesture, and agreement. *Sign Language and Linguistics* 16(2). 221–258.

Wilcox, Sherman. 2004. Cognitive iconicity: conceptual spaces, meaning, and gesture in signed language. *Cognitive Linguistics* 15(2). 119–148.

Wilcox, Sherman & Corrine Occhino. 2016. Constructing signs: *Place* as a symbolic structure in signed languages. *Cognitive Linguistics* 27(3). 371–404.

Wilcox, Sherman & Phyllis Wilcox. 1995. The gestural expression of modality in asl. In Joan Bybee & Suzanne Fleischmann (eds.), *Modality in grammar and discourse*, 135–162. Amsterdam: John Benjamins.

Zipf, George K. 1935. *The psychobiology of language: an introduction to dynamic philology*. Cambridge: MIT Press.

Chapter 24

Iconicity chains in sign languages

Donna Jo Napoli

Swarthmore College

> Stephen Anderson warns that approaches to linguistic universals that derive facts about language from the structure of the Language faculty or from external forces shaping the Primary Linguistic Data— where these two sources must be taken as mutually exclusive – not only are difficult to support since the two modes of explanation are entangled, but wrong (Anderson 2008). External forces shaping the Primary Linguistic Data can result in grammatical regularities – true properties of language – but, in order to recognize them, we must "take into account the filtering role of the perceptual systems through which these [brute physical facts] are presented to the mind for interpretation" (Anderson 2016: 13). In the communication systems of other species we find that particularities of biology are connected to pathways for messages. The same should be true for humans. "Why, in fact, might we be tempted to believe otherwise?" (Anderson 2011b: 364). Why, indeed? This paper argues for iconicity chains in sign languages, chains consisting of mappings from various perceptual systems into a visual realization and then into a semantic sense, allowing insight into why unrelated languages might exhibit similar signs for abstract concepts.

1 Introduction

Stephen Anderson has always been a brave intellect. He eschews theoretical blinders when he faces data. Had he been among those to investigate sign languages at the start, perhaps the present revolution in sign language analysis would never have needed to occur or would have occurred decades ago. For we are, indeed, in the middle of a revolution. Much of the early work in sign language linguistics was dedicated to showing how much sign languages are like spoken languages, in order to establish beyond a doubt that sign languages are *bona fide* languages (Vermeerbergen 2006). Having established that, present research is paying significant attention to modality-driven phenomena (Meier 2002; Woll 2003). In particular, the existence and extent of iconicity can now be studied outside the closet.

The number of investigations on iconicity in language is increasing exponentially, with international conferences occurring multiple times a year for the past few years. Given that iconic signs quickly get conventionalized to the point where they are processed by the brain in the same way as bundles of arbitrary features (Emmorey et al. 2004;

 Donna Jo Napoli. 2017. Iconicity chains in sign languages. In Claire Bowern, Laurence Horn & Raffaella Zanuttini (eds.), *On looking into words (and beyond)*, 517–546. Berlin: Language Science Press. DOI:10.5281/zenodo.495464

Fabisiak & Rutkowski 2011), there may be little cognitive difference between iconic and non-iconic signs. However, the recognition of iconicity is critical to understanding how it interacts with grammar (Meir et al. 2013). While many avenues of inquiry into iconicity are presently being explored, this paper is a call for scholars of sign languages to delve more deeply into the possibility of synesthesia as a source of iconicity. As Anderson (2011a; 2016) so rightfully alerts us, our perceptions can act as filters in communication systems. Here I propose an example: iconicity chains that map from any perception or other somatosensory information into a visual realization and from there into a semantic sense.

Sections 2 through 4 are a whirlwind introduction to iconicity in general. They are far from exhaustive, though I have attempted to be representative with respect to sign languages. References, in particular, are only a sampling, and I apologize to all the fine work I do not mention. §5 is an outline of the kinds of questions involving synesthesia that I hope to direct more attention to and an introduction to the notion of iconicity chain.

2 Background on iconicity

The term *iconicity* as it pertains to language was originally applied to non-arbitrary mappings from form to meaning; at the lexical level, essentially a sign that looked like what it meant, or a word that sounded like what it meant was labeled iconic. For example, with respect to action, in many (all?) sign languages the sign for 'eat' involves moving hand to mouth; the movement of the sign imitates an essential act in eating for humans (in most situations). The signer embodies the actor in the event. Likewise, with respect to concrete objects, the sign for 'deer' in many (not all) sign languages involves hands on either side of the head with one or more fingers extended (antlers as identification). The signer again embodies the referent, here mapping relevant parts of a deer onto the human body of the signer. For spoken languages, iconic words include imitations of animal sounds (*moo, peep*) and words whose sound evokes the sound of their sense (*bell, slam*). This phenomenon is labelled *onomatopoeia*, about which a great deal has been written.

Recent work gathers within the iconicity aegis a wider range of structural alignments – thus a sign/word can be called iconic if its articulation brings to mind its sense – that is, it is motivated (Russo 2004; Perniss, Thompson & Vigliocco 2010), where this extension of the concept is often culture-based (Adam et al. 2007). For example, joined arms swinging in front of the torso form the sign for 'baby' in many languages – bringing to mind rocking an infant. Again, we have embodiment – but not of the referent 'baby', rather of someone doing a typical action regarding a baby. Perhaps the long-recognized phonesthemes among the IndoEuropean languages (recognized for hundreds of years, in fact; see Drellishak 2006) should be included here. For example, words that start with the fricative [s] followed by the voiceless stop [t] often deal with lack of motion, including figurative motion (*stay, stand, stupid, stymie, stammer, stuck, stagnant, stutter,* ...), but not always (*start, stamp, stuff, stag*...), while words that start with the fricative

[f] followed by the liquid [l] often deal with quick motion, again including figurative motion (*fleet, flit, flick flow, fly, flutter, flame, floozy, flip* ...), but not always (*floor, flat, flab, flacid*...). This more catholic approach to iconicity allows one to assess its role in language development and language processing (Emmorey 2014; Perniss & Vigliocco 2014).

3 Iconicity involving the perception of vision only

3.1 Mappings outside language proper

Iconic mappings from a visually perceived message to meaning can belong to non-verbal communication (Argyle 1975; Knapp, Hall & Horgan 2013) or to language proper.

With respect to visual communication outside language proper, much gesture that accompanies speech (co-verbal gesture) or that occurs independently of speech communicates information of a general sort (such as attitude or emotional/intellectual involvement), or information supportive to the speech material (such as gesturing the shape of a vase as one talks about arranging flowers) (McNeill 1992; 2000; Goldin-Meadow 1999; Kendon 2004; Özyürek 2014), or information that promotes discourse coherence (Lascarides & Stone 2009). While typological categories for gestures can help us get a sense of the complexity involved in studying gesture, they are not discrete (Streeck 2009). And there are areas of gesture use that have been examined only briefly with a linguist's eye, but with such insight that they beg for further comparison to other uses, such as gestures in conducting orchestras (Boyes Braem & Braem 2000).

Other methods of visual communication can give precise information, including quantitative, though usually it is very limited in range, such as baseball signals (Komissaroff 2016), diving communication (Recreational Scuba Training Council 2005, and described in Mišković et al. 2016), and gestural systems used in hunting (Hindley 2014). Relevant mentions of systematic iconic mappings are found in work on semiotics with regard to flag signals, comics, the visual arts (all discussed in Berger 1984), auditory signals in military aircraft (Doll & Folds 1986), and others.

My call to arms in this paper is directed at scholars of language proper. Still, it might be relevant also to scholars of two other areas. One is mime, where the new and intriguing initial comparisons to sign languages in Sutton-Spence & Boyes Braem (2013) are suggestive. The other is gesture, for which there are multiple reasons to suspect that the directions of investigation suggested in §5 might be relevant. First, much research shows alignments between sign languages and gestural communication (such as Hall, Ferreira & Mayberry 2013). Second, home sign has many similarities to sign languages (Goldin-Meadow 2005, among many), and homesigning children at first base much of their communication on iconic gestures, but tend to modify them over time in much the same way that iconic signs change (such as going from two-handed gestures to one-handed ones; see Tomaszewski 2006). Third, emergent sign languages tend to quickly move from elaborate gestures to simplified signs (Kocab, Pyers & Senghas 2014), but iconicity manages to persist (Hwang et al. 2016). Fourth, children go through an intermediate stage in which they use gesture-word combinations as they transition from single-word utterances to more complex phrases (Capirci et al. 1996). And, fifth, there are arguments for a gestural origin of all manual linguistic systems (Ortega & Morgan 2015).

3.2 Mappings within language proper: Sign languages

Here we look at sign languages. There are also interesting observations to be considered about language represented in text, as noted briefly in the next subsection.

Meaning-form relationships are apparent across the grammar in sign languages, so much so that sign languages do, in fact, have much in common (Woll 2003). The discussion that follows is generally informed by the foundational work on metaphor of Wilcox (2000) and Taub (2001), both of whom suggested analyses that are only recently finding confirmation in the experimental work of others. For example, Meir (2010) shows that conceptual metaphors involve double mappings, one between source and target domains and the other between form and meaning iconicity – and both must "work" in order for the entire metaphor to "work". The pervasiveness of iconicity develops meta-linguistic skills that have been argued to be behind the fact that deaf people who use different sign languages can establish rich communication with each other much faster than hearing people who use different spoken languages (Zeshan 2015). Below I focus on the manuals, but the nonmanuals are often iconic, as well (as in Pizzuto et al. 2008).

In some signs the shape that the manuals assume mimics the shape of the referent or some visual form peculiar to the referent (Pizzuto et al. 1995; Pietrandrea & Russo 2007); in others the manuals draw outlines of the shape of the referent; in others the size of articulation corresponds to the size of the referent. The number of hands in a sign can be iconic: signs tend to recruit two hands for senses that encode relationship types (interaction, location, dimension, and composition) (Lepic et al. 2016). Lexical items cluster into families, with an under-specified meaning conveyed by the parts of the signs that are in common, which is typically iconic, and specific information added by the variable parts of the signs, which might or might not be iconic (Fernald & Napoli 2000). Lepic and Padden (this volume) go so far as to say that iconicity is morphology; internal structure of signs might be obfuscated by phonological change, but it will still be reinforced by the signers' knowledge of multiple related signs.

Sign languages vary in many ways on how they encode space (Perniss, Zwitserlood & Özyürek 2015), yet repeatedly the encoding is iconic (Vermeerbergen 2006). Point of view is expressed iconically through spatial alignments and relationships (Pyers, Perniss & Emmorey 2015). While there is debate over whether spatial loci are logical variables (Lillo-Martin & Klima 1990; Neidle et al. 2000) or purely iconic mechanisms that are not linguistic at all (Cuxac 1999; Liddell 2003), recent work allows insights from both camps in a formal semantics that "makes provisions for iconic requirements at the very core of its interpretive procedure" (Schlenker, Lamberton & Santoro 2013: 91, and see Giorgolo 2010). Likewise there is debate over whether agreement is morphological or, instead, iconic and non-linguistic, since locations in space represent locations in mental space, numbers of extended fingers can indicate numbers of referents, and direction of movement can indicate direction of change of transfer (Meier 1987; Janis 1995; Mathur 2000, vs. Liddell 1995; 2003; and for discussion relevant to this issue based on an atypical child signer, see Quinto-Pozos et al. 2013). Again, an appropriate formal semantics can make a comprehensive analysis based on the insights of both camps (Schlenker 2016).

Iconicity plays a role in delivering information about event structure, such as telicity (Wilbur 2003; 2008; Strickland et al. 2015; Schlenker 2016), and whether and at what rate an event is repeated (Kuhn & Aristodemo 2016). Path shape, speed, and other dynamics of movement can indicate location and dynamics of the action, particularly in classifier predicates, where languages can vary on how iconic they are (Aronoff et al. 2003; Tumtavitikul, Niwatapant & Dill 2009). Temporal ordering of signing corresponds to temporal ordering of visualization of the participants and action in events (Napoli & Sutton-Spence 2014; Napoli, Sutton-Spence & Quadros Forthcoming). Since there are multiple articulators in sign languages (that is, two manuals plus a variety of nonmanuals), more than one message can be conveyed at once (Vermeerbergen, Leeson & Crasborn 2007; Napoli & Sutton-Spence 2010). Simultaneous articulation of two events that occur simultaneously is a further kind of iconicity. Additionally, a signer can embody a participant in the event being conveyed, which is an iconicity similar in ways to pantomime (Metzger & Bahan 2001).

Meaning-form relationships are exploited across all components of the grammar in innovative creative language (Sutton-Spence & Kaneko 2016), as in poetry (Bauman, Nelson & Rose 2006; Sutton-Spence & Napoli 2010; Sutton-Spence & Napoli 2013), humor (Sutton-Spence & Napoli 2009), and taboo expressions (Mirus, Fisher & Napoli 2012; Napoli, Fisher & Mirus 2013). Much of this iconicity is founded on the cognitive topology involved in mapping the parts of a non-human entity onto the signer's body, since the poet/humorist will typically embody in turn the major characters in order to show how each referent's experience can be revelatory of the human (usually deaf) experience. Often attention is directed to the physical realities of the articulators. For example, one American Sign Language (ASL) joke concerns a woman on a diet tempted by a cookie. The sign TEMPT is made on the non-dominant elbow and the sign COOKIE is made on the non-dominant palm. In the joke the dominant hand "runs" from the elbow, along the forearm, to the palm of the non-dominant hand –exploiting the physiological connectedness of the two locations to show us the easy path from temptation to sweets.

Certainly, with respect to sign languages, the judgment of whether a sign is iconic or not can be so particular to a culture that it is non-obvious to those outside the culture. (Here and throughout this paper I offer speculative remarks on signs from different countries. If I do not cite a source, my information comes either from personal knowledge or from the website spreadthesign.com.) Iconic handshapes used in handling classifiers and object classifiers (otherwise known as entity classifiers), for example, express an agentive/non-agentive distinction in many sign languages; if the event is agentive, the handling classifier is used, and if it is non-agentive, the object classifier is used, where a recent comparison of the sign languages of Italy and America shows that cultural factors contribute to the conventionalization of which type of handshape will be used to convey a given event (Brentari et al. 2015). Iconicity involving temporal succession and cyclicity reflects cultural conceptions of time and thus presents similarities and distinctions across sign languages (Kosecki 2014).

A single example can help seal the point about culture. The sign for 'rent' in the sign language of Portugal (ALUGAR) is related to the sign for 'pay' (PAGAR) with an aspectual marker for repetition. Both are iconic. In the sign PAGAR the dominant hand taps the palm of the nondominant hand. This brings to mind putting payment in someone's waiting palm. In the sign ALUGAR the same handshape on the dominant hand makes a repeated circle going toward the addressee, bringing to mind paying repeatedly. Now let's compare to the sign RENT in America; it is morphologically related to the sign MONTH, neither of which at first looks iconic. In the sign MONTH a 1-handshape on the dominant hands move down the back of a 1-handshape on the nondominant hand. Only if you know that we read down the calendar's representation of the months in America and Canada (where this sign language is used) do you see the iconicity. The sign RENT is the sign MONTH with reduplication, so that the dominant hand circles back to repeat that downward motion. Only if you know the further fact that rent is generally paid on a monthly basis do you see the iconicity.

An additional complication to recognizing iconicity is that one language's sign may focus on certain visuals of the meaning while another's may focus on different visuals. Again, those visuals might be culture-based or not. The sign for 'dance', for example, can focus on movement of the torso (in the sign languages of Italy and Turkey, among others), of the legs (in the sign languages of America and Japan, among others), of the arms (in the sign languages of Germany and India, among others), of the whole person in relation to another person (in the sign languages of Austria and Estonia, among others), or maybe just on general movement (in the sign language of Iceland). Without knowing what the sign means ahead of time, one may be at a loss to guess its meaning just from seeing it, but once the meaning is given, one might quickly recognize its iconicity.

3.3 Mappings within language proper: Print

Written/print representations of spoken languages can use visual information iconically, as in concrete poetry, popular in Greek Alexandria during the Third and Second Centuries BCE and intermittently up to modern times (Newell 1976). But there are other, less obvious ways that print/writing can be iconic. Verbal constructions used in writing affect readers' ability to understand discussions of spatial relationships, the account being that the order in which verbal material is presented on the page can help or hinder as one tries to mentally construct spatial models (Moeser 1976; Morris & Bransford 1982; Ehrlich & Johnson-Laird 1982; Louwerse 2008; Zwaan & Yaxley 2003). In a reading test that involved static spatial relations, Zwaan (1993: 119) found, "If a text presents spatial information in a scattered way, spatial representations are relatively weak, even for subjects who are instructed to form spatial representations." When people read, they make a mental representation of the orientation (Stanfield & Zwaan 2001) and shape (Zwaan, Stanfield & Yaxley 2002) of objects. Readers "mentally simulate the visibility of objects during language comprehension" (Yaxley & Zwaan 2007: 229). Additionally, in understanding referents in reading, it appears that, if too much verbal material intervenes between two mentions of a referent, interpretation is hindered; again it looks like mentioning a referent foregrounds it in one's mental representation of the text (Sanford & Garrod 1981).

4 Iconicity involving the perception of sound only

Iconic mappings from an aurally perceived message to meaning are used in spoken languages, of course, but they are also used in Morse code (a code based on written language) and sound signals (whistles in baseball, sirens, melodies). Studies of iconicity in spoken language are experiencing a renaissance, just as studies of iconicity in sign language are (Perniss, Thompson & Vigliocco 2010). There is a growing consensus (Vigliocco, Perniss & Vinson 2014; Goldin-Meadow & Brentari 2015) that with respect to iconicity in order to really understand the extent of it in spoken language we should be considering speech plus gestures, not just speech. In this section, however, I discuss only mappings from auditory form.

In here falls onomatopoeia, mentioned in §2. Spoken languages can also play with intensity, duration, and pitch in iconic ways (say *angry* in a loud, angry voice; say *slow* with a drawn out syllable nucleus; say *little girl* with a very high pitch). But spoken languages can move beyond that to sound articulations that bring to mind a meaning – that is, associative iconicity (in the sense of Fischer 1999) – just as sign languages do (as in the discussion of signs meaning 'baby' in §2). In this regard, sometimes particular features of sounds are associated with meaning in a relatively stable way across several languages (Sapir 1929; Taylor 1963; Werner & Wapner 1952; Wertheimer 1958, among early studies, and Hinton, Nichols & Ohala 1994; Voeltz & Kilian-Hatz 2001, among more recent studies). For example, in many languages high pitch is associated with small size of referent, whether the referent be entity or action (Jespersen 1922; Nuckolls 1999). Perhaps a high pitch brings to mind the voices of smaller people (Evans, Neave & Wakelin 2006), and so the size association spreads from people to any referent. For English, some claim a back rounded vowel is gloomy while a front low vowel is brash – compare English *drip* (a relatively high pitch vowel) to *drop* and both to *droop* (a back rounded vowel); and *slip* (a relatively high pitch vowel) to *slap* (a front low vowel). Correspondences can be so strong that manufacturers capitalize on them when naming products (Spence 2012). Additionally, it's been shown that prosody works together with segmental information as cues for iconic interpetations of words (Dingemanse et al. 2016).

Just as in spoken languages, iconicity can be felt beyond the lexicon, where the discussion here is generally informed by Fabisiak & Rutkowski (2011). For example, morphology can be iconic: reduplication (Moravcsik 1978) can indicate plurality (Macdonald 1976) or intensification (Murane 1974). We can witness iconicity even in syntax. Moulton & Robinson (1981) show how a radio announcer can order and pace words to reflect the order of participants in an action and the timing of that action. The order of temporal subordinate clauses within the next adjacent clause up often reflects the temporal relationship between that clause and the action of the adjacent clause (Haiman 1985; Kortmann 1991; Diessel 2005).

Conventional judgments of iconicity in spoken languages are affected by cultural factors, just as they are in sign languages. That's obvious for things like phonesthemes, where a given speaker is making associations across multiple lexical items in a language. But it also occurs in onomatopoeia. It's instructive to peruse Derek Abbott's (2004) animal sound website in this regard. Granted, as Abbott points out, "a Swedish Vallhund is not an Anatolian Shepherd or a Japanese Spitz. But variations in dog breeds can't fully account for these differences..." (Friedman 2015). Sound iconicity runs the gamut from realistic to simply bizarre: words for animal sounds might actually ring true to a farmer (*kpok, kpok kpok kpok*) or other person with direct experience, while others don't ring true to anyone (*cockadoodledoo*). Often the same animal's sound is rendered distinctly differently in different languages. People simply somehow agree to accept a given sound in speech as the conventional rendering of the animal (or other type of) sound. Perhaps digging into the culture will allow a better understanding (as often happens in linguistic study, see Duranti 2009).

A huge gap in our discussion thus far is so-called mimetics. We now use them as a jumping off point to other types of iconicity in language in §5.

5 Cross-modal iconicity

5.1 Mimetics and iconicity chains

Mapping from a visual entity to a meaning that involves vision or from an auditory entity to a meaning that involves sound is relatively straightforward. But this is not the only kind of iconic mapping found in language. As we saw for both sign languages and spoken languages, associative (or motivated) iconicity can occur. At times these associations seem to belong fairly generally to the human experience, such as the sight of rocking layered arms meaning 'baby' and a high-pitched vowel adding small size to the meaning of a word. But, mostly, linguists seem to have assumed a cultural basis for these mappings, often pointing out how the mappings are particular to a specific language.

However, there are important challenges to that assumption. In some spoken languages recognizable patterns of sounds indicate a non-arbitrary relationship between form and sense – where the words with this property are labelled mimetic and the phenomenon is called sound symbolism. Korean, for example, exhibits correspondences between sound and subjective impressions or other modalities (smell, taste, vision) as well as "size, mood, movement, shape, and other perceptual and psychological experiences" (Cho 2006: 64), where changes in vowels and consonants systematically relate to meaning differences. Japanese, instead, uses templates (fixed patterns of consonants and vowels) to indicate mimetics (Hamano 1998) For example, the correspondence between an action (lick, roll) or a property (drunk, exhausted) and the sound of the word referring to that action/property feels non-arbitrary to Japanese speakers. Correspondences as precise as between a sound and an emotional reaction to a taste are felt to be firm (Kagitani et al. 2014). The surprising (perhaps at first astonishing) part is that adult speakers of English and Japanese as well as Japanese toddlers are sensitive to mimetic correspondences in novel verbs (Imai et al. 2008). Thus there is evidence of something going on that is not grounded fully in culture – something that allows cross-modal iconicity.

That something may be simply the physical nature of language – something that Stephen Anderson insists we acknowledge. Language is expressed through the body and governed by the brain – both complex physical entities. It's possible to step back for a wider perspective on iconicity, a biological perspective, which has the potential to offer a more comprehensive understanding. The contribution of biology to sign language iconicity has been recognized before: Woll (2009: 150) points out that since "the visual medium affords the identification of objects and their spatial locations as a function of their forms and locations on the retina and sensory cortex, it is not surprising that cortical systems specialised for such mappings are utilised when sign languages capture these relationships." Here I widen the perspective further based on recent findings in cognition that there is multisensory integration in the midbrain and cerebral cortex of mammals (Stein & Stanford 2008, among many).

It is important to recognize at the outset that abstract entities can have physiological effects on the human body. Our own emotions, for example, trigger bodily sensations through the somatosensory systems, including activation of cardiovascular, skeletomuscular, neuroendocrine, and autonomic nervous systems (Nummenmaa et al. 2014). Additionally, visual recognition of another's emotions (through observation of their facial expressions and body postures) can trigger somatosensory reactions (Rudrauf et al. 2009; Sel, Forster & Calvo-Merino 2014). This is why, all other things being equal, we smile when someone smiles at us (Niedenthal 2007). Additionally, emotions have a wide range of effects on our behavior and psyche, including our moral judgments (Charland & Zachar 2008), which might offer another way to recognize emotions in others.

For our purposes, the entities of the world can be organized into three groups:

- those that have a realization apparent in any way (to any part of the somatosensory system – such as wind or respect)

- those that have a realization apparent to sight (you could draw them, for example – such as cars)

- those that have a realization apparent to hearing (you could record them, for example – such as rain)

These three groups are not discrete; they relate as in the schema in Figure 1.

All iconic mappings between distinct entities rely on metaphor, metaphony, and/or analogy, all filtered through experience, so all of them are complex. However, some of the mappings are more complex than others. With respect to Korean and Japanese mimetics, for example, we can find mappings between a sound on the one hand and a taste or a mood on the other (Garrigues 1995; Iwasaki et al. 2013). That is, we have

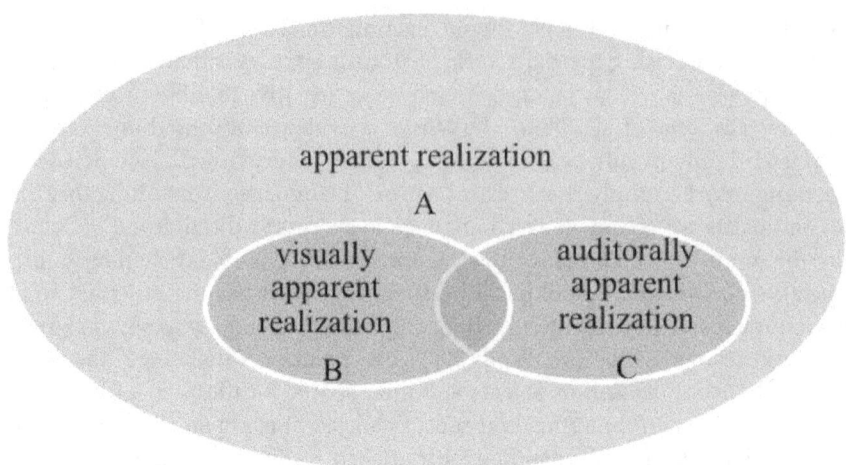

Figure 1: Entities of the world organized by type of realization

a mapping between something in the area C and something in the area A–C. So the mapping is cross-modal.

Iconic mappings in speech or sign into abstract meanings (which have neither visual nor auditory realizations) are necessarily cross-modal since they are mapping between elements in B or C and elements in A − (B ∪ C). Metaphor is the key mechanism used in sign languages for this kind of conceptual mapping (Borghi et al. 2014). Many conceptual metaphors hold both in spoken and sign languages (Roush 2016).

Metaphoric mappings that cross perceptual modalities are labeled synesthesia (Cytowic 1989, among many). We find mappings between many different senses, where a given sense S_1 can elicit a different sense S_2, and vice-versa. For example, texture can elicit visual forms (Simner & Ludwig 2012; Ludwig & Simner 2013) and visual forms can elicit textures (Albertazzi et al. 2016).

Many instances of synesthesia map a variety of senses onto auditory forms. Thus the odors of perfumery are mapped onto pitches (Belkin et al. 1997) and food smells are mapped onto the sounds of musical instruments (Crisinel & Spence 2012). Likewise, we find mappings from a variety of senses onto visual forms. With regard to odor again, Dematté, Sanabria & Spence (2006) examine odors mapped onto color hue, and Kemp & Gilbert (1997) show that intense smells are associated with darker colors. Hanson-Vaux, Crisinel & Spence (2013) look at the mappings from odors onto visual shape entities, where intense, unpleasant odors elicit angular shapes and other odors elicit rounded shapes.

Importantly, both hearing and deaf people can smile when a child says, "This tastes green." In fact, congenitally blind people and congenitally deaf people are sensitive to synesthesia, and in the same ways as sighted, hearing people (Ittyerah & Mitra 1988). A recent study shows that color-shape associations, in particular, are consistent across deaf and hearing people (Chen et al. 2014). Further, sign recognition involves reference to sensory-motor properties of one's own body (Corina & Gutierrez 2016), which would be compatible with sign formation likewise involving such reference. In sum, there is every reason to expect to find the effects of synesthesia in sign languages as much as in spoken languages.

Cross-modal mappings can have multiple layers of complexity. Let's say that we want to convey the sense of 'happy' in a sign language. What visual representation might we appeal to? A smile might come to mind. And some languages use the smile, though they draw it (in a variety of ways) rather than have the signer actually smile (such as the sign languages of Italy, Latvia, Portugal, and Turkey). The problem with using an actual smile is that that affective facial expression might conflict with other information in the message. If we ask in a sign language, "Are you happy?" we might well not smile, but use a neutral mouth as other nonmanuals articulate (such as the eyebrows raising). If we say in a sign language, "I'm not happy," it might be odd to smile (except in contrived circumstances). So the sense 'happy' has to be conveyed some other way. I conjecture that this way is through a chain of mappings, a chain which necessarily has precisely two cross-modal links – one from an entity that has a somatosensory realization other than visual to an entity that has a visual realization, and the next from that visual entity to a third entity that has a somatosensory realization other than visual (and see the distinction between two types of icons in Peirce 1932). An iconicity chain has complexity similar to that of the double metaphors of Meir (2010), but iconicity chains are culture independent, since they are grounded in biological properties.

In this regard, consider the sign HAPPY in ASL in Figure 2. (Figure from Lifeprint: http://www.lifeprint.com/asl101/pages-signs/h/happy.htm)

Figure 2: HAPPY in ASL

Here the hands hit the chest then circle away and hit again repeatedly. My conjecture is that this sign is built on the fact that physical activity correlates highly with happiness (Kahneman, Diener & Schwarz 1999) and with a heartbeat that we are conscious of. So it's like our heart is hopping inside our chests. The mapping is a chain from a hopping heart (which we cannot see, but we can feel) to an external representation of that heart (the visuals in Figure 2) and then to the abstract meaning 'happy'. So we are going from one somatosensory sense to vision and then from vision to a sense that is an emotion. Both links of the chain are cross-modal and both are iconic, as shown in Figure 3.

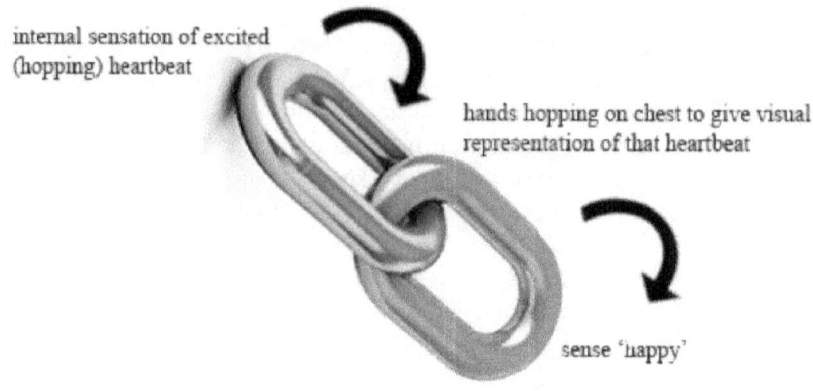

Figure 3: Schema of the iconicity chain for HAPPY in ASL

This iconicity chain between heart(beat) and happiness has its origins in our biological selves; it digs down inside our bodies. As such, it is culture-independent and we might expect to find sign languages using a chest-touching sign for 'happy' both among those that are genetically related to or have had contact with ASL (as happens in the sign languages of France and India) and among those that most likely developed independently (as happens in the sign languages of Austria, Germany, Iceland, and Sweden).

If we are alerted to likely possibilities for synesthesia in sign languages – that is, for iconicity chains – not only might we find them, but we might realize that signs we previously considered arbitrary are not. I contend this not only because of my own initial examinations, but because, on a theoretical basis, it should be true. Communication systems are subject to two potentially conflicting pressures: transmission efficiency, which drives them toward messages that are simple to produce (and perceive), and comprehension efficiency, which drives them toward messages that are semantically clear. As Roberts, Lewandowski & Galantucci (2015: 52) show in experimental work, "where iconicity was available, it provided scaffolding for the construction of communication systems and was overwhelmingly adopted." This goes hand-in-hand with work that shows that iconicity facilitates both recognition and production of signs (Vinson et al. 2015). In other words, comprehension efficiency trumps transmission efficiency. Rightly so. Non-arbitrary mappings, if they can be made, should be, since they enhance interpretability (and see Givón 1989). To do otherwise would be contrary to the overall goal of communication (and see Napoli, Sutton-Spence & Quadros Forthcoming).

In the rest of this section I briefly mention two areas for research in language synesthesia outside of speech, then focus on the area of potential sources for iconicity chains in sign languages.

5.2 Potential for iconicity chains in braille

Blind hearing people can access speech easily, thus, generally, language access is high, including access to all the mechanisms for synesthesia that speech uses. However, language represented in print is visual, thus inaccessible. The bumps in a braille cell allow print to be accessed tactilely and, because of this, a range of possibilities for cross-modal iconicity in language arise, where the connection between the two links in the iconicity chain is a tactile entity (comparable to the visual entity in sign language iconicity chains). So far as I know, such possibilities are not well-explored, though the iconic possibilities in rendering musical scores and literature on music theory are many (Pacun 2009; Johnson 2009). Given that cutaneous perception is high, it's no surprise that there's ongoing research on creating tactile icons (tactons) that include rhythm, location, frequency, amplitude, and duration of a tactile pulse, where iconicity influences the choices designers are making on attaching meaning to the various tactile factors (Brewster & Brown 2004), as well as V-Braille, a way to haptically represent Braille characters on a touch screen (such as on a mobile phone) (Jayant et al. 2010).

5.3 Potential for iconicity chains in tactile sign

The deaf-blind cannot access language visually or aurally. Thus, another area of exploration regarding synesthesia is tactile language for the deaf-blind, a complex of methods, such as fingerspelling, on-body signing, and hand-over-hand signing (Edwards 2012, and following). Research has shown that visual and tactile iconicity ratings of signs are similar across blind people, deaf people, and hearing-sighted people, allowing indications of which signs should be most salient to deaf-blind children (Griffith, Robinson & Panagos 1983).

5.4 Potential for iconicity chains in sign languages

Here I present the main course of this drawn-out feast in the form of a sampling of cross-modal associations that could serve as fertile ground for iconicity chains in sign languages. The iconic chains that interest me below involve mappings from an entity that is not visually apparent onto an entity that is visually apparent and then onto a meaning that is not visual in nature. Thus both links in these iconic chains are cross-modal. These are conceptually the most complex iconicity chains and, thus, might be the hardest to recognize.

The growing literature on synesthesia includes mappings involving forms that have realizations in various aspects of the somatosensory experience, including texture, temperature, weight, taste, smell, shape, emotions – the sorts of things that many of the mimetics in Korean and Japanese are based on. For humans, "meanings" associated with such forms, as discussed in the literature cited below, tend to be general and abstract rather than particular and concrete (to be contrasted with the "meanings" such forms might convey to nonhumans). For example, with respect to associations from a visual entity, a color might be associated with a broadly understood emotion (Johnson, Johnson & Baksh 1986), and with respect to associations from an auditory entity, pitch and tempo in music might be associated with a broadly understood emotion (Hevner 1937; Brower 2000). Often the emotion is hedonic, since the orbitofrontal cortex, which is involved in sensory integration, is also involved in hedonic experience (Kringelbach 2005). Evoking such general mappings has been claimed to be effective in psychopathology therapies (Lang 1979, and much work since).

Let's look at five potential sources for iconic chains in sign languages: mappings from texture, temperature, weight, taste, and smell.

5.4.1 Mappings from texture

Research on baby rhesus monkeys shows they choose soft models of their mothers over wire ones (Harlow 1959), which has been taken to show the importance of touch (particularly human touch) for human babies (Lynch 1970; Schneider 1996). Further, neonates in pain find comfort in skin-to-skin contact – which introduces a complex of factors, to be sure, but all transferred via that pliable skin (Kostandy et al. 2008). The potential, then, for an iconicity chain taking us from some relevant touch to the visuals related to that touch and then to the meaning 'safety' or 'love' arises. I believe that potential is realized. The sign GÜVENLI 'safe' in the sign language of Turkey uses two claw handshapes (the curled-5-handshape), which rake across the chest out to each side, one above the other (shown in the left side of Figure 4). This sign at first has no apparent iconicity. However, the sign KÜRK 'fur coat' is a compound of the sign for 'fur' and the sign for 'coat'. The sign for 'fur' has two claw handshapes raking out to each side from the center of the face (shown in the right side of Figure 4).

 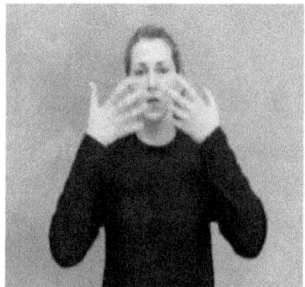

Figure 4: 'Safe' (left) and 'fur' (right) in the sign language of Turkey

The signs differ only by the parameter of location: one is on the chest, the other is on the face; one places one hand higher, the other has the hands at the same level. I suggest an iconicity chain mapping from the texture of softness onto the visual of fur or hair on the chest then onto the feeling of security and coziness that juvenile mammals (including humans) experience as they nestle against the chest of mature mammals (including male humans; i.e., daddy keeps us safe).

5.4.2 Mappings from temperature

Research on human emotional responses to changing a hand temperature show that changes of 6 degrees centigrade are distinctly unpleasant (Salminen et al. 2013). Thus one might associate warmth with pleasure/health/life, but extreme heat or cold with displeasure/fear/death. Consider here the sign TEAMA 'fear' in the sign language of Romania. The arms are bent and held close to the body, shaking them as if in a shiver (shown in the left side of Figure 5 – this is an embodiment sign, so the signer is shivering). Certainly, humans shake not only when they experience cold (where shivers occur because the drop in temperature signals the hypothalamus to stimulate muscle contractions to warm up the body) but when they experience fear (where adrenaline causes shivers) and a number of other emotions. And the sign STRACH 'fear' in the sign language of Poland is also built on an image of shaking, but this time it's the legs that shake (shown in the right side of Figure 5 – this is a classifier sign, so the dominant hand represents two legs that shake on the palm of the nondominant hand).

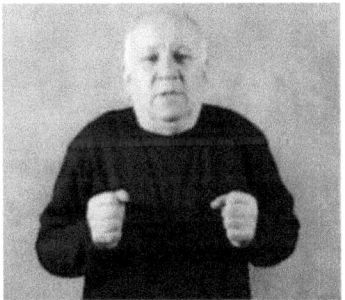 

Figure 5: 'Fear' in the sign languages of Romania (left) and Poland (right)

What makes me think the shaking is related directly to coldness in the sign in Romania is that this sign is identical to the sign for 'cold' in many sign languages (such as the sign languages of America, Austria, Britain, Czech Republic, Estonia, Germany, India, Italy, Japan, Russia, Spain, Turkey – a group that has three families in it, but also several languages that are unrelated to all others in that group). So the iconicity chain in the sign language of Romania would go from the sensation of coldness to the visually recognizable action of shivering to the emotion of fear (and see discussion on spoken languages in this regard in Atkins & Levin 1995).

5.4.3 Mappings from weight

There is little work in the literature regarding synesthesia and weight, however some work suggests a synesthetic link between weight and color brightness, where the darker a color is, the heavier it is perceived to be (Ward, Banissy & Jonas 2008). Any iconic chain of this sort in a sign language would have only one link being cross-modal.

Given my own experience with the world, however, I suspect other iconicity chains regarding weight exist where both links are cross-modal. For example, heavy might be associated with strong/substantial and light might be associated with weak/insubstantial in a broad range of contexts (such as judging food sources) while in other contexts heavy might be associated with dangerous/overwhelming and light with innocuous/possible (such as in lifting objects). My speculations might find confirmation. The signs for 'heavy' and 'strong' are close to identical to each other in the sign languages of Austria and Germany (which might or might not be independent facts – see Napoli & Sanders in preparation), where the visual image is related to lifting something heavy. In Figure 6 we see the sign for 'heavy' in Austria. In Figure 7 we see the sign for 'strong' in Austria. The handshapes and locations are the same. The orientation of the palms is upward in 'heavy' and the movement is relatively slow. The orientation of the palms is toward the signer in 'strong' and the movement is rapid (which is why the screenshot is blurred).

 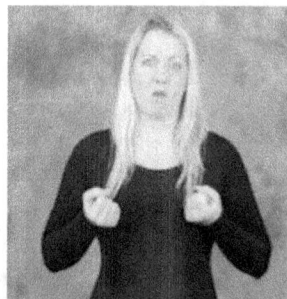

Figure 6: 'Heavy' in the sign language of Austria

Further, the signs for 'lightweight' and 'possible' are similar to one another in the sign language of India.

5.4.4 Mappings from taste

It appears that humans are born with a negative reaction (disgust) to acidic and a positive one to sweet (Fox & Davidson 1986). The sweet response is to taste rather than to a high-energy source, since neonates respond equally to sucrose as to artificial sweeteners (Ramenghi et al. 1996). The sign for 'sweet' is made at (or below or beside) the mouth in sign language after sign language, as expected (the only exception on spreadthesign.com being the sign language of Estonia, but it looks like the signer actually signed the sense of 'candy', rather than of the taste 'sweet'). Perhaps the association of sweetness with

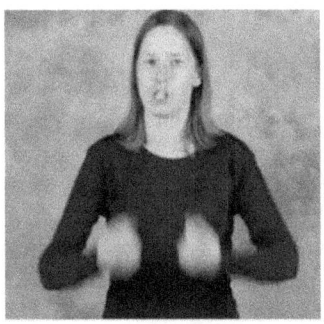 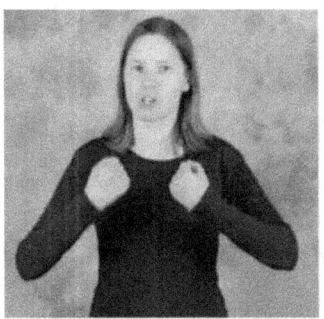

Figure 7: 'Strong' in the sign language of Austria

goodness is behind the fact that the sign for 'good' is made at the mouth in several languages (including those of America, Brazil, and France – all members of a single family). Of course, the reason here could as easily be that food and eating in general are associated with well-being (at least in that language family).

5.4.5 Mappings from smell

Some odors elicit pleasure and some displeasure (Alaoui-Ismaili et al. 1997), which might mean 'good/come close' (the smell of a hot bowl of pasta) versus 'bad/go away' (the smell of a skunk). Recent work suggests that affective experiences induced by odors are quite general, but allow for refinement of types, involving "well-being, social interaction, danger prevention, arousal or relaxation sensations, and conscious recollection of emotional memories" (Chrea et al. 2009: 49). Iconic chains mapping from odor to a visual form to an emotion occur. The sign REPUGNAR 'disgust' in the sign language of Brazil is clearly built on the perception of a bad smell (and is similar to CHIERO 'odor'), as is the sign ASQUEAR 'odor' in the sign language of Spain. In Figure 8 we see the Brazil sign, where the hand moves to the nose, then out to the ipsilateral side, then down and across to the contralateral side.

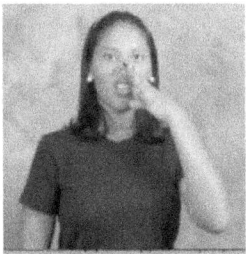 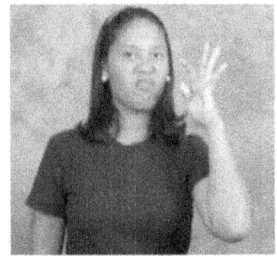 

Figure 8: 'Disgust' in the sign language of Brazil

6 Conclusion

Understanding iconicity in sign languages requires attention to cross-modal associations, which might be complex – involving an iconicity chain that has two mappings, rather than one. Thus the present work aims to alert researchers to such associations.

The benefits of a more (nearly) adequate approach to iconicity in communication are several. Understanding iconicity can help separate out what language is responsible for from what general communication is responsible for, and it might help us understand some of the more thorny areas in sign language studies, including why the signs for abstract concepts can be similar in unrelated languages.

Of particular interest to me is how languages change over time. Sign languages lack the regular changes typical of spoken language change (as discussed in any classical or more recent introduction to historical linguistics, such as Anttila 1972) but, instead, display only tendencies (Moser 1990). Thus diachronic changes motivated by the drive for ease of articulation (Napoli, Sanders & Wright 2014; Sanders & Napoli 2016b; Sanders & Napoli 2016a) apply erratically. The (near) insistence on maintaining iconicity might be at least partially responsible here, especially in light of the fact that iconic words in spoken language sometimes do not obey the same constraints that non-iconic words obey (as noted in Meir 2010). For example, well-formedness conditions and ordinary phonological rules do not always apply to Japanese mimetics (Itô & Mester 1995). And the onomatopoetic word *peep* in English (*pīpen* in Middle English) did not undergo the Great Vowel Shift perhaps because of the desire to maintain the [i] which connects to small size (Hock 1986: 294). Additionally, in West Papuan languages it looks like onomatopoeia in words meaning 'chicken' and 'cat' may have contributed both to the spread of these words among genetically unrelated languages and to their resistance to phonological change over time (Gasser in preparation). We find further evidence of onomatopoeia being ill-behaved in Italian (Marina Nespor, personal communication, December 2016). The horse in Italian goes *iiii* (that is [iiii], while the verb for this has consonants between the vowels: *nitrire*), and many parents reading to small children might enunciate four syllables here. But in the rest of the lexicon there are no words that contain a sequence of four uninterrupted vowels, except perhaps in other animal sounds. For example, the goat or sheep might go [be], [bee], [beee], or [beeee] (while the verb for this is well-formed: *belare*). Likewise, the mouse goes [skwit skwit], but elsewhere in Italian words do not end in [t], nor do syllables unless the [t] is part of a geminate (and, again, the verb for this is well-formed: *squittire*). And in the Turkic language Kazakh, we find onomatopoeic words with consonant clusters that fall outside the range of normally attested clusters (Washington in preparation). In sum, iconicity allows an alignment between form and meaning, and the pressure to establish it when it is possible and the subsequent pressure to maintain it once it is established are strong.

References

Abbott, Derek. 2004. *Animal sounds*. Accessed 11 January 2017. http://www.eleceng.adelaide.edu.au/Personal/dabbott/animal.html.

Adam, Meike, Wiebke Iversen, Erin Wilkinson & Jill P. Morford. 2007. Meaning on the one and on the other hand: Iconicity in native vs. foreign signed languages. In Elżbieta Tabakowska, Christina Ljungberg & Olga Fischer (eds.), *Insistent images (Iconicity in language and literature 5)*, 210–228. Amsterdam: John Benjamins.

Alaoui-Ismaili, Ouafae, Evelyne Vernet-Maury, Andre Dittmar, Georges Delhomme & Jacques Chanel. 1997. Odor hedonics: Connection with emotional response estimated by autonomic parameters. *Chemical Senses* 22(3). 237–248.

Albertazzi, Liliana, Francesca Bacci, Luisa Canal & Rocco Micciolo. 2016. The tactile dimensions of abstract paintings: A cross-modal study. *Perception* 7(45). 805–822.

Anderson, Stephen R. 2008. The logical structure of linguistic theory. *Language* 84(4). 795–814.

Anderson, Stephen R. 2011a. Clitics. In Marc van Oostendorp, Colin J. Ewen, Elizabeth Hume & Keren Rice (eds.), *The Blackwell companion to phonology*, 2002–2018. Chichester: Wiley-Blackwell.

Anderson, Stephen R. 2011b. The role of evolution in shaping the human language faculty. In Maggie Tallerman & Kathleen R. Gibson (eds.), *The Oxford handbook of language evolution*, 361–369. Oxford: Oxford University Press.

Anderson, Stephen R. 2016. The role of morphology in transformational grammar. In Andrew Hippisley & Gregory T. Stump (eds.), *The Cambridge handbook of morphology*, 587–608. Cambridge: Cambridge University Press.

Anttila, Raimo. 1972. *An introduction to historical and comparative linguistics*. New York: Macmillan.

Argyle, Michael. 1975. *Bodily communication*. London: Methuen & Co. Ltd.

Aronoff, Mark, Irit Meir, Carol A. Padden & Wendy Sandler. 2003. Classifier constructions and morphology in two sign languages. In Karen Emmorey (ed.), *Perspectives on classifier constructions in sign languages*, 53–83. Mahurah, NJ: Lawrence Erlbaum Associates.

Atkins, Beryl T. S. & Beth Levin. 1995. Building on a corpus: A linguistic and lexicographical look at some near-synonyms. *International Journal of Lexicography* 8(2). 85–114.

Bauman, H-Dirksen L., Jennifer L. Nelson & Heidi M. Rose. 2006. *Signing the body poetic: Essays on American Sign Language literature*. Vol. 1. Berkeley/Los Angeles: University of California Press.

Belkin, Kira, Robyn Martin, Sarah E. Kemp & Avery N. Gilbert. 1997. Auditory pitch as a perceptual analogue to odor quality. *Psychological Science* 8(4). 340–342.

Berger, Arthur Asa. 1984. *Signs in contemporary culture: An introduction to semiotics*. Salem, WI: Sheffield Publishing Co.

Borghi, Anna M., Olga Capirci, Gabriele Gianfreda & Virginia Volterra. 2014. The body and the fading away of abstract concepts and words: A sign language analysis. *Frontiers in Psychology* 5(811). DOI:10.3389/fpsyg.2014.00811

Boyes Braem, Penny & Thuering Braem. 2000. A pilot study of the expressive gestures used by classical orchestra conductors. In Harlan Lane & Karen Emmorey (eds.), *The signs of language revisited: An anthology to honor Ursula Bellugi and Edward Klima*, 143–167. Mahwah, NJ: Lawrence Erlbaum.

Brentari, Diane, Alessio Di Renzo, Jonathan Keane & Virginia Volterra. 2015. Cognitive, cultural, and linguistic sources of a handshape distinction expressing agentivity. *Topics in Cognitive Science* 7(1). 95–123.

Brewster, Stephen & Lorna M. Brown. 2004. Tactons: Structured tactile messages for non-visual information display. In *Proceedings of the Fifth Conference on Australasian User Interface; Volume 28*, 15–23. Sydney: Australian Computer Society, Inc.

Brower, Candace. 2000. A cognitive theory of musical meaning. *Journal of Music Theory* 44(2). 323–379.

Capirci, Olga, Jana M. Iverson, Elena Pizzuto & Virginia Volterra. 1996. Gestures and words during the transition to two-word speech. *Journal of Child Language* 23(3). 645–673.

Charland, Louis C. & Peter Zachar (eds.). 2008. *Fact and value in emotion*. Vol. 4. Amsterdam: John Benjamins.

Chen, Na, Kanji Tanaka, Daisuke Matsuyoshi, Yosuke Nagamori, Miki Namatame & Katsumi Watanabe. 2014. Color-shape association in deaf and hearing people. In *Proceedings of the 2014 6th International Conference on Knowledge and Smart Technology (KST)*, 112–115. Chonburi, Thailand: IEEE Computer Society.

Cho, Young-mee Yu. 2006. Sound symbolism in Korean. In Ho-min Sohn (ed.), *Korean language in culture and society*, 64–73. Honolulu: University of Hawaii Press.

Chrea, Christelle, Didier Grandjean, Sylvain Delplanque, Isabelle Cayeux, Bénédicte Le Calvé, Laurence Aymard, Maria Inés Velazco, David Sander & Klaus R. Scherer. 2009. Mapping the semantic space for the subjective experience of emotional responses to odors. *Chemical Senses* 34(1). 49–62.

Corina, David P. & Eva Gutierrez. 2016. Embodiment and American Sign Language. *Gesture* 15(3). 291–305.

Crisinel, Anne-Sylvie & Charles Spence. 2012. A fruity note: Crossmodal associations between odors and musical notes. *Chemical Senses* 37(2). 151–158.

Cuxac, Christian. 1999. French Sign Language: Proposition of a structural explanation by iconicity. In Annelies Braort (ed.), *Gesture-based communication in human-computer interaction*, 165–184. Berlin/Heidelberg: Springer.

Cytowic, Richard. 1989. *Synesthesia: A union of the senses*. Cambridge, MA: MIT Press.

Dematté, M. Luisa, Daniel Sanabria & Charles Spence. 2006. Cross-modal associations between odors and colors. *Chemical Senses* 31(6). 531–538.

Diessel, Holger. 2005. Competing motivations for the ordering of main and adverbial clauses. *Linguistics* 43(3). 449–470.

Dingemanse, Mark, Will Schuerman, Eva Reinisch, Sylvia Tufvesson & Holger Mitterer. 2016. What sound symbolism can and cannot do: Testing the iconicity of ideophones from five languages. *Language* 92(2). 67–83.

Doll, Theodore J. & Dennis J. Folds. 1986. Auditory signals in military aircraft: Ergonomics principles versus practice. *Applied Ergonomics* 17(4). 257–264.

Drellishak, Scott. 2006. *Statistical techniques for detecting and validating phonesthemes.* Seattle, WA MA thesis.

Duranti, Alessandro (ed.). 2009. *Linguistic anthropology: A reader.* Vol. 1. Chichester: John Wiley & Sons.

Edwards, Terra. 2012. Sensing the rhythms of everyday life: Temporal integration and tactile translation in the Seattle Deaf-Blind community. *Language in Society* 41(1). 29–71.

Ehrlich, Kate & Philip Johnson-Laird. 1982. Spatial descriptions and referential continuity. *Journal of Verbal Learning and Verbal Behavior* 21(3). 296–306.

Emmorey, Karen. 2014. Iconicity as structure mapping. *Philosophical Transactions of the Royal Society B: Biological Sciences* 369(1651). 20130301. DOI:10.1098/rstb.2013.0301

Emmorey, Karen, Thomas Grabowski, Stephen McCullough, Hanna Damasio, Laurie Ponto, Richard Hichwa & Ursula Bellugi. 2004. Motor-iconicity of sign language does not alter the neural systems underlying tool and action naming. *Brain and Language* 89(1). 27–37.

Evans, Sarah, Nick Neave & Delia Wakelin. 2006. Relationships between vocal characteristics and body size and shape in human males: An evolutionary explanation for a deep male voice. *Biological Psychology* 72(2). 160–163.

Fabisiak, Sylwia & Paweł Rutkowski. 2011. Iconicity in Polish Sign Language. In Ray Kunchev & Teresa Dobrzyńska (eds.), *Vision and cognition: Literary, linguistic and cultural aspects*, 237–257. Warsaw: Instytut Badan Literackich Polskiej Akademii Nauk (Institute of Literary Research of the Polish Academy of Sciences).

Fernald, Theodore B. & Donna Jo Napoli. 2000. Exploitation of morphological possibilities in signed languages: Comparison of American Sign Language with English. *Sign Language and Linguistics* 3(1). 3–58.

Fischer, Andreas. 1999. What, if anything, is phonological iconicity. In Olga Fischer & Max Nänny (eds.), *Form miming meaning: iconicity in language and literature*, 123–134. Amsterdam/ Philadelphia: John Benjamins.

Fox, Nathan A. & Richard J. Davidson. 1986. Taste-elicited changes in facial signs of emotion and the asymmetry of brain electrical activity in human newborns. *Neuropsychologia* 24(3). 417–422.

Friedman, Uri. 2015. How to snore in Korean: The mystery of onomatopoeia around the world. *The Atlantic*. Accessed 6 December 2016. http://www.theatlantic.com/international/archive/2015/11/onomatopoeia-world-languages/415824/.

Garrigues, Stephen L. 1995. Mimetic parallels in Korean and Japanese. *Studies in Language* 19(2). 359–398.

Gasser, Emily. in preparation. *Orange you glad I didn't say banana? Borrowed color and flora/fauna terminology in W. Papuan languages.* Manuscript, available by writing to the author. Swarthmore College.

Giorgolo, Gianluca. 2010. A formal semantics for iconic spatial gestures. In Maria Aloni, Harald Bastiaanse, Tikitu de Jager & Katrin Schulz (eds.), *Logic, language and meaning*, 305–314. Berlin/Heidelberg: Springer.

Givón, Talmy. 1989. *Mind, code and context: Essays in pragmatics*. Hillsdale, NJ: Lawrence Erlbaum Associates.

Goldin-Meadow, Susan. 1999. The role of gesture in communication and thinking. *Trends in Cognitive Sciences* 3(11). 419–429.

Goldin-Meadow, Susan. 2005. *The resilience of language: What gesture creation in deaf children can tell us about how all children learn language*. New York: Psychology Press.

Goldin-Meadow, Susan & Diane Brentari. 2015. Gesture, sign and language: The coming of age of sign language and gesture studies. *Behavioral and Brain Sciences* 39(1). 1–82.

Griffith, Penny L., Jacques H. Robinson & John H. Panagos. 1983. Tactile iconicity: Signs rated for use with deaf-blind children. *Research and Practice for Persons with Severe Disabilities* 8(2). 26–38.

Haiman, John (ed.). 1985. *Iconicity in syntax*. Amsterdam: John Benjamins.

Hall, Matthew L., Victor S. Ferreira & Rachel I. Mayberry. 2013. Investigating constituent order change with elicited pantomime: A functional account of SVO emergence. *Cognitive Science* 38(5). 943–972.

Hamano, Shoko. 1998. *The sound-symbolic system of Japanese*. Stanford CA: Center for the Study of Language & Information, Stanford University.

Hanson-Vaux, Grant, Anne-Sylvie Crisinel & Charles Spence. 2013. Smelling shapes: Crossmodal correspondences between odors and shapes. *Chemical Senses* 38(2). 161–166.

Harlow, Harry Frederick. 1959. *Love in infant monkeys*. San Francisco: WH Freeman.

Hevner, Kate. 1937. The affective value of pitch and tempo in music. *The American Journal of Psychology* 49(4). 621–630.

Hindley, Philip Colin. 2014. Nominal and imperative iconic gestures used by the Khoisan of North West Botswana to coordinate hunting. *African Study Monographs* 35(3). 149–181.

Hinton, Leanne, Johanna Nichols & John J. Ohala (eds.). 1994. *Sound symbolism*. Cambridge: Cambridge University Press.

Hock, Hans Henrich. 1986. *Principles of historical linguistics*. Berlin: Mouton de Gruyter.

Hwang, So-One, Nozomi Tomita, Hope Morgan, Rabia Ergin, Deniz İlkbaşaran, Sharon Seegers, Ryan Lepic & Carol A. Padden. 2016. Of the body and the hands: Patterned iconicity for semantic categories. *Language and Cognition*. 1–30. DOI:10.1017/langcog.2016.28

Imai, Mutsumi, Sotaro Kita, Miho Nagumo & Hiroyuko Okada. 2008. Sound symbolism facilitates early verb learning. *Cognition* 109(1). 54–65.

Ittyerah, Miriam & Dolly Mitra. 1988. Synesthetic perception in the sensorily deprived. *Psychological Studies* 33(2). 110–115.

Itô, Junko & Armin Mester. 1995. Japanese phonology. In John Goldsmith (ed.), *The handbook of phonological theory*, 817–838. Oxford: Blackwell Publishing.

Iwasaki, Noriko, Lucien Brown, Sotaro Kita & David Vinson. 2013. Japanese and Korean speakers' production of mimetic words. In Bjarke Frellesvig & Peter Sells (eds.), *Japanese/Korean linguistics, volume 30*, 199–213. Stanford, CA: CSLI.

Janis, Wynne D. 1995. A crosslinguistic perspective on ASL verb agreement. In Karen Emmorey & Judy Reilly (eds.), *Language, gesture, and space*, 195–224. Hillsdale, NJ: Lawrence Erlbaum Associates.

Jayant, Chandrika, Christine Acuario, William Johnson, Janet Hollier & Richard Ladner. 2010. V-braille: Haptic braille perception using a touch-screen and vibration on mobile phones. In *Proceedings of the 12th International ACM SIGACCESS Conference on Computers and Accessibility*, 295–296. Orlando, FL: ASSETS'10.

Jespersen, Otto. 1922. The symbolic value of the vowel i. *Philologica* 1. 1–19.

Johnson, Allen, Orna Johnson & Michael Baksh. 1986. The colors of emotions in Machiguenga. *American Anthropologist* 88(3). 674–681.

Johnson, Shersten. 2009. Notational systems and conceptualizing music: A case study of print and braille notation. *Music Theory Online* 15(3–4).

Kagitani, Tatsuki, Mao Goto, Junji Watanabe & Maki Sakamoto. 2014. Sound symbolic relationship between onomatopoeia and emotional evaluations in taste. In *Proceedings of the 36th Annual Meeting of the Cognitive Science Society*, 2871–2876.

Kahneman, Daniel, Edward Diener & Norbert Schwarz (eds.). 1999. *Well-being: Foundations of hedonic psychology*. New York: Russell Sage Foundation.

Kemp, Sarah E. & Avery N. Gilbert. 1997. Odor intensity and color lightness are correlated sensory dimensions. *American Journal of Psychology* 110(1). 35–46.

Kendon, Adam. 2004. *Gesture: Visible action as utterance*. Cambridge: Cambridge University Press.

Knapp, Mark L., Judith A. Hall & Terrence G. Horgan. 2013. *Nonverbal communication in human interaction*. 8th edn. Boston: Wadsworth Cengage Learning.

Kocab, Annemarie, Jennie Pyers & Ann Senghas. 2014. Referential shift in Nicaraguan Sign Language: A transition from lexical to spatial devices. *Frontiers in Psychology* 5. DOI:10.3389/fpsyg.2014.01540

Komissaroff, Bill. 2016. *Baseball signs: The game's secret underbelly*. Accessed 13 December 2016. https://howtheyplay.com/team-sports/Baseball-Signs-The-Games-Secret-Underbelly.

Kortmann, Bernd. 1991. *Free adjuncts and absolutes in English: Problems of control and interpretation*. London: Routledge.

Kosecki, Krzysztof. 2014. Time as a line and as a clock in signed languages: A view from cognitive linguistics. In *Practical Applications of Language Corpora Conference 2014*. Abstracted is found on *PALC 2014: Book of Abstracts*, p. 57. University of Lodz.

Kostandy, Raouth R., Susan M. Ludington-Hoe, Xiaomei Cong, Amel Abouelfettoh, Carly Bronson, Allison Stankus & Julia R. Jarrell. 2008. Kangaroo care (skin contact) reduces crying response to pain in preterm neonates: Pilot results. *Pain Management Nursing* 9(2). 55–65.

Kringelbach, Morten L. 2005. The human orbitofrontal cortex: Linking reward to hedonic experience. *Nature Reviews Neuroscience* 6(9). 691–702.

Kuhn, Jeremy & Valentina Aristodemo. 2016. Pluractionality, iconicity, and scope in French Sign Language. Accessed 15 December 2016. http://www.semanticsarchive.net/Archive/mQ4OWMyO.

Lang, Peter J. 1979. A bio-informational theory of emotional imagery. *Psychophysiology* 16(6). 495–512.

Lascarides, Alex & Matthew Stone. 2009. Discourse coherence and gesture interpretation. *Gesture* 9(2). 147–180.

Lepic, Ryan, Carl Börstell, Gal Belsitzman & Wendy Sandler. 2016. Taking meaning in hand: Iconic motivations in two-handed signs. *Sign Language and Linguistics* 19(1). 37–81.

Liddell, Scott K. 1995. Real, surrogate, and token space: Grammatical consequences in ASL. In Karen Emmorey & Judy Reilly (eds.), *Language, gesture, and space*, 19–42. Hillsdale, NJ: Erlbaum.

Liddell, Scott K. 2003. *Grammar, gesture, and meaning in American Sign Language*. Cambridge: Cambridge University Press.

Lillo-Martin, Diane & Edward S. Klima. 1990. Pointing out differences: ASL pronouns in syntactic theory. In Susan D. Fischer & Patricia Siple (eds.), *Theoretical issues in sign language research*, vol. 1, 191–210. Chicago: University of Chicago Press.

Louwerse, Max. 2008. Embodied relations are encoded in language. *Psychonomic Bulletin and Review* 15(4). 838–844.

Ludwig, Vera U. & Julia Simner. 2013. What colour does that feel? Tactile–visual mapping and the development of cross-modality. *Cortex* 49(4). 1089–1099.

Lynch, James J. 1970. Psychophysiology and development of social attachment. *The Journal of Nervous and Mental Disease* 151(4). 231–244.

Macdonald, R. Ross. 1976. *Indonesian reference grammar*. Washington, D.C.: Georgetown University Press.

Mathur, Gaurav. 2000. *Verb agreement as alignment in signed languages*. Massachusetts Institute of Technology PhD thesis.

McNeill, David. 1992. *Hand mind: What gestures reveal about thought*. Chicago: University of Chicago Press.

McNeill, David. 2000. *Language and gesture*. Cambridge: Cambridge University Press.

Meier, Richard P. 1987. Elicited imitation of verb agreement in American Sign Language: Iconically or morphologically determined? *Journal of Memory and Language* 26(3). 362–376.

Meier, Richard P. 2002. Why different, why the same? Explaining effects and non-effects of modality upon linguistic structure in sign and speech. In Richard P. Meier, Kearsy Cormier & David Quinto-Pozos (eds.), *Modality and structure in signed and spoken languages*, 1–25. Cambridge: Cambridge University Press.

Meir, Irit. 2010. Iconicity and metaphor: Constraints on metaphorical extension of iconic forms. *Language* 86(4). 865–896.

Meir, Irit, Carol Padden, Mark Aronoff & Wendy Sandler. 2013. Competing iconicities in the structure of languages. *Cognitive Linguistics* 24(2). 309–343.

Metzger, Melanie & Ben Bahan. 2001. Discourse analysis. In Ceil Lucas (ed.), *The sociolinguistics of sign languages*, 112–144. Cambridge: Cambridge University Press.

Mirus, Gene, Jami Fisher & Donna Jo Napoli. 2012. Taboo expressions in American Sign Language. *Lingua* 122(9). 1004–1020.

Mišković, Nikola, Marco Bibuli, Andreas Birk, Massimo Caccia, Murat Egi, Karl Grammer, Alessandro Marroni, Jeff Neasham, Antonio Pascoal, Antonio Vasilijević & Zoran Vukić. 2016. CADDY—Cognitive Autonomous Diving Buddy: Two years of underwater human-robot interaction. *Marine Technology Society Journal* 50(4). 54–66.

Moeser, Shannon D. 1976. Inferential reasoning in episodic memory. *Journal of Verbal Learning and Verbal Behavior* 15(2). 193–212.

Moravcsik, Edith A. 1978. Reduplicative constructions. In Joseph H. Greenberg, Charles A. Ferguson & Edith A. Moravcsik (eds.), *Universals of human language, Vol. 3: Word structure*, 297–334. Stanford, CA: Stanford University Press.

Morris, Donald & John Bransford. 1982. Effective elaboration and inferential reasoning. *Memory and Cognition* 10(2). 188–193.

Moser, Margaret G. 1990. The regularity hypothesis applied to ASL. In Ceil Lucas (ed.), *Sign language research: Theoretical issues*, 50–56. Washington, D.C.: Gallaudet University Press.

Moulton, Janice & George M. Robinson. 1981. *The organization of language*. Cambridge/New York: Cambridge University Press.

Murane, Elizabeth. 1974. *Daga grammar: From morpheme to discourse*. Vol. 43 (Summer Institute of Linguistics publications in linguistics and related fields). Norman: Summer Institute of Linguistics of the University of Oklahoma.

Napoli, Donna Jo, Jami Fisher & Gene Mirus. 2013. Bleached taboo-term predicates in American Sign Language. *Lingua* 123(1). 148–167.

Napoli, Donna Jo & Nathan Sanders. in preparation. *The Movement Parameter in the Historical Study of Sign Languages*. Manuscript, available by writing to the author. Swarthmore College.

Napoli, Donna Jo, Nathan Sanders & Rebecca Wright. 2014. On the linguistic effects of articulatory ease, with a focus on sign languages. *Language* 90(2). 424–456.

Napoli, Donna Jo & Rachel Sutton-Spence. 2010. Limitations on simultaneity in sign language. *Language* 86(3). 647–662.

Napoli, Donna Jo & Rachel Sutton-Spence. 2014. Order of the major constituents in sign languages: Implications for all language. *Frontiers in Psychology* 5. 376. DOI:10.3389/fpsyg.2014.00376

Napoli, Donna Jo, Rachel Sutton-Spence & Ronice Müller de Quadros. Forthcoming. Influence of predicate sense on sign order: Intensional and extensional verbs. *Language*.

Neidle, Carol, Judy Kegl, Dawn MacLaughlin & Benjamin Bahan. 2000. *The syntax of American Sign Language: Functional categories and hierarchical structure*. Cambridge, MA: MIT Press.

Newell, Kenneth B. 1976. *Pattern poetry: A historical critique from the Alexandrian Greeks to Dylan Thomas*. Boston, MA: Marlborough House.

Niedenthal, Paula M. 2007. Embodying emotion. *Science* 316(5827). 1002–1005.

Nuckolls, Janis. 1999. The case for sound symbolism. *Annual Review of Anthropology* 28. 225–252.

Nummenmaa, Lauri, Enrico Glerean, Riitta Hari & Jari K. Hietanen. 2014. Bodily maps of emotions. *Proceedings of the National Academy of Sciences* 111(2). 646–651.

Ortega, Gerardo & Gary Morgan. 2015. The effect of iconicity in the mental lexicon of hearing non-signers and proficient signers: Evidence of cross-modal priming. *Language, Cognition and Neuroscience* 30(5). 574–585.

Özyürek, Aslı. 2014. Hearing and seeing meaning in speech and gesture: Insights from brain and behaviour. *Philosophical Transactions of the Royal Society B: Biological Sciences* 369(1651). 20130296. DOI:10.1098/rstb.2013.0296

Pacun, David. 2009. Reflections on and some recommendations for visually impaired students. *Music Theory Online* 15(3–4).

Peirce, Charles Sanders. 1932. *Collected papers of Charles Sanders Peirce, Vol. 2: Elements of logic*. Cambridge, MA: Harvard University Press.

Perniss, Pamela, Robin L. Thompson & Gabriella Vigliocco. 2010. Iconicity as a general property of language: Evidence from spoken and signed languages. *Frontiers in Psychology* 1. 1–15.

Perniss, Pamela & Gabriella Vigliocco. 2014. The bridge of iconicity: From a world of experience to the experience of language. *Philosophical Transactions of the Royal Society B: Biological Sciences* 369(1651). 20130300.

Perniss, Pamela, Inge Zwitserlood & Aslı Özyürek. 2015. Does space structure spatial language?: a comparison of spatial expression across sign languages. *Language* 91(3). 611–641.

Pietrandrea, Paola & Tommaso Russo. 2007. Diagrammatic and imagic hypoicons in signed and verbal languages. In Elena Pizzuto, Paola Pietrandrea & Raffaele Simone (eds.), *Verbal and signed languages: Comparing structures, constructs and methodologies*, 35–56. New York/Berlin: Mouton de Gruyter.

Pizzuto, Elena, Elena Cameracanna, Serena Corazza & Virginia Volterra. 1995. Terms for spatio-temporal relations in Italian Sign Language (LIS). In Raffaele Simone (ed.), *Iconicity in language*, 237–256. Amsterdam: John Benjamins.

Pizzuto, Elena, Paolo Rossini, Marie-Anne Sallandre & Erin Wilkinson. 2008. Deixis, anaphora, and highly iconic structures: Cross-linguistic evidence on American (ASL), French (LSF), and Italian (LIS) signed languages. In Ronice Müller de Quadros (ed.), *Sign languages: Spinning and unraveling the past, present and future (TISLR9)*, 475–495. Petrópolis, Brazil: Editora Arara Azul.

Pyers, Jennie, Pamela Perniss & Karen Emmorey. 2015. Viewpoint in the visual-spatial modality: The coordination of spatial perspective. *Spatial Cognition and Computation* 15(3). 143–169.

Quinto-Pozos, David, Jenny L. Singleton, Peter C. Hauser, Susan Levine, Carrie Lou Garberoglio & Lynn Hou. 2013. Atypical signed language development: A case study of challenges with visual–spatial processing. *Cognitive Neuropsychology* 30(5). 332–359.

Ramenghi, Luca A., Gillian C. Griffith, Christopher M. Wood & Malcolm I. Levene. 1996. Effect of non-sucrose sweet tasting solution on neonatal heel prick responses. *Archives of Disease in Childhood— Fetal and Neonatal Edition* 74. 129–131. DOI:10.1136/fn.74.2.F129

Recreational Scuba Training Council, Inc. (RSTC). 2005. *Common hand signals for recreational scuba diving.* http://www.neadc.org/CommonHandSignalsforScubaDiving.pdf.

Roberts, Gareth, Jirka Lewandowski & Bruno Galantucci. 2015. How communication changes when we cannot mime the world: Experimental evidence for the effect of iconicity on combinatoriality. *Cognition* 141. 52–66.

Roush, Daniel R. 2016. The expression of the location event-structure metaphor in American Sign Language. *Sign Language Studies* 16(3). 389–432.

Rudrauf, David, Jean-Philippe Lachaux, Antonio Damasio, Sylvain Baillet, Laurent Hugueville, Jacques Martinerie, Hanna Damasio & Bernard Renault. 2009. Enter feelings: Somatosensory responses following early stages of visual induction of emotion. *International Journal of Psychophysiology* 72(1). 13–23.

Russo, Tommaso. 2004. Iconicity and productivity in sign language discourse: An analysis of three LIS discourse registers. *Sign Language Studies* 4(2). 164–197.

Salminen, Katri, Veikko Surakka, Jukka Raisamo, Jani Lylykangas, Roope Raisamo, Kalle Mäkelä & Teemu Ahmaniemi. 2013. Cold or hot? How thermal stimuli are related to human emotional system. In Ian Oakley & Stephen Brewster (eds.), *International workshop on haptic and audio interaction design,* 20–29. Berlin/Heidelberg: Springer.

Sanders, Nathan & Donna Jo Napoli. 2016a. A cross-linguistic preference for torso stability in the lexicon: Evidence from 24 sign languages. *Sign Language and Linguistics* 19(2).

Sanders, Nathan & Donna Jo Napoli. 2016b. Reactive effort as a factor that shapes sign language lexicons. *Language* 92(2). 275–297.

Sanford, Anthony & Simon Garrod. 1981. *Understanding written language: Explorations of comprehension beyond the sentence.* Chichester: John Wiley & Sons.

Sapir, Edward. 1929. A study of phonetic symbolism. *Journal of Experimental Psychology* 12. 225–239.

Schlenker, Philippe. 2016. *Visible meaning: Sign language and the foundations of semantics.* Accessed 14 December 2016. Institut Jean-Nicod & New York University. http://ling.auf.net/lingbuzz/002447.

Schlenker, Philippe, Jonathan Lamberton & Mirko Santoro. 2013. Iconic variables. *Linguistics and Philosophy* 36(2). 91–149.

Schneider, Elaine Fogel. 1996. The power of touch: Massage for infants. *Infants and Young Children* 8(3). 40–55.

Sel, Alejandra, Bettina Forster & Beatriz Calvo-Merino. 2014. The emotional homunculus: ERP evidence for independent somatosensory responses during facial emotional processing. *The Journal of Neuroscience* 34(9). 3263–3267.

Simner, Julia & Vera U. Ludwig. 2012. The color of touch: A case of tactile–visual synaesthesia. *Neurocase* 18(2). 167–180.

Spence, Charles. 2012. Managing sensory expectations concerning products and brands: Capitalizing on the potential of sound and shape symbolism. *Journal of Consumer Psychology* 22(1). 37–54.

Stanfield, Robert & Rolf Zwaan. 2001. The effect of implied orientation derived from verbal context on picture recognition. *Psychological Science* 12(2). 153–156.

Stein, Barry E. & Terrence R. Stanford. 2008. Multisensory intergration: Current issues from the perspective of the single neuron. *Nature Reviews Neuroscience* 9(4). 255–266.

Streeck, Jürgen. 2009. *Gesturecraft: The manu-facture of meaning*. Amsterdam: John Benjamins.

Strickland, Brent, Carlo Geraci, Emmanuel Chemla, Philippe Schlenker, Meltem Kelepir & Roland Pfau. 2015. Event representations constrain the structure of language: Sign language as a window into universally accessible linguistic biases. *Proceedings of the National Academy of Sciences* 112(19). 5968–5973.

Sutton-Spence, Rachel & Penny Boyes Braem. 2013. Comparing the products and the processes of creating sign language poetry and pantomimic improvisations. *Journal of Nonverbal Behavior* 37(4). 245–280.

Sutton-Spence, Rachel & Michiko Kaneko. 2016. *Introducing sign language literature*. London: Palgrave.

Sutton-Spence, Rachel & Donna Jo Napoli. 2009. *Humour in sign languages: The linguistic underpinnings*. Dublin: Centre for Deaf Studies at Trinity College Dublin.

Sutton-Spence, Rachel & Donna Jo Napoli. 2010. Anthropomorphism in sign languages: A look at poetry and storytelling with a focus on British Sign Language. *Sign Language Studies* 10(4). 442–475.

Sutton-Spence, Rachel & Donna Jo Napoli. 2013. How much can classifiers be analogous to their referents? *Gesture* 13(1). 1–27.

Taub, Sarah F. 2001. *Language from the body: Iconicity and metaphor in American Sign Language*. Cambridge: Cambridge University Press.

Taylor, Insup Kim. 1963. Phonetic symbolism re-examined. *Psychological Bulletin* 60. 200–209.

Tomaszewski, Piotr. 2006. From iconicity to arbitrariness: How do gestures become signs in peer-group pidgin. *Psychology of Language and Communication* 10(2). 27–59.

Tumtavitikul, Apiluck, Chirapa Niwatapant & Philipp Dill. 2009. Classifiers in Thai Sign Language. *SKASE Journal of Theoretical Linguistics [online]* 9. 27–44.

Vermeerbergen, Myriam. 2006. Past and current trends in sign language research. *Language and Communication* 26(2). 168–192.

Vermeerbergen, Myriam, Lorraine Leeson & Onno A. Crasborn (eds.). 2007. *Simultaneity in signed languages: Form and function*. Vol. 281. Amsterdam: John Benjamins.

Vigliocco, Gabriella, Pamela Perniss & David Vinson. 2014. Language as a multimodal phenomenon: Implications for language learning, processing and evolution. *Philosophical Transactions of the Royal Society B: Biological Sciences* 369(1651). DOI:10.1098/rstb.2013.0292

Vinson, David, Robin L. Thompson, Robert Skinner & Gabriella Vigliocco. 2015. A faster path between meaning and form? Iconicity facilitates sign recognition and production in British Sign Language. *Journal of Memory and Language* 82(1). 56–85.

Voeltz, F. K. Erhard & Christa Kilian-Hatz (eds.). 2001. *Ideophones*. Amsterdam: John Benjamins.

Ward, Jamie, Michael J. Banissy & Clare N. Jonas. 2008. Haptic perception and synaesthesia. In Martin Grunwald (ed.), *Human haptic perception: Basics and applications*, 259–265. Basel: Birkhäuser.

Washington, Jonathan. in preparation. *An assessment of the Split Margin Approach: Kazakh syllable margin phonology*. Manuscript, available by writing to the author. Swarthmore College.

Werner, Heinz & Seymour Wapner. 1952. Toward a general theory of perception. *Psychological Review* 59(4). 324–38.

Wertheimer, Michael. 1958. The relation between the sound of a word and its meaning. *The American Journal of Psychology* 71(2). 412–415.

Wilbur, Ronnie B. 2003. Representations of telicity in ASL. *Chicago Linguistic Society* 39. 354–368.

Wilbur, Ronnie B. 2008. Complex predicates involving events, time and aspect: Is this why sign languages look so similar? In Josep Quer (ed.), *Signs of the time*, 217–250. Hamburg: Signum.

Wilcox, Phyllis Perrin. 2000. *Metaphor in American Sign Language*. Washington, D.C.: Gallaudet University Press.

Woll, Bencie. 2003. Modality, universality and the similarities among sign languages: An historical perspective. In Ann E. Baker, Beppie van den Bogaerde & Onno Crasborn (eds.), *Crosslinguistic perspectives in sign language research: Selected papers from TISLR 2000*, 17–31. Hamburg: Signum Press.

Woll, Bencie. 2009. How the brain processes language in different modalities. In Anna Esposito, Amir Hussain, Maria Marinaro & Raffaele Martone (eds.), *Multimodal signals: Cognitive and algorithmic issues*, 145–163. Berlin/Heidelberg: Springer.

Yaxley, Richard & Rolf Zwaan. 2007. Simulating visibility during language comprehension. *Cognition* 105(1). 229–236.

Zeshan, Ulrike. 2015. "Making meaning": Communication between sign language users without a shared language. *Cognitive Linguistics* 26(2). 211–260.

Zwaan, Rolf. 1993. *Aspects of literary comprehension*. Amsterdam: John Benjamins.

Zwaan, Rolf, Robert Stanfield & Richard Yaxley. 2002. Do language comprehenders routinely represent the shapes of objects? *Psychological Science* 13. 168–171.

Zwaan, Rolf & Richard Yaxley. 2003. Spatial iconicity affects semantic relatedness judgments. *Psychonomic Bulletin and Review* 10(4). 954–958.

Chapter 25

Where, if anywhere, are parameters? A critical historical overview of parametric theory

Frederick J. Newmeyer
University of Washington, University of British Columbia, and Simon Fraser University

> Since the late 1970s, crosslinguistic variation has generally been handled by means of UG-specified parameters. On the positive side, thinking of variation in terms of parameterized principles unleashed an unprecedented amount of work in comparative syntax, leading to the discovery of heretofore unknown morphosyntactic phenomena and crosslinguistic generalizations pertaining to them. On the negative side, however, both macroparameters and microparameters have proven themselves to be empirically inadequate and conceptually nonminimalist. Alternatives to parameters are grounded approaches, epigenetic approaches, and reductionist approaches, the last two of which seem both empirically and conceptually quite promising.

1 Introduction

The existence of crosslinguistic variation has always been problematic for syntacticians. If there is a universal grammar, one might ask, then why aren't all languages exactly the same? In the earliest work in generative syntax, characterizing the space in which languages could differ, whether at the surface or at a deep level, was not a priority. At the time, surface differences between languages and dialects were generally attributed to language-particular rules or filters.

In the late 1970s, however, a strategy was developed that allowed the simultaneous development of a rich theory of Universal Grammar (UG) along with a detailed account of the limits of crosslinguistic morphosyntactic variation. In this view, syntactic complexity results from the interaction of grammatical subsystems, each characterizable in terms of its own set of general principles. The central goal of syntactic theory now became to identify such systems and to characterize the degree to which they might vary (be "parameterized") from language to language. Chomsky (1995) describes succinctly

Frederick J. Newmeyer. 2017. Where, if anywhere, are parameters? A critical historical overview of parametric theory. In Claire Bowern, Laurence Horn & Raffaella Zanuttini (eds.), *On looking into words (and beyond)*, 547–569. Berlin: Language Science Press. DOI:10.5281/zenodo.495465

how such variation might be accounted for in what, by the early 1980s, was called the "principles-and-parameters" (P&P) approach.

> Within the P&P approach the problems of typology and language variation arise in somewhat different form than before. Language differences and typology should be reducible to choice of values of parameters. A major research problem is to determine just what these options are, and in what components of language they are to be found. (Chomsky 1995: 6)

The first mention of parameters, I believe, was in Chomsky (1976):

> Even if conditions are language- or rule-particular, there are limits to the possible diversity of grammar. Thus, such conditions can be regarded as parameters that have to be fixed (for the language, or for the particular rules, in the worst case), in language learning ... It has often been supposed that conditions on applications of rules must be quite general, even universal, to be significant, but that need not be the case if establishing a "parameteric" condition permits us to reduce substantially the class of possible rules. (Chomsky 1976: 315)

An interesting question is why Chomsky at this point would propose parameters, since there is nothing in his 1976 paper that suggests that they need to be incorporated into the theory. A possible answer is that in the same year an MIT dissertation appeared (Kim 1976) that showed that Korean obeys a form of the Tensed-S-Condition, even though Korean does not distinguish formally between tensed and non-tensed clauses. That fact might have planted the seed for the idea of parameterized principles. At around the same time, an "external" inspiration for parameters was provided by the work of Jacques Monod and François Jacob (Monod 1972; "Darwinism reconsidered"). Their idea was that slight differences in timing and arrangement of regulatory mechanisms that activate genes could result in enormous differences. Berwick & Chomsky (2011: 28) has claimed that "Jacob's model in turn provided part of the inspiration for the Principles and Parameters (P&P) approach to language ..."

Whatever the direct inspiration for parameterized principles might have been, their adoption triggered an unprecedented explosion of work in comparative syntax. One unquestionably positive consequence of the P&P approach to linguistic theory was to spur investigation of a wide variety of languages, particularly those with structures markedly different from some of the more familiar Western ones. The explanation for this is straightforward. In earlier transformational grammar (oversimplifying somewhat), one worked on the grammar of English, the grammar of Thai, the grammar of Cherokee, and so on, and attempted to extract universal properties of grammars from the principles one found in common among these constructed grammars. But now the essential unity of all grammars, within the limits of parametric variation, was taken as a starting point. One could not even begin to address the grammar of some language without asking the question of how principles of Case, binding, bounding, and so on are parameterized in that language. And that in turn demanded that one have a rough feel for the degree of parameterization possible for the principle. As Chomsky noted, to delimit the domain of core grammar, we "rely heavily on grammar-internal considerations and comparative evidence, that is, on the possibilities for constructing a reasonable theory of UG and considering its explanatory power in a variety of language types, with an eye open to the eventual possibility of adducing evidence of other kinds" (Chomsky 1981: 9).

The core idea of the P&P approach is that both the principles of UG and the possible parameter settings are part of our genetic endowment:

> [W]hat we "know innately" are the principles of the various subsystems of S_0 [= the initial state of the language faculty – FJN] and the manner of their interaction, and the parameters associated with these principles. What we learn are the values of these parameters and the elements of the periphery (along with the lexicon, to which similar considerations apply). The language that we then know is a system of principles with parameters fixed, along with a periphery of marked exceptions. (Chomsky 1986: 150–151)

The original idea was that there are a small number of parameters and small number of settings. This idea allowed two birds to be killed with one stone. Parametric theory could explain the rapidity of acquisition, given the poor input, and explain the crosslinguistic distribution of grammatical elements. As Norbert Hornstein noted:

> The second reason in favor of parameter setting models has been their ability to provide (at least in principle) an answer to Plato's Problem [the fact that we know so much about language based on so little direct evidence – FJN]. The idea is that construing language acquisition as parameter setting eases the problem faced by the child, for setting parameter values is easier than learning the myriad possible rules of one's native language. In other words, the PLD [= Primary Linguistic Data – FJN] can be mined for parameter values more easily than it can be for rules. (Hornstein 2009: 165)

The need to base a theory of parametric variation on the investigation of a wide variety of languages resulted in what Bernard Comrie, always a major critic of the generative approach, referred to approvingly as "one of the most interesting recent developments in linguistic typology ... the entry of generative syntax into the field" (Comrie 1988: 458). Comparative studies of the distribution of null-subjects, binding domains, configurationality, and so on became routine by the 1980s and provided a generative interpretation of the kind of crosslinguistic typological studies that were initiated by the work of Joseph Greenberg. In this regard, it is instructive to observe Chomsky's changing rhetorical evaluation of Greenbergian typological work. His first reference to Greenberg was somewhat dismissive, noting that "Insofar as attention is restricted to surface structures, the most that can be expected is the discovery of statistical tendencies, such as those presented by Greenberg (1963)" (Chomsky 1965: 118). In 1981, Chomsky offered what was perhaps his first favorable reference to this line of research:

> Universals of the sort explored by Joseph Greenberg and others have obvious relevance to determining just which properties of the lexicon have to be learned in this

manner in particular grammars – and to put it in other terms just how much has to be learned as grammar develops in the course of language acquisition. (Chomsky 1981: 95)

By 1982 he was writing that "Greenbergian universals ... are ultimately going to be very rich. ... They have all the difficulties that people know, they are "surfacy," they are statistical, and so on and so forth, but nevertheless they are very suggestive" (Chomsky 1982: 111). And in 1986, they are "important, ... yielding many generalizations that require explanation ..." (Chomsky 1986: 21).

In this paper, I do not question the fertility of the research program that was launched by the P&P approach. What I do is to provide a critical review of the various approaches that have been taken to parameters since the late 1970s, discussing their *conceptual* strengths and weaknesses. Given space limitations, my overview will in places be unavoidably somewhat superficial. The paper is organized as follows. Sections 2 through 5 outline various approaches that have been taken with respect to parameters: UG-principle-based, microparametric, macroparametric, and interface-based, respectively. Some of the major conceptual and empirical problems with the classical view of parameters are outlined in §6, and §7 discusses alternatives to the classical approach. §8 is a brief conclusion.

2 Parameterized UG principles

All of the subsystems of principles in the Government-Binding Theory were assumed to be parameterized. Consider a few concrete examples:

(1) Examples of parameterized UG principles:
    a. BINDING (Lasnik 1991). Principle C is parameterized to allow for sentences of the form *John$_i$ thinks that John$_i$ is smart* in languages like Thai and Vietnamese.
    b. GOVERNMENT (Manzini & Wexler 1987). The notion "Governing Category" is defined differently in different languages.
    c. BOUNDING (Rizzi 1982). In English, NP and S are bounding nodes for Subjacency, in Italian NP and S'.
    d. X-BAR ("Origins of phrase structure"). In English, heads precede their complements; in Japanese heads follow their complements.
    e. CASE and THETA-THEORY (Travis 1989). Some languages assign Case and/or Theta-roles to the left, some to the right.

Fewer and fewer parameterized UG principles have been proposed in recent years for the simple reason that there are fewer and fewer widely accepted UG principles. The thrust of the Minimalist Program (MP) has been to reduce the narrow syntactic component and to reinterpret broad universal principles as economy effects of efficient computation. Economy principles are generally assumed not to be parameterized:

> There is simply no way for principles of efficient computation to be parameterized [...], it strikes me as implausible to entertain the possibility that a principle like "Shortest Move" could be active in some languages, but not in others. Put differently, [...] there can be no parameters within the statements of the general principles that shape natural language syntax. (Boeckx 2011: 210)

On the same page Boeckx proposes the "Strong Uniformity Thesis": Principles of narrow syntax are not subject to parameterization; nor are they affected by lexical parameters.

It should be noted that the very idea of looking for principles of UG has fallen into disrepute in recent years. For example, Chomsky has attributed to them what can only be described as negative qualities:

> [T]ake the LCA (Linear Correspondence Axiom) [Kayne 1994]. If that theory is true, then the phrase structure is just more complicated. Suppose you find out that government is really an operative property. Then the theory is more complicated. If ECP really works, well, too bad; language is more like the spine [i.e., poorly designed – FJN] than like a snowflake [i.e., optimally designed]. (Chomsky 2002: 136)

So if in theory there are very few UG principles and no parameters associated with them, then the question is where and how to capture systematic crosslinguistic variation. Given the organization of grammars in a P&P-type model, the simplest assumption to make is that one group of languages contains a particular feature attraction mechanism that another group lacks, thus allowing the presence or absence of this mechanism to divide languages into typological classes. Some early examples can be illustrated by whether or not a feature setting determines whether V moves to I in a particular language (Emonds 1978; Pollock 1989), whether V moves to C (to derive V2 order) (Besten 1977), and whether N incorporates into V (Baker 1988).

A major debate within parametric theory has centered on the host of the attracting feature. In "microparametric" approaches, the locus of variation lies in individual functional heads. "Macroparametric" approaches are not so restricted. They will be discussed in §3 and §4 respectively.

3 The Borer-Chomsky Conjecture and microparametric approaches

Hagit Borer, in *Parametric Syntax* (Borer 1984), made two proposals, which she may or may not have regarded as variants of each other. One is that parameters are restricted to the idiosyncratic properties of lexical items, the other that they are restricted to the inflectional system. Borer wrote:

> ...interlanguage variation would be restricted to the idiosyncratic properties of lexical items. These idiosyncrasies, which are clearly learned, would then interact with general principles of UG in a particular way. (Borer 1984: 2–3)

By way of example, she discussed a rule that inserts a preposition in Lebanese Arabic – a rule that does not exist in Hebrew:

(2) ø ------> *la* / [$_{PP}$ ... NP]

Along the same lines, Manzini & Wexler (1987) pointed to language-particular anaphors that have to be associated with parameters: *cakicasin* and *caki* in Korean; *sig* and *hann* in Icelandic.

Now every language has thousands of lexical items, but nobody ever entertained the possibility that every lexical item might be a locus for parametric variation. Borer's proposal that only inflectional elements provide the locus for parametric variation was designed to forestall this possibility. In the same book she wrote:

> It is worth concluding this chapter by reiterating the conceptual advantage that reduced all interlanguage variation to the properties of the inflectional system. The inventory of inflectional rules and of grammatical formatives in any given language is idiosyncratic and learned on the basis of input data. (Borer 1984: 29)

The restriction of parameters to the inflectional system is a somewhat different proposal than their restriction to lexical items. After all, not all lexical items are part of the inflectional system and not all inflections are lexical. However, Borer took "inflectional" in a pretty broad sense, namely, to encompass Case and agreement relations, theta-role assignment, and so on. She recognized an immediate problem here: Inflection-based parameters could not handle some of the best known cases of crosslinguistic variation such as differences in head-order and extraction possibilities.

In any event, the hypothesis that the locus of parametric variation is restricted to exclude major lexical categories came to be known as the "Borer-Chomsky Conjecture".

Borer (1984) appeared before the distinction between lexical and functional categories had been elaborated. Once this distinction had become well accepted, it seemed natural to associate parameters with functional heads, rather than with inflectional items. This idea was first proposed as The Functional Parameterization Hypothesis (FPH) in Fukui (1988). In this view, only functional elements in the lexicon (that is, elements such as Complementizer, Agreement, Tense, etc.) are subject to parametric variation.[1]

It is important to stress that FPH is not a simple extension of the idea that parameters are inflection-located. There have been countless functional categories proposed that have nothing to do with inflection, no matter how broadly this concept is interpreted. So adverbs, topic, focus, and so on are typically thought to be housed in functional categories, even though they are not in many languages "inflectional".

Associating parameters with functional heads has been claimed to have both methodological and theoretical advantages. Methodologically, it allows "experiments" to be constructed comparing two closely-related variants, thereby pinpointing the possible degree of variation. The ideal situation then would be to compare speech varieties that differ from each other only in terms of (most ideally) one or, failing that, only a few variables. Richard Kayne remarks:

---

[1] Fukui himself exempted ordering restrictions from this hypothesis.

> If it were possible to experiment on languages, a syntactician would construct an experiment of the following type: take a language, alter a single one of its observable syntactic properties, examine the result and see what, if any, other property has changed as a consequence. If some property has changed, conclude that it and the property that was altered are linked to one another by some abstract parameter. Although such experiments cannot be performed, I think that by examining pairs (and larger sets) of ever more closely related languages, one can begin to approximate the results of such an experiment. To the extent that one can find languages that are syntactically extremely similar to one another, yet clearly distinguishable and readily examinable, one can hope to reach a point such that the number of observable differences is so small that one can virtually see one property covarying with another. (Kayne 2000: 5–6)

In other words, in Kayne's view, this "microparametric variation" (as he called it) is the best testing ground for the hypothesis that syntactic variation can be reduced to a finite set of parameters.

Along more theoretical lines, it has been claimed that functional-category-situated microparameters impose a strong limit on what can vary, crosslinguistic differences now being reduced to differences in features, thereby restricting learning to the lexicon (Kayne 2000; Roberts 2010; Thornton & Crain 2013).[2] Indeed, Chomsky has often asserted that microparameters are necessary in order to solve Plato's Problem:

> Apart from lexicon, [the set of possible human languages] is a finite set, surprisingly; in fact, a one-membered set if parameters are in fact reducible to lexical properties [associated with functional categories – FJN] … How else could Plato's problem be resolved? (Chomsky 1991: 26)

4 Macroparameters

Not all minimalists have embraced the Borer-Chomsky Conjecture and consequent turn to microparameters. Mark Baker, in particular, while not denying that there are micro-level points of variation between languages, has defended what he calls "macroparameters" (Baker 1996), that is, parametric differences that cannot be localized in simple differences in attracting features of individual functional heads. He gives as examples, among others, the Head Directionality Parameter (i.e. VO vs. OV), where functional categories play no obvious role, the Polysynthesis Parameter, which in his account refers to the lexical category "Verb", and an agreement parameter (Baker 2008) distinguishing Niger-Congo languages from Indo-European languages, which, in opposition to a strong interpretation of the Borer-Chomsky Conjecture, applies to the full range of functional categories. Another example of a macroparameter is the compounding parameter of Snyder (2001: 328), which divides languages into those that allow formation of endocentric

---

[2] As an anonymous reviewer points out, this claim is highly dependent on the nature of the features and the role that they play in the system.

compounds during the syntactic derivation and those that do not. The NP/DP macroparameter of Bošković & Gajewski (2011) distinguishes "NP languages", which lack articles, permit left-branch extraction and scrambling, but disallow NEG-raising, from "DP languages", which can have articles, disallow left-branch extraction and scrambling, but allow NEG-raising. And Huang (2007) points to many features that distinguish Chinese-type languages from English-type languages, including a generalized classifier system, no plural morphology, extensive use of light verbs, no agreement, tense, or case morphology, no overt *wh*-movement, and radical pro-drop.

Baker and other advocates of macroparameters share the conviction long held by advocates of holistic typology that languages can be partitioned into macro-scope broad classes, typically (or, at least, ideally) where the setting of one feature entails a cascade of shared typological properties. As Baker puts it, "the macroparametric view is that there are at least a few simple (not composite) parameters that define typologically distinct sorts of languages" (Baker 2008: 355).

5 Parameters as being stated at the interfaces

Under the perspective that parameters are stated at the interfaces, lexical items are subject to a process of generalized late insertion of semantic, formal, and morphophonological features after the syntax, which is where all variation would take place. Or, as another possibility, the parametric differences would derive from the way in which such features are interpreted by the interfaces or by processes that manipulate the features on the path from spell out to the interfaces. There has been some debate as to whether there is parametric variation at the Conceptual-Intentional (C-I) interface. Angel Gallego remarks:

> ... it would be odd for semantic features to be a source of variation, which leaves us with formal and morphophonological features as more likely suspects. ... Considered together, the observations by Chomsky (2001) and Kayne (2005; 2008) appear to place variation in the morphophonological manifestation of closed classes (i.e. functional categories, which contain unvalued features)." (Gallego 2011: 543–544)

However, for Ramchand & Svenonius (2008) the narrow syntax provides a "basic skeleton" to C-I, but languages vary in terms of how much their lexical items explicitly encode about the reference of variables like T, Asp, and D.

6 Conceptual and empirical problems with parameters

Before moving on to nonparametric approaches to variation, it would be useful to highlight some of the main problems with the classic view of parameters as being innately-provided grammatical constructs (for an earlier discussion, see Newmeyer 2005).

6.1 No macroparameter has come close to working

The promise of parameters in general and macroparameters in particular is that from the interaction of a small number of simply-stated parameters, the vast complexity of human language morphosyntax might be derived. As Martin Haspelmath put it:

> According to the principles and parameters vision, it should be possible at some point to describe the syntax of a language by simply specifying the settings of all syntactic parameters of Universal Grammar. We would no longer have any need for thick books with titles like *The Syntax of Haida* (cf. Enrico 2003's 1300-page work), and instead we would have a simple two-column table with the parameters in the first column and the positive or negative settings in the second column. (Haspelmath 2008: 80)

Needless to say, nothing remotely like that has been achieved. The problem is that "few of the implicational statements at the heart of the traditional Principles-and-Parameters approach have stood the test of time" (Boeckx 2011: 216). The clustering effects are simply not very robust. The two most-studied macroparameters, I believe, are the Null Subject (Pro-drop) and the Subjacency parameters, neither of which is much evoked in recent work. As for the former: "History has not been kind to to the Pro-drop Parameter as originally stated" (Baker 2008: 352). And Luigi Rizzi notes that "In retrospect, [subjacency effects] turned out to be a rather peripheral kind of variation. Judgments are complex, graded, affected by many factors, difficult to compare across languages, and in fact this kind of variation is not easily amenable to the general format of parameters ..." (Rizzi 2014: 16).

6.2 "Microparameter" is just another word for "language-particular rule"

Let's say that we observe two Italian dialects, one with a *do*-support-like structure and one without. We could posit a microparametric difference between the dialects, perhaps hypothesizing that one contains an attracting feature that leads to *do*-support and one that does not. But how would such an hypothesis differ in substance from saying that one dialect has a rule of *do*-support that the other one lacks? Indeed, Norbert Hornstein has stressed that "microparameter" is just another words for "rule":[3]

> Last of all, if parameters are stated in the lexicon (the current view), then parametric differences reduce to whether a given language contains a certain lexical item or not. As the lexicon is quite open ended, even concerning functional items as a glance at current cartographic work makes clear, the range of variation between grammars/languages is also open ended. In this regard it is not different from a rule-based approach in that both countenance the possibility that there is no bound on the possible differences between languages. (Hornstein 2009: 165)

---

[3] See Rizzi (2014: 22–27) for a defense of the idea that microparameters are not merely rules under a different name and Boeckx (2014) for a reply to Rizzi.

Michal Starke has made a similar observation:

> Thirty years ago, if some element moved in one language but not in another, a movement rule would be added to one language but not to the other. Today, a feature "I want to move" ("EPP', "strength', etc.) is added to the elements of one language but not of the other. In both cases (and in all attempts between them), variation is expressed by stipulating it. Instead of a theory, we have brute force markers. (Starke 2014: 140)

6.3 There would have to be hundreds, if not thousands, of parameters

Tying parameters to functional categories was a strong conjecture in the 1980s, since there were so few generally recognized functional categories at the time. There were so few, in fact, that it was easy to believe that only a small number of parameters would be needed. Pinker (1994: 112), for example, speculated that there are just "a few mental switches'. Lightfoot (1999: 259) suggested that there are about 30 to 40 parameters. For Adger (2003: 16), "There are only a few parameters'. Roberts & Holmberg (2005) increased the presumed total to between 50 and 100. Fodor (2001: 734) was certainly correct when she observed that "it is standardly assumed that there are fewer parameters than there are possible rules in a rule-based framework; otherwise, it would be less obvious that the amount of learning to be done is reduced in a parametric framework'. At this point in time, many hundreds of parameters have been proposed. Gianollo, Guardiano & Longobardi (2008) propose 47 parameters for DP alone on the basis of 24 languages, only five of which are non-Indo-European, and in total representing only 3 families. Longobardi & Guardiano (2011) up the total to 63 binary parameters in DP. As Cedric Boeckx has stressed: "It is not at all clear that the exponential growth of parameters that syntacticians are willing to entertain is so much better a situation for the learner than a model without parameters at all" (Boeckx 2014: 157).

One way to circumvent this problem would be to posit nonparametric differences among languages, thereby maintaining the possibility of a small number of parameters. Let us examine this idea now.

6.4 Nonparametric differences among languages undercut the entire parametric program

Are all morphosyntactic differences among languages due to differences in parameter setting? Generally that has been assumed not to be the case. Charles Yang was expressing mainstream opinion when he wrote that "... it seems highly unlikely that all possibilities of language variation are innately specified ...' (Yang 2011: 191). From the beginning of the parameteric program it has been assumed that some features are extraparametric. Outside of (parametrically relevant) core grammar are:

> ... borrowings, historical residues, inventions, and so on, which we can hardly expect to – and indeed would not want to – incorporate within a principled theory

of UG. ... How do we delimit the domain of core grammar as distinct from marked periphery? ... [We] rely heavily on grammar-internal considerations and comparative evidence, that is, on the possibilities for constructing a reasonable theory of UG and considering its explanatory potential in a variety of language types ... (Chomsky 1981: 8–9)

In other words, some language-particular features are products of extraparametric language-particular rules. Consider, for example, the treatment of Hixkaryana in Baker (2001), based on an earlier proposal in Kayne (1994). This language for the most part manifests OVS word order:

(3) Hixkaryana (Derbyshire 1985)
Kanawa yano toto
canoe took person
'The man took the canoe.'

One's first thought might be that what is needed is a parameter allowing for OVS order. But in fact Baker rejects the idea that a special word order parameter is involved here. Rather, he argues that Hixkaryana is (parametrically) SOV and allows the fronting of VP by a movement rule:

(4) S[OV] → [OV]S

In other words, in this account word order is determined *both* by a parameter and a language-specific rule.

It is quite implausible that every syntactic difference between languages and dialects results from a difference in parameter settings. Consider the fact that there are several dozen systematic morphosyntactic differences between the Norfolk dialect and standard British English (Trudgill 2003), most of which appear to be analytically independent. If each were to be handled by a difference in parameter setting, then, extrapolating to all of the syntactic distinctions in the world's languages, there would have to be thousands – if not millions – of parameters. That is obviously an unacceptable conclusion from an evolutionary standpoint, given that the set of parameters and their possible settings is, by hypothesis, innate. Furthermore, many processes that can hardly be described as "marginal" have been assumed to apply in PF syntax (where the standard view, I believe, is that parameters are not at work), including extraposition and scrambling (Chomsky 1995); object shift (Holmberg 1999; Erteschik-Shir 2005); head movements (Boeckx & Stjepanovic 2001); the movement deriving V2 order (Chomsky 2001); linearization (i.e. VO vs. OV) (Chomsky 1995; Takano 1996; Fukui & Takano 1998; Uriagereka 1999); and even *Wh*-movement (Erteschik-Shir 2005).

I think that it is fair to say that, after 35 years of investigation, nobody has a clear idea about which syntactic differences should be considered parametric and which should not be.[4] But one thing seems clear: If learners need to learn rules anyway, very little is gained by positing parameters.

---

[4] But see Smith & Law (2009) for an interesting discussion of criteria for distinguishing parametric and nonparametric differences.

6.5 Parametric theory is arguably inherently unminimalist

There are a number of ways that the assumptions of the Minimalist Program have entailed a rethinking of parameters and the division of labor among the various components for the handling of variation. In one well-known formulation, "FLN [= the faculty of language in the narrow sense – FJN] comprises only the core computational mechanisms of recursion as they appear in narrow syntax and the mapping to the interfaces' (Hauser, Chomsky & Fitch 2002: 1573). Where might parameters fit into such a scenario? In one view, "… if minimalists are right, there cannot be any parameterized principles, and the notion of parametric variation must be rethought.' (Boeckx 2011: 206). That is, given that the main thrust of the minimalist program is the reduction to the greatest extent possible of the elements of UG, there would seem to be no place for innately-specified parameters.

Despite the above, a great deal of work within the general envelope of the MP is still devoted to fleshing out parameters, whether micro or macro. For example, Yang (2011: 202–203) writes that "a finite space of parameters or constraints is still our best bet on the logical problem of language acquisition'. Note also that in many approaches, "the mapping to the interfaces' encompasses a wide variety of operations. To give one example, "UG makes available a set **F** of features (linguistic properties) and operations C_{HL} … that access F to generate expressions" (Chomsky 2000: 100). In addition to features and the relevant operations on them, minimalists have attributed to the narrow syntax principles governing agreement, labelling, transfer, probes, goals, deletion, and economy principles such as Last Resort, Relativized Minimality (or Minimize Chain Links), and Anti-Locality. None of these fall out from recursion *per se*, but rather represent conditions that underlie it or that need to be imposed on it. To that we can add the entire set of mechanisms pertaining to phases, including what nodes count for phasehood and the various conditions that need to be imposed on their functioning, like the Phase Impenetrability Condition. And then there is the categorial inventory (lexical and functional), as well as the formal features they manifest. The question, still unresolved, is whether any of these principles, conditions, and substantive universals could be parameterized, in violation of the Strong Uniformity Thesis, but not of weaker proposals. If so, that would seem to allow for parametric variation to be manifested in the journey towards the interfaces.

7 Alternatives to the classic Principles-and-Parameters model

Chomsky (2005) refers to "the three factors in language design', namely, genetic endowment, experience, and principles not specific to the faculty of language. The last-named "third factor explanations', which include principles of data analysis and efficient computation, among other things, provide a potential alternative to the nonminimalist poliferation of parameters and their settings.[5]

The following subsections discuss alternatives to the classic P&P model, all appealing to one degree or another to third factor explanations. They are grounded approaches (§7.1), epigenetic (or emergentist) approaches (§7.2), and reductionist approaches (§7.3).

7.1 Grounded approaches

A grounded approach is one in which some principle of UG is grounded in – that is, ultimately derived from – some third factor principle. Along these lines, a long tradition points to a particular constraint, often an island constraint, and posits that it is a grammaticalized processing principle. One of the first publications to argue for grounded constraints was Fodor (1978), where two island constraints are posited, one of which is the Nested Dependency Constraint (NDC):

(5) The Nested Dependency Constraint: If there are two or more filler-gap dependencies in the same sentence, their scopes may not intersect if either disjoint or nested dependencies are compatible with the well-formedness conditions of the language.

As Fodor noted, the processing-based origins of this constraint seem quite straightforward.

Another example is the Final Over Final Constraint (FOFC), proposed originally in Holmberg (2000):

(6) Final Over Final Constraint: If α is a head-initial phrase and β is a phrase immediately dominating α, then β must be head-initial. If α is a head-final phrase, and β is a phrase immediately dominating α, then β can be head-initial or head-final.

As one consequence of the FOFC, there are COMP-TP languages that are verb-final, but there are no TP-COMP languages that are verb-initial. Holmberg and his colleagues interpret this constraint as the following UG principle:

(7) A theoretical reinterpretation of the FOFC: If a phase-head PH has an EPP-feature, then all the heads in its complement domain from which it is nondistinct in categorial features must have an EPP-feature. (Biberauer, Holmberg & Roberts 2008: 13)

Walkden (2009) points out that FOFC effects are accounted for by the processing theory developed in Hawkins (2004) and hence suggests that (7) is a good example of a grounded UG principle.[6]

---

[5] In what follows, I consider classical functional explanations of grammatical structure to be of the third factor type. It is not clear whether Chomsky shares that view.
[6] Mobbs (2014) builds practically all of Hawkins's parsing theory into UG.

Note that neither Fodor nor Walkden have reduced the number of UG constraints; they have merely attributed the origins of these constraints to what in Chomsky's account would be deemeed a third factor. Naturally, the question arises as to whether these principles would need to be parameterized. The answer is "apparently so', since the NDC does not govern Swedish grammar (Engdahl 1985: 75) and the FOFC is not at work in Chinese (Chan 2013). In other words, grounded approaches, whatever intrinsic interest they might possess, do not prima facie reduce the number of UG principles and parameters.

7.2 Epigenetic approaches

Let us turn now to "epigenetic' or "emergentist" approaches to variation, where parameters are not provided by an innate UG. Rather, parametric effects arise in the course of the acquisition process through the interaction of certain third factor learning biases and experience. UG creates the space for parametric variation by leaving certain features underspecified. There are several proposals along these lines, among which are Gianollo, Guardiano & Longobardi (2008); Boeckx (2011); and Biberauer et al. (2014) (preceded by many papers by the same four authors). For reasons of space, I focus exclusively on Biberauer et al. (2014). In their way of looking at things, the child is conservative in the complexity of the formal features that it assumes are needed (what they call "feature economy') and liberal in its preference for particular features to extend beyond the input (what they call "input generalization" and which is a form of the superset bias). The idea is that these principles drive acquisition and thus render parameters unnecessary, while deriving the same effects. Consider first their word order hierarchy, represented in Figure 1:

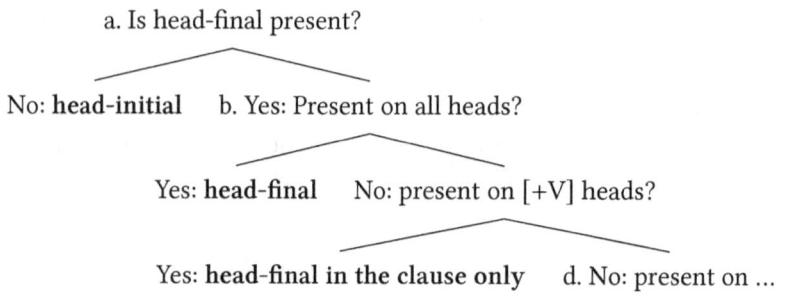

Figure 1: The Word Order Hierarchy of Biberauer et al. (2014: 110)

To illustrate with a made up example, let's say that a language is consistently head-initial except in NP, where the noun follows its complements. However, there is a definable class of nouns in this language that do precede their complements and a few nouns in this language behave idiosyncratically in terms of the positioning of their specifiers and complements (much like the English word *enough*, which is one of the few degree modifiers that follows the adjective). In their theory, the child will go through the following stages of acquisition, zeroing in step-by-step on the adult grammar. First it will assume that all phrases are head-initial, even noun phrases. Second, it will assume that all NPs are head-final. Third, it will learn the systematic class of exceptions to the latter generalization, and finally, it will learn the purely idiosyncratic exceptions.

The other hierarchies proposed in Biberauer et al. are more complex and depend on many assumptions about the feature content of particular categories. Consider for example their null argument hierarchy and the questions posed by the child in determining the status of such arguments in its grammar (Figure ??).

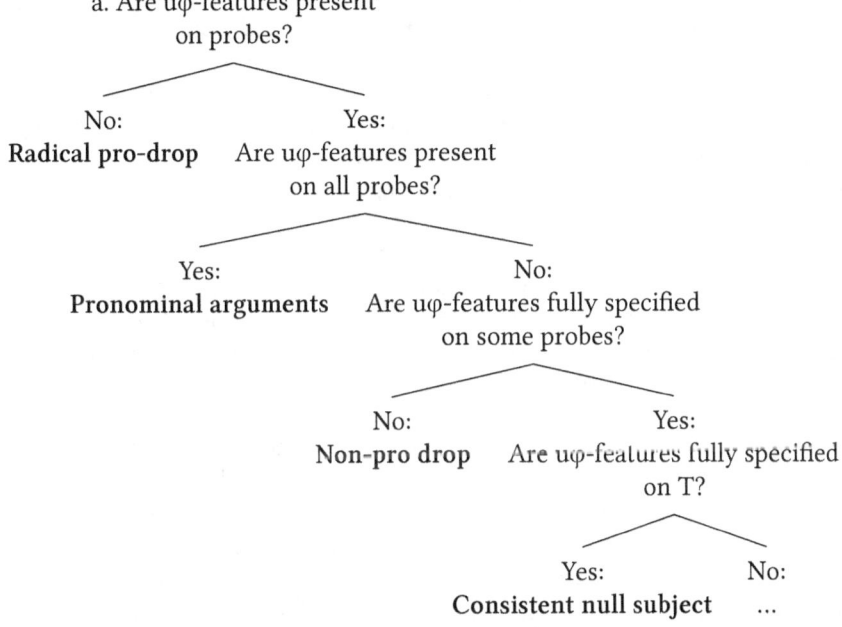

Figure 2: The Null Argument Hierarchy of Biberauer et al. (2014: 112)

There are many issues that one might raise about this acquisition scenario, the most important of which being whether children proceed from general to the particular, correcting themselves as they go, and gradually zero in on the correct grammar. Indeed, many acquisitionists argue for precisely the reverse set of steps, in which children learn idiosyncratic items before broad generalizations. Theresa Biberauer herself acknowledges (p.c., November 21, 2014) that these steps can be overridden in certain circumstances. For example, the early stages might correspond to a pre-production stage or possibly acquirers pass through certain stages very quickly if counterevidence to an earlier hypothesis is readily available. And finally, as they note, frequency effects can distort the smooth transition through the hierarchies.

One might also ask how much the child has to know *in advance* of the progression through the hierarchy. For example, given their scenario, the child has to know to ask

"Are unmarked phi-features fully specified on some probes?" That implies a lot of grammatical knowledge. Where, one might ask, does this knowledge come from and how does the child match this knowledge with the input?[7]

Despite these unresolved questions, the Biberauer et al. approach presents a view that preserves the major insights of parametric theory without positing UG-based parameters. As such, it needs to be taken very seriously.

7.3 Reductionist approaches and the need for language-particular rules

Reductionist approaches differ from epigenetic ones by reducing still further the role played by an innate UG in determining crosslinguistic variation. For example, returning to the FOFC, Trotzke, Bader & Frazier (2013) provide evidence that the best motivated account is to remove it entirely from the grammar, since, in their view, it can be explained in its entirety by systematic properties of performance systems. They also deconstruct the Head-Complement parameter in a similar fashion:

> [T]he physics of speech, that is, the nature of the articulatory and perceptual apparatus requires one of the two logical orders, since pronouncing or perceiving the head and the complement simultaneously is impossible. Thus, the head-complement parameter, according to this approach, is a third-factor effect. (Trotzke, Bader & Frazier 2013: 4)

Which option is chosen, of course, has to be built into the grammar of individual languages, presumably via its statement as a language-particular rule.

To take another example, Kayne (1994) provided an elaborate UG-based parametric explanation of why rightward movement is so restricted in language after language. But Ackema & Neeleman (2002) argue that the apparent ungrammaticality of certain "right-displaced" syntactic structures should not be accounted for by syntax proper (that is, by the theory of competence), but rather by the theory of performance. In a nutshell, such structures are difficult to process. A necessary consequence of their approach is that it is necessary to appeal to language-particular rules to account for the fact that languages differ from each other in the degree to which displacement to the right is permitted.

The microparametric approach to variation is well designed to capture the fact that even closely related speech varieties can vary from each other in many details. The question is why one would want to appeal to microparameters when the traditional term "rule" seems totally appropriate (see §6.2). The resistance to the idea of reviving the idea of (language-particular) rules is unsettling to some, perhaps because the idea of "rules" brings back the ghosts of pre-generative structuralism, where it was believed by

---

[7] An anonymous referee asks: "To be honest, I don't see how the approach sketched here is different from parameter setting. Perhaps it's my own ignorance of Biberauer et al.'s proposal, but if the hierarchy of questions that the learner must address is innate, how does this differ from parameters that are innately specified?" As I understand their proposal, the hierarchy of questions falls out from general learning principles, though I am hazy on the details of precisely how.

some that "languages could differ from each other without limit" (Joos 1957: 96), and the spectre of early transformational grammar, where grammars were essentially long lists of rules. But to call a language-particular statement a "rule" is not to imply that *anything* can be a rule. Possible rules are still constrained by UG. That of course raises the question of what is in UG. An obvious candidate is the Merge operation or something analogous, but surely there must be a lot more than that. For example, it is hard to see how the broad architecture of the grammar could be learned inductively. Consider the fact that syntactic operations have no access to the segmental phonology: There is no language in which displacement – Internal Merge, if you will – targets only those elements with front vowels. It seems probable that this state of affairs derives from UG.

However, if the general thrust of the work of John A. Hawkins is correct (see Hawkins 1994; 2004; 2014), the major constraints on the nature of rules derive from the exigencies of language processing. No language has a rule that lowers a filler exactly two clauses deep, leaving a gap in initial position. Such a rule, while theoretically possible, is so improbable (for processing reasons) that it will never occur. Norbert Hornstein's approach to variation, succinctly stated in the following passage, also stresses that it is not necessary to appeal to UG to explain why certain logically possible properties of grammars do not occur:

> There is no upper bound on the ways that languages might differ though there are still some things that grammars cannot do. A possible analogy for this conception of grammar is the variety of geometrical figures that can be drawn using a straight edge and compass. There is no upper bound on the number of possible different figures. However, there are many figures that cannot be drawn (e.g. there will be no triangles with 20 degree angles). Similarly, languages may contain arbitrarily many different kinds of rules depending on the PLD [= primary linguistic data – FJN] they are trying to fit. However, none will involve binding relations in which antecedents are c-commanded by their anaphoric dependents or where questions are formed by lowering a *Wh*-element to a lower CP. Note that this view is not incompatible with languages differing from one another in various ways. (Hornstein 2009: 167)

In my view, the idea that a grammar is composed of language-particular rules constrained by both UG principles and third factor principles is an appealing vision that stands to inform research on crosslinguistic variation in the years to come.

8 Conclusion

Since the late 1970s, crosslinguistic variation has generally been handled by means of UG-specified parameters. On the positive side, thinking of variation in terms of parameterized principles unleashed an unprecedented amount of work in comparative syntax, leading to the discovery of heretofore unknown morphosyntactic phenomena and crosslinguistic generalizations pertaining to them. On the negative side, however, both macroparameters and microparameters have proven themselves to be empirically inadequate and conceptually nonminimalist. Alternatives to parameters are grounded approaches, epigenetic approaches, and reductionist approaches, the last two of which seem both empirically and conceptually quite promising.

Acknowledgements

Earlier versions of this paper were presented at the Division of Labor Conference in Tübingen in January 2015 and at a University of Illinois Colloquium in February 2015. I would like to thank Laurence Horn, Robert Borsley, and an anonymous referee for their comments on the pre-final manuscript.

References

Ackema, Peter & Ad Neeleman. 2002. Effects of short term storage in processing rightward movement. In Sieb Noteboom, Fred Weerman & Frank Wijnen (eds.), *Storage and computation in the language faculty*, 219–256. Dordrecht: Kluwer.
Adger, David. 2003. *Core syntax: A minimalist approach*. Oxford: Oxford University Press.
Baker, Mark. 1988. *Incorporation: A theory of grammatical function changing*. Chicago: University of Chicago Press.
Baker, Mark. 1996. *The polysynthesis parameter*. Oxford: Oxford University Press.
Baker, Mark. 2001. *The atoms of language: The mind's hidden rules of grammar*. New York: Basic Books.
Baker, Mark. 2008. The macroparameter in a microparametric world. In Teresa Biberauer (ed.), *The limits of syntactic variation*, 351–374. Amsterdam: John Benjamins.
Berwick, Robert C. & Noam Chomsky. 2011. The biolinguistic program: The current state of its development. In Anna-Maria Di Sciullo & Cedric Boeckx (eds.), *The biolinguistic enterprise: New perspectives on the evolution and nature of the human language faculty*, 19–41. Oxford: Oxford University Press.
Besten, Hans den. 1977. On the interaction of root transformations and lexical deletion rules. In Werner Abraham (ed.), *On the formal syntax of the Westgermania*, 47–131. Amsterdam: John Benjamins.
Biberauer, Theresa, Anders Holmberg & Ian Roberts. 2008. Linearising disharmonic word orders: The Final-over-Final Constraint. In Kyoung Ae Kim & Jong Yurl Yoon (eds.), *Perspectives on linguistics in the 21st century (Proceedings of ICLK 2007)*, 301–318. Seoul.
Biberauer, Theresa, Anders Holmberg, Ian Roberts & Michelle Sheehan. 2014. Complexity in comparative syntax: The view from modern parametric theory. In Laurel B. Preston & Frederick J. Newmeyer (eds.), *Measuring grammatical complexity*, 103–127. Oxford: Oxford University Press.
Boeckx, Cedric. 2011. Approaching parameters from below. In Cedric Boeckx & Anna-Maria Di Sciullo (eds.), *Biolinguistic approaches to language evolution and variation*, 205–221. Oxford: Oxford University Press.

Boeckx, Cedric. 2014. What principles and parameters got wrong. In M. Carme Picallo (ed.), *Linguistic variation in the minimalist framework*, 155–178. Oxford: Oxford University Press.

Boeckx, Cedric & Sandra Stjepanovic. 2001. Head-ing toward PF. *Linguistic Inquiry* 32(2). 345–355.

Borer, Hagit. 1984. *Parametric syntax: Case studies in Semitic and Romance languages*. Vol. 13 (Studies in Generative Grammar). Dordrecht: Foris.

Bošković, Željko & Jon Gajewski. 2011. Semantic correlates of the NP/DP parameter. *North-Eastern Linguistics Society* 39. 121–134.

Chan, Brian Hok-Shing. 2013. Sentence-final particles, complementizers, antisymmetry, and the Final-over-Final Constraint. In Theresa Biberauer & Michelle Sheehan (eds.), *Theoretical approaches to disharmonic word order*, 445–468. Oxford: Oxford University Press.

Chomsky, Noam. 1965. *Aspects of the theory of syntax*. Cambridge, MA: MIT Press.

Chomsky, Noam. 1976. Conditions on rules of grammar. *Linguistic Analysis* 2. 303–351.

Chomsky, Noam. 1981. *Lectures on government and binding*. Vol. 9 (Studies in Generative Grammar). Dordrecht: Foris.

Chomsky, Noam. 1982. *The generative enterprise: A discussion with Riny Huybregts and Henk van Riemsdijk*. Dordrecht: Foris.

Chomsky, Noam. 1986. *Knowledge of language: Its nature, origin, and use*. New York: Praeger.

Chomsky, Noam. 1991. Linguistics and cognitive science: Problems and mysteries. In Asa Kasher (ed.), *The Chomskyan turn: Generative linguistics, philosophy, mathematics, and psychology*, 26–55. Oxford: Blackwell Publishing.

Chomsky, Noam. 1995. *The minimalist program*. Cambridge, MA: MIT Press.

Chomsky, Noam. 2000. Minimalist inquiries: The framework. In Roger Martin, David Michaels & Juan Uriagereka (eds.), *Step by step: Essays on minimalist syntax in honor of Howard Lasnik*, 89–155. Cambridge, MA: MIT Press.

Chomsky, Noam. 2001. Derivation by phase. In Michael Kenstowicz (ed.), *Ken Hale: A life in language*, 1–52. Cambridge, MA: MIT Press.

Chomsky, Noam. 2002. *On nature and language*. Cambridge: Cambridge University Press.

Chomsky, Noam. 2005. Three factors in language design. *Linguistic Inquiry* 36. 1–22.

Comrie, Bernard. 1988. Linguistic typology. In Frederick Newmeyer (ed.), *Linguistics: The Cambridge survey, 1: Linguistic theory: Foundations*, 447–461. Cambridge: Cambridge University Press.

Derbyshire, Desmond C. 1985. *Hixkaryana and linguistic typology*. Arlington, TX: Summer Institute of Linguistics.

Emonds, Joseph E. 1978. The verbal complex V' – V in French. *Linguistic Inquiry* 9(2). 151–175.

Engdahl, Elisabet. 1985. Interpreting questions. In David R. Dowty, Lauri Karttunen & Arnold M. Zwicky (eds.), *Natural language parsing: Psychological, computational, and theoretical perspectives*, 67–93. Cambridge: Cambridge University Press.

Enrico, John. 2003. *Haida syntax*. Lincoln: University of Nebraska Press.

Erteschik-Shir, Nomi. 2005. Sound patterns of syntax: Object shift. *Theoretical Linguistics* 31. 47–93.

Fodor, Janet D. 1978. Parsing strategies and constraints on transformations. *Linguistic Inquiry* 9. 427–473.

Fodor, Janet D. 2001. Setting syntactic parameters. In Mark Baltin & Chris Collins (eds.), *The handbook of contemporary syntactic theory*, 730–767. Oxford: Blackwell Publishing.

Fukui, Naoki. 1988. Deriving the differences between English and Japanese: A case study in parametric syntax. *English Linguistics* 5. 249–270.

Fukui, Naoki & Yuji Takano. 1998. Symmetry in syntax: Merge and demerge. *Journal of East Asian Linguistics* 7. 27–86.

Gallego, Ángel J. 2011. Parameters. In Cedric Boeckx (ed.), *Oxford handbook of linguistic minimalism*, 523–550. Oxford: Oxford University Press.

Gianollo, Chiara, Cristina Guardiano & Giuseppe Longobardi. 2008. Three fundamental issues in parametric linguistics. In Teresa Biberauer (ed.), *The limits of syntactic variation*, 109–142. Amsterdam: John Benjamins.

Greenberg, Joseph H. 1963. Some universals of grammar with special reference to the order of meaningful elements. In Joseph Greenberg (ed.), *Universals of language*, 73–113. Cambridge, MA: MIT Press.

Haspelmath, Martin. 2008. Parametric versus functional explanations of syntactic universals. In Teresa Biberauer (ed.), *The limits of syntactic variation*, 75–107. Amsterdam: John Benjamins.

Hauser, Marc D, Noam Chomsky & W Tecumseh Fitch. 2002. The faculty of language: What is it, who has it, and how did it evolve? *Science* 298(5598). 1569–1579.

Hawkins, John A. 1994. *A performance theory of order and constituency*. Vol. 73 (Cambridge Studies in Linguistics). Cambridge: Cambridge University Press.

Hawkins, John A. 2004. *Efficiency and complexity in grammars*. Oxford: Oxford University Press.

Hawkins, John A. 2014. *Cross-linguistic variation and efficiency*. Oxford: Oxford University Press.

Holmberg, Anders. 1999. Remarks on Holmberg's generalization. *Studia Linguistica* 53. 1–39.

Holmberg, Anders. 2000. Deriving OV order in Finnish. In Peter Svenonius (ed.), *The derivation of VO and OV*, 123–152. Amsterdam: John Benjamins.

Hornstein, Norbert. 2009. *A theory of syntax: Minimal operations and universal grammar*. Cambridge: Cambridge University Press.

Huang, C.-T. James. 2007. The macro-history of Chinese syntax and the theory of language change. Talk given at the University of Chicago.

Jacob, François. Darwinism reconsidered. *Le Monde* 1977-09-06.

Joos, Martin (ed.). 1957. *Readings in linguistics: The development of descriptive linguistics in America since 1925*. New York: American Council of Learned Societies.

Kayne, Richard S. 1994. *The antisymmetry of syntax*. Cambridge, MA: MIT Press.

Kayne, Richard S. 2000. *Parameters and universals*. Oxford: Oxford University Press.

Kayne, Richard S. 2005. *Movement and silence*. Oxford: Oxford University Press.

Kayne, Richard S. 2008. Some preliminary comparative remarks on French and Italian definite articles. In Robert Freidin, Carlos Otero & Maria-Luisa Zubizarreta (eds.), *Foundational issues in linguistic theory: Essays in honor of Jean-Roger Vergnaud*, 291–321. Cambridge, MA: MIT Press.

Kim, Wha-Chun M. 1976. *The theory of anaphora in Korean syntax*. Massachusetts Institute of Technology PhD thesis.

Lasnik, Howard. 1991. On the necessity of binding conditions. In Robert Freidin (ed.), *Principles and parameters in comparative grammar*, 7–28. Cambridge, MA: MIT Press.

Lightfoot, David W. 1999. *The development of language: Acquisition, change, and evolution*. Blackwell/Maryland Lectures in Language and Cognition, 1. Oxford: Blackwell Publishing.

Longobardi, Giuseppe & Cristina Guardiano. 2011. The biolinguistic program and historical reconstruction. In Cedric Boeckx & Anna-Maria Di Sciullo (eds.), *The biolinguistic enterprise: New perspectives on the evolution and nature of the human language faculty*, 266–304. Oxford: Oxford University Press.

Manzini, Maria Rita & Kenneth Wexler. 1987. Parameters, binding, and learning theory. *Linguistic Inquiry* 18. 413–444.

Mobbs, Iain. 2014. *Minimalism and the design of the language faculty*. University of Cambridge PhD thesis.

Monod, Jacques. 1972. *Chance and necessity*. London: Collins.

Newmeyer, Frederick J. 2005. *Possible and probable languages: A generative perspective on linguistic typology*. Oxford: Oxford University Press.

Pinker, Steven. 1994. *The language instinct: How the mind creates language*. New York: Morrow.

Pollock, Jean-Yves. 1989. Verb movement, Universal Grammar, and the structure of IP. *Linguistic Inquiry* 20(3). 365–424.

Ramchand, Gillian & Peter Svenonius. 2008. Mapping a parochial lexicon onto a universal semantics. In Teresa Biberauer (ed.), *The limits of syntactic variation*, 219–245. Amsterdam: John Benjamins.

Rizzi, Luigi. 1982. *Issues in Italian syntax*. Vol. 11 (Studies in Generative Grammar). Dordrecht: Foris.

Rizzi, Luigi. 2014. On the elements of syntactic variation. In M. Carme Picallo (ed.), *Linguistic variation in the minimalist framework*, 13–35. Oxford: Oxford University Press.

Roberts, Ian. 2010. Introduction: Parameters in minimalist theory. In Teresa Biberauer, Anders Holmberg, Ian Roberts & Michelle Sheehan (eds.), *Parametric variation: Null subjects in minimalist theory*, 1–57. Cambridge: Cambridge University Press.

Roberts, Ian & Anders Holmberg. 2005. On the role of parameters in Universal Grammar: A reply to Newmeyer. In Hans Broekhuis, Norbert Corver, Riny Huybregts, Ursula Kleinhenz & Jan Koster (eds.), *Organizing grammar: Linguistic studies in honor of Henk van Riemsdijk*, 538–553. Berlin: Mouton de Gruyter.

Smith, Neil & Ann Law. 2009. On parametric (and non-parametric) variation. *Biolinguistics* 3(4). 332–343.

Snyder, William. 2001. On the nature of syntactic variation: Evidence from complex predicates and complex word-formation. *Language* 77. 324–342.

Starke, Michal. 2014. Towards elegant parameters: Language variation reduces to the size of lexically-stored trees. In M. Carme Picallo (ed.), *Linguistic variation in the minimalist framework*, 140–152. Oxford: Oxford University Press.

Stowell, Timothy A. *Origins of phrase structure*. Cambridge, MA: Massachusetts Institute of Technology PhD thesis.

Takano, Yuji. 1996. *Movement and parametric variation in syntax*. University of California Irvine PhD thesis.

Thornton, Rosalind & Stephen Crain. 2013. Parameters: The pluses and the minuses. In Marcel den Dikken (ed.), *The Cambridge handbook of generative syntax*, 927–970. Cambridge: Cambridge University Press.

Travis, Lisa. 1989. Parameters of phrase structure. In Mark Baltin (ed.), *Alternative conceptions of phrase structure*, 263–279. Chicago: University of Chicago Press.

Trotzke, Andreas, Markus Bader & Lyn Frazier. 2013. Third factors and the performance interface in language design. *Biolinguistics* 7. 1–34.

Trudgill, Peter. 2003. *The Norfolk dialect*. Cromer, UK: Poppyland Publishing.

Uriagereka, Juan. 1999. Multiple spell-out. In Norbert Hornstein & Samuel Epstein (eds.), *Working minimalism*, 251–282. Cambridge, MA: MIT Press.

Walkden, George. 2009. Deriving the Final-over-Final Constraint from third factor considerations. 5. 67–72.

Yang, Charles D. 2011. Three factors in language variation. In Theresa Biberauer, Cedric Boeckx & Anna-Maria Di Sciullo (eds.), *The biolinguistic enterprise: New perspectives on the evolution and nature of the human language faculty*, 180–204. Oxford: Oxford University Press.

Chapter 26

Saussure's Dilemma: Parole and its potential

Alan Timberlake
Columbia University

> Saussure's account of the transformation of Latin to French stress leads to the unintended conclusion that *parole* has a life of its own: parole persists even after it is no longer dictated by *langue*; *parole* can prevent change or, conversely, presage potential change. Saussure's example is paralleled by intrusive r (*Cuba[r]against your friends*, not **day[r]and*) and the competition of *napron* and its near twin, and eventual successor, *apron*. Parole lives.

1 Saussure's Dilemma

It seems only fitting to begin this tribute to Steve Anderson, friend and erstwhile UCLA colleague, historian of linguistics and confirmed *helvétophile*, with Ferdinand de Saussure and his discussion of the history of stress from Latin to French (Chapter III.4–6 of the *Course*). That history presents a dilemma for Saussure's separation of synchrony from diachrony and linguistic activity (*parole*) from system (*système, langue*).

Here is Saussure's account of the transition from (ante)penultimate stress in Latin to final stress in French:

> In French, the accent always falls on the last syllable unless this syllable contains a mute *e* (ə). This is a synchronic fact, a relation between the whole set of French words and accent. What is its source? A previous state. Latin had a different and more complicated system of accentuation: the accent was on the penultimate syllable when the latter was long; when short, the accent fell back on the antepenult (cf. *amícus, ánĭma*). The Latin law suggests relations that are in no way analogous to the French law. Doubtless the accent is the same in the sense that it remained in the same position; in French words it always falls on the syllable that had it in Latin: *amícum → ami, ánimam →âme*. But the two formulas are different for the two moments because the forms of the words changed. We know that everything after the accent either disappeared or was reduced to mute *e*. As a result of the alteration of the word, the position of the accent with respect to the whole was

Alan Timberlake. 2017. Saussure's Dilemma: Parole and its potential. In Claire Bowern, Laurence Horn & Raffaella Zanuttini (eds.), *On looking into words (and beyond)*, 569–587. Berlin: Language Science Press. DOI:10.5281/zenodo.495466

> no longer the same; subsequently speakers, conscious of the new relation, instinctively put the accent on the last syllable, even in borrowed words introduced in their written forms (*facile, consul, ticket, burgrave*, etc.). Speakers obviously did not try to change systems, to apply a new formula, since in words like *amícum* → *ami*, the accent always remained on the same syllable; but speakers changed the position of the accent without having a hand in it. A law of accentuation, like everything that pertains to the linguistic system, is an arrangement of terms, a fortuitous and involuntary result of evolution. (Saussure 1959: 86)

To explain modern French final stress, Saussure goes back to its source in Latin, or rather to a stage of Romance subsequent to classical Latin but much earlier than modern French. He first defines the stress rules for French (final) and Latin ((ante)penultimate, depending on the quantity of the penult). That done, Saussure mentions in passing that the position of stress in French preserves the original position of stress from Latin, and illustrates the claim with examples of the two subcases of Latin stress, on a long penultimate (*amícum* → *ami*) and on the antepenultimate when the penult is short (*ánimam* →*âme*). It is worth mentioning that his formulation "the accent is the same in the sense that it remained in the same position" is not original; it repeats a standard observation from French philology in the middle of the nineteenth century. Thus in 1862 Gaston Paris (and seven other scholars he mentions, p. 11) stated the observation that stress falls on the same syllable in French as it did in Latin; for that phenomenon Paris in particular uses the apt term "persistence" (*persistance*) (Paris 1862: 28). Saussure does not use that term, but his formulation echoes this earlier tradition. Saussure then mentions the familiar fact that syllables after the syllable with the "persistent" stress are subject to stress reduction. At this point one might think he is preparing to explain how final stress in French arose, for example, perhaps by generalizing the word-final stress of words like *amícum* → *ami* that had undergone apocope. Saussure does not go in that direction. Instead, he declines to give a linguistic explanation for the development of final stress and places the burden on speakers acting "instinctively" and then on the vague assertion that "a diachronic fact was interposed." So although Saussure at the outset seemed prepared to explain modern French stress in terms of its source in Latin, the source is not relevant to Saussure's interpretation. He ends with a summary blaming the chaotic nature of change: "A law of accentuation, like everything that pertains to the linguistic system, is an arrangement of terms, a fortuitous and involuntary result of evolution."

Saussure seemed to recognize that the Latin rule of (ante)penultimate stress was lost as a rule. Further, it cannot have been a rule of the *système*; had it been rule of the *système*, it would have been maintained. Saussure's response was this:

> The synchronic law is general but not imperative. Doubtless it is imposed on individuals by the weight of collective usage..., but here I do not have in mind an obligation on the part of speakers. I mean that in language no force guarantees the maintenance of a regularity when established on some point. Being a simple expression of an existing arrangement, the synchronic law reports a state of affairs; it is like a law that states that trees in a certain orchard are arranged in the shape

of a quincunx. And the arrangement that the law defines is precarious precisely because it is not imperative. Nothing is more regular than the synchronic law that governs Latin accentuation...; but the accentual rule did not resist the forces of alteration and gave way to a new law, the one of French... In short, if one speaks of law in synchrony, it is in the sense of an arrangement, a principle of regularity. (Saussure 1959: 92–93)

This analysis, developed in connection with a discussion of six facts of Indo-European, is here applied to the Latin stress rule, which was downgraded to a descriptive observation about behavior maintained by social convention, analogous to the rule stating that "the trees in a certain orchard are arranged in the shape of a quincunx."

The phenomenon of Latin stress, with its properties of persistence, precariousness, and regularity presented a dilemma for Saussure. The phenomenon of persistence implies that usage (*parole*) has a life of its own; *parole* is maintained as parole, as habit, transmitted by imitation from one generation to the next. To invoke a metaphor, substituting "language" for "body" in Newton's first law, we could say: "a language at rest remains at rest unless it is acted on by an external force." Usage, such as the Latin stress rule, can exhibit coherent patterns (such as the elegant parallelism of length of the penultimate and antepenultimate position). Moreover, the patterns of *parole* are capable of defining the conditions for change (such as the "persistent" location of stress after Latin which conditions post-tonic apocope), and in this way patterns of *parole* act like elements of *système*.

Saussure's dilemma was that the more he insisted on the dominant, special, pure exclusionary status of *système*, the more ethereal and abstract system became, and that had the paradoxical effect of elevating *parole* to be the object of investigation.

2 "Law and Order" and sandhi doublets

To document the fate of /r/ in weak position (after a vowel, not before a vowel), Kurath & McDavid (1961) divided the eastern seaboard into four discontinuous zones, two northern and two southern, in which /r/ becomes [ə] in weak position: northern – including New England (Connecticut River east) and metropolitan New York; southern – including Upper South (Virginia, into northern North Carolina) and Lower South (South Carolina, Georgia). The four zones are separated by transitional belts which retain some form of r (presumably American [ɹ] or "velarized constricted" r [ɚ]). The largest of the transitional belts is Pennsylvania, from which rhoticism spread to Midwest and Midland dialects.

The discussion here focuses on the northern zones, which Kurath & McDavid (1961) treated as a single zone. As shown in Table 1, in the north /r/ is reflected in weak position as [ə] after mid and high vowels ([i, u, e, o]). After low vowels ([a/ɐ, ɒ/ɔ] and here [ə] as well) what must have been the earlier reflex [ə] was lost or absorbed by the vowel.

Alan Timberlake

Table 1: Postvocalic rhotic reflexes, North

high/mid V	low V
[ir], [ur], [er], [or] >	[ar/ɐr], [ɒr/ɔr], [ər] >
[iɚ], [uɚ], [eɚ], [oɚ]	[aɚ], [ɒɚ/ɔɚ], [ə] >
ear [iɚ]	[a/ɐ], [ɒ/ɔ], [ə]
poor [puɚ]	*far* [fa/fɐ]
care [keɚ]	*for* [fɒ/fɔ]
four [foɚ]	*father* [faðə]

Like northern dialects, southern dialects also absorbed [ɚ] after low-mid [a/ɐ, ɒ/ɔ, ə]. Furthermore: "In Southern folk speech, /ɚ/ is often lost, *door, four, poor* /doɚ, foɚ, poɚ/ thus becoming /do, fo, po/" (Kurath & McDavid 1961: 171a and map #156).[1]

Kurath and McDavid devoted special attention to sandhi contexts – contexts in which the word-final vowel which once had /r/ is used in a phrase with a following word. Then the word with original /r/ can be said to have two "sandhi doublets," depending on whether the second word begins with a consonant (when the original /r/ would have been in weak position) or with a vowel (when the original /r/ would have been prevocalic). They stated: "...*ear, poor, care, four* have... the positional allomorphs /iɚ ~ iɚr, puɚ ~ puɚr, kæɚ (keɚ) ~ kæɚr (keɚr), foɚ (fɔɚ) ~ foɚr (fɔɚr)/, and *car, for* (stressed), *father* the allomorphs /ka (kɐ) ~ kar (kɐr), fɒ (fə) ~ fɒr (fɔr), fað ~ faðər/." Note the difference between non-low vowels, in which the reflex is [Vɚ(r)], and low vowels, in which the reflex [V(r)] lacks [ɚ], since [ɚ] had been absorbed by the preceding low vowel. The idea of calling these doublets (and they provide a notation for doublets) suggests a model of the lexicon in which a lexical item is composed of multiple subunits, which could be written as an ordered pair such as {[iɚ]/sandhi before consonant; [iɚr] / sandhi before vowel}. One might, for example, write a doublet for the noun *Cuba* as pronounced by John F. Kennedy in his speech "in the Cuban Missile Crisis" generally as [kubə], as in *and then shall Cuba[ə] be welcomed* (16:07), but [kubər] in phrases such as *Soviet assistance to Cuba[r] and I quote* (4:32) and *turned Cuba[r] against your friends* (15:05).[2]

Examples constructed in the spirit of Kurath & McDavid (1961) are given in Table 2, top.

It is worth drawing attention to the fact that prevocalic sandhi examples with non-low vowels have the sequence [ɚr] (p. 171b); as in [iɚr, puɚr, kæɚr (keɚr), foɚr (fɔɚr)] from the list above. The sandhi sequence [VɚrV] has in effect two segments – [ɚ] and [r] – which reflect earlier /r/. Both cannot be original. There must have been an antecedent stage of [*irV, *purV, *kærV (*kerV), *forV (*fɔrV)] in sandhi position before a vowel. The [ɚ] we see now in [iɚr], etc., had to have been introduced by analogy from other forms to the sandhi forms before vowel.

---

[1] The lexeme *poor* is treated once as having a mid vowel (171a) and otherwise as a high vowel (170b, 171b, 172a, 172b). (One, also 171b, is ambiguous.)

[2] http://www.historyplace.com/speeches/jfk-cuban.htm.

Table 2: Sandhi /r/ and Intrusive /r/, North

context	high, mid V	low V
sandhi [V(ə)ɾV]	[iə], [uə], [eə], [oə] *ear and* [iərænd] *poor and* [puərænd] *care and* [keərænd] *four and* [foərænd]	[a/ɐ], [ɒ/ɔ], [ə] *far and* [farænd] *for all* [fɒral] *father and* [faðərænd]
intrusive [VɾV]	[i], [u], [e], [o] *three and* *[θrirænd] *two and* *[turænd] *day and* *[derænd] *know it* *[norɪt]	[a/ɐ], [ɒ/ɔ], [ə] *ma and* [marænd] *law and* [lɒrænd] *Martha and* [maθərænd]

Analogy is relevant to history in another respect (Sóskuthy 2013). Not uncommonly, words that ended originally in low vowels without /r/ acquired a non-etymological, or "intrusive," /r/ in sandhi, as in the familiar *law and order* [lɒrəndɒdə] and other examples in Table 2. As Kurath & McDavid (1961: 172a) state,

> On the analogy of such doublets as *for* /fɒ (fɔ) ~ fɒr (fɔr)/, *car* /ka (kɐ) ~ kar (kɐr)/, and *father* /faðə ~ faðər/, positional allomorphs ending in /r/ are often created in Eastern New England and Metropolitan New York for words that historically end in the vowels /ɒ ~ ɔ, a ~ ɐ, ə/, as *law, ma, Martha*. Thus one hears *law and order* /lɒr ənd ɒdə, lɔr ənd ɔdə/, *ma and pa* /mar ən(d) pa, mɐ ən(d) pɐ/, *Martha and I* /maθər (mɐθər) ənd ai/.

The examples of intrusive /r/ just cited involved only words which end in a low vowel – that is, they have the same vocalism in the non-sandhi environments as words that originally ended in /r/ but which absorbed the [ə] reflex of /r/; thus *law* /lɒ (lɔ)/ has the same vocalism as originally rhotic words like *for* /fɒ (fɔ)/. But words like *three, two, day, know*, which end in mid and high vowels, differ. Kurath & McDavid (1961: 172b) state:

> It is worth noting that after the normally upgliding free vowels /i, u, e, o/, as in *three, two, day, know*, an analogical "intrusive" /r/ never occurs. The reason for this is clear: since /θri, tu, de, no/ do not end like the phrase-final /r/-less allomorphs of *ear, poor, care, four* /iə, puə, keə, foə/, the basis for creating allomorphs ending in /r/ is lacking.

Thus according to Kurath & McDavid (1961), the development of intrusive /r/ involves the comparison of stem shapes, for example [lɒ] with [fɒ], which are similar and permit analogy, as opposed to *three* [θri] with [iə], which are dissimilar and do not permit analogy.

This distribution is interesting. What determines whether analogical intrusive /r/ develops is an arbitrary division of vowels inherited from the previous history of derhoticism; that is to say, a distinction in vowels involved in the earlier history of reflexes of /r/ in weak position continues to have an effect on later developments. Thus *parole* has the property of inertia (*persistance*), so that later changes (such as the analogical development of intrusive /r/) can be sensitive to properties of *parole* that persist. At the same time as *parole* is inertial and conservative, *parole* nevertheless carries with it the possibility of change. Thus original *r*-less words ending in low vowels have the potential to develop an intrusive sandhi /r/, as happened in northern dialects. Conversely, original *r*-full words had the potential to eliminate the second member of the "doublet" in which /r/ reappears in sandhi before a vowel; this is what happened in southern dialects (especially Upper South but even in the Lower South sandhi forms with /r/ are "only half as frequent as the variants without /r/", Kurath & McDavid 1961: 171b).

Parole, then, is inertial but carries the potential for change. This example is similar to what Saussure said about Latin stress, that it remained on the syllable where it had always been – by convention, or memory, or inertia – but eventually the stress was repositioned.

It might be objected that it would be easy to state a rule inserting /r/ that is sensitive to vowel height; insertion would happen only in position after low vowels. But why low vowels? Low vowels are not universally more likely than other vowels to adopt a phonotactic sequence [VCV] that other vowels. Intrusive /r/ develops only after low vowels because it is only low vowels that offered a model for analogical extension, and that is a distribution that goes back to a prior change; the restriction to low vowels can only be understood by viewing it as the hangover from a previous stage. Moreover, it is not just any consonant that reappears; it is just the one sound /r/. The /r/ can participate in "intrusive" analogy because the /r/, and only the /r/, was carried over from earlier history. The fact that /r/ is involved in analogy at all is a further instance of persistence of *parole*.

3 "Watergate" and its ilk

Against this background I want to discuss how innovations can arise directly out of speech. The word *Watergate* and its derivatives can serve as an illustration. As is familiar, *Watergate* is the name of a complex of five buildings built in Washington, D.C., over the period 1963–1971. An office building in this complex was used by the Democratic National Committee as headquarters leading up to the 1972 election. The Democratic offices suffered a break-in, for which staff members of the Republican administration were later discovered to be responsible. The break-in triggered an embarrassing scandal and, because of the attempt to cover up the original crime, led to the resignation of President Richard Nixon.

A modification of the name for this location keeps being applied to more events, which, like the original Watergate, include at least two events, layers of agency, times, places. The core is the pairing of two events: first, an event carried out in secret and, second, the fallout, including the embarrassment caused by the event for the participants and perhaps further developments (cover-up, disclosure). The whole scenario is a rich instance of the familiar trope of metonymy, which points to one event – here, the original transgression – which can invoke associated events (here, the fall-out) and the constituents of those events (locus, agents, patients). The name for this complex of events and constituents, which occurred in 1972, is of course *Watergate* – the name for the place is applied to the whole package of events, by the trope of *pars (locus) pro toto* (complex of events – crime, scandal, cover-up, further fall-out). The semantic operations involved in *Watergate* are familiar, banal tropes.

Event complexes similar to the original *Watergate* scenario can be named by the new compound {x+gate}, where {gate} refers to the existence of a scandalous event (and fall-out) and *x* refers to a focus – a constituent that is central to the events – such as the agent (*Billygate*) or causal entity (*nannygate*) or the patient (*contragate*).

The morphological structure and semantics of the new compound {x "focus"+gate} "event(s) leading to scandal" seem clear, and it seems clear that the compound is related to the origin *Watergate*. How? Given the apparent overlap of {gate} in both, one might imagine that the word *Watergate* was decomposed into two morphemes, {water} and {gate}, and that reanalysis provided the model for neologisms. But this cannot be: by itself "*water*" does not mean anything in this context; it is not the focus. And for that matter, *gate* doesn't mean scandal here in the compound *Watergate*. In the original word *Watergate*, there is no division; *Watergate* is the name for the complex as a whole, not for any of its constituents.

And yet *Watergate* was self-evidently the source for the formula {x+gate} and novel applications of the formula. What this means is that "Watergate" – the name for a whole complex of agents and events – allowed speakers to imagine a new structure {x+gate} whose semantics give overall semantics analogous to the meaning of *Watergate* (secret event and subsequent scandal, specific place or agents, etc.) but in which the event complex is broken into two constituents; one of them, {x}, refers to the focus of events, and the other part, {gate}, establishes the existence of a secret event and its attendant scandal involving the focus {x}, whereas in the source *Watergate*, the whole included all the components.

Two aspects of this change are significant. First, the new structure is motivated by the inherited word, but it is not a copy; it cannot be generated by a proportional analogy. Instead, what the example shows is that speech has the potential of providing motivation for creating new speech directly. To say it another way, speech is not just speech; speech invites modal possibilities. The second point is that the source here really is speech that actually occurred in real time: *Watergate* started as a single event complex that occurred at some time in history; it did not start as a pattern. That is, a singular event and the accompanying speech give rise to an innovation; speech creates speech. This new {x+gate} is a virtual structure which might exist indefinitely. We cannot verify its existence until it is acted on. Therein is a property of language that has eluded description: the fact that speech happens, that activity matters, it happens when a novel formation is used, and it happens to the extent that neologisms are created and used in speech.

575

This example, then, suggests a more active role for *parole* (performance, speech) than has usually been assumed. In this instance actual speech from a very specific historical time (1972) provided the model and created the potential for new speech, and that is what resulted. It is worth stating that speech is not just blind activity; speech comes with implicit patterns, whether firmly established or – as in this case – potential, possible, modal speech.

It could be mentioned that this formation, along with similar neologisms motivated by *alcoholic*, have distinctive stylistic overtones and spheres of usage – in the personal sphere, gentle mockery (*shopaholic, chocoholic*) and not-so-gentle journalistic irony for the former (*Camillagate*). The News History Gallery at the Newseum[3] in Washington, D.C., devoted to the history of journalism, has an exhibit called "The 'Gate' Syndrome," illustrated by five examples, starting with *Koreagate* (1976). [4]

4 "(N)apron" as dynamic doublet

A somewhat similar change is the change from *napron* to *apron* in Middle English. As is familiar, a dozen or so nouns which had once begun with an initial consonant *n* lost the *n* and came to begin with the vowel of the first syllable. According to the standard analysis, this happened because when such nouns were used with the indefinite article *a(n)*, a sequence of [anV] would result, and then it is unclear whether the intervocalic [n] belongs to the stem of the noun or to the article. The ambiguity opened up the possibility that the [n] could be attributed to the article and the noun could be reanalyzed as beginning with a vowel. Subsequently the stem shape without the vowel could be extended to all contexts; thus {a+napron} > [anapron] was analyzed as {an+apron} > [anapron], leading to the use of {apron} elsewhere. As is well known, the converse also occurs, where nouns beginning with an initial vowel (*an ewt*) acquired an initial *n* from the indefinite article (> *a newt*). It is not clear why the change of metanalysis should be able to go in either direction.

This standard analysis discusses only the end-points of this change – prior to metanalysis, after metanalysis – but does not describe how the change progressed. To get a sense of how this change actually proceeded, I attempted to trace the history of spellings *(n)apron* in Middle English with an eye to variation in the choice of the word form in different contexts. The task was rather more challenging than I had expected. The word *(n)apron* is quite specific. It occurs infrequently, primarily in wills and inventories of good to be bequeathed. (And also, as will be noted below, in a description of the rules of the household of Edward IV.) The item is mentioned only in a minority of the wills or inventories available, and usually when the deceased is a woman. For example, the extensive *Wills and Inventories of Bury St. Edmunds* has approximately 150 printed pages of wills from the beginning of the fifteenth century (one will from 1370, then 1418, etc.)

---

[3] http://www.newseum.org/
[4] Arnold Zwicky calls {gate} a "libfix" – "lib" in the sense of "liberated" – which captures the idea that a mental operation extracts a new affix (https://arnoldzwicky.org/2010/01/23/libfixes/). The author wishes to thank the editors for this and many other valuable and droll comments and corrections.

to the late sixteenth century (1570), and has no instances of the word in either variant, *napron* or *apron*. That, despite instances such as the will of one Agas Herte (a. 1522, pp. 114–18), who bequeathed about 50 distinct household objects to her son, including "*ij tabyll clothes, vj napkyns, iiij pleyne and to of diap, a salte saler of pewter...*" and about the same number to her daughter, including "*ij tabell clothes, vi napkyns, iiij pleyn and ij of diap, and a pleyn towel...*" Among all the items she bequeathed, including the items made of cloth just mentioned, no *(n)apron* was mentioned. This might because this household, and other households as well, did not use *(n)aprons*; it might be they were considered too insignificant to be mentioned in bequests (though towels and napkins and sheets are recorded regularly). In any event, the frequency with which *(n)apron* appears is modest. In short, it has proven difficult to find document sets in which *(n)apron* is mentioned multiple times; examples are isolated. To maximize the range of texts examined, I used Hathitrust/Google scans subjected to OCR. I searched for both *napron* and *apron*, both singular and plural, in variant spellings.

We can first take a quick look at chronology, using a ledger (*Fabric rolls*) kept by the York Minster which recorded miscellaneous expenses annually. The entries are written in Latin, though names for some items specific to the contemporary realia appear in English. Half a dozen times the rolls record payment for the costs of masonry, both for wages and equipment – aprons and gloves for masons (called "setters"). The earliest record from 1371 surprisingly has *n*-less *aprons* (*ij aprons et cirotecis* 'two aprons and gloves', 1371). Then at the beginning of the fifteenth century come two instances of *naprons: In remuneracione data cementariis vocatis setters ad parietes* **cum naprons** *et cirotecis, per annum 9s. 10d.* 'as compensation given to the masons known as setters at the wall with aprons and gloves, annually 9s. 10d.' (1404); *In ij pellibus emptis et datis eisdem* **pro naporons**, 'two hides were bought and given to them to serve as aprons' (1423). At the end of the fifteenth century there are two examples of Latin *limas* (**duobus limatibus**, 1497–98; **Pro ij limatibus**, 1499), and shortly thereafter, *aprons* (**pro ij le aprons** *de correo pro les setters per spacium ij mensium, 12d.* 'for two aprons of hide for the setters for the period of two months, 12 shillings' (1504). The use of *aprons* in 1371 seems anomalously early (could it be an error in transcribing the text?). This anomaly aside, the examples suggest a chronology: *napron* was used in the fifteenth century (1404, 1423) and shifted to *apron* the beginning of the fifteenth century (1504). Other texts suggest there was still some variation in the sixteenth century. By 1600 *apron* had taken over.

Against the background of generally skimpy attestation of *(n)apron* in the fifteenth and sixteenth century, there are two texts which offer enough examples to allow us to say something about usage. One is a single text, the so-called Liber Niger Domus Regis, which specifies the duties and compensation of the staff of King Edward IV's household in the last quarter of the fifteenth century (c. 1480). A modern edition compiles three manuscripts (discussion, Myers 1959: 51–60). The oldest is a manuscript from the end of the fifteenth century, which served as the basis for the famous 1790 publication by the Society of Antiquaries (abbreviated "A"); however, text A is now defective, and it also appears that the 1790 edition took some liberties, so the printed 1790 edition cannot be trusted to represented the oldest text A. In the accompanying Table 3 I've cited the location of readings from the 1790 reading edition in ||. The next oldest is a sixteenth-century manuscript (preserved in the Public Records Office, the Exchequer, abbreviated E), from the era of Henry VIII, is similar to A but fuller. Third, the youngest of the three manuscripts, known as Harleian 642 (here H), is a seventeenth-century copy made by Sir Simonds d'Ewers. In fact, differences recorded in footnotes by Myers in his edition are minimal and affect the analysis here in only one respect, mentioned below.

There are basically two contexts (with one additional outlier). Examples repeat over the descriptions of many different servants. The twelve examples of *(n)apron* are given in abbreviated form Table 3.

Table 3: *(n)apron* in Liber Niger of Edward IV

	type	text [variants]
§55 |49.7d|	MOD	they have part of the ᵅyeftesᵅ geuvn to the houshold... but **none aprons** [1790: ᵅgyftesᵅ]
§62 |52.28d|	DO	[takith] at euery of the iiij festes of the yere, **naprons** of the great spycery
§62 |52.28d|	DO	take **naprons** also at euerych of the iiij festes
§80 |71.6|	DO	etithe in the halle; taking for wages... and nyȝt lyuereye, **napors**, and parte of the generall giftes
§80	DO	taking for his wynter clothing chaunces, **napors**, parte of the giftes generall [extended passage, absent in 1790]
§74 |61.26d|	1DO	Eche of them takethe... **j napron** of lynyn cloth of ij ellez [1790: **a naperon**]
§77 |65.19d|	1DO	At euery of the iiij festes, **j napron** of j elle, price vjd. [1790: **one napron** of one elle]
§33 |36.10u|	PRP	[he takith]... ij elles of lynen clothe **for aprons**, price the elle, xijd.
§77 |64.25d|	PRP	ij ellez of lynyn cloth... **for naprons**
§77 |65.8d|	PRP	j elle of lynnyn clothe **for naprons**
§77 |64.41|	PRP	j elle **for naprons** of lynyn cloth
§80 |71.26d|	PRP	ᵅand for chaunces iiijs. viijd.ᵅ of **napors** at euerye [Hᵅᵅ; H **aprons**]

§ = section in Myers, || page in 1790 edition

In one isolated instance, the noun is preceded by *none*; the nasal might have elicited the following *apron*. The other eleven tokens are split between two contexts. In six instances the noun is the direct object of the verb 'take' (listed as "DO"). The entities taken have already been formed into garments; all have *napron*. Within this group of six examples, in two of these six, marked here as "1DO," the word *napron* is preceded in texts E and H by *j*, that is, Roman numeral 'one'. (The published 1790 version has the indefinite article *a napron* in one instance and the written word *one napron* in the other, rather than the numeral.) Both E and H use numerals consistently in discussions of compensation; prices of elles of linen cloth are cited with numerals, such as *j elle*. The numeral here must be original, thus *j napron* in both examples. I will return to these in a moment.

The second group of six examples involves the statement that servants receive compensation in the form of linen cloth which is supposed to be turned into *(n)aprons*, expressed by a preposition, usually *for*, once *of*. In this context the entity referred to as *(n)apron* does not yet exist; the noun has a future attributive sense: "the speaker wishes to assert something about whatever or whoever fits that description" of being (or becoming) an apron (Donnellan 1966: 285). An example is: *at eueryche of the iiij festes of the yere, of the clerk of greete spycery, ij elles of lynen clothe for **aprons**, price the elle, xij^d*. This one sentence has *aprons*, which seems to suggest that an attributive reading implies *aprons*. But this sentence is the only instance with *aprons* among the five tokens of this attributive context, so an attributive reading by itself can't explain *aprons* in this specific example. I return to this token below.

Let us turn to the second text, namely *Durham wills and inventories*. The second text is not, strictly speaking, a single text but a series of wills; still, they are all from one locale and one tradition over a short interval, from 1562 to 1570, and can be treated as a single text. (In fact, there is a string of four tokens of *(n)apron* in a row.) The tokens are given in Table 4.

Only two contexts occur in this small corpus. One context is represented by two tokens, in which the indefinite article and noun are separated by a modifier (*a linn Apron*, *a blewe apron*). The modifier makes these constructions novel. This pair of examples suggests two thoughts: that the innovative form *apron* is favored to the extent the context in which the noun is used is non-idiomatic, novel; and the concept of idiomaticity is a gradated (not discretely binary) parameter. To continue down this path, both in the example from 1562 and the 1570 example (from volume III of these documents), *an apron* occurs in the middle of a miniature list of three bequeathed items. Lists by their nature hint that a set of entities could be extended, so they promise a modal, possible, open-endedness. Thus it appears that open-endedness favors the innovative form *an apron*. In contrast, in the will of cook William Hawkesley (presented in Table 4 as a block of four tokens), the second through fourth tokens have a fixed phrase *a napron*, and the whole construction, 'I give to x *a napron*', is a standard idiom of bequests. Thus fixed idioms use the inherited older form *a napron*. In 1569 Alice Barnes receives two worsted items; possibly the parallel in material is the critical information, and the fact that one is a *(n)apron* is incidental.

Table 4: *(n)apron* in *Durham Wills and Inventories*

type	text
MOD	It' I bequith to Agnes Carter ***a linn Apron***. (I.277, 1567)
MOD	It'm I gyve to Helenor Huntley iiij^{or} blake patletts iiij^{or} cherches ***a blewe apron*** & ij^o velvett pattletts (I.343, 1570)
ART	to Thomas Burdon a busshell of wheat – to Jane Brantinga' a line kyrcheff ***an apron*** & a pair of hoose (I.198–99, 1562)
ART	I geve unto Elizabeth Hackforth a kerchif, a raill, a smock, ***an apron*** and all my workday rayment and in mony 3s. 4d. (III.56–57, 1570)
ART	It'm I gyve to katheryn barnes ij^s vj^d. It'm I gyve to thomeis hynde y^t was my p'ntice ***an apron*** & a new fyshe knyffe. | It'm I gyve to thomas capstone ***a napron***. | It'm I gyve to thomas boswell ***a napron***.|
ART	
ART	
ART	It'm I gyve to luke hanynge ***a napron*** & a fyshe borde. (I.327, 1570)
ART	And to alles Barnes a gowne of worsted & ***a napron of worsted*** (I.305, 1569)

The most interesting example is the first example of the 1570 set. Throughout this will of William Hawkesley, the recipients are identified in an unambiguous but not expansive fashion; the recipients are listed by name alone (22 xx) or with name and geographical location (3 xx) or name and relationship (9 xx), such as mother-in-law or midwife. That is, the recipients are presumed to be known by name with the briefest of descriptions, almost titles. Against that background, the description of the first recipient of aprons, *thomeis hynde y^t was my p'ntice*, stands out; given its relative clause *y^t* ('that'), the identification of Thomas is relatively elaborate. Indirectly, this means that the bequest – an apron and a fish knife – is out of the ordinary, atypical. In contrast, in the three bequests that follow immediately thereafter are idiomatic. It appears, then, that novel or unexpected bequests of aprons – the bequest itself or the recipient – are expressed by the innovative *(an) apron*, while less novel scenarios are expressed by the older form *a napron*.

This takes us back to the one example in the Liber Niger Domus Regis Edward IV which had *aprons* (other than *none aprons*): *[he taketh] at eueryche of the iiij festes of the yere, of the clerk of greete spycery, ij elles of lynen clothe **for aprons**, price the elle, xij^d*. In and of itself, the sentence is unremarkable and indistinguishable from the other examples with prepositions which had *naprons*. What might be atypical is the office described here, which is that of *sewar*, the highest ranking and first mentioned of the king's servants: A

SEWAR FOR THE KYNG, wich owith to be full cunyng, diligent, and attendaunt. He receueth the metes by sayez and saufly so conueyeth hit to the kinges bourde with saucez according therto, and all that commith to that bourde he settith and dyrectith (§33, p. 112). In this instance, although the act of taking aprons is not exceptional, the recipient – the *sewar* – is unique. This is then similar to *thomeis hynde y*^{t} *was my p'ntice* from *Durham wills and inventories*, in the sense that the non-idiomatic character of the example derives from the recipient, not the *(n)apron* phrase. That should not be surprising, since the act of bequeathing includes a recipient as well as the item bequeathed. The innovative *aprons* here acts effectively as an honorific to draw attention to the unusual status of the recipient, as it did with *thomeis hynde y*^{t} *was my p'ntice*.

In general, it appears the innovative form is favored if the transfer of *apron* is novel, not typical, and this extends to the recipient of the transfer (relative to other recipients). This principle applies to both example sets from different stages of the change. This distribution – unidiomatic context prefers the novel form – turns out to match other instances of the competition between equivalent morphological forms. Thus in contemporary Czech the locative singular (used with certain prepositions) can be either the traditional ending {-e} or a new ending {-u}. (That ending is original with nouns of the Indo-European *u*-stem declension, but its use with *o*-stem masculine nouns is new.) The parallel is that the traditional {-e} is used with "typical" combinations while innovative {-u} is used with atypical contexts (Bermel 1993).

There is another regularity of some interest that applies to both texts. We saw above that in Liber Niger there were two instances in which *(n)apron* followed the numeral *j* ('one'), and in both the older form *napron* was used. The examples are more or less equivalent in meaning to a true indefinite article as in *a napron*; the two examples of *j napron* (with *napron*) with the numeral invite the suspicion that true indefinite articles at this time might have *napron*, if they were attested. Conveniently, there is a contemporaneous will that has two tokens of an indefinite article one after the other: *Also I gyve to Margarete Holton my best kyrtill & **a napron**. Also I gyve to Elisabeth Wike a smok & **a napron*** (will of Jone Montor, 1489, *Surrey Wills*, p. 95). A slightly later example is consistent: *A jak & a salet, a gorget, ij gussettes, **a napron**, and iij gauntlettes* (*York wills*, p. 35, 1512). These examples at least suggest that the context with an indefinite article used the more conservative form.

To return to the other text under discussion here, *Durham wills and inventories*, there were two recognizable contexts. One involves an indefinite article split from the noun; it does show that the change had progressed to novel (unidiomatic) contexts. The other context had seven tokens with an indefinite article (not separated from the noun); the older form *napron* was used 4 times, the novel form time 3 times. That is to say, the novel form *apron* was slow to appear in the context in which the indefinite article immediately preceded the noun. For both periods (late 1400s, third quarter of 1500s) it appears that a construction with an indefinite article uses *apron* less (or at least not more) than other contexts.

Now the standard analysis is that the ambiguous combination of indefinite article and *napron* led to a reanalysis of {a+napron} to {an+apron}. If so, it would be natural to expect that *apron* would be used first in the context of reanalysis and only later in other contexts

– that is, it should appear earliest with the indefinite article. But we just saw that in both texts, *apron* was used in other contexts when *an apron* was not yet used (the first text plus the auxiliary wills) or not used as frequently (the second text).

This suggests a revision of the account of reanalysis. Since the appearance of *apron* is in fact not tied to the indefinite article, the unit *apron* appears to have some degree of autonomy. The reanalysis consists not of replacing the underlying shape of the noun, but it consists of imagining the possibility of an alternate word form {apron}, which co-exists, for a time, with an alternate sublexeme {napron}. Imagined {apron} becomes real only when it is actually used. Following the general principle that innovative forms appear first in novel contexts, {napron} was maintained with the indefinite article – in fact, the most conventional and idiomatized construction – while the sublexeme {apron} was used in novel contexts cited above, such as *[takith]... ij elles of lynen clothe* **for aprons** and *... to thomeis hynde y^t was my p'ntice* **an apron**. Over time, {apron} and {napron} compete; {apron} keeps on increasing, in a fashion that could be understood as the other half of Newton's first law: once in motion, a body, or linguistic subsystem, will remain in motion.

Semantically the new demilexeme {apron} must be basically similar to traditional {napron}. For example, both demilexemes refer to protective coverings, usually of cloth, though in artisanry, aprons could be sheepskins. In the York fabric rolls – the record of expenses of the York expenses, including irregular expenses of masons and their equipment – we observe naprons used at the beginning of the fifteenth century – *In ij pellibus emptis et datis eisdem pro naporons* 'two hides were bought and given to them to serve as aprons' (1423) – and then the form is *aprons* at the end of the fifteenth century]: **pro ij le aprons** *de correo pro les setters per spacium ij mensium, 12d.* 'for two aprons of hide for the setters for the period of two months, 12 shillings' (1504). That is only to say that *napron* and *apron* seem to have the same extension.

Still, despite the overlap in extension, there are indications that the two sublexemes began to develop slightly different connotations.[5] Two facts argue for this.

The first, perhaps unexpectedly, has to do with translations of the Bible. As is well-known, John Wyfcliffe translated much of the Bible from the Vulgate, around 1382. (His translation was finished by his followers after his death.) A passage of interest is Genesis 3:7 – the famous story of the nakedness of Adam and Eve – for which Wycliffe (or his followers) translated Vulgate *...cognovissent esse se nudos consuerunt folia ficus et fecerunt sibi perizomata* as *...and when they knew that they were naked, they sewed the leaves of a fig tree, and made breeches to themselves.*

Wycliffe's Bible became the model for an extended tradition of English translations thereafter, but with a difference in this passage. Starting with Tynsdale (1534), the subsequent translations have a different noun in Genesis 3:7: *...vnderstode how that they were naked. Than they sowed fygge leves togedder and made them apurns.* The translation with *aprons* continues through Cloverdale (1535), the Great Bible (1540), Matthew's Bible (1549), the Catholic Bishops' Bible (1568), the Geneva Bible (1587), and finally the King James (1604–1611). All have *aprons* (variant spellings) except for the Geneva Bible, a retrograde Protestant Bible which returned to Wycliffe's *breeches*.

---

[5] In a fashion consistent with Bréal's (1900: ch. 2) "law of differentiation" of synonyms.

The improvised fig-leaf garment of Genesis 3:7 wasn't exactly an apron in the sense of linen or hide aprons, but it was somewhat similar. Why was *apron* used instead of *napron*? One reason might be that *apron* was the innovative form, and innovative forms are more appropriate than conventional forms for encoding semantic extensions. There is another possibility. As we saw in the Liber Niger, *naprons* were something that would result from linen, and their value was defined by the price of the linen used to make them. In earlier wills *naprons* were classified with other items of cloth with different functions; *naprons* belonged to the *naperie* (the collection of similar cloths) along with *napkins* (same sense as modern) and *borde clothes* or *table cloths*. So the sublexeme {napron} emphasized the origin of the entity in cloth or hide; secondarily, such a flat piece of material could be donned for protection. With the sublexeme {apron} the dominant feature is not that it was made from material (or hide); the dominant feature is that it is a garment worn to provide protective covering. This difference in the ranking of features – MATERIAL as opposed FUNCTION – might be why the corrections to Wycliff's Bible used *apron*.

A second indication is the way items are grouped in *Chesterfield wills and inventories of household goods*. For example, from Derbyshire #177 (Margaret Capper, 1588) here is a partial list of items (omitting tools and animals). Items are listed in the inventory in natural classes. Categories are added here:

> <furniture> / 4 bedstids in the Chamber / 2 bedstids in the parlar with pented Cloates about them / 1 bed teaster of Cloathe / 3 bed stids in the nether Chamber / <bedding> / 8 pillobears / 8 hand towels / 4 shietes / <garment> / 1 smock / 2 aperns / 1 bruse and a grater / 1 Coat and a pear of house / 1 Gone and a for kertle [?] / 1 buckrame savgard / <utensils> / 2 Chamber pots / 1 morter and a Cressct / 3 Chaffindishes / 1 Skomar and a ladle of brase / 9 bear potes and 2 black potes / 1 falling bord in the house / 3 pans 2 ketles / 1 basson brase / 4 brase potes

Note that *aprons* is listed next to smock and other garments. (The listing of a "bruse and grater" below *aperns* seems out of place.) By this time, in the late sixteenth century, an {apron} was classified as a garment.

Does this explain why {apron} continued to displace {napron}? Possibly. The demilexeme {apron} removes aprons from the domain of the *naperie* (the collection of pieces of fabric) to the domain of garments. The extension may be the same, but the intension changes, by the re-ranking of the semantic features of the two demilexemes: {napron} ranks the material over the function, whereas {apron}, while it does not that fabric may be involved, ranks garment and its function of covering as more important.

There are several conclusions here. The two demilexemes have a certain autonomy: they have overlapping but not identical semantics; they have different preferred contexts in which they appear. From this it follows that the change of *napron* to *apron* is not a simple substitution of one form for the other. Next, the newer form *apron* seems not to appear in the context of an indefinite article ahead of other contexts, as might be expected if *apron* merely replaced *napron*. This again implies that *apron* and *napron* are somewhat separate entities. Third, the ambiguity of [anapron] made the change possible, but the change was the creation of two demilexemes here, {napron} and {apron}, not a reparsing.

5 Conclusion

The examples above suggest that *parole* exists, that it has a role in language. Saussure, as we saw, did his best to hide *parole* from view, but it ended up that *parole* has a life of its own: it required its own set of rules and it was maintained (the accent stayed on the same syllable as in Latin) without justification in the system.[6] All the action of stress in Romance was in *parole*, not *système*. In other examples, we saw that *parole* is maintained from one generation to the next, not because it is motivated by higher principles, but because it was the usage and it was then transmitted as usage. *Parole* can also shape other changes (such as the apocope of post-tonic vowels in the transition from Latin to French and the restriction on intrusive /r/ to low vowels). Variants of lexemes, such as {napron} and {apron}, have partially separate existences and properties, including semantics.

Parole is not always static and it is not one-dimensional. *Parole* is, after all, activity, and human activity implies the possibility of more activity and other paths of activity, which may differ from inherited activity. *Parole* is habit infused with potential.

---

[6] Boris Gasparov (2013) has argued that Saussure's thinking was more complex (and less rigidly categorial and structuralist) than the subsequent reception would have it (especially chapter 4, pp. 111–37).

Abbreviations and texts cited

Abbreviation	Explication of abbreviation
1790	Society of Antiquaries of London, 1790. *V. Liber Niger Domus Regis Edward IV. From a MS. in the Harleian Library, № 642, fol. 1–196*, A collection of ordinances and regulations for the government of the royal household, made in divers reigns. From King Edward III. to King William and Queen Mary. Also receipts in ancient cookery. Printed for the Society of Antiquaries by John Nichols.
Chesterfield wills and inventories	Bestall, J. M.; Fowkes, D. V., ed., a glossary by Rosemary Milward with an introduction by David Hey & an index by Barbara Bestall. 1977. *Chesterfield wills and inventories 1521–1603*. Vol. 1 (Derbyshire Record Society). Derbyshire: Derbyshire Record Society.
Durham wills and inventories	*Wills and inventories illustrative of the history, manners, language, statistics, &c., of the northern counties of England, from the eleventh century downwards.* 1835. Vol. I (Publications of the Surtees Society, vol. 2). London: J. B. Nichols & Son; 1906. Vol. III (Publications of the Surtees Society, 112.). London: J. B. Nichols & Son.
Fabric rolls	*The fabric rolls of York Minster with an appendix of illustrative documents.* 1859. Vol. 35. (Publications of the Surtees Society). Durham: Published for the Society by G. Andrews.
Surrey wills	*Surrey wills.* (Archdeaconry Court, Spage Register). 1922. Vol. 5 (Surrey Record Society). Surrey: Roworth & Co., for the Surrey Record Society.
Wills and inventories of Bury St. Edmonds	*Wills and inventories from the registers of the commissary of Bury St. Edmunds and the archdeacon of Sudbury.* 1850. London: Printed for the Camden Society.
York wills	*Testamenta eboracensia, or Wills registered at York: illustrative of the history, manners, language, statistics, &c., of the province of York, from the year MCCC downwards.* London: J. B. Nichols & Son, 1836–1902.

References

Bermel, Neil. 1993. Sémantické rozdíly v tvarech českého lokálu. *Naše řeč* 76. 192–198.

Bestall, Ed. J. M., a glossary by Rosemary Milward D. V. Fowkes with an introduction by David Hey & an index by Barbara Bestall. 1977. *Chesterfield wills and inventories 1521–1603*. Vol. 1 (Derbyshire Record Society). Derbyshire: Derbyshire Record Society.

Bréal, Michel. 1900. *Semantics: Studies in the science of meaning*. London: William Heinemann.

Donnellan, Keith. 1966. Reference and definite descriptions. *The Philosophical Review* 75(3). 281–304.

Gasparov, Boris. 2013. *Beyond pure reason: Ferdinand de Saussure's philosophy of language and its early Romantic antecedents*. New York: Columbia University Press.

Hodgson, J. C. (ed.). 1906. *Wills and inventories from the registry at Durham*. Vol. III (Publications of the Surtees Society, 112). London: Andrews.

Kurath, Hans & Raven I. McDavid. 1961. *The pronunciation of English in the Atlantic States. Based upon the collections of the Linguistic Atlas of the Eastern United States*. Ann Arbor, Mich: University of Michigan Press.

Minster, York. 1859. *The fabric rolls of York minster. With an appendix of illustrative documents*. Vol. 35 (Publications of the Surtees Society). Durham: Pub. for the Society by G. Andrews.

Myers, A. R. 1959. *The household of Edward IV. The Black Book and Ordinance of 1478*. Manchester: Manchester University Press.

Paris, Gaston. 1862. *Étude sur le rôle de l'accent latin dans la langue française*. Paris; Leipzig: A. Franck.

Raine, James (ed.). 1835. *Wills and inventories illustrative of the history, manners, language, statistics, &c., of the northern counties of England, from the eleventh century downwards*. Vol. I (Publications of the Surtees Society, 2). London: J. B. Nichols & Son.

Saussure, Ferdinand de. 1959. *Course in general linguistics. Ed. Charles Bailly and Albert Sechehaye, in collaboration with Albert Reidlinger. Transl. Wade Baskin*. New York: Ed. Charles Bailly & Albert Sechehaye, in collaboration with Albert Reidlinger Philosophical Library.

Society of Antiquaries of London. 1790. V. Liber Niger Domus Regis Edward IV. From a MS. in the Harleian Library, № 642, fol. 1–196. In *A collection of ordinances and regulations for the government of the royal household, made in divers reigns. From King Edward III. to King William and Queen Mary. Also receipts in ancient cookery*, 13–86. London: Printed for the Society of Antiquaries by John Nichols.

Surrey Wills. (Archdeaconry Court, Spage Register). 1922. Vol. 5 (Surrey Record Society). Surrey: Roworth & Co., for the Surrey Record Society.

Sóskuthy, Márton. 2013. Analogy in the emergence of intrusive-r in English. *English Language and Linguistics* 17(1). 55–84.

Name index

Abasheikh, Mohammad, 173
Abels, Klaus, 241
Abney, Steven, 313, 484
Abondolo, Daniel, 48
Ackema, Peter, 562
Ackerman, Farrell, 387, 490
Adam, Galit, 126, 127
Adam, Meike, 518
Adams, Matthew, 18, 20, 36
Adelaar, K.A., 509
Adger, David, 556
Agbayani, Brian, 236
Aissen, Judith, 235, 241, 243, 245–248, 250, 255
Alaoui-Ismaili, Ouafae, 533
Albertazzi, Liliana, 526
Albright, Adam, 89, 90, 220, 227
Alexiadou, Artemis, 250, 313, 329, 337
Alpher, Barry J., 62
Alter, Stephen G., 446, 447
Amador, Ana, 458, 459, 467
Amano, Shigeaki, 90
An, Duk-Ho, 247
Andersen, Paul Kent, 349
Anderson, Richard C., 220, 221
Anderson, Stephen R., 3–5, 17, 21, 23, 25, 28, 41, 43, 45–47, 49, 51–54, 59, 60, 62, 82, 92, 99, 101, 103, 110, 115, 116, 119, 129, 130, 135, 155–157, 162, 166, 168, 169, 171, 187, 189, 190, 192–196, 198–201, 203–205, 213, 227, 235, 241, 263, 270, 275, 289, 290, 294, 312, 316, 369, 381, 386, 398, 421, 422, 443, 453, 457, 458, 487, 489, 490, 495–497, 517, 518

Anderwald, Lieselotte, 218, 225
Angluin, Dana, 75
Anttila, Arto, 18, 20, 36, 325
Anttila, Raimo, 534
Arad, Maya, 117, 123, 126
Araujo, Veronica, 128
Argyle, Michael, 519
Aristodemo, Valentina, 521
Árnason, Kristján, 99, 100, 106
Arnott, D.W., 436
Aronoff, Mark, 118, 119, 126, 161, 205, 212, 213, 227, 396, 402, 437, 452, 490, 503, 521
Athanasopoulou, Angeliki, 29
Atkins, Beryl T. S., 531

Baayen, R. Harald, 90, 212, 490
Bach, Emmon, 4, 379
Bader, Markus, 562
Baerman, Matthew, 217, 220, 386
Bahan, Ben, 521
Baker, Carl L, 75
Baker, Mark, 311, 329, 332, 340, 484, 551, 553–555, 557
Baker, Mark C., 263, 266, 269, 283, 340
Baker, Robert, 216
Baksh, Michael, 530
Banissy, Michael J., 532
Barnes, Jonathan, 21
Baronian, Luc, 227
Bartholomae, Christian, 290
Bastin, Yvonne, 174, 175, 177
Bat-El, Outi, 117, 119–122, 127–129
Battison, Robbin, 491
Bauman, H-Dirksen L., 521
Baumann, Andreas, 37

Name index

Beard, Robert, 386, 413
Becker, Michael, 80, 89
Belkin, Kira, 526
Bellugi, Ursula, 491, 495
Benediktsson, Hreinn, 99
Bennett, Ryan, 236, 241, 249
Bennis, Hans, 374
Benua, Laura, 70
Berent, Iris, 5, 6, 128
Berg, Kristian, 452
Bergen, Benjamin K., 497
Berger, Arthur Asa, 519
Bermúdez-Otero, Ricardo, 236, 249, 250, 257
Berman, Ruth, 117, 127, 473
Bermel, Neil, 581
Bermudez-Otero, Ricardo, 21
Bermúdez-Otero, Ricardo, 72
Bernhardt, Barbara H., 68
Berrebi, Si, 128
Berwick, Robert, 220
Berwick, Robert C, 214
Berwick, Robert C., 548
Besten, Hans den, 551
Bhatt, Rajesh, 279
Biberauer, Theresa, 559–561
Bickel, Balthasar, 436
Blevins, James, 11
Blevins, James P., 312, 316, 490
Blevins, Juliette, 3, 4, 6, 11, 42, 45, 53, 54, 451
Bloch, Bernard, 211
Bloch, Jules, 350
Bloomfield, Leonard, 61, 91
Boas, Franz, 451
Boas, Hans C., 472
Bochner, Harry, 437, 490
Boeckx, Cedric, 551, 555–558, 560
Boer, Bart de, 451
Bohland, Jason W., 467
Bolinger, Dwight, 370
Bolozky, Shmuel, 119, 121
Bonami, Olivier, 396, 397, 436

Bonet, Eulàlia, 73
Bopp, 449
Borer, Hagit, 551, 552
Borghi, Anna M., 526
Borja, Manuel F., 273
Borroff, Marianne L., 373
Bošković, Željko, 236, 249, 257, 554
Bostoen, Koen, 185
Bowerman, Melissa, 212
Bowern, Claire, 62
Boyd, Robert, 452
Boyes Braem, Penny, 519
Braem, Thuering, 519
Brainerd, Barron, 223–225
Bransford, John, 522
Brentari, Diane, 511, 522, 523
Brereton, Joel, 298
Bresnan, Joan, 218
Bresnan, Joan W, 370, 378
Brewster, Stephen, 529
Broadbent, Judith M., 218
Broselow, Ellen, 5
Brower, Candace, 530
Browman, Catherine, 457
Brown, Dunstan, 217, 386
Brown, Dunstan P., 397
Brown, Gordon, 466
Brown, Lorna M., 529
Brown, Roger, 223
Brugmann, Karl, 448
Bubenik, Vit, 351, 364
Buckley, Eugene, 4
Bueasa, Noor Mohammed, 9
Bullock, Daniel, 459, 466, 467
Burrow, John W., 445
Burzio, Luigi, 205
Bybee, Joan, 17, 21, 212, 493, 494
Byrd, Dani, 461, 463

Calvo-Merino, Beatriz, 525
Campbell, Lyle, 4
Candrian, Johann Paul, 200
Capirci, Olga, 520

Carreiras, Manuel Jon Andoni Duñabeitia, 128
Carter, David M., 212
Carver, Norbert, 374
Casparis, Johannes de, 4
Chan, Brian Hok-Shing, 560
Charland, Louis C., 525
Chater, Nick, 466
Chen, Na, 527
Cho, Young-mee Yu, 524
Chomsky, Noam, 22, 61, 84, 91, 145, 147, 211, 212, 214, 220, 227, 311, 369, 378, 379, 381, 471, 547–551, 553, 554, 557, 558
Chrea, Christelle, 533
Chung, Sandra, 236, 250, 264, 265, 267, 272, 273, 276, 277, 279–281, 284
Cinque, Guglielmo, 147, 241
Clahsen, Harald, 213, 217
Clements, George, 120
Clements, George N., 91
Clercq, Eva de, 352, 355
Coats, Herbert S., 84
Coetzee, Andries W, 80
Collinder, Björn, 49
Collins, Christopher, 484
Comrie, Bernard, 347, 549
Condoravdi, Cleo, 349, 350
Corbett, Greville, 195
Corbett, Greville G., 217, 386
Corina, David P., 527
Cortelazzo, Manlio, 199
Cowan, Marion, 241
Crain, Stephen, 553
Crasborn, Onno A., 521
Crisinel, Anne-Sylvie, 526
Crowhurst, Megan, 62
Curtis, Emily, 50
Cutler, Ann, 128
Cutler, Anne, 212
Cuxac, Christian, 520
Cytowic, Richard, 526

Daland, Robert T., 220
Darwin, Charles, 444–446, 448
Davidson, Lisa, 6
Davidson, Richard J., 532
Davies, Mark, 218
Davis, Barbara L., 468
Davis, Stuart, 50
de Chene, Brent E., 4, 41, 43, 45–47, 49, 51, 52, 54
de Lacy, Paul, 51
Deal, Amy Rose, 313
Decurtins, Alexi, 192, 193, 196
Deese, James, 466
Dehé, Nicole, 256
Delancey, Scott, 348
Delaporte, Yves, 499, 500
Delgaty, Alfa Hurley, 241
Demattè, M. Luisa, 526
Deo, Ashwini, 349, 350
Derbyshire, Desmond C., 557
Deutsch, Avital, 119, 128
Di Sciullo, Anna-Maria, 150
Diener, Edward, 527
Diessel, Holger, 524
Dikken, Marcel den, 374
Dill, Philipp, 521
Dingemanse, Mark, 447, 497, 523
Dixon, Robert M. W., 42, 59–63, 65, 92, 347, 348
Dobzhansky, Theodosius, 451
Doke, C.M., 425–427
Doll, Theodore J., 519
Donnellan, Keith, 579
Doron, Edit, 120, 123
Dorsey, J. Owen, 7
Downing, Bruce, 249
Downing, Laura J., 174
Drellishak, Scott, 518
Dryer, Matthew S., 256
Dubinsky, Stanley, 473
Dungca, Bernadita C., 263, 266, 271, 274
Dupoux, Emmanuel, 5, 8–10
Duranti, Alessandro, 524

Name index

Durie, Mark, 263, 270

Éammon, 33
Ebbinghaus, Hermann, 466
Ebneter, Theodor, 199
Edmunds, David, 10
Edwards, Terra, 529
Egurtzegi, Ander, 4
Ehrlich, Kate, 522
Elfner, Emily, 236, 249
Ellis, N. C., 166
Embick, David, 136, 336
Emmorey, Karen, 491, 517, 519, 520
Emonds, Joseph E., 379, 551
Engdahl, Elisabet, 560
Enrico, John, 555
Ernestus, Mirjam, 90
Erteschik-Shir, Nomi, 557
Evans, Sarah, 523
Everett, Daniel, 128

Faarlund, Jan Terje, 186
Fabb, Nigel, 22, 28
Fabisiak, Sylwia, 517, 523
Faltz, Leonard M, 370
Fee, Michale S., 467
Fernald, Theodore B., 497, 520
Ferrand, J., 499
Ferreira, Victor S., 519
Fhailigh, Mhac An, 33
Finley, Sara, 69
Fischer, Andreas, 523
Fisher, Jami, 521
Fitch, W Tecumseh, 558
Flack, Kathryn, 70
Flack, Kathryn G., 70, 82, 90
Fleischhacker, Heidi, 5
Flemming, Edward, 21
Fodor, Janet D., 556, 559
Folds, Dennis J., 519
Forster, Bettina, 525
Forster, Kenneth I., 119, 128
Fort, Mathilde, 129
Fortson Benjamin W., IV, 6, 7

Fowler, Carol A., 459
Fox, Nathan A., 532
Frampton, John, 218
Francis, W. Nelson, 166
Frank, Robert, 248
Franks, Steven L., 19, 21, 31, 32, 34
Frazier, Lyn, 562
Friedman, Uri, 524
Frishberg, Nancy, 491, 493, 503, 504
Fromkin, Victoria, 216
Frost, Ram, 119, 128
Frye, Richard, 9
Fudge, Eric C., 92
Fukazawa, Haruka, 70
Fukui, Naoki, 552, 557

Gafos, Adamantios I., 119
Gajewski, Jon, 554
Galantucci, Bruno, 451, 528
Gallego, Ángel J., 554
Garrett, Andrew, 4, 54
Garrigues, Stephen L., 525
Garrod, Simon, 523
Gasser, Emily, 534
Gause, Georgy, 452
Gazdar, Gerald, 428
Geertz, Clifford, 452
Gerritsen, Nellike, 401
Gesenius, Wilhelm, 129
Gess, Randall, 41, 42, 47, 48
Gianollo, Chiara, 556, 560
Gibson, Courtenay St John, 100, 101
Gibson, Jeanne D., 263, 266–269, 278, 281, 282
Gilbert, Avery N., 526
Giorgolo, Gianluca, 520
Giridhar, Puttushetra Puttuswamy, 256
Gíslason, Indriði, 100
Givón, Talmy, 528
Goebl, Hans, 207
Goldberg, Adele, 471, 472
Goldin, Matías A., 463, 464
Goldin-Meadow, Susan, 519, 523
Goldstein, David M., 291, 292, 296

Goldstein, Louis, 457, 461–464
Goller, Franz, 458
Golston, Chris, 236
Gontier, Nathalie, 445
Good, Jeff, 174
Gough, Bonnie, 503
Gouskova, Maria, 59, 70–72
Grawunder, Sven, 4
Greenberg, Joseph H., 549
Gribanova, Vera, 336
Grice, Martine, 462
Griffith, Penny L., 529
Grisch, Mena, 192, 200
Grossberg, Stephen, 459
Guardiano, Cristina, 556, 560
Guenther, Frank H., 467
Guion, Susan, 216
Gutierrez, Eva, 527

Haeckel, Ernst, 445
Hagstrom, Paul, 248
Hahnloser, Richard H. R., 467
Haiman, John, 524
Hakulinen, Auli, 326, 327
Hale, Mark, 292, 294, 297, 304, 308
Hall, Judith A., 519
Hall, Matthew L., 519
Hall, Nancy, 6, 62
Halle, Morris, 22, 31, 61, 62, 84, 91, 126, 135, 211–213, 217
Halpern, Aaron, 236
Hamano, Shoko, 524
Hammond, Michael, 36, 82, 120, 129, 155, 158–161, 163, 168
Hanson-Vaux, Grant, 526
Hansson, Gunnar, 100, 101
Hansson, Gunnar Ó., 19
Harizanov, Boris, 336
Harley, Heidi, 136, 140, 329, 379
Harlow, Harry Frederick, 530
Harms, Robert, 4
Harms, Robert T., 42, 43, 48
Harris, Alice, 186
Harris, Alice C., 422

Harris, Marvin, 452
Hart, Betty, 221
Härtl, Holden, 477
Haspelmath, Martin, 388, 400, 555
Hausenberg, Anu-Reet, 41, 42, 48
Hauser, Marc D, 558
Haviland, John, 241
Hawkins, John A., 559, 563
Hay, Jennifer, 212, 490
Hayes, Bruce, 20, 26, 31, 42, 44, 49, 50, 62, 73, 90, 158, 212, 252
Heath, Jeffrey, 129
Heisenberg, August, 50, 51
Henderson, Robert, 251, 252
Hendrick, Randall, 370
Hermes, Anne, 462
Hetzron, Robert, 226
Hevner, Kate, 530
Hewitt, Mark, 62
Heycock, Caroline, 374
Himmelmann, Nikolaus, 509
Hindley, Philip Colin, 519
Hinton, Leanne, 523
Hippisley, Andrew, 217
Hoberman, Robert, 118
Hock, Hans Henrich, 41, 42, 293, 351, 534
Hockett, Charles F., 115, 130
Holmberg, Anders, 556, 557, 559
Hopper, Paul J., 141
Horgan, Terrence G., 519
Horn, George M., 379
Hornstein, Norbert, 549, 555, 563
Horvath, Julia, 129, 474, 476, 483, 484
Huang, C.-T. James, 554
Huddleston, Rodney, 313, 316, 321
Hudson, Richard, 218, 220, 227
Hulst, Harry van der, 91
Hume, Elizabeth, 54
Huonder, Josef, 200
Hwang, So-One, 511, 519
Hyde, Brett, 62
Hyman, Larry, 4, 18

Name index

Hyman, Larry M., 172–174, 177, 178, 183–186

Idsardi, William J., 6, 62
Imai, Mutsumi, 525
Indriðason, Þorsteinn G., 101
Ingason, Anton Karl, 100, 101
Inkelas, Sharon, 21, 61, 70, 72, 73, 186
Iordăchioaia, Gianina, 313, 329, 337
Ishii, Toru, 236
Itô, Junko, 534
Ittyerah, Miriam, 526
Itô, Junko, 5, 70
Iverson, Gregory, 101
Iwasaki, Noriko, 525

Jaberg, Karl, 204, 207
Jackendoff, Ray, 152, 490
Jackendoff, Ray S., 391
Jacob, François, 548
Jacobsen, Wesley M., 136, 140, 141, 151
Jamison, Stephanie, 298
Janis, Wynne D., 521
Jayant, Chandrika, 529
Jespersen, Otto, 223, 224, 523
Johnson, Allen, 530
Johnson, Kyle, 484
Johnson, Orna, 530
Johnson, Shersten, 529
Johnson-Laird, Philip, 522
Jonas, Clare N., 532
Joos, Martin, 563
Joseph, Brian D., 436
Joseph, John E., 449, 450
Jud, Jakob, 207
Jurgec, Peter, 70

Kabak, Barış, 6
Kager, René, 6, 62
Kager, René, 73
Kagitani, Tatsuki, 525
Kahneman, Daniel, 527
Kaisse, Ellen M., 18, 21, 22
Kaneko, Michiko, 521

Kang, Yoonjung, 5, 6
Karimi, Simin, 7
Karlsson, Fred, 326
Karttunen, Lauri, 327
Katamba, Francis, 186
Kathol, Andreas, 250
Katsanis, Nicolaos, 49
Katsika, Argyro, 42, 49–52, 463
Kaufman, Daniel, 371
Kaufman, Roger A., 466
Kavitskaya, Darya, 4, 42–45, 49–52, 54
Kaye, Steven, 201
Kayne, Richard S., 379, 551, 553, 554, 557, 562
Keenan, Edward L, 370, 376
Kehoe, Margaret, 216
Kelly, Michael H., 216
Kemp, Sarah E., 526
Kendon, Adam, 519
Kennedy, Christopher, 370, 373
Kenstowicz, Michael, 4
Ketrez, Nihan, 80, 89
Key, Greg, 9
Keydana, Götz, 291, 292, 296
Kilbury, James, 130
Kilian-Hatz, Christa, 523
Kim, Jong-Bok, 312, 325, 370, 373
Kim, Wha-Chun M., 548
Kiparsky, Paul, 19, 21, 22, 41, 42, 49–51, 53, 54, 61, 71, 72, 84, 99, 102, 103, 174, 213, 322, 325, 331–335, 337, 340
Kirby, Simon, 451
Kiss, Tibor, 250
Kjartansson, Helgi Skúli, 103
Klein, Thomas, 10
Klima, Edward, 491, 495
Klima, Edward S., 520
Knapp, Mark L., 519
Kocab, Annemarie, 519
Köhler, Wolfgang, 129
Komissaroff, Bill, 519
Koneski, Bozidar, 31, 32

Korhonen, Mikko, 53
Kornfilt, Jaklin, 311, 313
Kortmann, Bernd, 524
Kosecki, Krzysztof, 522
Kostandy, Raouth R., 530
Kouwenberg, Silvia, 509
Kozhevnikov, Alexay A., 467
Kramer, Johannes, 194
Kratzer, Angelika, 312, 325, 329
Kringelbach, Morten L., 530
Kristinsson, Ari Páll, 103
Kroch, Anthony, 374
Kubozono, Haruo, 30
Kučera, Henry, 166
Kuhn, Jeremy, 521
Kuo, Jonathan Cheng-Chuen, 141
Kurath, Hans, 571–574
Kurisu, Kazutaka, 156, 161, 252
Kuryłowicz, Jerzy, 451

Labov, William, 219, 451
Labrune, Laurence, 92
LaCharité, Darlene, 509
Ladefoged, Peter, 216
Laka, Itziar, 256
Lakoff, George, 84, 91
Laks, Lior, 125, 129
Lamb, Sydney M., 92
Lambert, L. M., 499
Lamberton, Jonathan, 520
Lang, Peter J., 530
Lascarides, Alex, 519
Lasnik, Howard, 550
Laughlin, Robert, 236–238, 241, 244–248, 253–255
Law, Ann, 557
Lederman, Shlomo, 129
Lees, Robert B., 311
Leeson, Lorraine, 521
Legate, Julie A., 212, 216
Lepic, Ryan, 501, 520
LeSourd, Phil, 387
Lev, Shaul, 123, 125, 129
Levin, Aryeh, 130

Levin, Beth, 531
Levin, Theodore, 331
Lewandowski, Jirka, 528
Liberman, Mark, 30, 158
Liddell, Scott K., 520, 521
Lieber, Rochelle, 390
Lightfoot, David W., 227, 556
Lillo-Martin, Diane, 496, 520
Lindsay, Mark, 452
Lipiński, Edward, 118
Lloret, Maria-Rosa, 73
Lombardi, Linda, 68
Long, Michael A., 464, 467
Longobardi, Giuseppe, 556, 560
Lotka, Alfred J., 452
Louwerse, Max, 522
Lowe, John, 400
Lowe, John J., 291, 292, 296, 332
Łubowicz, Anna, 68
Ludwig, Vera U., 526
Luís, Ana, 437
Lunt, Horace G., 17, 19, 21, 31, 32
Lynch, Galen F., 467
Lynch, James J., 530
Lytkin, V. I., 43, 48

Macdonald, R. Ross, 523
MacNeilage, Peter F., 468
MacWhinney, Brian, 212, 216, 218, 221, 223
Maeda, Kingoro, 149
Mahanta, Shakuntala, 70
Maiden, Martin, 189, 190, 192, 194, 195, 197, 199–201, 203, 205, 206, 227
Malchukov, Andrej L, 399
Malouf, Robert, 312, 490
Manzini, Maria Rita, 550, 552
Marantz, Alec, 126, 135, 136, 138, 140, 142, 143, 145, 148, 151, 211, 213, 217, 283, 336, 340
Marcus, Gary, 128, 212, 216
Margariti-Rogka, Marianna, 51
Margoliash, Daniel, 459

Name index

Marin, Stefania, 462
Markússon, Jón Símon, 101
Martin, Alexander, 129
Martin, Andrew T., 20
Mascaró, Joan, 73
Masica, Colin, 364
Mathur, Gaurav, 521
Matthews, Peter, 443
Matthews, Peter H., 119, 386
Matushansky, Ora, 373
Mayberry, Rachel I., 519
McCarthy, John, 67, 68, 84, 119–121, 129, 252
McCarthy, John J., 68, 117, 123, 220, 252, 253
McClelland, James L., 211, 212
McCloskey, James, 381
McCloskey, Jim, 236, 249
McDavid, Raven I., 571–574
McGowan, Richard S., 458
Mchombo, Sam, 173
McNeill, David, 519
Meeussen, Achille E., 172
Mehler, Jacques, 128
Meier, Richard P., 496, 517, 521
Meir, Irit, 496, 518, 520, 527, 534
Meltzer, Aya, 484
Merchant, Jason, 370, 373
Merchant, Nazarré Nathaniel, 82
Mester, Armin, 70, 73, 534
Metzger, Melanie, 521
Miller, Philip, 241
Miller, Philip H., 387
Miner, Kenneth, 8
Mirus, Gene, 521
Mišković, Nikola, 519
Mitra, Dolly, 526
Mobbs, Iain, 559
Moeser, Shannon D., 522
Mofokeng, S.M., 425–427
Molinaro, Nicola, 128
Monod, Jacques, 548
Moravcsik, Edith A., 523

Moreton, Elliott, 59, 82, 90
Morgan, Gary, 520
Morin, Yves-Charles, 41, 42
Morris, Donald, 522
Moscati, Sabatino, 117, 126
Moser, Margaret G., 534
Moulton, Janice, 523
Muecke, Doris, 462
Müller, Gereon, 250
Müller, Max, 446, 447
Murane, Elizabeth, 523
Muriungi, Peter Kinyua, 174
Myers, A. R., 577
Myers, Scott, 37, 70

Nagy, William E., 220, 221
Nam, Hosung, 462
Napoli, Donna Jo, 491, 492, 497, 520, 521, 528, 532, 534
Nazzi, Thierry, 128
Neath, Ian, 466
Neave, Nick, 523
Neeleman, Ad, 562
Neidle, Carol, 520
Nelson, Jennifer L., 521
Nespor, Marina, 128, 249, 256
Nevins, Andrew, 80, 89
Nevis, Joel A., 436
New, Boris, 128
Newell, Kenneth B., 522
Newmeyer, Frederick J., 554
Newport, Elissa, 215, 224
Newport, Elissa L., 508
Newton, Brian, 49, 50
Ng, E-Ching, 8
Nichols, Johanna, 523
Nida, Eugene A., 212
Niedenthal, Paula M., 525
Nikolaeva, Irina A., 388
Nivens, Richard, 509
Niwatapant, Chirapa, 521
Niyogi, Partha, 220
Norde, Muriel, 186
Nordlinger, Rachel, 387

Name index

Noyer, Rolf, 336, 379
Nuckolls, Janis, 523
Nummenmaa, Lauri, 525
Nunberg, Geoffrey, 484
Nzang-Bie, Yolande, 185

O'Hara, Robert J, 445
O'Neill, Paul, 227
Obata, Kazuko, 25
Occhino, Corrine, 496
Ohala, John, 3
Ohala, John J., 21, 523
Öhman, Sven E. G., 21
Omer, 331
Omodaka, Hisataka, 149
Ono, Susumu, 144, 149
Ooijen, Brit van, 128
Orešnik, Janez, 101, 103
Orgun, Cemil, 72
Ornan, Uzzi, 119
Ortega, Gerardo, 520
Osherson, Daniel N., 220
Osthoff, Hermann, 448
Özyürek, Aslı, 519, 520

Pacun, David, 529
Padden, Carol A., 504, 509, 510
Padgett, Jaye, 37
Panagos, John H., 529
Paolo, Zolli, 199
Paris, Gaston, 570
Parks, Douglas, 8
Partee, Barbara H., 378
Pater, Joe, 59, 61, 69–71, 80, 84
Patterson, Karalyn, 212
Paul, Hermann, 448
Payne, John, 236, 249, 250, 257, 313
Peirce, Charles Sanders, 527
Peña, Marcela, 128
Peperkamp, Sharon, 5, 21, 23, 24, 26, 129
Perea, Manuel, 128
Perlmutter, David, 504, 509
Perniss, Pamela, 491, 518–520, 523
Perry, John, 7, 9

Pertsova, Katya, 220
Pesetsky, David, 241
Peters, Stanley, 370, 378
Peterson, John M., 349
Pfister, Joel, 10
Picardo, Michel A., 467
Pierrehumbert, Janet, 220
Pietrandrea, Paola, 520
Pinker, Steven, 211, 212, 215–217, 220, 556
Pires, Acrisio, 313, 328
Pischel, Richard, 350, 355
Pizzuto, Elena, 520
Plag, Ingo, 33
Plank, Frans, 347
Polian, Gilles, 241
Pollock, Jean-Yves, 551
Pons-Moll, Clàudia, 24, 27
Pope, Mildred K., 45–47
Poplack, Shana, 89
Popova, Gergana, 397
Portner, Paul, 328
Poser, William, 30
Postal, Paul, 91
Pouplier, Marianne, 462
Pousada, Alicia, 89
Preminger, 331
Prince, Alan, 6, 67, 68, 72, 75, 84, 119, 120, 129, 130, 158, 217, 251–253
Pruitt, Kathryn, 62
Pullum, Geoffrey, 316, 321
Pullum, Geoffrey K., 22, 218, 221, 227, 239, 313
Pult, Caspar, 194
Punske, Jeffrey, 484
Pustejovsky, James, 313
Pyers, Jennie, 519, 520
Pylkkänen, Liina, 143

Quadros, Ronice Müller de, 521, 528
Quinto-Pozos, David, 521

Radin, Paul, 10
Raffelsiefen, Renate, 122

Name index

Ralli, Angela, 29
Ramchand, Gillian, 554
Ramenghi, Luca A., 532
Rankin, Robert, 8
Ratcliffe, Robert R., 129
Ravid, Dorit, 127
Recreational Scuba Training Council, Inc. (RSTC), 519
Reinhart, Tanya, 477, 484
Rhodes, Bradley J., 459, 466
Rice, Curt, 220
Richerson, Peter J., 452
Riede, Tobias, 458
Ringen, Catherine O., 100, 101
Risley, Todd R, 221
Ritt, Nikolaus, 37
Rizzi, Luigi, 550, 555
Roach, William, 47
Robert, Boyd, 452
Roberts, Gareth, 528
Roberts, Ian, 484, 553, 556, 559
Robinson, George M., 523
Robinson, Jacques H., 529
Rogers, Kenneth, 194
Rögnvaldsson, Eiríkur, 100, 101, 103
Rose, Heidi M., 521
Ross, John, 324
Round, Erich R, 64, 73
Round, Erich R., 62
Roush, Daniel R., 526
Rudrauf, David, 525
Rumelhart, David E., 211
Russell, Kevin, 82, 161
Russo, Tommaso, 518, 520
Rutkowski, Paweł, 517, 523
Ruwet, Nicolas, 473, 484
Ryan, Kevin, 50

Sadler, Louisa, 387, 397
Safford, William Edwin, 263, 266, 271
Sag, Ivan, 484
Sag, Ivan A., 387
Sahlins, Marshall D., 451
Salminen, Katri, 531

Saltzman, Elliot, 461–463
Saltzman, Elliot L., 458
Samvelian, Pollet, 436
Sanabria, Daniel, 526
Sánchez, Agustín Ruíz, 241
Sanders, Nathan, 491, 492, 532, 534
Sanford, Anthony, 523
Sankoff, David, 89
Santoro, Mirko, 520
Sapir, Edward, 451, 523
Satake, Akihiro, 149
Saussure, Ferdinand de, 449, 450, 570, 571
Schachter, Paul, 378
Schleicher, August, 444–446
Schleicher, Ernst, 446
Schlenker, Philippe, 520, 521
Schneider, Elaine Fogel, 530
Schorta, Andrea, 200
Schuler, Kathryn, 215, 224
Schütze, Carson T., 212
Schwarz, Norbert, 527
Sel, Alejandra, 525
Selkirk, Elisabeth, 249
Selkirk, Elisabeth O., 21, 23, 378, 379
Sells, Peter, 370, 373
Senghas, Ann, 519
Sezer, Engin, 91
Shaw, Emily, 499, 500
Shaw, Jason, 6, 462
Shih, Stephanie S., 18, 20, 36
Shimron, Joseph, 128
Shklovsky, Kirill, 241
Sibanda, Galen, 176
Signorell, Faust, 192, 198, 203, 204
Siloni, Tal, 474, 476, 483, 484
Simango, Silvester Ron, 473
Simeon, Gion Pol, 192, 204
Simner, Julia, 526
Simpson, Andrew, 241
Sims, Andrea, 189, 207, 386
Sims, Andrea D., 220, 227
Skopeteas, Stavros, 235, 239, 241, 244,

255
Smith, Jennifer, 51
Smith, Jennifer L., 82
Smith, Neil, 557
Smith, Philip, 216
Smolensky, Paul, 6, 67, 72, 74, 119, 130, 158, 217, 251, 252
Snyder, William, 553
Soare, Elena, 313, 329, 337
Solèr, Clau, 200
Sóskuthy, Márton, 573
Spence, Charles, 523, 526
Spencer, Andrew, 385–390, 392–397, 399, 400, 412, 437
Speriosu, Michael, 18, 20, 36
Stanfield, Robert, 522
Stanford, Terrence R., 525
Starke, Michal, 556
Stavi, Jonathan, 370, 376
Stein, Barry E., 525
Stein, Heidi, 9
Stemberger, Joseph P., 68
Steriade, Donca, 119, 220
Stewart, Thomas, 387
Stirtz, Timothy, 256
Stjepanovic, Sandra, 557
Stob, Michael, 220
Stockwell, Robert, 378
Stoel-Gammon, Carol, 216
Stokoe, William C., 491
Stone, Matthew, 519
Stone, Megan, 484
Stowell, Timothy A., 550
Strain, Jeris, 7
Streeck, Jürgen, 519
Strickland, Brent, 521
Stump, Gregory, 217, 386, 387, 392, 396, 397, 421, 428–430, 436, 437
Stürzinger, Jakob, 194, 200
Sumner, Megan, 42, 49
Supalla, Ted, 491, 508
Sussman, Gerald J., 215, 216
Sutton-Spence, Rachel, 519, 521, 528

Švedova, Natalija Ju., 405
Svenonius, Peter, 318, 554

Tagliavini, Carlo, 194
Takano, Yuji, 557
Taub, Sarah F., 491, 495, 496, 520
Taylor, Insup Kim, 523
Tenaillon, Olivier, 446
Teplyashina, T. I., 43, 48
Tesar, Bruce, 74, 75
Tesar, Bruce B., 74, 82
Thompson, Robin L., 491, 518, 523
Thompson, Sandra A., 141
Thornton, Anna, 194, 199, 386
Thornton, Rosalind, 553
Thráinsson, Höskuldur, 100, 101, 105–109
Tomaszewski, Piotr, 519
Toosarvandani, Maziar, 331, 337
Topintzi, Nina, 42, 49, 50
Topping, Donald M., 263, 266, 271, 274
Torrego, Esther, 241
Torrence, Harold, 256
Torres-Tamarit, Francesc, 24, 27
Tranel, Bernard, 73
Travis, Lisa, 550
Trevisan, Marcos A., 458
Troseth, Erika, 375
Trotzke, Andreas, 562
Trudgill, Peter, 557
Tsolaki, Maria, 51
Tsunoda, Takasu, 348
Tumtavitikul, Apiluck, 521
Tylor, Edward B., 451

Uffmann, Christian, 6
Uriagereka, Juan, 557
Ussishkin, Adam, 119, 129

Vaknin, Vered, 128
Vale, Ramchandra N., 355
Valfells, Sigrid, 101
van Driem, George, 424, 429, 430
Van Oostendorp, Marc, 84

Name index

Vaux, Bert, 4
Vergnaud, Jean-Roger, 31, 212, 321
Verhoef, Tessa, 451
Vermeerbergen, Myriam, 517, 520, 521
Vigliocco, Gabriella, 491, 518, 519, 523
Vijay-Shanker, K., 248
Vikner, Sten, 375
Vinokurova, Nadezhda, 341
Vinokurova, Nadya, 311, 329, 332, 340
Vinson, David, 523, 528
Voeltz, F. K. Erhard, 523
Vogel, Irene, 29, 249, 256
Volpe, Mark, 136, 138, 140, 148, 151
Volterra, Vito, 452

Wackernagel, Jacob, 289, 290
Wade, Terence, 404, 405
Wagers, Matthew, 273
Wakelin, Delia, 523
Walkden, George, 559
Wapner, Seymour, 523
Ward, Jamie, 532
Warner, Anthony, 224
Washington, Jonathan, 534
Wasow, Thomas, 476, 484
Wechsler, Stephen, 387
Wedel, Andrew, 11
Weinstein, Scott, 220
Weldon, Tracey, 219
Werner, Heinz, 523
Wertheimer, Michael, 523
Westerståhl, Dag, 370, 378
Wexler, Kenneth, 550, 552
Weyer, Jeroen van de, 91
Whitman, John, 311, 313
Whitney, William Dwight, 447, 449
Wiese, Richard, 213, 217
Wilbur, Ronnie B., 496, 521
Wilcox, Phyllis, 491, 495, 496
Wilcox, Phyllis Perrin, 520
Wilcox, Sherman, 491, 495, 496, 508
Williams, Edwin, 150, 437
Williams, Edwin S., 328
Wilson, Colin, 90
Wilson, Deidre, 227
Windfuhr, Gernot, 7
Winskel, Heather, 128
Wolf, Matthew, 73, 203, 220
Woll, Bencie, 517, 520, 525
Wood, Johanna L., 375
Wright, Joseph, 225
Wright, Rebecca, 491, 492, 534
Wright, William, 129
Wuethrich-Grisch, Mena, 192, 204
Wunderlich, Dieter, 316, 337

Xu, Fei, 212, 215
Xu, Zheng, 161

Yang, Charles, 211–218, 220, 224, 226
Yang, Charles D., 556, 558
Yaxley, Richard, 522, 523
Yip, Kenneth, 215, 216
Yoon, James Hye Suk, 315, 316
Yu, Albert C., 459

Zachar, Peter, 525
Zec, Draga, 51
Zeshan, Ulrike, 520
Zipf, George K., 493
Zoll, Cheryl, 70, 72, 73, 186
Zoll, Cheryl C., 59, 61, 70
Zonneveld, Wim, 61, 84
Zwaan, Rolf, 522, 523
Zwicky, Arnold, 235
Zwicky, Arnold M., 22, 218, 221, 239, 422
Zwitserlood, Inge, 520

Language index

Angami, 256^{13}
Arabic, 9, 552
Austronesian, 54, 263, 371^3, 381
Avestan, 6, 332^{22}

Bantu, 18^1, 172–176, 176^1, 177, 179–181, 181^5, 183, 185, 423, 425
Barcelona Catalan, 27
Basque, 4^1, 5, 51, 256^{13}
Bilua, 25, 34
British English, 557

Chamorro, 250, 257, 263, 264, 264^1, 265, 265^2, 266, 267, 270–273, 275–279, 279^{14}, 280–282, 282^{16}, 283–285, 285^{19}, 286
Chichewa, 172–174, 177, 178^3, 179, 473
Chimwiini, 173
Chinese, 554, 560
Cibemba, 174

English, 5, 19–22, 26–28, 30, 33, 34, 37, 46, 143, 146^{12}, 148, 155–158, 161–169, 203, 211, 212, 215–218, 219^2, 220–223, 223^4, 224, 225, 225^6, 225^7, 237, 238^5, 241, 264^1, 286, 299, 313, 316, 318, 319, 321, 322, 328, 329, 333, 336, 337, 340, 341, 363, 370, 375^7, 386–388, 391, 394, 396, 397, 402, 405, 412, 413, 444^1, 445, 446, 473, 474, 474^3, 475, 476, 477^8, 478, 481, 481^{11}, 482, 493^1, 496, 500, 507, 523, 525, 534, 548, 550, 554, 560, 576, 577, 582

Faroese, 101, 102, 106, 106^8, 107, 107^{10}, 107^9, 108–110
Formentera Catalan, 24
French, 42, 45–47, 52, 55, 91, 241, 450, 473, 475, 475^4, 499, 569–571, 584

Gaahmg, 256^{13}
German, 192

Hebrew, 473–475, 477^8, 478, 481, 481^{11}, 482, 552
Hittite, 298, 451
Hixkaryana, 557

Icelandic, 99, 100, 100^1, 100^2, 101, 102, 102^5, 103, 103^6, 104–106, 106^8, 107^9, 108, 109, 109^{12}, 110, 226, 552
Indo-European, 6–8, 45, 290^1, 296, 332^{22}, 349^2, 400, 446, 449, 450^4, 451, 553, 556, 571, 581, 601
Indo-European languages, 445
Indo-Iranian, 290
Italian, 24, 26, 194, 198^8, 205, 206, 534, 550, 555

Japanese, 135

K'iche', 251, 252
Kinande, 174
Kitharaka, 174
Korean, 51, 524, 525, 529, 548, 552

Latin, 4^1, 5, 6, 45, 191, 193, 197, 203, 316, 317, 386, 387, 410, 421, 437,

Language index

446, 449, 569–571, 574, 577, 584
Literary Macedonian, 30–32, 34
Luganda, 174, 175, 181, 185, 186[8]
Lusoga, 172–176, 176[1], 177[2], 178[3], 179, 181–183, 185–187

Makua, 172
Mayan, 4[1], 235, 235[1], 236[4], 239, 241[7], 251
Modern Greek, 20, 24–26, 28[4], 29, 36
Modern Irish, 33

Ndebele, 176[1]
Niger-Congo, 256[13], 553
Nilo-Saharan, 256[13]
Norfolk English, 557
Nyakyusa, 174
Nyamwezi, 174

Old English, 437[13]
Old Icelandic, 100
Old Norse, 102, 107, 109[12]

Romance languages, 190, 191
Romanian, 191
Romansh, 189, 190
Rumantsch, 193, 381
Russian, 213, 218, 388, 389, 391, 400–410, 410[11], 412, 413, 415

Sanskrit, 4[1], 5, 293, 297, 308[9], 315–317, 329, 331[20], 332, 334, 337, 341, 349, 350, 352[5], 357, 363, 400, 449
Savognin, 190, 191
Serbo-Croatian, 249, 257
Shona, 172, 174
Spanish, 4[1], 5, 18, 42, 157, 218, 236[3], 255, 387
Surmiran, 189
Swedish, 524, 560

Tagalog, 141[7], 371[3]
Thai, 548, 550
Tongan, 47, 241

Tseltal, 241[7]
Tsotsil, 235, 236, 236[3], 236[4], 237–241, 241[7], 242, 243, 246–252, 254, 256–258
Turkish, 20, 21[3], 51[10], 89–91

Vedic, 6, 293, 298, 302–304, 307, 308, 316, 329, 332, 332[23], 333, 334, 336–338, 341, 342, 349
Vietnamese, 550

Welsh, 155, 156, 160, 161, 164, 165, 168
Wolof, 256[13]

Yidiny, 60–62, 62[4], 64–69, 71–74, 76–78, 81–83, 85

Zulu, 174

Subject index

A-morphous Morphology, 421
acquisition, 9, 10, 53, 211, 215–217, 220, 222, 223, 225, 227, 462, 549, 560–562
adjunction, 264, 275, 275^{11}, 277, 278, 282, 381
affix, 19, 21–23, 27, 28, 28^{4}, 30, 34–36, 117, 117^{2}, 117^{4}, 119, 122, 130^{6}, 162, 171, 172, 178, 179, 182, 183, 186, 218, 236^{4}, 239–241, 251, 264, 269, 270, 274^{10}, 282, 285, 315, 318, 321^{12}, 334, 337, 341, 342, 369, 370^{1}, 371, 375^{8}, 375^{9}, 376, 380, 381, 386, 395, 422, 423, 423^{4}, 424, 424^{5}, 425, 427–429, 429^{9}, 436, 437, 512, 576^{4}
affix doubling, 178
affix order, 436
affixation, 162, 163
agent, 141, 267^{4}, 312, 313, 315, 316, 323, 329, 331, 331^{21}, 332, 332^{23}, 333, 333^{25}, 334, 335, 335^{26}, 335^{27}, 336–341, 341^{29}, 342, 349, 350, 423, 423^{4}, 424, 424^{5}, 425, 429, 431, 435, 438, 511, 575
allomorph, 73, 139, 144^{11}, 151, 180–183, 190, 191, 195, 198, 200, 204, 349^{2}
allomorphy, 19, 155, 157, 163, 182, 186, 192, 194, 195, 199, 207, 239, 452
allophone, 54
alloseme, 137, 148^{16}
alternation, 36, 42, 48, 50, 60, 62, 89, 91, 99, 101, 101^{4}, 102, 104–107, 107^{11}, 109, 110, 123, 126, 151, 158, 189–193, 193^{2}, 194–200, 202, 204–207, 217–219, 221, 265^{3}, 389^{1}, 393, 400–402, 408, 477, 479, 480, 482, 483, 487, 505
analogical, 4, 11, 54, 101, 102, 109, 110, 183, 194, 196, 201^{11}, 206, 212, 348, 351, 356, 363, 451^{5}, 512, 525, 572–575
analogy, 4, 11, 54, 110, 147, 183, 351, 366, 445–447, 450, 451^{5}, 496, 525, 563, 572–575
Anti-Locality, 558
applicative, 173–175, 178, 178^{3}, 180, 181
arbitrariness, 203
archaic Indo-European languages, 296
argument, 141, 143, 143^{10}, 145
argument structure, 136, 150, 313^{5}, 363, 387, 389^{1}, 390, 393, 399, 405, 408, 414
arguments, 236^{4}, 254, 264, 266, 274, 282, 308, 313, 315, 316, 318, 319, 322, 342, 347–351, 351^{4}, 354–363, 365, 366, 375^{8}, 387, 389^{1}, 390, 391, 393, 395, 400, 405–408, 414, 425, 429, 436, 480, 561
aspect, 5, 20, 60, 197, 258, 265^{3}, 274, 275, 277, 278, 278^{13}, 279^{14}, 290, 312, 316, 317, 337, 338, 341, 350, 354, 387, 392, 400–402, 405, 410, 415, 490, 497, 512
assimilation, 3, 18, 48, 53, 101, 104, 107, 108, 159, 196, 493^{1}
Attic drama, 306
autonomy, 205, 582, 583
Avestan, 297

backness, 101, 107^{9}

Subject index

behavioral ecology, 452
binding, 202, 348, 548, 549, 563
biology, 451
blocking, 157, 421
bound morpheme, 21, 115, 116, 264
braille, 529
Burzio's generalization, 140

caesura, 305
Case, 548
case, 82, 109, 109^{12}, 141, 238^5, 264, 265, 277^{12}, 280–285, 312, 313, 315, 317–321, 321^{12}, 322, 322^{14}, 323, 325, 326, 326^{17}, 327–329, 331, 331^{21}, 332, 333, 337–342, 347, 348, 352, 354–356, 356^8, 359, 362–364, 366, 379–381, 387, 388, 392, 393, 400, 404, 405, 414, 548, 550, 552, 554
causative, 136–138, 140–143, 143^{10}, 145, 147–150, 173–177, 181^5, 182, 183, 183^7, 184, 186, 263, 264, 266, 267^5, 268, 268^6, 269, 270, 273, 276, 278^{13}, 279, 280, 282–285, 334, 336–338, 341, 360, 389^1, 393
CEG corpus, 166
change, 448, 491, 492, 495–497
circumfixion, 157
clausal idioms, 473, 474, 477–486
clitic, 23–27, 31, 34, 35, 65^9, 177, 178, 181^6, 235, 235^1, 236, 237, 239–241, 244, 245, 247–251, 254–258, 264, 275, 289, 290, 290^1, 291–298, 305, 306, 306^7, 307, 308, 358, 365, 366, 371^3, 378, 386, 401
    ordering, 291
clitic cluster, 293, 295, 296
clitic clusters, 292
clitics, 289, 290
    ordering, 293
coalescence, 42, 46, 47, 50, 51, 51^{10}, 52, 53, 55, 244

coda, 42–44, 46, 49–51, 51^{10}, 63–65, 65^9, 66–68, 81, 461, 462, 464, 465
compelxity, 68
compensatory lengthening, 4, 41–43, 177, 185
complement, 29, 34, 240, 241, 241^6, 243, 247, 248, 250, 255, 264, 274–279, 279^{14}, 280–282, 284^{18}, 312–314, 320–322, 324, 326, 328, 331, 336, 338, 341, 342, 371, 375, 375^8, 378, 379, 404, 405, 413, 414, 476, 484
complex, 157, 525, 534
complex determiners, 370, 376
complexity, 6, 8–10, 10^9, 11, 31, 60^1, 84, 151, 155–161, 163, 164, 166–169, 243, 247, 249, 268, 277, 278, 282, 283, 285, 334, 337, 370, 378, 462, 464–466, 489, 496, 507, 512, 520, 527, 547, 560
compositional, 21, 33, 137, 143, 147–150, 173, 174, 178, 179, 459, 472, 490, 497, 497^3, 498, 498^4
compound, 19, 20, 22, 23, 25, 26, 28, 28^4, 29–30, 33, 36, 64^7, 125, 183, 184, 187, 317, 333, 334, 335^{26}, 335^{27}, 381, 386, 412, 493^1, 554, 575
conjunction, 163, 375, 378, 485^{14}
conjunctive, 152, 300
conservativity, 370, 376
consonant mutation, 156
constraint, 11, 45, 67–72, 74–86, 86^{16}, 87–92, 130, 147, 156, 158–164, 168, 214–216, 227, 241, 241^6, 249–252, 252^{12}, 253–257, 294–296, 321, 387, 391^3, 396, 406, 415, 472, 480, 482, 483, 486, 492, 534, 558–560, 563
constraint violations, 68, 158, 159
constraints, 158, 162, 163, 295
constraints-based, 387, 391^3, 396, 406, 415

construct-i-con, 472, 480
Construction Grammar, 472, 472[1]
contrastiveness, 53
coordination, 238, 300, 301, 460, 462
coplexity, 529
copular construction, 374
corpus, 127, 166, 215, 216, 218, 221, 223, 224, 225[6], 579
crosslinguistic variation, 551, 552, 563
cultural anthropology, 451, 452
cultural evolution, 451, 452
culture, 452

Darwinian theory, 451
Darwinism, 447, 448
defectiveness, 192–195, 198, 213, 221, 386
definite determiners, 236, 237, 240
definiteness, 241, 378, 386, 388, 414
degree inversion, 372, 380
degree phrases, 370–372
deletion, 43, 44, 47, 48, 50, 50[8], 51, 51[10], 60–62, 62[3], 63, 63[6], 64, 65, 65[9], 66–70, 72–74, 76, 78, 81, 82, 85, 87, 88, 103, 104, 108, 196, 558
derivation, 22, 49, 66, 72, 101, 116, 117[1], 118–124, 126, 127, 129, 130, 135, 135[1], 136, 137, 151, 171, 172, 182, 202–204, 215, 263, 264, 266–270, 272–274, 274[10], 278, 279, 282, 285, 312, 313[3], 315, 318, 321, 337, 378, 379, 381, 386–389, 392, 393, 395–397, 397[6], 398, 399, 406–408, 413–415, 476, 483, 487, 490, 554
derivational, 490, 494–496, 498, 500, 509
derivational affixes, 22, 202
derived, 268
diachrony, 3, 7, 8, 42, 53, 137, 148, 186, 190, 195, 206, 348, 349, 351, 356, 399, 443, 444, 449, 450, 534, 569, 570
dialects, 31, 446–448, 547, 555, 557

diatheses, 472, 473, 477, 481–483, 485, 485[14], 486, 487
diathesis, 482
differential object marking, 9[8], 351, 361
discourse, 194, 255, 297, 299, 326[17], 519
Distributed Morphology, 135, 217, 336, 413, 484
dominance, 491, 492, 495, 497, 498, 502–505, 505[5], 506, 507, 510, 521, 522
doublets, 224, 572, 573
DP, 556
DP hypothesis, 371

epenthesis, 4–7, 7[3], 8–11, 50, 101–103, 103[6], 108
epenthetic, 7, 103, 104
epigenetic, 559, 560, 562, 564
EPP feature, 373
ergative, 82, 236[4], 340, 347–351, 351[4], 354, 355, 355[7], 356, 356[8], 357–366
ergativity, 348
etymological history, 491
evolution, 352, 443–453, 557, 570
evolutionary biology, 449, 452
exception, 60, 61, 64–74, 76, 78, 81–85, 89–92, 101, 101[4], 102, 108, 122, 212–218, 221–227, 549, 561
explanatory power, 549
exponence, 155, 157, 163, 171, 172, 182, 186, 277, 406, 423, 425, 429, 435
external argument, 141, 143, 143[10], 145
extraposition, 557

feature, 161, 238[5]
features, 53, 71, 84, 91, 100, 101, 162, 163, 172, 196, 214, 222, 224, 226, 236[4], 238, 238[5], 241, 250, 270–273, 277, 277[12], 279–282, 284, 285, 315, 318, 319, 329, 336, 337, 340–342, 356, 369, 372, 372[4], 373, 379, 380[16], 381, 392, 393,

Subject index

395, 397, 397⁵, 398–400, 403, 406–408, 410, 412, 412¹³, 415, 517, 551, 553, 553², 554–562, 583
feminine, 101⁴, 103, 157, 160, 164, 351⁴, 366
Final Over Final Constraint, 559
fingerspelling, 529
focus, 238, 244–246, 265, 284, 295, 552, 575
foot, 19, 21, 24, 26, 30, 31, 36, 37, 60, 62–65, 67, 68, 88
fractions, 376, 376¹⁰, 380
Franz Boas, 451
free clitics, 26, 34
frequency, 158, 160, 165–167, 214, 218, 219, 219², 220–222, 226, 370, 463, 464, 468, 493¹, 529, 561
fronting, 107⁹, 297, 298, 306, 328, 557
function words, 20, 20², 21, 22, 29, 31
functional categories, 238, 314, 386, 473, 552, 553, 556
functional explanations, 559⁵
functional morphemes, 136

gender, 157
generative phonology, 60, 84, 100³, 105, 106
generative syntax, 547, 549
genetics, 451, 549, 558
gerund, 206, 311, 313, 313³, 315, 316, 319, 319⁹, 320, 321, 326–328, 342, 366, 391, 402
gesture, 458–464, 499, 501, 519
Grimm's law, 448
grounded constraints, 559

haplology, 156, 157, 161, 163, 168
historical linguistics, 450, 451

iconicity chains, 518, 527–529, 532
ideophones, 497³

idiom, 472, 473, 473², 474–478, 478⁹, 479, 479¹⁰, 480, 481¹¹, 481¹², 482–485, 485¹⁵, 486¹⁶, 486¹⁷, 579
idiomatization, 148, 150
imbrication, 181
imperfective, 313³, 337, 337²⁸, 353–355, 357, 365, 366, 400–405, 407, 408, 410
inchoative, 136, 138, 140, 142, 143, 145, 147, 265³
Indo-European studies, 290
infix, 157, 265, 267⁴, 279, 280, 282, 282¹⁶
infixation, 157
inflection, 22, 49, 62, 66, 101⁴, 104, 109, 126, 135, 135¹, 136, 136², 151, 171, 172, 182, 183, 187, 193, 195, 197, 198, 204, 211, 217, 218, 220, 226, 239–241, 263, 264, 269–272, 272⁸, 273, 274, 278, 279, 279¹⁴, 285, 315, 317, 332, 350, 352, 355, 381, 386–393, 393⁴, 394–398, 400, 401, 405–408, 410, 413–415, 421–423, 425, 426, 429, 431, 435–437, 452, 496², 551, 552
inflectional, 496²
Inflectional morphology, 135
initial position, 9, 294, 295, 401, 563
innovation, 120, 121, 124, 127, 206, 348, 356, 364, 365, 521, 574, 575, 579–583
input, 67–70, 73, 76, 84, 119, 123, 127, 155, 156, 158–161, 214, 216, 220, 222, 226, 252, 253, 362, 500, 549, 552, 560, 562
input–output mappings, 155
input–output pairings, 160
Interfaces, 258
interfaces, 147¹⁴, 386, 554, 558
intervention, 256, 313⁴, 379, 380
Intonational Phrase, 297
intrusive /r/, 573, 574, 584
irregularity, 166, 211–217, 394, 395, 447

Subject index

island constraints, 559
isoradical, 136–138, 144, 149, 152
item and arrangement, 373

Jena, 444

language acquisition, 4, 54, 214, 215, 217, 220, 222, 225, 225[6], 550, 558
language change, 575
language evolution, 446
languages, 155
law (of language), 448
lexemic index, 397, 407, 408, 410
lexemic individuation, 386
lexical causatives, 143[9]
lexical integrity, 387–389, 414
lexical relatedness, 386, 388, 390, 393, 395, 406, 412, 413, 415
lexical stress, 20–23, 26, 37
lexicalization, 37, 215, 222
lexicalized, 21, 33, 148, 150, 181[5], 183[7], 204, 226, 485
lexicon, 33, 67, 72, 89, 90, 116, 125, 127, 128, 148, 150, 158, 164, 171, 214, 216, 311, 312[1], 316, 386, 387, 471, 472, 483–485, 487, 489, 549, 552, 553, 555, 572
Lexicon Optimization, 158
libfix, 576[4]
linguistics, 36, 101, 191, 211, 213, 214, 227, 377, 443–450, 450[4], 451–453, 490, 491, 512, 517, 534, 569
loanword, 4, 4[1], 5, 7, 8, 101[4], 109[13]

macroparameter, 553–555
mapping, 497–506, 509, 511
markedness, 6, 11, 68, 70[12], 75–77, 79, 80, 89, 155, 158, 162, 166, 348
Merge, 145, 214, 563
merger, 50, 52, 145, 197
metanalysis, 576
metathesis, 50, 53, 54, 175, 190
metonymy, 575
microparameters, 562

mimetics, 524, 525, 529, 534
Minimalist Program, 387, 550, 558
monophthongization, 43, 44, 46, 48, 52
mora, 44, 50
morpheme, 101, 101[4], 103, 116–118, 130[6], 136, 155, 156, 156[1], 157, 161, 163–166, 168, 172, 186, 252–254, 264, 269, 316, 329, 334, 336–338, 386, 387
morpheme-specific, 101, 254
morphemes, 155, 168
morpho-syntactic, 160
morphology, 49, 59, 60[1], 61, 69, 71, 72, 79, 82, 90, 92, 101, 101[4], 102, 105, 109, 110, 115–120, 122, 123, 127–131, 136, 151, 152, 155–157, 160–164, 168, 171, 172, 174, 183, 186, 187, 190, 193, 194, 197, 202, 203, 205, 206, 212, 212[1], 214, 217, 227, 241, 252, 264, 270, 279, 280, 283, 311, 315, 316, 318, 325–327, 329, 336, 337, 340, 348, 351, 362, 369–372, 380, 381, 386–389, 389[1], 390–396, 398, 399, 401–403, 406–408, 410, 410[12], 412, 412[13], 413, 415, 421[2], 423, 425, 426, 428[7], 429, 431, 435, 437, 452, 489, 490, 494, 496, 496[2], 497[3], 500, 507, 512, 520, 523, 554, 575
morphome, 190, 402
morphophonology, 163, 169
morphosyntactic, 9, 151, 161, 196, 202, 218, 263, 278, 314, 322[14], 325–327, 386, 387, 389, 391, 394, 395, 398, 399, 405, 414, 421, 422[3], 428, 430, 434, 438, 496[2], 547, 556, 557, 563
morphosyntax, 421
movement, 241, 241[6], 250, 280, 281, 281[15], 282, 297, 305, 336, 369–371, 373, 375[9], 378–380, 482, 491, 492, 495–505, 505[5], 506–512,

605

Subject index

518, 521, 522, 524, 532, 551, 554, 556, 557, 562
mutation, 160–162

natural, 490
Neogrammarians, 448, 449, 451
neologism, 109[12], 575
nominative-accusative marking, 351, 352
non-concatenative morphology, 157
NP, 560
number agreement, 263, 264, 265[3], 266, 269–273, 277, 277[12], 278, 279, 279[14], 285

onomatopoeia, 523, 524, 534
onset, 9, 18, 42, 49–51, 51[10], 240, 459, 461–463, 467
opacity, 107, 110, 389, 413–415, 474, 493[1]
opaque, 65[8], 108, 110, 388, 390, 412, 474, 491, 494
Optimality Theory, 294
orthographic, 46, 100
orthography, 102[5], 107, 241, 265, 265[2]

paradigm, 21[3], 101[4], 102, 104, 109, 116, 123, 126, 128, 189, 190, 192, 193, 193[2], 194, 195, 197, 198, 201, 204, 206, 217, 265, 270, 279, 317, 332, 351, 352, 373[6], 386, 387, 389–394, 396–403, 406, 407, 410, 412–415, 422, 430[12], 438, 512
parameter, 562
parameters, 169, 348, 457, 458, 466, 467, 548–555, 555[3], 556–560, 562, 562[7], 563, 564
parametric variation, 548, 549, 552, 553, 558, 560
participles, 201, 315–318, 321, 321[12], 322, 389, 391, 393, 396, 399, 400, 402–405, 405[9], 406–408, 410, 412, 412[14], 413, 415
partitives, 377, 378, 378[12]

passive, 151, 267, 267[4], 268, 268[6], 269, 277, 284[18], 349, 389[1], 396, 397, 400–402, 404–406, 408, 412[14], 422, 472–481, 484–486
past tense, 105, 109, 175, 211, 212, 215, 216, 224, 316, 389, 392, 393[4], 394, 401, 402, 404, 412, 436
pedigree of man, 445
perfectives, 401
periphrasis, 193, 350, 386, 387
person-and-number agreement, 270, 272
person-and-number agreement, 266, 270, 272, 272[8], 273, 277, 277[12], 279, 279[14], 280, 284, 285
Phase Impenetrability Condition, 558
phon(a)esthemes, 497[3]
phoneme, 53, 54, 102, 107, 217
phonesthemes, 518, 524
phonological complexity, 155, 156, 159–161
phonological word, 21, 22, 24, 62, 62[4], 64[7], 65[9], 220, 275, 275[11], 276–278, 282, 282[16], 299, 300, 386
phonologically conditioned allomorphy, 190, 195, 197, 203, 205
phonologization, 20, 21, 21[3], 33, 41, 42, 45, 52, 53, 55
phonology, 4, 5, 7–9, 11, 21, 23–25, 28, 36, 59, 60, 60[1], 61, 70–74, 76, 78, 81–85, 90–92, 100[3], 101, 101[4], 102, 103, 105, 106, 109, 110, 118, 120, 128, 130, 155, 157–160, 163, 174, 183, 190, 192, 193, 193[2], 195, 203, 205, 213, 215, 235, 236, 249, 251–253, 255, 257, 258, 297, 336, 395, 457, 459, 490, 496, 496[2], 510, 511, 520, 534, 563
phrasal idioms, 473, 474, 474[3], 475, 477–481, 481[11], 483–485, 486[16]
phrasal phonology, 139, 146
plural, 105, 157, 161–165, 165[2], 166–169,

180, 190¹, 196, 199, 200, 202, 205, 216, 265³, 266, 267⁴, 269–271, 271⁷, 272, 273, 274¹⁰, 277, 278, 313, 313³, 319, 325, 336, 352, 354, 367, 370², 376¹⁰, 387, 393⁴, 394, 396, 401, 412, 422, 423, 424⁵, 425, 429, 435, 437, 438, 554, 577

polysemous, 142, 151
polysemy, 140
post-syntactic, 49, 151, 371³
pre-syntactic, 151
prefixation, 157, 162
preposition, 35, 160, 258, 328, 380, 412, 485¹⁴, 552, 579
Principles and Parameters (P&P), 548
Pro-drop, 555
productive, 494, 500
productivity, 110, 174, 198, 212–216, 219², 222–227, 312¹, 452, 468, 477
prosodic contour, 372
prosodic word, 20, 22–24, 26, 27, 34, 72, 73, 239, 249, 306⁷, 372
prosodically deficient, 22, 24–26, 31, 34, 35, 240, 241, 264, 273, 275, 275¹¹, 276, 278, 279, 282
prosody, 62, 249, 277, 290, 291, 293, 297, 305–307, 381, 523, 570
proverbs, 478, 478⁹

ranking, 68–70, 70¹², 71, 72, 74, 75, 78, 80, 81, 83, 87, 90, 160, 162, 163, 254, 255, 295, 580, 583
reanalysis, 42, 43, 46, 50, 52, 183, 186, 257, 276, 359, 361–363, 366, 399, 494, 498–500, 505⁵, 575, 581, 582
reciprocals, 267
recursion, 75, 76, 558
reduplication, 162, 186, 275, 509, 522, 523
regularity, 151, 166, 212, 312¹, 375⁸, 448, 451⁴, 460, 477, 479, 570, 571, 581

Relativized Minimality, 558
restructuring, 179, 184, 186, 256, 272⁸, 279, 352, 505
right periphery, 235, 254, 255
Rigveda, 293⁴, 297, 298, 302
Romance, 157
root, 23, 24, 61–68, 70, 71, 73, 76, 78, 79, 81, 82, 86¹⁶, 90, 115–120, 123–128, 128⁵, 129, 130, 130⁶, 135–138, 140, 143–147, 148¹⁶, 149, 150, 172, 174, 176, 181–183, 186, 189, 190, 195, 197–201, 201¹¹, 202, 204, 241, 333, 333²⁵, 334, 335, 335²⁶, 336, 337, 395, 410, 414
rounding, 101, 107⁹
rule blocks, 422

Sandhi, 573
sandhi, 571
Saussurean sign, 489
scansion, 47, 52
Schleicher, 444
scope, 73, 90, 157, 161, 172 174, 178, 178³, 179, 186, 212, 220, 225, 250, 292, 297, 307, 308, 326¹⁷, 339, 350, 388, 448, 452, 463, 485¹⁴, 496², 554
scrambling, 554, 557
second position, 237, 239, 240, 250, 257, 276, 289–291, 293, 296, 297, 299, 299⁶, 300, 302, 304, 308, 369, 371, 373, 380¹⁶, 381
selection, 22, 24, 60, 73, 74, 87, 148¹⁶, 190, 203–205, 375, 375⁸, 379, 444, 447, 448, 451, 453, 459, 466
semantic change, 137, 150
semantics, 23, 24, 28, 29, 33, 138, 140, 141, 148¹⁶, 151, 183⁷, 308, 332²², 349, 363, 370, 388, 392, 399, 400, 404, 405, 410, 511, 520, 521, 575, 583, 584
Separationism, 386
simple clitics, 240, 308

singular, 164
social Darwinism, 451
sound change, 4, 6, 7, 7^3, 8, 10, 11, 11^{13}, 21, 41–45, 51–55, 195, 354, 448
sound symbolism, 524
special clitics, 22
species, 445, 446
specifier, 145, 241, 241^6, 250, 277, 279^{14}, 280, 313^5, 323, 371, 373, 373^6, 376, 378–380
split ergativity, 337
split morphology, 171, 182, 386–389, 392, 396, 406, 415
stative, 145, 174, 349^2, 351, 414, 473, 476
stem, 21, 24, 28, 49, 103, 115, 118–123, 126–128, 128^5, 129, 130, 130^6, 135–137, 137^3, 138–143, 145–152, 162, 164, 165, 172, 174, 183, 184, 186, 187, 189, 193, 194^3, 195, 196, 198, 200, 203, 204, 211, 214–216, 263, 270, 317, 334, 388, 392, 394, 397, 398, 402, 407, 410, 421^2, 427, 436, 437, 573, 576
stress, 19–28, 28^4, 29–37, 50^9, 51, 53, 62, 157, 158, 190, 192, 193, 193^2, 194, 194^3, 195, 195^7, 196–201, 201^{11}, 202–205, 207, 212, 216, 241, 241^7, 267^5, 275, 276, 278, 282, 507, 569–571, 574, 584
stress , 158
stress shift, 26, 51
Structuralism, 387
structure, 489–491, 494, 496, 497, 497^3, 498, 500, 503, 505, 511, 512, 575
structure preservation, 41, 53, 54
subcategorization, 22
subordination, 64^7, 237, 247, 297–304, 326^{17}, 523
subtractive morphology, 165^2
suffix, 280, 282
suffixation, 22, 28, 61–64, 64^7, 65, 66, 68, 72, 76, 86^{16}, 136–138, 140, 142–151, 157, 162, 163, 172, 173, 175–177, 178^3, 179, 181–186, 197, 202, 204, 213, 215–217, 240, 251, 251^{10}, 252, 311, 315, 318, 332, 334–336, 338, 342, 391, 401, 421–423, 423^4, 425, 427–429, 430^{12}, 431, 436, 494
suffixes, 136, 164
suppletion, 190, 192, 193, 195, 196, 205, 270, 378
suppletive, 149, 191–194, 194^5, 195, 195^6, 196, 197, 267^5
surface exception, 108
surface representations, 155
syllabic consonants, 43, 102, 103^6
syllabification, 8^5, 18, 47
syllable, 7, 9–11, 18–20, 21^3, 31, 35, 43, 47, 50^9, 51, 54, 54^{11}, 60–65, 68, 70, 91, 130, 155, 190, 216, 241, 242, 459, 461–468, 534, 569, 570, 574, 576, 584
syllable structure, 461, 462, 467
synchrony, 193, 444, 449, 450, 569, 571
syncretism, 200, 352, 354, 386, 391, 397
syntactic constituents, 297
syntactic head, 280, 283, 373, 377, 378
syntactic structures, 135
syntax, 135, 308, 490
synthetic comparatives, 371, 372

tableaux, 158
telicity, 337, 521
template, 294, 366
templates, 172–179, 181, 186, 293–524
tense, 109, 197, 218, 315, 317, 318, 324, 329, 337, 350, 392, 394, 398, 400–403, 405, 406, 413, 425, 432, 436, 474, 477, 548, 552, 554
theme vowel, 157
Tolerance Principle, 213–216, 218, 221, 222, 225, 227
topic, 305
topicalization, 297

traditional grammar, 449
transitivity, 123–124, 135–137, 139^5, 140, 141, 141^8, 142, 143, 143^{10}, 145, 147, 150, 151, 247, 251^{10}, 256, 265–267, 267^5, 268^6, 273, 274, 277, 277^{12}, 278, 279, 281, 284, 285, 311, 315, 319, 320, 329, 341, 342, 347–349, 351, 351^4, 355, 361, 363, 365, 400, 401, 408, 413, 423, 425, 472, 474, 477, 479–481, 484, 485
transitivizing suffixes, 142, 145
transparency, 102, 389, 413–415, 474, 491, 493
trimeter, 305
typology, 11, 11^{13}, 28^4, 155, 166, 296, 313, 316, 322, 329, 332, 338, 339, 421^2, 462, 548, 549, 554

umlaut, 53, 99, 100, 100^3, 101, 101^4, 102–106, 106^7, 107, 107^{10}, 107^9, 108, 109, 109^{12}, 110, 157, 163, 168
Universal Grammar, 214, 348, 547, 555
universal grammar, 547
Utterance Group, 297

variation, 21, 37, 126, 151, 183, 399, 447, 547, 548, 551–556, 558, 560, 562, 563
verb second, 369, 381
Verner's law, 448
vocalic alternations, 189, 190, 192, 195–197, 205
voiceless, 103^6, 518
vowel length, 4, 41–48, 48^7, 49, 51–53, 55, 62, 184

Wackernagel, 298
Wackernagel's Law, 290, 295, 299^6
Watergate, 574, 575
weakening, 43, 44, 46, 105, 106
wh-agreement, 273^9, 280–283, 285
Word Formation Rule, 496–498

word order, 21, 36, 236, 247, 254, 256, 264, 281, 352, 379, 521–523, 551, 557, 560
word-and-paradigm, 373^6, 386

/pod-product-compliance